Controversies in Constitutional Law

Collections of Documents and Articles on Major Questions of American Law

General Editor

Paul Finkelman
University of Tulsa School of Law

A ROUTLEDGE SERIES

Race, Voting, Redistricting and the Constitution

Sources and Explorations on the Fifteenth Amendment

Volume 3

Alternative Redistricting, Registering, and Voting Systems

Edited with introductions by

Marsha J. Tyson Darling, Ph.D.
Adelphi University

ROUTLEDGE
New York/London

Published in 2001 by

Routledge
29 West 35th Street
New York, NY 10001

Published in Great Britain by
Routledge
11 New Fetter Lane
London EC4P 4EE

Routledge is an Imprint of Taylor & Francis Books, Inc.

Printed in the United States of America on acid-free paper.

10 9 8 7 6 5 4 3 2 1

Library of Congress Cataloging-in-Publication Data

Race, voting and redistricting, and the constitution : sources and explorations on the Fifieenth Amendment / edited with introduction by Marsha J. Tyson Darling
p. cm. -- (Controversies in constitutional law)
Includes bibliographical references.
Contents: v. 1. The 14th & 15th Amendments and the Voting Rights Act of 1965 -- v. 2. Enforcing and challenging the Voting Rights Act of 1965 -- v. 3. Alternative redistricting, registering, and voting systems.
ISBN 0-8153-3719-1 (set) -- ISBN 0-8153-4065-6 (v.l) -- ISBN 0-8153-4066-4 (v.2) -- ISBN 0-8153-4067-2 (v.3)
1. Apportionment (Election law)--United States. 2. Election districts--United States. 3. Gerrymandering--United States. 4. Voting--United States. 5. Race discrimination--Law and legislation--United States. 6. United States. Constitution. 15th Amendment. I. Darling, Marsha J. Tyson (Marsha Jean Tyson) II. Series.

KF4905 .R33 2001
342.73'07--dc21

2001031995

ISBN 0-8153-3719-1 (set)
ISBN 0-8153-4065-6 (v.1)
ISBN 0-8153-4066-4 (v.2)
ISBN 0-8153-4067-2 (v.3)

Acknowledgments

I am very grateful to a few people who have assisted me with the preparation of this book. My most heartfelt thanks are to Dr. Gloria Grant Roberson, Associate Professor and Reference Librarian in the University Libraries at Adelphi University. In a wonderful gesture as a colleague, Gloria Roberson, who is also a Reference Librarian at Hofstra University's Law Library, located many cases and supplemental materials for my review, and generously agreed to read over my monographs for the three volumes. In addition, I thank my colleague, Dr. Peyton McCrary, Historian in the Civil Rights Division, Voting Rights Section of the Justice Department for kindly allowing me to use the extensive research materials in the DOJ Library. Finally, I thank Ms. Mena Sieber, Associate Professor, Coordinator of the John W. Wydler Government Documents Depository at Hofstra University for her assistance at the last minute, as I sought additional documents that some other libraries had lost or discarded. I thank the series editor, Dr. Paul Finkelman for asking me to develop the volumes, and for his patience, as my relocation to begin a new job interfered with the time I had to devote to preparing the volumes. Finally, I thank my patient and persistent staff at the Center for African American & Ethnic Studies at Adelphi University, Ms. Denise C. Bynes and Ms. Regina DiPietro for all the big and little things they did to help put the three volumes on race, redistricting and voting rights together.

Contents

Series Introduction

This ongoing series, *Controversies in Constitutional Law*, provides teachers, scholars, and students convenient access to the debates and scholarly literature surrounding major questions of constitutional law. Each set of books—from two to four volumes—consists of four elements: an extended introduction to the issue by the editor; reprints of the significant cases and briefs on the subject; congressional testimony, and other primary documents on the issue; and a selection of the best scholarly articles on the subject. By conveniently gathering all this material in one place, each set of volumes allows users to become familiar quite quickly with the arguments and positions surrounding a particular constitutional controversy.

Scholars and students interested in constitutional law and public policy are often overwhelmed by the sheer amount of material published on controversial subjects. The topics in *Controversies in Constitutional Law* are timely, politically significant, and intellectually compelling. They are the issues that bring the legal academy, courts, politicians, and general public together—although not always in harmony.

Many scholars are barely able to keep up with the material in their own fields. Yet there is a need to learn about issues beyond our own specialties. A new course may require an introduction to a problem; our own research may lead us to a new issue. The series *Controversies in Constitutional Law* is designed to meet these needs, enabling scholars and teachers to come up to speed quickly on the topics in each volume.

This series also serves students at all levels of higher education. Students often encounter controversial topics without the background in how the problem developed. These volumes provide such a background. The important cases are reprinted in full; the introductions provide students with a map of the issues; the briefs, congressional testimony, and scholarly articles give convenient access to the arguments and debates.

The volumes bring together in one place a wide variety of sources and materials that are unlikely to be found in any one library. The primary documents include cases, briefs, testimony from legislative committee hearings, and, on occasion, executive branch publications. Few law libraries, university libraries, or public libraries will have all these materials. The secondary literature comes from the scholarly literature of law, history, political science, economics, criminology, and other relevant fields. Some of the articles also may be from serious nonacademic journals.

The related government publications, briefs, and congressional testimony are particularly important. Too often scholars overlook them. There is a tendency to focus on court opinions—what the Supreme Court said. Obviously this is important for understanding doctrine, but briefs, especially amicus briefs, are also an important source of information about the larger constitutional controversy the case represents. The politics of a case are often more apparent in these briefs than in either the oral arguments or the Court's opinion. Similarly, congressional hearings illustrate the social, philosophical, and political dimensions of these questions.

The goal of limiting each collection— two to four focused volumes— and the occasional inability to secure a reasonable copyright permission fee for some important articles often forces hard and judicious choices. Important articles that are not reprinted here are listed in the further reading sections at the end of the introductions.

The ongoing series *Controversies in Constitutional Law* provides in one single place comprehensive introductions to topics that will satisfy most lawyers, scholars, and students. By combining cases, briefs, legislative debates, and testimony from committee hearings with secondary articles, it is hoped to facilitate access to the issue presented in each set of volumes.

Paul Finkelman

Volume Introduction

> Shape is not in the Constitution. They call it a horseshoe, I call it a wishbone, meaning opportunity.[1]

In the decades preceding the 1990s, the Voting Rights Act (VRA) of 1965, one of several legislative outcomes of the Civil Rights movement, had altered the political landscape of the nation. The VRA was extended or amended three times (in 1970, 1975, and 1982), and it was the centerpiece of voluminous and contentious litigation and prodding judicial review. The VRA's provisions that placed restrictions on certain jurisdictions and required preclearance of changes to the voting system, while also suspending or abolishing those mechanisms that effected minority disenfranchisement, changed voting behavior in the South and the nation. Section 5 (requiring declaratory judgment or preclearance) of the Voting Rights Act, which opened the political process to disenfranchised African Americans, was extended in 1975 to empower Asians, Latinos, Alaskan natives, and Native Americans in more than sixteen states across the country.

Because the VRA's provisions instituted federal enforcement procedures that superseded the ability of states to interfere with voter registration, the immediate effect of the VRA in its early days was to increase dramatically African American voter registration and electoral participation. Black voter registration in eleven Southern states shot up from 29 percent in 1960 to 64 percent in 1972. Black suffrage and representation suddenly became prominent forces in Southern and national politics.

In addition, a number of African Americans poised to take advantage of the opportunity to seek elected office did so. In some places African American attorneys, as well as ministers and civil rights activists, ran for and were elected to office in the South, often for the first time in a century. By 1965, 72 African Americans had been elected to public office; five years after passage of the Voting Rights Act, African Americans elected to public office in the South accounted for 39 percent of the 1,469 black officeholders in the nation. There were 1,944 black elected officials in 1976, and by the twenty-fifth anniversary of passage of the VRA 4,955 African American women and men had been elected to public office in the South. By the decade of redistricting battles, for example, in 1997, there were 8,658 black elected officials, of whom 2,812 were women.[2]

At the beginning of the 1990s litigation based on the VRA's initiative to eliminate practices that disenfranchised racial and language minorities focused the attention of the nation's courts on adjudicating allegations of section 2 violations.[3] The decade began with this and other VRA challenges as legislators engaged the apportionment process following the 1990 census. Mindful of how *Thornburg* v. *Gingles* (1986), or application of the three-pronged *Gingles* test, had turned the

Supreme Court's jurisprudence on minority vote dilution and challenged multimember districts and at-large voting, participants in redistricting debates focused attention on how to foster minority political representation and the development of voting districts that provided racial and language minorities a real opportunity to engage in participatory and representative government by casting ballots and having those ballots add up to electing public officials. Against the backdrop of the persistent "one person, one vote" doctrine earlier embraced by the Court, and with a focus on opening the political process to racial and language minority voters, single-member minority-majority districts were constructed as an alternative to multimember at-large districts in a number of states across the South and the nation.

The 1990 federal census undercount of racial and language minorities prompted strident litigation against the Census Bureau. The census also prompted state legislative redistricting committees to begin drawing new boundaries for legislative and congressional districts. Congressional redistricting as a consequence of the 1990 census dramatically affected the creation of majority black and Latino districts. Black, Latino, Asian, and Native American men and women were elected to office at many levels of government across the nation. For example, without question, the dramatic increase in the numbers of black elected officeholders in the South after one hundred years of exclusion is due entirely to the Voting Rights Act's mandate to actualize minority political representation in the South and to ensure enforcement by the Justice Department. Given Southern resistance and attempts to crush the Civil Rights movement, only an erudite legislation like the amended Voting Rights Act, structured to ensure local, state, and federal compliance, could have intervened to transform the egregious violations to voting systems in the South and elsewhere.

In 1992 the Voting Rights Act was expanded to include the requirement for bilingual ballots, other voting assistance, and the inclusion of Indian reservations. However, in the same year the Supreme Court signaled that it was going to curtail equal political rights for people of color. In a 6-3 decision in *Presley* v. *Etowah County Commission*, the Supreme Court ruled against African American plaintiffs in Alabama who showed that the responsibilities of county commissioners were changed when blacks were elected to serve as commissioners.[4] With this abrupt decision, the Court caused concern among many legal thinkers who feared the Court was beginning to falter on the issue of racial fairness.

In 1993 the Supreme Court decided two very important voting rights cases. Each case was decided with a different degree of consent or dissent on the part of the nine justices, but in each case Justice Sandra Day O'Connor wrote the opinion for the Court. In *Voinovich* v. *Quilter* all nine justices agreed to reverse a lower-court decision that voided the construction of minority-majority districts in Ohio.[5] In Justice O'Connor's words: "[T]he creation of majority-minority districts, does not invariably minimize or maximize minority voting strength. Instead, it can have either effect or neither. On the one hand, creating majority-black districts necessarily leaves fewer black voters and therefore diminishes black-voter influence in predominantly white districts. On the other hand, the creation of majority-black districts can enhance the influence of black voters. Placing black voters in a district where they constitute a sizeable and therefore 'safe' majority ensures that they are able to elect the candidate of choice."

In the same year the Supreme Court issued an ambiguous directive to legislators about the use of race as a redistricting criterion and the whimsical scrutiny of a voting district's shape. In *Shaw* v. *Reno* a bare majority of 5 to 4 (Justices Byron White, Harry Blackmun, John Paul Stevens, and David Souter dissenting) ruled against North Carolina's two new majority-black districts.[6] In describing the shape of North Carolina's twelfth district as "bizarre,"[7] and calling for "close scrutiny" of the use of race as a predominant factor in redistricting, the conservatives on the Court began what would become a litany of *Shaw*-like cases that struck down majority-minority districts all across the South. In North Carolina an African American had not been elected to Congress since 1901.[8]

Citing the ideal of "colorblindness" mentioned in Justice John Harlan's dissent in *Plessy* v. *Ferguson* in 1896,[9] and granting relief to white plaintiffs under the equal protection clause of the Fourteenth Amendment, the Court's split decision laid bare the tension between the Court's interest in promoting minority political representation on the liberal side and the conservative agenda to weaken the VRA's reach. Many in the legal and scholarly communities were apprehensive, because the Court's ruling invoked a "colorblind" ideal at the expense of minority political interests and representation.[10] In a society where race is inseparable from voting (racially polarized voting), the Court directed legislators to construct voting districts that fulfilled the VRA's mandate, while decrying the use of race as a predominant factor in redistricting. In the above-mentioned decisions the conservative members of the Court required legislators to construct and defend compelling reasons for using race as the predominant criterion in drawing districts. The Court also instructed judges to enjoin "strict scrutiny" in their evaluations of voting districts.

In what J. Morgan Kousser has called "colorblind injustice, the undoing of the second Reconstruction," majority-minority voting districts have fallen in one Southern state after another: *Holder* v. *Hall* (Georgia, 1994), *DeGrandy* v. *Johnson* (Florida, 1994), *Miller* v. *Johnson* (Georgia, 1995), *Louisiana* v. *Hays* (Louisiana, 1995), *Shaw* v. *Hunt* (1996), *Bush* v. *Vera* (Texas, 1996), *Abrams* v. *Johnson* (1997), and *Hunt* v. *Cromartie* (North Carolina, 1999).[11] In still other cases, like *Reno* v. *Bossier Parish School Board* (Louisiana, 1997, 2000), the Court's reactionary decisions have been cause for alarm that state and judicial progress and momentum following the twentieth century's long-overdue Reconstruction era are unraveling for want of clarity and commitment to equality for racial and language minorities. Many in the legal and scholarly community fear that the Supreme Court has devastated section 5, essentially ending preclearance. There are jurisdictions engaging in violations to sections 2 and 5, while they allege that the VRA's requirements are burdensome and strain resources. And, regrettably, under the *Shaw* rulings, the Justice Department has been harshly chastened for persisting in its attempts to enforce the provisions of the VRA that have been the most resisted by advocates of white supremacy.

Several other major voting rights issues developed during the 1990s. Responding to the fact that the United States has one of the lowest rates of national voting in the industrialized world, Congress in May 1993 enacted the

National Voter Registration Act (NVRA),[12] which is designed to increase voter registration of economically and politically vulnerable Americans, who often do not register to vote. Within two years of the act's passage, there was cause for both celebration and concern about its implementation and outreach to previously unregistered citizens.[13] As has often been the case, marginalized and ignored plaintiffs and advocacy groups concerned to promote civil rights for the poor and differently abled undertook litigation directed at compelling state compliance with the NVRA.[14]

In the early 1990s, noting that there are arguments on both sides of the issue of the disenfranchisement of felons, civil rights advocates and legal scholars began asking whether states might not reexamine laws that permanently disenfranchise all felon ex-offenders.[15] Out of a concern for the nation's history of racism and sexism in criminal justice sentencing, especially the felony sentencing of young black males, the Democratic congressman John Conyers introduced legislation (H.R. 906) intended to allow federal-level voting rights for felons and ex-felons.

Whenever true participatory democracy is at stake, the goals and reach of the Voting Rights Act will have a role. In the twenty-first century those groups of Americans who, like African Americans, have been pushed the furthest from the exercise of constitutional rights and human rights will seek the path opened by the VRA's emphasis on the intent and reach of the Fifteenth Amendment. Although challenging, litigation and voluntary district compliance are moving a voting rights empowerment agenda forward for Asian Americans and Latino Americans.[16]

While the civil rights and voting rights issues that African American, Asian American, and Latino American citizens confront often overlap, and draw attention to the issues and problems of urban and suburban communities, the geographic isolation and economic, social, and political marginalization of large numbers of Native Americans often intensify their second-class citizenship and make it difficult for other Americans to recognize the extent of their disempowerment.

Native American voting empowerment is a large part of the unfinished business of the amended Voting Rights Act, and Native Americans and their progressive allies are still reaching for the exercise of citizenship rights. Native Americans have a relatively short history as citizens of the United States (they became citizens in the mid-1920s) and have been marginalized from the exercise of civil and human rights for most of the nation's history. In the 1990s the VRA enabled Native American plaintiffs, the Indian Law Resource Center, the American Civil Liberties Union (ACLU), and other allies to bring a section 2 litigation challenge to Montana's 1990 state legislative apportionment. The case, *Earl Old Person* v. *Mike Cooney*, filed in 1996 in the United States District Court for Montana, charged that districts were drawn with the discriminatory purpose of diluting Native American votes. Plaintiffs did not prevail in the district court in 1998, and they subsequently appealed to the United States Ninth District Court of Appeals.[17]

As the twenty-first century dawned, the nation went to the polls to elect a new president. For the first time in more than one hundred years the popular vote and the electoral vote were at odds. In particular, there were charges of voting irregularity and allegations of fraud. Many people of color, particularly in Florida, a state not known for easily advancing civil rights protections for people of color, came forward with personal accounts that alleged the kinds of voting rights abuses that should compel proactive engagement by the Justice Department. Thousands of election ballots were voided and ignored in counties known to be favorable to Democrats. And by almost any measure, the Supreme Court's eleventh-hour political maneuvering on whether to count thousands of disputed election ballots in Florida essentially handed the presidential election to then governor of Texas, George W. Bush.

Official hearings conducted by the United States Commission on Civil Rights have revealed that there is still much unfinished business for the Voting Rights Act. The U. S. Commission on Civil Rights (created by the Civil Rights Act of 1957) is an independent, bipartisan investigative agency charged with the responsibility to subpoena witnesses and documents, and to convene fact-finding hearings. In investigating allegations of voting system irregularities and abuses in Florida, the Commission convened hearings in Tallahassee on January 11-12, 2001 to collect testimony from registered voters who had problems voting, and in Miami on February 16, 2001 to investigate voting problems in Broward, Miami-Dade, Monroe, and Palm Beach Counties.

The Commission collected 30 hours of sworn testimony after having talked with over 100 witnesses who testified under oath, including: Governor John Ellis (Jeb) Bush, Secretary of State Katherine Harris, the Attorney General, the director of the Florida Division of Elections, the general counsel of the Florida Elections Commission, the chair and executive director of the Select Task Force on Elections Reform (set up by Governor Jeb Bush on December 14, 2000), a representative from Database Technologies, Inc. [Choicepoint], a company hired by state officials to ensure that felons did not vote on November 7, 2000, elected and appointed county officials, an administrator of the Department of Motor Vehicles, law enforcement personnel, Members of Congress, members of the Florida State Legislature, registered voters, poll workers, and legal and scholarly voting rights experts. Witnesses produced over 118,000 pages of documents, computer discs, CD-ROMS, and tapes of data.[18]

The Commission' s inquiry sought to investigate numerous allegations. For instance, in Miami the Commission explored allegations that: "... the state failed to provide adequate training to its poll workers and committed inadequate funds to voter education.... .persons were improperly purged from voter roles due to erroneous reports of felony convictions; voter lists did not include names of persons who had registered; properly filed voter registrations were processed too late for names to appear on voter rolls; polling places were closed early; polling places were removed without notice; some ballots were defective and confusing; officials failed to provide language assistance as requested; and, officials failed to provide access to the polls for persons with disabilities."[19] A number of older Americans and Americans with disabilities also provided personal testimonies regarding voting rights irregularities and abuses.

The Commission also asked questions to "... uncover who made the critical decisions regarding resource allocations for Election Day activities, why were these decisions made and what specific impact these decisions had on distinct communities."

Voicing his concern about the voting rights problems in the state, Florida Governor Jeb Bush addressed the opening session of the 2001 Florida state legislature by calling for the approval of new technology for recording votes. In response to the governor's comments, Commission chairperson, Mary Frances Berry expressed concern that an array of voting rights problems require focused intervention and resolution.[20] Specifically, the Commission has determined that there have been section 2 violations. The "Status Report on Probe of Election Practices in Florida During the 2000 Presidential Election," finds "voter disenfranchisement appears to be at the heart of the issue," and offered evidence of the following problems:

- Key officials anticipated before Election Day, that there would be an increase in levels of voter turnout based upon new voter registration figures, but did not ensure that the precincts in all communities received adequate resources to meet their needs;

- At least one unauthorized law enforcement checkpoint was set up on Election Day, resulting in complaints that were investigated by the Florida Highway Patrol and the Florida Attorney General;

- Non-felons were removed from voter egistration rolls based upon unreliable information collected in connection with sweeping, state sponsored felony purge policies;

- Many African Americans did not cast ballots because they were assigned to polling sites that did not have adequate resources to confirm voting eligibility status;

- College students and others submitted voter registration applications on a timely basis to persons and agencies responsible for transmitting the applications to the proper officials, but in many instances these applications were not processed in a timely or proper manner under the National Voter Registration Act ("motor-voter law");

- Many Jewish and elderly voters received defective and complicated ballots that may have produced "overvotes" and "undervotes;"

- Some polling places were closed early and some polling places were moved without notice;

- Old and defective election equipment was found in poor precincts;

- Many Haitian Americans and Puerto Rican voters were not provided language assistance when required and requested;

- Persons with disabilities faced accessibility difficulties at certain polling sites;

- Too few poll workers were adequately trained and too few funds were committed to voter education activities.[21]

In response to the serious nature of the voting rights irregularities and abuses revealed during its hearings, including disenfranchisement of racial and language minority citizens, older Jewish citizens, and those differently abled, on March 9th the Commission announced that it would convene a future meeting in Florida to assess what legislative changes have been enacted. The Florida legislature discussed approximately ten Senate bills regarding absentee ballots, and Senate Bill 152, "Felons' Right to Vote" proposed restoration of a felon's voting rights. On May 4, 2001, a day prior to the Commission's follow-up meeting, the Florida legislature agreed to overhaul the state's voting system. On May 9, 2001, Governor Jeb Bush signed the Florida Elections Reform Act into law.[22]

Much work remains for the Voting Rights Act in Florida. But in 2000 the governor of Florida was the president's brother and was instrumental in influencing the decisions that handed the election to George W. Bush. Most important, the VRA's enforcement mechanisms are crucial in Florida, and the rest of the nation, where retrenchment and the continuing hostility of white plaintiffs (some of whom lost elections to minority candidates) actively seek to accomplish in the courts what white racially polarized voting cannot do to undermine minority-influenced or minority-majority districts, the VRA is still the law. As of 2001 it remained to be seen whether the Bush administration's Justice Department would enforce the VRA. A bright light finally began to appear in the Supreme Court's post-*Shaw* decisions about race. In a 5-4 decision in April 2001, in *Easley* v. *Cromartie* (with Justice Stephen G. Breyer authoring the majority opinion), the Court recognized the role of race in legislative districting, thereby giving clearer guidance to state legislators and judges.[23] The Court enjoined legislators and judges to balance racial and political factors in drawing lines.

There is much unfinished business for the amended Voting Rights Act. The 2000 census brought another round of state legislative apportionment forward with concerns about the undercount of racial and language minorities.[24] Some angry white plaintiffs and conservative justices on the bench continued seeking to thwart the effectiveness with which the VRA provides for the construction of districts that promote the election of minority representatives. There are increasing numbers of legal and social science scholars who support alternative voting systems. The legal scholar Lani Guinier and others have written at length about proportional representation voting systems and their role in the governance of many of the world's other democracies, including most of western Europe, Latin America, countries of the former Soviet bloc, Israel, and South Africa. Proportional representational voting systems remedy minority and women vote dilution, are race-neutral, and allow political or ideological minorities to elect candidates to public office.[25]

Proportional representation has been tried as an alternative to our present voting rights dilemmas. Some form of proportional representation, notably cumulative voting (Peoria, Illinois; Chilton County, Alabama), preference voting (Cambridge, Massachusetts), and limited voting, is already being used in a number of U.S. cities and counties,[26] and in the decades since enactment of the VRA the range of professionals who have served as expert witnesses now includes those who traditionally were called to testify before the courts, as well as historians and other social scientists. Lastly, in addition to legal databases that facilitate one's ability to examine legal decisions, and law and political science periodicals, there is a huge volume of voting rights scholarship and debate.

Voting, the guardian of every *right*, is and will continue to be the key that unlocks access to the exercise of the rights, privileges, and immunities that the state offers its citizens. From participation in electoral politics, to an interface with state governance and beyond, to actualizing greater, more significant levels of participation in the economic, social, and cultural life of the nation, voting is the right that must be claimed and exercised. Continuing into the twenty-first century, the state must be persistent in affording minority vote dilution protections for long-deprived and marginalized racial and language minorities. State interest in and protection and enforcement of the right to vote for racial and language minorities and for women must be furthered as a matter of effective democratic governance. The Voting Rights Act must be the vehicle that ensures that the civil rights progresses of the twentieth century's Reconstruction era (1960s) are not ambushed, stymied, and put on hold, as were those of the nineteenth century's Reconstruction era.

The legacy of the Voting Rights Act of 1965 has to be weighed against the backdrop of all that has happened thus far. The accumulation of the meaning of slavery and the legal, political, and social distance to emancipation; physical repression and administrative disenfranchisement; skin-color- and language-based exclusion; segregation and the denial of equality; civil rights protests; Southern resistance; and relative federal inaction produced the Voting Rights Act. Few prevented the act's effectiveness in enforcing the right to vote and, until the early 1990s, in promoting the proportional representation of minorities and women in public office.

The act remains the most effective legislative vehicle ever enacted for redistributing electoral and political power. Its beneficiaries are all Americans, including people of color, women, and smaller political parties. It is vitally important that all Americans become more interested in the issues of voter participation and representation. The first struggle involved eliminating the restrictive qualifications to the exercise of the franchise. Next came passage and enforcement of the right to vote for politically marginalized groups, including people of color, women, the disabled, language minorities, and young people. But the work, a labor of love, is far from done. The most important political challenge at the beginning of the twenty-first century is ensuring that people of color, women, and the poor are protected from electoral subterfuge, vote dilution, and racially polarized voting.

Essentially, in the final analysis what we are really talking about is whether we will take the cultural high ground, or the path less traveled. We have choices, a series of decisions to make about whether we enter the twenty-first century holding on to vestiges of the eighteenth century, a time when selective democracy prevailed and people of color struggled to be regarded as humans while women were *persona non grata* under the law. Implementation of the Fifteenth Amendment and its companion legislation, the Voting Rights Act, is about the protection and enforcement of voting rights; *the guardian of rights*. It is also about ensuring that the exercise of voting rights produces representational government for people of color, women, and smaller political parties. As we begin a new century we should prepare ourselves to understand and explore what changes our modern multiethnic, multicultural society needs in order to secure proportionate influence for all in the nation's federal, state, and local voting systems.

***

Between 1990 and 2000, the Voting Rights Act of 1965 continued transforming the nation's political terrain. By 1990, state apportionment following the 1990 Census occupied a central place in every concern about the construction of voting systems. Judges as well as state legislators were deeply involved in voting rights issues, particularly, redistricting. Race is inextricable from the evolution of American society, and so, race has been an essential element in the varied discourses, choices, decisions, and actions affecting voting rights. This volume's documents reflect the wide ranging, yet encompassing range of scholarship and commentary that enforcement of the Voting Rights Act has produced in the decade of the 1990s.

Notes

[1] Statement by Florida Democratic state representative Corrine Brown in Kenneth Cooper, "Dismantling Black Political Power," *Emerge*, April 1994, 34.

[2] See data from reports and files of the Joint Center for Political and Economic Studies, including *Black Elected Officials: A National Roster, 1993* (Washington, D.C.: Joint Center for Political and Economic Studies Press, 1994), and *Elected and Appointed Black Judges in the United States 1991* (Washington, D.C.: Joint Center for Political and Economic Studies and the Judicial Council of the National Bar Association).

[3] See *Garza* v. *County of Los Angeles Board of Supervisors*, 756 F. Supp. 1298 (C. D. Cal. 1990).

[4] See *Presley* v. *Etowah County Commission*, 112 S. Ct. 820 (1992).

[5] See *Voinovich* v. *Quilter*, 113 S. Ct. 1149 (1993).

[6] See *Shaw* v. *Reno*, 113 S. Ct. 2816 (1993).

[7] Note that bizarreness as well as beauty exists in the eye of the beholder. There are many districts across the country that are oddly shaped, being neither compact nor adhering to community boundaries. See Brenda Wright, "The Myths Behind *Shaw* v. *Reno*, Committee Report, 30th Anniversary Edition, 1963–1993," *Lawyer's Committee on Civil Rights Under Law* 5, nos. 5 and 6.

[8] See A. Leon Higginbotham Jr., Gregory A. Clarick, and Marcella David, "Shaw v. Reno: A Mirage of Good Intentions with Devastating Racial Consequences," *Fordham Law Review* 62, no. 6 (April 1994): 1593–1659.

[9] See *Plessy* v. *Ferguson*, 163 U.S. 537 (1896) (Harlan, J., dissenting).

[10] See Brenda Wright, "Reflections and Projections," in *Redistricting and Minority Representation: Learning from the Past, Preparing for the Future*, edited by David A. Bositis (Lanham, Md.: University Press of America, 1998), and David O'Brien, *Supreme Court Watch 1995: Highlights of the 1993–1995 Terms, Preview of the 1995–1996 Term* (New York: W. W. Norton & Co., 1996).

[11] *Holder* v. *Hall*, 114 S. Ct. 2581 (Ga., 1994); *Johnson* v. *DeGrandy*, 114 S. Ct. 2647 (Fla., 1994); *Miller* v. *Johnson*, 115 S. Ct. 2475 (Ga., 1995); *Hays* v. *Louisiana*, 839 F. Supp. 118 (W.D. La. 1993) (La., 1995); *Shaw* v. *Hunt*, 116 S. Ct. 1895, 1905 (1996); *Bush* v. *Vera*, 116 S. Ct. 1941 (Tex., 1996); *Abrams* v. *Johnson*, 117 S. Ct. 1925 (1997); *Hunt* v. *Cromartie*, 119 S. Ct. __ (N.C., 1999). See Bernard Grofman, ed., *Race and Redistricting in the 1990s* (New York: Agathon Press, 1998); J. Morgan Kousser, *Colorblind Injustice: Minority Voting Rights and the Undoing of the Second Reconstruction* (Chapel Hill: University of North Carolina Press, 1999); Bernard Grofman and Chandler Davidson, eds., *Controversies in Minority Voting: The Voting Rights Act in Perspective* (Washington, D.C.: Brookings Institution, 1992); Samuel Issacharoff, Pamela S. Karlan, and Richard H. Pildes, *The Law of Democracy: Legal Structure of the Political Process* (Westbury, N.Y.: The Foundation Press, 1998); and Chandler Davidson and Bernard Grofman, eds., *Quiet Revolution in the South: The Impact of the Voting Rights Act, 1965–1990* (Princeton, N.J.: Princeton University Press, 1994). Also see Melissa E. Austin, "Casenotes: *Shaw* v. *Reno*: A Beginning for Color-Blind Reapportionment," *George Mason Independent Law Review* (Summer 1994); Thomas C. Goldstein, "Unpacking and Applying *Shaw* v. *Reno*," *American University Law Review* (Spring 1994); Pamela S. Karlan, "Just Politics? Five Not So Easy Pieces of the 1995 Term," *Houston Law Review* (1997); Tricia Ann Martinez, "Comment: When Appearance Matters: Reapportionment Under the Voting Rights Act and *Shaw* v. *Reno*," *Louisiana Law Review* (May 1994); Paula D. McClain and Joseph Stewart Jr., "The Voting Rights Act After *Shaw* v. *Reno*," *PS: Political Science & Politics* 28, no. 1 (March 1995); Laughlin McDonald, "Can Minority Voting Rights Survive *Miller* v. *Johnson*?" *Michigan Journal Race & Law* 119 (1996); A. Leon Higginbotham Jr., "Brief: *United States* v. *Hays*: Brief for the Congressional Black Caucus as *Amicus Curiae* in Support of Appellants," *Howard Law Journal* (1995); Frank R. Parker, "Essay: Factual Errors and Chilling Consequences: A Critique of *Shaw* v. *Reno* and *Miller* v. *Johnson*," *Cumberland Law Review* (1996); and Brenda Wright, "*Johnson* v. *DeGrandy*: Mixed Messages on Equal Electoral Opportunity Under Section 2 of the Voting Rights Act," *District of Columbia Law Review* (Spring 1995).

[12] See Public Law 103-31, 103rd Congress, May 20, 1993, 107 *STAT.* 77–89.

[13] See "Voter Registration Not Working, Survey Says," *New York Times Metro*, October 1, 1995, and a report prepared for the National Motor Voter Coalition (League of Women Voters of the United States, NAACP, AFL-CIO, AFSCME, Human SERVE, Common Cause, People for the American Way, Disabled & Able to Vote, Lawyers Committee for Civil Rights Under Law, Mexican American Legal Defense & Education Fund, Association of Community Organizations for Reform Now/ACORN), "The National Voter Registration Act: The First Six Months of 1995, a Report Prepared by Human SERVE, with the assistance of ACORN," New York, August 1995.

[14] For example, see the civil action suit brought by Mississippi residents, *Thomas Young, Richard L. Gardner, Eleanor Faye Smith, Rims Barber, et al.* v. *Governor Kirk Fordice et al.*, heard in the United States District Court, Southern District of Mississippi, Jackson Division, March 2, 1995, and *Voting Rights Coalition et al.* v. *Governor Pete Wilson et al.*, heard in the United States District Court, Northern District of California, San Francisco, January 27, 1995.

[15] See Marc Mauer, *Race to Incarcerate* (New York: New Press, 1999), and the excellent work of the Sentencing Project.

[16] In the tradition established by the legal and civil rights advocacy work of the NAACP Legal Defense and Educational Fund, the Asian American Legal Defense and Education Fund, the Puerto Rican Legal Defense and Education Fund, and the Mexican American Legal Defense and Educational Fund are persistent legal advocates on behalf of constitutional enfranchisement and political empowerment for their respective communities.

[17] See Christopher Coates, Special Litigation Counsel, Voting Section, Civil Rights Division, U.S. Department of Justice, "An Overview of Section 2 Case Law," a report prepared for the Lawyers Committee for Civil Rights Under Law Conference, November 19–20, 1999.

[18] See *Draft Staff Report on Voting Irregularities in Florida During the 2000 Presidential Election*. June 2001, available online at http://www.usccr.gov/vote2000/stdraft/main.htm. Also, note that at the March 9th hearing, the Commission discussed a nationwide (including all 50 states and the District of Columbia) survey of election procedure, undertaken with the assistance of State Advisory Committees and the Commission's regional representatives.

[19] See Press Releases on February 6, 2001 -"U.S. Civil Rights Commission Emphasizes Public Testimony in Continuing Examination of Florida Voting Problems," and on March 9, 2001 -"U.S. Commission on Civil Rights Concludes that 'No Count" Is Real Issue in Florida Vote."

[20] See "Letter to Governor Bush from Chairperson Mary Frances Berry," March 8, 2001.

[21] See U.S. Commission on Civil Rights. *Status Report on Probe of Election Practices in Florida During the 2000 Presidential Election.* March 9, 2001.

[22] See Epilogue, *Draft Staff Report on Voting Irregularities in Florida During the 2000 Presidential Election.* June 2001.

[23] The Court reversed the lower-court ruling and upheld a redrawing of the Twelfth Congressional District in North Carolina. Seemingly, considerations of North Carolina's Twelfth Congressional District started with *Shaw* v. *Reno* (1993) and have come full circle with this ruling.

[19] See Benjamin E. Griffith, ed., *Census 2000: Considerations and Strategies for State and Local Government* (Chicago: American Bar Association, 2000), and "Special Voting Rights Review: Fair Representation in the 2000s," *Southern Changes* 22, no. 4 (Winter 2000).

[20] See Lani Guinier, *The Tyranny of the Majority: Fundamental Fairness in Representative Democracy* (New York: Free Press, 1994).

[21] See "Voting and Democracy Report, 1993 & 1995: A Report of the Center for Voting and Democracy" (Washington, D.C.: Center for Voting and Democracy, 1997); also see legislation proposed by Democratic congresswoman Cynthia McKinney (Ga.), Voter's Choice Act, H.R. 3068, 105th Congress, 1st Session, Introduced to the House on November 13, 1997. See Web site for Center for Voting and Democracy for additional sources of information.

Suggestions for Further Reading

Report

U.S. Department of Justice, Civil Rights Division. *Civil Rights Division Journal.* 1st ed. (December 1992).

Books

Abraham, Henry J., and Barbara A. Perry. *Freedom and the Court: Civil Rights & Liberties in the United States.* New York: Oxford University Press, 1994.

Arrington, Karen McGill, and William L. Taylor, eds. *Voting Rights in America.* Washington, D.C.: Leadership Conference Education Fund/Joint Center for Political and Economic Studies, 1992.

Ball, Howard. *Compromised Compliance: Implementation of the 1965 Voting Rights Act.* Westport, Conn.: Greenwood Press, 1992.

Bositis, David A. *Black Elected Officials: A Statistical Summary, 1993–1997.* Washington, D.C.: Joint Center for Political and Economic Studies, 1998.

———, ed. *Redistricting and Minority Representation: Learning from the Past, Preparing for the Future.* Washington, D.C.: Joint Center for Political and Economic Studies, 1998.

Calvi, James V., and Susan Coleman. *Cases in Constitutional Law: Summaries and Critiques.* Englewood Cliffs, N.J.: Prentice Hall, 1994.

Canon, David T. *Race, Redistricting, and Representation: The Unintended Consequences of Black Majority Districts.* Chicago: University of Chicago Press, 1999.

Carson, Clayborne, David J. Garrow, Gerald Gill, Vincent Harding, and Darlene Clark Hine, eds. *The Eyes on the Prize Civil Rights Reader: Documents, Speeches, and Firsthand Accounts from the Black Freedom Struggle, 1954–1990.* New York: Penguin Books, 1991.

The Center for Voting and Democracy. *Voting & Democracy Report 1995.* Washington, D.C. (1997).

Daniels, Lee A., ed. *The State of Black America 1998.* National Urban League, 1998.

Davidson, Chandler, and Bernard Grofman, eds. *Quiet Revolution in the South: The Impact of the Voting Rights Act, 1965–1990.* Princeton, N.J.: Princeton University Press, 1994.

Davis, James F. *Who Is Black?* University Park: Pennsylvania State University Press, 1991.

Egerton, John. *Speak Now Against the Day: The Generation Before the Civil Rights Movement in the South.* Chapel Hill: University of North Carolina Press, 1994.

Finkelman, Paul, ed. *Race, Law, and American History, 1700–1990.* Vol. 1, *African Americans and the Law.* New York: Garland, 1992.

———. *Race, Law, and American History, 1700–1990*. Vol. 6, *African Americans and the Right to Vote*. New York: Garland, 1992.

———. *Race, Law, and American History, 1700–1990*. Vol. 4, *The Age of Jim Crow: Segregation from the End of Reconstruction to the Great Depression*. New York: Garland, 1992.

———. *Race, Law, and American History, 1700–1990*. Vol. 5, *The Era of Integration and Civil Rights, 1930–1990*. New York: Garland, 1992.

Fisher, Louis. *American Constitutional Law* Vol. 2, *Constitutional Rights: Civil Rights and Civil Liberties*. New York: McGraw-Hill, 1990.

Franklin, John Hope, and Genna Rae McNeil, eds. *African Americans and the Living Constitution*. Washington, D.C.: Smithsonian Institution Press, 1995.

Graham, Hugh Davis. *Civil Rights and the Presidency: Race and Gender in American Politics, 1960–1972*. New York: Oxford University Press, 1992.

———, ed. *Civil Rights in the United States*. University Park: Pennsylvania State University Press, 1994.

Gray, Fred D. *Bus Ride to Justice*. Montgomery, Ala.: Black Belt Press, 1995.

Greenberg, Jack. Crusaders in the Court: How a Dedicated Band of Lawyers Fought for the Civil Rights Revolution. New York: Basic Books, 1994.

Griffith, Benjamin E., ed. Census 2000: Considerations and Strategies for State and Local Government. Chicago: American Bar Association, 2000.

Grofman, Bernard, ed. *Race and Redistricting in the 1990s*. New York: Agathon Press, 1998.

Grofman, Bernard, and Chandler Davidson, eds. *Controversies in Minority Voting: The Voting Rights Act in Perspective*. Washington, D.C.: Brookings Institute, 1992.

Guinier, Lani. *The Tyranny of the Majority: Fundamental Fairness in Representative Democracy*. New York: Free Press, 1994.

Hall, Kermit L., *The Magic Mirror: Law in American History*. New York: Oxford University Press, 1989.

———, ed. *Major Problems in American Constitutional History*. Vol. 2, *From 1870 to the Present*. Lexington, Mass.: D. C. Heath and Company, 1992.

Hall, Kermit L., William M. Wiecek, and Paul Finkelman. *American Legal History: Cases and Materials*. New York: Oxford University Press, 1991.

Hampton, Henry, and Steve Fayer. *Voices of Freedom*. New York: Bantam Books, 1990.

Higginbotham, A. Leon. *In the Matter of Color: Race & The American Legal Process: The Colonial Period*. New York: Oxford University Press, 1980.

———. *Shades of Freedom: Racial Politics and Presumptions of the American Legal Process*. New York: Oxford University Press, 1996.

Hurtado, Albert L., and Peter Iverson, eds. *Major Problems in American Indian History*. Lexington, Mass.: D. C. Heath and Company, 1994.

Issacharoff, Samuel, Pamela S. Karlan, and Richard H. Pildes. *The Law of Democracy: Legal Structure of the Political Process*. New York: The Foundation Press, 1998.

Jaynes, Gerald David, and Robin M. Williams Jr., eds. *A Common Destiny: Blacks and American Society*. Washington, D.C.: National Academy Press, 1989.

Kairys, David, ed. *The Politics of Law: A Progressive Critique*. New York: Pantheon Books, 1990.

Kousser, Morgan J. *Colorblind Injustice: Minority Voting Rights and the Undoing of the Second Reconstruction*. Chapel Hill: University of North Carolina Press, 1999.

Lawson, Steven F. *Black Ballots: Voting Rights in the South, 1944–1969*. New York: Columbia University Press, 1976.

Levy, Peter B., ed. *Let Freedom Ring: A Documentary History of the Modern Civil Rights Movement*. New York: Praeger, 1992.

Lopez, Ian F. Haney. *White by Law*. New York: New York University Press, 1996.

Lubiano, Wahneema, ed. *The House That Race Built*. New York: Pantheon Books, 1997.

National Civic League. *Communities & the Voting Rights Act: A Guide to Compliance in These Changing Times*. Denver, Colo., 1996.

Nieman, Donald G. *Promises to Keep: African-Americans and the Constitutional Order, 1776 to the Present*. New York: Oxford University Press, 1991.

1994/1995/1996 Directory of African American State Legislators. National Black Caucus of State Legislators, March 1994.

O'Brien, David M. *Constitutional Law and Politics*. Vol. 1, *Struggles for Power and Governmental Accountability*. New York: W. W. Norton & Company, 1995.

———. *Constitutional Law and Politics.* Vol. 2, *Civil Rights and Civil Liberties.* New York: W. W. Norton & Company, 1995.

———. *Supreme Court Watch 1995.* New York: W. W. Norton & Company, 1996.

Rogers, Donald W., ed. *Voting and the Spirit of American Democracy: Essays on the History of Voting and Voting Rights in America.* Urbana and Chicago: University of Illinois Press, 1992.

Tate, Katherine. *From Protest to Politics: The New Black Voters in American Elections.* Enl. ed. New York: Russell Sage Foundation, 1994.

Terborg-Penn, Rosalyn. *African American Women in the Struggle for the Vote, 1850–1920.* Bloomington: Indiana University Press, 1998.

Urofsky, Melvin I. *The Continuity of Change: The Supreme Court and Individual Liberties, 1953–1986.* Belmont, Calif.: Wadsworth Publishing Company, 1991.

Vargas, Zaragosa, ed. *Major Problems in Mexican American History.* Boston: Houghton Mifflin, 1999.

Articles

Aleinikoff, Alexander T. and Samuel Issacharoff. "Symposium: The Future of Voting Rights After *Shaw* v. *Reno*: Race and Redistricting: Drawing Constitutional Lines After *Shaw* v. *Reno*." 92 *Michigan Law Review* 588, December, 1993.

Alston, Chuck. "Democrats Court Minority to Counter GOP's Pit." *Congressional Quarterly Weekly Report* 49 (1991): 1103–5.

American Civil Liberties Union. "Reaffirmation or Requiem for the Voting Rights Act? The Court Will Decide: A Public Policy Alert." Medford, NY: American Civil Liberties Union, May, 1995.

Association of Community Organizations for Reform Now (ACORN) & Project Vote. "Cheating Democracy: Discrimination in the Implementation of Motor Voter Laws, An Investigative Report." (ACORN) & Project Vote, December, 1995.

Barron, Kathleen L. "Colorblind Lines: *Shaw* v. *Reno* and the Demise of Majority-Minority Districts." 31 *Houston Law Review* 889, Fall, 1994.

Blacksher, James U. "Dred Scott's Unwon Freedom: The Redistricting Cases As Badges of Slavery." 39 *Howard Law Journal* 633, Spring, 1996.

Blumstein, James F. "Symposium: Voting Rights after *Shaw* v. *Reno*: Racial Gerrymandering and Vote Dilution: *Shaw* v. *Reno* in Doctrinal Context." 26 *Rutgers Law Journal* 517, Spring, 1995.

Bositis, David A. "Redistricting and Representation: The Creation of Majority-Minority Districts and the Evolving Party System in the South." *Joint Center for Political and Economic Studies* (1995).

Cook, Rhodes. "Map-Drawers Must Toe the Line in Upcoming Redistricting." *Congressional Quarterly Weekly Report* 48 (September 1, 1990): 2786–94.

Darcy, R., Charles D. Hadley, and Jason F. Kirksey. "Election Systems and the Representation of Black Women in American State Legislatures." *Women & Politics* (1993): 73–89.

Darling, Marsha J. Tyson. "African American Women State Legislators in the South." In *Women and Elective Political Office: Past, Present, and Future,* edited by Sue Thomas and Clyde Wilcox. New York: Oxford University Press, 1997.

———. "What's Oral History Got to Do with Understanding Voting Rights? Reflections on the Methodology of the Voting Rights Act Documentation Project." In *HUArchivesNet,* edited by Ronald Walters. November 1999.

Day, Gary. "Notes: The Voting Rights Act of 1965: All Bark, No Bite?" 12 *St. John's Journal of Legal Commentary* 756, Summer, 1997

de la Garza, Rodolpho O. and Louis DeSipio. "Overview: the Link Between Individuals and Electoral Institutions in Five Latino Neighborhoods," in *Barrio Ballots: Latino Politics in the 1990 Elections,* edited by de la Garza, et. al. Boulder: CO: Westview Press, 1994.

Gelman, Andrew and Gary King. "Enhancing Democracy Through Legislative Redistricting." 88 *American Political Science Review* 541, September, 1994.

Goldstein, Thomas C. "Unpacking and Applying *Shaw* v. *Reno*." 43 *American University Law Review* 1135, Spring, 1994.

Grofman, Bernard and Lisa Handley. "1990s Issues in Voting Rights." 65 *Mississippi Law Journal* 205, Winter, 1995.

Guinier, Lani. "The Triumph of Tokenism: The Voting Rights Act and the Theory of Black Electoral Success." 89 *Michigan Law Review* 1077, March, 1991.

Guinier, Lani. "No Two Seats: The Elusive Quest for Political Equality." 77 *Virginia Law Review* 1413,

November, 1991.
Halpin, Jr., Stanley A. "Waves and Backwashes in Voting Rights Law: Recognition Without Implementation of a New Principle Opposing Gerrymandering." 22 *Southern University Law Review* 255, Winter, 1995.
Higginbotham, Jr. Leon A. "BRIEF: *United States* v. *Hays*: Brief for the Congressional Black Caucus as *Amicus Curiae* in Support of Appellants." 38 *Howard University Law Journal* 665, Summer, 1995.
Hill, Kevin A. "Does the Creation of Majority Black Districts Aid Republicans? An Analysis of the 1992 Congressional Elections in Eight Southern States." *Journal of Politics* 57, no. 2 (May 1995): 384–401.
Issacharoff, Samuel. "Groups and the Right to Vote." 44 *Emory Law Journal* 869, Summer, 1995.
Isaacharoff, Samuel. "Supreme Court Destabilization of Single-Member Districts." 205 *University of Chicago Legal Forum*,1995.
Issacharoff, Samuel. "Polarized Voting and the Political Process: The Transformation of Voting Rights Jurisprudence." *Michigan Law Review* 90 (June 1992): 1833–91.
Johnson, Marcia. "The Systematic Denial of the Right to Vote to America's Minorities." 11 *Harvard BlackLetter Journal* 61, 1994.
Kaplan, Dave and Phil Duncan. "Voting Rights v. Redistricting." *Congressional Quarterly Weekly Report*, Oct. 2, 1993, v51, n39, p2646.
Karlan, Pamela S. "Just Politics? Five Not So Easy Pieces of the 1995 Term." 34 *Houston Law Review* 289, Summer, 1997.
Kousser, J. Morgan. "Symposium: Voting Rights after *Shaw* v. *Reno*: *Shaw* v. *Reno* and the Real World of Redistricting and Representation." 26 *Rutgers Law Journal* 625, Spring, 1995.
Malone, Stephen J. "Recognizing Communities of Interest in a Legislative Apportionment Plan." *Virginia Law Review Association* (1997).
Martinez, Tricia Ann. "When Appearances Matters: Reapportionment Under the Voting Rights Act." 54 *Louisiana Law Review* 1335, May, 1994.
McCain, Paula D. "W(h)ither the Voting Rights Act after *Shaw* v. *Reno*: Advancing to the Past?" ." *PS: Political Science & Politics*, v28, n1, p47, March, 1995.
McCrary, Peyton. "The Dynamics of Minority Vote Dilution: The Case of Augusta, Georgia, 1945–1986." *Journal of Urban History* 25, no. 2 (January 1999): 199–225.
McDonald, Laughlin. "Racial Fairness— Why Shouldn't It Apply to Section 5 of the Voting Rights Act?" *Stetson Law Review* 21 (1992): 847–69.
McDonald, Laughlin. "Can Minority Voting Rights Survive *Miller* v. *Johnson*." 1 *Michigan Journal of Race & Law* 119, Winter, 1996.
McDowell, James L. "Law Making: 'One Person, One Vote' and the Decline of Community." 23 *Legal Studies Forum* 131, 1999.
Mulroy, Steven J. "The Way Out: A Legal Standard for Imposing Alternative Electoral Systems as Voting Rights Remedies." 33 *Harvard Civil Rights-Civil Liberties Law Review* 333, Summer, 1998.
Mulroy, Steven J. "Alternative Ways Out: A Remedial Road Map for the Use of Alternative Electoral Systems as Voting Rights Act Remedies." 77 *North Carolina Law Review* 1867, June, 1999.
Nixon, Ron. "Plantation Politics?" *Southern Exposure* (Spring 1995): 27–39.
Parker, Frank R. "Minority Voting Rights Have Strong Legal Backing Now." *Nation's Cities Weekly*, January 28, 1991, 8.
Parker, Frank R. "*Shaw* v. *Reno*: A Constitutional Setback for Minority Representation." *PS: Political Science & Politics*, v28, n1, p47, March, 1995
Parker, Frank R. "The Damaging Consequences of the Rehnquist Court's Commitment to Color Blindness Versus Racial Justice." *American University Law Review*, 45, 763, 1996.
Pawa, Matt. "When the Supreme Court Restricts Constitutional Rights, Can Congress Save Us? An Examination of Section 5 of the Fourteenth Amendment." *University of Pennsylvania Law Review* 141 (1992/1993): 1029–1101.
Pildes, Richard H. "Symposium: Group Conflict and the Constitution: Race, Sexuality, and Religion." 106 *Yale Law Journal* 2505, June, 1997.
Pildes, Richard H. and Richard G. Niemi. "Expressive Harms, 'Bizarre Districts,' and Voting Rights: Evaluating Election-District Appearances After *Shaw* v. *Reno*." 92 *Michigan Law Review* 483, December, 1993.

Pildes, Richard H. and Kristen A. Donoghue. "Cumulative Voting in the United States." 241 *University of Chicago Legal Forum*, 1995.
Pildes, Richard H. "Principled Limitations on Racial and Partisan Redistricting." *Symposium Group Conflict and the Constitution: Race, Sexuality, and Religion, Yale Law Journal* (June 1997).
PS: Political Science & Politics, v28, n1, p47, March, 1995.
Polsby, Daniel D. and Robet D. Popper. "Symposium: The Future of Voting Rights After *Shaw* v. *Reno*: Ugly: An Inquiry into the Problem of Racial Gerrymandering under the Voting Rights Act." 92 *Michigan Law Review* 652, December, 1993.
Raskin, Jamin B. "From 'Colorblind' White Supremacy to American Multiculturalism."19 *Harvard Journal of Law & Public Policy* 743, 1996.
Raskin, Jamin B. "The Supreme Court's Racial Double Standard in Redistricting: Unequal Protection in Politics and the Scholarship that Defends It." *Journal of Law & Politics*, 14, 591, Fall, 1998.
Rose, Marta. "Recent Decision: Civil Rights— Race Obliviousness and the Invisibility of Whiteness: The Court's Construction of Race— *Miller* v. *Johnson*, 115 S. Ct. 2475 (1995)." *Temple Law Review* (Winter 1996).
Rosen, Jeffrey. "Gerrymandered." *New Republic*, Oct. 25, 1993, v209, n17 p12.
Sebold, Edward J. "Applying Section 2 of the Voting Rights Act to Single-Member Offices." 88 *Michigan Law Review* 2199, June, 1990
Sheperd, Jay N. "Abridge Too Far: Racial Gerrymandering, the Fifteenth Amendment, and *Shaw* v. *Reno*." 14 *Boston College Third World Law Journal* 337, Summer, 1994.
Still, Edward. "Alternative Electoral Systems as Voting Rights Remedies." Washington, DC: Center for Voting and Democracy, 1995.
Swain, Carol M. "Commentary: Not 'Wrongful' by Any Means: The Court's Decisions in the Redistricting." *Houston Law Review* (Summer 1997).
Texas Trailblazer Series. Houston: Texas Trailblazer Preservation Association & Texas Commerce Bank, June 1996.
"Voting Rights Review." Atlanta: Southern Regional Council, 1990-2000.
Wright, Brenda. "Symposium: The Bench and the Ballot: Applying the Protections of the Voting Rights Act to Judicial Elections." 19 *Florida State University Law Review* 669, Winter, 1992.
Zaragoza, Nancy C. "Participation Without Representation: The Meaning of the Right to Vote After *Presley* v. *Etowah County Commission*." 67 *Washington Law Review* 1023, October, 1992.

Symposiums

"Voting Rights Act Symposium: 25th Anniversary." Smithsonian Institution and American University. Washington, D.C., April 1990.
"Civil Rights 2000: Redefining the Agenda. NAACP Legal Defense and Educational Fund." Howard Law Journal Symposium, Washington, D.C., February 8–9, 1995.
"Symposium: Voting Rights After *Shaw* v. *Reno*." *PS: Political Science and Politics* 28, no. 1 (March 1995): 24–55.
Rutgers University School of Law Symposium 1995.
"Voting Rights Act 30th Anniversary Conference: The Future of Minority Representation." Lawyers Committee for Civil Rights Under Law and Southern Regional Council. New Orleans, October 27–29, 1995.
"The African American and the Crisis in Voting Rights: Views from the Inside." Proceedings of the Fifth Symposium on African American Voting Rights. Johnson C. Smith University, July 5–6, 1996.
"A New Framework for Redistricting: The Prospects for Minority Representation Post-Miller Conference." Joint Center for Political and Economic Studies. Washington, D.C., January 9, 1997.
"Census 2000, Redistricting, and Minority Scholars: Linking the Academy to the Policy Process. Report of a Conference." Williams College, June 24–27, 1999.
"Voting Rights Conference." Lawyers Committee for Civil Rights Under Law and American University Washington College of Law. Washington, D.C., November 19–20, 1999.
"Securing the Promise of Democracy: Linking Race, Scholarship, Policy, and Threats to Empowerment." Minority Scholars Conference, North Carolina Central University Law School, June 25–27, 2000.

Race, Voting and Redistricting, and the Constitution

Sources and Explorations on the Fifteenth Amendment

Volume 3

Alternative Redistricting, Registering, and Voting Systems

COVER STORY

Map-Drawers Must Toe the Line In Upcoming Redistricting

Recent rulings place limits on gerrymandering, insist on representation for minorities

Overview

This review of legal issues and rulings that have shaped the current world of redistricting is another element in Congressional Quarterly's continuing coverage of the 1990 round of remapping. Included in this package is a story highlighting which states may gain or lose seats in reapportionment *(p. 2793)*

Additional background on the census undercount issue appears on Weekly Report pp. 1905, 1337-1341, 1215, 852-853, 776 and 254. Additional stories on minority districts appear on pp. 2605, 2462, 1740, 1739, 282 and 202. A comprehensive survey of the anticipated effect of 1990 legislative elections on redistricting appeared on 1989 Weekly Report pp. 2971-3004. A discussion of the notion of expanding the size of the House is on p. 2914 of the 1989 Weekly Report.

As the myriad players in the coming round of redistricting dust off their maps, plug in their computers and pore over preliminary 1990 population figures, they will also have to acquaint themselves with a legal landscape substantially altered since 1980.

For most of the nation's political community, the process of redrawing congressional district lines is a once-in-a-decade activity. But for the courts, it is an ongoing preoccupation. Judges have become the not-so-silent partners of the redistricting process.

In the past decade, the courts have underscored the "one-person, one-vote" doctrine by which states must divide their population equally among districts.

They have sharply increased the pressure on state mapmakers to assure minority representation, even to the brink of mandating the election of minorities.

Moreover, the Supreme Court has opened the door to suits alleging partisan gerrymandering — the politically one-sided, often tortured, line drawing that clearly gives one party an advantage over the other.

And weaving through the issues of population, race and political partisanship in the 1990s are questions regarding the accuracy of the 1990 census itself.

A new legal debate now focuses on whether the tally should be statistically adjusted to compensate for an anticipated minority undercount.

For anyone contemplating a congressional candidacy — or interested in the composition of Congress in the 1990s — these issues are far from academic concerns.

By Rhodes Cook

Uncertainties Abound

After any redistricting process, the first election spells electoral opportunity for parties and individuals waiting to make their move.

The stakes are even higher if such an election coincides with a presidential campaign, as in 1992.

The exact shape and composition of each district dictates candidates' strategy and tactics. So it can be excruciating enough for office-seekers to wait on legislatures and governors to work out their redistricting differences. The added round of recourse to the courts means, at minimum, a longer wait. Such extended uncertainty becomes one more obstacle for would-be candidates.

Minority candidates, for example, may begin a campaign by appealing across racial lines, only to learn that the district they are seeking will consist almost entirely of minority voters.

In many states, candidates may go well into the election year itself still wondering whether a given district will be hospitable to them — or even whether it will continue to exist.

No one is quite sure at this point how the courts will approach redistricting litigation in the 1990s. After a quarter-century of Supreme Court involvement in the issues of population equality and minority representation, the court would seem to be unable to disengage itself — even if it wanted to.

At the same time, the high court may be less eager than in the past to break new ground, particularly with the recent retirement of Justice William J. Brennan Jr.

Probably more than any other member, Brennan pushed the court into what Justice Felix Frankfurter (1939-62) warned was the "political thicket" of reapportionment and redistricting.

Brennan wrote the majority opinion in *Baker v. Carr*, the landmark 1962 case that brought the court into redistricting, as well as several other cases that subsequently established and tightened the interpretation of the one-person, one-vote doctrine.

His rulings were controversial, since they often forced states to split historical geographic entities such as cities and counties between districts in order to achieve the strict population equality the court now requires.

Yet even before Brennan announced his retirement in July, there were signs that the Supreme Court was becoming more selective in the cases it would hear, to the point of being described as a "take your problems elsewhere" court.

But that does not necessarily imply less legal action elsewhere. It could mean more running room for state and lower federal courts. And it may even provide an opening for Congress, if it wants one, to address aspects of redistricting law.

Mapping Los Angeles County

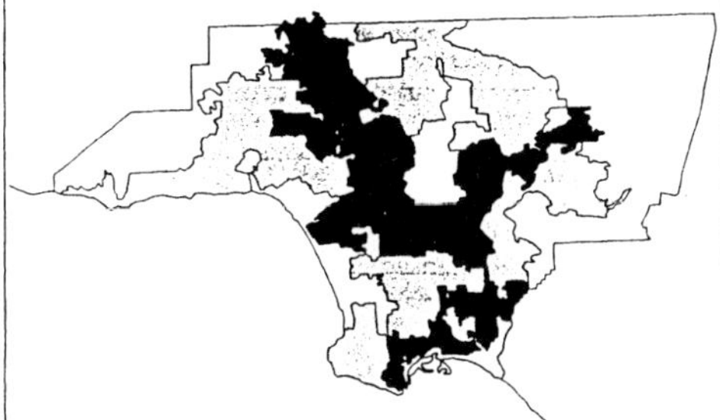

Partisan gerrymander: After the 1980 census, California Democrats drew convoluted House districts reaching in all directions for Democratic voters. This maximized the number of districts Democrats could win, while overstocking the remainder with Republican voters.

SOURCE: Elections Research Center

Population Equality

For most of its history, the court viewed redistricting as a political act that was essentially none of its business.

That attitude only gradually began to change in the 1950s as an activist court headed by former California Gov. Earl Warren began to take shape. By the early 1960s, it was clear that redistricting could be a ripe area for legal involvement.

By then, wide population disparity among congressional districts could no longer be ignored. Louisiana had not redrawn its district lines since 1912. Georgia, Wisconsin, Colorado and South Carolina had not done so since the early 1930s.

Rural areas generally benefited from the population disparity. In Florida, the most populous district was nearly three times as large as the least populated one. In both California and Illinois, the most populous district was nearly twice as large.

And by 1960, not a single state legislative body existed in which there was not at least a 2-to-1 population disparity between the most and least populous districts. In many legislatures, the disparity was huge: 223 to 1 in the Nevada Senate, 422 to 1 in the California Senate and 1,480 to 1 in the Vermont House.

In California, three mountain counties with a combined 1960 population of less than 15,000 had one state senator; so did Los Angeles County, with more than 6 million residents.

It was against this backdrop that a group of urban plaintiffs from Tennessee challenged the apportionment of their state legislature. While the Supreme Court did not rule on the merits of the case, the court did decide by a 6-to-2 vote in *Baker v. Carr* that the plaintiffs had raised a justiciable issue.

Bandwagon Rolls

In short order, other decisions followed. *Gray v. Sanders* in 1963 established the one-person, one-vote standard. *Wesberry v. Sanders* in 1964 extended the one-person, one-vote principle to congressional districts.

Had it acted, Congress might have slowed, if not stopped, the court's headlong march toward rigid population equality at this point.

Throughout the 1950s and early 1960s, House Judiciary Committee Chairman Emanuel Celler (D-N.Y., 1923-73) regularly introduced a bill to permit state lawmakers some flexibility regarding population in designing districts.

Celler's legislation went nowhere until after *Wesberry*. But in 1965, a version passed the House. It established 15 percent as the maximum percentage by which a congressional district's population might deviate from the average population of the state's districts.

There was little doubt that a major reason for House approval of Celler's bill was a fear that the courts would impose even more rigid criteria. But the measure died in the Senate without coming to a floor vote.

It stalled, in part, because it was overshadowed by the spirited reaction to another 1964 Supreme Court decision, *Reynolds v. Sims*. Applying the one-person, one-vote dictum to state legislative line drawing, the court ruled in *Reynolds* that legislative districts must be of substantially equal population.

Critics viewed the *Reynolds* decision as an invasion of states' rights. In Congress, Republicans and Southern Democrats joined forces. In both 1965 and 1966, Senate Minority Leader Everett McKinley Dirksen (R-Ill., House 1933-49, Senate 1951-69), pushed proposals for a constitutional amendment to allow states to apportion at least one house of their state legislature on a non-population basis.

In both years, Dirksen won a substantial majority for his proposal, but each time fell a few votes short of the two-thirds majority required for a proposed constitutional amendment.

The "substantially equal" standard of *Reynolds* led the court to accept state legislative plans with a population range of up to 10 percent.

Zero Tolerance

But after *Wesberry*, the population-equality standard for congressional districts was quantified and steadily tightened. In 1967, the court sent back Indiana and Missouri congressional redistricting plans that had allowed for as much as 20 percent deviation from the average district population.

Two years later, Missouri's revised plan returned to the court for full review (*Kirkpatrick v. Preisler*). It allowed a range of approximately 6 percent between the most and least populous districts. By a 6-3 vote, it was rejected.

The judicial rulings of the 1960s had their effect. A total of 385 of the 435 House members elected in 1972 were chosen from districts that varied less than 1 percent from their state's average congressional district population. The average variance from the ideal district size was less than 0.5 percent for the 93rd Congress (1973-75), compared with 17 percent for the

88th Congress (1963-65).

Any doubts in the political community about the courts' obsession with population equality were dispelled by the early 1980s, when a court-imposed map in Michigan created 16 districts with exactly equal population — 514,560. The state's other two districts listed a population just one person less — 514,559.

"Will we be faced with that kind of potential absurdity this time?" asks Kimball Brace, a Washington-based redistricting consultant. "I don't know."

Brace speculates that the court might be ready to take a more lenient view on population equality, particularly since the accuracy of the 1990 census has become a subject of controversy.

But Bruce Cain, a University of California-Berkeley political scientist, warns that no state should count on a change in the court's attitude in drawing new districts. "It's clear you have to get as close to zero as you can get," he says.

Any state that does not do so could find itself hauled into court. Plaintiffs with any number of agendas will know that population disparity gets the court's attention.

The late Democratic Rep. Phillip Burton (1964-83) also realized that in crafting a congressional district map for his home state of California in the early 1980s.

Partisan Gerrymandering

Burton's now-famous creation featured a number of odd-shaped districts that were drawn neither compactly nor with respect to community boundaries. But Burton could brag that his map was loyal to the court's edict: The average variance in population between districts was only 67 people.

To the national GOP's delight, the Supreme Court in 1986 decided that the entire area of partisan gerrymandering was open to legal challenge — even if the disputed districts met the one-person, one-vote test.

Ironically, the court's decision, in *Davis v. Bandemer*, resulted from a challenge by Indiana Democrats, who complained that the legislature's GOP majority unconstitutionally gerrymandered them out of legislative seats following the 1980 census. In 1984, a divided lower court agreed and voided the plan. Indiana Republicans appealed to the Supreme Court.

Two separate decisions followed in June 1986. The court first had to rule on whether partisan gerrymanders

1966 Mississippi Districts

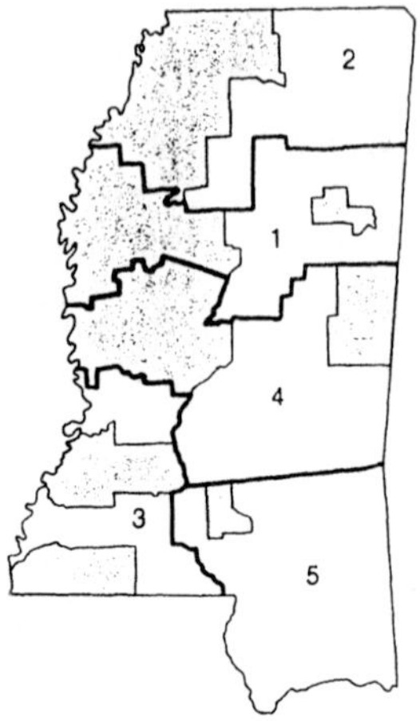

Minority representation: After the 1965 Voting Rights Act, Mississippi redrew its congressional map to split black counties among the districts and dilute black voting strength.

SOURCE: CQ Weekly Report 1966

should be subject to constitutional review. Six justices declared they were.

But the court rejected, by a 7-2 vote, the specific challenge by the Indiana Democrats. Left unclear were what standards the court would find necessary to prove a legally unacceptable partisan gerrymander.

National Republicans expressed delight with the *Bandemer* decision. The GOP had long held that Democratic control over most state legislatures had allowed them to draw congressional and legislative districts to their partisan advantage. In finding that partisan gerrymanders are open to constitutional challenge, the court gave the GOP a chance to fight those plans outside the electoral arena.

In particular, Republicans expressed confidence that the *Bandemer* decision lay the groundwork for overturning the Democratic-drawn congressional district map in California — a map, Republicans argued, that was as close to a classic partisan gerrymander as the political world can produce.

With the Burton creation in place for the 1982 election, the California congressional delegation went from a 22-21 Democratic edge to a 28-17 Democratic majority.

The map was redrawn slightly in 1983, after Republicans managed to get rid of the first version in a statewide referendum. In 1984, the GOP gained one seat. That was the only change in the delegation's party balance for the rest of the decade.

A Pattern of Exclusion?

The GOP's lawsuit against the Democratic plan was filed in federal district court in San Francisco by Rep. Robert E. Badham (1977-89) in 1983. The district court held a hearing on *Badham v. Eu* in the wake of the *Bandemer* decision but dismissed the Republican claim by a 2-1 vote.

Essentially, the district court ruled that a party seeking to overturn a remap must show a general pattern of exclusion from the political process, which the California GOP — in control of the governorship, a Senate seat and 40 percent of the House delegation — could not do.

The Republicans appealed to the Supreme Court, but the court refused to become involved, finally voting 6-3 in 1989 to reaffirm the lower court's decision without comment.

"I think the courts have shown they're cowards, and it's a cowardice I applaud," says Cain. In his opinion, "they have shown themselves wary of intervening and have set a threshold as high as possible without saying partisan gerrymandering is outside their jurisdiction" so that they will not get pulled into every politically charged case.

Jeffrey M. Wice, the counsel for the Democratic State Legislative Leaders Association, basically agrees: "The kind of proof that you have to show . . . is that the political party has been wiped off the face of the state's politics. That's a tough nut to crack."

Many in the political community believe that it would take distorted results from not one but several elections to make the case for partisan gerrymandering.

Even Republicans acknowledge that partisan gerrymandering is not easy to prove. "There is no doubt that the political gerrymandering claim is probably the most difficult of all redistricting claims to make," says Michael Hess, the deputy chief counsel for the Republican National Committee (RNC).

But Hess hopes the Supreme Court's refusal to hear GOP arguments in the *Badham* case was merely a matter of timing; the case reached the court at the end of the decade, shortly before lines were to be re-

Minority Districts

In the 1990s round of redistricting, the Justice Department and the courts are expected to demand that mapmakers prove they have done all they can to maximize the voting strength of minority groups.

Listed below are the current House districts that the 1980 census found were more than 30 percent black, those that are more than 30 percent Hispanic, and those where blacks, Hispanics and other minorities constitute 30 percent or more of the total population.

Key to abbreviations: A — Asian; B — black; H — Hispanic; I — American Indian; O — Other minorities.

Districts with more than 30% black population

District	% Black	House Member
Ill. 1	92	Charles A. Hayes (D)
N.Y. 12	80	Major R. Owens (D)
Pa. 2	80	William H. Gray III (D)
Md. 7	73	Kweisi Mfume (D)
Mich. 1	71	John Conyers Jr. (D)
Mich. 13	71	George W. Crockett Jr. (D)
Ill. 2	70	Gus Savage (D)
Ill. 7	67	Cardiss Collins (D)
Ga. 5	65	John Lewis (D)
Ohio 21	62	Louis Stokes (D)
La. 2	59	Lindy (Mrs. Hale) Boggs (D)
Miss. 2	58	Mike Espy (D)
N.J. 10	58	Donald M. Payne (D)
Tenn. 9	57	Harold E. Ford (D)
Mo. 1	52	William L. Clay (D)
Calif. 29	50 (H 37)	Augustus F. Hawkins (D)
N.Y. 6	50+	Floyd H. Flake (D)
N.Y. 16	49 (H 38)	Charles B. Rangel (D)
N.Y. 11	47 (H 38)	Ed Towns (D)
Miss. 4	42	Mike Parker (D)
S.C. 6	41	Robin Tallon (D)
Texas 18	41 (H 31)	Craig Washington (D)
N.C. 2	40	Tim Valentine (D)
Va. 4	40	Norman Sisisky (D)
Calif. 28	39 (H 28)	Julian C. Dixon (D)
La. 8	38	Clyde C. Holloway (R)
Ga. 2	37	Charles Hatcher (D)
Ga. 8	35	J. Roy Rowland (D)
Md. 5	35	Steny H. Hoyer (D)
N.C. 1	35	Walter B. Jones (D)
S.C. 2	35	Floyd D. Spence (R)
Ala. 6	34	Ben Erdreich (D)
Calif. 31	34 (H 25)	Mervyn M. Dymally (D)
Ga. 3	34	Richard Ray (D)
Ala. 7	33	Claude Harris (D)
Ga. 1	33	Lindsay Thomas (D)
La. 4	32	Jim McCrery (R)
Miss. 3	32	G. V. "Sonny" Montgomery (D)
Pa. 1	32	Thomas M. Foglietta (D)
S.C. 1	32	Arthur Ravenal Jr. (R)
S.C. 5	32	John M. Spratt Jr. (D)
Texas 24	32	Martin Frost (D)
Ala. 1	31	Sonny Callahan (R)
Ala. 2	31	Bill Dickinson (R)
La. 5	31	Jerry Huckaby (D)
Va. 1	31	Herbert H. Bateman (R)

Districts with more than 30% Hispanic population

District	% Hispanic	House Member
Texas 15	72	E. "Kika" de la Garza (D)
Calif. 25	63	Edward R. Roybal (D)
Texas 20	62	Henry B. Gonzalez (D)
Texas 27	62	Solomon P. Ortiz (D)
Texas 16	60	Ronald D. Coleman (D)
Texas 23	56	Albert G. Bustamante (D)
Calif. 30	54	Matthew G. Martinez (D)
Fla. 18	51	Ileana Ros-Lehtinen (R)
N.Y. 18	51 (B 44)	Jose E. Serrano (D)
Calif. 34	47 (O 5, B 2)	Esteban E. Torres (D)
N.M. 3	39 (I 21)	Bill Richardson (D)
N.M. 1	37	Steven H. Schiff (R)
Ariz. 2	36	Morris K. Udall (D)
N.M. 2	34	Joe Skeen (R)
Ill. 8	32	Dan Rostenkowski (D)

Other districts with 30% or more minority population

District	Minority	House Member
Calif. 5	A 22, H 14, B 11, O 1	Nancy Pelosi (D)
Calif. 8	B 27, A 8, H 7	Ronald V. Dellums (D)
Calif. 9	H 14, B 12, A 6	Pete Stark (D)
Calif. 10	H 28, A 10, B 6	Don Edwards (D)
Calif. 11	H 14, A 10, B 7	Tom Lantos (D)
Calif. 16	H 22, A 5, B 4	Leon E. Panetta (D)
Calif. 17	H 28, B 2	Charles "Chip" Pashayan Jr. (R)
Calif. 18	H 25, B 7	Richard H. Lehman (D)
Calif. 24	H 26, A 12, B 7	Henry A. Waxman (D)
Calif. 27	H 14, B 11, A 6	Mel Levine (D)
Calif. 32	H 23, B 9, A 5	Glenn M. Anderson (D)
Calif. 36	H 23, B 8	George E. Brown Jr. (D)
Calif. 38	H 28, A 7, B 3	Robert K. Dornan (R)
Calif. 44	H 27, B 14, A 8, O 1	Jim Bates (D)
Colo. 1	H 19, B 12	Patricia Schroeder (D)
Fla. 17	B 27, H 25	William Lehman (D)
Fla. 19	H 22, B 12	Dante Fascell (D)
Hawaii 1	A 65, H 6, B 2	Patricia Saiki (R)
Hawaii 2	A 56, H 9, B 2	Vacant
Ind. 1	B 24, H 8	Peter J. Visclosky (D)
N.J. 14	H 27, B 13	Frank J. Guarini (D)
N.Y. 7	H 20, B 12, A 7	Gary L. Ackerman (D)
N.Y. 15	H 15, A 10, B 5	Bill Green (R)
N.Y. 17	B 16, H 16	Ted Weiss (D)
N.C. 3	B 27, H 2, O 1	H. Martin Lancaster (D)
N.C. 7	B 27, I 8, H 2, O 1	Charlie Rose (D)
Texas 5	B 20, H 12, O 1	John Bryant (D)
Texas 8	B 17, H 13, O 1	Jack Fields (R)
Texas 9	B 21, H 8, O 2	Jack Brooks (D)
Texas 10	H 19, B 10, O 1	J. J. "Jake" Pickle (D)
Texas 14	H 20, B 12, O 1	Greg Laughlin (D)
Texas 19	H 25, B 5, O 1	Larry Combest (R)
Texas 25	B 25, H 14, O 2	Michael A. Andrews (D)
Va. 3	B 28, H 1 , O 1	Thomas J. Bliley Jr. (R)
Wis. 5	B 28, H 2, O 1	Jim Moody (D)

The Courts Warily Find Their Way . . .

While the federal judiciary has in recent years become a prominent, if somewhat unpredictable, player in the congressional redistricting process, for most of the nation's history the courts were content to be spectators, letting Congress set the ground rules for how district lines were drawn.

In the words of Justice Felix Frankfurter, congressional redistricting was a "political thicket" that the courts should avoid. It was not until the early 1960s that dramatic population shifts combined with a mood of judicial activism to shift the court's philosophy.

Frankfurter

Brennan

Over the course of the previous century, Congress did pass several pieces of legislation urging states to create districts of equal population, as well as of compact size and contiguous shape. But the prevailing attitude on Capitol Hill was that these standards were to serve as guidelines and were not binding on the states.

By the early 20th century, large population disparities had developed between lightly populated rural districts and heavily populated urban districts. But rural-dominated state legislatures often were reluctant to redraw the lines, and the courts provided no impetus for change. The Supreme Court maintained a hands-off attitude toward redistricting until well after World War II.

1932 — *Wood v. Broom* — In the first significant congressional redistricting case to reach the Supreme Court, a Mississippi law that had created congressional districts of unequal population is upheld. Four justices underscore the court's hands-off attitude by suggesting that it does not have jurisdiction over redistricting.

1946 — *Colegrove v. Green* — Supreme Court reaffirms its laissez faire attitude to redistricting in a case involving a challenge to the unequal population of Illinois districts (they ranged in size from barely 100,000 residents to more than 900,000). Justice Frankfurter warns that redistricting is a "political thicket" that courts should avoid. But the vote in *Colegrove* is only 4-3, and the dissenters argue that the court does have jurisdiction over redistricting.

1960 — *Gomillion v. Lightfoot* — Supreme Court strikes down the Alabama Legislature's attempt to redraw the city boundaries of Tuskegee to exclude virtually all black voters. This is one of a series of civil rights cases that begins to lay the groundwork for the Supreme Court's change of attitude. A commentator later describes the decision as amounting to a "dragon" in the "political thicket" of *Colegrove*.

1962 — *Baker v. Carr* — In a landmark 6-2 decision, the Supreme Court abandons its non-interventionist attitude by ruling in a case involving the apportionment of the Tennessee General Assembly that legislative redistricting (and by implication, congressional redistricting) is within its jurisdiction.

Justice William J. Brennan Jr. writes the majority opinion, emphasizing that the federal judiciary has the power to review the apportionment of state legislatures under the 14th Amendment's equal-protection clause.

Now in the minority, Justice Frankfurter writes that the decision is "a massive repudiation of the experience of our whole past" and is an assertion of "destructively novel judicial power."

1963 — *Gray v. Sanders* — The "one-person, one-vote" concept is enunciated by Justice William O. Douglas in this Supreme Court case striking down Georgia's weighted county unit system of voting in primary elections.

1964 — *Wesberry v. Sanders* — The Supreme Court applies the one-person, one-vote standard to congressional districts, striking down a Georgia map that has not been changed since 1931 and features a population disparity of 550,000 between the most and least populous districts.

In defending its decision, the court cites Article I, Section 2 of the Constitution, which states that "representatives shall be apportioned among the states according to their respective numbers" and be "chosen by the people of the several states." This language, the court states, means that "as nearly as is practicable," one person's vote in a congressional election is to be worth as much as another's.

The impact of *Wesberry* is sweeping: Nearly every state redraws its congressional district lines over the rest of the decade — sometimes more than once. By the end of the 1960s, 39 of the 45 states with more than one representative make adjustments.

1969 — *Kirkpatrick v. Preisler* — By a 6-3 vote, the Supreme Court reaffirms the strict application of one-person, one-vote to congressional redistricting, rejecting a Missouri plan that calls for a disparity of approximately 6

drawn.

"What the RNC will be doing and what we'll be encouraging Republican lawyers around the country to be doing," Hess says, "is to be aware that [partisan gerrymandering] is still a valid cause of action. The Supreme Court doesn't find that things are justiciable just for the heck of it."

Encouraging to Republicans is the fact that three members of the court were ready to hear arguments on *Badham*, one short of the number needed. All three — Chief Justice William H. Rehnquist and Justices Anthony M. Kennedy and John Paul Stevens — are still serving.

"If the court gives any sign of going to the Republican interpretation," predicts Cain, "you would see a flood of litigation at all levels. If it holds to *[Badham]*, there will probably be some cases to test the water and then they would fritter away."

. . . Into the 'Political Thicket'

percent between the most and least populous districts. The court decides that minor deviations from strict population equality are to be permitted only when the state provides substantial evidence that the variation was unavoidable.

1969 — *Wells v. Rockefeller* — Supreme Court rules as unacceptable a New York redistricting plan that had created congressional districts of nearly equal population within regions of the state, but not of equal population throughout the state.

1973 — *White v. Weiser* — Supreme Court continues to tighten its interpretation of the one-person, one-vote doctrine, rejecting a Texas congressional district map that calls for a disparity between the most and least populous districts of roughly 5 percent. The court rejects the argument that the disparity is an acceptable result of an attempt to avoid splitting political subdivisions.

1980 — *Mobile v. Bolden* — The reach of the 1965 Voting Rights Act is narrowed by this case concerning the city of Mobile's at-large system of electing city commissioners. Even though no black had been elected under the system, the Supreme Court rules that it does not violate the Voting Rights Act. It is not enough to find a voting system discriminatory in effect, the court says, unless there is also evidence that it was created with the intent to be discriminatory.

1982 — Reacting to the *Mobile* decision, Congress amends the Voting Rights Act to loosen the burden of proof in discriminatory vote cases. The new language states that discriminatory results are sufficient to demonstrate that a minority had been wronged.

1983 — *Karcher v. Daggett* — By a 5-4 vote, the Supreme Court rejects a New Jersey congressional district map that calls for a variation between the most and least populous districts of 0.7 percent. The court emphasizes that there is no uniform level of population disparity that is so small as to be acceptable, and that variations are permissible only if a state can prove that they are necessary to achieve some legitimate goal.

1986 — *Thornburg v. Gingles* — In a test of the 1982 Voting Rights Act, the Supreme Court agrees that a voting system that has the effect of discriminating against minorities is in violation of the law regardless of the lawmakers' intent. Specifically, the court rules that six multimember legislative districts in North Carolina violate the Voting Rights Act because they impermissibly dilute the strength of black voters. The decision is seen by many in the political community as a warning to states to create minority districts wherever possible.

1986 — *Davis v. Bandemer* — Supreme Court declares for the first time that partisan gerrymanders (line-drawing that blatantly gives one party an advantage over another) are subject to legal challenge. But the court decides that the specific case before it, involving a GOP-drawn legislative map in Indiana, does not constitute a partisan gerrymander.

1987 — Responding to charges that the 1990 census would undercount urban minorities, the Commerce Department announces that it will not make a statistical adjustment in the 1990 tally. Although no previous census count has been adjusted, the ruling fuels lawsuits and charges that the Republican administration is "playing politics" with the census.

January 1989 — *Badham v. Eu* — Supreme Court rules without comment that a Democratic-drawn congressional district map in California, long recognized as aggressively partisan, does not constitute an unacceptable partisan gerrymander. The court leaves unclear the question of what would be unacceptable. The vote to dismiss the Republican challenge is 6-3; three justices agree to hear the case, but the approval of four is needed.

July 1989 — Responding to a lawsuit brought by New York City (along with other cities, states and civil rights organizations), the Commerce Department agrees to keep the adjustment question open until July 1991. Other lawsuits are filed seeking to require Commerce to statistically adjust the census, or at least to make a final determination on the issue before mid-1991.

April 1990 — The nationwide census count begins. An initially low response rate heightens debate on the possibility of a serious undercount and the need for adjustment.

June 1990 — *Garza v. County of Los Angeles* — A federal district court judge in Los Angeles gives further impetus to the minority representation issue. He rules that the Los Angeles County Board of Supervisors had violated the Voting Rights Act by gerrymandering its districts to dilute the large Hispanic vote. In August, the judge approves a new map that creates a majority Hispanic supervisorial district in the nation's most populous county.

August 1990 — The U.S. Justice Department files suit against Georgia's "second primary" or election runoff system on the grounds that it discriminates against minority voters. The action is seen as an indicator that Justice may be an active ally of minority groups in redistricting cases.

—***Rhodes Cook***

Minority Representation

No aspect of redistricting law has changed more dramatically over the last decade than minority representation.

Ten years ago, the burden of proof was on minorities to show that lines were being drawn to dilute their voting strength. Now, the burden of proof has been shifted to the lawmakers to show that they have done all they can to maximize minority voting strength.

"We've gone from, 'Can you do something affirmative?' to 'Can you afford to avoid race?' " says Cain. "That's gone a long way in 10 years."

The cornerstone of minority representation cases is the Voting Rights Act of 1965, extended in 1970, 1975 and 1982. It bans redistricting plans that dilute the voting strength of minorities.

Originally aimed at those Southern states where blacks had long been targets of discrimination, the law was subsequently extended to other minorities, including Hispanics, Asian-Americans, American Indians and native Alaskans.

In 1980, the Supreme Court for the first time narrowed the reach of the Voting Rights Act in the case of *Mobile v. Bolden*, a challenge to the Alabama city of Mobile's at-large system of electing city commissioners.

By a vote of 6-3, the court ruled that proof of discriminatory intent by the commissioners was necessary before a violation could be found; the fact that no black had ever been elected under the challenged system was not proof enough.

The *Mobile* decision set off an immediate reaction on Capitol Hill. In extending the Voting Rights Act in 1982, Congress amended it to outlaw any practice that has the effect of discriminating against blacks or other minorities — regardless of the lawmakers' intent.

The congressional mandate in the Voting Rights Act is so specific, says Cain, that the court would find it virtually impossible to reverse direction even if it wanted to. "I think Congress tied their hands," he says.

Expanding Results Test

The Justice Department later adopted a similar "results test" for another part of the act (Section 5), which requires certain states and localities with a history of discrimination to have their electoral plans "precleared" by the department.

In 1986 the court applied this test in *Thornburg v. Gingles*, ruling that six of North Carolina's multimember legislative districts impermissibly diluted black voting strength.

Sharply departing from *Mobile*, the court held that since very few blacks had been elected from these districts, the system must be in violation of the law.

The court also used the *Thornburg* decision to develop three criteria that, if met, should lead to the creation of a minority legislative district: The minority group must be large and geographically compact enough to constitute a majority in a single-member electoral district, the group must be politically cohesive, and the white majority must vote as a bloc to the degree that it usually can defeat candidates preferred by the minority.

Legal action since *Thornburg* has increased the pressure for fuller minority representation.

In June, Los Angeles Federal District Judge David V. Kenyon ruled in *Garza v. County of Los Angeles* that the Los Angeles County Board of Supervisors had violated the Voting Rights Act by gerrymandering its districts to dilute the Hispanic vote.

No Hispanic has ever held a seat on the five-member governing board of the nation's most populous county (which has an estimated 8.7 million residents), even though the county is about one-third Hispanic. In August, Kenyon ordered the creation of a majority Hispanic district.

Also, the Justice Department in August filed a lawsuit against the Georgia election runoff system on the grounds that it discriminates against minority voters.

Runoffs are almost exclusively a feature of Southern politics. Civil rights activists have long argued that they dilute minority voting power because even if a black finishes first in a primary, he usually falls to united white opposition in the runoff.

Assistant Attorney General John R. Dunne, the head of Justice's Civil Rights Division, which enforces the Voting Rights Act, had signaled such a move in a speech to a National Conference of State Legislatures' redistricting conference in June.

> **"Our staff serves as watchdogs. ... Read my lips: No minority dilution."**
>
> **—John R. Dunne**

"Our staff serves as watchdogs of minority voting rights," he said, and its basic approach to redistricting could be summed up in the words: "Read my lips: No minority dilution."

But Dunne has not tipped his hand as to how far his office might go in requiring the creation of minority districts.

A 24-year veteran of the New York Senate, Dunne has expressed appreciation for the rough and tumble nature of the redistricting process, and he has said that incumbent protection is not impermissible as long as it does not impair minority voting strength.

Justice's responsibility "is to call them as we see them," he says. "There are so many variables that go into making this sausage."

Many observers expect minority representation cases to be the most active area of redistricting litigation in the 1990s, and not just because minority plaintiffs have an improved chance of winning.

Minority groups have traditionally viewed the courts as their prime avenue of redress. "The courts brought me to the table, not the parties," says Tony Harrison, the project director of voter participation for the Southern Regional Council.

Harrison speaks from personal experience. He was elected to the Alabama Legislature in 1974, he says, from a court-drawn district that the Legislature had refused to create.

Other litigation is inevitable because the legal landscape surrounding minority representation is still being defined.

A case being watched closely is *Armour v. Ohio*, which focuses on the issue of whether "minority influenced" districts should be created in areas where a district with a majority of minorities cannot be drawn.

The plaintiffs have asked that black populations that are split between two state legislative districts be combined into one district to maximize their political influence — even though the black population (which is 11 percent in one district and 25 percent in the other) would not constitute a majority in the new district. The case is before the 6th U.S. Circuit Court of Appeals in Cincinnati.

Still a Hot Button

The courts may also revisit the question of how large a proportion of a district's population must be of a particular minority group to give that minority a fair chance of winning the seat. For years, the rule of thumb has been that the minority population of a district needs to be at least 65 percent to compensate for lower rates of minority voter registration and turnout.

But it is possible that so high a minority population is not needed. Sixteen of the 17 House districts with a 1980 population at least 50 percent black have black representatives — the exception being the New Orleans-based Louisiana 2nd, where retiring Democrat Lindy (Mrs. Hale) Boggs holds the seat.

And eight of the nine majority Hispanic districts have Hispanic representatives — the exception being Democrat Ronald D. Coleman in the El Paso-based Texas 16th. *(Chart, p. 2789)*

Efforts to increase minority representation have spawned talk of enlarging the size of a variety of legislative bodies. A possible solution advanced by one of the plaintiffs in the *Garza* case, for instance, was to expand the number of seats on the Los Angeles County Board of Supervisors.

Expansion, they argued, is a way to promote racial and ethnic diversity on the board and shrink the size of districts in a huge jurisdiction such as Los Angeles County, where a single supervisorial district is as populous as three congressional districts.

It is a prospective solution that is also being voiced by some state legislators, who must apply new minority-representation rules in drawing their own state legislative lines. Many of them see expansion of legislative bodies as a relatively painless way to allow incumbents to retain their seats while facilitating minority representation.

Proposals have even been made to expand the U.S. House, which has had 435 seats for nearly 80 years, but which can change its size by statute.

Population Undercount

The building block of the whole redistricting process is the census count, and concern about the accuracy of the 1990 tally has already been the subject of litigation.

The core issue is whether the count should be left as is or be statistically adjusted to compensate for a population undercount. No such adjustment has been made in previous censuses.

An undercount is nothing new. In 1980 the Census Bureau estimated that it counted about 99 percent of the white population but only about 94 percent of blacks. This year's count, it is estimated, may fall even further short.

Calls for an adjusted count are not new either. Several cities with large minority populations sought but failed to win adjustment of the 1980 census count.

The latest debate began in 1987, when the Commerce Department (which includes the Census Bureau) announced that it would not adjust the 1990 count.

That fueled charges that the Republican administration was undercounting a Democratic constituency. And it was not long before a lawsuit was brought by New York City (along with other cities, states and civil rights organizations), calling on the Census Bureau to make a statistical adjustment of the tally to account for people who were missed.

In response to the lawsuit, the Commerce Department last year agreed to defer a final judgment on the adjustment question until as late as mid-July 1991.

This concession did not mollify Commerce critics, who see that scenario as opening the door to chaos. Enumerated census counts are to be reported to the states by April 1, 1991. It is estimated that by mid-July 1991 the deadlines for finishing the redistricting process will have passed in close to 20 states. And if states were given two sets of population figures — one adjusted, one not — that could lead to innumerable logistical, political and legal headaches in the redistricting process.

Earlier this year, the plaintiffs in the New York City case reopened their lawsuit in an effort to get the Commerce Department to draft new guidelines that would require the department to adjust the count in 1991, unless it could demonstrate that a statistical change would not be more accurate than the actual tally.

In something of a split decision, a federal district court in New York ruled in June that an adjustment would be constitutional and that the Commerce Department would "clearly incur a heavier burden" to explain an anti-adjustment decision in 1991. But it also ruled that the Commerce Department's guidelines on the matter were not inadequate or biased.

Meanwhile, an avalanche of litigation on the question seems inevitable. There has to be some form of adjustment and relief, says Harrison, and relief "has to come from the judiciary." ■

THE CENSUS

Final Count Will Shift Seats To Far West, Southeast

Preliminary results of the 1990 census generally confirm the flow of U.S. population and political power from the Northeast and Midwest to the Southeast and Far West.

The numbers show that in reapportionment, 13 states with declining or stagnant populations may lose 19 House seats to eight fast-growing states, mostly in the Sun Belt.

As expected, the big gainer is California, where 5.6 million new residents likely mean seven new seats, for an unprecedented total of 52. *(Story, p. 2761)*

Also likely to gain seats are Florida (four) and Texas (three). One new seat each would go to Arizona, Georgia, North Carolina, Virginia and Washington.

Most of the 13 states slated to lose House seats in the 103rd Congress have expected to see their delegations diminished. This includes New York, which would lose three seats, and two-seat losers Illinois, Michigan, Ohio and Pennsylvania.

But the preliminary population figures — the last of which were released by the Census Bureau on Aug. 29 — also featured unpleasant surprises for some.

Rural areas, a comeback story in the 1970s, experienced renewed deterioration in the 1980s. Big cities, braced for bad news, were nonetheless disturbed at the magnitude of their decline. Mayor David N. Dinkins of New York called the head count for his city "unadulterated nonsense."

An apparent exodus of about one-fifth of Detroit's residents dropped that city below 1 million in population, and from sixth-largest city in the nation to ninth.

Such eye-catching losses (Chicago and Philadelphia each dropped about 9 percent) may fuel court challenges to the Census Bureau's methods of counting. *(Story, p. 2786)*

Unexpected Losses

Moreover, several states that had not anticipated losing a House seat suddenly have found that they may.

New Jersey, for example, learned from the preliminary census numbers that it could lose one of its 14 seats, despite a 3.4 percent population growth in the 1980s. Much of the state's poor showing results from low numbers from Essex (Newark) County.

In Louisiana, once part of the Sun Belt boom, the oil downturn seems to have pinched the state enough in the late 1980s to reduce its House delegation in the '90s to seven seats from eight.

As recently as this spring, Oklahoma and Tennessee seemed safe

1990 Reapportionment: Projected Gainers and Losers

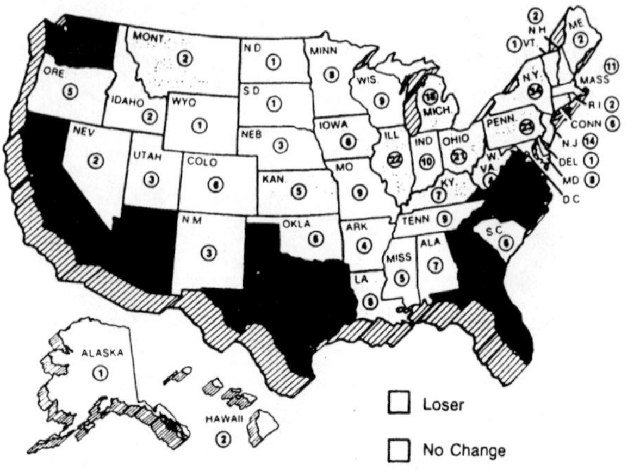

NOTE: Current number of House seats in circle.

GAINERS	
Arizona	1
California	7
Florida	4
Georgia	1
North Carolina	1
Texas	3
Virginia	1
Washington	1
LOSERS	
Illinois	2
Iowa	1
Kansas	1
Kentucky	1
Louisiana	1
Massachusetts	1
Michigan	2
Montana	1
New Jersey	1
New York	3
Ohio	2
Pennsylvania	2
West Virginia	1

NOTE: Chart based on projections from preliminary Census Bureau data, subject to revision prior to final reapportionment. Seat redistribution projected by consulting firm of Election Data Services, Inc.

from losing House seats. But disappointing numbers from the rural areas of both states mean that either could fall just below the population needed to keep their delegations intact. If either does drop a seat, the beneficiary might well be Maryland, which grew by more than 12 percent in the 1980s and might gain a ninth seat.

Kentucky, which last winter saw no danger of dropping its seventh seat, may indeed lose it. The Bluegrass State is in a close race with Mississippi, which was within 2,747 residents of losing one of its seats. If later adjustments alter that score, Kentucky could keep its seven seats and Mississippi could drop to four.

Montana, which had campaigned actively to increase its population on the eve of the census, may fall just shy of the number needed to keep its second House seat. In the reapportionment arithmetic by which the 435th seat will be assigned, the state could keep two seats if it had 8,157 more residents.

Texas grew by 2.6 million, but that was less than some had expected. The state apparently will not gain a fourth new House seat, which would have given it a delegation equal in size to New York's.

The preliminary population figures are now subject to four months of tabulation, review and legal challenges. They have been mailed by the Census Bureau to 39,000 state and local governments, which have three weeks to provide evidence of error or omission by census enumerators.

"The local governments have a real opportunity to have an impact," says Kimball W. Brace of Election Data Services. "Because a little work on their part now in local review and finding people the Census Bureau has missed can go a long way in swinging some of these seats."

The final, official counts are to be released Dec. 31. In the meantime, the Census Bureau will continue to search out residents in hard-to-count areas and to allocate overseas military personnel and dependents. The bureau announced in July that it would count such personnel in their "home of record" states, rather than where they were last posted before going overseas. *(Weekly Report, p. 2343)*

The census data to date have generated special attention for the burgeoning California delegation. But while no state has ever had more than California's current 45 seats (New York had the same number in the 1930s and '40s), some states have had larger delegations in proportion to the overall House.

A 52-member California delegation would be nearly 12 percent of the whole House in the 1990s. But when Congress first convened in 1789, Virginia's 10 members constituted 15 percent of the first House. And after the first census in 1790, Virginia was apportioned 19 of the 106 seats — nearly one in five.

When immigration began pumping up New York's population, it also enlarged the state's delegation to a peak of 17 percent of the House.

Although it is now clearer which states will be winners or losers in reapportionment, experts are sharply divided over the impact of redistricting on the partisan ratio in the House.

The Sun Belt beneficiaries of the reapportionment shift recently have leaned strongly Republican in presidential races. In each of the past three presidential elections, at least seven of the eight states have preferred the GOP nominee.

But most of the eight have legislatures dominated by Democrats. Half have Democratic governors, too, and as many as seven could have Democratic governors when remapping begins in 1991.

Moreover, partisan change will also be shaped by redistricting in states losing seats. In 12 of these 13 states, Democrats now control either the governorship or at least half the legislature. ∎

Voluntary Constituencies: Modified At-Large Voting as a Remedy for Minority Vote Dilution in Judicial Elections

Edward Still†

The Supreme Court has recently held in two cases that judicial elections are covered by section 2 of the Voting Rights Act of 1965[1], and that trial judges are not exempt from the Act because they happen to hold "single person offices"—that is, exercise an authority independent of others who hold a similar office.[2] The immediate, practical effect of the decision will be to remove a jurisdictional hurdle for the Blacks and Latinos who have suits

---

† Attorney at law, Birmingham AL. B.A. University of Alabama, 1968; J.D. University of Alabama, 1971. I am grateful to Rolondo Rios, Frank R. Parker, Robert B. McDuff, Pamela Karlan, Elizabeth Johnson, Lani Guinier, Richard L. Engstrom, Chandler Davidson, Dayna L. Cunningham, and James U. Blacksher for their assistance and constructive criticism of an earlier draft of this article. The foregoing list of names is in reverse alphabetical order as my affirmative effort to fight alphabetical bias in this country.

1. 42 U.S.C. § 1973 (1988):

> (a) No voting qualification or prerequisite to voting or standard, practice, or procedure shall be imposed or applied by any State or political subdivision in a manner which results in a denial or abridgement of the right of any citizen of the United States to vote on account of race or color, or in contravention of the guarantees set forth in section 1973b(f)(2) of this title, as provided in subsection (b) of this section.
>
> (b) A violation of subsection (a) of this section is established if, based on the totality of circumstances, it is shown that the political processes leading to nomination or election in the State or political subdivision are not equally open to participation by members of a class of citizens protected by subsection (a) of this section in that its members have less opportunity than other members of the electorate to participate in the political process and to elect representatives of their choice. The extent to which members of a protected class have been elected to office in the State or political subdivision is one circumstance which may be considered: *Provided*, That nothing in this section establishes a right to have members of a protected class elected in numbers equal to their proportion in the population.

2. Chisom v. Roemer, 111 S.Ct. 2354 (1991); Houston Lawyers' Ass'n v. Attorney Gen. of Texas, 111 S.Ct. 2376 (1991).

pending in several states[3] charging that multimember judicial elections violate section 2.

The plaintiffs in suits challenging the election of trial judges from multi-member districts still face the necessity of proving that the "totality of circumstances" outweighs the state's asserted interest in using multi-member districts. The *Houston Lawyers' Association* Court noted in dictum,

> we believe that the State's interest in maintaining the electoral system—in this case, Texas' interest in maintaining the link between a district judge's jurisdiction and the area of residency of his or her voters—is a legitimate factor to be considered by courts among the "totality of circumstances" in determining whether a § 2 violation has occurred. A State's justification for its electoral system is a proper factor for the courts to assess in a racial vote dilution inquiry . . . .[4]

Thus, the defendants in cases attacking the election of trial judges will assert that their present system (using jurisdiction-wide elections) outweighs the interests of the plaintiffs in having a judiciary which is less dilutive of the minority's voting strength. This article asserts that the use of two modified at-large election plans—limited voting and cumulative voting—as remedies would "maintain[ ] the link between a district judge's jurisdiction and the area of residency of his or her voters," while satisfying the dilution claims of the Black and Latino plaintiffs.[5] Modified at-large rules are, as the name implies, at-large election rules with modifications to allow political or racial minorities to elect *some* of the members of a legislative body or *some* judges, in contrast to the winner-take-all rules of most American elections which allow a bare majority to elect *all* the members of a multi-member body.[6]

---

3. The pending cases are listed below. Unless otherwise noted, the suit challenges the at-large election of trial judges in a large number of jurisdictions in the entire state.

Alabama—SCLC v. Siegelman, 714 F. Supp. 511 (M.D. Ala. 1989) (at-large elections and numbered places for trial judges);

Arkansas—Hunt v. Arkansas, No. PB-C-89-406 (E.D. Ark. 1989);

Florida—Nipper v. Martinez, No. 90-447-Civ-J-16 (M.D. Fla. 1990) (three counties); Davis v. Martinez, C.A. No. 9040098-MP (N.D. Fla. 1990) (six counties);

Georgia—Brooks v. State Bd. of Elections, Civ. No. 288-146 (S.D. Ga. 1989);

Louisiana—Chisom v. Roemer, 839 F.2d 1056 (5th Cir. 1988), *cert. denied*, 488 U.S. 955 (1988), 917 F.2d 187 (5th Cir. 1990), *rev'd* 111 S.Ct. 2354 (1991) (two-judge district used for election of state supreme court judges); and Clark v. Edwards, 725 F.Supp. 285 (M.D. La. 1988) (trial and intermediate appeals court judges);

Ohio—Mallory v. Eyrich, 666 F. Supp. 1060 (S.D. Ohio 1987), *rev'd*. 839 F.2d 275 (6th Cir. 1988) (countywide election of municipal judges in Cincinnati; issue of remedy pending after admission of liability);

Texas—LULAC v. Clements, 902 F.2d 293 (5th Cir. 1990) (panel decision later withdrawn), 914 F.2d 620 (5th Cir. 1990) (en banc), *rev'd sub nom.*, Houston Lawyers' Ass'n v. Attorney Gen. of Texas, 111 S.Ct. 2376 (1991) (at-large elections and numbered posts).

4. *Houston Lawyers' Ass'n*, 111 S.Ct. at 2381.

5. "Modified at-large" is a term coined by Prof. Lani Guinier. I concur in its use because it emphasizes the commonalities of modified at-large rules with at-large plans more usually found in the United States. Guinier, *No Two Seats: The Elusive Quest for Political Equality*, 77 VA. L. REV. (forthcoming Nov. 1991) (on file with author).

6. *See infra* part II for a discussion of the rules of these systems.

Minorities object to at-large voting in judicial elections because it dilutes minority voting strength. State officials object to subdividing judicial districts because it will result in narrowly drawn, racially defined single-member districts, and many think this will undermine judicial objectivity (or, at least, the appearance of such objectivity). Modified at-large plans are a compromise that give something to each side in the present controversy: minority voters will be able to elect candidates of their choice, but districts will not be used.

In this Article, I use the facts and arguments from cases in three states—Mississippi, Texas, and Alabama—as the basis of the discussion. The Mississippi and Texas cases have gone to judgment after a trial on the merits. The parties settled the Mississippi case on appeal, and it has provided the basis for new elections. The United States Supreme Court has remanded the Texas case to the Fifth Circuit for that court to consider the appeal by the Texas trial judges from the decision on the merits. In contrast, the Alabama case is still pending and had been stayed during the pendency of the Texas case in the Supreme Court. The Alabama case has been chosen for discussion in this Article because of the policy arguments made by the defendants.

In part I, I discuss the nature of the judge's job as a representative of the public and the necessity of a racially inclusive bench. Part II explains the mechanics of modified at-large elections. Part III of this Article discusses the method of electing judges and the progress of the above three lawsuits. In Part IV, I consider one of the arguments made by the defendants in Alabama regarding problems of judicial favoritism if small districts elect judges. Part V discusses the impediment to the adoption of modified at-large voting presented by the constraints the Supreme Court has placed on the definition of actionable vote dilution. In part VI, I discuss the benefits of modified at-large rules over single-member districts. In the final part, I deal with several objections that have been raised to modified at-large plans.

I. Judges As "Representatives"

The majority in *LULAC* held that section 2 of the Voting Rights Act applied only to "representatives," and that judges are not representatives because they do not represent the people, but serve them by making decisions based on principles higher than the popular will.[7] The Supreme Court rejected this reading of the Act and held that

> the better reading of the word "representatives" describes the winners of representative, popular elections. If executive officers, such as prosecutors, sheriffs, state attorneys general, and state treasurers, can be considered "representatives" simply

7. *LULAC*, 914 F.2d at 625-28.

because they are chosen by popular election, then the same reasoning should apply to elected judges.[8]

I suggest a slightly different rationale. "Represent" also means "to act for"; judges represent (act for) the people in enforcing and interpreting the law. The political scientist Hanna Pitkin noted this in discussing the judge as representative:

> This sense of representing may be illustrated by considering the question of whether judges are representatives . . . . It can take various forms, depending on the view of representation a writer adopts. From a formalistic standpoint, a judge is an agent of the state like all government officials. His pronouncements are not private expressions of opinion, but official utterances of the state. Hence he represents the state. In a democracy where all agencies of the government are servants of the sovereign people, the judge might be said to represent the people.[9]

Under this theory, the public views the judge's orders as legitimate because she is acting for the people, not because they believe she has any personal, non-judicial power over the litigants. Indeed, many white southerners of the last thirty-five years have considered federal judges' orders to be illegitimate exactly because they did not reflect the societal views of the dominant group in the region.[10] As discussed more fully in part IV, it appears that the defenders of the status quo believe that legitimacy attaches only to judges elected by a majority, rather than by some smaller group.

Even in non-legislative contexts, it is important that representatives be viewed as the legitimate stand-ins for the people. For instance, I suggest that the legitimacy of the courts is enhanced if all major groups in society see some of "us" on the court, even if one of "them" tries a particular case. This concept is known as "civic inclusion."

Professor Pamela Karlan has explained the nature of civic inclusion in a recent article:

> [T]he *Reynolds [v. Sims]*[11] majority's emphasis on equal political access for all voters . . . rests on a belief in the distinctive values that inclusion in governmental decisionmaking brings: a sense of connectedness to the community and of greater political dignity; greater readiness to acquiesce in governmental decisions and hence broader consent and legitimacy; and more informed, equitable and intelligent governmental decisionmaking . . . . [Civic inclusion] accepts the bedrock diversity of modern America and seeks to bring diverse groups into the governing circle because, quite simply, the best way to ensure that all points of view are taken into account is to create decisionmaking bodies in which all points of view

---

8. *Chisom*, 111 S.Ct. at 2366.

9. HANNA F. PITKIN, THE CONCEPT OF REPRESENTATION 116-17 (1967) (footnote omitted).

10. "The Supreme Court of the United States is not the Court of last resort. The citizens of the sovereign states are the court of last resort. If the citizens of the South are determined to maintain segregation in their schools and in their social order, then their will shall prevail." HERMAN E. TALMADGE, YOU AND SEGREGATION 76 (1955).

11. 377 U.S. 533 (1964). The *Reynolds* Court held that the equal protection clause requires that seats in both houses of the state legislature be apportioned on the basis of population.

are represented by people who embody them. It is not enough that there are people who can only imagine what minority interests might require.[12]

II. The Rules of Modified At-Large Elections

The special rules of modified at-large elections allow a minority group to have a better chance of electing candidates of its choice than the group would have in the typical at-large system. For instance, in the usual at-large election to fill five seats, each voter would have five votes to cast for five different candidates; in a cumulative voting system, the voter could cast all five votes for one candidate or split them among several candidates. In limited voting plans, the voter would have fewer votes to cast than the number of seats to be filled.

By allowing voters to cast their ballots in this way, modified at-large rules lower the "threshold of exclusion," the proportion of the voters at which a particular group will be able to elect one candidate, assuming that all other voters vote strategically.[13] The equation for the threshold of exclusion is $1/(1+S)$ for cumulative voting, and $V/(V+S)$ for limited voting, where V is the number of votes cast by each voter, and S is the number of seats to be filled.[14] In contrast, at-large elections (and single-member district elections,

12. Pamela S. Karlan, *Maps and Misreadings: The Role of Geographic Compactness in Racial Vote Dilution Litigation*, 24 HARV. C.R.-C.L. L. REV. 173, 180 & n.27 (1989). The idea of "power sharing" in governing bodies is not new. In 1875, the governor of South Carolina commended the idea to the legislature:

> I am confident, from various indications, that the principle of minority representation is growing in favor among all the people of the State. It offers in theory, certainly, and in practice, so far as yet tested, a mode of reaching that highest result of our representative system, the true proportional influence of each class or party into which our voting population may be divided. The rule of the majority is not thereby destroyed, while the voice and influence of the minority are not wholly suppressed.

N.Y. Times, Nov. 29, 1875, at 2. Since South Carolina had a black majority at the time, white conservatives (that is, those who were not associated with the radical wing of the Republican Party) had proposed cumulative voting as early as 1871 on the grounds that "[u]nder [cumulative voting] the true office of suffrage, which is to collect the sense of a whole community, will be subserved . . . . The proposition is that the cumulative system secures thorough and general representation of all the interests in the political body." Committee Report, Taxpayers' Convention, Columbia, S.C., May 1871, quoted in JAMES S. PIKE, THE PROSTRATE STATE: SOUTH CAROLINA UNDER NEGRO GOVERNMENT 239 (1874).

13. Assuming that all voters vote strategically, a minority group casting ballots equal to the threshold of exclusion will be able to elect one person. If the non-minority group does not vote strategically, the minority group may be able to win a seat with a proportion of the votes less than the threshold. For instance, black candidates for the Chilton County, Alabama Commission were able to win even though Blacks had less than the threshold of exclusion because the white majority came nowhere close to its optimum strategy of spreading votes evenly among seven candidates for seven seats. Edward Still, *Cumulative and Limited Voting in Alabama*, *in* THE IMPACT OF ELECTORAL SYSTEMS ON MINORITIES AND WOMEN (W. Rule & J. F. Zimmerman, eds., forthcoming 1992).

14. *See* Karlan, *supra*, note 12, at 224, 232; Edward Still, *Alternatives to Single-Member Districts*, *in* MINORITY VOTE DILUTION 253-58 (Chandler Davidson, ed., 1984).

as well) have a threshold of exclusion of 50%, if there is a majority-vote runoff requirement.[15]

While most Americans are unfamiliar with modified at-large rules, corporations use cumulative voting often.[16] Since most elections in the United States are winner-take-all rather than inclusive, election plans are defended and attacked by reference to winner-take-all principles. As long as the debate continues to be expressed in winner-take-all terms, the participants will not think about inclusive plans like modified at-large voting. For instance, during oral argument in *Chisom v. Roemer,* Justice Kennedy responded to a mention of limited voting by calling it "proportional representation" in a tone of voice that suggested proportional representation was a ridiculous proposition. Such hostility, I have found in talking to others, is usually based on the hearer's assumption that proportional representation foreordains the result of the election and eliminates usual decisionmaking by voters. These otherwise intelligent people fail to see that at-large winner-take-all elections foreordain that the racial minority will be excluded from representation if there is racially polarized voting, which is the usual situation in the United States. Unfortunately, many people accept such outcomes as the natural state of affairs. In contrast, modified at-large allows voters to form voluntary constituencies rather than have constituencies imposed upon them by legislative action.

Plaintiffs in vote dilution suits are beginning to breach this barrier by using concepts of civic inclusion,[17] even though they still couch their complaint in terms of "equal access" and usually want or settle for single-member districts.[18] Single-member district plans usually result in greater diversity in the legislative body while preserving the form of winner-take-all elections; thus, they provide a remedy with which both sides can usually be comfortable.

Modified at-large voting meets the goals of civic inclusion better than districts. Empirical studies of recent modified at-large elections show that racial minorities win elections at a level close to the minority percentage in the

15. The general formula for the threshold of exclusion for all four election plans mentioned in this paragraph is $V/(V+S)$. In a majority-vote single-member district or at-large system, V and S have the same value, resulting in a threshold of ½. The same threshold formula applies to cumulative voting if one thinks of the voter as having only one vote divided into V fractional parts. If the limited vote rules give the voter only one vote—sometimes called the single non-transferable vote—the threshold of exclusion is the same as for Cumulative Voting. *See* Karlan, *supra* note 12, at 223-25, 232.

16. *See,* ABA Model Business Corporation Act § 33. *See also,* Lani Guinier, *The Triumph of Tokenism: The Voting Rights Act and the Theory of Black Electoral Success,* 89 MICH. L. REV. 1077, 1139 n.298 (1991) (collecting sources).

17. *See* Karlan, *supra* note 12, 221-22.

18. In LULAC v. Clements, 902 F.2d 293, the Latino plaintiffs have steadfastly championed single-member districts, while the black intervenors have mentioned modified at-large elections as a possible remedy in their intervention papers. In oral argument before the Court of Appeals, the Latinos described modified at-large as "experimental," while the black intervenors argued that these plans provided a viable alternative to single-member districts. Telephone Interview with Sherrilyn Ifill, counsel for Houston Lawyers' Association (Mar. 18, 1991).

population.[19] Modified at-large plans allow voters to form "voluntary districts" with like-minded voters.[20] While a districting plan is imposed on the voters by an outside group (the legislature, the city council, a court) and may last for a decade or more, modified at-large elections allow voters to make grouping decisions for themselves at each election. Districting plans are based on the implicit assumption that voters have an identity of interest with their geographical neighbors. While my neighbors and I may have a common interest in whether the city repaves the street in front of our houses or rezones the lot on the corner for use as a fraternity house, on other issues we probably have no commonality. Districting relies on geographical proximity, while modified at-large plans are based on a community of perceived interest. Under a modified at-large plan, a like-minded group of voters has a greater chance of electing a legislator than under traditional at-large voting.

III. The Background to the Suits

Alabama, Mississippi, and Texas share common features relating to the election and powers of the judges of the general jurisdiction trial courts. The judges are nominated in partisan primaries and elected in general elections.[21] Where a particular district or circuit elects more than one judge, the candidates must run for a designated position, but are elected by the voters at large. Once elected, judges of the general trial courts have jurisdiction over the matters arising within the judicial power of the state, but generally sit in the jurisdiction that elected them. Each state has some provision for the temporary assignment of a judge from her home territory to another to handle docket overloads or recusals by the judges who would normally sit.[22]

Alabama: The Southern Christian Leadership Conference's suit complains about the election of judges in ten of the state's circuit courts and several

---

19. Edward Still, Cumulative and Limited Voting in Alabama: The Aftermath of Dillard v. Crenshaw County, (1988) (unpublished paper); Richard L. Engstrom et al., *Cumulative Voting as a Remedy for Minority Voter Dilution: The Case of Alamogordo, New Mexico*, 5 J. LAW & POLITICS 469 (1989); Leon Weaver, *Semi-Proportional and Proportional Representation Systems in the United States*, *in* CHOOSING AN ELECTORAL SYSTEM: ISSUES AND ALTERNATIVES 191 (Arend Lijphart & Bernard Grofman eds. 1984); Karlan, *supra* note 12, 173, 227 n.226; Delbert A. Taebel et al., *Alternative Electoral Systems as Remedies for Minority Vote Dilution*, 11 Hamline J. Pub. L. & Pol'y 19 (Spring 1990); Richard L. Cole et al., *Cumulative Voting in a Municipal Election: A Note on Voter Reactions and Electoral Consequences*, 43 W. POL. Q. 191 (1990). These studies involve only a few modified at-large systems in relatively small jurisdictions.

20. Karlan, *supra* note 12, at 226 & n.224 and accompanying text.

21. All three states began popular election of judges before the Civil War. In 1832, Mississippi was the first state in the nation to require popular election of all judges. Alabama and Texas followed suit in 1849 and 1850, respectively. RALPH A. WOOSTER, THE PEOPLE IN POWER: COURTHOUSE AND STATEHOUSE IN THE LOWER SOUTH, 1850-1860, 73-76 (1969).

22. ALA. CODE § 12-17-25, -27 (1986); MISS. CODE ANN. § 9-1-105 (Supp. 1990); TEX. GOVT. CODE ANN. § 74.052-.061 (1988); TEX. RULES OF COURT (1990).

district courts.[23] Although U.S. District (now Circuit) Judge Joel Dubina rejected Alabama's motion to dismiss,[24] he has stayed the trial of the case because of the pendency of *Houston Lawyers Association v. Mattox*[25] in the Supreme Court.[26]

Mississippi: In 1987, United States District Judge William Henry Barbour, Jr. held that Mississippi's at-large judicial elections violated section 2 of the Voting Rights Act in four chancery court districts, three circuit court districts, and one county court.[27] After remedy proceedings lasting nearly eighteen months, the court ordered single-member district elections for these courts.[28] The court did not change the boundaries of the chancery or circuit court districts, but simply set up nonresidential electoral subdistricts. Put another way, the judges stand for election in subdistricts in which the candidates do not have to live; the candidate is only required to be a resident of the larger circuit or chancery district in which she will serve.[29] The court rejected the plaintiffs' proposal to use modified at-large voting on the grounds that it was "experimental and contrary to most election laws of Mississippi."[30]

The affected counties held special elections in June 1989 and five Blacks were elected to judgeships. An incumbent black judge was defeated in the same election.[31]

Texas: Hispanic voters brought suit attacking the countywide election of judges in nine districts containing 172 judges out of 375 in the whole state.[32] After a bench trial, United States District Judge Lucius Desha Bunton, III found that this method of election violated section 2 of the Voting Rights Act and enjoined the state defendants from holding further elections under the at-large winner-take-all system. As an interim remedy for the 1990 elections, the court utilized a remedy similar to that in Mississippi: the court divided the nine districts into nonresidential electoral subdistricts for the purpose of electing judges, but retained the countywide district as the venue of each court. The

23. First Amended Complaint, SCLC v. Siegelman, 714 F.Supp. 511 (M.D. Ala. 1989) (No. 88-D-462-N). Circuit courts are general jurisdiction trial courts, while district courts handle misdemeanors and a limited group of civil claims.

24. SCLC v. Siegelman, 714 F. Supp. 511 (M.D. Ala. 1989).

25. Houston Lawyers' Association v. Mattox, *cert. granted,* 111 S.Ct. 775 (1991) (No. 90-813), *rev'd. sub nom.* Houston Lawyers' Ass'n v. Attorney Gen. of Texas, 111 S.Ct. 2376 (1991).

26. SCLC v. Siegelman, C.A. 88-D-462-N (M.D. Ala. filed Dec. 5, 1990).

27. Martin v. Allain, 658 F. Supp. 1183, 1187 (S.D. Miss. 1987). The court also rejected challenges to one chancery district, two circuit districts, and two county courts.

28. Martin v. Mabus, 700 F. Supp. 327 (S.D. Miss. 1988).

29. *Id.* at 332. The court noted that subdistricts with district-wide residency requirements were already used in Mississippi for the Supreme Court and justice courts.

30. *Id.* at 336-37.

31. FRANK R. PARKER, BLACK VOTES COUNT: POLITICAL EMPOWERMENT IN MISSISSIPPI AFTER 1965, 204 (1990); *Mississippi Elects Black Judges,* N.Y. Times, June 22, 1989, at A16. As a result of the *Martin* case, there are now eight black circuit and chancery court judges in Mississippi. Letter from Frank Parker to Edward Still, July 15, 1991 (on file with the YALE LAW & POLICY REVIEW).

32. Eight of the districts are coextensive with one county each: Harris, Tarrant, Dallas, Bexar, Travis, Jefferson, Hector, and Midland. The ninth district contains Lubbock and Crosby Counties.

court based its interim order on an agreement between the plaintiffs and the state attorney general, but the district judge went beyond the agreement to abolish partisan judicial elections.[33]

Several intervening Harris County judges appealed and obtained a stay of the interim remedial order. The state appealed from the finding of liability and from the abolition of partisan elections for judges. A panel of the Fifth Circuit reversed by a vote of 2-1 on the basis that section 2 of the Voting Rights Act did not reach single office holders, such as trial judges, although it did cover collegial courts.[34] The panel distinguished *Chisom v. Edwards* in which the Fifth Circuit had held that section 2 of the Voting Rights Act applied to the election of judges on the Louisiana Supreme Court.[35]

On rehearing, the Fifth Circuit sitting *en banc* reversed the district court by a vote of 12-1.[36] A seven-member majority overruled *Chisom v. Edwards* and held that section 2 did not apply to the election of any judges "for the cardinal reason that judges need not be elected at all . . . ."[37] Four judges, in an opinion by Judge Higginbotham, agreed with the panel opinion on the single-office holder exception.[38]

The Supreme Court disagreed with Judge Higginbotham's single-office holder theory as a jurisdictional bar, but held such concerns "relate to the question whether a vote dilution violation may be found or remedied rather than whether such a challenge may be brought."[39] In this way, the Court held that suits against at-large judicial elections may be heard by federal courts, but left in place at least a potential defense for the states. The Supreme Court reversed the judgment of the court of appeals and remanded the case.[40]

IV. The Problem of Judicial Favoritism

Plaintiffs in judicial election cases seek to tear down the barriers preventing the election of Blacks to judicial office. For instance, the *SCLC v. Siegelman* complaint alleges that "[t]he numbered place, at-large election system plan for circuit and district judges was enacted and has been maintained by the State of Alabama for the purpose and with the intent of diluting the voting strength

33. Houston Lawyers' Ass'n v. Attorney Gen. of Texas, 111 S.Ct. 2376, 2379 (1991).

34. LULAC v. Clements, 902 F.2d 293, 308 (5th Cir. 1990)(panel decision later withdrawn), 914 F.2d 620 (5th Cir. 1990) (en banc), *rev'd sub nom.*, Houston Lawyers' Ass'n v. Attorney Gen. of Texas, 111 S.Ct. 2376 (1991).

35. 839 F.2d 1056, *cert. denied*, 488 U.S. 955 (1988), *vacated sum nom.*, Chisom v. Roemer, 853 F.2d 1186 (5th Cir. 1988), *reh'g denied*, 857 F.2d 1473 (5th Cir. 1988)(en banc), 917 F.2d 187 (5th Cir. 1990), *and rev'd*, 111 S.Ct. 2354 (1991).

36. LULAC v. Clements, 914 F.2d 620 (5th Cir. 1990) (en banc).

37. *Id.* at 622.

38. *Id.* at 634.

39. Houston Lawyers' Ass'n v. Attorney Gen. of Texas, 111 S.Ct. 2376, 2381 (1991).

40. *Id.*

Blacks."[41] To remedy this situation, the plaintiffs asked the court to rder the State to develop an election system for circuit and district judges h will provide equal access to the political process and will not dilute the g strength of Black citizens of the State of Alabama."[42]

he attorneys representing the Alabama state judges contend that the cure f k of representation of Blacks will be worse than the disease:

> Single-member district systems would tie judges to election from small ricts composed of many fewer people than would constitute the electorate in -large election system. The temptation—some would say the need—for judges k after constituents in the courtroom would increase enormously: this system d represent the apotheosis of "home cooking."[43] . . . As for the effect on li ts, ironically the constitutional protection of unpopular minorities might su most, outside of minority districts. In short, a single-member district system w create enormous pressure for constituency-based justice at its worst.[44]

Th aintiffs and defendants are not even talking about the same problems. The pla ffs complain about the discrimination inherent in at-large elections and ask court to reform the election system; the defendants say any cure to this p em will inevitably lead to other problems, such as judicial favoritism and ' me cooking." Since the defendants oppose single-member judicial subdistric s well as modified at-large plans, we need to determine whether modified arge plans would meet many goals of both the plaintiffs and the defendants he civic inclusion principle and the winner-take-all principle.[45]

I doubt sincerity of this judicial favoritism objection because it includes a self-indict nt of the fairness of the people making the assertion. The *SCLC v. Siegelman* fendants probably would not admit that trial judges presently hold a bias ainst residents of another county or racial group. Why then should the def dants argue that judges will become biased if a smaller group elects them? I aving fewer people vote for a judge is more likely to make the judge unfai then the judges of the smaller circuits in Alabama are more likely to be unf than those elected in the large urban areas. For instance, the Seventeenth rcuit (Greene, Marengo, and Sumter Counties) has 49,411 people, while the enth Circuit (Jefferson County) has 651,525.[46] Obviously, according to the a ument of the Alabama defendants, residents of the Seventeenth Circuit are re likely to get "home cooking" from their judges. Taking

---

41. First Amended Co laint at 18, SCLC v. Siegelman, 714 F.Supp. 511 (M.D. Ala) (No. 88-D-462-N).

42. *Id.* at 21.

43. "Home cooking" is la yers' slang (at least in Alabama) for local favoritism by courts and juries.

44. Brief in Support of M tion for Reconsideration at 2-3, SCLC v. Siegelman, 714 F. Supp. 511 (M.D. Ala.) (No. 88-D-462-N).

45. Subdistricts need not b single-member districts. For instance, a remedial plan could call for dividing an urban county in two r more districts, each electing several judges.

46. The population per judge varies because of the greater number of lawsuits in commercial centers such as Jefferson County.

the defendants' argument to its extreme, they would have to adv the statewide election of judges.

The defenders of the status quo are apparently satisfied with the e-to-constituent ratio in the Seventeenth Circuit. Under modified at-lar ting, the same number of people would choose one judge in the Tenth uit as currently choose the single judge in the Seventeenth. Under eithe dified at-large or winner-take-all rules, the threshold of exclusion for the tion of the one judge in the Seventeenth Circuit is 50%. Thus (assum hat the whole population could and did vote) the threshold of exclusio ould be 24,706. If modified at-large were used in the Tenth Circuit to ele twenty-four judges, the threshold of exclusion would be 26,061 (1/25 the total population).

While modified at-large elections cannot meet all winner-ta ll criteria, they may be able to meet some goals of the defenders of the st quo. Like the Mississippi subdistricts, modified at-large plans will all less than a majority of all the voters of the judicial district to choose a judg r the whole district. However, more voters will have elected each judge i m dified at-large election than in an election using subdistricts. If the Ala a defendants are sincere in their objection to having a small number of vot elect a judge, they should consider modified at-large plan. For example, constituency were to elect ten judges, the threshold of exclusion would b % if the election were by traditional at-large rules, 9% under a modifie t-large system, and 5% of the total electorate (and 50% of each district) i bdistricts were used.[47]

V. The Problem of "Geographically Compact Minorities

In describing the proof plaintiffs must present in racia ote dilution cases, the Supreme Court has stated,

> unless there is conjunction of the following circumstances, th e of multimember districts generally will not impede the ability of minority vote o elect representatives of their choice. Stated succinctly, a bloc voting majority ust *usually* be able to defeat candidates supported by a politically cohesive, g graphically insular minority group. . . . First, the minority group must be abl to demonstrate that it is sufficiently large and geographically compact to con tute a majority in a single-member district. . . . Second, the minority group mu be able to show that it is politically cohesive. . . . Third, the minority group ust be able to demonstrate that the white majority votes sufficiently as a bloc enable it . . . usually to defeat the minority's preferred candidate.[48]

The "geographically compact" requirement (which i not found in section 2) makes sense only if one assumes that the sole alte native to a multimember

---

47. For a discussion of the formula for the threshold of exclusi . *see supra* note 15.
48. Thornburg v. Gingles, 478 U.S. 30, 48-51 (1986) (footnot and citations omitted).

plan is a single-member district plan. Certainly, if a minority group cannot show that it can form a single-member district, and if single-member districts are the only remedy a court will impose, there is not much point in fighting over whether the white voters are consistently defeating candidates supported by the minority group.[49]

On the other hand, if a court could adopt a remedy that would not require a geographically compact minority group, it could focus on the size and political strength, not the compactness, of the minority group. Modified at-large election plans are such remedies.

In *Martin v. Allain* the district judge followed the *Thornburg* analysis and found that

> [a]lthough evidence has established that throughout the state the minority group is politically cohesive and the white majority votes sufficiently as a bloc to usually defeat the minority's preferred candidate, only in a few districts have the plaintiffs established that the minority group is sufficiently large and geographically compact in the [judicial] district to constitute a majority in a single-member district.[50]

Fifteen months after the decision on the merits, the court reopened the record to receive evidence about modified at-large plans.[51] The court rejected modified at-large plans, holding "there is an adequate remedy in single-member sub-districts without imposing a radically new, judge-made process."[52]

Thus, we have a chicken-and-egg problem. The court held that the plaintiffs had to prove that single-member districts could solve their problems, and then held that single-member districts were an adequate solution to those problems that could be remedied by single-member districts. If the district court had not felt constrained by the *Thornburg* formulation of the proof "generally" needed, it probably could have found additional Mississippi judicial districts diluted black voting rights and might have welcomed the solution that modified at-large elections could provide.

The blindness to modified at-large as a remedy affects the way litigants present cases as well. The plaintiffs in the Alabama and Texas suits at first complained about a large number of multi-judge jurisdictions, but later amended their complaints to focus only on districts in which they would be able to

---

49. The preference for single-member districts is based on Connor v. Johnson, 402 U.S. 690 (1971).

> The lawyers for the [Connor v. Johnson] plaintiffs had made a strong case that multimember districts in Hinds County [Mississippi] were racially discriminatory. . . . [T]he Supreme Court could order single-member districts without departing from its repeatedly expressed position that multimember districts are not per se unconstitutional or from the line of precedent rejecting Fourteenth Amendment challenges to such districts.

Parker, *supra* note 31, at 114. The irony of the "Connor rule" is that it was a boost for the black and Latino plaintiffs at the time but now restricts the relief to which they are entitled.

50. Martin v. Allain, 658 F. Supp. 1183, 1204 (S.D. Miss. 1987).

51. Martin v. Mabus, 700 F. Supp. 327, 336 (S.D. Miss. 1988).

52. *Id.* at 337.

prove that Blacks or Latinos were "sufficiently large and geographically compact to constitute a majority in a single-member district."[53]

VI. The Benefits of Modified at-large Elections for Minorities and Majorities

While single-member districts are usually preferable for minorities over at-large elections, modified at-large rules can solve one practical problem that bedevils districting plans. Any election depending on districts is subject to gerrymandering and dilution (and sometimes inflation) of a minority group's voting power.[54] The remedial decision in *Martin v. Mabus* is an example of the problems caused by drawing single-member subdistricts. The plaintiffs sought subdistricts with 65% black majorities. The usual rule of thumb is that Blacks need a 65% population majority in a district to get a real voting majority because of "the discrepancy between black total population and black voting age population, . . . low voter registration and . . . low voter turnout among minorities . . . ."[55] The district court rejected much of the plaintiffs' plan for subdistricts on the grounds that it "over-emphasized black voting strength and provided for proportional representation of Blacks."[56] The court drew its own plan based on the idea that Blacks needed only a 60% majority in a district to win and that districts with more than 65% black majorities would constitute "packing of all minority voters into one sub-district [and] leav[ing] them without influence in other sub-districts and would further racially polarize these judicial elections."[57]

Of the fourteen majority black subdistricts the district court created, only three had black majorities of 65% or more. Frank Parker has described the result of these elections and the judge's decision to use 65% as a ceiling rather

53. Petition for Writ of Certiorari at 5 n.2, Houston Lawyers' Ass'n v. Mattox, No. 90-813 (suit against 44 counties, amended to attack only 10); First Amended Complaint, SCLC v. Siegelman, No. 88-D-462-N (M.D. Ala. filed Oct. 27, 1988).

54. Subdistricting of judicial elections presents an additional problem associated with geographical dispersion of lawyers. To put it simply, only lawyers may become judges, and lawyers may be geographically maldistributed in urban areas. To alleviate this problem, the jurisdiction must either abandon the usual residency requirement which makes the electoral district and the venue of the court coextensive or retain some form of at-large elections, either traditional or one of the alternative election plans discussed in this article. This may not be much of a problem because in urban areas (the most likely targets of judicial election suits) there are generally a higher number of lawyers per judge. According to statistics provided by the Alabama State Bar, there are 113 lawyers per circuit judge in the Tenth Judicial Circuit (Jefferson County, the most populous county in the state). Compare this to the 22 lawyers per circuit judge in the First Judicial Circuit (Choctaw, Clarke, and Washington counties). Relatively, the Tenth has more choice or a greater pool of potential candidates than the First, but perhaps we should focus on how little choice each has. We would be quite concerned if there were only 20 people constitutionally eligible to be mayor, or governor, or president.

55. *Martin*, 700 F. Supp. at 333. *See also* United Jewish Organizations v. Carey, 430 U.S. 144, 164 (1976).

56. *Martin*, 700 F. Supp. at 330.

57. *Id.* at 333-34.

than a floor: "Although seventeen Black candidates ran for state court judgeships, only five were elected. Three of the five who won were elected in districts that were over 65% Black."[58] We can only guess at how many might have won if the subdistricts had been drawn another way. The court made an inherently political decision when it decided to avoid concentrating Blacks. In a modified at-large system, the court would not have to group the voters geographically; instead the voters would group themselves behind their favored candidates.

While modified at-large rules will usually be adopted because there is polarized voting in the society, the success of modified at-large does not depend upon continued polarized voting, and it does not institutionalize the divisions in society by drawing a "black district," a "Latino district," and a "white district." In a district which is 65% or more black and in which there is racially polarized voting, the minority of Whites is likely to feel as closed out of the political process as Blacks felt when they were the minority in the multimember at-large plan. Modified at-large elections would allow those Whites to form voluntary constituencies with their ideological allies in the same way that Blacks or Latinos could. Thus, the burden of the election plan would not be shifted from a minority group in a multimember district to the new minorities in each of the single-member districts or subdistricts. The members of the county-wide majority who are minorities in their own districts may harbor a resentment at the "affirmative action" that has placed them in a powerless minority.[59]

Finally, modified at-large elections allow biracial coalitions to form as racially polarized voting decreases. Racially homogenous single-member districts tend to freeze the racial divisions of society by making it unnecessary for candidates to appeal to any group other than their own.[60] In these single-member districts, all compromises (if any) must take place in the legislative arena, rather than among the public.

VII. Possible Objections to Modified At-Large

In *Chapman v Meier*,[61] the Supreme Court mentioned several objections to at-large elections. While the Court was not dealing with modified at-large elections, it is instructive to consider these objections. The Court listed four objections—three it termed "practical weaknesses." "First," the Court said,

58. Parker, *supra* note 31, at 204.

59. Note, *Affirmative Action and Electoral Reform*, 90 Yale L. J. 1811, 1828-29 (1981).

60. *See* United Jewish Organizations v. Carey, 430 U.S. 144 at 172-73 (Brennan, J., concurring) (racially safe districts may frustrate "potentially successful efforts at coalition building across racial lines"); *see also* Guinier, *supra* note 16, at 1139 & n.300, 1148 & n.331. Prof. Guinier offers a stinging criticism of single-member districts in her forthcoming article. Guinier, *supra* note 5.

61. 420 U.S. 1 (1975).

"as the number of legislative seats within the district increases, the difficulty for the voter in making intelligent choices among candidates also increases."[62] This same problem will arise with modified at-large, but will be no greater—and perhaps less—than under winner-take-all rules. If limited voting were used, voters would be able to narrow their attention to a small number of candidates rather than having to make a large number of bilateral choices for each judicial position.

"Second, when candidates are elected at large, residents of particular areas within the district may feel that they have no representative specifically responsible to them."[63] As noted in part IV, this feature is considered an asset by the defenders of the status quo. Under modified at-large, a voter might feel she has someone on the bench looking after her interests, but the judge is unlikely to know which voters actually elected her. To the extent that the judge attempts to please all potential voters, modified at-large will be the same as the present plans.

"Third, it is possible that bloc voting by delegates from a multimember district may result in undue representation of residents of these districts relative to voters in single-member districts."[64] This objection is not applicable to the election of trial judges.

Finally, the Court discussed the possibility that at-large voting will "operate to minimize or cancel out the voting strength of racial or political elements of the voting population."[65] Modified at-large rules are designed to counteract this winner-take-all tendency in at-large elections.

The status quo defenders might raise the objection that modified at-large is confusing to voters. A study of a recently-adopted cumulative voting plan shows that nearly all the voters understood the proper way to cast a ballot and that only a small minority found the system more complex than other election rules.[66]

The minority group might also legitimately oppose modified at-large elections because the minority group will have to vote more or less uniformly to avoid splitting its strength. Take, for example, a judicial circuit electing five judges and having a 25% black population. At least 80% of the Blacks must vote for one candidate in a modified at-large election to get that candidate elected (assuming similar registration and turnout rates for the minority and majority). If the circuit were divided into five single-member districts—one with a 65% or more majority of Blacks—the Whites would not be able to

62. *Id.* at 15.

63. *Id.* at 15-16.

64. *Id.* at 16.

65. *Id.* at 17, quoting Fortson v. Dorsey, 379 U.S. 433, 439 (1965).

66. Engstrom et al., *supra* note 19, at 194. Ninety-five percent of the voters knew they could cast all three votes for one candidate; 13% found the cumulative voting plan "more difficult to understand" than other local elections in which they had voted.

defeat a black-preferred candidate in that one district if there were a runoff. In the absence of a runoff, two or more candidates seeking the black vote might splinter that vote sufficiently to allow a white-preferred candidate to be elected. In this situation, Blacks would be dependant upon runoffs to preserve their choices, even though Blacks have brought suits against runoffs in at least two jurisdictions.[67]

VII. CONCLUSION

Modified at-large plans are admittedly not used widely in the United States. However, advocates on both sides of judicial election cases should consider modified at-large plans as antidotes to racial and ethnic exclusion from the judiciary. Plaintiffs will find that modified at-large meets their goals of civic inclusion; defendants will discover that modified at-large election plans do not justify their fears of abandoning the present system. Finally, the knowledge that such alternatives to single-member districts or subdistricts are available may change courts' perceptions. Workable remedies *do* exist for the problem of dilution of minority voting strength in judicial elections and thus for violations of section 2 of the Voting Rights Act of 1965.

67. Whitfield v. Democratic Party of Arkansas, 902 F.2d 15 (8th Cir. 1990) (per curiam), *cert. denied sub nom.* Whitfield v. Clinton, 111 S.Ct. 1089 (1991); Butts v. City of New York, 779 F.2d 141 (2d Cir. 1985), *cert. denied*, 478 U.S. 1021 (1986).

VIRGINIA LAW REVIEW

VOLUME 77 | FEBRUARY 1991 | NUMBER 1

ARTICLE

UNDOING THE RIGHT THING: SINGLE-MEMBER OFFICES AND THE VOTING RIGHTS ACT

*Pamela S. Karlan**

> *We lived many lives in those swirling campaigns . . . yet when we achieved and the new world dawned, the old men came out again and took our victory to remake in the likeness of the former world they knew. . . . We stammered that we had worked for a new heaven and a new earth, and they thanked us kindly and made their peace.*
>
> *Lawrence of Arabia*[1]

THE relationship between the American political system and the Voting Rights Act of 1965 is somewhat more ambivalent than it might appear at first glance. Of course, the Act and its amendments reflect profound democratic impulses: They represent a national political consensus about the need to take extraordinary measures to bring about the effective inclusion of black Americans in the political sys-

* Associate Professor of Law, University of Virginia.

Many of my colleagues, both at Virginia and in the voting rights community, have improved this article with their suggestions and insights. I especially appreciate the comments of Ken Abraham, Jim Blacksher, Dick Engstrom, Lani Guinier, Gerry Hebert, Sherrilyn Ifill, Alex Johnson, Dan Ortiz, George Rutherglen, Elizabeth Scott, and Bill Stuntz. Lee Ashmore provided helpful research assistance.

1 J. Mack, A Prince of Our Disorder: The Life of T.E. Lawrence 272 (1976) (quoting Oriental Assembly 142-43 (A. Lawrence ed. 1939)).

tem.[2] At the same time, however, the Act has a deeply nonmajoritarian cast: It demands the intimate involvement of the courts in state and local electoral systems, even to the extent of setting aside longstanding political arrangements. The Act has been invoked to strike down literally thousands of practices throughout the nation over the last quarter century. Truly, it has served as a linchpin of the "Second Reconstruction."[3]

As with the First Reconstruction, however, the threat of judicial retrenchment is ever present. The First Reconstruction effectively ended with the *Civil Rights Cases*.[4] The United States Supreme Court took that opportunity to announce that

> there must be some stage in the progress of [the black citizen's inclusion] when he takes the rank of a mere citizen, and ceases to be the special favorite of the laws, and when his rights as a citizen, or a man, are to be protected in the ordinary modes by which other men's rights are protected.[5]

Recent developments in voting rights law suggest that a second Redemption is upon us.[6] The courts seem to have seized upon the

---

[2] The Supreme Court first recognized the Act's extraordinary character in South Carolina v. Katzenbach, 383 U.S. 301 (1966).

The Act protects a number of groups: racial minorities such as blacks, see, e.g., Thornburg v. Gingles, 478 U.S. 30 (1986); language minorities, specifically Hispanics, Native Americans, Asian Americans, and Alaskan Natives, see Gomez v. City of Watsonville, 863 F.2d 1407 (9th Cir. 1988) (challenge by Hispanic voters), cert. denied, 109 S. Ct. 1534 (1989); Buckanaga v. Sisseton Indep. School Dist., 804 F.2d 469 (8th Cir. 1986) (claim by Native Americans); 42 U.S.C. §§ 1973aa-1a (1988); and the disabled, see 42 U.S.C. §§ 1973aa-6 (1988). For the sake of simplicity, as well as because the political inclusion of blacks has been a primary concern of the Act since its original passage, this Article focuses on the application of the Act to claims by black voters.

[3] See Kousser, The Undermining of the First Reconstruction: Lessons for the Second, *in* Minority Vote Dilution 27 (C. Davidson ed. 1984) (viewing the Voting Rights Act as a central part of the "Second Reconstruction").

[4] 109 U.S. 3 (1883).

[5] Id. at 25.

[6] "Redemption" refers to the effective end of Reconstruction through the reassertion of white control in the South. See C. Woodward, The Strange Career of Jim Crow 4 n.* (2d rev. ed. 1966).

This phenomenon is hardly limited to the area of voting rights. Last year, for example, the Supreme Court dramatically restricted the scope of both 42 U.S.C. § 1981 (1988), a key civil rights provision of the First Reconstruction, see Patterson v. McLean Credit Union, 109 S. Ct. 2363 (1989), and Title VII of the Civil Rights Act of 1964 (codified as amended at 42 U.S.C. §§ 2000e to e-17 (1988)), a key civil rights provision of the Second Reconstruction, see Lorance v. AT & T Technologies, 109 S. Ct. 2261 (1989); Martin v. Wilks, 109 S. Ct. 2180 (1989); Wards Cove Packing Co. v. Atonio, 109 S. Ct. 2115 (1989).

Act's silver anniversary to announce that it is time for a return to normalcy and the ordinary modes of politics; once again, although "[b]lacks may vote . . . it is whites who will govern."[7]

To understand the depth of this retreat, one must first understand the vision of politics that animates the Voting Rights Act of 1965. In Part I of this Article, I will describe a central aspect of that vision: its nonmajoritarian character. The central substantive provision of the Act, amended section 2,[8] decisively rejects the conception of electoral politics as merely a means by which a numerical majority may arrogate to itself all governing power. Instead, it expresses a vision of electoral politics that demands the development of political institutions embodying racial pluralism.

Against the backdrop of Part I, Part II looks at a central vehicle that the courts have been using to restrict the Act's scope: the so-called "single-member office" doctrine. Under this doctrine, elections to fill single-member positions—such as mayor,[9] county chief execu-

---

[7] Guinier, Keeping the Faith: Black Voters in the Post-Reagan Era, 24 Harv. C.R.-C.L. L. Rev. 393, 394 (1989).

[8] Voting Rights Act of 1965, § 2 (as amended), 42 U.S.C. § 1973 (1988). Section 2 provides:

> (a) No voting qualification or prerequisite to voting or standard, practice, or procedure shall be imposed or applied by any State or political subdivision in a manner which results in a denial or abridgement of the right of any citizen of the United States to vote on account of race or color, or in contravention of the guarantees set forth in section 1973b(f)2 of this title [section 4(f)(2) of the original Act], as provided in subsection (b) of this section.
>
> (b) A violation of subsection (a) of this section is established if, based on the totality of circumstances, it is shown that the political processes leading to nomination or election in the State or political subdivision are not equally open to participation by members of a class of citizens protected by subsection (a) of this section in that its members have less opportunity than other members of the electorate to participate in the political process and to elect representatives of their choice. The extent to which members of a protected class have been elected to office in the State or political subdivision is one circumstance which may be considered: *Provided*, That nothing in this section establishes a right to have members of a protected class elected in numbers equal to their proportion in the population.

Section 2 was amended in 1982 to eliminate the requirement that plaintiffs show that the challenged electoral system was enacted or maintained for the purpose of denying or diluting the voting strength of a racial minority. See S. Rep. No. 417, 97th Cong., 2d Sess. 15-16, *reprinted in* 1982 U.S. Code Cong. & Admin. News 177, 192-93 [hereinafter Senate Report]; Parker, The "Results" Test of Section 2 of the Voting Rights Act: Abandoning the Intent Standard, 69 Va. L. Rev. 715 (1983).

[9] Butts v. City of New York, 779 F.2d 141 (2d Cir. 1985), cert. denied, 478 U.S. 1021 (1986).

tive,[10] or a designated seat on the state trial bench[11]—cannot be attacked under the "results test" of section 2.[12] According to the courts, it simply makes no sense to talk about vote dilution in a situation that is *inherently* winner-take-all.[13] I will show, however, that these situations are *not* inherently winner-take-all. First, governmental structures are themselves quite plastic; the so-called single-member office can often be recast in ways that increase the potential for racial pluralism. Second, the electoral structures themselves are equally malleable; election rules can be reshaped to dampen their exclusionary features. In particular, I claim that runoff requirements[14] exacerbate the tendency toward discredited forms of winner-take-all majoritarianism. Considered in this light, the single-member office doctrine represents a restrictive distortion of section 2.

In the final Part, I return to the broader question of *why* the courts have manufactured this doctrine. I will argue that under the guise of judicial deference to "democratic" choices and remedial circumspection the courts are seeking to re-entrench precisely the notion of politics that the Voting Rights Act of 1965 was intended to repudiate.

---

10 Whitfield v. Democratic Party, 686 F. Supp. 1365 (E.D. Ark. 1988), aff'd on reh'g en banc by an equally divided court, 902 F.2d 15 (8th Cir. 1990), petition for cert. filed sub nom. Whitfield v. Clinton, 59 U.S.L.W. 3180 (U.S. Aug. 31, 1990) (No. 90-383).

In the interest of full disclosure, I should note that I have represented Mr. Whitfield throughout the pendency of this litigation.

11 See League of United Latin American Citizens [LULAC] v. Clements, 914 F.2d 620, 647-49 (5th Cir. 1990) (en banc) (Higginbotham, J., concurring in the judgment), petition for cert. filed sub nom. Houston Lawyers' Ass'n v. Mattox, 59 U.S.L.W. 3406 (U.S. Nov. 21, 1990) (No. 90-813).

12 Section 2 forbids states and their political subdivisions from using voting schemes which "result[ ] in a denial or abridgement" of the right to vote, regardless of the intent behind such schemes. According to the Supreme Court, "[t]he essence of a § 2 claim is that a certain electoral law, practice, or structure interacts with social and historical conditions to cause an inequality in the opportunities enjoyed by black and white voters to elect their preferred representatives." Thornburg v. Gingles, 478 U.S. 30, 47 (1986); see also infra text accompanying notes 25-27 (discussing the functional view of the political process instituted by the amended section 2).

13 See, e.g., *Butts*, 779 F.2d at 149.

14 Runoff requirements have been much in the news of late. See, e.g., Isikoff, U.S. Sues Georgia over Voting Law; Racial Bias Alleged; Wide Effect Seen if Runoff Measure is Voided, Wash. Post, Aug. 10, 1990, at A1, col. 1 (reporting on a lawsuit filed by the Department of Justice challenging Georgia's majority-vote runoff statutes); Smothers, U.S. Files Suit Against Georgia, Charging Bias in Election Laws, N.Y. Times, Aug. 10, 1990, at A1, col. 1 (same).

I. Transformation and the Voting Rights Act

The right to vote clearly must be central to any theory of why American democracy is a legitimate form of government.[15] The right has both formal and functional importance. Its formal importance lies in how voting, regardless of whether one's views prevail, announces that the voter is a full member of the political community.[16] Its functional importance lies in the way that voting influences

---

[15] See, e.g., Wesberry v. Sanders, 376 U.S. 1, 17 (1964) ("No right is more precious in a free country than that of having a voice in the election of those who make the laws under which, as good citizens, we must live. Other rights, even the most basic, are illusory if the right to vote is undermined."); J. Rawls, A Theory of Justice 61, 221-22 (1971) ("The principle of equal liberty . . . requires that all citizens are to have an equal right to take part in, and to determine the outcome of, the constitutional process that establishes the laws with which they are to comply. Justice as fairness begins with the idea that where common principles are necessary and to everyone's advantage, they are to be worked out from the viewpoint of a suitably defined initial situation of equality in which each person is fairly represented."); see also Abrams, "Raising Politics Up": Minority Political Participation and Section 2 of the Voting Rights Act, 63 N.Y.U. L. Rev. 449, 480-81 (1988) (arguing that the opportunity to participate in the political process, broadly defined, is central to the "legitimacy of our governmental system").

It was precisely the stabilizing, legitimacy-conferring aspect of voting that provided the initial impetus for the voting rights movement of the early 1960s. The Kennedy Administration pressed civil rights groups to pursue voter registration both because it thought that an attack on black disenfranchisement provided the strongest moral claim in civil rights and because voter registration drives presented an alternative to more confrontational civil rights strategies (such as the Freedom Rides) that might prompt a white backlash. See T. Branch, Parting the Waters: America in the King Years, 1954-63, at 382, 404-06, 479-89 (1988).

[16] For a recent examination of the relationship between the right to vote and full membership in the community, see Note, The Disenfranchisement of Ex-Felons: Citizenship, Criminality, and "The Purity of the Ballot Box," 102 Harv. L. Rev. 1300, 1304-17 (1989).

This symbolic aspect of the right to vote is illustrated by cases such as Bell v. Southwell, 376 F.2d 659 (5th Cir. 1967). In *Bell*, the town of Americus, Georgia's practice of using three separate voting booths—one for white men, one for white women, and one for black persons—was challenged. Mary F. Bell (an unsuccessful black candidate for justice of the peace) and several other black voters sued to have the results of the election set aside, claiming that the use of segregated voting booths violated the Constitution. Id. at 660-61. The district court denied their request, in part because it found that regardless of the effects segregated booths may have had on voting (to the court this was limited to the narrow idea of participation among black voters), the outcome of the election would have been unchanged. Id. at 660. The Fifth Circuit, however, rejected this approach, reversed the district court, and ordered it to set the election aside. The Fifth Circuit stated "that there are certain discriminatory practices which . . . so infect the processes of the law" that they render the results invalid by their very presence. Id. at 662-63. "What [these plaintiffs] sought was an election conducted free of such indefensible, racial distinctions. That being so, it was not the usual simple case of counting votes and denying relief for want of affirmative proof of a different result." Id. at 664-65.

government: Realistically speaking, most citizens participate in the process of governing primarily by selecting representatives, and voting aggregates their preferences to declare a winner.[17] In this Part, I first describe how our understanding of the formal and functional aspects of the right to vote has evolved during the first twenty-five years of the Voting Rights Act. I then identify as a central feature of this understanding the Act's unequivocal rejection of winner-take-all majoritarianism as an appropriate rule of aggregation, and conclude by locating this feature within the longstanding debate over the so-called "countermajoritarian difficulty."

A. *From Formalism to Functionalism*

The first great achievement of the Voting Rights Act of 1965 lay in its radical expansion of *formal* voting rights. On the eve of the Act's passage, blacks were completely excluded from the registration rolls in large parts of the South, and economic and physical harassment kept even those blacks who had managed to register from actually casting ballots. A series of stringent measures, including the use of federal registrars and election observers,[18] the abolition of literacy tests nationwide,[19] and the invalidation of restrictive registration policies generally,[20] resulted in an exponential increase in black registration and voting.

But this expansion of formal voting rights was an incomplete response to the barriers preventing full black political empowerment. The courts soon recognized that even when black citizens were added to the rolls and voted, they were often still unable to elect the candidates of their choice: The states, in direct response to the appearance of black voters, adopted election schemes that aggregated voters' preferences in ways that minimized the impact of black votes.[21]

---

[17] See Reynolds v. Sims, 377 U.S. 533, 565 (1964) ("[E]ach and every citizen has an inalienable right to full and effective participation in the political processes of his State's legislative bodies. Most citizens can achieve this participation only as qualified voters.").

[18] 42 U.S.C. §§ 1973d-1973f (1988).

[19] Id. § 1973aa.

[20] See, e.g., Mississippi State Chapter, Operation Push v. Allain, 674 F. Supp. 1245 (N.D. Miss. 1987), appeal docketed, No. 89-4627 (5th Cir. Aug. 29, 1989).

[21] For discussions of the strategies used to offset increased black participation, see, e.g., Allen v. State Bd. of Elections, 393 U.S. 544, 550-53 (1969); Senate Report, supra note 8, at 6; F. Parker, Black Votes Count: Political Empowerment in Mississippi After 1965, at 34-77 (1990).

In reaction, the courts turned to protecting the *functional* integrity of black votes by striking down election systems that "diluted"[22] the collective power of black voters. The primary object of the courts' attention was the widespread use of multimember electoral districts and at-large elections.[23] For a variety of reasons—ranging from overt residential segregation to the continuing effects of socioeconomic disparities to communal preferences—blacks often live in a discrete portion of a particular jurisdiction, such as a city or county. If the jurisdiction were to be carved into smaller electoral districts, then blacks could form a majority of the electorate in one or more of those smaller districts and elect their preferred candidates. If the jurisdiction is left as a single, undivided district, however, the preferences of black voters can be "submerged in the larger pool of white vote[s],"

22 The concept of "dilution" can be traced back to the dawn of modern federal oversight of the election process. See, e.g., United States v. Saylor, 322 U.S. 385, 389 (1944); United States v. Classic, 313 U.S. 299, 315, 321-22 (1941); United States v. Mosley, 238 U.S. 383, 386 (1915). It first gained widespread currency, however, during the "apportionment revolution" of the early 1960s. See, e.g., Reynolds v. Sims, 377 U.S. 533, 555 n.29 (1964) ("The right to vote freely for the candidate of one's choice is of the essence of a democratic society, and any restrictions on that right strike at the heart of representative government. And the right of suffrage can be denied by a debasement or dilution of the weight of a citizen's vote just as effectively as by wholly prohibiting the free exercise of the franchise.").

For a general discussion of racial vote dilution, see, e.g., Thornburg v. Gingles, 478 U.S. 30, 42-51 (1986); Senate Report, supra note 8, at 6, 9-15; Davidson, Minority Vote Dilution: An Overview, *in* Minority Vote Dilution, supra note 3, at 1-23; Derfner, Racial Discrimination and the Right to Vote, 26 Vand. L. Rev. 523, 552-60 (1973).

23 See McCrary & Hebert, Keeping the Courts Honest: The Role of Historians as Expert Witnesses in Southern Voting Rights Cases, 16 S.U.L. Rev. 101, 102 (1989).

A multimember electoral district is any district that elects more than one official to fill a given office. Thus, for example, the States are multimember districts with respect to the United States Senate as each state elects two Senators. When a district selects only one person to fill a given office, the district is referred to as a single-member district. For example, each congressional district within a state is a single-member district because each is served by only one Representative. See 2 U.S.C. § 2c (1988) (requiring that each state establish a separate district for each of its Representatives and that each district elect one and only one Representative).

At-large elections are a subset of multimember district elections. In an at-large election, the entire jurisdiction forms a single electoral district from which all the officials are chosen. For example, a city with a five-member city council, each of whose members is selected by the votes of every voter within the city, is elected at large. See generally Abrams, supra note 15, at 451 n.13 (briefly describing the characteristics of multimember and at-large districts); Davidson, supra note 22, at 1-5 (describing at-large elections); Note, Alternative Voting Systems as Remedies for Unlawful At-Large Systems, 92 Yale L.J. 144, 144 nn.1-3 (1982) (same).

votes that have traditionally reflected preferences contrary to those of black voters.[24]

In amending section 2, Congress required courts to adopt "the functional view of 'political process' . . . rather than the formalistic view."[25] It delineated nine "[t]ypical factors," largely concerned with present socioeconomic and political conditions, to channel the inquiry.[26] The clear import of the nine so-called "Senate factors," as well as of the test for dilution through submergence set out by the Supreme Court in *Thornburg v. Gingles*,[27] is that systems for aggre-

---

[24] McCrary & Hebert, supra note 23, at 103; see Thornburg v. Gingles, 478 U.S. 30, 46 (1986); see also Rogers v. Lodge, 458 U.S. 613, 616 (1982) (describing the dilutive effects of at-large elections); F. Parker, supra note 21, at 63-64 (describing the use of multimember districts to dilute black voter strength in Mississippi); Davidson, supra note 22, at 1-2, 5 (describing the dilutive effects of multimember districting in Taylor, Texas).

[25] Senate Report, supra note 8, at 30 n.120; see *Gingles*, 478 U.S. at 45 (stating that the question of whether or not the political processes are " 'equally open' " depends on a "functional" view of both past and present conditions and the political process as a whole (quoting Senate Report, supra note 8, at 30 & n.120)).

[26] Senate Report, supra note 8, at 28-29. These factors, occasionally called the *White-Zimmer* factors because they were drawn from the Supreme Court's analysis in White v. Regester, 412 U.S. 755 (1973), as further refined by Zimmer v. McKeithen, 485 F.2d 1297 (5th Cir. 1973) (en banc), aff'd per curiam on different grounds sub nom. East Carroll Parish School Bd. v. Marshall, 424 U.S. 636 (1976), include: (1) the history of voting-related discrimination in the jurisdiction; (2) the presence of racial bloc voting; (3) the use of practices that enhance the opportunity for discrimination, such as majority-vote requirements and anti-single shot rules; (4) minority access to candidate slating processes; (5) the continuing socioeconomic effects of past and present discrimination; (6) the presence of overt or subtle racial appeals in campaigns; (7) the extent of minority electoral success; (8) the responsiveness of elected officials to minority concerns; and (9) the strength of the justification for the challenged practice. See Senate Report, supra note 8, at 28-29. It should be noted that only one of these nine factors deals with discrimination "that touched the right . . . to register [or] to vote." See id. at 28.

Initially, the factors set out in *White* and *Zimmer* were essentially treated as definitional. If these factors were present, then the challenged system was deemed to have denied minority voters an equal opportunity to participate in the political process and to elect their preferred candidates. See, e.g., *White*, 412 U.S. at 766-67 (considering proof of these factors as sufficient to uphold the district court's judgment invalidating the multimember districts and ordering new single-member districts to be drawn). With the decisions in Washington v. Davis, 426 U.S. 229 (1976), Nevett v. Sides, 571 F.2d 209 (5th Cir. 1978), cert. denied, 446 U.S. 951 (1980), and City of Mobile v. Bolden, 446 U.S. 55 (1980), which required proof of a discriminatory purpose rather than merely a discriminatory effect, the factors no longer served as sufficient proof; they became merely circumstantial evidence of an underlying discriminatory purpose. See, e.g., Rodgers v. Lodge, 458 U.S. 613, 623-27 (1982). The 1982 amendments to section 2 restored the factors to their original status as indicators of a practice violative of the results test. See Senate Report, supra note 8, at 15-16, 27-30.

[27] 478 U.S. 30, 50-51 (1986). The Court identified three circumstances that it saw as "necessary preconditions" for a section 2 challenge to at-large elections:

gating individual votes, and not simply rules for deciding who votes, are subject to searching analysis under section 2.

B. Nonmajoritarianism and the Voting Rights Act

To say that aggregation rules that submerge black voters' preferences are illegitimate because they allow a (white) majority to achieve an officeholding monopoly represents a decisive repudiation of the pervasive winner-take-all "instincts"[28] that govern what Congress has described as "the everyday rough-and-tumble of American politics—tactics used traditionally by the 'ins' against the 'outs.' "[29] This repudiation of majority monopolization is powerfully illustrated by the language consistently used by Congress and the Supreme Court to refer to the people whose functional voting rights section 2 was intended to protect: "members of the minority group."[30] That phrase has two not entirely overlapping meanings. On the one hand, "minority" reflects a numerical understanding of the position of black voters: There are fewer black than white voters in the relevant jurisdiction.[31]

> First, the minority group must be able to demonstrate that it is sufficiently large and geographically compact to constitute a majority in a single-member district. . . . Second, the minority group must be able to show that it is politically cohesive. . . . Third, the minority must be able to demonstrate that the white majority votes sufficiently as a bloc to enable it—in the absence of special circumstances . . . —usually to defeat the minority's preferred candidate.

Id. (footnotes omitted). Several recent cases have treated the three *Gingles* factors as threshold issues whose absence can absolutely bar a section 2 lawsuit. See, e.g., Solomon v. Liberty County, 899 F.2d 1012 (11th Cir. 1990) (en banc), cert. denied, 59 U.S.L.W. 3460 (U.S. Jan. 7, 1991) (No. 90-102); Brewer v. Ham, 876 F.2d 448 (5th Cir. 1989); McNeil v. Springfield Park Dist., 851 F.2d 937 (7th Cir. 1988), cert. denied, 109 S. Ct. 1769 (1989); cf. City of Carrollton Branch of NAACP v. Stallings, 829 F.2d 1547, 1550 (11th Cir. 1987) ("*Gingles* not only followed the results test mandated by Congress, but also established a new three-part test for analyzing minority vote dilution claims under Section 2 of the Voting Rights Act"), cert. denied, 485 U.S. 936 (1988).

28 See R. Dworkin, Law's Empire 178-79 (1986).

29 Senate Report, supra note 8, at 12.

30 See, e.g., *Gingles*, 478 U.S. at 49, 50-51 (using the term "minority" in articulating each of the three *Gingles* factors); Senate Report, supra note 8, at 28-29 (using the phrase "members of the minority group" in five of the nine factors, and using the shorter phrase "the minority group" in a sixth).

31 This is not to say, as one court has suggested, that no section 2 claim can be raised by black voters who form a numerical majority in the relevant jurisdiction. See Whitfield v. Democratic Party, 686 F. Supp. 1365, 1376 (E.D. Ark. 1988) ("[I]t occurs to the Court that, absent state-created barriers to registering and voting, there should be both some low threshold, as well as some high threshold of *minority* voting age population needed in order to trigger a consideration of any argument that a run off device results in a denial or an

On the other hand, "[i]n the context of the Constitution's guarantee of equal protection, 'minority' does not have a merely numerical denotation; rather it refers to an identifiable and specially disadvantaged group."[32]

Several scholars have expressed reservations about using the term "minority" precisely because "it implies a certain delegitimacy in a majoritarian system" by evoking an image that suggests that black persons are normatively, as well as descriptively, expected to lose in a system that is often, if imprecisely, described as being based on "majority rule."[33] That criticism may be well placed in general, but in the context of the Voting Rights Act, the repeated use of the term "minority," in implicit opposition to the term "majority," represents

---

abridgement of the right of any citizen to vote or to participate in the political processes of the state."), aff'd on reh'g en banc by an equally divided court, 902 F.2d 15 (8th Cir. 1990), petition for cert. filed sub nom. Whitfield v. Clinton, 59 U.S.L.W. 3180 (U.S. Aug. 31, 1990) (No. 90-383). Contra Monroe v. City of Woodville, 819 F.2d 507, 508-09 (5th Cir. 1987) (rejecting the district court's award of a summary judgment which had been based on the city's argument that "because blacks already constitute a 60.5 percent majority of the voting age population of Woodville, they accordingly currently possess any remedy they might receive pursuant to . . . Section 2 of the Voting Rights Act") (citation omitted). By its terms, section 2 condemns voting systems that "are not equally open to participation by members of a class of citizens protected by subsection (a)." 42 U.S.C. § 1973(b) (1988). Its terms do not condition the violation upon the relative size of that class.

Further, the legislative history of the Act supports providing protection to black numerical majorities. Congress relied principally on two cases—White v. Regester, 412 U.S. 755 (1973), and Zimmer v. McKeithen, 485 F.2d 1297 (5th Cir. 1973) (en banc), aff'd per curiam on other grounds sub nom. East Carroll Parish School Bd. v. Marshall, 424 U.S. 636 (1976)—in articulating the "results test" of amended section 2. See Senate Report, supra note 8, at 23, 27-28. Neither of these cases involved plaintiffs who were actually a numerical minority of the affected jurisdiction. See *Zimmer*, 485 F.2d at 1301 (jurisdiction was roughly 59% black in total population); Graves v. Barnes, 343 F. Supp. 704, 730 (W.D. Tex. 1972) (three-judge court) (involving a jurisdiction in which Mexican-Americans constituted "about half the population"), aff'd in relevant part and rev'd in part on other grounds sub nom. *White*, 412 U.S. 755; see also *White*, 412 U.S. at 767-70 (finding that the district court had properly treated the plaintiffs as a minority).

[32] *Graves*, 343 F. Supp. at 730.

[33] Williams, Alchemical Notes: Reconstructing Ideals from Deconstructed Rights, 22 Harv. C.R.-C.L. L. Rev. 401, 404 n.4 (1987); accord Karlan, Maps and Misreadings: The Role of Geographic Compactness in Racial Vote Dilution Litigation, 24 Harv. C.R.-C.L. L. Rev. 173, 214 n.174 (1989); L. Guinier, The Triumph of Tokenism: The Voting Rights Act and the Theory of Black Electorial Success 3 n.1 (1990) (unpublished manuscript on file with the author).

As Professor J.M. Balkin explains, this process of definition through opposition is critical to the way the legal system deals, through abstract categories, with social reality. Balkin, Deconstructive Practice and Legal Theory, 96 Yale L.J. 743, 746-49, 751-55, 763-64 (1987).

a critical, if somewhat subconscious, recognition by the Act's framers, amenders, and interpreters that section 2 rejects a simplistic equation of modern American democratic politics with a majority stranglehold on elective offices. In short, if members of a "minority group" cannot be given "less opportunity . . . to elect representatives of their choice" than can members of the "majority,"[34] then clearly we have moved beyond crude majority rule.[35]

---

[34] Voting Rights Act of 1965, § 2(b) (as amended), 42 U.S.C. § 1973(b) (1988).

[35] Of course, this movement is not entirely the creature of the Voting Rights Act. As the Supreme Court remarked in Gordon v. Lance, 403 U.S. 1, 6 (1971), "there is nothing in the language of the Constitution, our history, or our cases that requires that a majority always prevail on every issue," even when an issue is subject to decision by vote.

Moreover, there is a significant, albeit purely descriptive, difficulty with using the shorthand phrase "majority rule": it may not specify the voting rule that in fact determines the winner. It is often the case that candidates win without obtaining the support of a majority of the electorate. The simplest example of this fact is the existence of low voter turnout. For a penetrating examination of the phenomenon of nonvoting, particularly its ideological functions, see F. Piven & R. Cloward, Why Americans Don't Vote (1988). Given the level of turnout, it is often the case that the winning candidate has received far less than one half of the *potential* votes. The results of modern presidential elections illustrate this fact. Leaving aside the artificial majority created by the Electoral College, the winning candidate failed to obtain a majority of the popular votes cast in three of the last eleven elections (1948, 1960, and 1968). See Elections Research Center, Congressional Quarterly, America Votes 18: A Handbook of Contemporary American Election Statistics 5 (R. Scammon & A. McGillivray eds. 1989). Moreover, low registration and turnout meant that, in 1988, although George Bush received 53.4% of the votes cast, this represented the support of only 38% of registered voters and of a mere 27% of the eligible electorate. See Bureau of the Census, Statistical Abstract of the United States 1990, at 246, 263-64 (110th ed. 1990). In contrast to political elections, other elections often require some absolute level of support through the use of a quorum provision. See Jaconelli, Majority Rule and Special Majorities, 1989 Pub. L. 587, 588-89.

Voting rules may also often mean that the winning candidate or result was not the choice even of the majority of the voters who cast ballots. On the one hand, in most jurisdictions a candidate may be the winner even though he or she received only a plurality of the votes. See McDonald, The Majority Vote Requirement: Its Use and Abuse in the South, 17 Urb. Law. 429, 429-30 (1985) (pointing out that a "majority vote requirement is little used outside the South"). In such situations, it will often be the case that a *majority* of the voters in fact oppose the winning candidate. Indeed, this consideration is precisely the justification used by supporters of runoff requirements. See, e.g., *Whitfield*, 686 F. Supp. at 1367-70 (discussing the history of and motivations for Arkansas' primary run-off requirement).

On the other hand, many decisions require the support of a supermajority—more than 50% plus 1 of the relevant electorate. See generally Jaconelli, supra, at 587 (discussing the use of supermajorities generally and with reference to specific examples); Karlan, supra note 33, at 245-46 (generally discussing supermajority provisions and citing examples of their use in the state and federal systems); Revesz & Karlan, Nonmajority Rules and the Supreme Court, 136 U. Pa. L. Rev. 1067, 1109-31 (1988) (discussing the Supreme Court's "Rule of Three" under which the votes of only three justices suffice to postpone consideration of a petition for certiorari pending decision of another case, effectively requiring the votes of six justices to

C. *Countermajoritarianism and Voting Rights*

There is an ironic convergence of the twain[36] in the simultaneous emergence over the past quarter century of a nonmajoritarian perspective on voting rights—which rejects the idea that the majority's preferences as to how officials should be elected ought to be immunized from judicial scrutiny—and a preoccupation, in the academic and judicial communities, with the so-called "countermajoritarian difficulty"—which addresses the conditions under which a court can legitimately set aside the acts of elected officials. As Alexander Bickel has succinctly put it, a court that strikes down legislative or executive actions "thwarts the will of representatives of the actual people of the here and now; it exercises control, not on behalf of the prevailing majority, but against it."[37]

One of the major attacks leveled against the Voting Rights Act is its assertedly countermajoritarian character. According to one critic, section 2 leads courts to "undo the work of a democratic process" by overturning the use of the electoral scheme preferred by the majority

---

compel immediate consideration—a two-thirds supermajority). In such situations, the preferences of an electoral *minority* trump those of the majority.

[36] I borrow this phrase from Thomas Hardy's famous poem, "The Convergence of the Twain," which recounts how the Titanic and the iceberg that ultimately sank it developed independently of one another before their fateful collision. See T. Hardy, The Complete Poems of Thomas Hardy 306-07 (J. Gibson ed. 1978).

[37] A. Bickel, The Least Dangerous Branch 16-17 (1962).

To my mind, there is something faintly ironic in Bickel's analysis, particularly given his reservations about the reapportionment revolution. See A. Bickel, supra, at 189-97. At the time Bickel identified the countermajoritarian difficulty, there was in fact no reason to believe that the legislative majorities in many of the state legislatures corresponded at all to popular majorities. Due to tremendous population differences among state legislative districts, it was the case across the country that a majority of a state legislature could be composed of legislators elected from districts whose combined population was far less than a majority of a state's population. For example, in Maryland, 14.1% of the population could elect a majority of the State Senate and 24.7% could elect a majority of the State House of Representatives, see Maryland Comm. for Fair Representation v. Tawes, 377 U.S. 656, 665-66 (1964); in Delaware, the respective numbers were approximately 22% for the Senate and 18.5% for the House, see Roman v. Sincock, 377 U.S. 695, 705 (1964); in Colorado, the respective numbers were 29.8% for the Senate and 32.1% for the House, see Lucas v. Colorado Gen. Assembly, 377 U.S. 713, 725 (1964); in New York, the numbers were 41.8% for the Senate and 34.7% for the Assembly, see WMCA, Inc. v. Lomenzo, 377 U.S. 633, 647 (1964); and in Virginia, the numbers were 41.1% for the Senate and 40.5% for the House, see Davis v. Mann, 377 U.S. 678, 688-89 (1964). See also Eule, Judicial Review of Direct Democracy, 99 Yale L.J. 1503, 1526-27 (1990) (claiming that the Framers established a representative democracy rather than a direct democracy because they thought it would moderate and ultimately better reflect real public preferences).

in the jurisdiction.[38] Such concerns have in fact influenced the development of judicial doctrines under the Act. For example, the requirement that defendant jurisdictions be given an opportunity to develop and propose a remedial plan, and that the court defer to such a plan (assuming that it fully cures the violation),[39] can clearly be seen to rest on consideration of the "countermajoritarian difficulty": "Reapportionment produces a fundamental change in [the defendant] government and affects who will represent the people. Consequently, that determination is best left to the people rather than the federal judiciary."[40]

In taking this attack too much to heart, judges have misperceived the issue in two respects. First, it is simply wrong to see judicial oversight under the Act as countermajoritarian. Unlike a court faced with a constitutional challenge to a voting procedure, a court faced with a section 2 challenge is not asked to substitute *its* judgment for that of an elected body. Rather, it is called on only to substitute the views of the "national political culture," as expressed by the majority in Congress who supported the 1982 amendments, for the "views of a local

---

38 A. Thernstrom, Whose Votes Count?: Affirmative Action and Minority Voting Rights 78 (1987); see also LULAC v. Clements, 914 F.2d 620, 622 (5th Cir. 1990) (en banc) (holding that "because of the highly intrusive nature of federal regulation of the means by which states select their own officials, legislation doing so should not be pushed beyond its clear language"), petition for cert. filed sub nom. Houston Lawyers' Ass'n v. Mattox, 59 U.S.L.W. 3406 (U.S. Nov. 21, 1990) (No. 90-813); Voting Rights Act: Hearings on S. 53, S. 1761, S. 1975, S. 1992, & H.R. 3112 Before the Subcomm. on the Constitution of the Senate Comm. on the Judiciary, 97th Cong., 2d Sess. 228-29 (1982) [hereinafter 1982 Senate Hearings] (statement of Professor Walter Berns, resident fellow at the American Enterprise Institute) (stating that section 2 will have the effect "of abridging the electoral power of a group of voters [to choose their own electoral system], and it of course will make the Federal courts the supreme electoral lawgivers"); id. at 1644 (statement of Sen. Orrin W. Hatch) (stating that section 2 provides no "assurances that the citizens of Boston and Cincinnati and Baltimore are not going to have their own judgment about how they wish to run their own affairs overturned in deference to the judgment of the attorneys for the Lawyers Committee for Civil Rights [which represents plaintiffs in section 2 cases] here in Washington").

39 See, e.g., Wise v. Lipscomb, 437 U.S. 535, 540 (1978); see generally Ortiz, Federalism, Reapportionment, and Incumbency: Leading the Legislature to Police Itself, 4 J.L. & Pol. 653 (1988) (providing an overview of the roles played in the reapportionment process by state legislatures and federal courts).

40 Tallahassee Branch of NAACP v. Leon County, 827 F.2d 1436, 1438 (11th Cir.), cert. denied, 488 U.S. 960 (1988); see also Connor v. Finch, 431 U.S. 407, 414-15 (1977) (holding that a court must satisfy a higher standard than a legislature in formulating a reapportionment plan because the court "lack[s] the political authoritativeness that the legislature can bring to the task. . . . [and thus] the court's task is inevitably an exposed and sensitive one that must be accomplished circumspectly").

. . . political majority."[41] Put somewhat differently, the criticism attempts to dress up a discredited federalism concern in majoritarian clothing; whatever the policy arguments supporting local control over electoral arrangements, Congress clearly has the power under the enforcement provisions of the fourteenth and fifteenth amendments (the "*Morgan* power") to set federal statutory standards for local election procedures.[42] Second, as the preceding section has shown, the countermajoritarian criticism fails to account for the central insight of section 2's functional test: that when a numerical majority chooses a plan that shuts out a numerical minority, that plan is not in fact "democratic."[43]

In sum, the real danger in the preoccupation with countermajoritarianism is that courts will assume that election schemes adopted long ago by lily-white legislative bodies will in fact comport with our modern, post-Voting Rights Act understanding of the limits of the winner-take-all, majoritarian instinct. In Part II, I will show how, in one critical area of voting rights case law, that danger has come to fruition.

II. The Emergence and Contours of the Single-Member Office Exception

As an historical matter, both the Supreme Court and Congress have understood that the way in which an office held by a single individual is filled can unfairly minimize the political strength of distinct groups in the electorate. The Supreme Court's first modern decision on the merits in a vote-dilution lawsuit involved the system for nomi-

---

[41] See R. Dworkin, supra note 28, at 377.

[42] In Katzenbach v. Morgan, 384 U.S. 641 (1966), the Supreme Court delineated Congress's broad power under the enforcement section of the 14th amendment. See also Senate Report, supra note 8, at 39-43 (setting out the case law that establishes the constitutionality of amended section 2 and declaring that "[b]y now the breadth of Congressional power to enforce these provisions is hornbook law"); cf. Oregon v. Mitchell, 400 U.S. 112 (1970) (holding that Congress's *Morgan* power supports a nationwide ban on literacy tests regardless of the presence or absence of a discriminatory purpose).

[43] See Note, Making the Violation Fit the Remedy: The Intent Standard and Equal Protection Law, 92 Yale L.J. 328, 346 (1982) (stating that deference to the political branches' judgment in vote dilution cases "is absurd on its face; the vindication of voting rights can hardly be trusted to the very representatives whose election is the result of the alleged vote dilution").

nating United States Senators and all statewide officers in Georgia.[44] And the Court's first interpretation of the scope of section 5 of the Voting Rights Act involved, among other things, changes in the method for selecting county school superintendents in Mississippi.[45] By its own terms, the Voting Rights Act applies to "*any* primary, special, or general election" in which votes are "cast with respect to candidates for public or party office."[46] Despite this broad beginning, the vast majority of voting rights cases brought during the first two decades of litigation concerned schemes for electing multimember bodies.[47] This was probably due in part to relatively favorable case law (at least prior to *City of Mobile v. Bolden*[48] and since the 1982 amendments), in part to the reapportionment revolution (which required many multimember bodies to adjust their selection mechanisms periodically in any event, thereby prompting minority plaintiffs to object to plans that diminished their voting strength), and in part, as we have already seen, to the elegant simplicity of concepts of dilution as applied to multimember offices. Until recently, that predominance has been so great that casual observers of voting rights litigation, and this includes most courts, might have assumed that the results test of section 2 was concerned solely with elections for multimember offices.

That assumption has, however, begun to be challenged in a serious way by a number of recent challenges to procedures used for filling single-member offices.[49] The single-member office doctrine represents a judicial response to this broadened scope of voting rights litigation. The single-member office doctrine is less an attempt to channel lower courts' factual inquiries into the equality of electoral opportunity than it is an attempt to pretermit the factual inquiry altogether by creating

---

[44] Gray v. Sanders, 372 U.S. 368 (1963) (holding that a county-unit delegate system diluted the impact of urban voters).

[45] Allen v. State Bd. of Elections, 393 U.S. 544 (1969).

[46] Voting Rights Act of 1965, § 14(c)(1), 42 U.S.C. § 1973*l*(c)(1) (1988) (emphasis added); see also Voting Rights: Hearings on H.R. 6400 Before Subcomm. No. 5 of the House Comm. on the Judiciary, 89th Cong., 1st Sess. 21 (1965) (testimony of Attorney General Nicholas Katzenbach) (stating that "[e]very election in which registered electors are permitted to vote" is covered by the Act).

[47] See Abrams, supra note 15, at 451-52.

[48] 446 U.S. 55 (1980) (plurality opinion).

[49] See supra notes 9-11.

a legal rule that removes certain kinds of elections from section 2's scope.

The doctrine has two aspects. The first is ostensibly descriptive: *Which* elective positions are "single-member offices?" The second is purportedly analytic: What is it about single-member offices (however these are defined) that exempts them from scrutiny under section 2's results test? Although the descriptive prong focuses largely on post-election conduct—that is, on what an official does after she is elected—I address it first because many of the weaknesses in the analytic facet of the doctrine are understandable only in light of the complete indeterminacy of the descriptive prong. As we shall see, however, neither prong of the doctrine delivers what it promises. The descriptive prong fails to recognize that the potential variety in the ways of allocating governmental authority makes it impossible really to say that any particular power must be lodged in a single official. The analytic prong fails to account for the fact that different vote-aggregation rules may have dramatically different effects on the political strength of minority groups.

A. Single-Member Offices

The first case to raise the specter of a single-member office exception was *Butts v. City of New York*.[50] *Butts* concerned a challenge to a state statute governing the percentage of votes required to win the primaries for three city-wide offices in New York City: the mayor, the city council president, and the comptroller. If no candidate received at least forty percent of the votes cast for that office, then a second election would be held between the two candidates who had received the largest number of votes in the first primary.[51]

---

[50] 779 F.2d 141 (2d Cir. 1985), cert. denied, 478 U.S. 1021 (1986). The rationale behind *Butts*'s adoption of the single-member office doctrine is discussed infra text accompanying notes 79-83.

[51] N.Y. Elec. Law § 6-162 (McKinney 1978).

The more common form of such laws involves so-called "majority-vote requirements," under which a runoff election is required whenever no candidate receives an outright majority of the votes cast in the first election. For general discussions of such requirements, see, e.g., Voting Rights Act: Runoff Primaries and Registration Barriers: Oversight Hearings Before the Subcomm. on Civil and Constitutional Rights of the House Comm. on the Judiciary, 98th Cong., 2d Sess. (1984) [hereinafter Runoff Primaries]; Butler, The Majority Vote Requirement: The Case Against Its Wholesale Elimination, 17 Urb. Law. 441 (1985); McDonald, supra note 35, at 429; Note, Assessing the Legality of Runoff Elections Under the Voting Rights Act, 86

It is easy to see, in a case like *Butts*, what is meant by a single-member office. Within any given geographical jurisdiction there is only one mayor, one comptroller, or one city council president.[52] But the issue of whether or not a position is a single-member office is neither always so clear nor, even in apparently clear cases, really immutable.

The most recent examination of the single-member office doctrine, *League of United Latin American Citizens v. Clements*,[53] presents one aspect of this question. *LULAC* involved a challenge to the election process for state trial court judges in several Texas counties, specifically several counties in which the trial bench has more than one judgeship. In some senses, each of these judges occupies a single-member office. Each competes for one, and only one, position at election time.[54] Each exercises, in many settings, the undivided power of

---

Colum. L. Rev. 876 (1986) [hereinafter Note, Assessing Legality]; Note, The Primary Runoff: Racism's Reprieve?, 65 N.C.L. Rev. 359 (1987).

52 See Southern Christian Leadership Conf. v. Siegelman, 714 F. Supp. 511, 518 & n.16 (M.D. Ala. 1989) (defining a single-member office as "a situation where under no circumstances will there ever be more than one such position in a particular geographic voting area").

53 914 F.2d 620 (5th Cir. 1990) (en banc), vacating 902 F.2d 293 (5th Cir. 1990), petition for cert. filed sub nom. Houston Lawyers' Ass'n v. Mattox, 59 U.S.L.W. 3406 (U.S. Nov. 21, 1990) (No. 90-813).

54 Within each Texas judicial district, usually a county, there may often be more than one judicial position. A voter is entitled to vote for a candidate for each position within that district. *LULAC*, 902 F.2d at 307. Some judges are elected to handle specific types of cases, such as juvenile cases or family law cases, and they handle all such cases within the district. Many of the judges, however, handle the same types of cases. Id. at 306. Within such groups, cases are assigned by local administrative judges, who are elected by a majority vote of all the judges within the district. Id. at 305. Once a case is assigned to a judge, that judge becomes responsible for deciding it. Id. at 303.

Numbered-place provisions require that each candidate declare his or her candidacy for a designated position. If, for example, there were five judgeships to be filled, they might be called "Civil Court Judge No. 1," "Civil Court Judge No. 2," "Civil Court Judge No. 3," and so on. Each candidate would decide which seat to seek and each voter would be entitled to vote for one candidate to fill each place. See Davidson, supra note 22, at 7.

Numbered-post provisions have often been considered to enhance the discriminatory potential of multiposition elections, by preventing single-shot, or bullet, voting. See Senate Report, supra note 8, at 29. Single-shot voting occurs when a voter (or a group of voters) casts votes for fewer than all the seats for which he or she is entitled to vote. For example, in an election in which voters are entitled to vote for five judicial candidates, a voter who bullet votes will cast a vote for only his or her first-choice candidate. By denying other candidates any electoral support, the single-shot voter will have increased the share of the total votes received by his or her first-choice candidate. A cohesive racial minority may be able to use this strategy to elect some of its preferred candidates. See, e.g., City of Rome v. United States, 446 U.S.

the judicial office: Before rendering a verdict, issuing an opinion, or imposing a sentence, a judge does not usually consult with colleagues or obtain their approval.[55]

But in a number of respects, this structure is both contingent and incomplete. First, there is nothing about the function that judges perform once in office that *requires* their being elected to designated posts. Consider, for example, a trial court with five judgeships. It would obviously be possible to allow all of the candidates to compete in one pool with the five candidates who received the most votes being elected. In this sense, it is entirely contingent that each judgeship is denominated a separate office. Indeed, at this level, the election of judges is really no different than the election of a legislature from single-member districts. Once the district lines have been drawn, each legislative seat is a single-member office: There is only one state senator, for example, from the Seventh Senatorial District.[56] And with respect to a number of functions, such as constituent services, a state senator may act unilaterally, without consulting other legislators. Yet no court has ever suggested that the position of state senator is a single-member office.[57]

Ultimately, then, the fact that each judge formally fills a distinct post cannot be the basis for a conclusion that trial judgeships are single-member offices. Instead, the real basis for the characterization must be that each judge exercises undivided judicial power.[58] This explanation is, however, also fallacious. Although trial judges do perform many functions by themselves, those functions are not unique in the same way that a mayor's or a comptroller's are. Judges are essentially interchangeable, as practices such as the random assignment of cases and the ready transfer of cases among judges illustrate. More-

---

156, 184 n.19 (1980) (explaining the mechanics of single-shot voting); U.S. Comm'n on Civil Rights, The Voting Rights Act: Ten Years After 207 (1975) (same); cf. Karlan, supra note 33, at 223-31 (describing "limited" voting systems in which each voter is limited to voting for fewer candidates than there are seats to be filled and under which a majority cannot shut out a cohesive minority as essentially forcing bullet voting).

[55] *LULAC*, 914 F.2d at 649 (Higginbotham, J., concurring in the judgment).

[56] See id. at 661 (Johnson, J., dissenting) ("Every state legislator exercises full responsibility over his or her office; in that respect the legislator is no different from a judge.").

[57] See Southern Christian Leadership Conf. v. Siegelman, 714 F. Supp. 511, 519 & n.20 (M.D. Ala. 1989) (a position is a single-member office only when the boundaries of the district are immutable).

[58] See *LULAC*, 914 F.2d at 647-49 (Higginbotham, J., concurring in the judgment).

over, each judge relies on, and is often bound by (in the case of precedent), the work done by other judges on the court. In addition, the existence of three-judge district courts,[59] twelve-person juries, and collegial appellate courts[60] shows that there is nothing inherent in the process of adjudication that *requires* that it be performed by one person. Thus, to view each judge as an atomistic official is to misperceive the everyday function of the office.

Indeed, even the idea that executive power must be vested in a single individual is contingent. Federal judges and scholars are so accustomed to the federal constitutional model—with an individual president as the elected repository of executive authority—that they often forget the rich diversity of forms that exist in local government. The city commission in *Bolden* provides a prime example. The commission consisted of three commissioners who "jointly exercise[d] all legislative, executive, and administrative power in the municipality."[61] And, although they designated one of their number as the mayor after the election, "no formal provision [was] made for allocating specific executive or administrative duties among the three."[62] Along the same lines, many states divide executive power among various independently elected officials, each of whom may follow his or her own agenda and may respond to different constituencies.[63]

---

59 See 28 U.S.C. § 2284 (1988) (requiring three-judge district courts in, inter alia, statewide apportionment challenges); 42 U.S.C. § 1973b(a)(5) (1988) (requiring three-judge district courts in certain cases under the Voting Rights Act). See generally, Williams, The New Three-Judge Courts of Reapportionment and Continuing Problems of Three-Judge-Court Procedure, 65 Geo. L.J. 971 (1977) (discussing the jurisdiction and principles governing federal three-judge-court statutes).

60 See Kornhauser & Sager, Unpacking the Court, 96 Yale L.J. 82, 82 (1986) (noting that appellate judges "almost always sit and act together").

61 446 U.S. at 59 (Stewart, J., plurality opinion).

62 Id. Ultimately, Mobile's system was found to have been adopted for the purpose of diluting black voting strength, Bolden v. City of Mobile, 542 F. Supp. 1050, 1077 (S.D. Ala. 1982), and was replaced with a "mayor-council form of government". See Ala. Code § 11-44C-11 (1989). For a discussion of some unique structural aspects of the remedy, see Karlan, supra note 33, at 246-47.

63 See, e.g., Ala. Const. art. V, § 114; Idaho Const. art. IV, §§ 1, 2; La. Const. art. IV, §§ 1, 3 (1974, amended 1986); Va. Const. art. V, §§ 2, 13, 15. This consideration is neatly illustrated in the Thornburg v. Gingles, 478 U.S. 30 (1986) litigation. In North Carolina, the governor and the attorney general are both elected positions. N.C. Const. art. III, §§ 2, 7 (1970, amended 1987). While Lacy Thornburg, the attorney general and lead defendant in *Gingles*, prosecuted the appeal and argued the case in the Supreme Court, see *Thornburg*, 478 U.S. at 33, James G. Martin, the governor, filed an amicus brief in support of the black plaintiffs, see id. at 34 n.*.

Moreover, the decision to vest governmental power in a single person may itself be vulnerable to attack under section 2. For example, in *City of Carrollton Branch of the NAACP v. Stallings*,[64] the Court of Appeals for the Eleventh Circuit held that the plaintiffs could challenge Carroll County's use of a single commissioner form of government,[65] instead of a three- or five-member commission that would enable blacks to elect a commissioner.[66] And in *Dillard v. Crenshaw County*,[67] the district court rejected a proposed section 2 remedy that would have dissolved the old commission, placing its executive power in a single county commission chairperson elected at-large and its legislative power in a new commission elected by district.[68] The court found that such a division of authority would violate section 2 because the enhanced authority given the chairperson would mean that "the members elected by a racially fair district election method would have their voting strength and influence diluted" and would lose "the practical political powers that commissioners normally enjoy."[69] Further, the court held that the continued use of at-large elections for the chairperson's position would effectively create "a public office completely beyond the reach of the counties' black citizens and thus reserved exclusively for the white citizens of the counties."[70] In place of a chairperson selected through an at-large election, the district court ordered that the chairperson's position be rotated among the commissioners.[71] In this way, the court guaranteed that the powers of the chairperson's office would, at least some of the time, be exercised by the commissioner elected from the majority black district.[72] The case stands as a paradigm of the variety possible

---

[64] 829 F.2d 1547 (11th Cir. 1987), cert. denied, 485 U.S. 936 (1988).

[65] The single commissioner, elected by a majority vote of the county's electorate, was the "entire governing body for the county" and was empowered to "direct, control and convey the county property . . . [and] to select and appoint all minor offices of the county, whose election or appointment is not otherwise fixed by law." Id. at 1551 n.7.

[66] See id. at 1551 (reviewing Georgia law and history to show that three- and five-member commissions were permitted and had existed at various times in the history of Carroll County).

[67] 649 F. Supp. 289 (M.D. Ala. 1986), aff'd in part and rev'd in part, 831 F.2d 246 (11th Cir. 1987), on remand, 679 F. Supp. 1546 (M.D. Ala. 1988).

[68] See id. at 292-94.

[69] Id. at 296.

[70] Id. at 297.

[71] Id. at 299; see *Dillard*, 679 F. Supp. at 1547 (reaffirming, on remand, the court's prior order mandating that the chairperson's position be rotated among the commissioners).

[72] For a discussion of rotation in office, see Karlan, supra note 33, at 241-44.

in the structuring of governmental powers. The fact that a multi-member commission had exercised executive power for over a century shows that such power need not be vested in one individual. Even if a particular power is to be vested in a single office, the opportunity clearly exists for arrangements under which that power may be rotated among several elected officials.[73]

Thus, the single-member office doctrine faces a serious uncertainty from the very outset. A court faced with a section 2 challenge can never simply assume that a particular position represents a single-member office. Rather, it must consider whether the position's power is in fact exercised by a single official and whether it is functionally necessary that a *single* official exercise it, given the available alternatives.

B. The Analytic Bankruptcy of the Single-Member Office Doctrine

As I have just shown, the insight that drives the descriptive prong of the single-member office doctrine focuses on a *post*-election consideration: Some offices are held by a single person and thus involve, in some fashion, the exercise of undivided power. By contrast, the analytic prong of the doctrine focuses on the electoral process itself to explain why there can be no denial of equal electoral opportunity when a single-member position is up for election. Put simply, the doctrine equates the equal opportunity to participate and to elect promised by section 2 with the ability to provide simultaneous proportionality (that is, to provide proportional representation across the range of offices at any specific position), and holds that when the latter concept is meaningless, that is, when there is only a single position

---

[73] Cf. Eu v. San Francisco County Democratic Cent. Comm., 109 S. Ct. 1013, 1016-18 n.8 (1989) (describing a California statute, struck down on first amendment grounds, that required the chairmanship of major political parties to rotate between residents of northern and southern California). Another traditional way of rotating officeholders is to limit the term any one person may serve. See, e.g., U.S. Const. amend. XXII, § 1 (limiting the President to a maximum of two elected terms).

Fear that an unchanging ruling group will otherwise emerge has historically underlaid term limitations and rotation requirements. See A. Jones, Athenian Democracy 106 (1969) (observing that in ancient Athens each of the ten tribes ran city government for 35 days each year); G. Wood, The Creation of the American Republic, 1776-1787, at 87, 521 (1969) (recounting the era's public antipathy toward leaders who "behaved as though they thought they had some sort of fee simple" in their offices and the public's concern that the Senate would become "a fixed and unchangeable body of men and the president a king for life" (citation omitted)).

at issue, no violation of the former could possibly have occurred either.

The most thorough exposition of this concept came in *Butts*, where the plaintiffs advanced two distinct theories.[74] First, they claimed that the statute represented an intentional effort to prevent the nomination of a black or Hispanic candidate. In their view, the statute was a direct response to the strong showing of a Puerto Rican candidate, and the forty percent threshold was specifically established so that it would just exceed the combined minority population of New York City at that time.[75] Second, they claimed that, whatever its purpose, the statute would *result* in minority voters being unable to nominate their preferred candidate:[76] The combination of the refusal of white voters to support minority candidates and the city's demographic breakdown would preclude the possibility of a minority candidate receiving the forty percent required to gain the nomination in the initial primary, and in the runoff the white electorate would coalesce behind whichever white candidate was left and outvote the combined black-Hispanic electorate.[77]

Ultimately, the court of appeals rejected both theories. Its rationale for concluding that the statute was not enacted for a discriminatory purpose, while debatable, turned on a situation-specific interpretation of conflicting factual accounts of legislative motivation.[78] With

---

[74] *Butts*, 779 F.2d 141 (upholding the legality of the runoff laws for certain "single-member offices" in New York). Political observers agreed that the runoff statute had been passed largely in response to the 1969 Democratic mayoral primary. Id. at 143. New York was an overwhelmingly Democratic city and in the usual course of events, the Democratic nominee could expect to win the mayoralty easily. In a five-way primary contest, Mario Procaccino, by far the most conservative candidate, had finished first with 33% of the votes. Two mainstream liberal candidates (how ironic that term now seems)—Robert Wagner and Herman Badillo, a Puerto Rican congressman from the Bronx—finished second and third, with 29% and 28% of the vote respectively, and two splinter candidates (also liberals) each received 5% of the vote. *Butts*, 614 F. Supp. at 1529-30. In the general election, John Lindsay, a liberal Republican who was running under the banner of the Independent and Liberal Party, defeated Procaccino for the mayoralty. Id. at 1530. See generally McKay, Butts v. City of New York: Race, Politics and the Run-Off Primary, 53 Brooklyn L. Rev. 499, 501-02 (1987) (discussing the operation of New York's runoff primary law).

[75] See *Butts*, 779 F.2d at 144-45.

[76] Id. at 145.

[77] *Butts*, 614 F. Supp. at 1536-37.

[78] The court concluded that the runoff statute was a response to Procaccino's plurality victory, rather than Badillo's performance, and that it reflected a desire to ensure that the candidate emerging from the primary represented an ideological, as opposed to a racial, majority of the party. *Butts*, 779 F.2d at 146. The tenability of the distinction between

regard to the plaintiffs' results claim, however, the court announced a broad legal rule: It held that there were only certain "kind[s] of electoral arrangements that can violate the Act."[79] The court identified two general classes of actionable arrangements: those that "deter members of the class from voting" and those that "diminish a class's opportunity to elect representatives in proportion to its numbers."[80]

The court recognized that runoff requirements could exacerbate the dilution of black voting strength in elections for multimember bodies.[81] It went on to conclude that it would be improper to

> take the concept of a class's impaired opportunity for equal representation and uncritically transfer it from the context of elections for multi-member bodies to that of elections for single-member offices. There can be no equal opportunity for representation within an office filled by one person. Whereas, in an election to a multi-member body, a minority class has an opportunity to secure a share of representation equal to that of other classes by electing its members from districts in which it is dominant, there is no such thing as a "share" of a single-member office. . . .

---

ideological and racial minorities drawn by the court is beyond the scope of this Article. But cf. Thornburg v. Gingles, 478 U.S. 30, 38 (1986) (White, J., concurring) (suggesting that when race and party coincide, defeat of a minority group's preferred candidates may represent interest-group politics not racial vote dilution); Whitcomb v. Chavis, 403 U.S. 124, 149-60 (1971) (same).

79 *Butts*, 779 F.2d at 148.

80 Id.

81 Id. In support of this proposition, the court cited City of Rome v. United States, 446 U.S. 156 (1980). In 1966, Rome, Georgia changed its manner of electing city commissioners from a plurality-win rule to a system that contained a majority-vote requirement, numbered posts, and staggered terms. Id. at 160. The Court, in affirming the Attorney General's denial of § 5 preclearance for the changes, explained how the adoption of a majority-vote requirement diluted black voting strength:

> [U]nder the pre-existing plurality-win system, a Negro candidate would have a fair opportunity to be elected by a plurality of the vote if white citizens split their votes among several white candidates and Negroes engage in "single-shot voting" in his favor. The 1966 change to the majority vote/runoff election scheme significantly decreased the opportunity for such a Negro candidate since, even if he gained a plurality of votes in the general election, [he] would still have to face the runner-up white candidate in a head-to-head runoff election in which, given bloc voting by race and a white majority, [he] would be at a severe disadvantage.

Id. at 183-84 (citation omitted). Note that the use of numbered posts and staggered terms had already created a set of discrete offices for which candidates were competing, and thus *City of Rome* itself involved the application of the majority-vote requirement to a set of (artificially created) "single-member offices." See supra note 57 and accompanying text.

> . . . [S]o long as the winner of an election for a single-member office is chosen directly by the votes of all eligible voters, it is unlikely that electoral arrangements for such an election can deny a class an equal opportunity for representation. . . . The rule in elections for single-member offices has always been that the candidate with the most votes wins, and nothing in the Act alters this basic political principle. Nor does the Act prevent any governmental unit from deciding that the winner must have not merely a plurality of the votes, but an absolute majority . . . or at least a substantial plurality, such as the 40% level required by § 6-162.[82]

Put simply, *Butts* and its progeny hold that when only one position is up for grabs, the rule used for selecting that position cannot be held discriminatory as long as it provides for majority rule.

A close examination of *Butts's* language and reasoning reveals, however, that its analysis rests on two serious distortions of section 2. First, the standard it uses for unimpaired electoral success linguistically and logically mangles part of section 2's results test. Second, the standard entirely ignores one of the two political rights protected by section 2—the right to "participate in the political process."[83]

1. Errors of Omission and Transposition

Section 2 is violated when "the political processes leading to nomination or election are not equally open to participation by members of a [protected class] in that its members have less opportunity than other members of the electorate to participate in the political process and to elect representatives of their choice."[84] *Butts* pulls three words out of this test—"opportunity," "equally," and "representatives"—and rearranges them into the phrase an "opportunity for equal representation,"[85] a phrase that appears nowhere in section 2.

This rephrasing, however, reflects more than the condensation of a somewhat wordy standard: It fundamentally narrows the substantive reach of section 2. It is simply not the case that it is only when a group has been denied an "opportunity for equal representation" that

---

[82] *Butts*, 779 F.2d at 148-49.

[83] 42 U.S.C. § 1973(b) (1988).

[84] Id.

[85] *Butts*, 779 F.2d at 148 ("We cannot, however, take the concept of a class's impaired opportunity for equal representation and uncritically transfer it from the context of elections for multi-member bodies to that of elections for single-member offices.").

its members have had "less opportunity than other members of the electorate . . . to elect representatives of their choice." Ironically, majority-vote runoff requirements offer perhaps the most striking example of why the equation in *Butts* is wrong.

Two concepts are critical to understanding why this is so: the normal process of coalition-building and the corrosive effect of racial bloc voting. Quite often, more than two candidates will seek a party's nomination for a given position.[86] If a majority-vote requirement exists, it will be necessary for a numerical minority within the party to form a coalition with other elements of the party in order for its candidate to win the nomination.[87] The dynamics of coalition-building mean that coalitions are usually relatively fluid: Their makeup will change from election to election as issues and candidates change or as out-groups offer incentives to defect to members of the winning coalition.[88] Thus, in the normal course of events, a relatively large, relatively cohesive voting bloc can expect to have significant opportunities to become part of a winning coalition.[89]

Such expectations will be defeated, however, if the minority is faced with racial bloc voting. If black voters in a majority-white jurisdiction are faced with white voters who *consistently* refuse to support black candidates, then they will have been denied the opportunity to build a

---

[86] The following discussion concentrates on the nomination process—which is explicitly covered by section 2, see 42 U.S.C. § 1973(b) (making the results test applicable to "the political processes leading to nomination or election")—in large part because majority-vote requirements are simply more common at the nomination stage than at the election stage. Compare, e.g., Ark. Stat. Ann. § 7-7-102 (1987) (requiring majority of votes cast for, inter alia, gubernatorial nomination) with Rockefeller v. Matthews, 249 Ark. 341, 459 S.W.2d 110 (1970) (holding that the state constitution bars the imposition of a majority-vote requirement on the actual gubernatorial election). But the same analysis is likely to apply to a large number of local elections, since over 70% of these are nonpartisan, see International City Management Ass'n, 1982 Mun. Y.B. 181, and thus will often have more than two realistic candidates.

[87] For a general discussion of coalition building, see W. Riker, The Theory of Political Coalitions (1962). For discussions of certain kinds of coalition building in the context of the Voting Rights Act, see Albritton, Voting Rights, 21 Tex. Tech L. Rev. 565, 570-72 (1990); Butler & Murray, Minority Vote Dilution Suits and the Problem of Two Minority Groups: Can a "Rainbow Coalition" Claim the Protection of the Voting Rights Act, 21 Pac. L.J. 619, 674-86 (1990).

[88] See J. Buchanan & G. Tullock, The Calculus of Consent: Logical Foundations of Constitutional Democracy 120-24 (1962); W. Riker, supra note 87, at 102-23;

[89] See J. Ely, Democracy and Distrust 84, 135 (1980); Ackerman, Beyond Carolene Products, 98 Harv. L. Rev. 713, 727-28 (1985).

winning coalition for their candidate of choice.[90] In such a case, black voters are rendered politically discrete and insular by the runoff requirement.[91]

Keeping these two concepts in mind, let us return to how majority-vote requirements operate. In a jurisdiction where black voters, although a numerical minority, form a significant proportion of the electorate, there may often be occasions when the black community backs a single candidate while the white community's support is divided among a number of candidates.[92] In such elections, the black candidate may well receive a plurality of the votes cast. If there is no majority-vote requirement, he or she will automatically receive the nomination, along with its concomitant advantages.[93] If, however, there is a majority-vote requirement and racial polarization, the black candidate will be unable to gain the additional votes needed to win the runoff; the white community will coalesce behind the remaining white candidate and, since white voters outnumber black voters, the white candidate will become the party's nominee.[94] In this way, a majority-vote requirement has the effect of creating a *de facto* "white primary":

---

[90] See Thornburg v. Gingles, 478 U.S. 30, 51, 57 (1986). Technically, of course, the question is whether the white community will vote for "the minority's preferred candidate." I use the phrase "black candidate" here because, in contests involving both black and white candidates, it is frequently the case that the black voters' preferred candidates are black while white voters' preferred candidates are white. See id. at 54, 59; id. at 68 (opinion of Brennan, J.). For general discussions of this issue, see, e.g., A. Thernstrom, supra note 38; Guinier, supra note 7, at 420-24; Note, Defining the Minority-Preferred Candidate Under Section 2, 99 Yale L.J. 1651 (1990).

[91] See Ackerman, supra note 89, at 718-37.

[92] For general discussions of the operation of majority-vote requirements, see, e.g., City of Rome v. United States, 446 U.S. 156, 183-84 (1980); Runoff Primaries, supra note 51, at 3-8 (discussing the effect of minority-vote requirements on the ability of black primary candidates to be nominated and pointing, as a prime example of this phenomenon, to the case of H. M. Michaux, a black candidate who led the first primary in the 1982 Democratic Congressional race in North Carolina's second district with 44.5% of the vote but lost the runoff when white voters coalesced behind a white candidate who had received only 32.7% of the votes in the first election).

[93] These advantages include funding in the general election from state and national party sources and support from straight-ticket white voters. In general election situations, candidates elected by a plurality will enjoy the advantages of incumbency. Anecdotal evidence suggests that black incumbents normally receive a significantly higher percentage of the white vote than black challengers or black candidates for open seats. See, e.g., J. Conyers & W. Wallace, Black Elected Officials 143-45 (1976); Guinier, supra note 7, at 425 n.138.

[94] Moreover, such factors as the relative poverty of the black community may exacerbate the black candidate's disadvantage. See Senate Report, supra note 8, at 29 & n.114. To begin with, there is the obvious economic strain of having to finance two primary efforts.

In the first election, white party members choose among the white candidates, and in the runoff they unite behind the surviving white candidate.[95] In this way, by increasing their relative chances of getting elected, majority-vote requirements serve as "an electoral steroid for white candidates."[96]

In short, the existence of racial bloc voting—which both Congress and the Supreme Court have treated as a central issue under the results test[97]—denies black voters the opportunity enjoyed by numerically equivalent groups of white voters to win nominations through

---

> When poorer black candidates are required to finance two campaigns rather than one, get out the vote twice rather than once, aid and provide illiterate black voters with voting assistance on two occasions rather than one, the resulting drain of finances and other resources makes the dual primary a real threat to equal participation in both party and general electoral politics.

Runoff Primaries, supra note 51, at 30-31, 47. Additionally, income and educational levels have traditionally been correlated to the levels of turnout and participation:

> [T]he frozen-in advantage provided whites who have not suffered from historical discrimination results in substantially higher white election turnouts when compared to blacks similarly situated. When these white turnout figures are combined with historic white racial bloc voting, the white community becomes a formidable force, able to disproportionately control and dominate every aspect of the political arena even in areas where blacks represent a substantial majority of the population.

Id. at 31.

95 The Supreme Court has unequivocally held the use of white primaries to be unconstitutional. Smith v. Allwright, 321 U.S. 649 (1944). Terry v. Adams, 345 U.S. 461 (1953), suggests that even de facto white primaries offend the principles of justice underlying the Voting Rights Act. *Terry* invalidated a preprimary "straw poll" conducted by the Jaybird Association of Fort Bend County, Texas, a private all-white organization. While the Court was unable to adopt a single rationale for its decision, Justice Black's opinion for himself and Justices Douglas and Burton found that the Jaybird Association's poll was "[t]he only election that has counted" since its winner always won the Democratic primary and general election, and that as such, "[t]he effect of the whole procedure, Jaybird primary plus Democratic primary plus general election, is to do precisely that which the Fifteenth Amendment forbids—strip Negroes of every vestige of influence in selecting the officials who control the local county matters that intimately touch the daily lives of citizens." Id. at 469-70. Justice Clark, in an opinion joined by Chief Justice Warren and Justices Reed and Jackson, similarly found that the Fifteenth Amendment reached the Jaybird poll because "[o]ver the years its balloting has emerged as the locus of effective political choice." Id. at 484. But see id. at 484-90 (Minton, J., dissenting) (arguing that both of these opinions failed to locate with any specificity the actual state action that brought the Jaybird poll within the ambit of the Fifteenth Amendment).

The Voting Rights Act should prohibit practices that are the functional equivalent of a white primary—whether adopted intentionally to replicate that repudiated device or not.

96 Isikoff, supra note 14, at A1, col. 1 (quoting John Dunne, assistant attorney general in charge of the Civil Rights Division).

97 See, e.g., Thornburg v. Gingles, 478 U.S. 30, 47-48 & n.15 (1986); Senate Report, supra note 8, at 33.

coalition-building.[98] Consider, for example, a town with one hundred Democratic voters, forty of whom are black. The forty black voters simply have less opportunity than a group of forty, similarly situated white voters to nominate and elect the mayoral nominee of their choice. While the forty white voters may have the opportunity to coalesce with voters of originally differing preferences in order to gain the required majority of votes, the forty black voters will not. In fact, the forty black voters have even less electoral opportunity than a far *smaller* group of white voters. Regardless of the size of the coalition supporting the white candidate who received the largest percentage of votes *among white candidates*, that candidate can depend on the rest of the white community coalescing behind him in the runoff and providing him with the additional votes needed to win the nomination.[99]

Although the preceding discussion explains how a runoff can deprive black voters of the chance to elect their preferred candidate, that deprivation is independent of any notion of proportionality. The

---

[98] See Butler & Murray, supra note 87, at 641 ("Racist attitudes prevent the minority group from engaging in the same coalition building as other interest groups . . . ."); Guinier, supra note 7, at 427 (arguing that a meaningful right to vote is frustrated if whites "refuse to work with or vote for a black candidate"); cf. Senate Report, supra note 8, at 29 (including as a factor that will be probative of a section 2 violation the denial of minority access to "a candidate slating process" and "a significant lack of responsiveness on the part of elected officials to the particularized needs of the members of the minority group"); Abrams, supra note 15, at 460 & n.69 (noting testimony regarding minorities' inability to participate in informal political alliances).

[99] To put this in concrete terms, return to our town of 100 Democratic voters, 40 of whom are black. Now imagine that there is a single black candidate who receives 40 votes and five white candidates who split the remaining 60 votes, the most popular of whom receives 15 votes. In the runoff, this group of 15 white voters will be able to form a coalition with the rest of the white community and nominate its candidate of choice. Obviously, the numbers could be adjusted to make the example even more stark. The point, however, remains the same: A group of white voters, although substantially smaller, will have considerably more opportunity to nominate its candidate of choice than will the group of black voters.

Moreover, the interplay of the runoff and racial bloc voting may have another, insidious effect. A white voter is free to vote for his or her first-choice candidate in the first primary, even if that candidate is not likely to be the most popular candidate among all white voters, secure in the knowledge that, at worst, a less-preferred white candidate will make the runoff and, ultimately, receive the nomination. Thus, the white community can field a number of candidates in the first round, giving white voters a broad range of choices. In the black community, however, black voters will have to coalesce behind a single candidate *before* the first primary to give that candidate a chance of making the runoff. Thus, each black voter is required to consider electability (to some extent, the potential to attract some level of white crossover voting) before considering his or her absolute candidate preference, since otherwise there will be no black candidate in the runoff at all.

fact that black voters make up forty percent of a given electorate will not mean that the black community's candidate will finish first forty percent of the time. He or she may finish first far less often if the white community normally gives real support to only a single candidate.[100] If the white community frequently fragments its support among several candidates, however, he or she may succeed far more frequently. Thus, the relationship between relative size and electoral success may be far less predictable than is true in many cases involving at-large elections, where residential segregation permits creating a districting scheme that achieves virtually perfect proportionality. Put somewhat differently, in the runoff context it is not the denial of an opportunity for representation proportional to the group's presence in the electorate that is at issue; rather it is the denial of an opportunity for representation commensurate with the opportunity enjoyed by similarly-sized groups. Next, I shall explain how this focus on proportionality overlooks a fundamental aspect of the political rights protected by section 2. After that, I shall return to the question of why courts have elevated proportionality to this talismanic status.

2. *The Centrality of Participation in Its Own Right*

A solitary focus on the potential for formal proportional outcomes reflects far too cramped a reading of the Voting Rights Act. Section 2 protects more than black voters' ability to "elect representatives of their choice"; it guarantees as well their right to "participate in the political process."[101]

The precise contours of, and relationship between, these two rights are never spelled out, and the courts have consistently failed to come to grips with the issue. It is not surprising to find, therefore, that one of the signal weaknesses of the emerging jurisprudence of section 2 in general, and of the single-member office doctrine in particular, is the way courts have turned the ability to elect into a threshold inquiry.[102] Courts have come to treat the companion right to "participate in the political process" as nothing more than the elemental ability to cast a

---

100 In the example, if more than two-thirds of the white electorate supports one candidate, that candidate will receive more votes than the black-sponsored candidate and will win, with either a majority or a plurality of the vote.

101 42 U.S.C. § 1973(b) (1988).

102 See infra notes 107-09, 112-16, and accompanying text. For a penetrating criticism of this tendency, see L. Guinier, supra note 33.

ballot.[103] While the ability to cast a ballot is unquestionably of fundamental importance, narrowing the view of the right to participate in this manner has the pernicious effect of condoning practices that impair the practical political influence of black voters. The structure of section 2[104] and frequent references in the legislative history to the broader political process[105] belie such a cramped vision. If anything, the ability to elect is a subset of the right to participate, for electing representatives is but one way of taking part in the political process.[106]

The elevation of the ability to elect to talismanic status has its genesis in *Thornburg v. Gingles*.[107] The evidence in that case showed that if the challenged multimember legislative districts were disaggregated and the boundaries of two single-member legislative districts were redrawn, it would be possible to create several new districts with effective black voting majorities.[108] In each of these proposed majority-black districts, a cohesive black community would be able to elect its preferred candidate regardless of the voting behavior of white voters. The Court noted, therefore, that

> [t]he claim we address in this opinion is one in which the plaintiffs alleged and attempted to prove that their ability *to elect* the representatives of their choice was impaired by the selection of a multimember electoral structure. We have no occasion to consider whether § 2 permits, and if it does, what standards should pertain to, a claim brought

---

103 See, e.g., *Butts*, 779 F.2d at 148-49; cf. *Bolden*, 446 U.S. at 65 (asserting that, because blacks in Mobile are able to "vote without hindrance," they have no claim under the 15th amendment or original section 2).

104 Section 2 covers "the political *processes* leading to nomination or election." 42 U.S.C. § 1973(b) (emphasis added). That language surely implies that more than mere balloting is covered. Cf. 28 C.F.R. § 51.13 (1987) (describing the broad range of "[c]hanges affecting voting" for purposes of triggering preclearance requirements under section 5).

105 See, e.g., Senate Report, supra note 8, at 29 (among the factors relevant to determining whether or not minorities have an equal opportunity to participate in the political process are whether they are denied access to slating processes and whether elected officials are responsive to the particularized needs of the minority community); H.R. Rep. No. 227, 97th Cong., 1st Sess. 14 (1981) (noting that among the consequences of minority exclusion "from all stages of the political process" is the failure to receive an equitable share of government services).

106 For discussions of this broader concept of political participation, see Abrams, supra note 15; Karlan, supra note 33; L. Guinier, supra note 33; cf. *LULAC*, 914 F.2d at 625 n.5 ("Not all aspects of [the political] process pertain to elections, e.g., the celebrated New England town meeting.").

107 478 U.S. 30 (1986).

108 Id. at 38.

> by a minority group, that is not sufficiently large and compact to constitute a majority in a single-member district, alleging that the use of a multimember district impairs its ability *to influence* elections.[109]

As Justice O'Connor pointed out in her concurrence, however, there is a certain "artificiality" in distinguishing between claims involving the ability to elect and claims involving an ability to influence.[110] In fact, as she noted, "the Court recognizes that when the candidates preferred by a minority group are elected . . . the minority group has *elected* those candidates, even if white support was indispensable to these victories." It therefore follows that

> if a minority group that is not large enough to constitute a voting majority in a single-member district can show that white support would probably be forthcoming in some such district to an extent that would enable the election of the candidates its members prefer, that minority group would appear to have demonstrated that, at least under this measure of its voting strength, it would be able to elect some candidates of its choice.[111]

Since *Gingles*, however, the courts of appeals have repeatedly rejected "influence" claims.[112] Their primary vehicle for doing so has been the first prong of *Gingles*—the requirement that the plaintiffs show that it would be possible to draw one or more single-member districts in which the minority group will predominate.[113] When plaintiffs are unable to satisfy this relatively formal demographic test, courts have refused to consider whether other alternatives to the present system would provide the minority group with a greater say in the

---

[109] Id. at 46 n.12.

[110] Id. at 90 n.1 (O'Connor, J., concurring).

[111] Id.

[112] See, e.g., Brewer v. Ham, 876 F.2d 448 (5th Cir. 1989); McNeil v. Springfield Park Dist., 851 F.2d 937 (7th Cir. 1988), cert. denied, 109 S. Ct. 1769 (1989).

[113] It is not enough, the lower courts have declared, for the minority group to constitute a population majority in the proposed district: It must also constitute a majority of the voting age population (VAP). *Brewer*, 876 F.2d at 452. The theoretical underpinning for this augmentation of the *Gingles* requirement is that, without a majority of VAP, the minority in fact will not control electoral outcomes since it may still be outvoted by whites. See Albritton, supra note 87, at 572-80. For a critical analysis of the first prong of *Gingles*, see generally Karlan, supra note 33, at 199-213 (contending that the first prong of the *Gingles* test establishes a bright line geographic focus that does not reflect the Voting Rights Act's commitment to a broader measure of civic inclusion).

decisionmaking process;[114] nor do they ask whether an alternative to the present system would give black voters a better *chance* of electing their preferred candidate or would give black voters a better prospect of building a successful biracial coalition.[115] Rather, they simply ask whether it is mathematically possible to devise an alternative under which blacks would control the outcome solely by virtue of their numerical predominance.[116]

This exclusive focus on whether an alternative redistricting plan creates a guaranteed ability to elect has blinded the courts to the way in which many practices deny minority voters a substantial opportunity to elect. This effect is not limited to the districting process; it also appears in the single-member office doctrine. No group that constitutes less than an outright majority of the electorate is ever *guaranteed* that its candidate can win an election to fill a single-member position.[117] But, as we have already seen, real-life politics in a partic-

---

[114] See, e.g., *Brewer*, 876 F.2d at 454-56; *McNeil*, 851 F.2d at 946-47.

The one appellate decision not to require a showing of an ability to elect was vacated when a petition for rehearing en banc was granted. Armour v. State of Ohio, 895 F.2d 1078 (6th Cir. 1990), vacated upon grant of petition for reh'g en banc (6th Cir. Feb. 7, 1990) (No. 88-4040). In *Armour*, the court of appeals reversed the dismissal of a section 2 lawsuit challenging the configuration of two single-member state legislative districts. One of the districts was 11% black, while the other was 25% black. The plaintiffs argued that it would be possible to redraw the districts to make one district 36% black, while leaving fewer than 1000 of the district's black residents in the other district. Id. at 1080. The panel held that it would be "incongruous" to require section 2 plaintiffs to show the ability to elect before permitting them to proceed in light of the fact that the statute "specifically excludes [from the remedial array] an unqualified right to elect a number of representatives equal to its proportions of the population." Id. at 1086.

[115] See Karlan, supra note 33, at 202-04.

[116] See, e.g., *McNeil*, 851 F.2d at 947 ("We cannot accept the appellants' contention that they can avoid the *Gingles* criteria by arguing that the multi-member districts impair their ability to influence elections. Given the Court's decision to draw a bright line for summary judgment purposes, it seems counterproductive to permit plaintiffs who cannot satisfy the threshold *Gingles* tests to make alternative claims that would obliterate the bright line."). It is ironic that black-white coalitions are irrelevant to the section 2 inquiry while other biracial coalitions, for example, black-Hispanic coalitions, can be relevant. See generally Butler & Murray, supra note 87, at 674-87 (addressing the issues raised by the efforts of minority groups to form coalitions with other minorities in order to satisfy the first prong of *Gingles*).

[117] The point at which a group *is* guaranteed that it can elect the candidates of its choice, regardless of the voting strategies adopted by the rest of the electorate, is termed the "threshold of exclusion." See Dillard v. Chilton County Bd. of Educ., 699 F. Supp. 870, 874 (M.D. Ala. 1988), aff'd without opin. sub nom. Dillard v. Chilton County Comm'n, 868 F.2d 1274 (11th Cir. 1989); Karlan, supra note 33, at 222. For single-seat elections, the threshold of exclusion is 50% plus 1: A group of this size can absolutely control the outcome and no

ular jurisdiction—the number of white candidates who file, divisions within the white community, the level of white crossover voting for black candidates, or the value of a party's nomination in the general election—may give a black-sponsored candidate a realistic possibility of obtaining a plurality of the votes cast. A majority-vote requirement, however, may operate in tandem with many of the same factors to render it an absolute certainty that the black candidate will be defeated.[118]

This rejection of influence claims in section 2 cases is particularly ironic in light of the simultaneous emergence of a richer understanding of the many forms of political influence in the analogous area of political gerrymandering. On the same day that the Court announced its decision in *Gingles*, four of the Justices who had joined the Court's opinion recognized the salience of extra-ballot influence to claims of unconstitutional political (as opposed to racial) vote dilution.[119] In *Davis v. Bandemer*,[120] a plurality of the Court rejected a claim by Indiana Democrats that the state's legislative districting scheme represented an unconstitutional partisan gerrymander that diluted the voting strength of Democratic voters. Although the apportionment scheme might make it more difficult for particular groups to elect their preferred representative,

> the power to influence the political process is not limited to winning elections. An individual or a group of individuals who votes for a losing candidate is usually deemed to be adequately represented by the winning candidate and to have as much opportunity to influence that candidate as other voters in the district. We cannot presume in such a situation, without actual proof to the contrary, that the candidate elected will entirely ignore the interests of those voters. . . . [U]nconstitutional discrimination occurs only when the electoral sys-

smaller group is assured of winning. Of course, there are often cases where smaller groups *do* win the election. But that happens solely because the majority does not unite to shut them out.

118 See supra notes 86-99 and accompanying text (discussing the relationship between the ability to elect and the ability to form coalitions).

119 See Davis v. Bandemer, 478 U.S. 109 (1986) (White, J., joined in Parts I, III, & IV by Brennan, Marshall, and Blackmun, JJ.). For general discussions of political vote dilution, see, e.g., Grofman, Criteria for Districting: A Social Science Perspective, 33 UCLA L. Rev. 77 (1985); Niemi, The Relationship Between Votes and Seats: The Ultimate Question in Political Gerrymandering, 33 UCLA L. Rev. 185 (1985); Schuck, The Thickest Thicket: Partisan Gerrymandering and Judicial Regulation of Politics, 87 Colum. L. Rev. 1325 (1987).

120 478 U.S. 109 (1986).

> tem is arranged in a manner that will consistently degrade a voter's or a group of voters' influence on the *political process as a whole.*[121]

In the *Bandemer* Court's view, a variety of structural factors gave even voters who had backed losing candidates "influence" in this larger "political process." Their presence affected the terms of the political debate; their potential support in future elections created an incentive for responsive representation.[122]

I am not suggesting that *Bandemer*'s insight can be folded into section 2 wholesale. After all, *Bandemer*'s ultimate holding was that the existence of "influence on the political process as a whole" pretermitted a claim that the challenged system was invalid because it denied Democrats an equal opportunity to *elect* state legislators of their choice.[123] Viewing some form of "influence" as sufficient to avoid section 2 liability has already been squarely rejected.[124] But if "influence" is one component of full civic participation, then surely its diminution or denial should be subject to scrutiny. When an election system is structured in a fashion that allows candidates to ignore black voters' concerns (and we have seen how runoffs permit this disregard), then black voters' influence has been degraded because they cannot affect the terms of the political debate.

One lower court's interpretation of *Bandemer* gives a sense of how this broader notion of participation could temper the single-member office doctrine. In *Badham v. Eu,*[125] the three-judge court dismissed a challenge brought by California Republicans to California's admittedly partisan congressional districting, holding that the plaintiffs had failed to allege facts sufficient to support a finding of discriminatory effect under *Bandemer.*[126] Although the reapportionment had reduced the number of seats held by Republicans from twenty-one (of forty-three) to seventeen (of forty-five),[127] Republicans still controlled

---

[121] Id. at 132 (plurality opinion) (emphasis added); see also id. at 152-53 (O'Connor, J., concurring) (adopting the plurality's judgment that the political process may be influenced by more than simply winning an election).

[122] See id. at 132.

[123] Id. at 132-34.

[124] See, e.g., Gingles v. Edmisten, 590 F. Supp. 345, 356-57 (E.D.N.C. 1984) (three-judge court), aff'd in relevant part and rev'd in part on other grounds sub nom. *Gingles,* 478 U.S. 30. But see A. Thernstrom, supra note 38, at 224-27.

[125] 694 F. Supp. 664 (N.D. Cal. 1988) (three-judge court), aff'd, 488 U.S. 1024 (1989).

[126] Id. at 670.

[127] Id. at 666.

"a sizeable bloc that is far more than mere token representation."[128] Moreover, the court continued:

> California has a Republican governor, and one of its two senators is a Republican. Given also that a recent former Republican governor of California has for seven years been President of the United States, we see the fulcrum of political power to be such as to belie any attempt of plaintiffs to claim that they are bereft of the ability to exercise potent power in "the political process as a whole" because of the paralysis of an unfair gerrymander.[129]

Thus, *Badham* looks beyond the question of whether any individual elective position was held by a Republican to consider whether the *overall distribution* of positions gives Republicans a fair voice in the political process as a whole. *Badham* recognizes that each elective position represents a "share" of the available political power.[130] Notably, *all* of the positions to which the *Badham* court refers are, in some sense, single-member offices: Senators and representatives are elected to fill single openings,[131] and governors and presidents fill the paradigmatic single-member office of chief executive. What *Badham* suggests is that a group's effective strength in the political process can be assessed by looking at its representation in the array of single-member offices.[132] As one commentator has noted, "[t]here may be 'no such thing as a "share" of a single-member office.' However, minorities are entitled to the opportunity to elect representatives to a 'share' of all single-member *offices*."[133]

This insight is hardly new. It underlies a well-known historical practice, the so-called "balanced ticket." Party officials (or aspirants for office themselves) would take the available positions and divide them among candidates who appealed to different constituencies in the belief that each member of the slate would attract his followers to

---

128 Id. at 672.

129 Id.

130 Cf. United Jewish Orgs. v. Carey, 430 U.S. 144, 166 (1977) (holding that as long as 70% of legislative seats were controlled by white voters, white voters who were placed in predominantly minority districts could not complain about racial vote dilution).

131 See supra note 23.

132 Cf. A. Thernstrom, supra note 38, at 72-73 (suggesting that it should have been a "crucial fact" in White v. Regester's analysis of state legislative districts in Bexar County, Texas, that the county was represented in Congress by Henry Gonzalez, a Mexican-American).

133 Note, Assessing Legality, supra note 51, at 882 (quoting *Butts*, 779 F.2d at 148).

vote for the slate as a whole. The balance might be ideological, geographical, or ethnic. The result, however, is that each constituency, though not large enough to guarantee that its preferred candidates will win election to *every* available position, is able to obtain a share of the total political power.

Ironically, the same array of elective offices that prompted the first detailed articulation of the single-member office doctrine—New York City's mayor, comptroller, and city council president—provides a pointed illustration of this phenomenon. As Nathan Glazer and Daniel Patrick Moynihan noted in their study of ethnic groups in New York City:

> Ethnic considerations have always been primary in New York City politics, where the three top spots of each party [the three city-wide offices mentioned above] are regularly divided among a Jew, an Italian, and an Irishman (sometimes a white Protestant noses out one of the others, most recently the Irishman, who now represents the smallest of the three major white ethnic groups) [and] where the Borough Presidency of Manhattan has been reserved to Negroes for some years . . . .[134]

The upshot of this ticket balancing is to mimic, among ostensibly single-member offices, the same kind of representativeness and proportionality that districting creates within a legislature or other multimember body.

It is a further irony that election—ostensibly the most democratic method of filling governmental positions—can also be the most racially exclusionary. There are, crudely speaking, three ways of selecting who should perform governmental functions: (1) offices can be subject to formally apolitical, "merit" selection; (2) they can be allocated as patronage—where a winning candidate can fill them with

---

[134] N. Glazer & D. Moynihan, Beyond the Melting Pot: The Negroes, Puerto Ricans, Jews, Italians, and Irish of New York City xxvii-xxviii (2d ed. 1970). Glazer and Moynihan give one particularly striking example of the balanced ticket conforming to this stereotype "almost to the point indeed of caricature": In 1961, the Republican slate of Lefkowitz, Gilhooley, and Fino faced a Democratic slate of Wagner, Screvane, and Beame, that had defeated Levitt, Mackell, and Di Fede in the primary. Id. at 305.

The ethnically balanced ticket survives to this day. Consider the following example: In 1987 Harold Washington, the black mayor of Chicago, endorsed a slate of candidates running for single-member offices in Cook County: One candidate was black, one was Hispanic, and two were whites (one of these being ex-Mayor Richard Daley's son). Washington termed the ticket "made in heaven." Guinier, supra note 7, at 425 n.138.

her supporters; or (3) they can be filled by actual election. If they are filled by the first means, federal antidiscrimination law prohibits the use of selection practices that have either a racially exclusionary purpose or a demonstrable (and unjustified) racially disparate impact.[135] If they are filled by the second method, the scope of which has been radically restricted by the Supreme Court,[136] black aspirants will often receive a significant share of the jobs in communities where black voters are part of a winning coalition—even if the official actually elected is not herself black.[137] Only if they are filled through the last method, direct election, are blacks effectively excluded from occupying any positions at all. Thus, the very decision to make positions elective rather than either merit-based or subject to patronage can itself preclude blacks from participating in the policymaking process.

And so we arrive back at the point I was making with regard to the artificiality of denominating positions as "single-member" in the first place. It is entirely possible to think of any particular office as part of a matrix of political offices, each with some distinct attributes but all sharing some fundamental characteristics, including the electorate that selects them. Moreover, the history of balanced tickets exemplifies how blacks often do not enjoy an equal ability to participate in the political process and elect the candidates of their choice: Candidates

---

135 The Equal Employment Opportunity Act of 1972, Pub. L. No. 92-261, 86 Stat. 103 (codified at 42 U.S.C. § 2000e-2(a) (1988)), extended the coverage of Title VII of the Civil Rights Act of 1964 to employees of state and local governments. For a general discussion of the substantive standards for showing discrimination under Title VII, see Rutherglen, Disparate Impact Under Title VII: An Objective Theory of Discrimination, 73 Va. L. Rev. 1297 (1987).

136 See Rutan v. Republican Party, 110 S. Ct. 2729 (1990).

137 See id. at 2746 (Scalia, J., dissenting). According to Justice Scalia, patronage is an important way of "achieving the social and political integration of excluded groups." Id. at 2754-55. A study of political patronage in New York noted that

> "[e]very ethnic group that has achieved political power in American cities has used the bureaucracy to provide jobs in return for political support. It's only when Blacks begin to play the same game that the rules get changed. Now the use of such jobs to build political bases becomes an 'evil' activity, and the city insists on taking the control back 'downtown.' "

Hamilton, The Patron-Recipient Relationship and Minority Politics in New York City, 94 Pol. Sci. Q. 211, 212 (1979) (quoting New York Amsterdam News, Apr. 1, 1978, at A-4).

sponsored by other groups of comparable size are slated while blacks are not.[138]

The interesting thing to note about the single-member office doctrine in this context is how it completely fails, despite the explicit mention of candidate slating among the Senate factors,[139] to consider what "slating" means. Instead, the courts implicitly seem to view slating as relevant only when a slate of candidates for fungible positions is being put together.

The overall impression a careful reader takes away from the cases that develop and interpret the single-member office doctrine is that the doctrine was developed in a vacuum. The Supreme Court has directed the courts, in evaluating section 2 claims, "to consider the totality of the circumstances and to determine, based upon a searching practical evaluation of the past and present reality, whether the political process is equally open to minority voters."[140] The Court goes on to emphasize that "[t]his determination is peculiarly dependent upon the facts of each case and requires an intensely local appraisal of the design and impact of the contested electoral mecha-

---

[138] For a discussion of the relationship between slating practices and section 2, see Note, Applying Section 2 of the Voting Rights Act to Single-Member Offices, 88 Mich. L. Rev. 2199, 2205 (1990).

Of course, while the existence of balanced tickets is illustrative of how effective participation should not be equated solely with the ability to elect through the unaided strength of the group alone, it does not provide much direct insight into a difficult remedial question: *If* blacks have been denied access to slating processes for ostensibly single-member offices, what should be done? I confess that the remedial question is a hard one. Ultimately, it is probably impossible, without radical restructuring of the political process, to provide black voters with proportionate influence, even if they do attain proportional representation. The ramifications of that issue are explored in Lani Guinier's provocative essay. See L. Guinier, supra note 33; see also Note, supra, at 2237-47 (making tentative remedial suggestions). But what does seem clear to me is that we should not allow the risk that no failsafe remedy can be devised to justify the continued use of election systems that exacerbate the likelihood of black exclusion. Cf. Note, Discriminatory Purpose and Mens Rea: The Tortured Argument of Invidious Intent, 93 Yale L.J. 111, 134 & n.133 (1983) (stating that honesty about remedial imperfection may provide "other actors with moral authority and the impetus to seek a fuller realization of the right than the courts are able or willing to provide"). Given that section 2 speaks about providing blacks with equal "opportunity," 42 U.S.C. § 1973(b), the fact that, in some cases, remedies may provide simply "opportunity" and not an absolute guarantee should hardly cause the courts to refuse to do anything.

[139] Senate Report, supra note 8, at 29 (stating that "if there is a candidate slating process, whether the members of the minority group have been denied access to that process" is relevant to whether § 2 has been violated).

[140] *Gingles*, 478 U.S. at 79 (citation omitted).

nisms."[141] In response, however, the lower courts have announced a bright-line legal rule that reflects little or no consideration of how politics actually works. It remains to consider why.

III. Judicial "Redemption" of the Voting Rights Act

The Voting Rights Act was intended to bring about a radical realignment of political control.[142] This intention appears most dramatically in two areas of the Act that are not the direct subject of this Article: the nationwide abolition of literacy tests[143] and the preclearance regime.[144] In each instance, Congress took from local gov-

---

141 Id. (citation omitted).

142 See A. Thernstrom, supra note 38, at 15 ("Critics and supporters alike agreed that [the Voting Rights Act] was 'radical.' ")

143 Despite the Supreme Court's prior holding that literacy tests were not a per se violation of the 14th or 15th amendments, Lassiter v. Northampton County Bd. of Elections, 360 U.S. 45 (1959), Congress used its enforcement powers to suspend such requirements nationwide in 1970, Voting Rights Act Amendments of 1970, Pub. L. No. 91-285, § 201, 84 Stat. 314 (1970), and to ban them permanently in 1975, Voting Rights Act Amendments of 1975, Pub. L. No. 94-73, § 102, 89 Stat. 400 (1975) (codified, as amended, at 42 U.S.C. § 1973aa (1988)).

In Oregon v. Mitchell, 400 U.S. 112 (1970), the Court upheld the nationwide suspension of literacy tests. Although the Court did not unite behind a single opinion (Justice Black's opinion on this point—the lawsuit also involved expanding voting rights for Americans overseas and lowering of the minimum voting age from 21 to 18—was joined by Chief Justice Burger and Justices Stewart and Blackmun; Justice Brennan's opinion was joined by Justices White and Marshall), the general reasoning seems to have been that Congress's factual conclusions regarding the discriminatory impact of literacy tests were sufficient to justify a nationwide ban without a specific judicial finding of discriminatory application in each state. See id. at 132-34 (Black, J.); id. at 233-36 (Brennan, J.). For a general discussion of Congress's enforcement power, see Carter, The Morgan "Power" and the Forced Reconsideration of Constitutional Decisions, 53 U. Chi. L. Rev. 819 (1986).

144 Section 5 of the Voting Rights Act requires specified jurisdictions to seek federal approval ("preclearance") of any changes in their electoral practices prior to implementation. 42 U.S.C. § 1973c (1988). A triggering formula based on depressed political participation and the use of certain "devices" that Congress found to be discriminatory (e.g., literacy tests) brings a jurisdiction within section 5's coverage. See id. § 1973b(b). Most of the Deep South, many areas with high concentrations of Hispanics (such as Arizona and Texas), and three boroughs of New York City are among the covered jurisdictions. See 28 C.F.R. § 51 app. (1989) (listing the covered jurisdictions).

A covered jurisdiction has two options for getting federal approval: (1) it can seek a declaratory judgment from the District Court for the District of Columbia that its proposed changes have neither a discriminatory purpose nor a discriminatory effect; or (2) it can submit the change to the Attorney General and if he does not object within 60 days, it can proceed to use the new practice. See 42 U.S.C. § 1973c. For general discussions of section 5, see Days & Guinier, Enforcement of Section 5 of the Voting Rights Act, *in* Minority Vote Dilution, supra note 3, at 167-80; Motomura, Preclearance Under Section Five of the Voting Rights Act, 61 N.C.L. Rev. 189 (1982).

ernments their autonomy over electoral practices. In the case of literacy tests, the ban substituted a national judgment for localized decisions; in the case of preclearance, the Act sharply restricted the ability of localities to change their electoral practices.[145] Just as unprecedented, however, is the extent to which Congress also took away some of the *judiciary's* control over electoral practices. The literacy test ban rejected the Supreme Court's approach in *Lassiter v. Northampton County Board of Elections*.[146] Even more radically, section 5 denied local district and circuit courts the power to determine whether changes complied with federal law.[147]

In a somewhat less flamboyant fashion, section 2 represents a similar realignment. First, section 2 represents Congress's "dispositiv[e]" rejection of *City of Mobile v. Bolden* and the purpose requirement.[148] Second, and more critically, section 2 rejects the notion that it is acceptable for states and localities to choose winner-take-all political arrangements when those arrangements result in the diminution of black voting strength.[149] A government's interest in strict majoritarianism and its own preferred electoral forms are trumped by what section 2 identifies as a more compelling, immediate concern—political opportunity for minority voters.

The immediate wake of the 1982 amendments saw an intensive assault on existing electoral practices across the nation. At first, the litigation focused on legislative or quasi-legislative bodies. The success rate in these cases was exceptionally high, somewhere over ninety percent.[150] With regard to these electoral practices, the combination of the Senate Report, with its nine typical factors, and the Supreme

---

[145] See South Carolina v. Katzenbach, 383 U.S. 301, 334 (1966) (terming preclearance "an uncommon exercise of congressional power"); see also id. at 360 (Black, J., dissenting) (preclearance marks "a radical degradation of state power").

[146] 360 U.S. 45 (1959).

[147] 42 U.S.C. § 1973*l*(b) (1988). Local district courts are limited to deciding the issue of whether or not a practice constitutes a change. If it does constitute a change, then the court must enjoin the practice until preclearance has been received from either the Attorney General or the District Court for the District of Columbia. See, e.g., Perkins v. Matthews, 400 U.S. 379, 383-86 (1971). One of Congress's central concerns in denying local federal courts jurisdiction over section 5 proceedings on the merits was that local district courts would tend to favor governmental plaintiffs at the expense of black voters' rights. See Senate Report, supra note 8, at 58-59.

[148] Thornburg v. Gingles, 478 U.S. 30, 43 (1986).

[149] See supra text accompanying notes 28-35 and infra text accompanying notes 162-69.

[150] See A. Thernstrom, supra note 38, at 228.

Court's three-pronged *Gingles* test left lower courts with little room to maneuver.[151] But as plaintiffs have begun to widen their focus, the courts have increasingly resisted attempts to eradicate other electoral practices that diminish black political power. If the Voting Rights Act was a keystone of the Second Reconstruction, then these courts are bent on moving us into "Redemption II."[152]

The single-member office doctrine can be placed in the broader context of this Thermidorian reaction. In the remainder of this Part, I will discuss why the courts are so resistant to the transformative possibilities of the Voting Rights Act. I conclude that the single-member office doctrine expresses a deeply felt, if unconscious, need to maintain white political control in the guise of protecting democratic values.

A. Remedial Considerations

Courts find the eradication of winner-take-all racial majoritarianism easiest, and most palatable, when multiposition elections are at stake. There are essentially two reasons for this. The first is a matter of practical feasibility. Simply stated, there already exist a variety of tried and true techniques for eliminating the white officeholding monopoly on multimember offices, including the creation of single-member districts or the adoption of a set of voting rules that prevents the majority from capturing all the seats.[153]

A second, deeper factor is the knowledge or tacit understanding that giving blacks a few seats on a multimember body poses no immediate threat to continued majority predominance in the political process. Although section 2 squarely rejects the idea that black voters

---

151 That is not to say, however, that they haven't tried. For a particularly egregious example, consider Chief Judge Tjoflat's special concurrence in Solomon v. Liberty County, 899 F.2d 1012, 1021-37 (11th Cir. 1990) (en banc) (Tjoflat, C.J., concurring specially), cert. denied, 59 U.S.L.W. 3460 (U.S. Jan. 7, 1991) (No. 90-102), where he and four other judges propound the theory that section 2 contains a discriminatory purpose requirement: Plaintiffs must show, in essence, that individual white voters are racists. Id. at 1030-32 (Tjoflat, C.J., concurring specially).

152 Note, supra note 43, at 350 (quoting Eric Foner, Redemption II, N.Y. Times, Nov. 7, 1981, at 23, col. 2.); see Engstrom, The Reincarnation of the Intent Standard: Federal Judges and At-Large Election Cases, 28 How. L.J. 495, 498 (1985) (contending that some federal judges have recently begun to require plaintiffs to show "intent" in order to establish a finding of racially polarized voting).

153 For a discussion of such alternative systems, see Karlan, supra note 33, at 221-36.

are entitled to proportional representation,[154] *Thornburg v. Gingles* implicitly treated proportionality as a ceiling on the political rights of black voters.[155] As long as blacks are a numerical minority within the jurisdiction, the white majority can retain control over the majority of the seats.[156] As long as a court is not faced with the prospect that control of the decisionmaking process will be wrested from the white majority, the remedy can be viewed as the removal of a discrete imperfection in the political process rather than as a fundamental reworking of the political system.[157]

---

[154] 42 U.S.C. § 1973(b) (1988) ("[N]othing in this section establishes a right to have members of a protected class elected in numbers equal to their proportion in the population.").

One of the major arguments, both at the time of the 1982 amendments and since, has been over the salience of proportionality to voting rights claims. For representative views on this controversy, see, e.g., Senate Report, supra note 8, at 30-31, 34-35; id. at 193-95 (views of Sen. Robert Dole); 1982 Senate Hearings, supra note 38, at 3-4 (statement of Sen. Orrin W. Hatch); id. at 735-37 (statement of Michael Levin, professor of philosophy, City University of New York); id. at 796, 819-22 (testimony and statement of Armand Derfner, civil rights attorney); id. at 1401 (statement of Drew S. Days III, former Assistant Attorney General for Civil Rights); F. Parker, supra note 21, at 195-96; A. Thernstrom, supra note 38, passim.

[155] 478 U.S. 30, 77 (1986). The Court reversed the finding of liability with respect to one multimember district because blacks had achieved sustained proportional representation within the district. Id. at 77. The Court's earlier decision in City of Richmond v. United States, 422 U.S. 358 (1975), a section 5 case, buttresses this conclusion. There, the Court permitted Richmond to annex outlying, predominantly white areas despite the fact that this would render the city majority white. The Court held that a simultaneous switch from at-large to ward elections for the city council, with four of the nine wards being predominantly black, would give blacks fair representation. Id. at 371-72. The Court rejected the black voters' argument that a plan with five predominantly black wards should have been adopted instead, id. at 366-67, 372, although it would have been possible, demographically, to draw anywhere between zero and seven majority-black wards, Freeman, Legitimizing Racial Discrimination Through Antidiscrimination Law: A Critical Review of Supreme Court Doctrine, 62 Minn. L. Rev. 1049, 1088 (1978). The Court stated that requiring the city to adopt five black wards would "permanently . . . underrepresent other elements in the community." *City of Richmond*, 422 U.S. at 373. For the Court to use "underrepresent" to describe the condition of Richmond's new white majority necessarily "implies an expectation of racial proportionality." Freeman, supra, at 1088.

[156] See D. Bell, And We Are Not Saved: The Elusive Quest for Racial Justice 73 (1987) (ours is "a majoritarian system" in which "[w]hites are still the majority in most electoral districts"); Freeman, supra note 155, at 1107; cf. United Jewish Orgs. v. Carey, 423 U.S. 945 (1975) (holding that the remedial districting plan did not violate the rights of white voters because whites continued to retain 70% of the available seats).

[157] See LULAC v. Clements, 914 F.2d 620, 630 (5th Cir. 1990) (en banc) ("It is hard to envision any area lying closer to the core of state concerns than the process by which it selects its own officers and functionaries. Any federal trenching here strikes at federalism's jugular . . . ."), petition for cert. filed sub nom. Houston Lawyers' Ass'n v. Mattox, 59 U.S.L.W. 3406 (U.S. Nov. 21, 1990) (No. 90-813).

This is not to suggest that the presence of black elected officials is only symbolic. There are powerful tangible benefits to a black presence, even a numerically small one, within the council chamber.[158] But the voluminous literature on "tipping points"[159] suggests that whites see a substantial gulf between black presence and black predominance.

The reform of selection processes governing single-member offices does not share this reassuring characteristic. It would obviously be easy enough to replace majority-vote runoff systems with plurality-win ones. But this would create situations in which the white majority would find itself governed by a black person whom it did not choose.[160] Faced with this prospect—and the litigated cases in fact present such a scenario, since black plaintiffs would hardly have brought them otherwise—the courts have retreated to protecting the expectations of white voters at the expense of the aspirations of black voters.[161]

---

158 See Karlan, supra note 33, at 213-19.

159 The "tipping point" refers to the point at which the black presence within a particular setting prompts whites to leave, presumably because whites do not want to remain in a system in which they do not predominate. The term has received its greatest currency in school desegregation cases, where the tipping point is the point at which substantial "white flight" from the schools occurs. This point is generally estimated at between 25 and 50%, depending on such factors as the nature of the desegregation program, the strength of racist feelings, and the availability of alternatives. See Gewirtz, Remedies and Resistance, 92 Yale L.J. 585, 630 (1982). Tipping also occurs as housing is desegregated. See Goering, Neighborhood Tipping and Racial Transition: A Review of Social Science Evidence, 44 J. Am. Inst. Planners 68 (1978); Note, Tipping the Scales of Justice: A Race-Conscious Remedy for Neighborhood Transition, 90 Yale L.J. 377, 379-82 (1980); cf. Bell, Application of the "Tipping Point" Principle to Law Faculty Hiring Policies, 10 Nova L.J. 319, 323-24 (1986) (suggesting that law school faculties may be restricting the number of minority professors to preserve their traditional, majority-white character).

160 And unlike white voters in a previously multimember district who now find themselves in a predominantly black single-member district, these whites would not have virtual racial representation since there would be no offsetting majority-white districts electing representatives.

161 Cf. Steel, Nine Men in Black Who Think White, N.Y. Times, Oct. 13, 1968, at 56, 112 (Magazine) (describing the Supreme Court as "a white court which would protect the interests of white America in the maintenance of stable institutions"). Both Alan Freeman and Abigail Thernstrom, though obviously from diametrically opposed points of view, have remarked on the role of whites as "innocent white victims." See A. Thernstrom, supra note 38, at 78; Freeman, supra note 155, at 1055.

B. The Racial Character of Majority Control

The single-member office doctrine lies at the convergence of two notions of majoritarianism, one numerical and the other racial. The courts that have embraced the doctrine *say* that they are protecting majoritarian American democracy.[162] But what they *mean* by majority rule is not just control by a numerical majority, but control by the white majority. The single-member office doctrine reflects a belief that there is nothing unusual or troubling about a political system in which, whenever there is only one position up for grabs, whites occupy it. White control is seen as the normal, and normatively desirable, state of affairs. "Blacks may vote, but it is whites who will govern."[163] In light of this powerful preservationist instinct, it is hardly surprising that the doctrine has been hopelessly stretched to foreclose a section 2 challenge. This is especially true when the issue is how state trial judges are elected:[164] It would threaten white federal judges' sense of their *own* legitimacy to admit that there is something wrong with a court system in which, because of the means of selection, the law is decided solely by white people.[165]

The emergence of the single-member office doctrine bears some uncanny resemblances to the earlier emergence of the purpose requirement in *Bolden*. Once again, the courts have embraced a narrow view of the right to vote,[166] a faith in the race-neutral merit of

---

162 See, e.g., Butts v. City of New York, 779 F.2d 141, 149 (2d Cir. 1985), cert. denied, 478 U.S. 1021 (1986); Whitfield v. Democratic Party, 686 F. Supp. 1365, 1373-74 (E.D. Ark. 1988), aff'd on reh'g en banc by an equally divided court, 902 F.2d 15 (8th Cir. 1990), petition for cert. filed sub nom. Whitfield v. Clinton, 59 U.S.L.W. 3180 (U.S. Aug. 31, 1990) (No. 90-382).

163 Guinier, supra note 7, at 394.

164 See LULAC v. Clements, 914 F.2d 620, 636 (5th Cir. 1990) (en banc) (Higginbotham, J., concurring in the judgment) (arguing that the majority's holding that judicial elections are not covered by section 2 "is an undisguised effort by judges to claim for judges an exemption from the Voting Rights Act"), petition for cert. filed sub nom. Houston Lawyers' Ass'n v. Mattox, 59 U.S.L.W. 3406 (U.S. Nov. 21, 1990) (No. 90-813).

165 Cf. Record at 2215, New York Times v. Sullivan, 376 U.S. 254 (1964) (reprinting article from Ala. J., Feb. 1, 1961) (quoting the judge at the libel trial as saying "We will now continue with the trial of this case . . . in the belief and knowledge that the white man's justice, a justice born long centuries ago in England, brought over to this country by the Anglo-Saxon Race, and brought to its full flower here . . . will give the parties at the bar of this court, regardless of race or color, equal justice under law.").

166 Compare *Bolden*, 446 U.S. at 65 (plurality opinion) (holding that since "Negroes in Mobile 'register and vote without hindrance,'" the lower courts had erred in treating the dilution claim as cognizable under the 15th amendment and section 2) with Butts v. City of

existing forms of government,[167] and a deep sense that acceptable conditions of politics can produce monoracial outcomes.[168] And once again, the courts have ignored the language and legislative history of section 2 in favor of advancing their own vision of voting rights.[169] At least in *Bolden*, the Court could claim that it was interpreting the Constitution; today's judicial guardians of traditional notions of politics have to set aside a clear congressional command in order to reach their goal. In the guise of protecting the old notions of democracy, the courts are refusing to enforce the new, more inclusionary understanding of democracy that the democratic process itself has produced in amended section 2. The court's treatment of "majority rule" is countermajoritarianism with a vengeance.

New York, 779 F.2d 141, 149 (2d Cir. 1985) (rejecting a test for section 2 that "condemns any electoral arrangement that makes it more difficult for a minority class to elect one of its members to office"), cert. denied, 478 U.S. 1021 (1986).

[167] Compare *Bolden*, 446 U.S. at 70 (plurality opinion) (claiming that it "would nearly always be true where, as here, an entire system of local governance is brought into question" that "the character of a [challenged] law is readily explainable on grounds apart from race") and id. at 81-82 (Blackmun, J., concurring) (stating that the district court should not order so drastic a change as abandoning the commission form of government) with supra text accompanying note 38 (setting out the argument that the Voting Rights Act is countermajoritarian because it seeks to set aside the democratically expressed views and preferences of the majority in favor of those of a minority) and *LULAC*, 914 F.2d at 622, 630-31 (concluding that § 2 should not be used to undermine a state's longstanding arrangement of its judiciary). See also Note, supra note 43, at 336 (1982) (arguing that the imposition of an intent requirement in *Bolden* was best understood as anxiety over the scope of potential remedies). In fact, on remand, the *Bolden* plaintiffs succeeded in proving that the at-large commission form of government was adopted precisely because it diluted black voting strength. Bolden v. City of Mobile, 542 F. Supp. 1050 (S.D. Ala. 1982).

[168] Compare *Bolden*, 446 U.S. at 73 (plurality opinion) (dismissing the significance of the fact that no blacks had ever been elected to the city commission) and Note, supra note 43, at 350 (quoting Justice Stewart, author of the *Bolden* plurality, as saying "reconstruction is over") with Solomon v. Liberty County, 899 F.2d 1012, 1022-30 (11th Cir. 1990) (en banc) (Tjoflat, J., specially concurring) (stating that section 2 plaintiffs must ultimately prove that white voters who do not vote for black candidates refuse to do so *because* they are racially biased; it is not enough merely to show that white voters in fact do not support the black community's candidates of choice) and Engstrom, supra note 152, at 500 (stating that courts have tried to require that plaintiffs show that "voting is racist, not just racial or racially conscious").

[169] See *Bolden*, 446 U.S. at 60-61 (holding, with virtually no discussion, that section 2 merely recapitulates the 15th amendment standard).

A CASE FOR RACE-CONSCIOUSNESS*

*T. Alexander Aleinikoff***

> I believe that [whites] today, raised white in a racist society, are often ridden with *white solipsism*—not the consciously held *belief* that one race is inherently superior to all others, but a tunnel-vision which simply does not see nonwhite experience or existence as precious or significant, unless in spasmodic, impotent guilt-reflexes, which have little or no long-term, continuing momentum or political usefulness.[1]

> [W]hen a white man says he's white, . . . the impression that the nonwhite person gets is that *he means more than color*.[2]

Debate over the appropriateness of race-conscious measures has dominated discussions of civil rights law over the past two decades. In the mid-1980s, one could say with confidence that, despite a number of differing justifications and constitutional analyses, the Supreme Court had generally ratified race-conscious programs and policies aimed at ameliorating the continuing social and economic consequences of several centuries of American racism. *Fullilove v. Klutznick*[3] typified the "consensus" that the Court had reached: despite an absence of agreement on the standard for constitutional review, a majority of the Court voted to uphold a federal statute requiring that at least ten percent of federal funds granted for local public works projects be used to procure services or purchase supplies from minority businesses.[4] In light of this decision, as well as the Court's other "affirmative action" cases, federal, state, and local units of government—as well as scores of colleges and universities—continued or adopted programs that earmarked expenditures or "set aside" employment or admissions opportunities for nonwhites.

The muddiness of the Court's opinions never permitted a clear-cut sense of victory for the proponents of race-conscious programs. A normative principle of "colorblindness" runs deep in the American civil

---

* I dedicate this Article to the memory of Elizabeth Wise Aleinikoff (1919–1991), my earliest teacher and most honest critic, and, in many ways, the soul of this piece.

I would like to thank the many friends who read and commented on earlier drafts, and participants at faculty workshops at the University of Kentucky College of Law and the Yale Law School.

** Professor of Law, University of Michigan Law School.

1. A. Rich, Disloyal to Civilization: Feminism, Racism, Gynephobia, *in* On Lies, Secrets, and Silence 275, 306 (1979). Rich's Comment is made specifically about "white feminists," but I think the statement is clearly generalizable—hence my substitution of "whites" for "white feminists."

2. Malcolm X, quoted in P. Goldman, Death and Life of Malcolm X 168 (2d ed. 1979).

3. 448 U.S. 448 (1980).

4. Id.

rights narratives, from the first Justice Harlan's dissent in *Plessy v. Ferguson*[5] to Martin Luther King, Jr.'s hope that his children would be judged by the "content of their character" rather than by the "color of their skin." To the extent colorblindness represents the goal of antidiscrimination law, race-conscious measures must always be defended as temporary and transitional.

The Reagan Administration, through its arguments in court and its judicial appointments, launched an attack on race-conscious policies that achieved its first major success in the Court's 1989 decision in *City of Richmond v. J.A. Croson Co.*[6] In *Croson*, the Court invalidated a Richmond set aside program for minority business enterprises that virtually mirrored the federal program approved nine years earlier in *Fullilove*. Although *Croson* distinguished (and apparently reaffirmed) *Fullilove* by drawing a sharp, if unpersuasive, distinction between race-conscious programs that are adopted by Congress and those adopted by state or local authorities, its language and emotion were grounded in a metaphor of colorblindness. *Fullilove*, it seemed, was vulnerable.

The Court's decision last Term in *Metro Broadcasting, Inc. v. FCC*,[7] then, came as somewhat of a surprise. There the Court, in a five to four decision, upheld several explicitly race-conscious policies of the Federal Communications Commission that sought to increase nonwhite ownership of radio and television stations. Writing for the Court, Justice Brennan—in an act of "turnabout-is-fair-play"—took *Croson* at its word that federal authorities adopting race-conscious policies were entitled to deference not accorded state and local officials.[8] And it may well have been this federal/state distinction that motivated Justice White to join the prevailing side in both *Croson* and *Metro Broadcasting*.[9] (One cannot be certain, since White did not write an opinion in either case.) But it is apparent that this distinction carried little weight in the considerations of the other Justices: the majority opinion in *Metro Broadcasting* is largely a replay of the dissents in *Croson*; and the dissents in *Metro Broadcasting* read like the opinions that constitute the majority in *Croson*.[10]

---

5. 163 U.S. 537, 559 (1896) (Harlan, J., dissenting).

6. 109 S. Ct. 706 (1989). See Devins, Affirmative Action after Reagan, 68 Tex. L. Rev. 353, 355–57 (1989).

7. 110 S. Ct. 2997 (1990).

8. Id. at 3008–09.

9. See Fried, *Metro Broadcasting, Inc. v. FCC*: Two Concepts of Equality, 104 Harv. L. Rev. 107, 126 (1990). White had also voted to sustain the federal set aside statute in *Fullilove*.

10. Justice Stevens was the only Justice to join the judgment of the Court in *Croson*, 109 S. Ct. at 730 (concurring in part and concurring in the judgment), and the majority opinion in *Metro Broadcasting*, 110 S. Ct. at 3028 (concurring). Stevens's votes can be explained as turning on two considerations: (1) because race is so rarely relevant to a legitimate governmental purpose, race-based statutes must be subjected to close scrutiny, *Fullilove*, 448 U.S. at 537 (Stevens, J., dissenting); and (2) race-based policies may

Of course, Justice Brennan's departure from the Court adds further uncertainty about doctrinal developments in this area, including the longevity of *Metro Broadcasting*. Justice Souter's confirmation hearings, in characteristic fashion, do not provide clear answers to how he would vote in cases involving race-conscious measures.[11] At the very least it is safe to say that there is a deep division on the Court about the underlying presuppositions of antidiscrimination law.

I want, in this Article, to consider and critique "colorblindness"—the version of antidiscrimination law adopted by a majority of the Court in *Croson* and by the dissenters in *Metro Broadcasting*. I will not replay the well-worn debate on affirmative action; indeed, in great part I wish to suggest that advocacy for race-conscious programs is more than a call for "affirmative action," as that phrase is usually understood in current political and legal discourse. Nor will I propose a new "mediating principle"[12] for the equal protection clause that will justify race-conscious measures. My attack on colorblindness is stated more in cognitive and cultural terms; and my defense of color-consciousness is made more in terms of political principle than constitutional argument.

Specifically, I will argue that we are not currently a colorblind society, and that race has a deep social significance that continues to disadvantage blacks and other Americans of color. While the legal strategy of colorblindness achieved great victories in the past, it has now become an impediment in the struggle to end racial inequality. At the base of racial injustice is a set of assumptions—a way of understanding the world—that so characterizes blacks as to make persistent inequality seem largely untroubling. A remedial regime predicated on colorblindness will have little influence at this deep level of social and legal consciousness because it cannot adequately challenge white attitudes or recognize a role for black self-definition. In the pages ahead I will explain and justify this somewhat paradoxical claim that a norm of colorblindness supports racial domination. I will conclude that in order to make progress in ending racial oppression and racism, our political and moral discourse must move from colorblindness to color-consciousness, from antidiscrimination to racial justice.

I. Colorblindness and Race-Consciousness: Clarifying the Categories

The norm of colorblindness is invariably traced to Justice Harlan's

pursue other than remedial grounds, *Croson*, 109 S. Ct. at 730–31 & n.1; accord *Metro Broadcasting*, 110 S. Ct. at 3028.

11. See S. Exec. Rep. 32, 101st Cong., 2d Sess. 23–25 (1990) (statement by nominee Souter that definition of scope of congressional power to adopt race-conscious "remedies" remains to be worked out).

12. Fiss, Groups and the Equal Protection Clause, 5 Phil. & Pub. Aff. 107, 108 (1976).

dissent in *Plessy v. Ferguson*.[13] A typical modern rendering appears in a 1987 report of the Department of Justice that criticizes the use of "effects tests" in the enforcement of civil rights laws: "The non-discrimination principle, simply put, forbids *race-dependent* decisions and conduct. By race-dependent, it is meant decisions and conduct that would have been different but for the race of those benefitted or disadvantaged by them."[14] While the constitutional norm of colorblindness applies only to the acts of governments, it is usually deemed an appropriate norm of conduct for most arms-length private transactions as well; and civil rights laws prohibiting race-dependent decisions in employment, contracting, and the sale or rental of real and personal property are hardly controversial.

In the colorblind world, race is an arbitrary factor—one upon which it is doubly unfair to allocate benefits and impose burdens: one's race is neither voluntarily assumed nor capable of change. For nearly all purposes, it is maintained, the race of a person tells us nothing about an individual's capabilities and certainly nothing about her moral worth. Race-consciousness, from this perspective, is disfavored because it assigns a value to what should be a meaningless variable. To categorize on the basis of race is to miss the individual.[15]

Adhering to a strategy of colorblindness does not make race a prohibited classification. Violations of the colorblind principle cannot be recognized and remedied without "noticing" the race of the harmed individual or racial group. But, to be true to the model, race-conscious measures must be limited to identified instances of past

---

13. 163 U.S. 537, 559 (1896) (Harlan, J., dissenting) ("Our Constitution is color-blind, and neither knows nor tolerates classes among citizens."). For a revisionist reading of Harlan's dissent, see Tribe, In What Vision of the Constitution Must the Law be Color-blind?, 20 J. Marshall L. Rev. 201, 203 (1986) ("color-blind ideal . . . was only shorthand for the concept that the Fourteenth Amendment prevents our law from enshrining and perpetuating white supremacy").

14. U.S. Dep't of Just., Off. of Legal Pol'y, Rep. to the Att'y Gen., Redefining Discrimination: "Disparate Impact" and the Institutionalization of Affirmative Action 4 (Nov. 4, 1987) [hereinafter DOJ Report]; see also Brest, The Supreme Court 1975 Term—Foreword: In Defense of the Antidiscrimination Principle, 90 Harv. L. Rev. 1, 6 (1976) ("The antidiscrimination principle disfavors race-dependent decisions and conduct, at least when they selectively disadvantage the members of a minority group"); Strauss, The Myth of Colorblindness, 1986 Sup. Ct. Rev. 99, 116–17 ("[I]t is easy to see why affirmative action is . . . in tension with the prohibition against discrimination: affirmative action relies on racial generalizations, but the point of the prohibition against discrimination is precisely to forbid racial generalizations.").

15. Gary Peller puts this idea in a broader intellectual and social context:

> The meaning of race has been grafted into other central cultural images of progress, so that the transition from . . . race consciousness to race neutrality mirrors movements from myth to enlightenment, from ignorance to knowledge . . . and most importantly, the historical self-understanding of liberal society as representing the movement from status to individual liberty.

Peller, Race Consciousness, 1990 Duke L.J. 758, 774.

discrimination.[16]

The debate over colorblindness and race-consciousness has usually appeared in the cases and literature discussing programs that give preferences in employment or other opportunities to nonwhites. In now familiar terms, advocates of colorblindness characterize affirmative action programs as unjustifiably altering meritocratic standards and requiring a distribution of social goods that reflects the proportionate representation of minority groups in the population as a whole.[17]

The presuppositions of supporters of affirmative action may be closer to those of their opponents than is usually recognized. Many advocate "goals" of rough proportional representation upon the claim that since race is, or ought to be, an irrelevant factor in the distribution of the good in question, deviation from proportionate shares is the result either of present discrimination or the continuing effects of past discrimination. That is, the justification for affirmative action programs is usually stated in terms of remedying past and present violations of the colorblind principle. What separates most of the participants in the debate is not so much the goal of colorblindness, but rather differing views about the cause of current inequality and of the efficacy of race-blind or race-conscious remedies in reaching a colorblind future.[18]

In this Article, I will use the term "race-consciousness" to apply to more than just "affirmative action" programs intended to help bring about a colorblind world or remedy past discrimination.[19] There are

---

16. There is a surface logic here that falls apart on analysis. No doubt it does make sense to notice race even in a colorblind world in order to be able to remedy violations of the norm: if a black is denied a job because of her race, the plaintiff must show her race and the race of the person hired to prove the violation; and to remedy the violation requires that relief be directed to her because of her race. This reasoning cannot, however, explain the remedial programs the Court seems willing to permit because the beneficiaries of such programs are not necessarily the victims of the discrimination. See Sullivan, Sins of Discrimination: Last Term's Affirmative Action Cases, 100 Harv. L. Rev. 78, 92–94 (1986); Hazard, Permissive Affirmative Action for the Benefit of Blacks, 1987 U. Ill. L. Rev. 379, 381 (1987). Justice White's opinion for the Court in Firefighters Local Union No. 1784 v. Stotts, 467 U.S. 561, 578–82 (1984), created panic in the civil rights community by hinting at the narrower view of justifiable remedial uses of race, but the Court—at least in *Croson*—appears to have rejected that stance. City of Richmond v. J.A. Croson Co., 109 S. Ct. 706, 717–19 (1989) (opinion of O'Connor, J.) (apparently affirming *Fullilove*). The Court is not unanimous on this point, however, since Justices Kennedy and Scalia seem open to the claim that race-conscious measures may only be used to provide remedies to specific victims of discrimination. Id. at 734 (Kennedy, J., concurring in part and concurring in the judgment); id. at 735 (Scalia, J., concurring in the judgment).

17. See Abram, Affirmative Action: Fair Shakers and Social Engineers, 99 Harv. L. Rev. 1312, 1312–13 (1986).

18. See Regents of the Univ. of Cal. v. Bakke, 438 U.S. 265, 407 (1978) (Blackmun, J., dissenting) ("In order to get beyond racism, we must first take account of race. There is no other way.").

19. Stephen Carter adopts the word "racialist" to designate color-conscious decisions (as opposed to "racist," which he uses to refer to virulent forms of race-conscious-

many other situations in which race *qua* race might be seen as relevant to the pursuit of a legitimate and important governmental goal. These include: ensuring the presence of persons of color on juries;[20] taking race into account in allocating radio and television licenses;[21] seeking nonwhites to fill positions in social service agencies that deal largely with minority populations;[22] requiring voting rules and districts that improve the chances of electing minority representatives;[23] fostering integration by adopting race-based school assignment plans and housing programs;[24] taking measures to integrate police forces;[25] adding the works of minority authors to the "literary canon" taught to college students;[26] and giving weight to the race of applicants for teaching positions in higher education.[27] In each of these situations, the race-consciousness of the program may be justified in other than remedial (and colorblind) terms.[28]

II. THE DIFFERENCE THAT RACE MAKES[29]

We live in a world of racial inequality. In almost every important

ness). Carter, When Victims Happen to be Black, 97 Yale L.J. 420, 430 (1988). Paul Brest uses the term "race-dependent decisions" (which may or may not be based on an intent to harm blacks). Brest, supra note 14, at 6. "Race-consciousness," to me, goes beyond identifying whether or not race played a noticeable role in reaching a particular decision. It refers to a precognitive stance, a set of assumptions and mental filters that channel and influence what we label a problem, how we perceive it, and how we gather and analyze data. My usage is close to Charles Lawrence's "unconscious racism." Lawrence, The Id, the Ego, and Equal Protection: Reckoning with Unconscious Racism, 39 Stan. L. Rev. 317, 322–23 (1987). However, I, like Carter, would reserve a more specific meaning for "racism." See Carter, supra, at 433–39.

20. See Holland v. Illinois, 110 S. Ct. 803, 809 (1990).

21. See Metro Broadcasting, Inc. v. FCC, 110 S. Ct. 2997, 3009 (1990).

22. A State of Michigan official has reported to me that state social service agencies informally pursue such policies.

23. See Voting Rights Act, 42 U.S.C. § 1973(b) (1990).

24. See United States v. Starrett City Assocs., 840 F.2d 1096, 1101 (2d Cir.), cert. denied, 488 US 946 (1988).

25. City of Richmond v. J.A. Croson Co., 109 S. Ct. 706, 731 n.2 (Stevens, J., concurring).

26. See generally Redefining American Literary History (A.L.B. Ruoff & J.W. Ward eds. 1990).

27. See Matsuda, Affirmative Action and Legal Knowledge: Planting Seeds in Plowed-Up Ground, 11 Harv. Women's L.J. 1, 4 (1988).

28. This is hardly a novel suggestion. See, e.g., Sandalow, Racial Preferences in Higher Education: Political Responsibility and the Judicial Role, 42 U. Chi. L. Rev. 653, 682–89 (1975).

29. This phrase was sparked by Catharine MacKinnon's claim that "[o]ne of the most deceptive antifeminisms in society, scholarship, politics, and law is the persistent treatment of gender as if it truly is a question of difference, rather than treating the gender difference as a construct of the difference gender makes." C. MacKinnon, Introduction, *in* Feminism Unmodified 1, 8–9 (1987). However, while I agree with her assessment of sex discrimination law, I would turn it around for race-discrimination law: one of the most deceptive antiracial equality principles in society, scholarship, politics,

category, blacks as a group are worse off than whites. Compared to whites, blacks have higher rates of unemployment, lower family incomes, lower life expectancy, higher rates of infant mortality, higher rates of crime victimization, and higher rates of teenage pregnancies and single-parent households. Blacks are less likely to go to college, and those who matriculate are less likely to graduate. Blacks are underrepresented in the professions, in the academy, and in the national government.[30]

Of course there has been progress. Comparing the situation of blacks half a century ago to their situation today shows a difference that is startling, and even encouraging, although the last decade evidences a slowing progress and some backsliding. But when the comparison is made between whites and blacks today, it is impossible to ignore the deep and widening difference that race makes.[31]

To say that race makes a difference means more than simply identifying material disadvantages facing people of color in contemporary America. It also recognizes that race may have an influence on how members of society understand their worlds and each other, and how such understandings may serve to perpetuate racial inequalities in our society. The next two sections pursue these psychological and cultural claims.

A. *Race and Cognition*

Race matters. Race is among the first things that one notices about another individual. To be born black is to know an unchangeable fact about oneself that matters every day. "[I]n my life," wrote W.E.B. Du Bois in his autobiography *Dusk of Dawn*, "the chief fact has been race—not so much scientific race, as that deep conviction of myriads of men that congenital differences among the main masses of human beings absolutely condition the individual destiny of every member of a group."[32] To be born white is to be free from confronting one's race on a daily, personal, interaction-by-interaction basis.[33] Being white, it has been said, means not having to think about it. Understandably, white people have a hard time recognizing this difference.[34] Most blacks have to overcome, when meeting whites, a set of assumptions older than this nation about one's abilities, one's marriageability, one's

---

and law is the persistent treatment of race as if there is no difference that need be noticed between the races, rather than seeing the difference that race makes.

30. See A Common Destiny: Blacks & American Society 3–32 (G. Jaynes & R. Williams, Jr. eds. 1989) [hereinafter A Common Destiny].

31. For data to support the assertions in the preceding two paragraphs, see id. at 122–23, 278, 280–81, 293, 295, 302–03, 399, 416–17, 465, 524, 530.

32. W.E.B. Du Bois, Dusk of Dawn 139 (1940).

33. See Freeman, Racism, Rights and the Quest for Equality of Opportunity: A Critical Legal Essay, 23 Harv. C.R.-C.L. L. Rev. 295, 357–58 (1988).

34. Much as men have a difficult time understanding the routine and ever-present fears that women have for their physical safety.

sexual desires, and one's morality. Most whites, when they are being honest with themselves, know that these racial understandings are part of their consciousness.

Race matters with respect to the people we choose to spend time with or marry, the neighborhoods in which we choose to live, the houses of worship we join, our choice of schools for our children, the people for whom we vote, and the people we allow the state to execute. We make guesses about the race of telephone callers we do not know and about persons accused of crimes. While not every decision we make necessarily has a racial component, when race is present it almost invariably influences our judgments. We are intensely—even if subconsciously—race-conscious.

It is common to speak of racial attitudes as being based on "stereotypes"—an incorrect or unthinking generalization applied indiscriminately to individuals simply on the basis of group membership. From this perspective, stereotypes can be overcome by supplying more information about an individual or the group to which that individual belongs.

But this explanation fails to recognize race-consciousness as an entrenched structure of thought that affects how we organize and process information.[35] Social science research suggests that stereotypes serve as powerful heuristics, supplying explanations for events even when evidence supporting nonstereotypical explanations exists,[36] and leading us to interpret situations and actions differently when the race of the actors varies.[37] It is often more likely that our mental schema will influence how we understand new information than it is that the new information will alter our mental schema.[38]

A troubling example can be found in *Larry P. by Lucille P. v. Riles*,[39] a case challenging the use of IQ tests that disproportionately assigned black children to special classes for the "educable mentally retarded." In discussing the expert testimony presented on the adequacy of the tests, the court of appeals observed:

> Since the 1920's it has been generally known that black persons perform less well than white persons on the standardized

35. See Hamilton & Trolier, Stereotypes and Stereotyping: An Overview of the Cognitive Approach, *in* Prejudice, Discrimination, and Racism 127 (J. Dovidio & S. Gaertner eds. 1986) [hereinafter Prejudice], and studies cited therein.

36. See, e.g., Bodenhausen & Wyer, Effects of Stereotypes on Decision Making and Information-Processing Strategies, 48 J. Personality & Soc. Psychology 267, 267–82 (1985).

37. See, e.g., Sagar & Schofield, Racial and Behavioral Cues in Black and White Children's Perceptions of Ambiguously Aggressive Acts, 39 J. Personality & Soc. Psychology 590, 590–98 (1980).

38. Note that the usual response to another's use of a stereotype is that "not all Xs are Ys." The response does not deny (or correct) the stereotype; by stating an exception to the stereotype, it implicitly affirms it.

39. 793 F.2d 969 (9th Cir. 1984).

> intelligence tests. IQ tests had been standardized so that they yielded no bias because of sex. For example, when sample tests yielded different scores for boys and girls, the testing experts assumed such differences were unacceptable and modified the tests so that the curve in the standardization sample for boys and girls was identical. No such modifications on racial grounds has ever been tried by the testing companies.[40]

The testing companies received two sets of data and chose to act on just one. Their assumptions made one set of data "surprising" and the other "expected" or "natural."[41]

Because cognitive racial categories predispose us to select information that conforms to existing categories and to process information in such a way that it will fit into those categories, they are self-justifying and self-reinforcing. And because we adopt racial categories more through a process of cultural absorption than rational construction, we are likely to be unaware of the role that the categories play in the way we perceive the world. As Charles Lawrence has noted, "racially prejudiced behavior that is actually the product of learned cultural preferences is experienced as a reflection of rational deduction from objective observation, which is nonprejudicial behavior."[42]

Consider two recent incidents at the University of Michigan Law School:

(1) During a class discussion of the Bernhard Goetz case, a student commented that New York newspapers helped fan the view that Goetz's actions were a justifiable response of a white person confronted by black youths in a New York City subway. When it was suggested that there is a vibrant nonwhite press in New York that discussed the Goetz case in quite different terms, the student responded: "Yes, I know. I am from New York and have read those papers. And they have some very intelligent articles."

(2) The law school student newspaper published a column written by a white student calling for the abolition of a law school program established to provide academic and nonacademic support to nonwhite students. The program, asserted the student, "implicitly brands every minority student with a scarlet 'D.' I can't believe so many bright people allow themselves to be insulted and stigmatized in such an obnoxious way . . . ." Broadening his attack to reach affirmative action programs in general, he stated: "I see stirrings of resentment everywhere. If a black student makes a silly classroom comment (and we all do), some white students—not racists, mind you—will think in their

40. Id. at 975–76; see generally S. Gould, The Mismeasure of Man (1981).

41. Cf. MacKinnon's attack on the use of the term "stereotype" as negating the reality of the oppression of women. C. MacKinnon, Women, Self-Possession, and Sport, *in* Feminism Unmodified, supra note 29, at 118–19.

42. Lawrence, supra note 19, at 339.

heart of hearts about affirmative admissions policies."[43]

These examples provide glimpses at the underlying assumptions, the mental filters, through which whites view and process social data.[44] Why must a white student feel compelled to comment that some articles in nonwhite periodicals are "intelligent"? Why do "silly classroom comments" by black students trigger different responses than the silly comments "we all" make?

This deeply imbedded race-consciousness has a distressing effect on discourse between the races. In many ways, whites and blacks talk past each other. The stories that African-Americans tell about America—stories of racism and exclusion, brutality and mendacity[45]—simply do not ring true to the white mind. Whites have not been trained to hear it, and to credit such accounts would be to ask whites to give up too much of what they "know" about the world. It would also argue in favor of social programs and an alteration in power relations that would fundamentally change the status quo. White versions of substantial progress on racial attitudes are also likely to ring hollow for many blacks.[46] One might see an equality of missed communication here. But there is actually a great inequality because it is the white version that becomes the "official story" in the dominant culture.

B. *The Power of Definition*

In our society, race has not been a benign mode of classification. The designation of one's race has had a double function, both defining social categories and assigning characteristics to members of those categories.[47] The predominant power of social and cultural definition has, from the start, been exercised by and for whites.

The theme of invisibility that permeates black literature portrays white erasure of black attempts at self-definition.[48] Listen to Audre

---

43. Goldberg, MAP Does More Harm Than Good, Res Gestae, Feb. 8, 1989, at 3, col. 1.

44. Of course, this assumption/construction process is not limited to racial matters. We all have been the victims of assumptions preceding data. I recall a weekend morning walking down a law school corridor wearing an army jacket that my father had obtained in Australia during World War II. A colleague commented, "I bet that's an Israeli army jacket."

45. For a concise version of the story, see Delgado, Derrick Bell and the Ideology of Racial Reform: Will We Ever Be Saved? (Review Essay), 97 Yale L.J. 923, 928–47 (1988).

46. As Thomas Pettigrew notes, white ideas about progress are, counter-intuitively, supported by segregation. Few whites spend much time with blacks, and those blacks who are most visible—particularly to elite whites—are successful. Pettigrew, New Patterns of Racism: The Different Worlds of 1984 and 1964, 37 Rutgers L. Rev. 673, 686 (1985).

47. The content and meaning of "blackness" has changed over time, but has been deeply derogatory in all historical eras. See G. Fredrickson, The Black Image in the White Mind xix, 325–32 (1971).

48. See, e.g., R. Ellison, Invisible Man 4 & passim (1952); Morrison, Unspeakable

Lorde:

> . . . I can recall without counting
> eyes
> cancelling me out
> like an unpleasant appointment
> postage due
> stamped in yellow red purple
> any color
> except Black[49]

Blacks are "invisible" not in the sense that whites do not see them; they are "invisible" in the sense that whites see primarily what a white dominant culture has trained them to see.[50] In a curious yet powerful way, whites create and reflect a cultural understanding of blackness that requires little contribution from blacks. The dominant and dominating story excludes or ignores black representations of blackness not out of vindictiveness or animus but because the black stories simply do not register.[51] Robert Berkhofer's description of the process by which whites understand American Indians applies here: "preconception became conception and conception became fact."[52]

In *Black Skin, White Masks*, Frantz Fanon described the power of definition whites hold over African-Americans—a power that was used to serve white needs and perpetuate white myths, and whose exercise has drowned out black attempts at self-definition:

> I came into the world imbued with the will to find a meaning in things, my spirit filled with the desire to attain the source of the world, and then I found that I was an object in the midst of other objects.
>
> Sealed in to that crushing objecthood, I turned beseechingly to others. Their attention was a liberation, running over my body suddenly abraded into nonbeing, endowing me once more with an agility that I had thought lost, and by taking me out of the world, restoring me to it. But just as I reached the

---

Things Unspoken: The Afro-American Presence in American Literature, 28 Mich. Q. Rev. 1, 11–12 (1989); Williams, The Obliging Shell: An Informal Essay on Formal Equal Opportunity, 87 Mich. L. Rev. 2128, 2140–43 (1989).

49. A. Lorde, To the Poet Who Happens to Be Black and the Black Poet Who Happens to Be a Woman, *in* Our Dead Behind Us 6–7 (1986).

50. See B. Hook, Ain't I a Woman: Black Women and Feminism 51–86 (1981); Crenshaw, Race, Reform, and Retrenchment: Transformation and Legitimation in Antidiscrimination Law, 101 Harv. L. Rev. 1331, 1358 (1988) ("The most significant aspect of Black oppression seems to be what is believed *about* Black Americans, not what Black Americans believe.").

51. Cf. Lears, The Concept of Cultural Hegemony: Problems and Possibilities, 90 Am. Hist. Rev. 569, 577 (1985) ("As Gramsci understood, the hegemonic culture depends not on the brainwashing of the 'masses' but on the tendency of public discourse to make some terms of experience readily available to consciousness while ignoring or suppressing others.").

52. R. Berkhofer, The White Man's Indian 71 (1978).

> other side, I stumbled, and the movements, the attitudes, the glances of the other fixed me there, in the sense in which a chemical solution is fixed by a dye. . . .
>
> . . . .
>
> "Look at the nigger! . . . Mama, a Negro! . . . Hell, he's getting mad. . . . Take no notice, sir, he does not know that you are as civilized as we. . . ."
>
> My body was given back to me sprawled out, distorted, recolored, clad in mourning in that white winter day. The Negro is an animal, the Negro is bad, the Negro is mean, the Negro is ugly; look, a nigger, it's cold, the nigger is shivering, the nigger is shivering because he is cold, the little boy is trembling because he is afraid of the nigger, the nigger is shivering with cold, that cold that goes through your bones, the handsome little boy is trembling because he thinks that the nigger is quivering with rage, the little white boy throws himself into his mother's arms: Mama, the nigger's going to eat me up.[53]

Continued white ignorance of blacks and lack of contact in daily life makes white understandings of race difficult to alter.[54] Whites are only dimly aware of how blacks live or what it means to be black in America. Despite attempts to bring African-American history into the classroom, most whites do not understand the role of black slavery in the economic development of the United States, nor are they familiar with major trends in black political and social thought, or even the contributions of Frederick Douglass, W.E.B. Du Bois, and Malcolm X.[55] Absence of knowledge is compounded by physical and social segregation.[56] Blacks and whites rarely get to know each other in neighborhoods, schools, or churches; and interracial friendships remain surprisingly rare. As a result, most of what a white person in America

---

53. F. Fanon, Black Skin, White Masks 109, 113–14 (C. Lammarkmann trans. 1967).

54. This is not to say that simply putting white and black folks together will end discrimination. As social science studies have suggested, such contacts may actually increase prejudice unless the contact occurs under particular conditions—such as when there are superordinate goals or institutional support in the form of superordinate norms and sanctions. For a review of the "contact" literature, see Amir, The Role of Intergroup Contact in Change of Prejudice and Ethnic Relations, *in* Towards the Elimination of Racism 245, 245–308 (P.A. Katz ed. 1976).

55. See School Reading Lists Shun Women and Black Authors, N.Y. Times, June 21, 1989, at B6, col. 1 (reporting study by the Center for Learning and Teaching of Literature, SUNY, Albany).

The recent designation of Martin Luther King, Jr.'s birthday as a national holiday has generated a fair amount of discussion about King and the civil rights movement of the 1960s. Interestingly, it is the "I have a dream" speech—with its resonant and reassuring message of colorblindness—that seems to get the most attention.

56. See Massey & Denton, Hypersegregation in U.S. Metropolitan Areas: Black and Hispanic Segregation Along Five Dimensions, 26 Demography 373, 388–89 (1989) (degree of black/white segregation worse than previous studies reported).

knows about blacks is likely to have been learned from white family, friends, or the white-dominated media.

That the white-created image of African-Americans should remain largely unchallenged by black conceptions is troubling not only because the white version reflects stereotypes, myths, and half-truths, but also because of the role the white definition plays in explaining the historical treatment and current condition of blacks. Given strong incentives to absolve whites and blame blacks for existing social and economic inequalities, the white story about blacks has never been flattering. As Kimberle Crenshaw has powerfully argued, when the white image of blacks is combined with other American stories—such as equality of opportunity—it becomes "difficult for whites to see the Black situation as illegitimate or unnecessary." It works this way:

> Believing both that Blacks are inferior and that the economy impartially rewards the superior over the inferior, whites see that most Blacks are indeed worse off than whites are, which reinforces their sense that the market is operating "fairly and impartially"; those who should logically be on the bottom are on the bottom. This strengthening of whites' belief in the system in turn reinforces their beliefs that Blacks are *indeed* inferior. After all, equal opportunity *is* the rule, and the market *is* an impartial judge; if Blacks are on the bottom, it must reflect their relative inferiority.[57]

In sum, racial inequality has many faces. Social and economic statistics paint a clear and distressing picture of the differences among racial groups. Yet other inequalities are less obvious, based on nearly inaccessible and usually unchallenged assumptions that hide power and explain away domination. The next section examines alternative legal responses to this complex web of inequalities based on race.

III. Legal Strategies of Colorblindness and Race-Consciousness in a Color-Conscious World

In each of the past two Terms, the Supreme Court considered the constitutionality of a race-conscious program aimed at overcoming entrenched racial inequality in a particular economic context. The first, adopted by Richmond, Virginia, provided a set aside for minority businesses competing for city contracts;[58] the second, promulgated by the Federal Communications Commission, sought to increase the number of minority-owned radio and television stations.[59]

In 1983 the City Council of Richmond, Virginia took notice of one small aspect of racial inequality. In previous years, the city had paid millions of dollars to contractors to undertake public construction projects. Yet in a city in which blacks constitute about fifty percent of

57. Crenshaw, supra note 50, at 1380 (footnote omitted).
58. City of Richmond v. J.A. Croson Co., 109 S. Ct. 706, 713 (1989).
59. Metro Broadcasting, Inc. v. FCC, 110 S. Ct. 2997, 3002 (1990).

the population, less than one percent of the public funds spent by Richmond went to general contracting companies owned by blacks and other nonwhite groups. In 1980 the Supreme Court had upheld a federal program aimed at directing public funds to nonmajority-owned contractors,[60] and a number of states and cities around the country had by that time also adopted similar set aside programs for minority-owned enterprises.[61] The Richmond City Council decided to follow suit and adopted an ordinance requiring contractors awarded city contracts to ensure that thirty percent of the city funds go to Minority Business Enterprises (MBEs) engaged as subcontractors for the projects. Contractors could obtain a waiver of the set-aside requirement from the City's Department of General Services, but only upon a showing that "every feasible attempt ha[d] been made to comply" and that qualified MBEs were "unavailable or unwilling to participate in the contract."[62] The program lasted only five years, and it had expired before the case testing its constitutionality reached the Supreme Court.[63]

One need have only the dimmest idea of American history to have a sense of why African-Americans were underrepresented in the construction industry in Richmond, Virginia. Two hundred and fifty years of slavery were followed by four score years of legally enforced subordination of blacks. Jim Crow unionism and social norms about what kind of work was "appropriate" for African-Americans kept blacks in the lowest status, least remunerative jobs, and denied them the chance to move up the occupational ladder.[64] For more than a decade after the *Brown*[65] decision, Richmond tenaciously fought desegregation of its schools.[66] In 1966, the Supreme Court struck down Virginia's poll tax, a levy "born of a desire to disenfranchise the Negro."[67] One year later, the Court invalidated Virginia's antimiscegenation law, which the

60. Fullilove v. Klutznick, 448 U.S. 448, 492 (1980).

61. See Days, *Fullilove*, 96 Yale L.J. 453, 474–76 (1987); Amicus Brief of the National League of Cities at 1a–50a, *Croson*, 109 S. Ct. 706 (No. 87-998).

62. *Croson*, 109 S. Ct. at 713.

63. The case was not mooted by the expiration of the program because the plaintiff contractor alleged that it had suffered damages when it was not awarded a contract due to its failure to meet the set-aside requirement.

64. See generally P. Foner, Organized Labor and the Black Worker 1619–1973, 45–46, 351 (1974) (union apprentice system that excluded blacks from construction in 1870 still did so in 1964); R. Gavins, The Perils and Prospects of Southern Black Leadership, 55–58 (1977) (blacks denied access to unions and apprenticeship programs because of race); Payton, Redressing the Exclusion of and Discrimination Against Black Workers in the Skilled Construction Trades: The Approach of the Washington Lawyers' Committee for Civil Rights Under Law, 27 How. L.J. 1397 (1984) (discrimination against black workers in construction trades due more to outright exclusion by white unions than to subtler forms of racism).

65. Brown v. Board of Educ., 347 U.S. 483 (1954).

66. See School Bd. v. State Bd. of Educ., 462 F.2d 1058, 1061 (4th Cir. 1972), aff'd by an equally divided court, 412 U.S. 92 (1973).

67. Harper v. Virginia Bd. of Elections, 383 U.S. 663, 666 n.3 (1966) (quoting Harman v. Forssenius, 380 U.S. 528, 543 (1965)).

State's highest court defended as a reasonable regulation intended to prevent the "mongrelization" of the races.[68] When black political strength in the city grew following passage of the 1965 Voting Rights Act, Richmond attempted to annex neighboring white areas in order to dilute black voting power.[69] The cumulative impact of such public and private discrimination seriously disadvantaged blacks seeking entry into economic spheres by making it difficult for them to accumulate capital, contacts, and experience.[70]

The FCC policies, too, were aimed at nonwhite entrepreneurs, but the justifications used by the FCC for the race-conscious measures were quite distinct from those offered in support of the Richmond set-aside program. In the mid-1970s, minorities owned less than one percent of the television and radio stations in the United States. Concerned about the lack of broadcast diversity, the Commission established a task force on minority ownership and conducted a conference on ownership policies. The investigations of the task force culminated in a 1978 *Statement of Policy on Minority Ownership of Broadcasting Facilities*, in which it announced the adoption of several measures to increase the number of minority-owned stations. The Commission based its new policies upon its conclusion that:

> [t]he views of racial minorities continue to be inadequately represented in the broadcast media. This situation is detrimental not only to the minority audience but to all of the viewing and listening public. Adequate representation of minority viewpoints in programming serves not only the needs and interests of the minority community but also enriches and educates the non-minority audience.[71]

In 1986, following judicial invalidation of an FCC policy that gave "enhancement credits" to women owners in comparative license proceedings,[72] the FCC announced that it would reconsider its racial, ethnic, and gender preference policies. Congress prevented completion of the FCC's new study, however, by prohibiting the Commission from spending any appropriated funds on the re-examination or alteration of its

68. Loving v. Virginia, 388 U.S. 1, 7 (1967). Writing for the majority, Chief Justice Warren held that the statute was "designed to maintain White Supremacy." Id. at 11.

69. See City of Richmond v. United States, 422 U.S. 358, 372–74 (1975).

70. Cf. Fullilove v. Klutznick, 448 U.S. 448, 505–06 (1980) (Powell, J., concurring) (quoting congressional reports that concluded that low minority rates of participation in business were a result of past social and economic discrimination). Justice O'Connor likewise recognizes that "past societal discrimination in education and economic opportunities" is a factor in explaining "extremely low" membership of MBEs in local contractors' associations. City of Richmond v. J.A. Croson Co., 109 S. Ct. 706, 726 (1989).

71. Statement of Policy on Minority Ownership of Broadcasting Facilities, 68 F.C.C.2d 979, 980–81 (1978) (footnotes omitted) (quoted in Metro Broadcasting, Inc. v. FCC, 110 S. Ct. 2997, 3004 (1990)).

72. Steele v. FCC, 770 F.2d 1192, 1199 (D.C. Cir. 1985).

minority ownership policies.[73] The Senate report on the legislation noted that "[t]he Congress has expressed its support for such policies in the past and has found that promoting diversity of ownership of broadcast properties satisfies important public policy goals."[74] Congress has twice extended the ban on using appropriated funds for re-examination of the policies.[75]

When a city council attempts to overcome some of its city's history, to move toward erasing the gross disparity in grant awards by directing funds towards a group singled out and subordinated because of its race for almost four hundred years, to provide the means by which African-Americans can begin the economic development promised but denied during Reconstruction, to say to blacks that the city recognizes the harms inflicted on blacks as blacks by white supremacy and white economic and political power, how should race discrimination law respond? When a federal agency, following intensive study, concludes that nonwhite programming is significantly underrepresented on American airwaves, and that such underrepresentation harms both minority and majority consumers, and Congress—also of the view that broadcasting diversity is in the public interest—three times instructs the FCC not to alter its racial, ethnic, and gender preference policies, how should race discrimination law respond?

A. *Colorblindness and Antidiscrimination Law*

One response is that if past categorization based on race has created the problem, then the best solution might simply be to now forbid categorization altogether. Justice Scalia suggests this colorblind approach in his opinion in *Croson*: "The difficulty of overcoming the effects of past discrimination is as nothing compared with the difficulty of eradicating from our society the source of those effects, which is the tendency—fatal to a nation such as ours—to classify and judge men and women on the basis of . . . the color of their skin."[76]

73. Continuing Appropriations Act for Fiscal Year 1988, Pub. L. No. 100-202, 101 Stat. 1329–31 (1988).

74. S. Rep. No. 182, 100th Cong., 1st Sess. 76 (1987).

75. Judiciary and Related Agencies Appropriations Act, Pub. L. No. 100-459, 102 Stat. 2216 (1989); Judiciary and Related Agencies Appropriations Act, Pub. L. No. 101-162, 103 Stat. 1020 (1990).

The Commission ultimately defended the preference policies in the *Metro Broadcasting* litigation. See 110 S. Ct. at 3006 n.8; accord Devins, *Metro Broadcasting, Inc. v. FCC*: Requiem for a Heavyweight, 69 Tex. L. Rev. 125, 152–53 (1990) (noting how President Bush's appointment in 1989 of three commissioners supportive of diversity preferences inspired the FCC to change course).

76. City of Richmond v. J.A. Croson Co., 109 S. Ct. 706, 735 (1989) (Scalia, J., concurring in the judgment); cf. William Van Alstyne's declamation: "[O]ne gets beyond racism by getting beyond it now: by a complete, resolute and credible commitment *never* to tolerate in one's own life—or in the life or practices of one's government—the differential treatment of other human beings by race." Van Alstyne, Rites of Passage: Race, the Supreme Court, and the Constitution, 46 U. Chi. L. Rev. 775, 809 (1979).

The allure of colorblindness is strong. It is rooted in the dissenting opinion of the case that ratified American apartheid.[77] And it fits with liberal, individualistic principles that each person should be assessed on individual merits, not upon the basis of group membership. Color-consciousness, under this account, is irrational and immoral[78] because it is so rarely relevant to acceptable purposes.

Colorblindness also has powerful strategic appeal. In a world of white supremacy, most classifications based on race will have the intent or effect of harming blacks. Colorblindness sweeps these away. Furthermore, since whites are likely to look after their own, insisting that blacks get precisely what whites get will materially advance black interests.[79] Colorblindness also keeps white guilt and anxiety at an acceptable level. As Alan Freeman has noted, colorblindness designates as "wrongdoers" only those "racists" who continue to take race into account; colorblind whites are absolved even if they continue to benefit from an unequal state of affairs.[80] Finally, there is the risk that noticing race, even for a "benign" purpose, will only serve to affirm the view of racial differences that supported racial domination in the past.[81]

---

77. Plessy v. Ferguson, 163 U.S. 537, 554–55 (1896) (Harlan, J., dissenting).

78. See, e.g., A. Bickel, The Morality of Consent 133 (1975) ("The lesson of the great decisions of the Supreme Court and the lesson of contemporary history have been the same for at least a generation: discrimination on the basis of race is illegal, immoral, unconstitutional, inherently wrong, and destructive of democratic values.").

79. Interestingly, the first civil rights law was worded in this way: "[A]ll . . . citizens . . . shall have the same right[s] . . . as . . . white citizens . . . ." Act of Apr. 9, 1866, ch. 31, § 1, 14 Stat. 27.

80. Freeman, Legitimizing Racial Discrimination Through Antidiscrimination Law: A Critical Review of Supreme Court Doctrine, 62 Minn. L. Rev. 1049, 1054–56, 1067 (1978).

Colorblindness has never meant that race should be or can be totally ignored. Consistent with the individualist underpinnings of colorblindness, it remains permissible for persons to make personal, intimate choices based on race. The idea here is not so much that it is a good thing that race influence private choices, but rather that it is a bad thing for the state to seek to control such choices. While the scope of the unconstrained private choice has shrunk noticeably in the past twenty-five years, it clearly still includes decisions about marriage and association.

81. W.E.B. Du Bois recognized this problem almost a century ago:

> The American Negro has always felt an intense personal interest in discussions as to the origins and destinies of races: primarily because back of most discussions of race with which he is familiar, have lurked certain assumptions as to his natural abilities, as to his political, intellectual and moral status, which he felt were wrong. He has, consequently, been led to deprecate and minimize race distinctions, to believe intensely that out of one blood God created all nations, and to speak of human brotherhood as though it were the possibility of an already dawning to-morrow.

W.E.B. Du Bois, The Conservation of the Races 5 (1897). Although he expressly rejected the claim, Du Bois reported that many thought that:

> our sole hope of salvation lies in our being able to lose our race identity in the commingled blood of the nation; and that any other course would merely increase the friction of races which we call race prejudice, and against which we have so long and so earnestly fought.

The opinions in *Croson* and *Metro Broadcasting* show that four Justices believe that colorblindness should be the animating vision for antidiscrimination law.[82] Justice O'Connor's plurality opinion in *Croson* identifies the central constitutional norm as prohibition of the use of racial classifications:

> The Richmond Plan denies certain citizens the opportunity to compete for a fixed percentage of public contracts based solely upon their race. To whatever racial group these citizens belong, their "personal rights" to be treated with equal dignity and respect are implicated by a rigid rule erecting race as the sole criterion in an aspect of public decisionmaking.[83]

The concurring opinions of Justices Scalia and Kennedy are equally explicit. Justice Scalia writes: "I share the view expressed by Alexander Bickel that '. . . discrimination on the basis of race is illegal, immoral, unconstitutional, inherently wrong, and destructive of democratic society.' "[84] Justice Kennedy agrees: "The moral imperative of racial neutrality is the driving force of the Equal Protection Clause."[85]

The Justices adopting a colorblind approach do not suggest that the Constitution prohibits all racial classifications; their invocation of "strict scrutiny" review leaves them space to uphold race-conscious measures that remedy violations of the colorblind principle[86] or, perhaps, when the use of race is necessary in responding to a "social emergency" such as a prison race riot.[87] To allow other justifications for color-conscious state action, however, would undermine, in Justice O'Connor's words, "[t]he dream of a Nation of equal citizens in a society where race is irrelevant to personal opportunity and achievement."[88]

Justice O'Connor's opinion captures the essence of a colorblind approach: equality as a personal, individual right to equal opportunity,

---

Id. at 10.

82. Given the fact that Justice White joined Justice O'Connor's *Croson* opinion, there are apparently five votes for a colorblind approach—at least as far as nonfederal programs are concerned. See City of Richmond v. J.A. Croson Co., 109 S. Ct. 706, 712 (1989).

83. Id. at 721. Justices White and Kennedy joined O'Connor with respect to this part of the opinion. Id. at 712.

84. Id. at 735 (Scalia, J., concurring) (quoting A. Bickel, supra note 78, at 133).

85. Id. at 734 (Kennedy, J., concurring).

86. The linkage between the underlying norm of equal protection and the test the Court uses for vindication of this norm—strict scrutiny—has been subject to much scholarly comment and speculation. See, e.g., J. Ely, Democracy and Distrust 145–70 (1980) (strict scrutiny analysis "flushes out" impermissible purpose). Although it is not generally recognized, a colorblind approach provides a persuasive account. By limiting permissible ends to the remedying of past discrimination and requiring a close fit between means and ends, strict scrutiny can assure that race is used only to remedy previous breaches of the colorblind norm.

87. *Croson*, 109 S. Ct. at 735 (Scalia, J., concurring).

88. Id. at 727.

and race-consciousness as an irrational impediment to the creation of a just society. In the same stroke that O'Connor condemns race-consciousness as a serious violation of fundamental American norms, she promises us that colorblindness is the road to the future we all seek. Those who attack colorblindness, therefore, are put in the position of arguing for an approach that rings false to widely held norms and also moves us away from our utopian ideal. Here is the power of a dominant legal consciousness. It supports the legitimacy of the current set of norms both by privileging certain accounts of the way the world is and by promising a better world tomorrow.[89]

B. *From Colorblindness to Race-Consciousness*

Colorblindness may seem to be a sensible strategy in a world in which race has unjustly mattered for so long. Yet the claim that colorblindness today is the most efficacious route to colorblindness tomorrow has always been controversial. Justice Blackmun's paradoxical aphorism in *Bakke* reflects the usual counterclaim: "In order to get beyond racism, we must first take account of race. There is no other way. And in order to treat some persons equally, we must treat them differently."[90] To those who agree with Blackmun, the invalidation of Richmond's set-aside program in *Croson* amply demonstrates how a demand for means that are colorblind will retard the remedying of racial inequality.

The claim I wish to press here is different from Blackmun's familiar stance in the affirmative action debate. I will argue in this section that a legal norm of colorblindness will not end race-consciousness; rather, it will simply make the unfortunate aspects and consequences of race-consciousness less accessible and thus less alterable. Furthermore, colorblind strategies are likely to deny or fail to appreciate the contribution that race-consciousness can make in creating new cultural narratives that would support serious efforts aimed at achieving racial justice.

Before these claims can be made, however, two varieties of colorblindness should be distinguished. The first, which I will call "strong colorblindness," argues that race should truly be an irrelevant, virtually unnoticed, human characteristic. Richard Wasserstrom has described this "assimilationist ideal":

> [A] nonracist society would be one in which the race of an individual would be the functional equivalent of the eye color of individuals in our society today. In our society no basic political rights and obligations are determined on the basis of eye color. No important institutional benefits and burdens are

89. See Lears, supra note 51, at 590; Cf. Lawrence, supra note 19, at 324–25 (discussing use of law to create utopian images that serve to justify status quo).

90. Regents of Univ. of Cal. v. Bakke, 438 U.S. 265, 407 (1978) (Blackmun, J., dissenting).

> connected with eye color. Indeed, except for the mildest sort of aesthetic preferences, a person would be thought odd who even made private, social decisions by taking eye color into account.[91]

The second type, "weak colorblindness," would not outlaw all recognition of race, but would condemn the use of race as a basis for the distribution of scarce resources or opportunities and the imposition of burdens. Under "weak colorblindness," race might function like ethnicity: an attribute that could have significance for group members, and one that society as a whole could recognize, but not one upon which legal distinctions could be based. Furthermore, individuals would be able to choose how important a role race would play in their associations and identifications, but their race would not be used by others to limit their opportunities or define their identities. Thus, college courses on "African-American literature" might well be permissible under a weak colorblindness regime, but such a regime would not tolerate allocating places in the class based on race or allowing race to be used as a factor in the choice of an instructor. In the sections that follow, I will argue that strong colorblindness is impossible and undesirable, and that weak colorblindnes—although perhaps able to be implemented as a legal strategy—is an inadequate response to current manifestations of racial inequality.

1. *Masking Race-Consciousness.* — It is apparently important, as a matter of widespread cultural practice, for whites to assert that they are strongly colorblind, in the sense that they do not notice or act on the basis of race. One can see this at work in such statements as: "I judge each person as an individual." Of course, it cannot be that whites do not notice the race of others. Perhaps what is being said is that the speaker does not begin her evaluation with any preconceived notions. But this too is difficult to believe, given the deep and implicit ways in which our minds are color-coded. To be truly colorblind in this way, as David Strauss has shown, requires color-consciousness: one must notice race in order to tell oneself not to trigger the usual mental processes that take race into account.[92]

The denial of race-consciousness occasioned by the desire to be strongly colorblind is described in a recent study of a desegregated junior high school by psychologist Janet Schofield. She reports that teachers, apparently concerned that acknowledging racial awareness would be viewed as a sign of prejudice, claimed not to notice the race of their students. In pursuit of colorblindness, teachers rarely used the words "white" or "black," and avoided racial topics and identifications in

91. R. Wasserstrom, Philosophy and Social Issues 24 (1980) (footnote omitted). Wasserstrom is careful to point out that his use of the term "assimilationist" is "stipulative" and is not intended to suggest the incorporation of dominated groups into dominant culture. Id. at 47 n.25.

92. See Strauss, supra note 14, at 114.

class.[93]

This act of denial is troubling not only because it distorts reality, but also because it will make less accessible the ways in which color-consciousness influences our understanding of the world and of others.[94] Strong colorblindness will perpetuate the white image of blacks by rendering irrelevant the kind of race-based discussion and data necessary for a serious critique of white definitions. Schofield's study documents how teachers' desires to act in a colorblind fashion harmed the educational experience by ignoring or denying race when it would have been appropriate to notice it:

> [One] teacher included George Washington Carver on a list of great Americans from which students could pick individuals to learn about but specifically decided not to mention he was black for fear of raising racial issues. In the best of all worlds, there would be no need to make such mention, because children would have no preconceptions that famous people are generally white. However, in a school where one white child was surprised to learn from a member of our research team that Martin Luther King was black, not white[!], it would seem reasonable to argue that highlighting the accomplishments of black Americans and making sure that students do not assume famous figures are white is a reasonable practice.[95]

Certainly such conduct creates possibilities for serious miscommunication. There is significant evidence of cultural differences between whites and blacks. Although the relative contributions of race and class to these differences remain in dispute and wide variations within groups occur, few doubt that race plays a substantial, independent role.[96] Thomas Kochman has suggested a number of ways in which modes and styles of communication differ widely between inner-city blacks and middle class whites,[97] producing substantial misunderstanding when forms of argumentation and presentations of self are misread. An ethnographic study by Shirley Brice Heath notes significant differences in the kinds and number of questions that black and white children are asked at home. When white teachers, unaware of such differences, ask questions in a way that conforms to white middle-class practice, they unwittingly disadvantage black school children.[98]

But the problem runs deeper than the level of miscommunication.

---

93. Schofield, Causes and Consequences of the Colorblind Perspective, *in* Prejudice, supra note 35, at 231.

94. For example, a person's desire to reach decisions in a race-neutral manner may lead him or her to believe that race-neutral reasons provided the basis for a decision and to leave undisclosed the actual role that race played in the decision making process. Id. at 247.

95. Id. at 249.

96. See, e.g., Jones, Racism: A Cultural Analysis of the Problem, *in* Prejudice, supra note 35, at 279–314.

97. See T. Kochman, Black and White Styles in Conflict 8 (1981).

98. See S. Heath, Questioning at Home and at School: A Comparative Study, *in*

Whites believe that they can act in a colorblind fashion merely by acting as they always have. Colorblindness puts the burden on blacks to change; to receive "equal" treatment, they must be seen by whites as "white."[99] Hence, the "compliment" that some whites pay to blacks: "I don't think of you as black."[100] Colorblindness is, in essence, not the absence of color, but rather monochromatism: whites can be color-blind when there is only one race—when blacks become white.

2. *Local Knowledge: Race-Consciousness as Cultural Critique.* — Strong colorblindness, I have argued, is unlikely to produce the result it promises—a world in which race does not matter. In this section, I want to make the case for race-consciousness more direct by focusing on the benefits of race-consciousness in undermining and shifting deep cultural assumptions and ultimately, perhaps, making progress in overcoming racism. In presenting these claims, I hope also to undermine the case for weak colorblindness. To be effective, strategies for attacking racism may well demand affirmative race-conscious governmental policies.

Clifford Geertz, in a collection of his essays entitled *Local Knowledge*, has stated that:

> To see ourselves as others see us can be eye-opening. To see others as sharing a nature with ourselves is the merest decency. But it is from the far more difficult achievement of seeing ourselves amongst others, as a local example of the forms human life has locally taken, a case among cases, a world among worlds, that the largeness of mind, without which objectivity is self-congratulation and tolerance a sham, comes.[101]

Colorblindness operates at Geertz's level of "merest decency." It begins and ends with the observation that there is something, under the skin, common to all human beings. I do not want to discount the deep humanism underlying this perspective. Indeed, it is a significant improvement over the racist ideologies that have been prevalent throughout United States history and that have denied the "inner" equality of the races. But Geertz clearly seeks more than this; he would reorient the usual hierarchical relationship between dominant and subordinate cultures by rotating the axis through its center point, making the verti-

---

Doing the Ethnography of Schooling: Educational Anthropology in Action 105, 110 (G. Spindler ed. 1982).

99. James Baldwin commented on the

> tone of warm congratulation with which so many [white] liberals address their Negro equals. It is the Negro, of course, who is presumed to have become equal—an achievement that not only proves the comforting fact that perseverance has no color but also overwhelmingly corroborates the white man's sense of his own value.

J. Baldwin, The Fire Next Time 127 (1962).

100. See Lawrence, supra note 19, at 318, for a description of this maladroit white behavior.

101. C. Geertz, Local Knowledge: Further Essays in Interpretive Anthropology 16 (1983).

cal horizontal. This shift requires two related transformations: the first is to appreciate the contingency, the nonuniversalism of one's own culture—to view it as an example of "local knowledge;" the second is to recognize and credit the "local knowledges" of other groups. Of course, these two efforts are related. By valorizing the dominated, one is likely to cast doubts on the dominant group's characterizations or definition of the dominated group, which, in turn, tells us something new about the dominant group as well.

My claim outlined in the pages that follow is that race-consciousness can aid in these cultural transformations. This is, to be sure, hardly a new claim. The calls for "black pride" and "black power" in the 1960s represented a reorienting demand of race-consciousness.[102] Stokely Carmichael and Charles Hamilton's manifesto put it this way:

> [W]hile color blindness *may* be a sound goal ultimately, we must realize that race is an overwhelming fact of life in this historical period. There is no black man in this country who can live "simply as a man." His blackness is an ever-present fact of this racist society, whether he recognizes it or not. . . .
>
> "Integration" as a goal today speaks to the problem of blackness not only in an unrealistic way but also in a despicable way. It is based on complete acceptance of the fact that in order to have a decent house or education, black people must move into a white neighborhood or send their children to a white school. This reinforces, among both black and white, the idea that "white" is automatically superior and "black" is by definition inferior. . . .
>
> "Integration" also means that black people must give up their identity, deny their heritage. . . . The fact is that integration, as traditionally articulated, would abolish the black community. . . .
>
> The racial and cultural personality of the black community must be preserved and that community must win its freedom while preserving its cultural integrity. Integrity includes a pride—in the sense of self-acceptance, not chauvinism—in being black, in the historical attainments and contributions of black people.[103]

---

102. Malcolm X told white America:

> What you don't realize . . . is that black people today don't think it is any victory to live next to you or enter your society. This is what you have to learn—that the black man has finally reached the point where he doesn't see what you have to offer. Today you haven't got anything to offer. Your own time has run out, your own ship is sinking, the seas are stormy, and now that your boat is rocking and on its way down, you're offering the black man a chance to integrate into your doomed society. And those Uncle Tom, brain-washed, white-minded Negroes who love you may do it, but the masses of black people want a society of their own in a land of their own.

(quoted in P. Goldman, supra note 2, at 66–67).

103. S. Carmichael & C. Hamilton, Black Power 54–55 (1967). Also during this

The consequences wrought by the race-conscious advocates were startling. They were able to take the term "black"—which for more than three hundred years had symbolized degradation and stigma—and turn it into an assertion of a group's humanity and solidarity.[104] But African-American self-pride does not necessarily penetrate white cultural norms and narratives. Indeed, a dominant culture can be relatively unconcerned with a subordinated group's definition of itself if that definition either does not get air time or can be dismissed as romantic, self-serving, or fictional.

Rotating the axis helps us to be open to other accounts and perspectives, and in doing so it reminds us of the fictional or constructed nature of "local knowledges"—including our own. Once white Americans shed the false assumption that "they know all they need to know" about African-Americans,[105] they will begin to learn as much about themselves as about others.[106]

a. *Understanding Domination.* —

> The American Negro has the great advantage of having never believed that collection of myths to which white Americans cling . . . .[107]
>
> — James Baldwin

"[T]he quickest way to bring the reason of the world face to face [with white racism]," Du Bois wrote, "is to listen to the complaint of those human beings today who are suffering most from white attitudes,

---

time, some blacks urged increased financial support for, and black control of, black schools rather than busing to achieve racial balance, which would undermine attempts at black community building. See Congress on Racial Equality, School Segregation: Its True Nature, *in* Education for Whom? 199, 205 (C. Tesconi & E. Hurwitz eds. 1974) (reprint of CORE's amicus brief filed in Swann v. Charlotte-Mecklenburg Bd. of Educ., 402 U.S. 1 (1971)).

104. "Black is beautiful" may sound like a cliché today, but it was a brave and dramatic declaration in the 1960s. See also P. Goldman, supra note 2, at 398–402 (explaining core of Malcolm X's philosophy as "altering the terms in which [black people] thought and the scale by which they measured themselves"; "his most important legacy was his example, his bearing, his affirmation of blackness").

105. Similarly, Said can claim in Orientalism that a study of the Occident's views of the East reveals much about the West and very little about the East. E. Said, Orientalism 6 (1978).

106. Many will find my argument problematic to the extent that it postulates an "essential" black or white "voice" and thereby suppresses the diversity between and among whites and blacks that we seem to experience daily. The attack on "essentialism" is shared by both proponents and opponents of the "different voice" claim. Compare Kennedy, Racial Critiques of Legal Academia, 102 Harv. L. Rev. 1745, 1802–03 (1989) (attacking essentialism by arguing that racial status in itself is inadequate intellectual credential since white scholars can advance "black" arguments and vice-versa) with Harris, Race and Essentialism in Feminist Legal Theory, 42 Stan. L. Rev. 581, 585 (1990) (questioning the unitary concept of "woman" in some feminist scholarship by analyzing the voices of black women). I will take up this critique below. See infra notes 152–166 and accompanying text.

107. J. Baldwin, supra note 99, at 136.

from white habits, from the conscious and unconscious wrongs which white folk are today inflicting on their victims."[108] Du Bois's suggestion is a persistent theme in recent nonmajority scholarship. Mari Matsuda, in her sympathetic critique of the Critical Legal Studies movement, has urged legal scholars to "look to the bottom" to discover the "distinct normative insights" of "victims of racial oppression."[109] Catharine MacKinnon has argued that "the standpoint from which legal method has been designed and injuries have been defined . . . has not been women's standpoint"; when one "[d]efin[es] feminism in a way that connects epistemology with power as the politics of women's point of view," a "whole shadow world of previously invisible silent abuse has been discerned."[110]

The claim here is limited, but important. One need not believe that subordinated groups hold world views thoroughly differentiated from the dominant culture in order to give credit to the claim that the views of subordinated groups on the extent and nature of subordination are likely to differ from those of majority groups. This is so for a number of reasons.

Dominant groups may have neither the inclination nor the ability to be fully aware of their domination. Dominant groups generally do not consider themselves to be oppressive, particularly in a society in which tolerance for diversity is valued, and they can provide descriptions of themselves and the disadvantaged that explain inequality as either justified or natural. To the extent that these descriptions effectively absolve dominant groups of responsibility for inequality, and therefore from bearing any of the costs of ameliorating inequality, there is little motivation for the dominant culture to question them.

Furthermore, the dominant culture's conceptions of the dominated are often not explicit. They are likely to be rooted, as Du Bois notes, in "long followed habits, customs, and folkways; [in] subconscious trains of reasoning and unconscious nervous reflexes."[111] These assumptions and mental structures, as noted above, may well have a significant influence on conduct and attitudes, yet they are rarely subjected to careful scrutiny because they seem so natural, so much a part of us.[112]

---

108. W.E.B. Du Bois, supra note 32, at 172.

109. Matsuda, Looking to the Bottom: Critical Legal Studies and Reparations, 22 Harv. C.R.-C.L. L. Rev. 323, 326 (1987); see also id. at 325 ("The technique of imagining oneself black and poor in some hypothetical [Rawlsian or Ackermanian] world is less effective than studying the actual experience of black poverty and listening to those who have done so.").

110. C. MacKinnon, Francis Biddle's Sister, *in* Feminism Unmodified, supra note 29, at 169.

111. W.E.B. Du Bois, supra note 32, at 172; see also Lawrence, supra note 19, at 317–18 (Lawrence's own experiences with race-based habits of thought); id. at 328–44 (explaining various theories of psychoanalysis and their views of unconscious racism).

112. See G. Fredrickson, The Black Image in the White Mind: The Debate on Afro-American Character and Destiny, 1817–1914, at 331–32 (1971) ("consciousness of

Finally, since dominant groups are not the direct victims of their acts toward dominated groups, they may underestimate the burdens suffered by the dominated groups. This problem is compounded if dominant and dominated groups inhabit separate geographical and social spaces, so that the extent and harms of domination remain largely hidden from the dominant groups.

For these reasons, accounts of domination by those outside the dominant culture ought to be seen as an important check on what the dominant culture thinks it knows. To be sure, such "outsider" accounts should be subjected to critical scrutiny. Every group will have reasons for constructing narratives that reflect well on it and poorly on its perceived oppressors. Furthermore, the power of a dominant culture may well reside in large part in its ability to convince subordinated groups that the stories told about them are true.[113] But if these kinds of reasons are viewed as sufficient cause for not privileging black accounts of domination, then they should also be seen as undermining the claims of objectivity and neutrality that are usually accorded white accounts.

Unfortunately, however, accounts of domination by the dominated are often discounted because the dominated are seen as having a self-interested motive in exaggerating the degree of harm.[114] Scholarship done by minority scholars on minority issues is frequently greeted with skepticism from majority members of the academy.[115] María de la Luz Reyes and John Halcón write that,

> [t]he assumption is that minority researchers cannot be objective in their analyses of those problems which are so close to their life experiences. . . . White-on-White research is accorded legitimacy, but "brown-on-brown" research is questioned and challenged at the same time that many White social scientists are establishing their professional careers as experts on minority issues.[116]

As George Fredrickson has shown (with detail and insight painful

---

color is combined, as it is in the United States, with a tradition of slavery and caste so deeply rooted in the white psyche that it often seems impervious to rational argument.").

113. Cf. C. MacKinnon, Difference and Dominance, *in* Feminism Unmodified, supra note 29, at 38–39 (arguing that "different" moral reasoning of women suggested by Carol Gilligan may be "what male supremacy has attributed to us for its own use").

114. A particularly insensitive example was Ronald Reagan's comment in 1989—reported the day before the national holiday celebrating Martin Luther King Jr.'s birthday—that civil rights leaders overstate the existence of racism in order to keep themselves in business.

115. Minority scholarship has also been harmed by white assumptions that nonmajority scholars are not as capable as whites.

116. De la Luz Reyes & Halcón, Racism in Academia: The Old Wolf Revisited, 58 Harv. Educ. Rev. 299, 307 (1988); accord Williams, Alchemical Notes: Reconstructing Ideals from Deconstructed Rights, 22 Harv. C.R.-C.L. L. Rev. 401, 413 (1987) ("[W]hite statements of black needs suddenly acquire the sort of stark statistical authority which

to the reader), the image of blacks in the white mind has historically been what whites needed to tell themselves in order to justify racial oppression and inequality.[117] Such justificatory schemes—particularly ones that support the continued existence of great inequality—should be constantly subjected to re-evaluation. Nonmajority perspectives have an important role to play in the uncovering and critiquing of the dominant culture's assumptions and explanations about domination.[118]

b. *Understanding the Dominant.* — The recognition of a nonmajority presence may also provide important perspectives on matters not generally associated with race.[119] This point has been made persuasively by scholars interested in the relationship of law and literature. James Boyd White has argued that

> [r]eading texts composed by other minds in other worlds can help us see more clearly (what is otherwise nearly invisible) the force and meaning of the habits of mind and language in which we have been brought up, as lawyers and as people, and to which we shall in all likelihood remain unconscious unless led to perceive or imagine other worlds.[120]

White uses the word "invisible" to describe the reader's implicit assumptions. But there is another kind of invisibility as well, one that has denied the presence of blacks and the issue of race in American history and culture. Toni Morrison has urged a re-examination and reinterpretation of the American literary canon for "the ghost in the machine": "the ways in which the presence of Afro-Americans has shaped the choices, the language, the structure—the meaning of so much American literature."[121] She demonstrates her claim by offering a powerful reinterpretation of *Moby Dick* that sees a critique of "whiteness as ideology" as central to the novel.[122]

I will leave to literary critics the task of evaluating Morrison's analysis. But there is ample evidence of "unspeakable things unspoken" in the texts of constitutional law. In most constitutional law casebooks,

---

lawmakers can listen to and politicians hear. But from blacks, stark statistical statements of need are heard as 'strident,' 'discordant,' and 'unharmonious . . . .' ").

117. See G. Fredrickson, supra note 112, at 320–32; G. Fredrickson, Social Origins of American Racism, *in* The Arrogance of Race: Historical Perspectives on Slavery, Racism, and Social Inequality 189 (1988).

118. As Barrington Moore, Jr. has written, "sympathy with the victims of historical processes and skepticism about the victors' claims provide essential safeguards against being taken in by the dominant mythology." Quoted in Woodward, Clio with Soul, 56 J. Am. Hist. 5, 20 (1969).

119. See, e.g., Peters v. Kiff, 407 U.S. 493, 503–04 (1972) ("[W]e are unwilling to make the assumption that the exclusion of Negroes has relevance only for issues involving race . . . . [Their] exclusion deprives the jury of a perspective on human events that may have unsuspected importance in any case that may be presented.")

120. White, What Can a Lawyer Learn from Literature? (Book Review), 102 Harv. L. Rev. 2014, 2023 (1989).

121. Morrison, supra note 48, at 11.

122. Id. at 16.

for example, the commerce power provides the major vehicle for the examination of the nature and scope of federal legislative authority. The canon includes several cases from the pre-Civil War era from which modern constitutional understandings are said to trace.[123] Yet a number of leading texts make no mention of the fact that crucial to the early conflict over the scope of the commerce power was the explosive question of Congress's power to regulate the internal slave trade.[124] This recognition immediately puts the constitutional debate in a different light;[125] and it helps establish linkages between the nationalist opinions of Chief Justice Marshall in *Gibbons v. Ogden*[126] and Justice Story in *Prigg v. Pennsylvania*,[127] in which exclusive federal powers are asserted in an attempt to prevent interstate rivalries that could threaten the Union.[128]

c. *Recognizing the Dominated.* — Finally, recognizing race validates the lives and experiences of those who have been burdened because of their race. White racism has made "blackness" a relevant category in our society. Yet colorblindness seeks to deny the continued social significance of the category, to tell blacks that they are no different from whites, even though blacks as blacks are persistently made to feel that difference. Color-consciousness allows for recognition of the distinct and difficult difference that race has made; it facilitates white awareness of the efforts of African-Americans to describe and examine that difference. This is not simply the telling of a story of oppression. Color-consciousness makes blacks subjects and not objects, undermining the durability of white definitions of "blackness." It permits recognition of

123. E.g., Willson v. Blackbird Creek Marsh Co., 27 U.S. (2 Pet.) 244 (1829); Brown v. Maryland, 25 U.S. (12 Wheat.) 419 (1827); Gibbons v. Ogden, 22 U.S. (9 Wheat.) 1 (1824).

124. For example, E. Barrett, W. Cohen & J. Varat, Constitutional Law (8th ed. 1989); G. Gunther, Constitutional Law: Cases and Materials (11th ed. 1985); and W. Lockhart, Y. Kamisar, J. Choper & S. Shiffrin, Constitutional Law: Cases, Comments and Questions (6th ed. 1986); virtually ignore slavery, except as a backdrop to a discussion of the fourteenth amendment. This failure to mention slavery seems particularly unreasonable given the high profile afforded the "founding" commerce clause cases. To see these cases as turning simply on competing models of federalism is to distort their significance in American constitutional history and theory; what was at stake was the survival of a political, economic, and social system. P. Brest & S. Levinson, Processes of Constitutional Decisionmaking: Cases and Materials (2d ed. 1983) was the early exception here. See id. at 120–25, 153–81. G. Stone, L. Seidman, C. Sunstein & M. Tushnet, Constitutional Law (1986), have followed suit, and admirably report in a note to *Gibbons v. Ogden* that "[c]ontroversies over the scope of the commerce clause, and over the breadth of Congress's powers generally, were inextricable from the issue of slavery in the antebellum period." Id. at 137.

125. See G. Stone, L. Seidman, C. Sunstein & M. Tushnet, supra note 124, at 137 ("Southerners feared that broad affirmations of congressional power would license Congress to regulate slavery as a form of commerce.").

126. 22 U.S. (9 Wheat.) 1 (1824).

127. 41 U.S. (16 Pet.) 539 (1842).

128. See *Gibbons*, 22 U.S. (9 Wheat.) at 209; *Prigg*, 41 U.S. (16 Pet.) at 622–25.

the strength and adaptive power of a black community able to survive slavery and oppression;[129] and it acknowledges the contributions of black culture—not simply as windows on "the race question" but as distinct (if varied) voices and traditions, worthy of study in their own right.[130]

It is difficult to improve upon Adrienne Rich's insight:

> I used to envy the "colorblindness" which some liberal, enlightened, white people were supposed to possess; raised as I was, where I was, I am and will to the end of my life be acutely, sometimes bitterly, aware of color. Every adult around me in my childhood, white or black, was aware of it; it was a sovereign consciousness, a hushed and compelling secret. But I no longer believe that "colorblindness"—if it even exists—is the opposite of racism; I think it is, in this world, a form of naiveté and moral stupidity. It implies that I would look at a black woman and see her as white, thus engaging in white solipsism to the utter erasure of her particular reality.[131]

Here is the turn of the axis, the recognition of others that helps one to see one's own culture as "a world among worlds."

3. *Weak Colorblindness and Its Costs.* — It is common for advocates of affirmative action to point out that a legal strategy dedicated to "equality of opportunity" is likely to replicate deeply imbedded inequalities. The familiar metaphor is of a race between two runners, one of whom starts many yards back from the starting line, or is encumbered by ankle weights.[132] Color-conscious policies are said to remove the advantage that has for several centuries been granted to whites. The simplicity of this argument should not disguise its soundness or moral power.[133]

---

129. See generally E. Foner, Reconstruction: America's Unfinished Revolution, 1863–1877, at 102 (1988) ("Blacks brought out of slavery a conception of themselves as a 'Working Class of People' who had been unjustly deprived of the fruits of their labor."); E. Genovese, Roll Jordan, Roll: The World the Slaves Made 658 (1974) ("Accommodation and resistance developed as two forms of a single process by which the slaves accepted what could not be avoided and simultaneously fought individually and as a people for moral as well as physical survival."); H. Gutman, The Black Family in Slavery and Freedom, 1750–1925, at 36 (1976) ("[T]he developing Afro-American culture had at its core common adaptive slave domestic arrangements and kin networks and . . . enlarged slave communities emerged over time out of these adaptive kin arrangements.").

130. Cf. Gates, Introduction: Writing "Race" and the Difference It Makes, *in* "Race," Writing, and Difference 1, 13 (H.L. Gates, Jr. ed. 1986) ("The Western critical tradition has a canon, as the Western literary tradition does. I once thought it our most important gesture to *master* the canon of criticism, to *imitate* and *apply* it, but I now believe that we must turn to the black tradition itself to develop theories of criticism indigenous to our literatures.").

131. A. Rich, supra note 1, at 300.

132. See M. King, Jr., Why We Can't Wait 134 (1964); Commencement Address of Pres. Lyndon Johnson at Howard University, June 4, 1965, *in* 2 Public Papers of the Presidents: Lyndon B. Johnson, 1965, at 635, 636 (1966).

133. But see, e.g., Abram, supra note 17, at 1314–23.

Unfortunately, however, affirmative action programs based on the objective of overcoming past societal discrimination are deemed to run afoul of the Court's model of weak colorblindness.[134] To the extent race conscious policies help ameliorate material disadvantage due to societal discrimination, the negative injunction of weak colorblindness imposes heavy costs.

Beyond this familiar terrain in the affirmative action debate, there are other advantages to race-conscious programs that also call into question the adequacy of weak colorblindness. As Justice Stevens has noted, there are a number of situations in which it seems eminently reasonable for government decision makers to take race into account.[135] For example:

> in a city with a recent history of racial unrest, the superintendent of police might reasonably conclude that an integrated police force could develop a better relationship with the community and thereby do a more effective job of maintaining law and order than a force composed only of white officers.[136]

Similar claims could be made about integrated civil service and school administrations. That situations exist that could benefit from race-conscious policies should hardly be surprising, given the prominent role that race has played in allocating benefits and burdens throughout American history. Indeed, Justice Powell's famous "diversity" argument in *Bakke*[137] implicitly acknowledges the reasonableness of some manner of color-conscious decision making in a world in which race has mattered and continues to matter. To the extent that weak colorblindness makes these forms of race-consciousness problematic, it is simply nearsighted social policy.

Most fundamentally, weak colorblindness sacrifices much of the cultural critique that race-consciousness can provide. If the task is to subject dominant views to scrutiny and challenge through the investigation and acceptance of nondominant perspectives,[138] then it would appear sensible to permit decision makers to adopt facilitative programs that necessarily take notice of race. *Metro Broadcasting*[139] is a significant case in this respect. The FCC policies upheld in this case are important not only because they channel economic resources— broadcasting licenses—to African-Americans, but also because these resources both

---

134. See, e.g., City of Richmond v. J.A. Croson Co., 109 S. Ct. 706, 720–23 (1989); Wygant v. Jackson Bd. of Educ., 476 U.S. 267, 277–78, 293–94 (1986). This point is discussed at length infra text at notes 167–239.

135. See *Wygant*, 476 U.S. at 314–15 (Stevens, J., dissenting); see also Sullivan, supra note 16, at 96–98 (analysis of *Wygant* reveals that a forward-looking justification for affirmative action would be more effective than treating it as a remedy for past wrongs).

136. *Wygant*, 476 U.S. at 314 (Stevens, J., dissenting).

137. Regents of Univ. of Cal. v. Bakke, 438 U.S. 265, 315–19 (1978).

138. See supra notes 101–106 and accompanying text.

139. Metro Broadcasting, Inc. v FCC, 110 S. Ct. 2997 (1990).

support minority cultural self-definition and provide a means for penetrating mainstream culture.[140] As the Court recognized, "[T]he benefits of [increased] diversity are not limited to the members of minority groups who gain access to the broadcasting industry by virtue of the ownership policies; rather, the benefits redound to all members of the viewing and listening audience."[141]

The explicitly race-conscious goal of promoting broadcast diversity sends a very different message than would alternative policies justified in terms of remedying past discrimination against minorities. Take, for example, a policy mentioned by Justice Scalia in his *Croson* opinion that gives preference not to racial groups per se but rather to "the disadvantaged."[142] It may well be true, as Scalia suggests, that blacks would disproportionately benefit from such a program. But to the extent that the policy is characterized as "remedial," it maintains the standard (white) broadcaster as the norm to which benefitted minority applicants cannot measure up without the FCC's "loosening" of standards. The policy in *Metro Broadcasting*, however, rotates the axis, not measuring the nonmajority applicant's deviation from or congruence to the standard (white) broadcaster, but rather viewing minority owners as equal contributors to an integrated broadcasting spectrum.[143]

To return to a previous example, universities need more than African-American literature classes; they need a diversity of students in all literature classes, and not simply to show white students that students of color can perform as well as white students,[144] but also to help all

---

140. See Williams, *Metro Broadcasting, Inc. v. FCC*: Regrouping in Singular Times, 104 Harv. L. Rev. 525, 537 (1990) ("Participation in ownership of . . . broadcast stations or other tools of mass communication . . . is the gateway to our greatest power as Americans . . . . It provides the opportunity to propagate oneself in the marketplace of cultural images.").

141. *Metro Broadcasting*, 110 S. Ct. at 3010–11. This view is consistent with the FCC's reasons for establishing its race-conscious policies. See supra notes 71–72 and accompanying text.

142. City of Richmond v. J.A. Croson Co., 109 S. Ct. 706, 739 (1989) (Scalia, J., concurring).

143. See Williams, supra note 140, at 529 ("a real notion of diversity includes a concept of multiculturalism").

Arguably, it would be possible to construct a program dedicated to increasing diversity that does not draw an explicit race line. The FCC might, for example, review the content of broadcasters' proposed programming. But such a policy would create difficult evaluation, monitoring, and enforcement problems and, as Justice Brennan notes in *Metro Broadcasting*, would raise serious first amendment issues as well. 110 S. Ct. at 3019–24, 3019 n.35, 3022 n.42.

144. Thus, Justice Stevens provides quite a limited justification for race-conscious measures in Wygant v. Jackson Bd. of Educ., 476 U.S. 267, 315 (1986), when he suggests that

> a school board may reasonably conclude that an integrated faculty will be able to provide benefits to the student body that could not be provided by an all-white, or nearly all-white, faculty. . . . It is one thing for a white child to be taught by a white teacher that color, like beauty, is only "skin deep"; it is far

students become more self-conscious of the underlying assumptions with which they approach the world.[145] To be sure, there are risks. Given the power of imbedded ways of thinking, new information may simply be "processed" in accordance with pre-existing views; or, white students may make the error of assuming that comments by black students express "the" black perspective. But to students and faculty open to a Geertzian moment, the intellectual rewards are enormous.

C. *Two Objections to Race Consciousness*

Two objections to race-conscious policies are frequently posed: the first suggests that such policies can actually increase racial stereotyping and intolerance; the second questions the "essentialist" underpinnings of the case for race-consciousness presented here.

The first objection, one that figures prominently in the attack on affirmative action, is that race-consciousness is self-defeating to the extent that it reinforces rather than undermines racism.[146] Affirmative action, it is argued, may have this effect because it inevitably creates the impression of a lowering of standards in order to benefit minorities. Furthermore, as Shelby Steele argues, the "implication of inferiority in racial preferences" has a demoralizing effect on blacks, contributing to "an enlargement of self doubt."[147]

One response is that we ought to run this claim by those who have been the victims of racism. Despite assertions by whites that race-conscious programs "stigmatize" beneficiaries, blacks remain overwhelmingly in favor of affirmative action.[148] Would we not expect blacks to be the first to recognize such harms and therefore to oppose affirmative action if it produced serious stigmatic injury? It might be argued, however, that individual blacks are willing to participate in affirmative action programs because of the direct benefits they receive, yet those blacks who are not beneficiaries suffer the stigmatic harm without the compensating gains. But, again, one would expect that if

---

> more convincing to experience that truth on a day-to-day basis during the routine, ongoing learning process.

This argument is ultimately grounded on the colorblind claim that race is, and should be, irrelevant.

145. My judgment here, I must confess, is influenced by my own teaching experiences. Some of the richest classes I have taught have been those in which students of color have challenged white assumptions and presumptions. See Aleinikoff, Multicultural and Anti-Racist Teaching in a Law School Class, *in* Multicultural Teaching in the University (D. Schoem, L. Frankel, X. Zuniga & E. Lewis eds. forthcoming).

146. See, e.g., *Metro Broadcasting*, 110 S. Ct. at 3029 (O'Connor, J., dissenting) ("Racial classifications, whether providing benefits to or burdening particular racial or ethnic groups, may stigmatize those groups singled out for different treatment and may create considerable tension with the Nation's widely shared commitment to evaluating individuals upon their individual merit.").

147. S. Steele, The Content of Our Character 116–17 (1990).

148. D. Kinder & L. Sanders, Pluralistic Foundations of American Opinion on Race 9 & n.6 (August 1987) (unpublished paper) (on file with Columbia Law Review).

this were the case, then blacks as a class would oppose affirmative action since the vast majority of blacks are not beneficiaries of affirmative action. Furthermore, Randall Kennedy provides a convincing argument that affirmative action, on balance, is more likely to reduce stigma than to impose it:

> It is unrealistic to think . . . that affirmative action causes most white disparagement of the abilities of blacks. Such disparagement, buttressed for decades by the rigid exclusion of blacks from educational and employment opportunities, is precisely what engendered the explosive crisis to which affirmative action is a response. . . . In the end, the uncertain extent to which affirmative action diminishes the accomplishments of blacks must be balanced against the stigmatization that occurs when blacks are virtually absent from important institutions in the society.[149]

Confident measures of the costs and benefits of affirmative action do not exist. Given the material gains afforded minorities by race-conscious programs and the fact that these gains are likely, as Kennedy notes, to counteract "conventional stereotypes about the place of the Negro,"[150] I would put the burden of proof on those who claim that affirmative action contributes more to racism than it diminishes racism. Significantly, the case for race-consciousness suggested here would affect the evaluation of the costs and benefits because it would count as one of the benefits—as colorblindness cannot—the gains to white society of increased association with minorities and greater awareness of nondominant cultures. Thus, in *Wygant*, in which the Court invalidated a lay-off plan that provided for the discharge of white teachers with greater seniority than black teachers who were not discharged,[151] a color-conscious analysis would recognize the benefits accruing to white students from a program that increases (or preserves) the number of nonmajority faculty.

The second challenge argues that building a case for color-consciousness on, in part, notions of "subordinated cultures" runs the risk of repeating the objectification of minorities that such an approach strives to undermine. According to this view, support for race-conscious measures must be based on an implicit or explicit foundational claim that something unites all members of each race and that races may be differentiated on the basis of these common elements of identity or culture. This "essentialist" description[152] is seen as deeply troubling because, as Randall Kennedy has argued (in the context of legal academic scholarship), it "homogenize[s] the experience of per-

149. Kennedy, Persuasion and Distrust: A Comment on the Affirmative Action Debate, 99 Harv. L. Rev. 1327, 1331 (1986) (footnotes omitted).

150. Id.

151. 476 U.S. 267 (1986).

152. See Harris, supra note 106, at 585.

sons of color and . . . minimize[s] the heterogeneity of opinions held and articulated by persons of color."[153] Kennedy adds:

> [R]acial groups are not monolithic and . . . social divisions generate differences in interests and consciousness within racial groups. [The assertion that victims of racial oppression share a distinct experiential commonality] wraps in one garment of racial victimization the black law professor of middle-class upbringing with a salary of $65,000 and the black, unemployed, uneducated captive of the ghetto. In the overwhelming majority of cases, however, these two social types will inhabit radically dissimilar social universes . . . . Even during the eras of slavery and de jure segregation, the structure and experience of racial oppression often varied along class lines *within* black communities. There are, moreover, other important cross-cutting variables . . . that diversify the experiences of persons of color, including gender, region, and differing group affiliations within the catch-all category "people of color."[154]

Thus, race-conscious measures, to the extent that they are based on assertions that blacks bring a distinctive "voice" to the academy, may be as objectifying, as demeaning, as the oppressive racial views of difference that colorblindness was constructed to combat.[155] To credentialize race is to make every black a representative of all blacks, to oversimplify the richness and diversity of the black community into "*a* black perspective."[156]

Kennedy's description of the complexity of racial experience in the United States is surely correct. Furthermore, the claim that there is a distinctive black voice seems to ignore the fact that majority and nonmajority cultures have been forged together, each influencing and responding to the other.[157] But it is far from clear that Kennedy's insights—or similar "postmodern" claims about the fluidity and open-ended nature of culture—provide strong support for colorblindness.

Kennedy's attack on "race credentializing" is an argument against hiring a nonmajority person for an academic position upon the belief that the person will or should provide "*the*" nonmajority perspective.

---

153. Kennedy, supra note 106, at 1782.

154. Id. at 1782–83 (footnotes omitted); see also Carter, The Best Black, & Other Tales, *in* 1 Reconstruction 6, 7 (1990) (personal illustrations of the "best black" syndrome).

155. See also Cousins v. City Council, 466 F.2d 830, 852 (7th Cir.) (Stevens, J., dissenting) ("Respect for the citizenry in the black community compels acceptance of the fact that in the long run there is no more certainty that these individuals will vote alike than will individual members of any other ethnic, economic, or social group."), cert. denied, 409 U.S. 893 (1972).

156. Kennedy, supra note 106, at 1782–87.

157. See J. Clifford, The Predicament of Culture: Twentieth-Century Ethnography, Literature, and Art 11–17 (1988); A. Ross, No Respect: Intellectuals and Popular Culture 68 (1989).

But I do not understand him to deny the central claims of this section: that dominant white society would come to understand itself better by seeing itself through the eyes of a diverse range of nonmajority members of society and that respect for nonmajority members must be based on an understanding and appreciation of their lives as nonmajority members. To say that the black community is pluralistic is, to my mind, to demand greater attention to such diversity, to see the number of ways in which members of nonmajority groups have attempted to mediate oppression in their lives. Indeed, for whites to understand the diversity of the black community is simply to accord to nonmajority groups the same nonreductionist respect majority groups accord to themselves.[158] But it is precisely that appreciation that colorblindness denigrates; one may only approach another as "an individual," for whom race is an irrelevant factor in his or her experience and identity. Of course, *how* one's race has had such an influence will vary according to all sorts of other factors.[159] But this hardly denies that race has had an influence.[160]

Furthermore, to reject "essentialism" is not to deny the significance of the color line in American life. It was precisely this issue that the Court faced in *Metro Broadcasting*. The dissents asserted that the FCC's assumption that increasing minority ownership of television and radio stations would create greater diversity in programming was based "on the demeaning notion that members of the defined racial groups ascribe to certain 'minority views' that must be different from those of other citizens"[161] and "impermissibly equat[ed] race with thoughts and behavior."[162] But Justice Brennan's response to these claims is plainly more accurate:

---

158. Cf. Kennedy, A Cultural Pluralist Case for Affirmative Action in Legal Academia, 1990 Duke L.J. 705, 729 (1990) (emphasis omitted):

> [I]t seems likely that an increase in minority scholarship would change the framework of ideological conflict within which issues in the race area but also in other areas are discussed. I do not mean by this that there is a black (or other minority) ideology. The point is rather that there are historic, already established debates within the minority intelligentsias that are obviously relevant to law, but that have been largely absent from legal scholarship.

159. As Duncan Kennedy sensibly argues, "[r]ecognizing culture doesn't annihilate the individual." Id. at 743 (emphasis omitted). Rather, "culture and ideology provide a vocabulary from which 'individuals' pick and choose to produce themselves, constrained by their situation in time and space but with plenty available, even in the most apparently 'disadvantaged' position, from which to make something that has the stamp of unpredictable humanity." Id. at 745.

160. Patricia Williams, while recognizing that "the categories of 'white' and 'black' do not begin to capture the richness of ethnic and political diversity," notes: "the simple matter of the color of one's skin so profoundly affects the way one is treated, so radically shapes what one is allowed to think and feel about this society, that the decision to generalize from this division is valid." Williams, supra note 116, at 404 n.4.

161. Metro Broadcasting, Inc. v. FCC, 110 S. Ct. 2997, 3046 (1990) (Kennedy, J., dissenting).

162. Id. at 3036 (O'Connor, J., dissenting).

> While we are under no illusion that members of a particular minority group share some cohesive, collective viewpoint, we believe it a legitimate inference for Congress and the Commission to draw that as more minorities gain ownership and policymaking roles in the media, varying perspectives will be more fairly represented on the airwaves.[163]

To sustain the claim that a race-based investigation is intellectually unwarranted, one would have to show that there is no reason to believe that the experiences of members of racial minorities in this nation have not, to some extent, diverged from the experiences of whites.[164] I simply find this an implausible suggestion, given a three hundred year social history of having so much turn on one's racial identification.[165] Is it conceivable that the meaning of race and American racism has been the same for whites and blacks, or that a maddeningly resilient social and geographical separation of the races has not produced race-based experiential differences?[166]

IV. Colorblindness and the Affirmative Action Cases

The critique of colorblindness sketched above provides critical purchase on the plurality and concurring opinions in *Croson* and on the *Metro Broadcasting* dissents. Much has been written on the doctrinal aspects of the cases as well as their practical and political implications.[167] Much remains to be written.[168] I will examine here two issues that best

163. Id. at 3018.

164. This is not a claim that the variation within black culture may not be as great as the variation between white and black cultures.

165. See Sandalow, supra note 28, at 685–89.

166. Social science investigations have identified a number of significant differences in views and experiences between racial groups that cut across class lines. See R. Farley & W. Allen, The Color Line and the Quality of Life in America 148–50 (1987) (black/white residential segregation significant at every economic level); A Common Destiny, supra note 30, at 136 (alienation of blacks from white society is not concentrated within any particular segment of black community); D. Kinder & L. Sanders, Divided by Color: Race, American Politics, and the American Ideal (forthcoming from University of Chicago Press). These findings contradict seat-of-the-pants assumptions that class, not race, is the significant dividing line. Such studies describe aggregate differences and cannot (and would not) demonstrate that no black and no white share similar views on social and political issues.

167. See, e.g., Bendick, The *Croson* Decision Mandates Set-Aside Programs Be Tools of Business Development, 1 George Mason U. Civ. Rts. L.J. 87 (1990); Devins, supra note 6; Fried, supra note 9; Payton, The Meaning and Significance of the *Croson* Case, 1 George Mason U. Civ. Rts. L.J. 59 (1990); Rosenfeld, Decoding *Richmond*: Affirmative Action and the Elusive Meaning of Constitutional Equality, 87 Mich. L. Rev. 1729 (1989); Sullivan, *City of Richmond v. J.A. Croson Co.*: The Backlash Against Affirmative Action, 64 Tul. L. Rev. 1609 (1990); Williams, supra note 140; Note, *City of Richmond v. J.A. Croson Co.*: A Federal Legislative Answer, 100 Yale L.J. 451 (1990).

168. For example, what standard will be applied to affirmative action programs for women? If, following *Croson*, all lines drawn on the basis of gender will be judged by the same standard, then gender-based affirmative action programs, which have been sub-

exemplify the problems of imposing colorblindness on a color-conscious world: (1) the rendering suspect of the goal of remedying "societal discrimination"; and (2) the reluctance of those who insist on colorblindness to recognize other than remedial goals for race-conscious measures. As I have puzzled through the recent cases, I have noticed the significant influence that legal scholarship written by nonmajority members of the academy has had on my evaluation and understanding of the Court's work.

A. *The Hesitancy to Remedy "Societal Discrimination"*

As previously mentioned,[169] a colorblind approach is understood to permit the use of race-conscious measures to remedy violations of the colorblind principle. Given several centuries of intense and continuous race discrimination in the United States, a legal principle authorizing race-consciousness to remedy past discrimination could take us quite far. Justice Marshall's dissent in *Croson* provides a clear example. Working well within the remedying-past-discrimination model (and therefore remaining consistent with a colorblind model), he concludes that Richmond's set-aside program is sustainable.[170]

But two aspects of the opinions that form the majority in *Croson* limit the scope of the remedial justification for race-consciousness. The first demands that a solid factual record be built demonstrating past discrimination in the construction industry.[171] This burden may well raise political problems for localities since city councils might be loathe to put together a record of racism that tars influential members of the community, but it is not theoretically insurmountable.

More troubling is the limitation on the kind of discrimination that the city is permitted to seek to remedy. Affirmative action programs, the Court has said, may not attempt to remedy the effects of past and present "societal discrimination."[172] Sometimes societal discrimination appears to refer to the acts of persons and groups other than the

---

jected to mid-level scrutiny, would seemingly be subjected to a lower level of scrutiny than race-based plans. This conundrum cannot go unaddressed.

169. See supra note 16 and accompanying text.

170. City of Richmond v. J.A. Croson Co., 109 S. Ct. 706, 750–52 (1989) (Marshall, J., dissenting).

171. Importantly, Justice O'Connor rejects the argument that the city itself must have discriminated, id. at 717–20; and in recognizing that "[i]n the extreme case, some form of narrowly tailored racial preference might be necessary to break down patterns of deliberate exclusion," id. at 729, Justice O'Connor implicitly accepts that such programs may reward persons who themselves were not victims of past discrimination and may impose costs on white contractors who may not have been past violators. Since it may be safely assumed that the dissenters in *Croson* agree with these propositions, they should be understood as reflecting the views of the Court, despite Justice Scalia's nonacquiescence. See id. at 735–39 (Scalia, J., concurring).

172. See Metro Broadcasting, Inc. v. FCC, 110 S. Ct. 2997, 3034 (1990) (O'Connor, J. dissenting) ("In *Croson*, we held that an interest in remedying societal discrimination cannot be considered compelling.").

target of the affirmative action program. In *Wygant*, for example, the school system was not permitted to remedy discrimination in which it had not participated.[173] But *Croson* suggests a slightly broader meaning, because in that case a majority of the Court appeared willing to accept a plan that covered all contractors—provided that an adequate factual predicate had been laid—whether or not particular contractors burdened by the program had themselves discriminated in the past and even if the city had not so discriminated.

The best reading of societal discrimination, therefore, seems to be discrimination, past and present, that prevents nonmajority individuals and groups from getting to the playing field and that is attributed to groups other than those already on the field. Thus, if the contractors had created barriers to the entry of black firms, that discrimination could be remedied by imposing burdens on the contracting industry as a whole. However, if poor schools, segregated living patterns, and bank loan policies have resulted in a lack of skills, contacts, and capital necessary for entry into the contracting business, that discrimination could not be remedied by imposing burdens on contractors (although, conceivably, narrowly tailored programs directed at each of the specific areas of discrimination might be acceptable).

Why is it not a permissible goal for a state or locality to seek, by race-conscious measures, to overcome the debilitating effects of societal discrimination?[174] From the perspective of the excluded groups, the source of the discrimination should hardly matter: if discrimination (even when defined as a violation of the colorblindness principle) has prevented them from getting a fair shot at competing with white contractors, remedies for the discrimination are appropriate. The Court's worries appear to be three: the "amorphousness" of the goal of remedying societal discrimination, the possibility that current inequality is not a function of discrimination, and the influence of "racial politics" in the crafting of race-conscious programs. I will consider these in turn.

1. *The "Amorphousness" of the Goal.* — The first of the Court's concerns, often termed the "amorphousness" of remedial programs, relates to the scope and the duration of the plan under consideration and the burdens imposed by it on "innocent" whites. Here, the Court *concedes* the existence of societal discrimination, yet appears to conclude that the personal rights of those burdened by the plan outweigh the

173. See Wygant v. Jackson Bd. of Educ., 476 U.S. 267, 274 (1986) (plurality opinion) ("This Court never has held that societal discrimination alone is sufficient to justify a racial classification. Rather, the Court has insisted upon some showing of prior discrimination by the governmental unit involved before allowing limited use of racial classifications in order to remedy such discrimination.").

174. For Justice Scalia, it appears to be a matter of definition: "racial discrimination" is violative of the colorblind principle, and is distinct from "social disadvantages, whether they have been acquired by reason of prior discrimination or otherwise." *Croson*, 109 S. Ct. at 735 (Scalia, J., concurring). I find the tag "or otherwise" to be laden with unfortunate connotations.

state interest in ridding society of the effects of past discrimination. Justice Powell noted in *Wygant*:

> No one doubts that there has been serious racial discrimination in this country. But as the basis for imposing discriminatory *legal* remedies that work against innocent people, societal discrimination is insufficient and over-expansive. In the absence of particularized findings, a court could uphold remedies that are ageless in their reach into the past, and timeless in their ability to affect the future.[175]

These sentences are terrifically disturbing.[176] Use of the word "innocent" coupled with an attempt to paint racial discrimination as a thing of the past ("there *has been* serious racial discrimination in this country") permits Powell, in essence, to invoke the moral injunction that it is wrong to visit the sins of prior generations on present generations.[177] On this account, societal discrimination becomes an "amorphous" justification for race-conscious policies because its past omnipresence can always overwhelm the harms done to current (purportedly nondiscriminating) whites. But, as I will suggest below,[178] the very "agelessness" of racial discrimination—which has instilled within the dominant culture seemingly ineradicable racism—argues *in favor* of serious remedies. Furthermore, as Stephen Carter has argued, opponents of affirmative action have been remarkably successful at transforming black victims into perpetrators and white beneficiaries of past discrimination into victims.[179] It would clearly be wrong to argue that whites are not harmed by affirmative action programs.[180] But it would

175. 476 U.S. at 276 (emphasis in original).

176. A small but interesting question is why Powell uses the word "legal" and chooses to italicize it. What is he suggesting?

177. In this way, Powell echoes the view he expressed in cases involving discrimination against illegitimate children. See, e.g., Weber v. Aetna Casualty & Sur. Co., 406 U.S. 164, 175 (1972) (visiting "society's condemnation of irresponsible liaisons" on an infant is "illogical and unjust").

178. See infra notes 217–223 and accompanying text.

179. See Carter, supra note 19, at 435–37.

180. It is possible for the harm occasioned by affirmative action plans to rise to the level of a constitutional injury. At least two sorts of claims might be made: First, businesses that are severely injured by a set-aside plan (such as those that have grown dependent upon public contracts) or tenured white teachers who are laid-off before untenured black teachers (as in *Wygant*), may have suffered constitutional injuries to property interests, and therefore may be entitled to compensation of some sort. It is crucial to see, however, as Laurence Tribe has argued, that this principle is external to antidiscrimination law. That is, the injured white is not a victim of race discrimination. See L. Tribe, American Constitutional Law § 16-22, at 1536–37 (2d ed. 1988) ("Distinguishing between otherwise justified affirmative action plans on the basis of the degree of sacrifice they extract from equally innocent white workers unnecessarily confounds takings and equal-protection analyses and subordinates the achievement of racial justice to whatever pattern of economic distribution our discriminatory past happens to have produced."); see also Fiss, supra note 12, at 159 (arguing for a distinction between unfair treatment and "disadvantaging" treatment in racially conscious conduct). Second, affirmative action plans might be so arbitrary, either because based on an impermissible

be difficult to construct a plausible case for the proposition that the harms to whites adversely affected by affirmative action programs *outweigh* the harms imposed on *innocent* black beneficiaries[181] by a history of racism.[182]

Nor is Powell's claim about unbounded remedies reaching into the future understandable. Affirmative action programs have generally been linked to achieving black participation in employment or education in rough proportionality to a defined pool of available black candidates. There is no reason why norms established by courts in interpreting antidiscrimination statutes would not set appropriate boundaries for affirmative action programs.[183] Arguably, attention to societal discrimination would expand the relevant pool of black candidates. Thus, in *Croson* the issue would not be the percentage of contracting dollars received by *existing* MBEs, but rather the extent to which discrimination elsewhere blocked the formation of MBEs.[184] Yet this seems perfectly appropriate, once we recognize the importance of ending societal discrimination.[185] Moreover, there will always be an upper limit on minority participation established by the overall nonmajority population of a locality.[186]

---

purpose, such as a bare desire to injure whites, or because of a miserable fit between means and ends, as to violate the due process clause.

Seeing these claims as arising outside of an equal-protection analysis is important because an injured white person would have to demonstrate the existence of an independently guaranteed constitutional right that is infringed by the program. Clearly, under existing constitutional doctrine, not every burden visited upon a person by a social program constitutes a constitutional harm.

181. Justice White characterized the affirmative action program in *Wygant* as calling for dismissal of white teachers "to make room for blacks, none of whom has been shown to be a victim of any racial discrimination." Wygant v. Jackson Bd. of Educ., 476 U.S. 267, 295 (1986) (White, J., concurring). Do we really believe that there is a black person in this society who has not been the victim of any racial discrimination? The responses of blacks should be sobering.

182. See Crenshaw, supra note 50, at 1342.

Note also that the affirmative action plan struck down in *Croson* was substantially less burdensome than the lay-off program discussed in *Wygant*, because of the low percentage of total contracting dollars affected by the former. Indeed, Powell suggested as much in *Wygant* by comparing it to the set-aside program upheld in *Fullilove*. See *Wygant*, 476 U.S. at 282; *Fullilove*, 448 U.S. at 484.

183. See, e.g., Title VII of the Civil Rights Act of 1964, 42 U.S.C. §§ 2000e–2000e-17 (1988); cf. *Wygant*, 476 U.S. at 291–94 (O'Connor, J., concurring) (Public employers may make the determination that affirmative action is warranted when, for example, there is "demonstrable evidence of a disparity . . . sufficient to support a prima facie Title VII pattern or practice."). See generally Note, Finding a "Manifest Imbalance": The Case for a Unified Statistical Test for Voluntary Affirmative Action Under Title VII, 87 Mich. L. Rev. 1986 (1989).

184. See Note, supra note 167, at 454–55 (comparing number of qualified MBEs to percentage of contracts awarded to minority firms "may preclude the use of race-based remedies" when past discrimination has impeded the establishment of MBEs).

185. See supra notes 29-57 and accompanying text.

186. Cf. Metro Broadcasting, Inc. v. FCC, 110 S. Ct., 2997, 3025 (1990) ("greater

It seems that what is really behind the "amorphousness" claim is neither the inability to recognize the continuing effects of past discrimination nor the impossibility of establishing limits on relief. Rather, the justices are concerned that, *given the extent and consequences of past and present discrimination*, recognizing societal discrimination as a basis for race-based programs would leave the Court helpless in screening out improper purposes and in assuring that programs are "narrowly tailored." Because it could always be asserted that, absent discrimination, African-Americans would attain a proportion of jobs or other opportunities roughly commensurate with their representation in the population as a whole, an interest in remedying societal discrimination would support programs that demand both achievement and maintenance of proportional representation[187]—a result, as Justice O'Connor asserts in her dissent in *Metro Broadcasting*, that would "support measures that amount to the core constitutional violation of 'outright racial balancing.' "[188] But again, it would seem far more appropriate to require careful proof of the effects of past and present discrimination or to permit those challenging a race-conscious program to show why one would not expect proportionate representation of racial groups in the area covered by the program than to hold that such discrimination, in effect, *counts against* the legitimacy of race-conscious measures. Thus, even from within the colorblind model, the limit on remedying societal discrimination seems inexplicable.

2. *Nonexistence of Discrimination.* — The Court has repeatedly stated that mere underrepresentation of nonmajorities does not demonstrate the presence of discrimination. Consistent with the suggestions of Thomas Sowell, Nathan Glazer, and others,[189] Justice O'Connor asserts that "it is completely unrealistic to assume that individuals of each race will gravitate with mathematical exactitude to each employer or union absent unlawful discrimination."[190]

---

programming diversity . . . carries its own natural limit, for there will be no need for further minority preferences once sufficient diversity has been achieved").

It would also be reasonable to allow those attacking a plan to show why we should not expect rough proportionality (for example, because of choice).

187. But see Johnson v. Transportation Agency, 480 U.S. 616, 664–68, 673–75 (1987) (Scalia, J., dissenting).

188. 110 S. Ct. at 3035 (quoting City of Richmond v. J.A. Croson Co., 109 S. Ct. 706, 728 (1989) (O'Connor, J., dissenting)). The same objection has been made in school desegregation cases. See, e.g., Columbus Bd. of Educ. v. Penick, 443 U.S. 449, 486–89 (1979) (Powell, J., dissenting); id. at 508–13 (Rehnquist, J., dissenting); Dayton Bd. of Educ. v. Brinkman, 443 U.S. 526, 542–44 (1979) (Rehnquist, J., dissenting).

189. See N. Glazer, Affirmative Discrimination: Ethnic Inequality and Public Policy 67–68 (1975); T. Sowell, Civil Rights: Rhetoric or Reality? 42–48 (1984); Abram, supra note 17, at 1315–16; Loury, Why Should We Care About Group Inequality?, 5 Soc. Phil. & Pol. 249, 249–50 (1987); DOJ Report, supra note 14, at 5–6.

190. Sheet Metal Workers v. EEOC, 478 U.S. 421, 494 (1986) (O'Connor, J., concurring in part and dissenting in part) (quoted in United States v. Paradise, 480 U.S. 149, 197 (1987) (O'Connor, J., dissenting)).

But if discrimination is not the cause of underrepresentation, what is? One answer might be ability. Blacks may be less qualified or less competent than whites for two reasons—either past societal discrimination, which the Court ought, but refuses, to accept as a sufficient justification; or natural inferiority, which the Court no doubt would consider an unacceptable explanation. To finesse the issue of ability, the Justices have recently introduced the notion of "choice" to accompany societal discrimination in explaining the underrepresentation of nonmajority firms, teachers, and students.[191]

Fair enough. It is plausible that group membership might influence one's choice of job, neighborhood, or school and that all disparities are not ipso facto proof of discrimination. But given the history of racial discrimination that this nation has witnessed and given the undeniable impact of that history on limiting black opportunities, one would expect the Court to shift the burden of persuasion to those opposing a plan to demonstrate that underrepresentation is a product of choice. More importantly, is it remotely conceivable that the lack of black contractors in Richmond is due to the "choice" of the city's black population? Minority set-aside programs around the nation have demonstrated that when efforts are made, black entrepreneurs are eager to form firms and enter the industry covered by the program.[192] What has kept them out? A perverse desire not to earn a share of the locality's public spending? Similarly, is it reasonable to believe that black entrepreneurs have not been interested in owning television and radio stations?

It seems likely that the Court is willing to accept, without being willing to state, that underrepresentation is a function of capability or "culture."[193] But even if that were so, why is it an impermissible state objective to make equality of opportunity a reality by helping blacks to be more competitive? One answer might be that affirmative action works at the wrong place and time. Attempts to remedy disadvantage should come earlier so that the same rules apply to all parties during the competition. This, however, is a question of social policy, and it is hard to see why a legislature is not entitled to conclude that direct intervention in the market is the surest way to improve minority opportunities.[194]

---

191. See, e.g., *Croson*, 109 S. Ct. at 726 ("[T]here are numerous explanations for [the] dearth of minority participation [in local contractors' associations], including past societal discrimination in education and economic opportunities as well as both black and white career and entrepreneurial choices."); see also DOJ Report, supra note 14, at 6 (stressing "demographic, cultural, and geographical variables" as nondiscriminatory causes of "statistical imbalance").

192. See Suggs, Rethinking Minority Business Development Strategies, 25 Harv. C.R.-C.L. L. Rev. 101, 112–13 (1990); Smothers, Affirmative Action Booms in Atlanta, N.Y. Times, Jan. 27, 1989, at 10, col. 4.

193. See DOJ Report, supra note 14, at 6.

194. Another aspect of the "capability" concern is that the Court, along with many

Moreover, if notions of race-based capability or culture do in fact influence the Justices' views, then they are relying on unexamined race-consciousness to support a colorblind approach. Yet the colorblind rhetoric of the opinions, identifying disproportionality as the product of the actions of "individuals" exercising "choice," obfuscates the implicit assumptions being made about racial groups. Thoughtful attention to color-consciousness could help the Justices move beyond blame-the-victim justifications for colorblindness.

3. *"Racial Politics."* — A final concern of the Court may be that localities are using the label of "past discrimination" to mask political handouts. Echoing Justice Stevens's concerns in *Fullilove*,[195] Justices O'Connor, Scalia, and Kennedy appear to suggest that the set-aside program in *Croson* was adopted by a black-dominated city council, not to further the interests of the city as a whole, but as a pay-off to black enterprises.[196] Allowing the mere assertion of "past societal discrimination" to justify such programs would give the green light to political self-dealing that is doubly troubling: it violates principles of good government by not distributing contracts on the basis of lowest cost and it lends the Court's sanction to exercises of "racial politics." Again, in a perverse way, the extent of previous discrimination works against blacks: because past societal racial discrimination is recognized by all, virtually any program could be justified by reference to it and illicit, self-dealing motives could thereby be hidden.

Whether or not the Justices' concerns are justified, the rejection of remedying "societal discrimination" as a legitimate goal is overkill. The insistence on the creation of an adequate record of past discrimination should serve to allay fears that race-conscious programs are simply "naked preferences."[197]

More significantly, the apparent assumption that any program adopted by black elected officials to help black entrepreneurs is an exercise in self-dealing seems to violate the colorblind principles under which the Justices profess to be operating. Justice O'Connor mentions the racial composition of Richmond's City Council in her discussion of the level of scrutiny that ought to be applied to affirmative action programs. Responding to John Hart Ely's argument that race-conscious programs adopted by whites to help nonwhites are less suspicious than policies adopted by whites that harm whites, she states:

---

white Americans, may believe that affirmative action secures benefits for "unqualified" minorities. But that objection (whatever its merit) does not explain why remedying societal discrimination is not an appropriate goal.

195. Fullilove v. Klutznick, 448 U.S. 448, 541–48 (1980) (Stevens, J., dissenting).

196. See infra text accompanying notes 198–204.

197. See, e.g., Cygnar v. City of Chicago, 865 F.2d 827, 836–40 (7th Cir. 1989) (no record of past discrimination); accord Days, supra note 61, at 479–80. See generally Sunstein, Naked Preferences and the Constitution, 84 Colum. L. Rev. 1689, 1710–17 (1984) (equal protection clause in accord with general constitutional principle that prohibits the distribution of entitlements solely on the basis of a group's political power).

> In this case, blacks comprise approximately 50% of the population of the city of Richmond. Five of the nine seats on the City Council are held by blacks. The concern that a political majority will more easily act to the disadvantage of a minority based on unwarranted assumptions or incomplete facts would seem to militate for, not against, the application of heightened judicial scrutiny in this case.[198]

Recognition of the racial composition of the city council is not crucial to the Court's decision. Even if this factor knocked out *Ely's* justification for lower scrutiny of affirmative action programs, there are, after all, other sensible justifications.[199] And nothing in the Court's opinion suggests that its decision would be any different if the Richmond program had been adopted by a white-dominated city council. In fact, the plan was adopted by a vote of six to two, with one abstention—indicating that at *least* one white council member supported it.

But several of the opinions nonetheless raise suspicions that the fact that blacks held a majority on the city council was the "ghost in the machine." This is evident in Justice O'Connor's opinion, which identifies impermissible racial classifications as those "motivated by illegitimate notions of racial inferiority *or simple racial politics*."[200] A paragraph later she argues that unless race-based classifications "are strictly reserved for remedial settings, they may in fact promote notions of racial inferiority *and lead to a politics of racial hostility*."[201] And in her concluding paragraph, she again asserts that, absent appropriate findings of prior discrimination, "there is a danger that a racial classification is merely the product of unthinking stereotypes *or a form of racial politics*."[202]

The opinions of Justices Kennedy and Scalia are more explicit. Kennedy finds that the city council provided an inadequate factual predicate for the set-aside program and concludes:

> We are left with an ordinance and a legislative record open to the fair charge that it is not a remedy but is itself a preference which will cause the same corrosive animosities that the Constitution forbids in the whole sphere of government and that our national policy condemns in the rest of society as well.[203]

Scalia, after quoting from James Madison's warning in *The Federalist* No. 10 that majority tyranny may reign in small polities, asserts that

> in Richmond . . . the enactment of a set-aside [was] clearly and directly beneficial to the dominant political group, which hap-

198. City of Richmond v. J.A. Croson Co., 109 S. Ct. 706, 722 (1989).

199. See, e.g., Brest, supra note 14, at 16–17 (affirmative action programs not likely to stigmatize whites); Fiss, supra note 12, at 157–64 (equal protection clause should be understood as protecting historically oppressed groups).

200. *Croson*, 109 S. Ct. at 721 (emphasis added).

201. Id. (emphasis added).

202. Id. at 730 (emphasis added).

203. Id. at 735 (Kennedy, J., concurring).

> pens also to be the dominant racial group. The same thing has no doubt happened before in other cities . . . and blacks have often been on the receiving end of the injustice. Where injustice is the game, however, turn-about is not fair play.[204]

There can be little doubt, then, as to the story that a majority of the Court told itself about Richmond. After attaining political power (thanks to the Voting Rights Act), blacks on the city council acted according to one of the oldest American political traditions of rewarding one's friends out of public coffers. The lack of an adequate record, in the Court's eyes, demonstrated that the program was simply an exercise of raw political power. From this perspective, for the Court to accept the city's claim that the program was intended to remedy past societal discrimination would allow black-dominated political bodies to disguise their political handouts. Recognition of the Court's concern with the racial composition of the city council also sheds light on the troubling distinction that the majority draws between congressional power and the authority of states and localities to adopt race-conscious programs:[205] blacks may increasingly come to dominate local governments (thereby gaining significant power to exercise "racial politics"); however, they are exceedingly unlikely to attain a majority position in Congress.

On the surface, the Court's reasoning is consistent with a colorblind model. Favoring one's political friends can be seen as a regular feature of politics, irrespective of the race of the elected official.[206] Furthermore, the majority's concern about "racial politics" is ultimately helpful to its colorblind approach because it provides grounds for equal treatment of white and black decision makers. Justice

---

204. Id. at 737 (Scalia, J., concurring).

205. An entire article could be written about the Court's curious distinction between congressional and state power to remedy the effects of past discrimination. To note just a few of my disagreements with the majority in *Croson*: (1) Prior to the fourteenth amendment nothing prohibited states from taking action to ameliorate the effects of past discrimination; is it sensible to say that the fourteenth amendment prohibited accomplishment of a thirteenth amendment goal? (2) Except for the peculiar case of immigration regulations, the Court applies the same standards to federal and state regulations in other areas of fourteenth amendment jurisprudence. Compare, e.g, Mathews v. Lucas, 427 U.S. 495, 505–06 (1976) (federal statute classifying on basis of legitimacy) with Weber v. Aetna Casualty & Sur. Co., 406 U.S. 164, 172–76 (1972) (state statute doing same); and compare Craig v. Boren, 429 U.S. 190, 197 (1976) (applying mid-level scrutiny to state statute discriminating on the basis of gender) with Califano v. Webster, 430 U.S. 313, 316–17 (1977) (same test applied to federal statute). (3) Federalism values, to which a conservative Court might be expected to be sympathetic, suggest that local governments may be far better positioned to identify past discrimination and craft remedies. (4) If the concern of the Court was the ability of minorities to dominate local governing units, it overestimated the power of black officials in a white economy and underestimated the power of minority blocs in Congress (*Fullilove* being a prime example).

206. See Cygnar v. City of Chicago, 865 F.2d 827 (7th Cir. 1989), for evidence that both blacks and whites can "play the game" in Chicago.

O'Connor asserts that strict scrutiny of white-adopted, race-conscious measures is necessary to ensure that they are not based on "illegitimate notions of racial inferiority."[207] Since it is far less likely that blacks will establish programs benefitting blacks for such a reason, she needs some other justification to support strict scrutiny for black-adopted plans. The fear of "racial politics" guarantees symmetry by providing a reason to be suspicious of black elected officials.

But crucial to the Court's analysis is an unstated and unexamined set of assumptions about black officials. The majority implicitly assumes that all blacks are part of a cohesive, self-identified group— that is, that black officials adopting a program to aid blacks are necessarily helping their friends (the "naked preference/racial politics" claim). In so doing, the Court implicitly questions the ability of black politicians to be "other-directed," interested in improving the condition of disadvantaged members of the community, whatever their race. Any action taken on behalf of the black community is presumed to be racial self-dealing and therefore a serious violation of antidiscrimination law. Similar programs adopted by a white-dominated council would be less likely to be so characterized, although they might also violate a colorblind test. Just as the academy approaches the research of nonwhite scholars on racial problems with a skepticism not accorded white-on-black scholarship, so too the Court is suspicious of programs adopted by black elected officials that aid the black community.

The *Croson* Court's analysis is also oddly colorblind when it should be color-conscious. The majority does not appear to recognize the different power relations faced by white and black office-holders.[208] Even in cities where blacks attain electoral success, they are still unlikely to possess major economic power and may be subject to pressures from white-dominated state governments. Black officials, therefore, must constantly be aware of how their behavior affects dominant white economic and political forces, who may well view affirmative actions programs as being against their interests. Adoption of the set-aside program in Richmond cannot, therefore, be automatically equated with the legendary actions of Chicago's first Mayor Daley. Yet the differences in political power—grounded in a history of racial oppression and inequality—elude the abstract symmetry of colorblindness.

Ultimately, Justice Marshall is correct that the majority's story insults the black elected officials of Richmond. The Court seems to view the Richmond city council in the way that earlier historians viewed the Reconstruction governments: black elected officials who are simply not up to the task of governing fairly and in the best interests of all.[209] It is a spectacular irony that black electoral successes are used to deny black

207. *Croson*, 109 S. Ct. at 721.

208. This argument was suggested to me by Lisa Freeman.

209. For a summary and critique of the earlier historiography, see E. Foner, Reconstruction xix–xx (1988).

elected officials an equal opportunity to fashion what they believe to be effective programs for ending second-class citizenship based on race.

I have argued that identification of the possibility of racial politics provided the Court with a justification for subjecting both white- and black-adopted affirmative action programs to strict scrutiny. There is another, far more troubling, "equality" implicit in the Court's analysis: colorblindness sees no difference between whites hurting blacks and blacks (or whites) helping blacks. That is, the paradigmatic violation of antidiscrimination law—white racism—is subjected to the same scrutiny as efforts aimed at ameliorating the effects of racism. This equal treatment of racial classifications seems wholly mistaken in light of a history of racial oppression and continued inequality. The discussion of racial preferences ought not to take as its starting point a hypothetical world in which race is largely irrelevant. A program designed to advance black economic development possesses a prima facie social legitimacy that cannot be accorded to programs that funnel money to whites qua whites. Furthermore, if, as discussed above, whites may be less able or willing to identify racial inequalities or to view them as important targets of governmental programs, then it ought to be white opposition to affirmative action rather than black support for such programs that raises a presumption of self-dealing.

This is not to suggest that racial self-dealing, by both white and black politicians, is not possible. Accordingly, as Drew Days has urged, a requirement of a factual record may be sensible to ensure the "other-directedness" of the program.[210] But such concerns are not an adequate ground for holding that the remedying of societal discrimination is an impermissible basis for race-conscious programs.

By disallowing the justification of remedying societal discrimination, the Court severely limits the ability of antidiscrimination law to overcome the deepest and most long-lasting effects of racial discrimination.[211] The set-aside program in *Croson* was a small, appropriate step in the direction of recognizing the harms that society-wide discrimination has imposed on people of color. It is difficult to deny that it would be a limited but effective way of fostering black economic development, thereby moving toward the goal—promised, but never delivered by Reconstruction—of full membership for blacks in the American community. A more radical position—that the Civil War Amendments *mandate* affirmative action—was not urged on the Court. The Court was simply asked to allow the political branches to take action on behalf of persons that no one denies have been victims. Yet colorblindness, which makes the use of race a constitutional harm, sees the Richmond program as a major breach of individual rights. In *Croson*, antidiscrimination law has

---

210. See Days, supra note 61, at 480–83.

211. There is an interesting parallel to Justice Holmes's troubling opinion in Giles v. Harris, 189 U.S. 475, 483–84, 488 (1903) (because State of Alabama had so thoroughly suppressed the opportunity of blacks to vote, Court was powerless to prevent it).

stopped focusing on the national shame over the difference that race has made.

The Court's answer to the charge that it is destroying state and local power to aid victims is that nothing prevents the establishment of race-neutral programs that benefit the "disadvantaged." The Court is eager to point out that blacks may well be overrepresented among the disadvantaged, so "a race-neutral program of city financing for small firms would, *a fortiori*, lead to greater minority participation."[212] Such programs would not only avoid the use of racial criteria, but would also reduce the overinclusiveness of race-conscious programs that help minority entrepreneurs whether or not they have been the victims of race discrimination.

But the Court's "solution" hardly avoids the self-dealing problem that seems to motivate its rejection of societal discrimination as a justification for affirmative action. If minorities are likely to be overrepresented among the disadvantaged, then the clever city council will adopt a program to help the disadvantaged knowing that it will largely channel funds to minorities. Interestingly, such programs are unlikely to receive rigorous scrutiny from the Court since they are not based on a suspect classification. Thus, with a wink and a nod, local governments can accomplish much of what the Richmond city council sought with *less* of a burden of justifying its program.

B. *Beyond Remediation*

For sound strategic reasons, supporters of affirmative action may choose to defend race-conscious governmental programs largely in terms of remedying past discrimination. Since, as noted above, race-conscious remedies can be fitted into a colorblind model, remedial justifications for affirmative action provide less of a challenge to the underlying principles of the opponents of such programs. It is therefore not surprising to see Justice Marshall in *Croson* playing on the majority's ball field, urging that "Richmond has proffered satisfactory proof of past racial discrimination to support its twin interests" of "eradicating the effects of past racial discrimination" and "preventing the city's own spending decisions from reinforcing and perpetuating the exclusionary effects of past discrimination."[213]

Metro Broadcasting, in holding that the FCC's goal of increasing broadcast diversity is constitutionally permissible, clearly suggests that race-conscious programs may pursue goals other than simply remedying past discrimination.[214] But with the departure of Justice Brennan from the Court, *Metro Broadcasting* is unlikely to be the last word.

212. City of Richmond v. J.A. Croson Co., 109 S. Ct. 706, 728 (1989).

213. Id. at 743–45 (Marshall, J., dissenting). The majority in *Croson* accepts both of these goals as legitimate.

214. Metro Broadcasting, Inc. v. FCC, 110 S. Ct. 2997, 3010 (1990).

Justice O'Connor, joined by three other justices in her *Metro Broadcasting* dissent, explicitly rejects the FCC's justification for its policies:

> Under . . . strict scrutiny, only a compelling interest may support the Government's use of racial classifications. Modern equal protection doctrine has recognized only one such interest: remedying the effects of racial discrimination. The interest in increasing the diversity of broadcast viewpoints is clearly not a compelling interest.[215]

It thus appears that Justice Souter's views here will provide the decisive vote with respect to the Court's future position as to what goals may provide the basis for an affirmative action program.[216]

I have already mentioned a range of situations in which nonremedial race-conscious policies appear to be sensible.[217] But beyond these situations, in which race is rationally related to the pursuit of a governmental objective because of the way race functions in this society, race-consciousness can also be a part of the struggle against racism.[218] This suggestion, of course, is hard to square with the claim that colorblindness represents the absence or vanquishing of racism. Yet, as discussed above,[219] that claim appears quite wrong. White perceptions of black inferiority cannot be overcome by repressing our implicit recognition of race. Racism can be challenged only when whites *see* blacks as equals.

---

215. Id. at 3034 (O'Connor, J., dissenting). Of course, O'Connor's language leaves some room for the future recognition of other goals, and at times she has seemed open to "diversity"-type claims. See Wygant v. Jackson Bd. of Educ., 476 U.S. 267, 284–94 (O'Connor, J., concurring) (apparently accepting Powell's view in *Bakke* that assuring classroom diversity is a legitimate state interest). In *Croson*, she seems to have moved away from *Wygant*: in justifying her conclusion that affirmative action programs must be subjected to "strict scrutiny," she states that unless classifications based on race "are strictly reserved for *remedial* settings, they may in fact promote notions of racial inferiority and lead to a politics of racial hostility." 109 S. Ct. at 721 (emphasis added).

216. Justice Souter's testimony before the Senate Judiciary Committee was unclear on this point. He appears willing to approve the Court's holding in *Metro Broadcasting*, but, as the Senate Report notes, he mischaracterizes it as follows:

> Judge SOUTER . . . . The proposition which *Metro* stands for is that the congressional power to engage in . . . limited remedial action, which does indeed take some account of race, is to be judged under the middle-tier standard of scrutiny. . . .
>
> Therefore *Metro* is one step in what I assume will be a long line of cases that is going to result in the definition of the scope of congressional power over . . . remedial legislation with race conscious references.

S. Exec. Rep. 101-32, 101st Cong., 2d Sess. 23 (1990) (citation omitted). The Court in *Metro Broadcasting*, however, expressly denied that the FCC's policies were justified as "remedies for victims of . . . discrimination." 110 S. Ct. at 3010.

217. See supra text accompanying notes 19–28.

218. I try to use this term carefully. By "racism" I mean a belief system (or ideology) of one group that asserts the inferiority of another group based on that group's race. I distinguish it from "racial discrimination," by which I mean conduct that adversely affects a person or group based on race.

219. See supra text accompanying notes 92–100.

There are two parts to this revisioning. First, whites must see blacks in positions of power, authority, and responsibility—as teachers, police officers, elected officials, and fellow employees.[220] Second, whites must begin to recognize and credit self-definition by subordinated groups.

Equality among groups depends upon shared recognition of the equal moral status of groups of which one is not a part. When we ask others to respect us, we are asking that they understand us in and on our own terms, even if they disagree with us. We do not ask others to like us for the image *they* have of us, but for the image we have of ourselves. For others to do less than this for us is to create an unequal situation—one in which they seek to exercise power over us. For example, I may not share my wife's commitment to religious traditions, but it is incumbent upon me to appreciate what those traditions mean to her. Otherwise, I am not according her the respect I accord myself. Equality among groups requires intersubjectivity: a recognition by each of the power of the other to define itself and have its definitions taken seriously.

Such self-definitions are contingent, fluid, the product of negotiations between and among groups. And even persons eager and willing to appreciate another's self-definition will do so in light of his or her own culture and psychology.[221] There is thus no assurance of an intersubjective meeting of the minds even between people (or groups) of good will. But neither agreement nor closure is the goal; rather, what is sought is an on-going joint search for self and others in which all groups can participate as equals.

This argument for race-consciousness goes beyond reparations and beyond recognizing victimhood. Affirmative action as a remedy for past wrongs may be perfectly consistent with a continued belief in inferiority. It is the reconceptualization of blacks as subjects rather than objects—a project at the core of recent scholarship on slavery and race relations[222]—that holds out promise for undermining racism.

Race-consciousness, therefore, should play a double role in ending black invisibility. It demands that people of color attain visible and important positions in society that challenge traditional views of where they "belong"; and it demands that whites recognize the holders of such positions as people of color.[223] Such use of race, I believe, will

220. Social science evidence supports the claim that altering expected social roles can have an effect on attitudes. See, e.g., Eagly & Steffen, Gender Stereotypes Stem from the Distribution of Men and Women into Social Roles, 46 J. Personality & Soc. Psychology 735, 752 (1984).

221. Cf. Kennedy, supra note 158, at 745 (difficulty in discerning the true "individuality" of others due to constraints of personal perceptions).

222. See, e.g., A. Meier & E. Rudwick, Black History and the Historical Profession, 1915–1980, at 175-237 (1986); B. Quarles, Black Mosaic: Essays in Afro-American History and Historiography 80–213 (1988).

223. See I. Young, Justice and the Politics of Difference 194 (1990).

help remove the effects of past discrimination. Yet it is not "remedial" in the sense used by the Court; it is not a response to discrete discriminatory acts. Rather, it attempts to attack the underlying structure of thought that supports inequality and that allows society to define discrimination in a way guaranteed to ensure no material change in the lives of black people.

C. *Congressional Race-Consciousness*

Congress and executive branch agencies have adopted race-conscious measures aimed both at overcoming the effects of societal discrimination and achieving other than remedial goals. The congressional set-aside program in *Fullilove*, for example, was premised on remedying broad societal discrimination that had kept minority businesses from equal participation in state and local public works contracts. Following *Fullilove*, Congress and executive agencies adopted additional set-aside programs that passed constitutional scrutiny in the courts.[224] So, too, Executive Order 11,246,[225] requiring affirmative action efforts by federal contractors, was justified in terms that go far beyond remedying specific violations by covered employers of the colorblind principle.[226]

Indeed, the persistent complaint of many opponents of affirmative action is that federal statutes and regulations have demanded that virtually all employers and recipients of federal funds achieve work forces that roughly reflect the percentages of minorities in the general population.[227] Congress has not indicated dissatisfaction with the executive branch rules, nor have the courts held them unconstitutional.[228]

The FCC's policies sustained in *Metro Broadcasting* are an example of race-conscious federal policies pursuing other than remedial goals. As the Court noted,

> Congress and the Commission do not justify the minority ownership policies strictly as remedies for victims of this dis-

---

224. See Days, supra note 61, at 471–77.

Of course, the numerous state and local set aside programs fashioned after the congressional program upheld in *Fullilove* are now vulnerable because of the Court's decision in *Croson*. For an attempt at damage control, see Constitutional Scholars' Statement on Affirmative Action After *City of Richmond v. J.A. Croson Co.*, 98 Yale L.J. 1711 (1989).

225. Exec. Order No. 11,246 (1965), 3 C.F.R. 339 (1964–1965), reprinted in 42 U.S.C. § 2000e app. at 28–31 (1990); accord 41 C.F.R. part 60-30 (obligation to remedy underutilization of protected groups).

226. See Contractors Ass'n v. Secretary of Labor, 442 F.2d 159, 177 (3d Cir.), cert. denied, 404 U.S. 854 (1971) (Executive Order within implied authority of President to reduce costs by ensuring that largest possible pool of qualified workers available to undertake work on government contracts).

227. See, e.g., N. Glazer, supra note 189, at 51–57; T. Sowell, supra note 189, at 48–60.

228. See, e.g., *Contractors Ass'n*, 442 F.2d at 176–77 (upholding Plan enacted pursuant to Exec. Order No. 11,246).

> crimination . . . . Rather, Congress and the FCC have selected the minority ownership policies primarily to promote programming diversity, and they urge that such diversity is an important governmental objective that can serve as a constitutional basis for the preference policies.[229]

The 1982 amendments to the Voting Rights Act provide the most dramatic example of federal race-consciousness. In 1980, the Court had read section two of the Voting Rights Act as incorporating simply the fifteenth amendment's protection against the deprivation of the right to vote on the basis of race.[230] Since the Court understood the fifteenth amendment as prohibiting only intentional discrimination, this standard was applied to section two as well. Two years later, Congress rejected the Court's intent standard by amending section two to prohibit any voting qualification, rule, or procedure "which *results* in a denial or abridgement of the right . . . to vote on account of race or color."[231]

The substitution of a results test for an intent test was strenuously opposed by some members of Congress and the Reagan Administration, who argued that the new section two, in effect, demanded proportional representation.[232] Proponents of the amendment denied the charge[233] and accepted a proviso to section two, which declares that "nothing in this section establishes a right to have members of a protected class elected in numbers equal to their proportion in the population."[234] The proviso, however, has not prevented courts, upon finding a violation, from ordering relief that virtually guarantees injured groups a proportionate share of elected offices.[235]

More importantly, the animating purpose of the amendment to section two was to afford minority voters "an equal opportunity to participate *and to elect candidates of their choice*."[236] Under the revised section two, the relevant question is not whether the political system has been responsive to the needs of minorities; it is, instead, whether voting rules (including district line drawing) have allowed those candidates who are preferred by protected groups to win elections. In a society as

229. Metro Broadcasting, Inc. v. FCC, 110 S. Ct. 2997, 3010 (1990).

230. See City of Mobile v. Bolden, 446 U.S. 55, 60–61 (1980).

231. 42 U.S.C. § 1973(b) (1988) (emphasis supplied).

232. See, e.g., S. Rep. No. 417, 97th Cong., 2d Sess. 96 (1982) (statement of Sen. Hatch).

233. Id. at 193–94 (statement of Sen. Dole).

234. Voting Rights Act Amendments of 1982, Pub. L. No. 97-205, § 3, 96 Stat. 131, 134 (1982) (codified as amended at 42 U.S.C. § 1973(b)).

235. See, e.g., United States. v. Dallas County Comm'n, 850 F.2d 1433, 1440–41 (11th Cir. 1988). This result appears to have been anticipated by the drafters (if one reads between the lines): "The court should exercise its traditional equitable powers to fashion the relief so that it completely remedies the prior dilution of minority voting strength and fully provides equal opportunity for minority citizens to participate and to elect candidates of their choice." S. Rep., supra note 232, at 31.

236. S. Rep., supra note 232, at 30 (emphasis added).

racially divided as ours, it is more than likely that minority groups will choose representatives drawn from among their own ranks. Section two, as amended, therefore, must be understood as being primarily about helping minority groups elect minority office-holders.

There can be little doubt that supporters of the amendment to section two hoped and anticipated that the revitalized provision would produce more minority elected officials.[237] The straightforward reasoning was that black office-holders will be better able and more likely to represent the interests of black voters. Section two, in sum, is based on a race-conscious theory and was written to achieve race-conscious results. And despite the fact that the 1982 amendment, in effect, rejected a constitutional judgment of the Court, no challenge to its constitutionality has succeeded.[238]

The history of the Voting Rights Act illustrates an additional point. The amendment to section two was predicated upon the congressional finding that there exists persistent racial bloc voting in many jurisdictions. Under colorblindness, such voting patterns would be condemned as an irrational (or at least unfortunate) aspect of our political system that ought to be overcome. In crafting a voting rights strategy, legislators who are "colorblind" would not think it appropriate to reinforce or rely upon bloc voting; rather, they would be more likely to favor measures that prohibited intentional deprivation of the right to vote on the basis of race. Senator Orrin Hatch explicitly urged this view in his comments appended to the Senate report on the 1982 amendments:

> In place of the traditional focus upon equal *access* to registration and the ballot, the amendments would focus upon equal *outcome* in the electoral process. Instead of aiming ultimately at the nonconsideration of race in the electoral process as did the original Act, the amendments would make race the overriding factor in public decisions in this area. Instead of directing its protections toward the individual citizen as did the original Act—and as does the Constitution—the amendments would make racial and ethnic *groups* the basic unit of protection.[239]

But in a society in which blacks constitute a minority in most election districts and in which racial bloc voting is a fact of life, colorblindness will neither make bloc voting go away nor will it provide sufficiently for minority representation in the political system. The intensely race-

---

237. See Karlan, Maps and Misreadings: The Role of Geographic Compactness in Racial Vote Dilution Legislation, 24 Harv. C.R.-C.L. L. Rev. 173, 213–14 (1989).

238. See, e.g., United States v. Marengo County Comm'n, 731 F.2d 1546, 1556–63 (11th Cir.), cert. denied, 469 U.S. 976 (1984). The Court has not expressly passed on the constitutional issue. However, in its only major decision on section two, the Court gave no hint that it thought the section raised a serious constitutional question. See Thornburg v. Gingles, 478 U.S. 30 (1986).

239. S. Rep., supra note 232, at 94 (emphasis in original).

conscious Congress that amended section two understood that comforting theories must sometimes yield to practical facts, that colorblindness can be an inadequate response to a color-conscious world.

V. From Antidiscrimination to Racial Justice

Discussion about the appropriateness of race-conscious measures is but the doctrinal manifestation of a broader debate regarding the animating principle of race discrimination law. The strategy of colorblindness follows from an understanding of discrimination law that views the use of racial classifications as morally and politically objectionable. In contrast, support for broad race-conscious policies is usually imbedded in a description of race discrimination law as aimed at ending the second-class citizenship of African-Americans and other subordinated minorities.

It is commonplace today to speak of the body of law dealing with issues of race as "antidiscrimination law" and to see the constitutional norms of antidiscrimination as grounded in the fourteenth amendment's guarantee of "equal protection of the laws." While the terms "antidiscrimination" and "equal protection" do not entail a colorblind approach, they signal an abstractness and a symmetry that makes colorblindness a natural-seeming doctrinal instantiation of the concepts. It is fair to say that modern antidiscrimination law—at least at the constitutional level—has largely become a fourteenth amendment story about drastically curtailing the use of racial classifications. From this perspective, affirmative action is a problematic exception to the rule, requiring sophisticated theories to establish the legitimacy of race-conscious measures. What is the origin and justification for the antidiscrimination-as-colorblindness model? Certainly, it is difficult to locate in the "original intent" of the fourteenth amendment.[240] Nor can it be based on a claim that race is always "irrelevant" to rational decision making. Colorblindness—as a constitutional or moral norm—seems to be the product of a successful litigation strategy that buried Jim Crow. Yet *Brown v. Board of Education*[241] can quite sensibly be read to proscribe not the mere use of race, but rather systemic state practices that impose harm on a subordinated group.[242]

Starting fresh, it appears obvious that an antidiscrimination model that sees the use of racial classifications as the central problem to be addressed ill-fits this society's current racial situation. There is no symmetry in either the use of racial classifications or the experiences of different racial groups. To see the problem of race discrimination as the problem of using racial criteria is to wrench legal theory out of so-

240. See Tribe, supra note 13, at 204-06.

241. 347 U.S. 483 (1954).

242. See Brest, supra note 14, at 9; Tribe, supra note 13, at 204-05; see also Black, The Lawfulness of the Segregation Decisions, 69 Yale L.J. 421, 430 n.25 (1960).

cial reality.[243]

The view that race discrimination law ought to be about ending the second-class citizenship of blacks (and other persons disadvantaged on the basis of historical group oppression) is at the core of the Civil War Amendments from which antidiscrimination norms derive. There is no dispute that blacks, at the close of the Civil War, suffered from severe legal disabilities and economic privation in both the North and South.[244] The 1866 Civil Rights Act, in language that looks curious to us today, sought to guarantee to "all persons" the same civil rights "as [are] enjoyed by white citizens."[245] The great problem of the day was not the use of racial criteria, but rather the existence of a class of Americans who had been exploited and degraded for two centuries. Indeed, there is substantial evidence that proponents of the fourteenth amendment supported race-conscious federal programs directed at improving the condition of freed slaves.[246]

But to state the motivating purposes behind the Civil War Amendments is not necessarily to provide a standard for interpretation today. It could be plausibly argued that the civil rights revolution of this century has redefined antidiscrimination norms, much as the commerce power has taken on new meaning in the twentieth century in light of the demands of a national economy. *Brown* could be understood as the paradigm-shifting case that, responding to modern notions of equality, ushered in colorblindness.

The choice among race discrimination law principles is, in the deepest sense, moral and political. Arrayed on the side of the antidiscrimination-as-colorblindness model is the knowledge of the terrible wrongs that color-consciousness has wrought in our history, the ending of legal segregation effectuated by colorblindness, an ideology of individualism that stresses evaluation and rewards based on individual effort and personal characteristics over which a person has control, and the antagonisms that race-based preferences may breed. These, of course, are not trivial arguments, which suggests why colorblindness has had such significant appeal.[247]

But the claim that race should be ignored would be far more per-

---

243. To its advocates, colorblindness remains an instrumental strategy for achieving racial justice. I do not mean to imply that supporters of colorblindness have no regard for the real-world consequences of their theoretical positions.

244. On the Northern history of racism and oppression, which rarely makes it into the American history textbooks, see L. Litwack, North of Slavery: The Negro in the Free States, 1790–1860 (1961).

245. Act of Apr. 9, 1866, ch. 31, § 1, 14 Stat. 27.

246. See Schnapper, Affirmative Action and the Legislative History of the Fourteenth Amendment, 71 Va. L. Rev. 753, 754 (1985).

247. See supra notes 76–89 and accompanying text. Other consequences of colorblindness may make it attractive to whites, such as its failure to demand significant change in the allocation of resources and opportunities away from whites. I do not credit this argument in the discussion that follows.

suasive if the difference that race had made in the past had been overcome. What cannot be denied—even if it is often ignored—is that blacks, as a class, have never attained economic or social equality with whites. Reconstruction ended long before it achieved its (some would say limited[248]) set of goals. The "Second Reconstruction" of the 1960s wiped away some of the additional legal insults added by the race hysteria of the late nineteenth century, but it did little to fundamentally alter the material well-being of blacks. The narrowing of the economic gap between blacks and whites that occurred in the 1950s and 1960s—due primarily to the overall growth in the economy—stalled by the middle of the 1970s[249] and did not improve during the Reagan years.[250] A prodigious study sponsored by the National Academy of Sciences has recently concluded that the United States faces "an unfinished agenda: many black Americans remain separated from the mainstream of national life under conditions of great inequality."[251]

A colorblind strategy might still be advisable if it could be shown that it would materially advance racial equality. But whatever the contribution colorblindness made in striking down segregation laws, the *Croson* majority and the *Metro Broadcasting* dissents make all to clear that a colorblind norm is no longer primarily concerned with ending the difference that race has made. It is therefore not surprising that instrumental arguments for colorblindness are now cast in terms not of ending material inequality, but in terms of serving the ultimate goal of colorblindness (that is, acting in a colorblind fashion will help bring about a colorblind future) or of avoiding both the stigma purportedly imposed by race-conscious policies and white resentment of such measures.[252] Or, instrumental arguments are dropped altogether, and colorblindness is asserted as an a priori moral principle.[253]

The weakness of these arguments, combined with the adverse consequences of colorblindness detailed above, suggest to me that there are strong reasons for continuing the struggle to fulfill the initial goals

---

248. See, e.g., B. Fields, Ideology and Race in American History, *in* Region and Reconstruction 143, 164–68 (1982); P. Foner, supra note 64, at xxiii n.8 (collecting sources).

249. See R. Farley & W. Allen, supra note 166, at 313.

250. A Common Destiny, supra note 30, at 7.

251. Id. at 4.

252. See, e.g., City of Richmond v. J.A. Croson Co., 109 S. Ct. 706, 735–39 (1989) (Scalia, J., concurring); Abram, supra note 17, at 1312. Of course, this is a contested claim. See, e.g., Regents of the Univ. of Cal. v. Bakke, 438 U.S. 265, 402–08 (Blackmun, J., concurring in the judgment in part and dissenting in part) (in order to get past racism, society must be race-conscious now).

Supporters of colorblindness also assert that color-consciousness produces bad results (such as a lowering of standards, a divisive racial spoils system, and imposition of stigma on beneficiaries of affirmative action).

253. See, e.g., A. Bickel, supra note 78, at 133; DOJ Report, supra note 14, at 4–5.

of race discrimination law. Whether phrased as "anti-caste,"[254] "anti-group disadvantage,"[255] or "anti-subjugation,"[256] the task remains where it began: the ending of second class status of an historically oppressed group and the achieving of racial justice.

There are two interrelated aspects to this agenda for race discrimination law. The first supports programs that would produce material improvements in the lives of black people: programs promoting jobs, medical care, and decent housing. Such programs, it should be noted, need not be race-based. A "racial justice" perspective need not entail explicitly race-conscious policies.[257] It seems clear, however, that a racial justice perspective is friendly to race-conscious policies directed at overcoming the effects of past and present societal discrimination. The set-aside programs in *Fullilove* and *Croson* are modest examples of the kind of state intervention that is needed.

The second aspect of a racial justice perspective is an attack on the set of beliefs that makes existing inequalities untroubling. What must be addressed is not just old-fashioned racism,[258] but also the deeply ingrained mental structures that categorize and define race to the disadvantage of blacks and other nonwhite groups.[259] As suggested above, altering the image of blacks in the white mind requires paying

---

254. Dimond, The Anti-Caste Principle—Toward A Constitutional Standard for Review of Race Cases, 30 Wayne L. Rev. 1 (1983).

255. Fiss, supra note 12, at 157, 160.

256. L. Tribe, supra note 180, § 16–21, at 1515.

257. The Court's interpretation of Title VII in Griggs v. Duke Power Co., 401 U.S 424 (1971), provides an example. There, the Court invalidated a testing requirement for employment that had a disproportionate impact on minority applicants because the test had not been shown to be sufficiently job-related. Id. at 432. *Griggs* clearly goes beyond the colorblind/antidiscrimination model because it rejects the claim that discriminatory intent is necessary to make out a violation of Title VII and strikes down an employment prerequisite that did not include an explicit racial classification. The Court seriously narrowed *Griggs* in Wards Cove Packing Co. v. Atonio, 109 S. Ct. 2115, 2121 (1989), but it did not overturn the effects test. Title VII also allows private affirmative action plans, see Johnson v. Transportation Agency, 480 U.S. 616, 637–40 (1987); United Steelworkers v. Weber, 443 U.S. 193, 200–08 (1979), but it is not clear that *Johnson* will survive the departures of Justices Powell and Brennan.

Other federal antidiscrimination statutes and regulations permit the invalidation of policies causing disproportionate impact in the absence of proof of discriminatory intent. See, e.g., Resident Advisory Bd. v. Rizzo, 564 F.2d 126, 147–48 (3d Cir. 1977), cert. denied, 435 U.S. 908 (1978); Fair Housing Act (Title VIII of the Civil Rights Act of 1968), 42 U.S.C. §§ 3601–3631 (1988); 42 U.S.C. §§ 2000d–d-7 (1988) (regulations implementing the Civil Rights Act's disproportionate impact policies).

258. For an excellent discussion contrasting the traditional conception, i.e., that discrimination is a product of prejudice, with institutional and other conceptions of discrimination, see J. Feagin & C. Feagin, Discrimination American Style: Institutional Racism and Sexism (2d ed. 1986).

259. To the extent that a "racial justice" approach condemns racism, it may be difficult to square with the original intent of the thirteenth amendment. But even the current Court has allowed a broader, more up-to-date reading of this amendment. See Patterson v. McLean Credit Union, 109 S. Ct. 2363, 2377–79 (1989).

attention to, and crediting, black voices, and to refashioning institutions in ways that will allow those voices to be heard. Here race-conscious programs may be crucial, and the FCC's policies upheld in *Metro Broadcasting* provide an important example.

Underlying this two-pronged attack on racial inequality is a conception of the field of race discrimination law that is broader in two ways than prevailing descriptions.[260] First, it effaces the line drawn by colorblindness between "antidiscrimination law" (understood as prohibitions against irrational prejudice) and "social policy" (understood as programs directed at ameliorating disadvantage).[261]

Second, the reconceptualization of race discrimination law proposed here is not stated as a constitutional principle. Rather, my claim is that the pursuit of racial justice ought to be recognized as a fundamental social and political commitment in this society.[262] There is a troubling tendency in modern constitutional law to see judicial interpretation of the Constitution as defining the political and moral ideals for society.[263] Constitutional law may well reflect and support such ideals, but legal discourse necessarily distorts and alters political principles. In an attempt to arrive at rules for judicial application, constitutional antidiscrimination law proceeds by identifying an underlying norm that sorts out permissible and impermissible uses of race. Even asymmetrical antidiscrimination principles rarely describe any sort of political duty to undo the effects of past discrimination. These negative injunctions, to my mind, seriously understate the proper content of antidiscrimination norms.

Furthermore, a focus on constitutional norms is likely to be influenced by considerations of the judicial role. The persistent debate about whether the fourteenth amendment condemns "intentional discrimination" or policies with "disproportionate impact" is, at bottom, a

---

260. Cf. Torres, Local Knowledge, Local Color: Critical Legal Studies and the Law of Race Relations, 25 San Diego L. Rev. 1043, 1064 (1988) (noting that "choice of terms used to characterize the legal struggle against racism reveals particular conceptions of law and social relations").

261. Justice Scalia implicitly adopts this distinction in *Croson*:

> The benign purpose of compensating for social disadvantages, whether they have been acquired by reason of prior discrimination or otherwise, can no more be pursued by the illegitimate means of racial discrimination than can other assertedly benign purposes we have repeatedly rejected.

City of Richmond v. J.A. Croson Co., 109 S. Ct. 706, 735 (1989).

262. This would mean a dramatic shift in law school studies. The focus would be on historical and social science materials demonstrating the difference that race makes, rather than on discussions of the appropriate level of scrutiny by which the judiciary ought to judge governmental programs that draw racial lines.

263. Cf. West, Progressive and Conservative Constitutionalism, 88 Mich. L. Rev. 641, 717–18 (1989) (noting "pervasiveness of the perceived equation of public morality with constitutionalism," and suggesting "recharacteriz[ing] our progressive understanding of the constitutional guarantees of liberty and equality as political ideals to guide legislation, rather than as restraints on legislation").

fight over the appropriateness of the use of judicial power to remedy inequality.[264] There is far less dispute that Congress has the *power* to remedy disproportionate impact, even if there is a dispute about whether it should act to do so.[265]

Although a racial justice perspective goes beyond explication of a constitutional norm, it still needs some constitutional mooring in order to provide federal authority for action. The usual place to turn to in looking for this authority is section five of the fourteenth amendment, but I think there would be significant advantages to an "amendment shift"—away from the fourteenth amendment's commitment to equal treatment based on race and toward reliance on the thirteenth amendment for a call to an end of second-class status for racial minorities. Such a move would recolor our antidiscrimination law, making its central concern not race-neutral norms but rather the social and economic conditions of historically disadvantaged racial groups.

I should not be understood as asserting that the thirteenth amendment *proprio vigore* mandates certain governmental programs. Rather, the "amendment shift" is more symbolic. It is an attempt to anchor a redefinition of race discrimination on an important legal and cultural artifact, thereby demonstrating that the reconceptualization is well within the bounds of constitutional tradition and discourse.

The Supreme Court itself has recognized this role for the thirteenth amendment. In *Jones v. Alfred H. Mayer Co.*[266], the Court held that Section 1982's[267] prohibition against private discrimination in the sale of property was appropriate legislation under the thirteenth amendment. Writing more than a century after the enactment of the statute that it was interpreting, the Court adopted a present-minded view of the "badges and incidents" of slavery that the thirteenth amendment authorized Congress to condemn: "when racial discrimination herds men into ghettos and makes their ability to buy property turn on the color of their skin, then it too is a relic of slavery."[268] In effect, the Court identified a constitutional provision that plausibly provided the historical and moral force necessary for its conclusion, demanded by the times, that Congress has the power to prohibit private discrimination.[269]

264. See, e.g., Justice White's penultimate paragraph in Washington v. Davis, 426 U.S. 229, 252 (1976), and Justice Powell's majority opinion in McCleskey v. Kemp, 481 U.S. 279, 314–19 (1987), both suggesting that "impact tests" would have drastic societal consequences.

265. See West, supra note 263, at 717–21.

266. 392 U.S. 409 (1968).

267. 42 U.S.C. § 1982.

268. 392 U.S. at 442–43.

269. In language more rhetorical than analytical, the Court declared:

> At the very least, the freedom that Congress is empowered to secure under the Thirteenth Amendment includes the freedom to buy whatever a white man can buy, the right to live wherever a white man can live. If Congress cannot say that

The "amendment shift" suggested here would put the fourteenth amendment back where it belongs: between the thirteenth and the fifteenth. Under a colorblind framework, the fourteenth amendment serves as the font of antidiscrimination law, while the thirteenth amendment is reduced to simply prohibiting the reinstitution of slavery. But this is a most curious flip. Slavery had ended by the time the North conquered the South, and not even unreconstructed Confederates thought it could be reinstituted.[270] As the passage of the 1866 Act after ratification of the thirteenth amendment demonstrated, Congress clearly believed that the amendment was about more than freeing the slaves from their masters.[271] It makes a great deal of sense to see the fourteenth amendment as an extension and generalization of the themes of the thirteenth. But it is odd, to say the least, to read the fourteenth amendment as constraining attempts to fulfill the promise of the thirteenth.

Some might claim that a thirteenth amendment approach will prove unpersuasive because white America is simply unwilling to see the current condition of blacks as a legacy of slavery. Indeed, just fifteen years after adoption of the thirteenth amendment, the Supreme Court held in the *Civil Rights Cases*[272] that the amendment did not authorize congressional legislation prohibiting racial discrimination in public accommodations and theatres. To give such a scope to the thirteenth amendment, wrote Justice Bradley for the majority, "would be running the slavery argument into the ground."[273] Opponents of affirmative action today are quick to make the same argument: whatever the sins of slavery, surely time and subsequent events (including the civil rights movement of the 1960s) have vitiated any plausible claim that slavery is a proximate cause of current inequality.

> being a free man means at least this much, then the Thirteenth Amendment made a promise that the Nation cannot keep.

Id. at 443.

When the Court recently re-examined the applicability of the 1866 statute to private discrimination, it held that "whether . . . [our decision] is right or wrong as an original matter, it is certain that it is not inconsistent with the prevailing sense of justice in this country." Patterson v. McLean Credit Union, 109 S. Ct. 2363, 2371 (1989).

270. See H. Hyman & W. Wiecek, Equal Justice Under Law: Constitutional Development 1835–1875, at 397 (1982); J. ten Broek, The Antislavery Origins of the Fourteenth Amendment 141–43 (1951).

271. See H. Hyman & W. Wiecek, supra note 270, at 391–403; J. ten Broek, supra note 270, at 140–80; Kaczorowski, Reconstructing Reconstruction: The Enforcement Provisions of the Civil Rights Act of 1866: A Legislative History in Light of *Runyon v. McCrary*, 98 Yale L.J. 565, 569–73 (1989).

272. 109 U.S. 3 (1883).

273. Id. at 24; see also City of Memphis v. Greene, 451 U.S. 100, 128 (1981) (street closing that separated white and black communities did not violate thirteenth amendment: "to regard [disparate impact of city's action] as a form of stigma so severe as to violate the Thirteenth Amendment would trivialize the great purpose of that charter of freedom.").

A strong case, I believe, could be made for a proximate relationship between slavery and current racial conditions.[274] But there is another linkage as well. Slavery left a legacy of racism that this society has never overcome. Although historians continue to debate the cause and effect relationship of slavery and the belief in black inferiority,[275] there can be no doubt that the American system of slavery—from at least the 1830s on—was justified in terms of the subhumanness of blacks. As George Fredrickson has explained, "[e]xplicit racism, a public ideology based on the doctrinaire conception of the black man as a natural underling, developed . . . directly out of the need to defend slavery against nineteenth-century humanitarianism."[276] That slavery was undergirded by a belief in the inherent inferiority of blacks should hardly be surprising—society needed some story to tell itself in order to justify its enslavement of several million human beings.

Over the past 150 years, the terms and explanations have shifted, primarily from a biological to a cultural basis for black inferiority. But the message of inferiority has not been extirpated. "The persistence of negative stereotypes about blacks," Kent Greenawalt has suggested, "can be argued to be an 'incident' of slavery in the extended sense of a debilitating effect of slavery and also an 'incident' in the narrower sense of a feature that accompanied slavery itself and continues to disadvantage blacks."[277] To see this legacy of slavery, whites need simply to peer into their own minds and watch as they confront blacks on the street, in a classroom, or on television. Only the rarest white person will be able to honestly deny race-consciousness. Most, I believe, will be forced to come to grips with the fact that for whites race-consciousness most often takes the form of racism.

Relying on the thirteenth amendment as authorization for governmental action to combat racial inequality, then, provides a number of advantages. The amendment is expressly aimed at ameliorating the second class status of blacks, it reaches private action, and its condemnation of slavery forces us to recognize historical facts and consequences that are too easily dismissed as remote. It helps redefine the issue as one not simply of preventing racial discrimination, but of achieving racial justice.[278]

---

274. See Williams v. City of New Orleans, 729 F.2d 1554, 1577 (5th Cir. 1984) (Wisdom, J., concurring in part and dissenting in part) (affirmative action program in police department justified by thirteenth amendment since "present discriminatory effect upon blacks as a class can be linked with a discriminatory practice against blacks as a race under the slavery system"); Loury, supra note 189, at 253–59 (concept of inherited disabilities).

275. See Vaughan, The Origins Debate: Slavery and Racism in Seventeenth-Century Virginia, 97 Va. Mag. Hist. & Biography 311, 311 & nn.1–2 (1989).

276. G. Fredrickson, supra note 112, at 189.

277. Greenawalt, Judicial Scrutiny of "Benign" Racial Preference in Law School Admissions, 75 Colum. L. Rev. 559, 592 (1975).

278. Cf. Binder, Negating Slavery, *in* Recognizing Freedom: Slavery and Emanci-

VI. Conclusion: Toward an Inclusive American Story

In the current political and social climate, a call for color-consciousness poses real risks. For several centuries of American history, noticing race provided the basis for a caste system that institutionalized second-class status for people of color. It was precisely this oppressive use of race that colorblindness sought to overcome. Furthermore, central to white opposition to affirmative action is the belief that blacks have attained equality of opportunity, and therefore any assistance directed to minorities qua minorities affords them an undeserved benefit and an unfair advantage.[279]

Perhaps these considerations suggest that it would be politically wise, much as the Supreme Court suggested in *Croson*, for civil rights advocates to turn their attentions toward race-neutral goals.[280] It may be time, some might reasonably suggest, to reinitiate the struggle, abandoned in the 1970s, for a recognition of the constitutional status of "fundamental rights" such as housing, jobs, medical care, and a decent education that a just society ought to provide to its members.[281] Although this prong of the civil rights movement withered when the Supreme Court made clear that it would not read the Constitution to require that governments provide certain minimal levels of support to those in need,[282] and there is little chance that the current Court will retreat from this position, it is possible that a Democratically dominated Congress—well aware of the disastrous impact that the policies of the Reagan Administration had on the least advantaged members of our society—might be moved to increase support for social programs.[283]

I do not claim to be a savvy political analyst and would not predict the chances of success for such a strategy. But I wish to identify several important issues with which a race-neutral civil rights program must come to grips. A "fundamental rights" approach will not get at the

---

pation After Hegel (G. Binder, J. Bush & K. Thomas eds., forthcoming 1992)(suggesting interpretation of the thirteenth amendment based on the conception of freedom held by African-American beneficiaries of the amendment).

279. See J. Kluegel & E. Smith, Whites' Beliefs about Black Opportunity, 47 Am. Soc. Rev. 518, 523 (1982).

280. This proposal has received support from some African-American scholars. See, e.g., S. Steele, supra note 147, at 19–20; W. Wilson, The Truly Disadvantaged: The Inner City, the Underclass, and Public Policy 109–24 (1987).

281. For theoretical possibilities, see Baker, Outcome Equality or Equality of Respect: The Substantive Content of Equal Protection, 131 U. Pa. L. Rev. 933 (1983); Michelman, The Supreme Court, 1968 Term—Foreword: On Protecting the Poor Through the Fourteenth Amendment, 83 Harv. L. Rev. 7 (1969).

282. See Maher v. Roe, 432 U.S. 464, 480 (1977); San Antonio Indep. School Dist. v. Rodriguez, 411 U.S. 1, 36 (1973).

283. A fundamental rights strategy has other potential strengths. It provides opportunities for coalition building across race lines, and may well bring back to the civil rights movement those who supported earlier political action but lost faith during the fight over affirmative action.

underlying assumptions and structures of thought that support second-class status for blacks in this society.[284] It will not change the American belief that all it takes to make it in this society is hard work, and that those who do not make it fail because of their own character (or cultural) flaws. And it may, in fact, reinforce stereotypes to the extent that minority members are overrepresented in programs directed at the disadvantaged.

Race-neutral strategies simply postpone our society's inevitable rendezvous with its history of racism. Constant liminal and subliminal messages of the difference that race makes take their toll—no matter what justificatory rhetoric enshrouds official governmental action—and will ultimately breed a powerful claim of enough-is-enough. Such a call can take the form of a national commitment to end racial injustice, or it can take the form of "by any means necessary"[285] in the minds and hands of the victims of discrimination who know that colorblindness is a descriptive lie and a normative mistake.

Race-conscious programs alone will not end racism. At best, they represent a small step toward changing social relations and structures of thought and perception. What is needed is direct, self-conscious scrutiny of the way we think and of the assumptions about race that each of us holds and upon which we act. Attention to black constructions of reality can provide a counterbalance to the white construction of blacks in the white mind.

The walls that separate whites from blacks are based on more than ignorance, myth, and fear. Despite American myths about "one nation, indivisible" and "e pluribus unum," blacks remain strangers in the land, identified by a skin color that is still a badge of otherness.[286] In reflecting on his life in his autobiography, W.E.B. Du Bois wrote, "I was not an American; . . . I was by long education and continual compulsion and daily reminder, a colored man in a white world."[287]

How can blacks living in the United States not "be Americans"? Historical facts are clearly to the contrary. With the virtual closing of the slave trade at the time of the American Revolution, the ancestors of

284. Indeed, one of the ironies of affirmative action is that it allows whites to be exposed to successful blacks, and, given the nonintersecting worlds of whites and blacks, thereby leads whites to overestimate the opportunities available to blacks. See Kluegel & Smith, supra note 279, at 519.

285. The famous phrase of Malcolm X. E.g., Speech of Dec. 20, 1964 at the Audubon Ballroom, reprinted in Malcolm X Speaks 116 (G. Breitman ed. 1965) ("Our objective is complete freedom, complete justice, complete equality, by any means necessary.").

286. The most infamous rendering of this view is Chief Justice Taney's opinion in Dred Scott v. Sandford, 60 U.S. (19 How.) 393 (1856). Taney is properly castigated for his historical, legal, and logical errors, but he may have been closer to the mark with his claim that many white Americans did not consider blacks to be full members of the new nation.

287. Du Bois, supra note 32, at 135.

most black Americans came to this country in colonial times, long before the waves of immigration that brought the Irish, the Jews, and Eastern and Southern Europeans to America. African-Americans were present at the creation; their forced labor, ended only by civil war, was a crucial component in the construction of the American economy. Black soldiers have fought and died in every American war—and in recent wars, in disproportionate numbers. Given this history, one would think it reasonable for blacks to be seen as integral to the American story.

But one can be *in* a nation, and still not be *of* that nation. Writing of Jews in France, Jean-Paul Sartre noted that despite years of residence and significant economic and cultural achievements, Jews remain "the unassimilated at the very heart of [French] society":

> [The Jew] accepts the society around him, he joins the game and he conforms to all the ceremonies, dancing with the others the dance of respectability. Besides, he is nobody's slave; he is a free citizen under a regime that allows free competition; he is forbidden no social dignity, no office of the state. He may be decorated with the ribbon of the Legion of Honor, he may become a great lawyer or a cabinet minister. But at the very moment when he reaches the summits of legal society, another society—amorphous, diffused, and omnipresent—appears before him as if in brief flashes of lightning and refuses to take him in. . . . [H]e never encounters any particular resistance; people seem, rather, to be in flight before him; an impalpable chasm widens out, and, above all, an invisible chemistry devaluates all he touches.
>
> . . . .
>
> . . . Everything is accessible to him, and yet he possesses nothing; for, he is told, what one possesses is not to be bought.[288]

As Frantz Fanon has pointed out, the situation of blacks in a white society is analogous, but worse. "[T]he Jew can be unknown in his Jewishness. . . . His actions, his behavior is the final determinant. He is a white man, and . . . can sometimes go unnoticed." But as a black, Fanon is "given no chance": "I am the slave not of the 'idea' that others have of me but of my own appearance."[289]

The claim that one can penetrate to the core and still be an outsider is a statement about culture and about a society's self-conception. It means that even after we end all the forms of physical exclusion (slavery, lynching, Jim Crow, housing, and employment discrimination), and after we discredit all the justifications for subordination (bestiality, genetic inferiority, and cultural depravity), there may still be another kind of exclusion that ultimately makes blacks the "unassimilated at the very

288. Jean-Paul Sartre, Anti-Semite & Jew 83 (G. Becker trans. 1948).
289. F. Fanon, supra note 53, at 115–16.

heart of American society." It is the story that America tells about itself that keeps blacks in the position of outsiders.

The crudest version is that America is a white man's country. While it can hardly be denied that there are white Americans who continue to believe this, I think there is a more genteel version that better describes the complex ways in which this society has included some and excluded others. This version portrays America's story as the immigrant's story. True to our individualistic orientation, the predominant myth America tells about Americans is the story of *those who chose* (because of political, religious, or economic persecution) to come to this country.

One would think that a "nation of immigrants" would be open to a humanitarian pluralism, and therefore expanding the immigrant tale to include all previously excluded groups would be a simple task.[290] But the invitation that the Statue of Liberty holds in her hand does not read "come as you are." It has always been an offer to join us on our terms. The immigrant story is one of assimilation, not multi-culturalism.

African-Americans do not fit either aspect of the immigrant account. The vast majority of those who came to America did not do so voluntarily; they arrived not on immigrant ships, but on slave ships. Nor were blacks thought to be candidates for assimilation. Indeed, when the ingenious American devices for excluding blacks from society are contrasted with the assimilationist welcome accorded immigrants, one can quickly begin to formulate a sensible answer to the question that lies deep in many white minds: why can't blacks do what my immigrant ancestors did?

Racial equality will not be attainable until American myths include

290. Kenneth Karst's book, Belonging to America, can be read in this fashion. K. Karst, Belonging to America: Equal Citizenship and the Constitution (1989). But I think the task is far more difficult than Karst allows.

blacks as full members and equal partners in society.[291] A new set of stories is needed to provide the impetus for self and social re-examination, and to provide the foundation upon which support for race-conscious measures can be based. For example, we might develop an historical narrative not about those who *chose* America, but rather about those who *built* America. This account would be about slaves and free blacks in the South in the nineteenth century and blacks in the twentieth century who migrated to work in Northern factories; about women who worked in the factories and (unnoticed and uncompensated) in the home; and about Chinese laborers who built the railroads, Mexican workers who harvested the crops, and European immigrants who built the great cities of the East. Such a narrative would acknowledge the deep and lasting contributions of African-Americans and other groups usually marginalized in the traditional account and would focus attention on the injustice of continued inequalities founded on racial oppression.[292]

Blacks as blacks have had an unique history in this country. It is a history that whites and blacks confront every day and will continue to confront into the indefinite future. In pretending to ignore race, this society denies itself the self-knowledge that is demanded for eradicating racism and achieving racial justice.

---

291. It will require that Langston Hughes's celebrated poem be a statement of fact, rather than a dream:

I, Too

I, too, sing America
I am the darker brother

They send me to eat in the kitchen
When company comes,
But I laugh,
And eat well,
And grow strong.

Tomorrow,
I'll be the table
When company comes.
Nobody'll dare
Say to me,
"Eat in the kitchen,"
Then.

Besides,
They'll see how beautiful I am
And be ashamed—

I, too, am America.

L. Hughes, Selected Poems 275 (1959).

292. It might be objected that this narrative is also inadequate to the extent that it is based on a set of values (that "building" and "accumulating" are the appropriate measures of worth) not shared by all Americans.

☒ Redistricting of the State Legislature: 1991-1992

The first redistricting of the Mississippi Legislature after the passage of the 1965 Voting Rights Act took 14 years and 7 trips to the United States Supreme Court to complete. The redistricting effort had been a strictly legal battle without the effective participation of the community in whose name the battle was fought.

When the second redistricting process began in the Fall of 1990, the state population was 35 percent African-American, there were only 19 African-Americans in the State House of Representatives out of 122 (approximately 15 percent), and 2 in the State Senate out of 52 (less than 4 percent).

Southern Echo, in collaboration with a number of other organizations and individuals, formed the Mississippi Redistricting Coalition to work with and on behalf of the African-American community in connection with the redistricting of the Mississippi Legislature. At the urging of *Southern Echo* staff members, the Mississippi Redistricting Coalition committed to the systematic involvement of the community in the planning and decision-making process. The goal was to avoid the past experience of years of expensive litigation which left the community out of the process, uninformed and powerless.

Key to the strategy was rooting the decision-making in the grassroots organizations and ensuring that the attorneys agreed not to make policy or settlements without direction and approval from the grassroots community!

This meant that while plans were being developed and negotiated at the legislative level, the grassroots communities across the state would be kept informed and a vehicle created to ensure that community people had an effective voice in the process at every stage.

In the Fall of 1990 the redistricting of the Mississippi Legislature began with a series of public hearings across the state conducted by the Joint Standing Committee on Legislative Reapportionment of the State Legislature. The

Redistricting Coalition, with the assistance of ***Southern Echo*** staff, brought hundreds of community people to these hearings. Through a series of meetings community people came prepared to support a five fundamental points:

1. that any redistricting plan adopted by the Legislature create the maximum number of electable black districts to rectify the history of systematic exclusion of African-Americans from the political process;

2. Since the Joint Committee of 25 legislators had only 3 African-Americans (12 percent), the Committee should be reconstituted to increase the number of African-Americans to reasonably reflect that African-Americans are 35 percent of the population;

3. that the Joint Committee hire African-American demographers on their staff who have experience representing the African-American community in redistricting cases;

4. that the Joint Committee hire as counsel to the Joint Committee African-American attorneys, who have experience representing the African-American community in redistricting cases, to represent and advise the Joint Committee as to its constitutional and legal obligations;

5. that African-American demographers, attorneys, and members of the Legislative Black Caucus working with the grassroots community have access to the same computers and census data in the possession of the State, and to the same computer operators used by the State, to prepare and draw proposed redistricting plans.

For the first time in Mississippi history, the Joint Committee adopted as part of its groundrules, three of the five demands presented by the Redistricting Coalition:

1. Any plan adopted by the Committee would have to create electable black districts wherever possible (Prior to this time, the Joint Committee had not conceded this principle of law.)

2. The Joint Committee retained as one of the counsel to the Committee, former Supreme Court Justice Reuben Anderson, the first African-American to serve on Mississippi's High Court (A majority of the Committee surely thought he would be more accommodating than the civil rights attorneys proposed by the Redistricting Coalition. But Justice Anderson proved to be tough and unyielding in his advice to the Joint Committee on its obligations under the Voting Rights Act); and

3. The Joint Committee authorized a procedure for the public to have effective access to the same computers, computer operators and census data that was to be used by the State in the preparation of proposed redistricting plans.

The Legislature responded to the pressure from the active involvement in the process of the grassroots community!

The three concessions made by the Joint Committee meant that for the first time in Mississippi history the leadership of the Legislature acknowledged that the African-American community had an inherent right to participate in the formation of critically important public policy. This was the direct result of the apprehension caused by the mass turnout of the people at the public hearings and the continuing unity of the Coalition representatives and the Legislative Black Caucus members in the negotiation process.

As a result of the pressure generated by the community at these hearings and subsequent Joint Committee meetings at the Capitol, the three members of the Legislative Black Caucus on the Committee, and other members of Caucus, began to coordinate with the efforts of the Mississippi Redistricting Coalition on behalf of the community. This was a major development because, traditionally, the incumbent black legislators, using the white legislators as a model and with considerable encouragement from the white leadership in the

House and Senate, looked at the redistricting process as an opportunity to tighten up their own districts to ensure their own individual electability.

The Redistricting Coalition presented three principles to members of the Legislative Black Caucus:

1. that the legislative seats belonged to the people, not the incumbents;

2. that the black legislators needed to view all black people in the State as their constituents, not just those who lived within their district lines; and

3. that the Black Caucus had to fight to create electable black districts wherever possible in order to maximize the size of the Black Caucus in order to increase the input from and impact of the African-American community on the formation of public policy.

Many of the black legislators were initially skeptical that the vision of the Redistricting Coalition was viable, or that the community could be mobilized to provide the democratic basis and support to the Caucus in a process that historically had been controlled by the consummate *insiders*, the legislative leadership.

The Legislative Black Caucus also responded to pressure from the active involvement of their constituents in the process!

One factor that won over many of the black legislators was the active involvement of the community in the redistricting process at the county level which state representatives could observe and which resulted from the extensive county-level redistricting workshops described above.

Another factor was the turnout of people at the legislative redistricting hearings and their impact in gaining three major concessions from the Joint Committee in the early stages of the process.

An additional factor was the formation of the Delta Redistricting Working Group, a Coalition of representatives from each of the ten county redistricting committees which were formed in the Delta during the redistricting workshops in the winter of 1991. The Working Group held a series of meetings during 1991, attended by as many as 50 persons from across the Delta. These meetings had two functions:

Sharing information through good communication enables the community to develop skills, knowledge, confidence, unity and organization.

1. The Redistricting Coalition shared knowledge and information about the legislative redistricting process with the delegates from each of the county committees. The delegates, in turn, took that information back to their respective communities to keep people at the local level informed. This network process proved invaluable as a means of raising the consciousness of community people regarding progress in the legislative redistricting process. At the same time, Coalition staff assured the grassroots people that their viewpoints would be shared with the members of the Black Caucus to keep pressure on the Caucus by providing members with the views of their constituents.

2. The delegates from the counties had an opportunity at each meeting to make presentations about county redistricting developments in their respective counties and to obtain feedback from the delegates from other counties about how to deal with the variety of obstacles and problems they were encountering. This cross-fertilization process helped to reduce the sense that people were struggling in isolation, broadened everyone's awareness regarding strategies and tactics, and began to forge the links of an African-American empowerment network that could operate at the state level, without compromising the work at the county level.

This process actually emboldened the Black Caucus members because, historically, the missing ingredient against the most powerful forces in the white community had been the active involvement of the grassroots in the redistricting struggle. **The involvement of the community actually had the effect of empowering the Legislative Black Caucus!**

The Legislative Black Caucus had never come together around a major issue of importance to the African-American community, except for the vote on the adoption of Martin Luther King day. The white leadership was caught off guard by the degree of unity and commitment within the Black Caucus. The white leadership did not anticipate the forging of an alliance between the grassroots, speaking through the Redistricting Coalition, and the Black Caucus. This had never happened before and it had a powerful psychological impact on white legislators and the white community. It provided to the Caucus and the Coalition a powerful hand in the negotiation process.

With the community behind them, the Coalition and the Caucus were able to state in the negotiations that community people had defined the vision and the goals of the negotiation process, and therefore, could not yield these fundamental principles. The theme in negotiations became: *Democracy for the African-American community means creating the maximum number of electable black districts in the legislature!*

Above all, the white community feared the development of *unified, independent black political action.* The white strategy had always been to try to prevent that from happening at all cost. That could lead to real leverage and power in the political process. The white community was accustomed to keeping the black community off-balance with "divide and conquer", "carrot and stick", and massive resistance techniques. The white-dominated legislature had spent millions of dollars over 14 years just to delay the process in the previous redistricting battle. It appeared that the legislature would be prepared once again to spend any amount of money to minimize the ability of African-Americans to have an impact on the formation of public policy.

The legislative redistricting vision was clear: legislative accountability means adopting a redistricting plan which creates the maximum number of electable black districts. The essence of the strategy was simple: *any proposed*

The Legislative Black Caucus realized that it, too, could build strength through unity and unity through organization!

settlement had to have the approval of the grassroots people involved in the process. The commitment to build strength through unity and unity through organization shifted the center of gravity of the redistricting fight away from the legislative "smoke-filled backrooms" into the community for the first time in the history of Mississippi.

Southern Echo staff were part of the negotiating team for the Redistricting Coalition on both the House and Senate teams, and provided legal and technical assistance in support of the negotiation process. ***Southern Echo*** staff, in conjunction with other community organizations, also had primary responsibility in this process for keeping the community informed and to ensure that the white leadership could not trap and back down the negotiating or legal teams representing the African-American community.

A strong base rooted in the community is the best defense against the military strategy to identify, isolate and destroy those who would fight for the needs of the people!

As the Black Caucus and the Coalition became aware of the strength which their unity had created in the process, they also found that weaknesses within the ranks of the white community had developed. The Caucus and Coalition leadership anticipated that any attempt to exploit the divisions within the white community would be met with a furious, broad-based attack on the leadership of the Caucus and the Coalition. Therefore, in order to take advantage of the situation and protect their leaders, the black community would have to remain unified behind a clear vision of what constituted the best interests of the black community.

The split within the ranks of white legislators emerged over the election of the Speaker of the House which would take place shortly after the November, 1991 legislative election. House legislators split into two factions, one supporting the incumbent Speaker and one supporting the representative aspiring to the post. The legislators in the Black Caucus held the balance of power on this issue and both factions sought the support of Caucus members by approaching them as individuals.

A shift in power had occurred: If the Caucus remained sufficiently unified, even if not unanimously so, it had enough votes to retain the balance of power on both the determination of a redistricting plan and the selection of the Speaker of the House and the Speaker Pro-Tempore of the House.

The Caucus, supported by the Coalition, determined that support of a Speaker-candidate should turn on which candidate was willing to support the redistricting goals of the African-American community. Furthermore, the Speaker-candidate should be judged by concrete commitments to change in the status of African-American legislators and other employees in the legislative process.

The faction supporting the challenger for the Speaker's post was a group of primarily young, white legislators who characterized themselves as "progressives". The self-described "progressives" characterized the faction supporting the incumbent Speaker as "conservatives". These labels proved to be meaningless. In a nutshell, the sequence of key events was as follows:

Never Assume! Don't rely on labels! Investigate to find out what you need to know to understand where people are really coming from. You need a clear vision of your long-term and short-term goals to determine whether the policies of others are really in the best interest of the community

In the Spring of 1991, the Joint Committee, dominated by legislators committed to the values of the past, ignored the several plans submitted by the Redistricting Coalition and adopted a plan designed to create the "least change" possible.

In the early summer the Justice Department rejected the plan and a combination of Redistricting Coalition and Black Caucus members brought suit in federal court to vindicate the rights of the African-American community under the 1965 Voting Rights Act, and the 14th and 15 Amendments to the United States Constitution.

The Federal Court refused to enjoin the elections and urged the parties to try to settle the case rather than going through a complex, protracted trial.

For the first time in Mississippi the plaintiffs in the redistricting case were represented entirely by Mississippi lawyers, without the participation of any national civil rights lawyers. This demonstrated that the African-American community in Mississippi had the resources to sustain this kind of fight without dependency on outside organizations. The white legislative leadership did not believe that the legal fight in federal court could be sustained by the black community without the involvement of a national civil rights organization.

In the late summer, 1991, when the federal court refused to enjoin the legislative elections, the Coalition lawyers were dubious about the value of taking an appeal to the United States Supreme Court. The issue was brought back to the community for consideration, where the clear sentiment was to take every step available to show the Legislature that the community was determined and unyielding in its unity and commitment to create the maximum number of electable black districts. Two appeals were taken to the United States Supreme Court as a result of the input of the grassroots people.

This proved to be an important turning point in the relationship with the legislative leadership, who came to understand that they were facing the specter of protracted, expensive litigation again at a time when the white factions were jockeying for support of the Black Caucus in relation to the Speaker's race.

The Black Caucus held the balance of power. It could use its power for community interest or self-interest. In this instance it used its power for the community interest. The community was able to make sure of that because the community was organized!

Both factions conceded that the Caucus had the balance of power and each faction sought support for a plan which provided sufficient advantage to that faction to guarantee victory in the Speaker's race. As a result, each faction appeared willing to agree to a plan which created the maximum number of electable black districts.

Which faction, which plan, which Speaker-candidate should the Black Caucus *support?*

As the negotiations wore on a pattern emerged. On the Senate side, the negotiators for the Joint Committee became intransigent. At one point, the Chair of the Joint Committee, from Washington County in the Delta, stated that he would not preside over the demise of his colleagues in the Delta. Therefore, he would not consider any plan which created a meaningful number of electable black districts in the Delta.

On the House side, the *conservative* faction made significant concessions to the creation of electable black districts where possible. But the *progressive* faction began to seek to *reduce* the number of electable black districts in order to maximize the number of safe districts for the incumbents in their faction. Eventually, the tripartite negotiations between the two factions and the Coalition/Caucus forces fell apart.

The *progressive* faction contended that it was the duty of the black community to subordinate its goal of creating electable black districts to the desire of the *progressive* faction to take power in the Legislature. The *progressive* faction argued that the black community could only achieve its goals if the *progressive* faction took power. The Redistricting Coalition and Black Caucus representatives, with support from the grassroots, absolutely rejected the position of the so-called *progressive* faction.

The Coalition and Caucus representatives made the determination to agree on a plan with the *conservative* faction in the House because that faction did not waiver in its support for the black districts sought by the Coalition and Caucus. The districts configured in this plan may have given an advantage to one white faction over another, but it preserved the goals of the African-American community to create the maximum number of electable black districts.

The white liberals (in the context of Mississippi) in and out of the Legislature exposed their true position: they still saw black people in a fundamentally subordinate, supportive role to white needs, and rejected outright any independent black political vision of progress. Ironically, the so-called conservatives had adopted a very practical approach to the retention of power. They accepted the inevitability of the increase in electable black districts in the House and embraced it.

The outcome of the Speaker's race was still in doubt after the 1991 legislative elections were held. The Black Caucus held the balance of power now that it was proceeding in a largely unified manner. Both factions still sought the support of Caucus members. The Caucus sent representatives to the leadership of each white faction seeking to control the seat of the Speaker to present specific demands.

These demands included the election of the first African-American as Speaker Pro-Tempore of the House of Representatives, the first African-American Clerk of the House, important committee chairs and vice-chairs for African-Americans, including Finance, Judiciary, etc., and significant job security for the predominantly African-American security, maintenance and janitorial staff of the House, who up to that point had no job security at all.

The incumbent Speaker, head of the so-called *conservative* faction, agreed to the demands of the Black Caucus. The challenger for the Speaker's seat, head of the so-called *progressive* faction, rejected all of the demands of the Black Caucus on the grounds that he had already made his commitments on each of these issues and would not change his position.

Most of the Black Caucus members supported the incumbent Speaker, ensuring his victory at the opening of the Legislative session in January, 1992. As a result, the first African-American Speaker Pro-Tempore was elected, significant chairs and co-chairs were awarded to African-American House members, and a job security package was created for the House staff for the first time.

There was a demonstrable shift of power in the House of Representatives. The empowerment process was underway. The black community had access to the system in ways it never had before, and had an opportunity to impact on the formation of public policy unseen in Mississippi since Reconstruction.

Remarkably, white liberals were in a frenzy of recrimination. They accused the Black Caucus leadership of being racist and as having injected racial considerations into the Legislative process where it did not belong. In other words, white liberals were promoting the concept that black community efforts to implement the Voting Rights Act by creating electable black districts wherever possible were *racist*.

This was and continues to be a serious attempt to turn the meaning of racism on its head and intimidate the black community into moderating its efforts to bring real democracy to the process. Racism is about domination, control, exclusion and separation: touchstones of the Mississippi system. It cannot be racist to fight to climb out of the abyss of exclusion and participate effectively in the democratic system on the same basis as any other group in society.

At the beginning of the Legislative session in 1992 the redistricting fight was still not resolved. The Federal Court was pressing the parties to prepare for trial. The House side was settled, as demonstrated by an overwhelming vote in favor of the plan supported by the Black Caucus. But the Senate still would not adopt a plan acceptable to the Caucus, although the vote was much closer than it had been the year before.

Another dramatic turn took place in the Senate, reflecting the material shift in power that resulted from the redistricting fight. A black candidate for Lt. Governor in the 1991 race (former Sen. Henry Kirksey) accomplished his major objective by taking enough votes from the incumbent Lt. Governor (Brad Dye) to enable the challenger (Rep. Eddie Briggs) to win.

In early 1992, the new Lt. Governor asked the attorneys for the Coalition and Caucus what it would take to resolve the redistricting battle on the Senate side, which was bringing a great deal of bad publicity for a State trying to attract new industry. The attorneys made it clear that the grassroots people would not permit a compromise on the creation of the maximum number of electable black districts. But replacing the Chair of the Joint Committee with a Senator committed to settlement might enable an acceptable plan to be agreed upon.

The Lt. Governor accepted the approach recommended by the Coalition/Caucus attorneys. That could not have happened without the perception on the part of the white leadership that the Black Caucus was essentially unified, had obtained a position of power in the legislative process, and was supported by the grassroots community in its goals in the redistricting process.

Within two months an acceptable plan was agreed upon in the Senate. With the House and Senate in agreement on the plan. the federal voting rights litigation could also be brought to conclusion with the adoption of the plan by the three-judge federal panel hearing the case.

The court proceeding was dramatic because it was an historic moment. The past redistricting effort was dominated by the spirit of massive resistance to change. At this proceeding all of the white factions, white public officials, and the two political parties had to represent to the Federal Court that they supported a plan which was acceptable to the Black Caucus and the

Redistricting Coalition. The plan was acceptable to the Caucus and Coalition because it created the maximum number of electable black districts.

In an extraordinary moment of candor, the Court noted that the plan created the maximum number of electable black districts and the members of the federal panel publicly expressed their outrage and dismay that the white legislators and other public officials had agreed to such a plan. In fact, the three white judges indicated from the bench, and later in a written opinion, that they had told the white legislative leadership that this panel would never have adopted such a plan because they did not subscribe to an interpretation of the Voting Rights Act which would require the creation of electable black districts wherever possible.

If the white legislative leadership knew the federal court would not adopt a plan which incorporated the vision of the black community, why did the white legislative leadership and public officials agree to such a plan?

The African-American community, through effective community organizing, had established a solid base within the political framework which could not go unrecognized any longer. The strength generated by the unity and organization of the African-American community, most visibly embodied in the unity within the Black Caucus, and between the Caucus and the Redistricting Coalition, had fractured the political foundation of the white community.

The second redistricting fight, based on community control through effective community organizing, had taken only 1½ years and resulted in a settlement in which the community played a major role in fashioning the redistricting plan. The community avoided years of protracted, expensive litigation during which the organizing work would likely have stalled, and saved the taxpayers of the state, black and white, millions of dollars in expenses and attorney's fees.

The legislative redistricting struggle had demonstrated that an alliance could be created between the members of the Legislative Black Caucus, community organizations, and grassroots people, based on the goal of community empowerment, guided by a standard of accountability for public officials, and rooted in the reality of control and support from the grassroots.

The work of the alliance demonstrated that it could obtain access to the system and an opportunity to impact the formation of public policy that would have been unthinkable 30 years ago when the voting rights movement began in Mississippi.

The adoption of the legislative redistricting plan created 50 electable black districts: 12 in the Senate and 38 in the House. But the Court created a very short timetable for the special election, with the qualification deadline for candidates only 33 days from the date of the court order setting the schedule. This appeared to give an enormous advantage to incumbents who were already aware of the configuration of their new districts, but little time for the community to learn about the new districts, generate accountable candidates, raise money with which to campaign and fashion campaign organizations for all these new districts.

There was no time to spare, but the ***Southern Echo*** staff was ready. The Federal Court Order was issued May 2, 1992. ***Southern Echo*** staff had been preparing since the end of March for the possibility of a court order that would create a short election schedule.

On May 9, 1992, ***Southern Echo*** staff, working under the umbrella of the Mississippi Empowerment Project, a Coalition of community-based organizations committed to the empowerment of the African-American community, held the first of a series of 6 workshops strategically located in every area of concentration of black population.

The primary purpose of these workshops was to share with the people specific information about each of the new legislative districts and to keep the vision of empowerment through accountability at the forefront of the process. The *Legislative Redistricting Manual* prepared by the Mississippi Empowerment Project for the workshops provided each participant with a map of each new electable black district with all of the census data needed by a prospective candidate to analyze the composition of the district.

Armed with solid information, grassroots people could determine:

► the location of their district lines,

► who lived in which districts,

► who might be interested in being a candidate,

► develop a unity process for selecting the candidate most likely to be accountable to the needs and interests of the African-American community,

► make sure candidates filed their papers on or before the qualification deadline,

► and work to unify the community behind one accountable candidate to win the primary and general election.

It is clear that the consciousness of the African-American community had been raised substantially across the entire state by the 1½ year redistricting fight. African-American candidates emerged in every district. Most of them were younger, more activist-oriented than in past election years, and across the state the theme of black candidates was the importance of electing accountable representatives to the legislature who would be responsive to the needs of the community.

Once the candidates qualified, there was an immediate need to ensure that community people had effective knowledge of how to get out the vote, handle the absentee ballot process, and use poll watchers to ensure that the election at the polls is conducted fairly.

Under the umbrella of the Mississippi Empowerment Project, ***Southern Echo*** staff prepared and conducted a residential, 2-day Get Out the Vote school at Tougaloo College in July, 1992. The school was attended by more than 60 African-American community activists representing more than 20 counties.

It is important to note, unfortunately, that the Legislative Election workshops and the Get Out the Vote School were the only efforts of the kind to share with the community the information needed to participate effectively in the democratic election process. No governmental agency, political party, or non-profit organization prepared any material to inform the community about the new districts.. In fact, the Mississippi Democratic Party, several labor unions, the national office of the NAACP, and the Southern Regional Council lauded the manual when they saw it and requested copies either for use during the election process or as models for other states to follow.

The 1992 special legislative election shocked Mississippi. ***African-American candidates won 42 of the 50 electable districts, increasing African-American representation in the State Legislature from 21 in 1991 to 42 in 1993.*** That meant that in 1993 there would be 10 African-Americans in the State Senate and 32 in the State House of Representatives.

The black community had turned out in record numbers. Most of the victories were won in the first primary, which meant the candidate had to obtain more than 50 percent of the vote, regardless of the number of candidates. Traditionally, the black community has a drastically reduced turnout if there is a second primary. But in 1992 the black turnout actually increased in the second primary.

Black candidates swept the Delta, the historic stronghold of massive resistance to effective black participation in the political process. Black candidates in every section of the state defeated white incumbents or experienced white political candidates running in new districts.

Two days after the election, the senior State Senator, 29-year veteran Robert Crook of Sunflower County, and veteran President Pro-Tempore of the Senate, Sen. Ollie Mohamed, of Humphreys County, both from hardcore Delta Senate districts, complained to Secretary of State Dick Molpus that the Secretary had failed in his duty to the white legislators to alert them in advance of the election that there was going to be a record turnout in the black community.

One thing is clear: the community organizers from ***Southern Echo*** and other community organizations, and the incumbent members of the Legislative Black Caucus did *not* get out the record vote all over the state by themselves. The extraordinary voter turnout could only have resulted from the heightened consciousness and enormous grassroots organizational work that was undertaken, guided and implemented at the local level by grassroots people.

What the Coalition and Caucus members did accomplish was to share with the community across the state an exciting, credible vision, combined with an effective strategy for achieving it, to which the people responded. In addition, ***Southern Echo*** staff, working with others, shared with the community at the community level the information and skills which they needed to do the organizing work at the local level. *The people did the rest!* The empowerment process works.

ARTICLES

SHAW V. RENO: A MIRAGE OF GOOD INTENTIONS WITH DEVASTATING RACIAL CONSEQUENCES

A. LEON HIGGINBOTHAM, JR. *
GREGORY A. CLARICK **
MARCELLA DAVID ***

In this Article the authors critically examine the Supreme Court's recent decision in Shaw v. Reno, *which held that a North Carolina minority-majority voting district of "dramatically irregular" shape is subject to strict scrutiny, absent sufficient race-neutral explanations for its boundaries. While the authors assert that such race-conscious redistricting will meet the burdens of strict scrutiny, given the peculiar history of the southern states, they here argue that* Shaw *is fundamentally flawed. They examine the history of political racism in North Carolina leading up to the 1991 redistricting plan. They then examine the Court's misguided presumptions that race-conscious districting plans are akin to political apartheid and segregation, reinforce racial stereotypes, and damage our system of democracy. The authors argue that minority-majority congressional districts—unlike apartheid and segregation—are intended to include racial minorities in the politics from which they were for so long locked out, thereby furthering pluralism in Congress. The authors therefore call on the Court to modify* Shaw *before its misguided reliance on shape and appearance over intent and history results in a rollback of recent political gains by African-Americans, gains which have brought America a step closer to the ideal of a truly representative democracy.*

TABLE OF CONTENTS

* Chief Judge Emeritus, United States Court of Appeals for the Third Circuit (Retired); Of Counsel to Paul, Weiss, Rifkind, Wharton & Garrison; Professor, John F. Kennedy School of Government, Harvard University. B.A., Antioch College, 1949; L.L.B., Yale Law School, 1952.

Judge Higginbotham has been appointed Special Counsel by the Congressional Black Caucus to file *amicus curiae* briefs in the redistricting cases pending in the federal courts of North Carolina, Louisiana, Texas, Georgia, Florida, and South Carolina.

** A.B., Princeton University, 1986; J.D., New York University Law School, 1990; Associate, Paul, Weiss, Rifkind, Wharton & Garrison.

*** B.S., Rensselaer Polytechnic Institute, 1986; J.D., University of Michigan Law School, 1989; Associate, Paul, Weiss, Rifkind, Wharton & Garrison.

BACKGROUND: STATEMENTS OF NORTH CAROLINA PUBLIC OFFICIALS

CONGRESSMAN George White of North Carolina, African-American, farewell speech to the United States Congress, January 29, 1901:

> I want to enter a plea for the colored man, the colored woman, the colored boy, and the colored girl of this country. . . .
>
> . . . .
>
> . . . This, Mr. Chairman, is perhaps the negroes' temporary farewell to the American Congress; but let me say, Phoenix-like he will rise up some day and come again. These parting words are in behalf of an outraged, heart-broken, bruised, and bleeding, but God-fearing people, faithful, industrious, loyal people—rising people, full of potential force.
>
> . . . .
>
> The only apology that I have to make for the earnestness with which I have spoken is that I am pleading for the life, the liberty, the future happiness, and manhood suffrage for one-eighth of the entire population of the United States.[1]

North Carolina Governor Charles Brantley Aycock, December 1903:

> I am proud of my State, moreover, because there we have solved the negro problem. . . . *We have taken him out of politics* and have thereby secured good government under any party and laid foundations for the future development of both races. We have secured peace, and rendered prosperity a certainty.[2]

North Carolina Governor Thomas Walter Bickett, August 23, 1920:

> In North Carolina we have definitely decided that the happiness of both races requires that *white government shall be supreme and unchallenged in our borders*. Power is inseparably linked with responsibility; and when we *deny to the negro any participation in the making of laws*, we saddle upon ourselves a peculiar obligation to protect the negro in his life and property, and to help and encourage him in the pursuit of happiness.[3]

John Parker, upon accepting the 1920 Republican Party nomination for governor of North Carolina:

> I have attended every state convention since 1908 and I have never seen a Negro delegate in any convention that I attended. The Negro as a class does not desire to enter politics. The Republican party of North Carolina does not desire him to do so. *We recognize the fact that he has not yet reached the stage in his development when he can*

---

1. 34 Cong. Rec. 1635, 1638 (1901) (statement of Rep. White).
2. Charles B. Aycock, Speech before the North Carolina Society, Baltimore (Dec. 18, 1903), *in* The North Carolina Experience: An Interpretive and Documentary History 415 (Lindley S. Butler & Alan D. Watson eds., 1984) (emphasis added).
3. Thomas W. Bickett, Message to the General Assembly of 1920, *in* Public Letters and Papers of Thomas Walter Bickett, Governor of North Carolina 1917-1921, at 72 (R.B. House ed. 1923) (emphasis added).

> *share the burdens and responsibilities of government.* This being true, and every intelligent man in North Carolina knows that it is true, the attempt of certain petty Democratic politicians to inject the race issue into every campaign is most reprehensible. I say it deliberately, there is no more dangerous or contemptible enemy of the state than the man who for personal or political advantage will attempt to kindle the flame of racial prejudice or hatred.[4]

Campaign literature of Willis Smith,[5] successful North Carolina candi-

---

4. John Parker, An Address Upon Accepting the Republican Nomination for Governor (Apr. 18, 1920), *quoted in* Richard L. Watson, *The Defeat of Judge Parker: A Study in Pressure Groups and Politics*, 50 Miss. Valley Hist. Rev. 213, 218 (1963) (emphasis added).

Parker, appointed to the U.S. Court of Appeals for the Fourth Circuit in 1925, was nominated by President Hoover on March 21, 1930, for appointment as an associate justice of the United States Supreme Court.

> Walter White, executive secretary of the NAACP, telegraphed Judge Parker on March 26, 1930, inquiring if he had actually made the [above] statement, and if so whether he still held the same views. . . . [H]e apparently did not answer the telegram, and thus the NAACP launched a vigorous campaign against Parker's confirmation. The NAACP was aided by some two hundred Negro newspapers and the National Association of Colored Women. The official protest was filed with the Senate Judiciary Committee, and the senators were bombarded with telephone calls, telegrams, letters, petitions, and visitations . . . .
>
> . . . .
>
> . . . Walter White argued that no one who favored keeping the Negro out of politics, as Parker seemed to have done in 1920, could approach Fourteenth Amendment questions with that 'dispassionate, unprejudiced, and judicial frame of mind which would enable him to render a decision according to the Constitution.'

Id. at 218-19. Parker's nomination was defeated on May 7, 1930 by two votes. *See id.* at 230.

Some years later, as a court of appeals judge in Briggs v. Elliott, 98 F. Supp. 529 (E.D.S.C. 1951), Judge Parker voted to deny the integration of South Carolina schools, reasoning that South Carolina could lawfully offer "separate but equal" schools for that state's white and black schoolchildren. *Id.* at 533-37. He denied plaintiff's assertion that "separate but equal" violated the equal protection guarantee, holding that

> [t]he federal courts would be going far outside their constitutional function were they to attempt to prescribe educational policies for the states in such matters . . . . For the federal courts to do so would result, not only in interference with local affairs by an agency of the federal government, but also in the substitution of the judicial for the legislative process in what is essentially a legislative matter.

Id. at 536. Judge Waring filed a vigorous dissent to Parker's position, writing:

> From [the] testimony, it was clearly apparent, as it should be to any thoughtful person . . . that segregation in education can never produce equality and that it is an evil that must be eradicated. . . . [A]ll of the legal guideposts, expert testimony, common sense and reason point unerringly to the conclusion that the system of segregation in education . . . must go and must go now.
>
> *Segregation is per se inequality.*

Id. at 547-48 (Waring, J., dissenting). In Brown v. Board of Education, 347 U.S. 483 (1954), the Supreme Court overruled Judge Parker's holding.

5. Willis Smith ran against and defeated Dr. Frank Graham, a distinguished educator and former president of the University of North Carolina. *See* Julian M. Pleasants & Augustus M. Burns III, Frank Porter Graham and the 1950 Senate Race in North Caro-

date for United States Senate, 1950:[6]

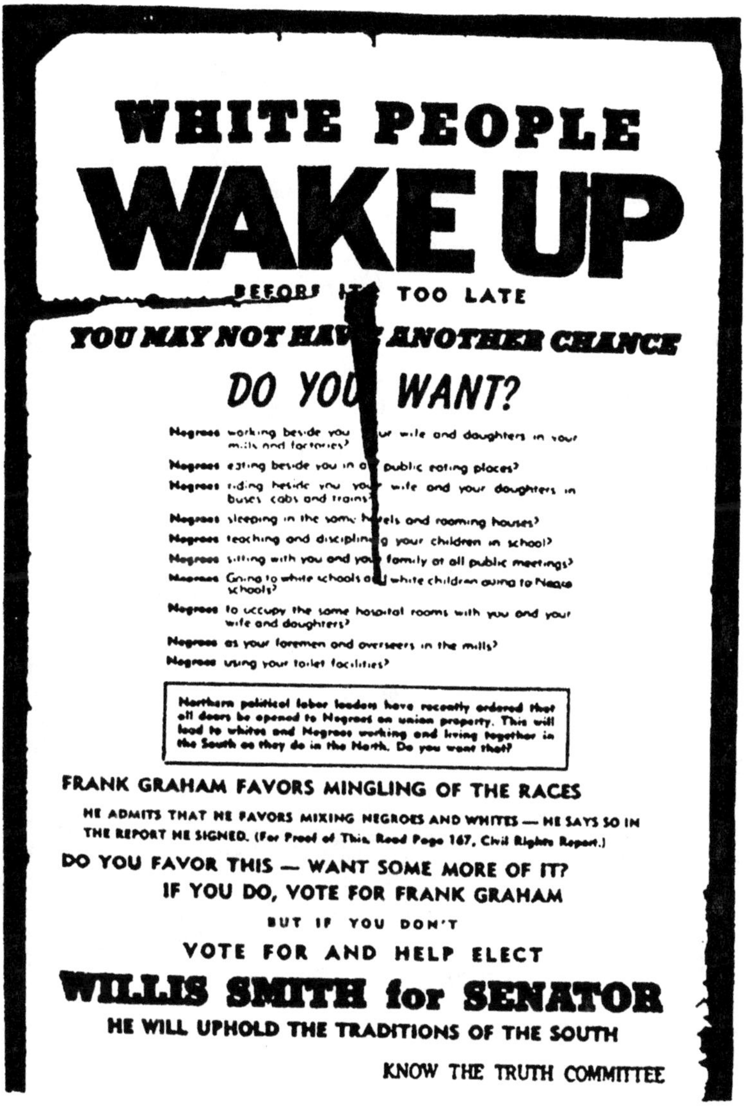

lina (1990); *see also* Samuel Lubell, The Future of American Politics 106-17 (3d ed. 1965). Jesse Helms, who was a campaign worker for Smith, was later elected to the United States Senate, using racist, though more subtle, campaign literature. *See* Kathleen H. Jamieson, Dirty Politics 80 (1992).

6. Campaign literature of Willis Smith, 1950, *reproduced in* Lubell, *supra* note 5, at 109.

The final oppositional campaign ad of North Carolina Senator Jesse Helms, 1990:

> The . . . ad . . . showed the plaid-shirted arms and white hands of a male, a simple gold wedding ring on the third finger of his left hand, opening, presumably reading and then crumpling a rejection letter as the announcer says, 'You needed that job, and you were the best qualified. But they had to give it to a minority because of a racial quota. Is that really fair? Harvey Gantt says it is. Gantt supports Ted Kennedy's racial quota law that makes the color of your skin more important than your qualifications. You'll vote on this issue next Tuesday. For racial quotas: Harvey Gantt. Against racial quotas: Jesse Helms.'[7]

Excerpts from the United States Supreme Court majority opinion in *Shaw v. Reno*,[8] written by Justice Sandra Day O'Connor, 1993:

> Put differently, we believe that reapportionment is one area in which appearances do matter. A reapportionment plan that includes in one district individuals who belong to the same race, but who are otherwise widely separated by geographical and political boundaries, and who may have little in common with one another but the color of their skin, bears an uncomfortable resemblance to *political apartheid*. . . .[9]
>
> . . . .
>
> . . . [A]ppellants have stated a claim under the Equal Protection Clause by alleging that the North Carolina General Assembly adopted a reapportionment scheme so irrational on its face that it can be understood only as an effort to *segregate* voters into separate voting districts because of their race, and that the separation lacks sufficient justification. . . . Accordingly, we reverse the judgment of the District Court and remand the case for further proceedings consistent with this opinion.[10]

I. From Darkness to a New Dawn?

From 1901 to 1992, the one constant in North Carolina congressional politics was the triumph of white supremacy. For that state's African-Americans, these were nine decades of exclusion (or absence) from the United States Congress.[11] Similarly, for all of these years, African-Americans were absent from the congressional delegations of Alabama, Florida, South Carolina, and Virginia.[12]

When in 1992, North Carolinians elected Eva Clayton and Mel Watt, two African-Americans, to the House of Representatives of the United

7. Jamieson, *supra* note 5, at 97 (quoting campaign advertisement of Jesse Helms).
8. 113 S. Ct. 2816 (1993).
9. *Id.* at 2827 (emphasis added).
10. *Id.* at 2832 (emphasis added).
11. *See* African-Americans in the U.S. Congress, 1870-1993, *infra* app. A.
12. *See id.* African-Americans were absent from the congressional delegations of Louisiana until 1991, of Mississippi until 1987, of Tennessee until 1975, and of Georgia and Texas until 1973. *See id.*

States Congress, many Americans—black and white—were ecstatic, believing they were experiencing a new dawn in American congressional racial politics.[13] Not since 1901 had an African-American represented North Carolina in Congress, despite the candidacy of numerous, qualified black individuals and the fact that more than 20% of North Carolinians are and were African-American.[14] Absent representation, throughout this period, the rights of North Carolina's African-Americans were stripped and their interests ignored; for decades, North Carolina politics were marred by the forcible exclusion of African-Americans from the political process,[15] by race-baiting[16] and by extreme racial polarization at the polls,[17] in short, by the marginalization of the political power and interests of African-Americans.

The 1991 North Carolina congressional redistricting[18] was a significant step toward correcting these past injustices. Pursuant to that enactment, in two of North Carolina's twelve congressional districts, African-Americans comprise a slight majority—approximately 53%—of eligible voters.[19] In the 1992 congressional election, voters in those two districts chose African-American representatives, Eva Clayton and Mel Watt, two veterans of North Carolina politics, highly regarded by their constituents and congressional peers.

Notwithstanding these representatives' service, a suit, *Shaw v. Barr*,[20] was brought by two white Duke University law professors and local voters,[21] challenging the pluralism occurring in North Carolina's congressional delegation. These plaintiffs have sought to invalidate the 1991 redistricting which enabled Representatives Clayton and Watt to take office, claiming that the redistricting violates the Equal Protection

---

13. *See, e.g.*, Steve Berg, *Court Will Get Case of 'Racial Gerrymandering,'* Star Tribune, Mar. 27, 1994, at 1A; Affidavit of Representative Mel Watt, ¶ 2 (sworn to Mar. 23, 1994) (submitted as evidence in Shaw v. Hunt, 92-202-CIV-5-BR (E.D.N.C.)).

14. *See* African-Americans in the U.S. Congress, 1870-1993, *infra* app. A; Shaw v. Reno, 113 S. Ct. 2816, 2820 (1993) (20% of North Carolina's voting population is African-American); *infra* notes 110-23 and accompanying text (discussing electoral difficulties faced by black candidates).

15. *See infra* notes 64-96 and accompanying text.

16. *See infra* notes 99-109, 120-25 and accompanying text.

17. *See infra* notes 110-26 and accompanying text.

18. 1991 N.C. Extra Sess. Laws, Ch. 7.

19. *See* Southern U.S. Congressional Districts by Party and Black Vote, 103rd Congress, First Session, *infra* app. B. The First and Twelfth Districts (like other similar districts) are commonly referred to as "minority-majority districts" because, in these, minorities comprise the majority of voters.

20. Shaw v. Barr, 808 F. Supp. 461 (E.D.N.C. 1992), *rev'd sub nom.* Shaw v. Reno, 113 S. Ct. 2816 (1993).

21. Professors Robinson O. Everett (lead counsel) and Melvin G. Shimm (plaintiff) teach at Duke University School of Law, where this year there is only one African-American on the school's full-time faculty. Their colleague, Professor Jerome McCristal Culp, Jr., has written often about his lonely experience at that school. *See, e.g.*, Jerome M. Culp, Jr., *Autobiography and Legal Scholarship and Teaching: Finding the Me in the Legal Academy*, 77 Va. L. Rev. 539 (1991).

Clause.[22] Plaintiffs have focused their attack on the Twelfth District's shape, contending that its untraditional configuration renders it constitutionally infirm.[23]

Initially, a three-judge district court panel dismissed the case. The district court majority held that plaintiffs failed to state a claim as they failed to allege (and could not prove) discriminatory intent, a prerequisite to an equal protection claim:

> Simply put, . . . the plaintiffs here have not alleged—nor could they prove under the circumstances properly before us on this record—an essential element of their equal protection (and parallel Fifteenth Amendment) claim: that the redistricting plan was adopted with the purpose and effect of discriminating against white voters such as plaintiffs on account of their race. The requisite intent, for equal protection and Fifteenth Amendment purposes, is a legislative intent to deprive white voters, including plaintiffs, of an equal opportunity with all other racial groups of voters—on a statewide basis—to participate in the political process and to elect candidates of their choice.[24]

The three-judge panel further held that plaintiffs could not prove constitutional injury:

> The plan demonstrably will not lead to proportional underrepresentation of white voters on a statewide basis. Within the specifically challenged districts . . . the mere fact that white voters (assuming the sad continuation for yet another season of racial bloc voting) will elect fewer candidates of their choice than if they were in white-majority districts is not a cognizable constitutional abridgement of their right to vote, and the two plaintiffs who alone are registered to vote in one of the challenged districts, the Twelfth, will suffer no cognizable constitutional injury if her or his particular candidate should lose by virtue of the district's racial composition.[25]

The court concluded by recognizing that "questions about the political and social wisdom of the North Carolina congressional redistricting plan's creation of two tortuously configured black-majority districts . . . are in the end political ones."[26]

Plaintiffs' assault on racial pluralism, however, was resuscitated on appeal. The Supreme Court reversed the district panel, stating that "ap-

---

22. *See Barr*, 808 F. Supp. at 467-68.

23. *See id.* A prior challenge brought by the Republican Party of North Carolina, objecting to the district as a political gerrymander, was dismissed. *See* Pope v. Blue, 809 F. Supp. 392, 395 (W.D.N.C.), *aff'd*, 113 S. Ct. 30 (1992). The *Barr* court described District Twelve as "a thin band, sometimes no wider than Interstate Highway 85, some 160 miles long, snaking diagonally across piedmont North Carolina . . . ." *Barr*, 808 F. Supp. at 464. The plan divides precincts, counties, and towns. *See id.* A map of the Twelfth District is appended to the Supreme Court majority opinion. *See Shaw*, 113 S. Ct. at 2833.

24. *Barr*, 808 F. Supp. at 472 (citations omitted).

25. *Id.* at 473 (citation omitted).

26. *Id.*

pearances do matter,"[27] and questioning race-conscious districting that results in bizarre districts such as North Carolina's Twelfth District.[28] The Court held that such "dramatically irregular" districts[29] are subject to strict scrutiny, absent sufficient race-neutral explanations for their boundaries.[30] Under strict scrutiny, such districts would be upheld only where they are narrowly tailored to serve a compelling state interest.[31]

To support its conclusion, the Court identified three potential "harms" that might result from "dramatically irregular" districting plans: the "uncomfortable resemblance to political apartheid," the reinforcement of racial stereotypes, and possible damage to "our representati[onal] democracy" that might result from politicians' assuming that they represent the interests of only one race.[32]

Implicitly equating racial classification with racial discrimination, the Court's "harm" analysis abandoned settled principles of equal protection law.[33] Yet the distinction between classification and discrimination underlies all cases considered by the Court since its decision in *Regents of the University of California v. Bakke*[34] addressing state attempts to remedy past racial discrimination. Indeed, the *Shaw* Court tacitly acknowledged the significance of the distinction by stressing that "[t]his court never has held that race-conscious state decisionmaking is impermissible in *all* circumstances."[35] The internal tension between the Court's "harm" analysis and its recognition that race-conscious remedial legislation can be justified and legal was left unresolved.[36]

This tension was created because the Court abandoned the requirement of proving direct constitutional injury—here voter dilution.[37] The concept of voter dilution is well established:

27. Shaw v. Reno, 113 S. Ct. 2816, 2827 (1993).

28. *See id.* at 2832.

29. *Id.* at 2820.

30. *See id.* at 2832.

31. *See id.*

32. *See id.* at 2827. Proceeding in the context of an appeal from the grant of 12(b)(6) dismissal, the Court did not find such harms, but rather posited their potential existence.

33. *See The Supreme Court, 1992 Term—Leading Cases*, 107 Harv. L. Rev. 144, 199-204 (1993) ("[T]hese . . . analytical moves enabled the Court to substitute an ideal of color-blindness for the anti-discrimination principle at the core of the Equal Protection Clause.") (citations omitted).

34. *See* Regents of the Univ. of Cal. v. Bakke, 438 U.S. 265 (1978) (race-conscious admissions not based on set racial quotas are constitutionally permissible).

35. *Shaw*, 113 S. Ct. at 2824. The classification/discrimination distinction had been maintained in a variety of circumstances. For example, in Metro Broadcasting, Inc. v. FCC, 497 U.S. 547, 566 (1990), the Court found permissible racial classifications intended to promote diversity and remedy past discriminatory practices. *See also* Laurence H. Tribe, American Constitutional Law 1577-85 (2d ed. 1988) (discussing circumstances in which the Supreme Court has appropriately upheld gender distinctions).

36. Revealingly, the Court describes the notion of a "color-blind" constitution as an "ideal." *Shaw*, 113 S. Ct. at 2824. In trying to accomplish that ideal, the Court had previously sanctioned race-conscious remedies. *See Bakke*, 438 U.S. at 320.

37. *See Shaw*, 113 S. Ct. at 2824. The plaintiffs' failure to allege dilution was key to the district court panel's dismissal of the action. *See* Shaw v. Barr, 808 F. Supp. 461, 473

> The essence of racial vote dilution . . . is this: that primarily because of the interaction of . . . racial polarization . . . with a challenged electoral mechanism, a racial minority with distinctive group interests . . . is effectively denied the political power to further those interests that numbers alone would presumptively give it in a voting constituency not racially polarized.[38]

Yet the Court here specifically noted that the plaintiffs failed even to allege voter dilution:

> [A]ppellants did not claim that the General Assembly's reapportionment plan unconstitutionally 'diluted' white voting strength. Rather, appellants' complaint alleged that the deliberate segregation of voters into separate districts on the basis of race violated their constitutional right to participate in a 'color-blind' electoral process.[39]

The theoretical right to "participate in a 'color-blind' electoral process," never before recognized by the Court, was accepted as a substitute for the direct injury of voter dilution.[40] But what sets lawful classifications apart from outright discrimination is the fact that discrimination injures those adversely classified.[41]

Absent injury—and the Supreme Court accepts there was no voter dilution here—the classification should be lawful. The *Shaw* Court's abandonment of the touchstones of discriminatory harm and purpose in

(E.D.N.C. 1992), *rev'd sub nom.* Shaw v. Reno, 113 S. Ct. 2816 (1993), discussed *supra* notes 20-26 and accompanying text.

38. Gingles v. Edmisten, 590 F. Supp. 345, 355 (E.D.N.C. 1984) (citations omitted), *modified sub nom.* Thornburg v. Gingles, 478 U.S. 30 (1986).

39. *Shaw*, 113 S. Ct. at 2824.

40. *Id.* The majority states that racial classifications " 'are by their very nature odious to a free people whose institutions are founded upon the doctrine of equality.' " *Id.* (quoting Hirabayashi v. United States, 320 U.S. 81, 100 (1943)). However, the very cases relied upon by the majority in support of permitting a claim to proceed *without* allegations of direct harm were cases in which *extreme* harm was alleged by plaintiffs. *See, e.g.*, *Hirabayashi*, 320 U.S. at 86-88 (loss of liberty and property through wartime internment of Japanese American citizens); Loving v. Virginia, 388 U.S. 1 (1967) (denial of right to marry across racial lines).

41. For example, it was the allegations of direct constitutional injury which gave white plaintiffs standing to raise "reverse" discrimination claims in Wygant v. Jackson Bd. of Educ., 476 U.S. 267 (1986) (white teachers laid off before black teachers with less seniority raised valid equal protection claim); *see also Shaw*, 113 S. Ct. at 2845-49 (Souter, J., dissenting) (criticizing majority's abandonment of traditional injury requirement and discussing cases).

In addition, under the Court's analysis, plaintiffs need not show discriminatory purpose. Since deciding Washington v. Davis, 426 U.S. 229 (1976), however, the Court has required plaintiffs alleging indirect harms—there, adverse impact—to allege discriminatory purpose. *See, e.g.*, Village of Arlington Heights v. Metropolitan Housing Dev. Corp., 429 U.S. 252, 270 n.21 (1977) (challenge to village rezoning plan adversely impacting black residents required proof of discriminatory intent); Hunter v. Underwood, 471 U.S. 222, 227-28 (1985) (challenge to criminal provision which resulted in disproportionate numbers of black convictions required proof that statute was enacted with that purpose); McClesky v. Kemp, 481 U.S. 279, 298 (1987) (challenge to death penalty statute's disproportionate impact on black defendents required proof that statute was enacted "*because of* an anticipated racially discriminatory effect").

voting rights cases where a congressional district's shape does not comport with some obscure notion of regularity lacks any principled basis under its equal protection precedent.[42]

With plaintiffs' urging, the Court has created law that could make *Shaw v. Reno* equivalent for the civil rights jurisprudence of our generation to what *Plessy v. Ferguson*[43] and *Dred Scott v. Sandford*[44] were for prior generations. In the specific context of voting-rights jurisprudence, the Court has made it possible that North Carolina's (and other states' as well) congressional representation might once again become lily white by providing the basis for invalidating all minority-majority districts.[45] Many districts will fail through the difficulty of applying strict scrutiny. For example, one court's application of the narrowly tailored standard to minority-majority districting has proved fatal to a districting plan. *Hays v. Louisiana*,[46] the first case to apply strict scrutiny to minority-majority districts, held that a black voting population of 63% was in excess of that "adequate to ensure that blacks could elect a candidate of their choice."[47] The guidance provided by that court was that a percentage of "55%—and *probably less*" would be adequate.[48] We fear that the Supreme Court, faced with the unworkable application of an inappropriate standard, will next move to invalidate *all* minority-majority

42. Moreover, the Court recognized that traditional principles of compactness and contiguity in congressional districting *are not* constitutionally required. *See Shaw*, 113 S. Ct. at 2827. Justice Souter aptly pointed out that, because these are not constitutionally required, "their absence cannot justify the distinct constitutional regime put in place by the Court today." *Id.* at 2849 (Souter, J., dissenting). Indeed, Congress itself has considered and rejected compactness requirements several times since 1929, when the last apportionment statute requiring compactness, the 1911 Apportionment Act, expired. *See* Wood v. Broom, 287 U.S. 1, 6-8 (1932) (citing congressional debate concerning compactness requirement); *see also* H.R. 970, 89th Cong., 1st Sess. (1965); H.R. 2349, 97th Cong., 1st Sess. (1981). Congress has consistently determined that effective representation of a district is not dependent upon the shape of the district.

There is no reasoned basis for concluding that politically similar but geographically diverse voters cannot be adequately represented in Congress by the same representative. Indeed, our national government is based on the opposite assumption. National legislators typically campaign on issues transcending local political boundaries. For example, Congressman Watt's campaign was pro-labor and pro-urban development. Presidential and senatorial candidates are elected by widely dispersed coalitions responding to common issues and concerns such as health care and fiscal responsibility.

43. 163 U.S. 537 (1896) (determining that "separate but equal" treatment of African-Americans is lawful).

44. 60 U.S. (19 How.) 393, 404-05, 407 (1856) (determining that blacks, as "a subordinate and inferior class" of beings, had no rights of citizenship and noting that "at the time of the Declaration of Independence, and when the Constitution of the United States was framed and adopted . . . . [blacks] had no rights which the white man was bound to respect. . . .").

45. Again, the term "minority-majority" refers to districts—like North Carolina's First and Twelfth Districts—where racial minorities comprise the majority of voters.

46. 839 F. Supp. 1188 (W.D. La. 1993).

47. *Id.* at 1206-08.

48. *Id.* (emphasis added). *Cf.* Gingles v. Edmisten, 590 F. Supp. 345, 358 n.21 (E.D.N.C. 1984) (discussing testimony that 60% or 65% minority voting-majority is required), *modified sub nom.* Thornburg v. Gingles, 478 U.S. 30 (1986).

districts.[49]

Accordingly, we believe that *Shaw* is one of the most important civil rights cases decided by the United States Supreme Court since *Brown v. Board of Education*[50] and *Baker v. Carr.*[51] While the majority opinion undoubtedly was written with good intentions, unwittingly it has created the potential for devastating racial consequences.[52]

In this Article, we analyze *Shaw v. Reno* to determine whether it was "wrongly decided."[53] We evaluate the potential adverse political consequences of *Shaw* and whether it could lead to the significant diminution throughout the South of recent gains by African-Americans in Congress.[54] In our analysis, we focus on the *Shaw* case itself and on North Carolina's history of political oppression of African-American citizens, both because *Shaw* arose in North Carolina and because that state is a fair proxy (and even a beneficent one) for the histories of other southern states. In light of that history and for the good of the American democratic ideal, the standards set by this "wrongly-decided" decision must be modified and its application in North Carolina and other states must be strictly limited.

History illuminates the flaws of the Supreme Court's decision, in particular the Court's purported reliance on doctrines of oppression. In *Shaw*, the Supreme Court for the first time used the term "political

---

49. As Professors Aleinikoff and Issacharoff note:

> So we are left with an unsatisfactory theory that yields an unsatisfactory standard for its implementation. *Shaw* does not adequately instruct lower courts as to how they should review subsequent claims, it does not resolve the ongoing claims of the filler people, and it does not answer the more troubling questions that lie close to the heart of any system of districting.

T. Alexander Aleinikoff & Samuel Issacharoff, *Race And Redistricting: Drawing Constitutional Lines After* Shaw v. Reno, 92 Mich. L. Rev. 588, 651 (1993).

50. 347 U.S. 483 (1954) (rejecting "separate but equal" in context of public schools), *supplemented by* 349 U.S. 294 (1955).

51. 369 U.S. 186 (1962) (stating that representatives must be fairly apportioned across the population).

52. *Shaw* has created a cottage industry for its critics. *See, e.g.*, Richard H. Pildes & Richard G. Niemi, *Expressive Harms, "Bizarre Districts," and Voting Rights: Evaluating Election-District Appearances After* Shaw v. Reno, 92 Mich. L. Rev. 483, 485 (1993) ("*Shaw* will not only constrain the districting process constitutionally but, through its radiating effects on statutory interpretation, may reshape the districting process at its core."); Aleinikoff & Issacharoff, *supra* note 49, at 650 ("At the end of the day, *Shaw* remains an enigmatic decision . . . .").

53. In Fullilove v. Klutznick, 448 U.S. 448, 522 (1980), Justice Rehnquist joined Justice Stewart's view that "*Plessy v. Ferguson* was wrong" when decided. This view has been endorsed by two members of the *Shaw* majority. *See* Planned Parenthood of Southeastern Pa. v. Casey, 112 S. Ct. 2791, 2813 (1992) ("[W]e think *Plessy* was wrong the day it was decided."). We submit that *Shaw* was similarly wrong when decided, and must be promptly modified.

54. Notably, elections in the past few years have nearly doubled the number of African-American members of Congress. *See* African-Americans in the U.S. Congress, 1870-1993, *infra* app. A; Congressional Representation (House and Senate), 1871-1993, *infra* app. C.

apartheid."[55] Yet the Court's comparison of North Carolina's voting districts to political apartheid is based on a profound misperception of apartheid and of those districts.[56] The *Shaw* majority's concern that minority-majority districts will polarize the nation and work to the detriment of African-Americans is unfounded. In congressional districts throughout America, white congressmen represent the majority of African-Americans without unduly polarizing the nation.[57] Enabling African-American congressmen to represent some African-Americans—as well as whites in their districts—does not raise concerns different from those raised by white congressmen representing blacks and is not, as the Supreme Court hints, political apartheid.[58]

Nor does minority-majority districting perpetuate stereotyping, or foster segregation. Rather, it is a modest policy of inclusion appropriately considered by the North Carolina legislature.

Designed so that North Carolina Governor Aycock's promise to take the Negro "out of politics"[59] and North Carolina Governor Bickett's plan that "white government shall be supreme and unchallenged"[60] would not return, there is compelling justification for the creation of North Carolina's challenged districts. Under any scrutiny, the flaws in *Shaw* limit its value, yet, even under the strict scrutiny that *Shaw* appears to require, North Carolina's 1991 redistricting, which serves to remedy the ills of lingering historic discrimination, is constitutionally sound.

II. "A Page of History"—1896-1945

In *Shaw v. Reno*,[61] the Supreme Court held that race-conscious redistricting is lawful if "narrowly tailored to further a compelling govern-

55. *Shaw*, 113 S. Ct. at 2827.

56. As did the dissenters, we submit that "it strains credulity to suggest that North Carolina's purpose in creating a second majority-minority district was to discriminate against members of the majority group by 'impair[ing] or burden[ing their] opportunity . . . to participate in the political process.' " *Id.* at 2838 (White, J., dissenting and quoting the majority) (alteration in original).

57. Approximately 8.66 million, or 42.5%, of the country's 20.38 million voting age blacks are represented by African-American congresspersons. *See* David A. Bositis, Joint Center for Pol. & Econ. Stud., The Congressional Black Caucus in the 103rd Congress, tbl. 16 (1993) (for number of black voters) (copy on file with the *Fordham Law Review*); U.S. Dep't of Commerce, 1990 Census Population and Housing Profile: Congressional Districts of the 103rd Congress (Census Doc. No. 1990 CPH-L-117), tbl. 2 (for number of black voters in minority-majority districts) (copy on file with the *Fordham Law Review*).

58. We agree with Justice Blackmun:

> It is particularly ironic that the case in which today's majority chooses to abandon settled law and to recognize for the first time this 'analytically-distinct' constitutional claim, . . . is a challenge by white voters to the plan under which North Carolina has sent black representatives to Congress for the first time since Reconstruction.

Shaw, 113 S. Ct. 2843 (Blackmun, J., dissenting).

59. *Supra* note 2 and accompanying text.

60. *Supra* note 3 and accompanying text.

61. 113 S. Ct. 2816 (1993).

mental interest."[62] The phrases "race conscious," "narrowly tailored," and "compelling governmental interest" do not have the specificity of scientific description. The only way to wisely evaluate minority-majority districting plans in light of these specific terms is to view them in proper historical perspective, applying the maxim of Justice Oliver Wendell Holmes: "a page of history is worth a volume of logic."[63]

The redistricting plan at issue in *Shaw v. Reno*, for example, is permissible in view of the historic circumstances of North Carolina's extensive legitimization of racism in every sphere of public and private life during the post-Reconstruction era. The North Carolina plan is justified by the State-imposed racism—imbedded in the laws of North Carolina regulating housing, marriage, employment, public conduct and indeed every facet of life—that was reinforced and exacerbated by the private and public use of fraud and violence to deter African-Americans in North Carolina from voting.[64]

In fact, the very housing patterns that define the shape of the challenged districts emerged as a product of North Carolina's history. To avoid white disapprobation and violence even when not state imposed, African-Americans in North Carolina conducted their lives and settled in communities where it was thought they would minimize physical hostility by whites and maximize the few economic options permitted by racially discriminatory hiring practices. Accordingly, the dispersal of blacks throughout North Carolina demands a district shape different from that which would protect the interests of white voters. Otherwise, black voters will once again be penalized by North Carolina law and culture, which forced them to live in distinct communities where most black North Carolinians continue to reside.[65] In short, North Carolina and white North Carolinians caused the "circumstances" that now make constitutionally permissible the relatively modest race consciousness of the 1991 redistricting legislation.

The post-Reconstruction era of racial suppression in North Carolina began with the "White Supremacy Campaign" of 1898. Professor

62. *Id.* at 2824, 2832.

63. New York Trust Co. v. Eisner, 256 U.S. 345, 349 (1921).

64. A list of North Carolina's numerous, patently racist statutes is on file with the *Fordham Law Review*.

65. In Louisiana, a snake-like district that follows the riverbeds was recently invalidated. *See* Hays v. Louisiana, 839 F. Supp. 1188, 1199-1200 (W.D. La. 1993). Amazingly, the court ignored the historical significance of the district's economic base: "[c]otton and soybean plantations, centers of petrochemical production, urban manufacturing complexes, timberlands, saw mills and paper mills, river barge depots and rice and sugar cane fields." *Id.* These "segments" of the state economy, viewed by the *Hays* court as diverse, have the acknowledged commonality of disadvantage. *Id.* at 1203 n.48 ("At this momemt in history black people in the South (and generally in America) are—on average—poorer and less well-educated than their white counterparts. Moreover, blacks in largely segregated communities are probably poorer—on the average—than blacks in more integrated communities.").

Prather's description of the violence and intimidation of the 1898 election, at the hands of racist "Red-Shirts," is instructive:

> [C]rowds of Red-Shirts were waiting for Governor Russell at Laurinburg on his return from voting in Wilmington. Anticipating that some violence would be inflicted upon him, the train conductor suggested that he ride in the baggage car to avoid personal injury, and the Governor obligingly took a prepared seat among the baggage. When the train stopped at Laurinburg, it was surrounded and boarded by Red-Shirts, shouting: 'Where is Russell?' 'Where is the Governor?' 'Bring him out!' Those outbursts were accompanied by all sorts of vulgar language. There were rumors of threats to assassinate Governor Russell, and a race riot in the state appeared imminent. It was pathetic, indeed, to see a chief executive of a state subjected to such crass humiliation. This incident not only made a mockery out of the two-party tradition, but the democratic process as well.[66]

That the Republican governor was so intimidated by race-mongers that he hid in a baggage car so that his fellow white citizens would not assassinate him serves only to underscore the legitimacy of the fear felt by African-Americans were they, against the wishes of the white community, either to exercise their franchise rights or to move into white residential areas.

The Red-Shirts' tactics of violence and intimidation dominated the election of 1898, when "armed with Winchester rifles and shotguns. . . . [t]hey stalked about, frightening Republicans, Fusionists, and blacks away from the polls."[67] Two years later, volatile elections again rocked North Carolina and resulted in passage of legislation disenfranchising African-Americans with the use of literacy tests and poll taxes:

> As in 1898, Red-Shirts with all types of guns could be seen throughout the Black Belt loitering around the polls in riotous manner. To avoid violence, blacks as a body just did not vote. The elections were most gratifying to the Democrats. Aycock won the governorship against his Republican rival, Adams, by a decisive vote of 186,650 to 126,296, the largest majority ever given a gubernatorial candidate. Likewise, the [disenfranchisement] amendment was carried. To win the election, intimidation, physical terror, 'fraud and rascality have reigned supreme,' complained Senator Butler.[68]

After Governor Aycock was inaugurated, he made clear that the state's primary governmental obligation was to disenfranchise the Negro to assure white supremacy. The implementation of the Aycock disenfranchisement scheme in 1900 incorporated all means possible to defeat George White, the last African-American from North Carolina to serve

66. H. Leon Prather, Sr., *The Red Shirt Movement in North Carolina 1898-1900*, 62 J. Negro Hist. 174, 179 (1977) (citation omitted).

67. *Id.*

68. *Id.* at 182.

in the United States Congress until Eva Clayton and Mel Watt were elected in November 1992.

Congressman White's defeat was part of a pervasive conspiracy throughout the southern United States to keep the colored man "in his place" and to destroy his "manhood-suffrage."[69] White's defeat symbolized the use of governmental, vigilante and other forces that denied the African-American what he had pleaded for: "the same chance for existence."[70]

Governor Aycock of North Carolina was determined, at all costs, to deny blacks first class citizenship and to preclude them from the right to participate in the governmental process. In December 1903, Aycock spoke before the North Carolina Society of Baltimore and proclaimed:

> I am inclined to give to you our solution of this problem. It is, first, as far as possible under the Fifteenth Amendment *to disfranchise him*; after that let him alone, quit writing about him; quit talking about him, . . . Let the negro learn once for all that there is unending separation of the races . . . that they cannot intermingle; let the white man determine that no man shall by act or thought or speech cross this line, and the race problem will be at an end.[71]

Governor Aycock set the tone for his successors. Several years later, Governor Locke Craig described and supported a proposed amendment to the North Carolina Constitution under which "the white men of North Carolina shall make and administer *all* the laws."[72] And, in his presentation to the all white legislature of 1920, Governor Thomas W. Bickett said:

---

69. 34 Cong. Rec. 1635-38 (1901).

70. *Id.* at 1638.

71. Aycock, *supra* note 2, at 415 (emphasis added). Governor Aycock stressed his supposed "regard" for African-Americans:

> These things are not said in enmity to the negro but in regard for him. He constitutes one third of the population of my State: he has always been my personal friend; as a lawyer I have often defended him, and as Governor I have frequently protected him. But there flows in my veins the blood of the dominant race; that race that has conquered the earth and seeks out the mysteries of the heights and depths. If manifest destiny leads to the seizure of Panama, it is certain that it likewise leads to the dominance of the Caucasian. When the negro recognizes this fact we shall have peace and good will between the races.

Id.

72. Locke Craig, Campaign Speech on the Suffrage Amendment, *in* Memoirs and Speeches of Locke Craig: Governor of North Carolina, 1913-1917, at 34 (May F. Jones ed., 1923) (emphasis added). He further explained:

> This one section will wipe out the negro vote in North Carolina. Of the 120,000 negro voters it will disfranchise 110,000 of them, practically all of them. It will be good-bye to all negro office holders, and all those who base their hope of office on the negro vote. . . . There is only one kind of a white man in North Carolina that will be disfranchised, and that is the white man who . . . denies his race and his color . . . and swears that he is a negro or the son of a negro, or the grandson of a negro, and that white man will be disfranchised.

Id. at 36-38.

> Candor and my deep friendship for and my abiding interest in the permanent happiness of the negro race compel me to add that it is the settled conviction of the best people in all political parties in the South that it is necessary for the protection, the progress and the happiness of both races *for the government to be run by white people, and it is the unalterable determination of the whites to keep in their own hands the reins of government.*[73]

Some public officials in other states were even less subtle than North Carolina governors in declaring their hatred of the colored man, willfully manipulating the political process to exclude blacks from voting. Judge Chrisman of Lincoln County, Mississippi, for example, described his state's experience to its constitutional convention in 1890:

> Sir, it is no secret that there has not been a full vote and a fair count in Mississippi since 1875—that we have been preserving the ascendancy of the white people by revolutionary methods. In plain words, we have been stuffing ballot boxes, permitting perjury and here and there in the State carrying the elections by fraud and violence until the whole machinery for elections was about to rot down.[74]

The explicit racism in government spanned from almost every southern state public official to, at times, the White House. As an example, in 1896 President Grover Cleveland, distraught about a false rumor that a black had been present at an official White House function, made a frenzied denial: "It so happens that I have never, in my official . . . position, either when sleeping or waking, alive or dead, on my head or on my heels, dined, lunched, or supped, or invited to a wedding reception any colored man, woman, or child."[75]

Seven years after the Supreme Court decided *Plessy v. Ferguson*, incorporating segregation into our Constitution, President Theodore Roosevelt, who was less hostile on the race issue, invited the moderate Booker T. Washington for an informal lunch at the White House.[76] In response, the *Memphis Scimitar* wrote: "The most damnable outrage which has ever been perpetrated by any citizen of the United States was committed yesterday by the President, when he invited a nigger to dine with him at the White House."[77] Senator Benjamin Tillman of South Carolina said: "Now that Roosevelt has eaten with that nigger Washington, we shall have to kill a thousand niggers to get them back to their places."[78] Georgia's governor was sure that "no Southerner can respect

73. Bickett, *supra* note 3, at 292 (emphasis added).

74. Burke Marshall, Federalism and Civil Rights 13-14 (1964) (quoting remarks of Judge Chrisman).

75. George Sinkler, The Racial Attitudes of American Presidents: From Abraham Lincoln to Theodore Roosevelt 227 (1971) (emphasis omitted).

76. *See* William A. Sinclair, The Aftermath of Slavery 187-96 (2d ed. 1905).

77. *Id.* at 187.

78. *Id.*

any white man who would eat with a negro."[79]

Senator James K. Varderman of Mississippi, who often used Booker T. Washington as a foil for his racist rhetoric, once commented:

> I am just as much opposed to Booker Washington as a voter, with all his Anglo-Saxon reinforcements, . . . as I am to the coconut-headed, chocolate-covered, typical little coon, Andy Dotson, who blacks my shoes every morning. Neither is fit to perform the supreme function of citizenship.[80]

Contempt for African-American suffrage was well pronounced in the political arena.[81]

The courts were often as insensitive as the state governments on the issue of assuring equal justice for African-Americans.[82] In many cases, appellate courts upheld convictions despite prosecutors' references to black defendants and witnesses in such racist terms as "black rascal,"[83] "burr-headed nigger,"[84] "mean negro,"[85] "big nigger,"[86] "pickaninny,"[87]

---

79. *Id.* at 188. Not to be outdone by others in racist rhetoric, James K. Varderman, then governor of Mississippi, wrote in his newspaper:

> It is said that men follow the bent of their geniuses, and that prenatal influences are often potent in shaping thoughts and ideas in after life. Probably old lady Roosevelt, during the period of gestation, was frightened by a dog, and the fact may account for the qualities of the male pup that are so prominent in Teddy. I would not do either an injustice, but am disposed to apologize to the dog for mentioning it.

Id. at 196.

80. 1 Harvard Sitkoff, A New Deal For Blacks: The Emergence of Civil Rights As a National Issue 8 (1978) (citation omitted). *See also* David L. Lewis, W.E.B. Du Bois: Biography of a Race 1868-1919, at 257-61 (1993) (describing white rejection of Washington's conciliatory efforts).

81. African-Americans had few allies. Even the women's suffrage movement placed great reliance on the argument that the votes of white women would serve to dilute the "adverse" impact of black male suffrage mandated by the Fifteenth Amendment. Suffragettes Elizabeth Cady Stanton and Susan B. Anthony "opened the way to . . . bigotry" in their influential National Suffrage Association. Eleanor Flexner, Century of Struggle: The Woman's Rights Movement in the United States 316 (rev. ed. 1975). Indeed, the National Board of that organization issued a statement noting that "granting suffrage to women who can read and write and pay taxes *would insure white supremacy without resorting to any methods of doubtful constitutionality.*" *Id.* at 317 (citation omitted); *see also* William H. Chafe, The American Woman 15 (1972). The Equal Suffrage League of Raleigh, North Carolina—a chapter of the National American Woman's Suffrage Association—was particularly strident in its calls for women's suffrage, limited through the application of literacy tests to white women, to ensure white domination. *See* Glenda E. Gilmore, Gender and Jim Crow: Women and the Politics of White Supremacy in North Carolina, 1896-1920, at 439-47 (1993) (Ph.D. dissertation, University of North Carolina, Chapel Hill) (forthcoming UNC Press, 1995).

82. *See* A. Leon Higginbotham, Jr., *Racism in American and South African Courts: Similarities and Differences*, 65 N.Y.U. L. Rev. 479, 521-43 (1990).

83. State v. Miles, 98 S.W. 25, 31 (Mo. 1906).

84. Adams v. State, 216 S.W. 863, 864 (Tex. Crim. App. 1919).

85. Green v. State, 105 P.2d 795, 797 (Okla. Ct. App. 1940).

86. State v. Hubbard, 195 P.2d 604, 605 (Kan. 1948).

87. People v. Curry, 218 P.2d 153, 161 (Cal. Ct. App. 1950).

"mean nigger,"[88] "three nigger men,"[89] "niggers,"[90] and "nothing but just a common Negro, [a] black whore."[91]

Moreover, even the institution of the Supreme Court was not immune from racist influence:

> Mr. Hoover nominated as Justice of the United States Supreme Court John J. Parker of North Carolina, in spite of the fact that Parker had opposed the right of Negroes to vote. We have been told that Parker was willing to repudiate this stand but that the White House refused to let him; at any rate, while Mr. Hoover hastened to explain Parker's labor decisions, he treated his anti-Negro attitude with disdainful silence and despite advice and pleading, insisted upon sending this nomination to the Senate. It was finally defeated by a narrow margin by the influence of the Negro and labor vote and despite every effort of the administration to force it through.[92]

From birth to death, even in defense of the country, innumerable aspects of legitimized racism affected the lives of most African-Americans every day. In World War I, African-American soldiers fought abroad and lost their lives for what President Woodrow Wilson proclaimed was the war to make the world "safe for democracy." Yet, at home there was segregation, not democracy. During World War II, thousands of African-American soldiers lost their lives for what President Roosevelt said was the fight for the Four Freedoms. But at home, many African-Americans were denied the Four Freedoms, including the right to vote.

Nearly every achievement was gained only through struggle. For example, consider the experiences of John Hope Franklin, now the James B. Duke Professor Emeritus at Duke University, and a former colleague of the plaintiffs in *Shaw v. Reno*:

> [John Hope Franklin] has achieved all of [these academic honors] despite having had to cope with the outrageous indignities that can be visited on a black person in our society. When his father, who was an attorney in Indian Territory before it became Oklahoma, moved to Tulsa, the building in which he had acquired a law office was burned down by a white mob, and for months his father had to work out of a tent. As a boy riding on a Jim Crow train in Oklahoma, John Hope and his mother were put off the coach by a white conductor and left stranded in the dust.
>
> When as a graduate student he sought to pursue historical research at the archives in Raleigh, he was not permitted to sit with white researchers but was shunted off to an isolated chamber. The Library of Congress was still worse . . . [he] could not eat with . . . colleagues at

88. Quarles v. Commonwealth, 245 S.W.2d 947, 949 (Ky. 1951).

89. Thornton v. State, 451 S.W.2d 898, 903 (Tex. Crim. App. 1970).

90. Thornton v. Beto, 470 F.2d 657, 658 (5th Cir. 1972), *cert. denied*, 411 U.S. 920 (1973).

91. Hilson v. State, 258 S.W. 826, 826 (Tex. Crim. App. 1924).

92. W.E.B. Du Bois, *Herbert Hoover*, The Crisis 39 (Nov. 1932), *reprinted in* 2 Writings in Periodicals Edited by W.E.B. Du Bois 675 (1983) (Herbert Aptheker ed., 1983).

any downtown restaurant, not even at the greasiest People's Drug Store counter. Nor, after having fought a victorious war against fascism, was there a downtown movie a black person could go to, or a downtown hotel at which, in the nation's capital, a black person could stay. That was John Hope's experience as a young scholar.

During this same period, on a train journey in North Carolina from Greensboro to Durham, he was compelled to stand even though there were ample seats in an adjacent coach—for those coach seats were reserved for whites, who sat there grinning at his discomfort. They were Nazi prisoners of war.[93]

III. THE PERSISTENCE OF SIGNIFICANT POLITICAL RACISM IN NORTH CAROLINA IN THE LAST FOUR DECADES

Through the mid-20th century, voting by black North Carolinians was nearly non-existant, as literacy tests prohibited blacks from exercising their political rights.[94] Although voting slowly increased through the course of the century, by 1948 still only 15% of North Carolina's blacks were registered to vote.[95] Even as courts began to take action against *de jure* segregation, the displacement of African-Americans from America's and North Carolina's political life continued. After the North Carolina literacy requirement was eliminated in 1961, North Carolina continued to require voting registrants "of uncertain ability" to read and copy the North Carolina Constitution, a practice that continued for another decade, disproportionately disenfranchising black citizens.[96]

Even after the demise of Jim Crow *de jure* segregation, racial discrimination against blacks continued. Beyond the realm of political empowerment, discrimination governed all facets of life including neighborhood development, business development, employment patterns, schooling, and criminal justice. There can be little doubt that such discrimination was able to occur because African-Americans were excluded from civic life. Through the 1960s, every significant decision-making agency in the state—public and private—was completely dominated by whites even though their policy decisions had full effect in black communities.[97] In

93. William E. Leuchtenburg, *Tribute: John Hope Franklin*, 42 Duke L.J. 1022, 1023-24 (1993).

94. *See* Gingles v. Edmisten, 590 F. Supp. 345, 360 (E.D.N.C. 1984), *modified sub nom.* Thornburg v. Gingles, 478 U.S. 30 (1986). From 1900 through 1919, blacks also were prohibited from voting, as North Carolina enforced a voting poll tax. *See* John V. Orth, The North Carolina State Constitution—A Reference Guide 119 (1993).

95. *See* J. Morgan Kousser, After 120 Years: Redistricting in North Carolina 30-31 (Mar. 22, 1994) (submitted as sworn testimony in Shaw v. Hunt, No. 92-202-CIV-5-BR (E.D.N.C.)).

96. *Gingles*, 590 F. Supp. at 359 (quoting Bazemore v. Bertie County Bd. of Elections, 119 S.E. 2d 637 (N.C. 1961)).

97. *See* Alex Willingham, Report on Certain Questions Involving Race and North Carolina Congressional Redistricting with Reference to the 1990 Round 5-6 (Mar. 22, 1994) (submitted as sworn testimony in Shaw v. Hunt, No. 92-202-CIV-5-BR (E.D.N.C.)).

fact, North Carolina did not elect its first black state legislator until 1968, at a time when it refused to abolish patently discriminatory multimember districts.[98]

A. *The Return of Race-Baiting Campaigns*

After the Jim Crow Era closed, the exclusion of blacks from the political process took different forms; in particular, racial rhetoric once again inflamed North Carolina politics to divide voters along racial lines. In a 1950 Democratic Party senate primary, Willis Smith took on incumbent Frank Graham, appealing to white voters' racism. Smith supporters distributed leaflets warning: "WHITE PEOPLE WAKE UP! . . . FRANK GRAHAM FAVORS MINGLING OF THE RACES."[99] From that point forward, although direct barriers to voting fell, white North Carolinians increasingly appealed to white prejudice and fear to polarize the electorate and marginalize African-Americans and candidates who might protect their interests.

In 1954, supporters of Alton Lennon distributed a false endorsement of rival Ken Scott by a black political leader, in order to discredit him. Scott responded with an adamant endorsement of segregated schools.[100] In 1956, two of three North Carolina representatives who refused to endorse the "Southern Manifesto," which vowed to resist the desegregation order of *Brown v. Board of Education*, were defeated at the hands of segregationist groups.[101]

In 1960, I. Beverly Lake ran for North Carolina governor on a segregationist platform, while his opponent, Terry Sanford, was accused of being "soft" on the race issue.[102] In the 1964 gubernatorial election, Lake again defended segregation, prompting primary rivals to oppose the pending federal civil rights acts. Concurrently, presidential candidate Barry Goldwater, pressing for the support of North Carolina voters, asserted his opposition to civil rights legislation as well.[103]

B. *The Aftermath of the Civil Rights Act*

The passage of the Civil Rights Act in 1965 did little to quell racial appeals in North Carolina politics. Although the Act has encouraged black voter registration, which between 1960 and 1982 rose in North

98. *See* Kousser, *supra* note 95, at 21-22.
99. *Supra* note 5 and accompanying reproduction.
100. *See* Harry L. Watson, Race and Politics in North Carolina, 1865-1994, at 13 (submitted as sworn testimony in Shaw v. Hunt, 92-202-CIV-5-BR (E.D.N.C.)); *see also Alton Lennon Forces Flood State with 'Phony' Race Issue Leaflet*, Raleigh News & Observer, May 28, 1954, at 1. The fact that a supposed endorsement by a black leader proved such an effective tool for discrediting Scott is striking evidence of white voters' hostility to black candidates and black issues, an attitude that still prevails. *See infra* notes 104-33 and accompanying text.
101. *See* Watson, *supra* note 100, at 13.
102. *See id.* at 14.
103. *See id.* at 14-15.

Carolina from 39.1% to 50.9% of the black voting-age population,[104] not until the challenged redistricting has the Act enabled African-Americans in North Carolina to choose representatives who would protect their interests.

After passage of the Voting Rights Act, subtle (and not so subtle) appeals to white racism in elections persisted in North Carolina elections, intimidating African-American voters, punishing candidates for protecting "black" interests or for being African-American, and dividing voters along racial lines.

In 1966, two Democratic congressmen drew fire and were defeated for acceding to federal pressures for desegregation in an election marred by "violent intimidation against black families who proposed to register their children in formerly all-white schools."[105] George Wallace's 1968 presidential campaign appealed to voters' fears of court-ordered busing.[106] And, Jesse Helms, in his bid for Senate in 1972, signalled his racial animus with slogans like "He's one of us."[107]

In the 1960s, if not beyond, the North Carolina legislature continued to dilute African-American political rights with the redistricting process. Time and again the legislature approved gerrymanders to dilute the vote of African-Americans living in the well-organized, black community of Durham County. In 1965, for example, a proposal to create a "Research Triangle District" of Durham, Wake, and Orange Counties was rejected in favor of a gerrymander placing Durham with conservative Forsyth County.[108] This "solution" led to the 16-year-term of L.H. Fountain—a conservative who opposed the civil rights movement, ignoring the interests of Durham County's substantial African-American population.[109]

This district finally was broken up in 1982, after a protracted fight marred by neutral sounding, race-based appeals. But even in Durham County's new district, African-Americans fared no better.[110] Although black voters represented 40% of this district's Democratic Party electorate,[111] due to the extreme racial polarization of North Carolina politics,

---

104. *See id.* at 15.

105. *Id.* at 16.

106. In an ad placed in *The Charlotte News* by the Wallace Campaign, a school bus was pictured with the text:

> If you're wondering why more and more millions of your fellow Americans are turning to Governor Wallace: Follow, as your children are bused. All across town. Governor Wallace as President will let you and your local schools decide what is best for your children.

Charlotte News, Oct. 29, 1968, at 5C.

107. *See* Watson, *supra* note 100, at 17.

108. *See id.* at 23-24.

109. *See id.*

110. *See* Kousser, *supra* note 95, at 36-41; James M. O'Reilly, A Report Prepared for *Shaw v. Hunt* 4-5 (Mar. 22, 1994) (submitted as sworn testimony in Shaw v. Hunt, 92-202-CIV-5-BR (E.D.N.C.)).

111. *See* O'Reilly, *supra* note 110, at 5-6.

the African-American community was still unable to elect a representative who would support its interests.

In the Democratic primary for that seat, black candidate H.M. "Mickey" Michaux—a United States Attorney appointed by President Jimmy Carter—opposed Tim Valentine—a white Democrat, who did not hesitate to appeal to white voters' racist instincts.[112] In an initial primary, Michaux finished first among three candidates, with 44.1% of the racially polarized vote, receiving 88.6% of the black vote but only 13.9% of the white vote.[113] In a runoff between Michaux and Valentine, Valentine emphasized racial themes, warning against "the *well organized bloc vote*" and predicting that Michaux "will again be *busing his supporters* to the polling places in record numbers."[114] In a vote straight along racial lines, Valentine defeated Michaux by a spread of 6% and went on to win the general election.[115] Notably, Michaux received 91.5% of the black vote but only 13.1% of the white vote.[116] Two years later, in a vote similarly split along racial lines, black candidate Kenneth Spaulding also lost the district's primary election to Valentine.[117]

As the Michaux race demonstrates, candidates representing African-American interests and black candidates face an immense barrier in garnering white votes in North Carolina. Due to racial polarization alone, the prospect of winning 30-40% of the white vote for such candidates is remote if not inconceivable.[118] Where Michaux had the support of the district's 40% black voters, he still failed to garner sufficient white votes to win.[119]

In the 1980s and 1990s, race-baiting campaigns, marginalizing black voters, have been commonplace. In 1983, advertising supporting Jesse Helms' bid for governor against Jim Hunt showed Hunt beside Jesse Jackson. As one journalist described, "the primary motive is simply to make the association between Hunt and blacks and to raise fears among whites that Hunt is a captive of black voters."[120] Helms also used a multitude of racially oriented signals in his 1990 bid for reelection to the Senate against an African-American candidate, Harvey Gantt. Gantt

112. *See* Kousser, *supra* note 95, at 48.

113. *See id.* at 49.

114. Watson, *supra* note 100, at 25-26; *see also* Kousser, *supra* note 95, at 50.

115. *See* Watson, *supra* note 100, at 26.

116. *See* Kousser, *supra* note 95, at 50.

117. *See id.* at 53-54.

118. *See* O'Reilly, *supra* note 110, at 2.

119. Moreover, as J. Morgan Kousser demonstrates, the ability to elect a black representative is not merely symbolic. *See* Kousser, *supra* note 95, at 20. Black representatives more effectively and consistently present and protect the chosen interests of their black constituency. *See id.* at 20-23. This is neither surprising nor disturbing. Due to their unique history and state-enforced inequality in America, blacks tend to hold attitudes divergent from those of whites on the issues of most import to them, including race relations, remedies for discrimination, and other areas of civil rights policy. *See id.* at 24-27.

120. Watson, *supra* note 100, at 18.

had been leading in the polls until the final week of the race when the Helms campaign ran an advertisement showing a white man's hand crumpling a job rejection notice, with a voice-over explaining

> You needed that job, and you were the best qualified. But they had to give it to a minority because of a racial quota. Is that really fair? Harvey Gantt says it is. Gantt supports Ted Kennedy's racial quota law that makes the color of your skin more important than your qualifications.[121]

This advertisement galvanized white support for Helms, bringing him victory.[122]

More directly, an anonymous leaflet appeared in rural Columbus County in 1990, warning voters of "the Negro Vote" and that "more *Negroes* will vote in this election than ever before."[123] Representative J. Alex McMillan of the 9th District fanned racial fears with a 1990 fund-raising letter that warned of "the potential danger of a sophisticated get-out-the-vote effort among the core Gantt constituency—a constituency that particularly exists in substantial numbers in the most populous part of my district, Mecklenburg County."[124]

In the 1992 Presidential campaign, local Republican Party advertisements warned that "[i]f Bill Clinton is elected President, Jesse Jackson will be a U.S. Senator."[125] And, the Republican Party also engaged in a massive "postcard campaign," mailing postcards to black voters to discourage them from voting by threatening prosecution against voters who no longer lived at addresses registered with the Board of Elections.[126]

C. *North Carolina's Racial Politics Disproportionately Harm African-Americans*

There can be no dispute that race consciousness has been—and continues to be—central to North Carolina's politics. Racial appeals in campaigns are serious strategic tactics, designed to bring victory, that minimize the effectiveness of African-American participation in the electoral process. Race consciousness and racial polarization have regularly marginalized African-American voters—intimidating African-Americans from voting; fomenting fear among white voters of candidates who may forward interests of black citizens; suggesting that black candidates

121. Jamieson, *supra* note 5, at 97.

122. *See id.* at 99-100. The "white hands" commercial was not an isolated incident of the Helms campaign playing to racial fears and animus. The Helms campaign featured numerous advertisements highlighting Democratic Party Chairman Ron Brown, an African-American, as well as advertisements featuring Gantt's black campaign manager. *See* Watson, *supra* note 100, at 20.

123. Watson, *supra* note 100, at 21.

124. *Id.* at 26.

125. *Id.* at 21.

126. *See* Watt, *supra* note 13, ¶ 8; Affidavit of Charles E. Johnson, ¶¶ 8-13 (sworn to Mar. 18, 1994) (submitted as evidence in Shaw v. Hunt, No. 92-202-CIV-5-BR (E.D.N.C.)).

are unable to protect the interests of all constituents; and perpetuating animosity and political divisions along racial lines.

Moreover, a mere decade ago the federal courts found that North Carolina's *de jure* exclusion of African-Americans from the voting process—with, among other means, a poll tax, a literacy test, and a prohibition against bullet voting[127]—had contributed to the continued suppression of African-American participation in North Carolina's political process.[128] In 1982, there was approximately a 14% disparity between voter registration of white and black age-qualified citizens—66.7% of whites were registered as compared with 52.7% of blacks.[129] Although the Court expressed a hope that continued registration efforts would overcome the chilling effect of historic discrimination,[130] such efforts have not yet succeeded. The lingering effects of historic discrimination in voting (as well as in myriad other facets of civic life) continue to dilute the political power of African-Americans in North Carolina.[131] In fact, a significant disparity in voter registration alone—approximately 6.8%—between whites and blacks still persists, limiting the ability of African-Americans in North Carolina to assert their political interests.[132]

The exclusion from North Carolina politics that African-Americans have suffered has served only to reinforce the legacy of racial segregation in which many black North Carolinians have lived. For example, black North Carolinians suffer the harms of poverty, inadequate education and medical care, infant mortality, unemployment, and violent crime more acutely than their white counterparts.[133] The North Carolina legislature's 1991 redistricting is not only the first step toward recognizing that African-Americans disproportionately suffer these ills, but also the first step toward remedying them.

---

127. Bullet voting is a practice designed to maximize a group's voting strength in at-large voting schemes. In at-large districts—where multiple seats are filled in a single election—voters may cast one vote for as many candidates as there are seats available. Thus if there are five seats available each voter may cast a vote for any five candidates running. With bullet voting, voters decline to cast all of their votes—choosing instead to vote only for their "target" candidate—thereby avoiding the dilution of their vote that would accompany voting for a full slate. When done in concert, and particularly where racial bloc voting occurs, bullet voting provides gains to the "target" candidate relative to other candidates, and therefore increases the likelihood of minority representation.

128. *See* Gingles v. Edmisten, 590 F. Supp. 345, 359-60 (E.D.N.C. 1984), *modified sub nom.* Thornburg v. Gingles, 478 U.S. 30, 38-39 (1986).

129. *See Gingles*, 590 F. Supp. at 360. In North Carolina, 70.8% of voting-age whites are registered, while only 64% of voting age blacks are registered. *See* Jerry T. Jennings, U.S. Dep't of Commerce, Voting and Registration in the Election of November 1992, at 27 (on file with the *Fordham Law Review*).

130. *See Gingles*, 590 F. Supp. at 361.

131. *See* Willingham, *supra* note 97, at 30-31.

132. *See* Jennings, *supra* note 129, at 27.

133. *See* Willingham, *supra* note 97, at 28-30.

IV. The 1991 Redistricting Plan—A Step Towards Pluralism

In 1991, the North Carolina state legislature formulated the current redistricting plan. Armed with 1990 census data, the state redistricting committee implemented the guidelines set forth in the 1982 amendments to the Voting Rights Act that prohibit the dilution of minority voting power, both in intent and effect.[134] In addition, population shifts that allocated North Carolina an additional representative also altered the concentration of voters on the county level.[135] Accordingly, the legislature redrew the entire face of North Carolina's congressional districts.

In its initial formulation, the redistricting plan included one district of twelve as a minority-majority district.[136] That district, the First Congressional District, is located in eastern North Carolina, and is largely rural in character.[137] The other eleven districts, all drawn to account for, among other factors, the race and political concerns and party affiliations of the voters,[138] were white-majority districts with varying concentrations of black voters.

Because of North Carolina's history of inhibiting the political participation of its African-American citizens, forty of its counties are covered by Section 5 of the Voting Rights Act, requiring the state to submit all redistricting plans to the Justice Department for approval.[139] The Justice Department objected to the initial plan on the basis that an additional minority-majority district could be drawn to increase African-American representation. Although relatively "compact" in shape, the district suggested by the Justice Department lumped together black voters of all demographic and socio-economic backgrounds—urban and rural, middle-class and poor, white collar and blue collar.[140]

Rather than adopt the district suggested by the Justice Department,

---

134. 42 U.S.C. § 1973(c). The Voting Rights Act was enacted to ensure that the rights of voters are not abridged due to "race, color, or previous condition of servitude," 42 U.S.C. § 1971(a)(1) (1988), intimidation, 42 U.S.C. § 1971(b) (1988), or the devices of literacy tests and poll taxes, 42 U.S.C. § 1971(a)(2)(C) (1988). The Act falls within the class of statutes enacted by Congress to remedy the effects of past state discrimination. *See, e.g.*, Metro Broadcasting, Inc. v. FCC, 497 U.S. 547, 563-64 (1990) (congressional remedial efforts due particular deference); Fullilove v. Klutznick, 448 U.S. 448, 472 (1980) (same).

135. *See* Affidavit of William Hodges, former Chairman of First District Democratic Party, ¶ 9 (sworn to Mar. 21, 1994) (submitted as evidence in Shaw v. Hunt, No. 92-202-CIV-5-BR (E.D.N.C.)); *see also* Affidavit of Representative Eva M. Clayton, ¶ 2 (sworn to Mar. 22, 1994) (submitted as evidence in Shaw v. Hunt, No. 92-202-CIV-5-BR (E.D.N.C.)).

136. *See* Shaw v. Barr, 808 F. Supp. 461, 463 (E.D.N.C. 1992), *rev'd sub nom.* Shaw v. Reno, 113 S. Ct. 2816 (1993); Hodges, *supra* note 135, ¶ 15.

137. *See* Hodges, *supra* note 135, ¶ 16; Clayton, *supra* note 135, ¶ 2(A).

138. *See* Hodges, *supra* note 135, ¶¶ 6-8, 12-13, 15-16.

139. *See* Shaw v. Reno, 113 S. Ct. 2816, 2820 (1993).

140. This suggested district in the southeastern part of the state was to run from Charlotte toward Wilmington along the South Carolina border. It thus included both North Carolina's largest city and numerous poor, rural areas stretching toward the coast.

North Carolina legislators reconsidered the entire plan, taking into account not only the differentiating factors overlooked by the Justice Department, but also the political implications for incumbents. The resulting additional minority-majority district, the Twelfth District, was drawn along Interstate Highway 85, linking urban industrial areas across several counties.[141]

Although nominally "minority-majority" districts, the First and Twelfth Districts—as well as the plan as a whole—are more accurately characterized as "integrated."[142] The majority of North Carolina's eligible black voters do not live in the state's two minority-majority districts. In fact, less than one-half—only 43%—of North Carolina's eligible black voters live in these two districts.[143] Most of North Carolina's black voters—57%—vote in white-majority districts, with 45.8% in the state's six Democratic, white-majority voting districts and 11.2% relegated to the four Republican, white-majority districts.[144] African-American voters typically represent 18% of the eligible voting strength of the Democratic, white-majority districts.[145]

Furthermore, the fact that these districts are "minority-majority" by no means ensures minority representation, even assuming a viable African-American candidate seeks office. Once the voting profile is adjusted for voter turnout, the black voting strength is only 49.7%,[146] and no candidate can rely on receiving 100% of that voting bloc. In reality, the lines of the Twelfth District only ensure that its congressional representa-

141. Much has been made of the fact that the Twelfth District follows I-85, and crosses several counties. However, as redistricting veteran William Hodges points out, district lines are often drawn along or up to recognizable landmarks such as rivers or main streets, and "county-splitting" has been a fact of North Carolina's districting plans since the 1980s. *See* Hodges, *supra* note 135, ¶¶ 9, 10, 14. Moreover, a district's shape is not the only possible touchstone of legitimacy for a voting scheme. As discussed extensively, *supra*, the political outlook, economic experience, or common history of voters can provide an equally compelling, if not more compelling, basis for districting. Indeed, making these considerations paramount in districting (and rendering shape of little significance) would align the districting process with an effort to identify and give voice to a wider spectrum of political communities. *See* Dillard v. Baldwin County Bd. of Educ., 686 F. Supp. 1459, 1465-66 (M.D. Ala. 1988) (recognizing that compactness "does not mean that a proposed district must meet, or attempt to achieve, some aesthetic absolute, such as symmetry or attractiveness" but rather "that a district is sufficiently geographically compact if it allows for effective representation").

142. Indeed, when evaluated using two well-accepted measures of population distribution, these two districts are the most heterogeneous of North Carolina's districts. *See* David A. Bositis, Joint Center for Pol. & Econ. Stud., Statistical Measure of Racial Heterogeneity, U.S. Congressional Districts of the 103rd Congress, North Carolina (Apr. 1994) (prepared as part of the study, Redistricting and Representation) (on file with the *Fordham Law Review*).

143. *See* Southern U.S. Congressional Districts by Party and Black Vote, 103rd Congress, First Session, *infra* app. B.

144. *See id.*

145. *See id.*

146. *See* North Carolina 12 Voting-Age Population by Race, and by Race and Turnout, *infra* app. D.

tive—regardless of his or her race—will be more responsive to the needs of African-American voters than representatives have been in the past.

In a state with the reprehensible history, and continuing practice, of excluding and marginalizing African-Americans from the political process, as detailed above, this achievement is almost embarrassingly modest. Notably, these two districts—from which two African-Americans were elected to Congress—represent only 16.67% of North Carolina's congressional delegation, while African-Americans comprise 20.1% of North Carolina's voting-age citizens.[147] Ten of the twelve districts remain white-majority, and, through bloc voting by whites—often encouraged by race-baiting campaigns—are represented by white congressmen. The concerns of the black voters living in those districts have historically been ignored by the elected representatives,[148] and in those districts, black voters have little hope of electing more responsive leaders.

V. The Misguided Presumptions Underlying *Shaw v. Reno*

In *Shaw v. Reno*, the Supreme Court failed to focus on the realities of racial bloc voting and race-baiting campaigns. Instead, they impugned minority-majority districts, utilizing inexpert, inaccurate, and inappropriate analogies.

A. *"Political Apartheid"—A Profoundly Flawed Comparison*

Since *Guinn & Beal v. United States*,[149] the Supreme Court has developed a body of understandable and reasonably precise terminology in construing the Fourteenth and Fifteenth Amendments, and later, in construing the Voting Rights Act. Until its opinion in *Shaw*, however, the Supreme Court had never used the term "political apartheid." While

147. *See* Southern U.S. Congressional Districts by Party and Black Vote, 103rd Congress, First Session, *infra* app. B.

148. North Carolina Representatives Valentine (D-2nd Dist.) and Hefner (D-8th Dist.) represent districts with the largest share of African-American voters, 20.1% and 20.9% respectively. *See* Voting Scores, White Non Hispanic Democratic Congressmen, Southern States by District Black and Hispanic Voting-Age Populations, 103rd Congress, First Session, *infra* app. E. Both have consistently voted with the Conservative Coalition of Southern Democrats and Republicans, with Conservative Coalition voting support scores of 76% and 67% respectively. *See id.* Representative Valentine voted *against* the Democratic party for 28% of his votes cast during the first session. *See id.* In contrast, during the same period Representatives Clayton and Watt cast only 14% and 7%, respectively, of their votes with the Conservative Coalition. *See* Voting Scores, CBC Members, Southern States by District Black and Hispanic Voting-Age Populations, 103rd Congress, First Session, *infra* app. F.

149. 238 U.S. 347 (1915). In *Guinn* the Supreme Court invalidated an amendment to the Oklahoma constitution that had restricted suffrage to those who could read and write the state constitution, or who were descendants of someone entitled to vote in 1866. *See id.* at 365. Although the Court only relied on the provisions of the Fifteenth Amendment, it found the provision, intended to prevent most blacks from voting while permitting the right of illiterate whites to vote, constitutionally invalid. *See id.* at 364-65.

explaining the relevance of an irregularly shaped district's "appearance," the majority argued that

> [a] reapportionment plan that includes in one district individuals who belong to the same race, but who are otherwise widely separated by geographical and political boundaries, and who may have little in common with one another *but the color of their skin, bears an uncomfortable resemblance to political apartheid.*[150]

Whenever the Supreme Court uses a new term, scholars ask whether the term was chosen pursuant to a carefully considered analysis as to its meanings and implications, or merely in order to add a stylistic flourish to "liven up" an otherwise drab opinion. We assume that the phrase "resemblance to political apartheid" was used to convey some significant insight. In considering North Carolina's redistricting plan, however, the Court's analogy to political apartheid adds no insight but rather obscures the issues of whether North Carolina's minority-majority districts are justified and constitutionally permissible.

The most significant analysis of apartheid written in the last fifteen years is the report of the Study Commission on U.S. Policy Toward Southern Africa entitled *South Africa: Time Running Out.*[151] That work notes the words of Professor G.A. Cronjes of the University of Pretoria, a leading proponent of apartheid, in endorsing that policy:

> The racial policy which we as Afrikaners should promote must be directed to the preservation of racial and cultural variety. This is because it is according to the *Will of God,* and also because with the knowledge at our disposal it can be justified on practical grounds. . . .
>
> The more consistently the policy of apartheid could be applied, the greater would be the security for the purity of our blood and the surer our unadulterated European racial survival. . . . Total racial separation . . . is the most consistent application of the Afrikaner idea of racial apartheid.[152]

Apartheid required drastic social engineering, which in turn required political engineering:

> [A] Nationalist leader, spelled out the ways in which his government

---

150. *Shaw v. Reno,* 113 S. Ct. 2816, 2827 (1993) (emphasis added).

151. Study Comm'n on U.S. Policy Toward Southern Africa, South Africa: Time Running Out (1981) [hereinafter Time Running Out]. This classic treatise has had an Update Series of books: Pauline H. Baker, The United States and South Africa: The Reagan Years (1989); John Dugard et al., The Last Years of Apartheid: Civil Liberties in South Africa (1992); Robert S. Jaster et al., Changing Fortunes: War, Diplomacy, and Economics in Southern Africa (1992); Tom Lodge et al., All, Here, and Now: Black Politics in South Africa in the 1980s (1991); Robert Schrire, Adapt or Die: The End of White Politics in South Africa (1991).

The Commissioners of the study were: Franklin A. Thomas, Chair; Robert C. Good; Charles V. Hamilton; Ruth S. Hamilton; Alexander Heard; Aileen C. Hernandez; Constance Hilliard; C. Peter McColough; J. Irwin Miller; Alan Pifer; and Howard D. Samuel.

152. Time Running Out, *supra* note 151, at 41 (emphasis added) (quoting Professor G.A. Cronjes of the University of Pretoria).

> would apply apartheid. It would . . . abolish the Natives' Representative Council (which had refused to cooperate with the government) and the limited indirect African representation that still existed in the House of Assembly, treat the reserves as the true African homelands, control the African influx into the cities, protect white workers from African competition, prohibit African trade unions, and generally segregate whites and blacks as much as possible.
>
> The election took place on May 26, 1948. The results surprised almost everyone: Despite obtaining a minority of the popular vote, the Nationalists and their ally, the small, ephemeral Afrikaner party, won a working majority in Parliament. The word *apartheid* would soon become notorious around the globe.[153]

Other commentators similarly describe the far-reaching, invidious nature of apartheid. In his classic treatise, *Human Rights and the South African Legal Order*, John Dugard has defined the fundamentals of apartheid:

> Parliamentary supremacy is basic to the constitutional structure of South Africa. Parliament may make laws on any subject it pleases and no court of law may enquire into the validity of any act of Parliament except one which affects the equal language rights. . . .
>
> The twenty-one million black people enjoy no representation in the central Parliament. Nor are they represented in the Provincial Councils which have limited legislative powers over the provinces. African political power is confined to the six homelands, each of which has a legislative assembly with powers substantially similar to those of the Provincial Councils. The Colored Persons Representative Council, which has a very limited law-making capacity, caters for the political aspirations of the colored people, while a largely advisory body, the South African Indian Council, constitutes the Indian people's sole political institution in the body politic.[154]

As Professor Dugard makes clear, this discriminatory political structure was essential to the perpetuation of the supremacy of South Africa's white population:

> [T]he laws which constitute the foundation of modern South African society are discriminatory in the sense in which this term is generally understood. Some laws, such as the pass laws and the job-reservation laws, openly discriminate by allocating rights unequally to blacks. Some, such as the Reservation of Separate Amenities Act and the Group Areas Act, do not expressly provide for unequal treatment for blacks but in practice there is no question about their discriminatory effect, which has been acknowledged by the courts. Some, such as those dealing with education, create separate facilities for blacks that are either in fact inferior or produce a sense of inferiority among blacks. Others, such as the race classification laws, the Prohibition of

153. *Id.* at 41.

154. John Dugard, Human Rights and the South African Legal Order 6 (1978) (footnotes omitted).

> Mixed Marriages Act, and the Immorality Act, provide for racial separation but produce a sense of humiliation among blacks on account of their professed goal to preserve the "racial purity" of the whites. On the political front, too, there is discrimination. Even if the homelands policy is accepted as a genuine, fair political dispensation to Africans in the homelands, it is difficult to explain the grossly unequal allocation of land other than in terms of discrimination. As far as Africans in the common area, coloreds, and Indians are concerned, however, there is a clear denial of full political rights on account of their race.[155]

The effect of the laws of apartheid is to "create a sense of inferiority or humiliation among blacks stemming from their professed aim to promote the interests of the white group as a primary goal."[156]

Apartheid, as described above, is in no way analogous to minority-majority redistricting plans in North Carolina—however irregular the shape of the boundaries. The essence of South African apartheid has been the *exclusion* of vast numbers of the population—more than 85%—from having the right to vote for *any* representation in Parliament and the National Government. The first time Dr. Nelson Mandela, like all other black South Africans, had the opportunity to vote in a national election of that country was April 26, 1994.[157] "Coloured" and "Indian" South Africans, permitted to vote in South Africa only recently, were mandated to choose representatives of their own race to represent them in separate legislative bodies which could always be overruled by the national parliament.[158]

In sharp contrast, the minority-majority districts in the United States foster *inclusion* into political life; these districts do not exclude any segment of the population. Instead, race-consciousness is used as a means of

155. *Id.* at 102-03.

156. *Id.* at 103.

157. *See* Francis X. Clines, *After 300 Years, Blacks Vote in South Africa*, N.Y. Times, Apr. 27, 1994, at A1, A8.

158. In the late 1970s, notably after P.W. Botha became prime minister, the National Party government devised a new constitution that co-opted Coloureds and Indians into the parliamentary system while enabling the whites to maintain political control. The Republic of South Africa Constitution Act of 1983 enfranchised Coloureds and Indians—but not Africans—and established a tricameral Parliament consisting of separate legislative chambers for whites, Coloureds, and Indians. Although this constitution was heralded by the government as an exercise in democracy, it maintained white domination of the political system.

The 1983 Constitution established three chambers:

- House of Assembly, with 178 white members elected by whites to represent some five million whites;
- House of Representatives, with 85 Coloured members elected by Coloureds to represent three million Coloureds; and
- House of Delegates, with 45 Indian members elected by Indians to represent nine hundred thousand Indians.

Dugard, *supra* note 151, at 6. Although provision was made for joint sessions of the three houses, when adopting legislation, each chamber deliberated separately. In the event of disagreement, the will of the majority in the white House of Assembly—i.e., the ruling National Party—prevailed. *See id.* at 5-6.

enhancing the possibility that African-Americans, who constitute a significant percentage of the population, may have responsive representation and the chance of some members of their race elected to the United States Congress.[159]

In the course of his trial for inciting an illegal strike, Dr. Nelson Mandela made the following statement about the pervasiveness of apartheid:

> In its proper meaning equality before the law means the right to participate in the making of the laws by which one is governed, a constitution which guarantees democratic rights to all sections of the population, the right to approach the court for protection or relief in the case of the violation of rights guaranteed in the constitution, and the right to take part in the administration of justice as judges, magistrates, attorneys-general, law advisers and similar positions.
>
> In the absence of these safeguards the phrase "equality before the law," in so far as it is intended to apply to us, is meaningless and misleading. All the rights and privileges to which I have referred are monopolised by whites, and we enjoy none of them.
>
> The white man makes all the laws, he drags us before his courts and accuses us, and he sits in judgement over us.
>
> It is fit and proper to raise the question sharply, what is this rigid colour-bar in the administration of justice? Why is it that in this courtroom I face a white magistrate, am confronted by a white prosecutor, and escorted into the dock by a white orderly? Can anyone honestly

---

159. No one has analyzed this issue better than Professor Charles V. Hamilton who has said:

> The macro-historical perspective seems to me to be eminently sound. Looking at Justice Souter's language of dissent in *Shaw v. Reno*, and recognizing that very much will turn around the color-blind/color conscious debate, it is crucial to put this issue in well-grounded historical context. That is, to indicate precisely why it is important to take race into account. There are certain 'realities' of developments over time that should not be overlooked. The courts (in the earlier white primary cases, the dilatory voter registration practices of southern boards of registrars, *Gomillion v. Lightfoot*) have faced these matters head-on and honestly. When ostensibly race-neutral practices were adopted or district lines drawn, the courts were not blind to the historical purpose of continuing racial *exclusion*.
>
> Today (on the flip side), we should not be blind to the need to take race into account for the ultimate purpose of *inclusion*. It is this constitutional *intent*—INCLUSION—that remains the goal.
>
> A good macro-historical perspective on the districts involved will illuminate this argument.
>
> The purpose is not to exclude, but to include. This is the historical journey as it brings us to present circumstances. It is a route 'political realities' require our country to take. Neither do we want these to be prescriptions for all time, but for these evolving times.

Memorandum from Charles V. Hamilton, the Wallace S. Sayre Professor, Columbia University, to the Honorable A. Leon Higginbotham, Jr. (Mar. 4, 1994) (on file with the *Fordham Law Review*). *See also* Charles V. Hamilton & Adam C. Powell Jr., The Political Biography of an American Dilemma (1991); Charles V. Hamilton, The Bench and the Ballot: Southern Federal Judges and Black Voters (1973); Charles V. Hamilton, The Black Experience in American Politics (1973).

> and seriously suggest that in this type of atmosphere the scales of justice are evenly balanced?[160]

As Nelson Mandela recognized, political apartheid is the complete exclusion of one race from governance and the domination of that race by another. Anyone conversant with the origins and development of apartheid would be shocked with the Supreme Court's suggestion that the North Carolina plan resembles "political apartheid."[161] Apartheid in South Africa is totally dissimilar to the voting rights issues in *Shaw v. Reno*.[162]

B. *"Little in Common with One Another But the Color of Their Skin"*

Equally disturbing is the premise supporting the Court's political apartheid analogy—that skin color is, or should be, irrelevant. In suggesting that minority-majority districts bring together those "who may have little in common with one another but the color of their skin,"[163] the Court implicitly hypothesizes that skin color is not relevant in American politics. That supposition, however, is insupportable in light of this country's racial history, and the past and current socio-economic conditions afflicting large segments of the African-American population, all of which uniquely inform African-American politics. Blackness *is* culturally and politically relevant. To suggest otherwise is not only naive, but demeaning.

For African-Americans, there is a commonality in the immutable characteristic of the "color of their skin."[164] It is skin color that rationalized the enslavement of African-Americans, and since emancipation, race has remained more significant an identifying factor than religion, region, age, class, or status. The history of race has been more important to African-Americans than to any other component in this society.

The commonality of the African-American experience has its origins, of course, in the abducting of Africans for slave labor in the New World.[165] Color was the common denominator in the following advertisement, typical of thousands of advertisements posted in newspapers and bulletin boards throughout our land:

> One hundred and twenty Negroes for sale—The subscriber has just arrived from Petersburg, Virginia, with one hundred and twenty likely

---

160. Nelson Mandela, The Struggle is My Life 135 (1990).
161. Shaw v. Reno, 113 S. Ct. 2816, 2827 (1993).
162. 113 S. Ct. 2816 (1993).
163. *Id.* at 2827.
164. *Id.*
165. Critics of minority-majority districting have challenged the commonality of black interests, contrasting the experiences and concerns of those African-Americans who are descendants of American slaves and those emigrating from the West Indies and South America. *See* Supreme Court Amicus Brief of American Jewish Congress, Wetherell v. De Grandy (No. 92-519), at 5-6, 113 S. Ct. 1249 (1993). Of course, in all of the New World, Africans were kidnapped to serve as slaves and servants to those of European ancestry.

> young Negroes of both sexes and every description, which he offers for sale on the most reasonable terms. The lot now on hand consists of plough-boys, several likely and well-qualified house servants of both sexes, several women and children, small girls suitable for nurses, and *several small boys without their mothers*. Planters and traders are earnestly requested to give the subscriber a call previously to making purchases elsewhere, as he is enabled to sell as cheap or cheaper than can be sold by any other person in the trade.
>
> —Hamburg, South Carolina, Benjamin Davis.[166]

Even after slavery was abolished, simply because of "the color of their skin,"[167] blacks were denied all rights of citizenship, the *least* of which were rights to participate in the political process. As the tools for the economic advancement of the white population, blacks were systemically deprived of fair treatment by the legislatures, executives, and judiciaries of every level of government from the county-level to the country-level.[168] In the context of slave codes, criminal codes, and post-Reconstruction Jim Crow legislation, laws defining the races were enacted to ensure that anyone who was "black" would—simply because of the color of his or her skin—be relegated to second-class citizenship.[169]

---

166. A. Leon Higginbotham, Jr., In the Matter of Color: Race and the American Legal Process, The Colonial Period 12 (1978) (quoting Benjamin Davis advertisement). Similarly, a *New Orleans Bee* advertisement noted:

> Negroes for sale—a Negro woman, 24 years of age, and her two children, one eight and the other three years old. Said Negroes will be sold separately or together, as desired. The woman is a good seamstress. She will be sold low for cash, or exchange for groceries. For terms apply to Matthew Bliss and Company, 1 Front Levee.

Id.

167. *Shaw*, 113 S. Ct. at 2827.

168. A. Leon Higginbotham has written extensively on this subject. *See* A. Leon Higginbotham & Anne F. Jacobs, *The "Law Only As An Enemy": The Legitimization of Racial Powerlessness through the Colonial and Antebellum Criminal Laws of Virginia*, 70 N.C. L. Rev. 969 (1992); A. Leon Higginbotham, Jr. & Greer C. Bosworth, *"Rather than the Free": Free Blacks in Colonial and Antebellum Virginia*, 26 Harv. C.R.-C.L. L. Rev. 17 (1991); A. Leon Higginbotham, *Race, Sex, Education and Missouri Jurisprudence:* Shelley v. Kraemer *in a Historical Perspective*, 67 Wash. U. L.Q. 673 (1989); A. Leon Higginbotham, Jr. & Barbara K. Kopytoff, *Racial Purity and Interracial Sex in the Law of Colonial and Antebellum Virginia*, 77 Geo. L.J. 1967 (1989); A. Leon Higginbotham, Jr. & Barbara K. Kopytoff, *Property First, Humanity Second: The Recognition of the Slave's Human Nature in Virginia Civil Law*, 50 Ohio St. L.J. 511 (1989).

169. *See generally* John H. Franklin, From Slavery to Freedom, A History of African-Americans 236-77 (7th ed. 1994) (discussing the post-Civil War development of "Jim Crow" laws and "Black Codes"). In Plessy v. Ferguson, 163 U.S. 537 (1896), the plaintiff, Homer Plessy, who alleged that he was seven-eighths white, asserted that racial segregation by the state was *per se* unconstitutional and that being considered a white man was property "which [had] an actual pecuniary value" that could not be taken without due process of law. Brief for Plaintiff in Error at 8, *Plessy v. Ferguson*, 163 U.S. 537 (No. 210). He stated:

> How much would it be *worth* to a young man entering upon the practice of law to be regarded as a *white* man rather than a colored one? Six-sevenths of the population are white. Nineteen-twentieths of the property of the country is owned by white people. Ninety-nine hundredths of the business opportunities

Indeed, *de jure* segregation was the norm until very recently.[170] And, as the Supreme Court itself has recognized, African-Americans continue to suffer from the effects of slavery, segregation, and prejudice.[171] As a direct result of hundreds of years of oppression, African-Americans are at the bottom of every socio-economic indicator. For example, according to information about North Carolina collected by various state and federal agencies, 61% of black households are classified as low income or very low income, in comparison to 36% of the white population.[172] In North Carolina's five major metropolitan areas there are at least four black children living in poverty for every white child living in poverty even though blacks are only 21.9% of the state's population.[173] African-American mothers are more likely to be "at risk" than white mothers, and more likely to receive sub-standard health care during pregnancy.[174] Large numbers of North Carolina's African-American population are on public assistance;[175] the unemployment rate for blacks in North Carolina is disproportionately high;[176] and the scholastic achievements of blacks in North Carolina are disproportionately low.[177]

In the course of his trial for sabotage and treason, Dr. Nelson Mandela described the link between socio-economic deprivation and political empowerment:

> are in the control of white people. These propositions are rendered even more startling by the intensity of feeling which excludes the colored man from the friendship and companionship of the white man. Probably most white persons if given a choice, would prefer death to life in the United States *as colored persons*. Under these conditions, is it possible to conclude that *reputation of being white* is not property? Indeed, is it not the most valuable sort of property, being the master-key that unlocks the golden door of opportunity?

Id. at 9.

170. It is only forty years since the Supreme Court overruled *Plessy* in Brown v. Board of Education, 347 U.S. 483, 495 (1954), holding that in the context of public education, separateness fostered inequality. Statutes requiring segregation in a variety of other contexts remained in force for a significant period after *Brown* was announced.

171. *See* Wygant v. Jackson Bd. of Educ., 476 U.S. 267, 276 (1986) (Powell, J.) ("No one doubts that there has been serious racial discrimination in this country."); *see also* Gingles v. Edmisten, 590 F. Supp. 345, 361-62 (E.D.N.C. 1984) (discussing continuing effects of discrimination in North Carolina), *modified sub nom.* Thornburg v. Gingles, 478 U.S. 30 (1986).

172. *See* North Carolina Housing Finance Agency, 1994-98 Comprehensive Housing Affordability Strategy, tbl. 1A (1993) (on file with the *Fordham Law Review*).

173. *See* Children's Defense Fund, Child Poverty Data from 1990 Census (1992) (on file with the *Fordham Law Review*).

174. *See* Kathryn B. Surles et al., North Carolina Dep't of Env't, Health & Natural Resources, Special Report: Health Status of Blacks in North Carolina, tbls. 10, 12, 13, 19 (1993) (on file with the *Fordham Law Review*).

175. *See* North Carolina Div. of Social Servs., AFDC Case Profile Summary, Cases Active on January 1, 1994 (1994) (on file with the *Fordham Law Review*); North Carolina Dep't of Human Resources Food Stamp Info. Sys., Case Information Profile (1993) (on file with the *Fordham Law Review*).

176. *See* U.S. Dep't of Labor, Geographic Profile of Employment and Unemployment, 1992 (Bulletin #2428), tbl. 12 (1993) (on file with the *Fordham Law Review*).

177. *See* North Carolina Dep't of Pub. Instruction, The North Carolina 1993 Scholastic Aptitude Test Report 20 (1993) (on file with the *Fordham Law Review*).

> Africans want to be paid a living wage . . . to perform work which they are capable of doing, and not work which the government declares them to be capable of . . . to be allowed to live where they obtain work . . . to be part of the general population, and not confined to living in their own ghettos . . . . Africans want to be allowed out after eleven o'clock at night and not to be confined to their rooms like little children . . . to be allowed to travel in their own country . . . . Africans want a just share in the whole of South Africa; they want security and a stake in society.
>
> *Above all, we want equal political rights, because without them our disabilities will be permanent.*[178]

Even the cultural experience of African-Americans has political significance. African-Americans share a cultural tradition with roots reaching back to slavery. Black churches, which during slavery were centers for illicit learning and part of the network of freedom, nourished the civil rights movement and continue today as centers of political activism.[179] Black music, rooted in the tradition of slave spirituals of freedom, continues today as a means of communicating political and social ideas. Black writers, excluded from the white press, created separate newspapers and magazines, used to call the government to respond to the plague of lynching, to inform black citizens of significant political events, and to advertize civil rights activities, traditions which continue today.[180] Culturally and politically, it is likely that two African-Americans will have more in common simply because of the color of their skin than will random persons who happen to live within the same compact district.

Ultimately the Supreme Court majority accomplishes what it cautions the plaintiffs not to do: it confuses the ideal of a color-blind society with the reality of our race-conscious society.[181] The *Shaw* majority put on blinders to dream of a world that Langston Hughes once described:

I Dream a World

I dream a world where man
No other will scorn,
Where love will bless the earth
And peace its paths adorn.
I dream a world where all
Will know sweet freedom's way,
Where greed no longer saps the soul

---

178. Mandela, *supra* note 160, at 180-81 (emphasis added).

179. Notably, many of the civil rights movement's most influential leaders come from the tradition of African-American religion: Rev. Martin Luther King, Adam Clayton Powell Jr., Malcolm X, Rev. Jesse Jackson, and Rev. Al Sharpton are all products of black religious organizations. *See generally* Evelyn B. Higginbotham, Righteous Discontent: The Women's Movement in the Black Baptist Church, 1880-1920 (1993) (discussing role of activists in the Baptist church).

180. Journalist Ida Wells-Barnett regularly published articles chronicling the lynchings plaguing the South and calling for action. *See* Flexner, *supra* note 81, at 192-93. That tradition was continued by *Crisis*, the magazine of the NAACP.

181. *See* Shaw v. Reno, 113 S. Ct. 2816, 2824 (1993).

Nor avarice blights our day.
A world I dream where black or white,
Whatever race you be,
Will share the bounties of the earth
And every man is free,
Where wretchedness will hang its head,
And joy, like a pearl,
Attend the needs of all mankind.
Of such I dream—
Our world![182]

Though Langston Hughes dreamt of a world where race was irrelevant, he described the contrasting reality of being black in America:

Let America Be America Again

Let America be America again.
Let it be the dream it used to be.
Let it be the pioneer on the plain
Seeking a home where he himself is free.
(America never was America to me.)
Let America be the dream the dreamers dreamed—
Let it be that great strong land of love
Where never kings connive nor tyrants scheme
That any man be crushed by one above.
(It never was America to me.)
O, let my land be a land where Liberty
Is crowned with no false patriotic wreath,
But opportunity is real, and life is free,
Equality is in the air we breathe.
(There's never been equality for me,
Nor freedom in this "homeland of the free.")[183]

On another occasion he wrote:

Merry-Go-Round

Where is the Jim Crow section
On this merry-go-round,
Mister, cause I want to ride?
Down South where I come from
White and colored
Can't sit side by side.
Down South on the train
There's a Jim Crow car.
On the bus we're put in the back —
But there ain't no back
To a merry-go-round!
Where's the horse
For a kid that's black?[184]

182. American Negro Poetry 71-72 (Arna Bontemps ed., 1963).
183. *Id.* at 193.
184. *Id.* at 192.

For African-Americans in North Carolina, for most of their lives, there has been no "merry-go-round" to ride in national political life. The 1991 Redistricting Act, which finally made it possible to have a concerned congressman "for a kid that's black," was necessitated by the continuing race-consciousness in our country and by the bonds of history, economics, and culture that still inexorably link African-Americans.

In our society, there is racial bloc voting; campaigns focus on civil rights initiatives, and political ads play on the most blatant stereotypes and fears surrounding race relations.[185] We doubt that the immutable characteristic of skin color will ever become irrelevant to politics. But even if that ideal is motivating the *Shaw* majority, to deem irregularly shaped minority-majority districts subject to strict scrutiny as overly "race-conscious" is counter-productive. As Justice Blackmun stated in *Bakke*, "[i]n order to get beyond racism, we must first take account of race. There is no other way."[186] We submit that American society has not yet reached a moment where African-Americans have "little in common with one another but the color of their skin."[187] The Supreme Court's voting rights law should not be based on a politically appealing dream that denies all of American history. The law should not distort that history such that the concept of "color blindness" is used—like a surgeon's scalpel—to excise African-Americans from significant political power.

C. *"Segregation" . . . "Stereotypes" . . . "Representative Democracy" and Federalism*

The Supreme Court's majority opinion, with its comments on racial "segregation," "stereotypes," and "representative democracy" also suggests naiveté about the history of American race relations and the competence of African-American congresspersons. The majority concludes that "an effort to *segregate* voters into separate voting districts because of their race [violates equal protection if] the separation lacks sufficient justification."[188] The Court reasoned:

> If our society is to continue to progress as a multiracial democracy, it must recognize that the automatic invocation of race *stereotypes* retards that progress and causes continued hurt and injury. . . . By perpetuating such notions, a racial gerrymander may exacerbate the

185. *See supra* notes 99-133 and accompanying text.

186. Regents of the Univ. of Cal. v. Bakke, 438 U.S. 265, 407 (1978). Justice Blackmun continued:

> And in order to treat some persons equally, we must treat them differently. We cannot—we dare not—let the Equal Protection Clause perpetuate racial supremacy.

Id. See also David A. Strauss, *The Myth of Colorblindness*, 1986 Sup. Ct. Rev. 99, 114 ("[W]e do not have a choice between colorblindness and race-consciousness; we only have a choice between different forms of race-consciousness.").

187. Shaw v. Reno, 113 S. Ct. 2816, 2827 (1993).

188. *Id.* at 2832 (emphasis added).

> very pattern of racial bloc voting that majority-minority districting is sometimes said to counteract . . . .
>
> When a district obviously is created solely to effectuate the perceived common interests of one racial group, elected officials are more likely to believe that their primary obligation is to represent only the members of that group, rather than their *constituency as a whole*. This is altogether antithetical to our system of *representative democracy*."[189]

The Supreme Court majority also suggested the irregular shape of the Twelfth District was possibly *de jure* segregation, writing that "a reapportionment plan may be so highly irregular that, on its face, it rationally cannot be understood as anything other than an effort to '*segregat[e]* . . . voters' on the basis of race."[190]

The South's long-term oppression of African-Americans required and sanctioned racial separation and racial discrimination. This segregation involved, *inter alia*, denying blacks first-rate public accommodations in restaurants, hotels, and public facilities. It existed in housing, educational policies, and employment—in nearly every facet of life. It notoriously required black children to attend separate schools, and blacks to ride in the back of buses, use separate bathrooms, and drink from separate water fountains.[191]

Racist segregation, however, is not analogous to a white voter's residence in a congressional district where a slight majority of the voting population is African-American. No person residing in either District One or District Twelve is required to live in those districts; nor is anyone precluded from moving to any of the other ten congressional districts in North Carolina. Nor has any person had his or her vote diluted by reason of living in either District One or District Twelve.[192]

---

189. *Id.* at 2827 (quoting Edmonson v. Leesville Concrete Co., 111 S. Ct. 2077, 2088 (1991)) (emphasis added).

190. *Id.* at 2826-27 (citing Gomillion v. Lightfoot, 364 U.S. 339, 341 (1960)) (emphasis added). The majority went on to liken District Twelve to the district at issue in *Gomillion*:

> *Gomillion*, in which a tortured municipal boundary line was drawn to exclude black voters, was such a case. So, too, would be a case in which a State concentrated a dispersed minority population in a single district by disregarding traditional districting principles such as compactness, contiguity, and respect for political subdivisions.

Shaw, 113 S. Ct. at 2826-27. But as Justice Souter notes, *Gomillion* is distinguishable from *Shaw* in that the *Gomillion* plaintiffs alleged a constitutional harm—being excluded from voting within the municipality in which they lived. *See id.* at 2846 (Souter, J., dissenting) ("[R]ace-based discrimination places the disfavored voters at the disadvantage of exclusion from the franchise.").

191. *See* Regents of the Univ. of Cal. v. Bakke, 438 U.S. 265, 387-402 (1978) (Marshall, J., dissenting).

192. As Justice Souter explained:

> The majority's use of 'segregation' to describe the effect of districting here may suggest that it carries effects comparable to school segregation making it subject to like scrutiny. But a principal consequence of school segregation was inequality in educational opportunity provided, whereas use of race (or any other

White voters who live in District One or District Twelve have no fewer rights than African-Americans living in any of the ten other congressional districts of North Carolina, where the African-American population is less than 50%, but in some instances as high as 20%.[193] The use of the term "segregation" thus reveals a certain naiveté by the majority of the Court: as long as African-Americans constitute less than a majority of a district, the Court suggests, the district is "integrated," but once the black presence exceeds 50%—however slightly—the district is "segregated."[194] But it is not rational to equate districts having 53% black voters with the oppression of racial segregation that America sanctioned for decades.

D. *North Carolina's Integrated Districts Are Neither Apartheid Nor Segregation*

Suggestions that Districts One and Twelve amount to political apartheid or segregation are poorly reasoned. Apartheid, an official policy designed to exclude the members of one racial group from participating in government, is instituted by the promulgation of restrictive legislation *adversely impacting* a disenfranchised population.

By contrast, North Carolina's First and Twelfth Districts are not the black "homelands"—they are not isolated or segregated black ghettos. They are integrated districts, where African-Americans constitute only slight majorities and voters are not required to vote for representatives of a particular race. Indeed, candidates in these districts have as much of a probability of facing a diverse field of opponents as do candidates in any of the other ten districts. Once elected, all representatives sit in Congress, not in a separate legislative body, where they vote on a national legislative agenda. African-American representatives do not speak only to "black" interests, any more than representatives from Iowa farmlands speak only to "farming interests" and representatives from New York City or Chicago speak only to "urban interests." Indeed, Congressman Watt and Congresswoman Clayton have distinguished themselves with service in the House for their constituents on a broad range of issues.[195]

In this last regard, it is worth remembering that many of the interests

---

group characteristic) in districting does not without more deny equality of political participation.

Shaw, 113 S. Ct. at 2846 n.4 (Souter, J., dissenting).

193. *See supra* notes 141-45 and accompanying text.

194. The "tipping phenomenon" has been recognized by many courts and sociologists as a proven phenomenon, in which white flight is precipitated by the perception by whites of "over integration," when African-Americans are more than 33% of a neighborhood's population. *See, e.g.*, Burney v. Housing Auth. of County of Beaver, 551 F. Supp. 746, 766 (W.D. Pa. 1982) (discussing cases and commentaries).

195. In fact, Congresswoman Clayton was not only elected president of the Democratic freshman class but also was recently voted "most influential newcomer to the Hill." *See Michel Closes on Foley in 'Most Respected, Tally,'* Roll Call, Feb. 7, 1994, at 6.

One of the most disturbing aspects of the Court's opinion is its pejorative implications as to the capabilities of African-American public officials. The Court stressed:

of particular concern to North Carolina's African-American voters are shared by the state's whites of similar socio-economic deprivation. High unemployment and poverty, increased incidents of violent crime and police brutality, and limited health care resources—although issues that disproportionately impact the African-American community—are not issues limited to the black community. Indeed, in creating the First and Twelfth Districts, North Carolina legislators, while preserving the interests of incumbents and the balance of political power within the state, created districts that, although awkwardly shaped, gracefully unite a multi-racial coalition of interests.[196] What is significant then about the voters of the First and Twelfth districts is that their interests are similar on many key issues—regardless of race. These districts are not "black" districts, are not political apartheid, and are not racially segregated. In fact, the opposite is true.

At a minimum, the First and Twelfth Districts ensure representation that will fairly effectuate the concerns of African-American and white voters, without fear of neglect or intimidation. They cause in effect the

---

> When a district obviously is created solely to effectuate the perceived common interests of one racial group, elected officials *are more likely to believe that their primary obligation is to represent only the members of that group*, rather than their constituency as a whole. This is altogether antithetical to our system of representative democracy.

Shaw v. Reno, 113 S. Ct. 2816, 2827 (1993) (emphasis added). Mel Watt is a Phi Beta Kappa graduate of the University of North Carolina and a Yale Law School graduate. Eva Clayton holds Bachelor's and Master's degrees from Johnson C. Smith University and North Carolina Central University. Both are able to represent their "constituency as a whole," certainly as well as the white congressmen who for nine decades, the Supreme Court apparently assumes, represented their "constituency as a whole." Mel Watt and Eva Clayton, no doubt, will more steadfastly protect the rights of their white constituents than did Senators Willis Smith and Jesse Helms protect the rights of their black constituents. *See supra* notes 5, 99-107, 120-22 and accompanying text. Unless the Court truly believes that African-American representatives are inherently less capable than their white counterparts, it should exercise caution when making suggestions about black representatives' abilities "to represent only the members of [their] group." *Shaw*, 113 S. Ct. at 2827.

196. District One connects voters in several sparsely populated, largely rural counties. *See* Clayton, *supra* note 135, ¶ 2. The district's inhabitants include the state's largest concentration of small farmers, as well as many small business proprietors, government and military employees, and employees at several area colleges. The district has a large proportion of "working poor families." *Id.* ¶ 2.B. Economic development and increased community services, like health care, housing, and utilities delivery, are issues that unite the voters of the First District. *See id.* ¶ 2.B-C.

Similarly, the Twelfth District brings together voters with common socio-economic backgrounds and interests. These voters are largely urban and dependent upon an industrial economic base. *See* Affidavit of Jose F. Alvarez, ¶¶ 4-6, 9-14 (sworn to Mar. 23, 1994) (submitted as evidence in Shaw v. Hunt, No. 92-202-CIV-5-BR (E.D.N.C.)); Watt, *supra* note 13, ¶ 18. In addition to shared concerns about labor and foreign trade arising from the textile industry, which dominates the district, as urban dwellers the voters of District Twelve share concerns about crime, housing, and community investment. *See generally*, Lonni Guanier, *Groups, Representation, and Race-Conscious Redistricting: A Case of the Emperor's New Clothes*, 71 Tex. L. Rev. 1589, 1593 n.18 (1993) (criticizing *Shaw* and arguing that North Carolina's African-American constituency is politically cohesive).

inclusion of African-Americans in the political process. The presence of two representatives from North Carolina who are responsive to the concerns of their constituents will go far towards preventing the continued promulgation of policies that, at best, are insensitive to the plight of African-Americans, and, at worst, exacerbate the deteriorating condition of blacks in America.

VI. Pluralism in Congress: A Barrier to Perpetuating "Historic White Supremacy"[197]

In *Shaw*, the Supreme Court relies on an ideal of democracy that the United States has yet to, and might never, attain. Wielding this vision, the Court has created a dynamic that might undermine the recent strides toward pluralism made in Congress.

A. *Defining "Representative Democracy"*

In *Shaw*, the majority speaks of "our system of representative democracy,"[198] resurrecting a view of democracy expressed by Justice Douglas in his dissent in *Wright v. Rockefeller*.[199] Under this view, the 1991 redistricting puts at risk " 'the multiracial, multireligious communities that our Constitution seeks to weld together as one,' " by " 'emphasizing differences between candidates and voters that are irrelevant in the constitutional sense.' "[200] The Court's reliance on Justice Douglas's dissent is fitting, as he would have invalidated the districting plan that had enabled Adam Clayton Powell, Jr. to return to Congress. Justice Douglas, in the guise of ensuring that "race . . . creed or . . . color" would not be inappropriately interjected into the "democratic ideal,"[201] would have denied minority voters an important voice in Congress during the height of the Civil Rights movement, a time when race, creed, and color were of paramount concern to the nation. Those issues still inform American politics. Accordingly, the *Shaw* majority's belief in "our system of representative democracy" is no more realistic than Justice Douglas' faith in a democratic ideal in which "the individual['s] . . . race, his creed or his color" is not important.

What does the *Shaw* majority envision when it speaks of "our system of representative democracy"? Was our system a "representative democracy" when the Supreme Court declared in *Dred Scott* that a black man "had no rights which the white man was bound to respect"?[202] Was our system a representative democracy from 1901 to 1927 when there were no African-Americans in the United States House of Representatives, or

197. Franklin, *supra* note 169, at 259.
198. *Shaw*, 113 S. Ct. at 2827.
199. 376 U.S. 52, 59 (1964).
200. *Shaw*, 113 S. Ct. at 2827 (quoting Wright v. Rockefeller, 376 U.S. 52, 66-67 (1964) (Douglas, J., dissenting)).
201. *Wright*, 376 U.S. at 66-67 (Douglas, J. dissenting).
202. Dred Scott v. Sandford, 60 U.S. (19 How.) 393, 407 (1857).

from 1929 to 1944, when there was only one African-American voice in Congress?[203] The voice of that one representative, Congressman Arthur Mitchell, was all but drowned out by the antagonistic posturing of his white colleagues. During the 1936 Democratic convention, for example, his own party rejected his participation in the electoral process: "Congressman Mitchell's presence on the podium . . . was used as an excuse for a U.S. senator from South Carolina and eight other delegates to stage a walkout in protest. But even that demonstration was mild compared to what had happened in previous conventions . . . ."[204]

In fact, Congressman Mitchell was a second class citizen to Congress, his party, and his country. On April 30, 1937, he boarded a Pullman car in Chicago with a first class ticket to Hot Springs, Arkansas. When the conductor told him that he could no longer ride in the first class section (the train had crossed state lines), Mitchell, as he later testified, "thought it might do some good for me to tell him who I was."[205] After he identified himself as a United States Congressman, according to Mitchell, the conductor said "it didn't make a damn bit of difference who I was, that as long as I was a nigger I couldn't ride in that car."[206] Mitchell testified:

> [F]or a moment I decided that I wouldn't go, that I would let them put me in jail down there and see how the thing would finally come out.
>
> But I happened to think that I was in Arkansas, and sometimes they don't keep them in jail for trial down there, but they take them out and lynch them after they put them in jail; so I thought maybe I had better not; being the only negro in Congress, that I had better not be lynched on that trip.[207]

Mitchell retreated to the decrepit black coach.[208]

Was our system a representative democracy when from 1945 to 1955

---

203. *See* African-Americans in the U.S. Congress, 1870-1993, *infra* app. A.

204. William L. Clay, Just Permanent Interests: Black Americans in Congress 1870-1991, at 72 (1992).

205. Record from the United States Supreme Court, Mitchell v. United States Interstate Commerce Comm'n, 313 U.S. 80 (1941) (No. 577), at 79 (reprinting the testimony of Arthur W. Mitchell before the Interstate Commerce Comm'n, Mitchell v. Chicago, R.I. & Pac. Ry., 229 I.C.C. 703 (1938) (No. 27844)), *quoted in* A. Leon Higginbotham, Jr. & William C. Smith, *The Hughes Court and The Beginning of The End of The "Separate but Equal" Doctrine*, 76 Minn. L. Rev. 1099, 1103 (1992).

206. Higginbotham, *supra* note 205, at 1103 (testimony of Arthur W. Mitchell).

207. *Id.* at 1103-04 (testimony of Arthur W. Mitchell).

208. *See id.* "The conductor's behavior was in clear violation of a 1914 Supreme Court ruling that the denial of first class accommodations on trains to blacks violated the Fourteenth Amendment." *Id.* at 1103; *see* McCabe v. Atchison, T. & S.F. Ry., 235 U.S. 151, 161-62 (1914). "In 1941, the Supreme Court declared that the railroad's treatment of Mitchell violated his rights under the Interstate Commerce Act." Higginbotham, *supra* note 205, at 1103; *see* Mitchell v. United States Interstate Commerce Comm'n, 313 U.S. 80, 97 (1941). The *Mitchell* Court concluded that "the discrimination shown was palpably unjust and forbidden by the [Interstate Commerce] Act." *Mitchell*, 313 U.S. at 97. Mitchell eventually received $1,250 in settlement. *See* Higginbotham, *supra* note 205, at 1103.

there were only *two* African-Americans in the United States Congress?[209] The feelings of helplessness many African-Americans experienced in these decades was expressed poignantly by Richard Wright in his introduction to the classic sociological treatise, *Black Metropolis*.[210] Wright wrote:

> [I]n the 1920's, when racial hate was at a hysterical pitch, and after the grinding processes of history had forged iron in the Negro's heart, we hear a new and strange cry from another Negro, Claude McKay. In his sonnet, *If We Must Die*, he seems to snarl through a sob:
>
> If we must die—let it not be like hogs
> Hunted and penned in an inglorious spot,
> While round us bark the mad and hungry dogs,
> Making their mock at our accursed lot.
> If we must die—oh, let us nobly die,
> So that our precious blood may not be shed
> In vain; then even the monsters we defy
> Shall be constrained to honor us though dead!
> Oh, kinsmen! We must meet the common foe;
> Though far outnumbered, let us still be brave,
> And for their thousand blows deal one death-blow!
> What though before us lies the open grave?
> Like men we'll face the murderous, cowardly pack
> Pressed to the wall, dying, but—fighting back!
>
> What has America done to people who could sing out in limpid verse to make them snarl about being 'pressed to the wall' and dealing 'one death-blow?' Is this the result of a three-hundred-year policy of 'knowing niggers and what's good for 'em?' Is this the salvation which Christian missionaries have brought to the 'heathen from Africa?' That there is something wrong here only fools would deny.
>
> White America has reduced Negro life in our great cities to a level of experience of so crude and brutal a quality that one could say of it in the words of Vachel Lindsay's *The Leaden-Eyed* that:
>
> It is not that they starve, but they starve so dreamlessly,
> It is not that they sow, but that they seldom reap,
> It is not that they serve, but they have no gods to serve,
> It is not that they die, but that they die like sheep.[211]

The presence of two African-Americans in Congress contributed little towards efforts to shed the African-American community of its outsider status. Even in 1957, when *four* of 545 members of Congress were African-Americans, did not the significant lack of racial pluralism in Congress signify that America was not a representative democracy?[212] During that period, congressmen from the South almost uniformly joined the Southern Manifesto expressing in chorus resistance to *Brown*

209. *See* Congressional Representation (House and Senate), 1871-1993, *infra* app. C.
210. St. Clair Drake & Horace R. Clayton, Black Metropolis: A Study of Negro Life in a Northern City at xxxiii-xxxiv (1945) (introduction by Richard Wright).
211. *Id.*
212. *See* African-Americans in the U.S. Congress, 1870-1993, *infra* app. A.

and its anti-segregation signal.[213]

In 1965, Adam Clayton Powell, Jr., a representative of Congress (despite Justice Douglas' opposition in *Wright*), and three other sitting black congressmen, voted in support of the Voting Rights Act of 1965.[214] As a direct result of that Act, African-American voters were no longer barred from the polls, and the number of African-American representatives began to increase. The input of these representatives, who have included John Conyers, Jr. (D-Mich. 1965-present), William L. Clay (D-Mo. 1969-present), Shirley Chisholm (D-NY 1969-82), Charles Rangel (D-NY 1970-present), Ron Dellums (D-Ca. 1971-present), Barbara Jordan (D-Tx. 1973-78), and Andrew Young (D-Ga. 1973-77), among others, has been influential in focusing at least some attention on issues of importance to African-Americans.

Yet, these voices did not begin to make the Congress "look like America" until recent elections, which brought the tally of members of the Congressional Black Caucus to forty.[215]

These new congresspersons finally have the possibility of insuring that issues of African-American concern are brought before the Congress. For example, because of the influence of African-American voters in North Carolina's minority-majority districts, their representatives are responsive to issues of special concern to *all* black North Carolinians. As long as these districts remain minority-majority black, it is likely that the interests of the historically black colleges will be aggressively addressed,[216] and that redlining practices of banks affecting black neighborhoods will be closely scrutinized.[217] Funding for Head Start programs will be vigorously pursued, and cutbacks to social services will be challenged by representatives ready to dispute the stereotypes of lazy black men and "welfare mothers." Furthermore, unlike some of their predecessors who attempted to thwart the interests of African-American voters, these representatives can support civil rights initiatives without fear that taking a principled stand will end their political careers.

But the importance of a pluralistic Congress is not only bringing "African-American" issues to the fore; a pluralistic Congress, perhaps more importantly, also nurtures a truer representative democracy. A Congress with members of all colors brings more American citizens into the political system, as it announces that government is for *all* Americans, increases the confidence of *all* American voters in the government, and

213. Nineteen senators and 83 representatives from the South joined the Manifesto. *See* Norman Dorsen et al., 2 Political and Civil Rights in the United States 700 n.2 (4th ed. 1979).

214. 42 U.S.C. §§ 1971-1973 (1965).

215. *See* African-Americans in the U.S. Congress, 1870-1993, *infra* app. A.

216. *See* Affidavit of Dr. Robert Albright, ¶¶ 7-8 (sworn to Mar. 19, 1994) (submitted in Shaw v. Hunt, No. 92-202-CIV-5-BR (E.D.N.C.)).

217. *See* Affidavit of J.C. Harris, ¶¶ 7-8 (sworn to Mar. 23, 1994) (submitted in Shaw v. Hunt, No. 92-202-CIV-5-BR (E.D.N.C.)).

thereby cultivates political participation of *all* Americans.[218]

Thus, the challenge in these present voting rights cases is whether the significant racial pluralism finally occurring in the United States Congress will prevail—whether the voices and interests of minorities and, indeed, all Americans will be welcomed in the public debate—or whether the voices of minorities again will be silenced.

B. *The Problems of an Unrepresentative Congress*

Some people might ask what is wrong in having an unrepresentative Congress. They may prefer boundary lines that are compact and neatly drawn at the expense of racial pluralism in Congress. Minimizing pluralism in Congress, however, comes at a high cost: the confidence of large segments of the population in the government is undermined and the insight of the body is significantly limited. Those groups that are the most tolerant of an unrepresentative Congress, we believe, are composed primarily of individuals who have been the major beneficiaries of a congressional system that is not pluralistic in its composition.[219] They are content with the system as long as their "group" enjoys a more advantageous position than it would were the Congress more representative of the population. However, the adverse impact of an unrepresentative Congress on both the public's perception of the Congress and the Congress' perception of the public is significant.

The Armed Services, which are disproportionately black and poor, provide a palpable example of the necessity that all Americans have confidence in a government that they perceive to be representative, particularly when that government makes decisions impacting that group. As was noted in *The New York Times* during the Gulf War:

> Close to 30 percent of the Army's troops in Operation Desert Storm are black, though blacks are just 14 percent of the nation's population between the ages of 18 and 24. In a land war, black casualties will be similarly disproportionate. Is it fair? Is it inevitable? For answers, one must search the soul of American society.[220]

The decision to commit forces to combat bears much less legitimacy when the legislative body acting in support of that decision does not well represent soldiers sent to combat, in other words, when Congress is not pluralistic.[221]

---

218. For a thoughtful review of these and other issues, see Kathryn Abrams, *Raising Politics Up: Minority Political Participation and Section 2 of the Voting Rights Act*, 63 N.Y.U. L. Rev. 449 (1988).

219. As an example, in a somewhat different context, most Americans seemed oblivious or indifferent to the fact that until October 1992, Presidents Reagan and Bush between them had appointed 115 court of appeals judges, only two of whom were African-American. *See* A. Leon Higginbotham, Jr., *The Case of the Missing Black Judges*, N.Y. Times, July 29, 1992, at A21.

220. *The Killing Fields Aren't Level*, N.Y. Times, Jan. 28, 1991, at A2.

221. The fears of African-American servicemen and women and their families were surely lessened by the participation of General Colin Powell, America's first African-

Further, in the context of the Gulf War, the value of a pluralistic body deciding whether to send soldiers into combat was particularly acute. Public opinion was sharply divided on race (and gender) lines. In fact, although most black voters supported the war effort, twice as many blacks as whites—39% vs. 19%—thought President Bush should have given sanctions more time to work.[222]

Some persons might argue that it is possible to have a viable, fair, and effective congressional system even when there is no significant correlation between the composition of the Congress and the nation's population. Nevertheless, we submit that it is difficult to have a Congress that in the long run has the respect of most segments of the public unless it has significant pluralistic strands in its composition. Although the values held by each individual congressperson are important, and although mere pluralism does not guarantee an effective Congress, pluralism is nevertheless an important virtue, a *sine qua non* to building a Congress that is both substantively excellent and also respected by the general population. A pluralistic Congress brings a variety of backgrounds and experiences to pressing issues of social policies, which demand innovation to solve. More often than not, congressional homogeneity and exclusivity are deterrents to, rather than promoters of, such innovation.[223] In contrast, a pluralistic Congress raises the likelihood that that body will identify the concerns of *all* Americans. As was recently demonstrated in the debate over whether to retire at full rank the Navy's top admiral—who commanded that organization at the time of the infamous "Tailhook Scandal"—the presence of women in the Senate stirred unprecedented soul searching and insight on that gender-related issue.[224]

American Joint Chief of Staff, in the command decision-making process. General Powell's sentiment that the soldiers fighting in the Gulf "were family . . . [no matter] what color they were, where they came from, whether they were rich or poor" was a poignant statement, a marked departure from prior commanders of an institution which had perpetuated segregation in its ranks. African Americans: Voices of Triumph—Perseverance 177 (Time Life Books ed., 1993).

222. Suzanne Alexander et al., *Guns vs. Butter: Many Blacks Oppose America's Role in War Citing Domestic Needs*, Wall St. J., Jan. 25, 1991, at A1, A7.

> While some successful black businessmen support the war, for instance, others oppose it. Thomas Hightower, a businessman in Burbank, Calif., says, 'It's not about civil rights, but about oil. And look who's at the heart of the decision-making process: wealthy white males who are sending minorities to their death.'

Id.

223. The essence of pluralism in Congress is the influence of myriad individual experiences. As Justice Benjamin Cardozo has advised us with respect to judges:

> We do not pick our rules of law full-blossomed from the trees. Every judge [and congressperson] consulting his own *experience* must be conscious of times when a free exercise of will, directed of set purpose to the furtherance of the common good, determined the form and tendency of a rule which at that moment took its origin in one creative act.

Benjamin N. Cardozo, The Nature of the Judicial Process 103-04 (1921) (emphasis added).

224. *See* Maureen Dowd, *Senate Approves a 4-Star Rank for Admiral in Tailhook Af-*

Professor Charles Warren categorized the problem, with respect to courts, this way:

> The Court is not an organism dissociated from the conditions and history of the times in which it exists. It does not formulate and deliver its opinions in a legal vacuum. Its Judges are not abstract and impersonal oracles, but are men whose views are necessarily, though by no conscious intent, affected by inheritance, education and environment and by the impact of history past and present.[225]

Warren's analysis is equally applicable to a legislature and its members. A vastly unrepresentative legislature may articulate precepts or laws that seem appropriate to its members, who never imagine that their views may be nothing more than the "prejudices" they "share with [some of] their fellow-men."[226] The American experience is replete with examples of such legislative biases.[227]

The courts provide a provocative example of the problems of unrecognized prejudices. On a homogeneous court, no "outsider" challenges the biases the dominant group accepts as "self-evident" truths. As Justice Sandra Day O'Connor, the first woman on the U.S. Supreme Court, has

---

fair: 54-43 Vote Follows Heated Debate on Floor, N.Y. Times, Apr. 20, 1994, at A1, B10. As was reported:

> [A]ll seven women in the Senate joined in trying to stop Admiral Kelso, the Chief of Naval Operations from retiring at four-star rank. . . . The women in the Senate were angrily opposed in the debate by other Senators from both sides of the aisle . . . . There were vivid signs in the chamber of women's progress. . . . But the women in the chamber clearly felt more progress was needed.

Id. We need not spend much time wondering whether the result of that debate would have differed had women been closer to their 50% proportionate share of Senate members rather than merely 7%.

225. 1 Charles Warren, The Supreme Court in United States History 2 (1926).

226. Oliver W. Holmes, The Common Law 1 (1881) ("[E]ven the prejudices which judges share with their fellow-men, have had a good deal more to do than the syllogism in determining the rules by which men should be governed.") As Professor David A. Strauss has noted:

> If a person is prejudiced against black people, his prejudice will manifest itself whenever he deals with a black person. It follows that if a legislator is prejudiced, his prejudice will manifest itself whenever he votes on legislation affecting black people, at least so long as he knows it affects them. If, for example, he has—as one theory holds—a tendency to be insufficiently sympathetic to the burdens placed on blacks, this tendency will manifest itself whenever legislation places burdens on blacks. Whether the explicit terms of the legislation happen to mention blacks is immaterial.

David A. Strauss, *The Myth of Colorblindness*, 1986 Sup. Ct. Rev. 99, 121.

227. The Congressional Quarterly, describing the passage of the 1965 Voting Rights Act, detailed twelve critical civil rights initiatives defeated in Congress, including two anti-lynching statutes, five initiatives addressing poll taxes and literacy tests, three bills concerning fair employment practices, and two Civil Rights Acts. *See* Cong. Q. Almanac 551 (1965). Similarly, gender prejudice influenced Congress and state legislatures, which in 1871 incorporated gender in the Fifteenth Amendment to ensure women did not gain suffrage. *See* Flexner, *supra* note 81, at 152 (discussing greater support for black suffrage than for female suffrage). Sexist attitudes successfully thwarted efforts to incorporate women into the electorate until the passage of the Nineteenth Amendment in 1920.

recently written of Justice Thurgood Marshall, the first black on the Supreme Court:

> At oral arguments and conference meetings, in opinions and dissents, Justice Marshall imparted not only his legal acumen but also his life experiences, pushing and prodding us to respond not only to the persuasiveness of legal argument but also to the power of moral truth.[228]

Justice O'Connor concluded that the stories of such outsiders "made clear what legal briefs often obscure: the impact of legal rules on human lives."[229]

Pluralism allows a mutual education process between individuals. Minorities learn of the concerns and fears of majorities, while majorities learn of the lives of others and experiences that they may well be unable to imagine. The sharing of such life experience is indisputedly necessary if American democracy is to thrive.

We do not want to be misunderstood. Pluralism does not mean that only a person of one race will be able to legislate a matter fairly when his or her race is involved. Pluralism is not grounded on the premise that a person of a specific race, religion, ethnic background, gender, or region is able to decide an issue more appropriately than a person of another race, religion, ethnic background, gender, or region.[230] Instead, we are suggesting that pluralism guards against the influences of individual prejudice,[231] and further creates a milieu in which the entire congressional system benefits from the multi-faceted experiences of its members. A pluralistic Congress insures that the public does not perceive the legislature as having a vested interest in the preservation of the status quo, and all Americans, whether victims of discrimination or not, can believe that

228. Sandra D. O'Connor, *The Story Behind the Storyteller Thurgood Marshall*, Phila. Inquirer, July 5, 1992, at E7 [hereinafter O'Connor, *Story*]; *see also* Sandra D. O'Connor, *Thurgood Marshall: The Influence of a Raconteur*, 44 Stan. L. Rev. 1217, 1217 (1992) [hereinafter O'Connor, *Influence*].

229. O'Connor, *Story*, *supra* note 228, at E7.

230. Similarly, we are not suggesting that all persons of the same racial, religious, or ethnic background share a monolithic view of every issue. There is almost as much difference between the views of Justice Thurgood Marshall, the first African-American to serve on the U.S. Supreme Court, and Justice Clarence Thomas, the second African-American to hold that honor, as there is between what mathematicians would call the difference between infinity and zero. Justice Thomas's views, in fact, are antithetical to those of most African-Americans. *See Race-ing Justice, En-Gendering Power: Essays on Anita Hill, Clarence Thomas, and the Construction of Social Reality* (Toni Morrison ed., 1992).

231. As is detailed in one article, newly appointed Justice Ginsburg experienced the effects of discriminatory practices based on her ethnicity and gender. *See* Elizabeth E. Gillman & Joseph M. Micheletti, *Justice Ruth Bader Ginsburg*, 3 Seton Hall Const. L.J. 657, 657 (1993). When a Harvard student, she was considered a usurper of a seat more appropriately filled by a male, and in every class she was forced to prove her worth. Although a top student, she was refused work by New York law firms, who feared as a wife and mother she would not be able to devote her "full mind and time to a law job." *Id.* at 658. The New York law firms of today, now reflecting the influence of capable women associates and partners, would consider carefully before rejecting such an able graduate on the basis of outmoded "mommy" stereotypes.

the legislature is foremost concerned with advancing the good of the nation.

C. *Racial Pluralism and Leverage in Congress*

The number of African-Americans in the United States Congress became truly significant when their number rose from 26 in 1991 to 40 in 1993. Yet *Shaw v. Reno* and its progeny have challenged this progress. These lawsuits threaten to reduce the number of African-Americans in Congress by thirty percent, and once again, to diminish the political impact of black citizens.

Pluralism serves more than merely an educational function—it also has a leveraging factor and determines the scope of political influence, as Dr. David Bositis suggests:

> If all diversity of experience brings to the Congress are other voices and anecdotes that the traditional membership might sample and consider in their deliberations, that is not enough. Political leverage requires [that] those traditional members—typically white middle class males—must seriously regard those new representatives as full partners, and as in the past (principally in dealing with their white peers), fear the repercussions that come with overlooking the just and reasonable demands of these new and different members.[232]

A manifestation of leveraging has already occurred. The House Democratic Caucus met on July 11, 1993 to consider disciplining eleven Democratic subcommittee chairmen, who voted against President Clinton's budget. This meeting was summoned at the behest of eighty-one Democratic members, a majority of whom were minority group members and women. While no action was taken against these chairmen, this is the first time such an attempt was made, and further, it clearly signaled the new influence of the expanded Black and Hispanic caucuses.[233]

In the 103rd United States Congress there are twenty-two standing House committees.[234] Except for the Committee on Natural Resources, there is at least one African-American on each committee.[235] If the freshman congressmen of 1993 return in substantial numbers, with their seniority increasing, African-American congressmen will be a formidable group in assisting to shape the federal government's national policies. It is that breadth of power that *Shaw v. Reno* threatens.

---

232. Memorandum from Dr. David A. Bositis, April 20, 1994, to A. Leon Higginbotham, Jr. (on file with the *Fordham Law Review*).

233. *See id.*

234. Agriculture; Appropriations; Armed Services; Banking, Finance and Urban Affairs; Budget; District of Columbia; Education and Labor; Energy and Commerce; Foreign Affairs; Government Operations; House Administration; Judiciary; Merchant Marine and Fisheries; Natural Resources; Post Office and Civil Service; Public Works and Transportation; Rules; Science, Space and Technology; Small Business; Standards of Official Conduct; Veterans Affairs; Ways and Means.

235. *See* Bositis, *supra* note 57, at 6 & tbl. 8.

The 1969 report of the National Commission on the Causes and Prevention of Violence warned the nation:

> When in man's long history other great civilizations fell, it was less often from external assault than from internal decay. Our own civilization has shown a remarkable capacity for responding to crises and for emerging to higher pinnacles of power and achievement. But our most serious challenges to date have been external—the kind this strong and resourceful country could unite against. While serious external dangers remain, the graver threats today are internal: haphazard urbanization, racial discrimination, disfiguring of the environment, unprecedented interdependence, the dislocation of human identity and motivation created by an affluent society—all resulting in a rising tide of individual and group violence.
>
> The greatness and durability of most civilizations has been finally determined by how they have responded to these challenges from within. Ours will be no exception.[236]

The challenge to America is to solve our problems from within—in the legislative halls, in the courts, and in government, rather than to allow increased deterioration from within so that the rule of law becomes less relevant because the weak, the poor, and the dispossessed feel they have no advocates pleading their cause. We cannot close our eyes to crisis in American society today. When there is no dilution of the white vote, the Supreme Court should not preclude states from working toward significant minority representation, as a means of solving problems in legislatures.[237]

CONCLUSION

Ninety-eight years ago, the United States Supreme Court decided *Plessy v. Ferguson*,[238] triggering the legitimization of racism and retarding racial progress for almost a century. Last year, Justices Kennedy, O'Connor, and Souter said "we think *Plessy* was wrong the day it was decided."[239] Other justices, including Chief Justice Rehnquist, have

---

236. National Comm'n on the Causes & Prevention of Violence, To Establish Justice, To Insure Domestic Tranquility, at xxxii (1969).

237. As Justice O'Connor has noted:

> [S]tate innovation is no judicial myth. When Wyoming became a State in 1890, it was the only State permitting women to vote. That novel idea did not bear national fruit for another thirty years. Wisconsin pioneered unemployment insurance, while Massachusetts initiated minimum wage laws for women and minors. After decades of academic debate, state experimentation finally provided an opportunity to observe no-fault automobile insurance in operation. Even in the field of environmental protection, an area subject to heavy federal regulation, the States have supplemented national standards with innovative and far-reaching statutes.

FERC v. Mississippi, 456 U.S. 742, 788-89 (1982) (O'Connor, J., dissenting in part).

238. 163 U.S. 537 (1896).

239. Planned Parenthood of Southeastern Pa. v. Casey, 112 S. Ct. 2791, 2813 (1992).

agreed.[240] We feel strongly that *Shaw v. Reno* also "was wrong the day it was decided" and hope that the Court will correct this error and not perpetuate a questionable and newly-imposed legal standard[241] that one district court already has used to invalidate a congressional districting plan.[242] Absent a change in direction, as other courts struggle with applying strict scrutiny to legislative districting plans, *Shaw*, like *Plessy* before it, may have devastating racial consequences.

Shaw is fundamentally flawed. The decision, at least in part, is premised on the notion that irregularly shaped, minority-majority congressional districts are somehow akin to apartheid and segregation. But apartheid and segregation are invidious policies intended, at bottom, to exclude citizens from civic life because of their race. Minority-majority districts, intended to include racial minorities into the politics from which they were for so long locked out, are neither similar nor analogous to apartheid or segregation. *Shaw*'s misguided suggestion otherwise limits the legitimacy of that decision.

Yet, even under the strict scrutiny required by *Shaw*, we believe—in light of the peculiar history of the southern states where challenges to minority-majority districts are pending—that race-conscious redistricting used to insure the fair representation of African-Americans will meet the burdens of that standard. As the North Carolina experience well demonstrates, only such districting (or other effective means of empowering African-American voters) will unravel the burdens of history and nurture the experiment of a pluralistic democracy.

Until 1992, with respect to the United States Congress, North Carolina implemented for ninety years the wishes of its former governors to take the "negro . . . out of politics"[243] and to assure "that white government shall be supreme and unchallenged in [North Carolina's] borders."[244] When stripped to its essence, the fundamental issue in the current North Carolina voting case, as well as in similar cases in other states, is whether whites and blacks will share in political power. Either North Carolina—and our nation—will revert to politics akin to the former "historic white supremacy,"[245] where African-Americans were a relatively minuscule power in shaping and directing the policies of our government, or North Carolina will now—though belatedly—fulfill the vision expressed by Martin Luther King thirty-five years ago when he said:

240. *See supra* note 53.

241. As Justice White noted in *Shaw*, the Court's opinion that the redistricting plan "might have violated appellants' constitutional rights is both a fiction and a departure from settled equal protection principles." Shaw v. Reno, 113 S. Ct. 2816, 2834 (1993) (White, J., dissenting).

242. *See* Hays v. Louisiana, 839 F. Supp. 1188 (W.D. La. 1993).

243. *Supra* note 2.

244. *Supra* note 3.

245. Franklin, *supra* note 169, at 259.

> Give us the ballot and we will no longer have to worry the federal government about our basic rights.
>
> Give us the ballot and we will no longer plead to the federal government for passage of an antilynching law; we will by the power of our vote write the law on the statute books of the southern states and bring an end to the dastardly acts of the hooded perpetrators of violence.
>
> Give us the ballot and we will transform the salient misdeeds of bloodthirsty mobs into the calculated good deeds of orderly citizens.
>
> Give us the ballot and we will fill our legislative halls with men of good will . . . .
>
> Give us the ballot and we will place judges on the benches of the South who will 'do justly and love mercy' . . . .
>
> Give us the ballot and we will quietly and nonviolently, without rancor or bitterness, implement the Supreme Court's decision of May 17, 1954.[246]

The Supreme Court's majority opinion in *Shaw v. Reno*, applying the Equal Protection Clause to preclude African-Americans from attaining significant political power in this nation, turns the intent and meaning of the Fourteenth Amendment on its head.[247] In the 1873 case first construing the Fourteenth Amendment, the *Slaughter-house Cases*,[248] the Supreme Court declared:

> We repeat, then, in the light of this recapitulation of events, almost too recent to be called history, but which are familiar to us all; and on the most casual examination of the language of these amendments, no one can fail to be impressed with the one pervading purpose found in them all, lying at the foundation of each, and without which none of them would have been even suggested; we mean the freedom of the slave race, the security and firm establishment of that freedom, and the protection of the newly-made freeman and citizen from the oppressions of those who had formerly exercised unlimited dominion over him. It is true that only the fifteenth amendment, in terms, mentions the negro by speaking of his color and his slavery. But it is just as true that each of the other articles was addressed to the grievances of that race, and designed to remedy them as the fifteenth. . . .

246. Martin L. King, Jr., Give Us the Ballot—We Will Transform the South, Address to the Prayer Pilgrimage for Freedom, Washington, D.C. (May 17, 1957), *in* A Testament of Hope, The Essential Writings of Martin Luther King, Jr. 197, 197-98 (James M. Washington ed., 1986).

247. The only African-American scholar that we know who supports the majority's opinion is Carol Swain. In our opinion, her argument is flawed, and we agree with Professor Randall Kennedy's insightful analysis of her work. *See* Randall Kennedy, *Blacks in Congress: Carol Swain's Critique*, 2 Reconstruction, No. 2, at 34 (1993). *Cf.* Guanier, *supra* note 196 (generally critiquing minority-majority districts).

Of the disheartening factors in *Shaw v. Reno*, none is more so than the decisive vote of Justice Clarence Thomas—who succeeded Thurgood Marshall—in favor of the 5-4 decision. It is inconceivable that Justice Thurgood Marshall would have so interpreted the Fourteenth Amendment, risking a significant set-back to African-Americans' recent political progress.

248. 83 U.S. (16 Wall.) 36 (1873).

> We doubt very much whether any action of a State not directed by way of discrimination against the negroes as a class, or on account of their race, will ever be held to come within the purview of this provision. It is so clearly a provision for that race and that emergency, that a strong case would be necessary for its application to any other.[249]

Now, 120 years after the *Slaughter-house Cases*, the Fourteenth Amendment may be used to thwart rather than to assure effective use of the ballot by African-Americans. Now, ninety years after George White was driven from Congress, the Fourteenth Amendment may be used to undermine rather than to guarantee the racial pluralism that has been occurring in the Congress.

But, with respect to North Carolina, the history of state-imposed and state-condoned exclusion of African-Americans from meaningful participation in the political process is compelling justification for the creation of the two minority-majority congressional districts included in the 1991 redistricting, and the 1991 redistricting is narrowly tailored to meet that interest. The redistricting creates only two minority-majority districts that still provide African-Americans less than proportional representation. Further, these two districts are well-integrated—whites comprise just less than half of the voting-age citizens in each; they pool together individuals with similar political interests; they do not simply band together voters based on the color of their skin; and, only 43% of North Carolina's African-American citizens reside in these districts.

North Carolina's two minority-majority districts have brought to Congress two African-American legislators of particular acumen and experience, who are quite capable of representing all of their constituents. At the time of Reconstruction, racists distorted the truth to impugn the intelligence of African-American members of Congress. Today, the record establishes that the African-American representatives in Congress are every bit as talented and more diverse than their white peers,[250] as well as similarly committed to making the United States a land of freedom and basic justice.

The bizarreness in this case thus is not the shape of the district boundaries but rather the challenge itself, where the white vote is not diluted and where talented legislators represent the districts.[251] These cases

249. *Id.* at 71.

250. Of the 40 members of the Congressional Black Caucus, 10 are women. *See* African-Americans in the U.S. Congress, 1870-1993, *infra* app. A. A comparison of education levels of African-American and white members of Congress reveals that African-American members essentially match the accomplishments of their white peers. Nearly all have completed secondary education and over 60% have completed post-graduate degrees. *See* Bositis, *supra* note 57, at 4 & tbl. 4; Educational Background of CBC Members, 103rd Congress, *infra* app. G.

251. John Hope Franklin recently noted:

> It is curious, but characteristic I fear, that as the new apportionment of 1991 made it possible for more African Americans to gain seats in Congress in 1992, opposition to those gains would go all the way to the Supreme Court. Justice O'Connor called the 12th North Carolina Congressional District "bizarre" in

strike at the heart of race relations in America. While white America apparently approves of African-Americans serving in entertainment roles, such as basketball players Michael Jordan at the University of North Carolina and Grant Hill at Duke, anxiety appears to rise when avenues open for African-Americans to attain significant political power and to determine the public policy rather than the entertainment policy of this nation.

Shaw v. Reno notwithstanding, African-Americans have a right to full participation in American politics and a right to be heard in determining the public policy of the nation. Full participation includes the right to have African-American interests articulated, protected, and advanced in Congress. Minority-majority districting—like that of North Carolina—not only is one successful means of insuring these rights but also provides pluralism to Congress, a body instituted to serve *all* Americans. Encouraging pluralism in Congress, in turn, is a starting point toward bringing American politics a step closer to that democratic ideal.

> shape. Perhaps it is, but not merely because blacks live along I-85. It is also because industrial and urban developments trace that same route. Thus, it has a homogeneity that is as legitimate as a district that enjoys so-called compactness and contiguity. After all, in order to preserve six Democratic districts and four Republican districts, those responsible for redistricting the state and adher[ing] to the principles of the Voting Rights Act of 1965 had few choices. . . . One must remember, moreover, that gerrymandering was invented in 1810 in Massachusetts and not in 1992 in North Carolina.

John H. Franklin, Keynote Address at the American Issues Forum, National Humanities Center, at 16-17 (Mar. 24, 1994) (on file with the *Fordham Law Review*).

APPENDIX A:
AFRICAN-AMERICANS IN THE U.S. CONGRESS, 1870-1993

TABLE 1. African-Americans in the U.S. Congress, 1870-1993

Member	Party-State	Years
United States Senate		
Hiram R. Revels	R-MS	1870-71
Blanche K. Bruce	R-MS	1875-81
Edward W. Brooke	R-MA	1967-79
Carol Moseley-Braun	D-IL	1993-
United States House of Representatives		
Joseph H. Rainey	R-SC	1870-79
Jefferson F. Long	R-GA	1870-71
Robert B. Elliot	R-SC	1871-74
Robert C. De Large	R-SC	1871-73
Benjamin S. Turner	R-AL	1871-73
Josiah T. Walls	R-FL	1871-73
Richard H. Cain	R-SC	1873-75;1877-79
John R. Lynch	R-MS	1873-77;1882-83
James T. Rapier	R-AL	1873-75
Alonzo J. Ransier	R-SC	1873-75
Jeremiah Haralson	R-AL	1875-77
John A. Hyman	R-NC	1875-77
Charles E. Nash	R-LA	1875-77
Robert Smalls	R-SC	1875-79
James E. O'Hara	R-NC	1883-87
Henry P. Cheatham	R-NC	1889-93
John M. Langston	R-VA	1890-91
Thomas E. Miller	R-SC	1890-91
George W. Murray	R-SC	1893-95;1896-97
George W. White	R-NC	1897-1901
Oscar DePriest	R-IL	1929-35
Arthur W. Mitchell	D-IL	1935-43
U. S. House of Representatives, *continued*		
William L. Dawson	D-IL	1943-70
Adam C. Powell, Jr.	D-NY	1945-67;1969-71
Charles C. Diggs, Jr.	D-MI	1955-80
Robert N.C. Nix	D-PA	1958-78
Augustus F. Hawkins	D-CA	1963-90
John Conyers, Jr.	D-MI	1965-
William L. Clay	D-MO	1969-
Louis Stokes	D-OH	1969-
Shirley A. Chisholm	D-NY	1969-82
George W. Collins	D-IL	1970-72
Ronald V. Dellums	D-CA	1971-
Ralph H. Metcalfe	D-IL	1971-78
Parren H. Mitchell	D-MD	1971-86
Charles B. Rangel	D-NY	1971-
Walter E. Fauntroy	D-D.C.	1971-90
Yvonne B. Burke	D-CA	1973-79
Cardiss Collins	D-IL	1973-
Barbara C. Jordan	D-TX	1973-78
Andrew J. Young	D-GA	1973-77
Harold E. Ford	D-TN	1975-
Bennett M. Steward	D-IL	1979-80
Julian C. Dixon	D-CA	1979-
William H. Gray	D-PA	1979-91
Mickey Leland	D-TX	1979-89
Melvin Evans	R-V.I.	1979-80
George W. Crockett, Jr.	D-MI	1980-90
Mervyn M. Dymally	D-CA	1981-92

TABLE 1, *Continued*					
U. S. House of Representatives, *continued*			Maxine Waters	D-CA	1991-
Gus Savage	D-IL	1981-92	Lucien E. Blackwell	D-PA	1991-
Harold Washington	D-IL	1981-83	Sanford Bishop	D-GA	1993-
Katie B. Hall	D-IN	1982-84	Corrine Brown	D-FL	1993-
Major R. Owens	D-NY	1983-	Eva M. Clayton	D-NC	1993-
Edolphus Towns	D-NY	1983-	James E. Clyburn	D-SC	1993-
Alan Wheat	D-MO	1983-	Cleo Fields	D-LA	1993-
Charles A. Hayes	D-IL	1983-92	Alcee L. Hastings	D-FL	1993-
Alton R. Waldon, Jr.	D-NY	1986-87	Earl F. Hilliard	D-AL	1993-
Mike Espy	D-MS	1987-93	Eddie B. Johnson	D-TX	1993-
Floyd H. Flake	D-NY	1987-	Cynthia McKinney	D-GA	1993-
John Lewis	D-GA	1987-	Carrie Meek	D-FL	1993-
Kweisi Mfume	D-MD	1987-	Mel Reynolds	D-IL	1993-
Donald M. Payne	D-NJ	1989-	Bobby L. Rush	D-IL	1993-
Craig A. Washington	D-TX	1989-	Robert C. Scott	D-VA	1993-
Barbara R. Collins	D-MI	1991-	Walter R. Tucker, III	D-CA	1993-
Gary A. Franks	R-CT	1991-	Melvin Watt	D-NC	1993-
William J. Jefferson	D-LA	1991-	Albert R. Wynn	D-MD	1993-
Eleanor H. Norton	D-D.C.	1991-	Bennie G. Thompson	D-MS	1993-

JOINT CENTER FOR POLITICAL AND ECONOMIC STUDIES

APPENDIX B: SOUTHERN U.S. CONGRESSIONAL DISTRICTS BY PARTY AND BLACK VOTE, 103RD CONGRESS, FIRST SESSION

Table 40. Southern U.S. Congressional Districts By Party and Black Vote, 103RD Congress, First Session

State	Black Voting-Age Population (%)	Black Districts			White Democratic Districts			White Republican Districts		
		(N)	Share of Statewide Eligible Black Vote (%)	Average District Eligible Black Vote (%)	(N)	Share of Statewide Eligible Black Vote (%)	Average District Eligible Black Vote (%)	(N)	Share of Statewide Eligible Black Vote (%)	Average District Eligible Black Vote (%)
Alabama	22.7	1	38.1	63.5	3	27.3	14.4	3	34.6	18.4
Arkansas	13.7	0	0	0	2	54.2	15.0	2	45.8	12.6
Florida	11.4	3	52.1	50.1	7	23.8	9.1	2	Hispanic 3.0	3.9
								11	Anglo 21.1	5.0
Georgia	24.6	3	61.7	56.7	4	18.6	12.5	4	19.7	13.3
Louisiana	27.9	2	59.7	59.4	2	18.7	18.6	3	21.6	13.7
Mississippi	31.6	1	34.8	58.1	4	65.2	25.5	0	0	0
North Carolina	20.1	2	43.0	53.4	6	45.8	18.4	4	11.2	6.6
South Carolina	26.9	1	34.7	58.3	2	28.9	23.4	3	36.4	19.4
Tennessee	14.4	1	40.4	54.1	5	44.6	11.5	3	15.0	18.9
Texas	11.2	2	28.9	47.9	4	Hispanic 5.1	4.5	1	Hispanic 0.9	2.9
					15	Anglo 55.0	12.2	8	Anglo 10.1	4.3
Virginia	17.6	1	30.8	61.2	6	47.4	15.3	4	21.8	10.6
Totals 125 Districts		17	42.1	55.1	60	38.0	13.9	48	19.9	9.5

SOURCES: *1990 U.S. Census, Population and Housing Profile, Congressional Districts of the 103RD Congress*, CPH-L-117, pp. 9-16. Information identifying the partisanship, race, and district number for the 125 southern congressional districts is from *Politics in America, 1994*, pp. 12-38, 79-95, 317-420, 632-658, 835-856, 1111-1154, 1363-1387, 1400-1535, 1565-1601. Politics in America, 1994, Congressional Quarterly Press, Washington, D.C.

JOINT CENTER FOR POLITICAL AND ECONOMIC STUDIES

APPENDIX C: CONGRESSIONAL REPRESENTATION (HOUSE AND SENATE), 1871-1993

Table 3.1. Congressional Representation (House and Senate), 1871-1993

CONGRESS	YEAR	TOTAL MEMBERS OF CONGRESS	WHITE & OTHER MEMBERS OF CONGRESS	BLACK MEMBERS OF CONGRESS
42	1871	329	324	5
43	1873	386	379	7
44	1875	391	383	8
45	1877	385	381	4
46	1879	382	381	1
47	1881	396	394	2
48	1883	422	420	2
49	1885	416	414	2
50	1887	408	408	0
51	1889	446	443	3
52	1891	444	443	1
53	1893	474	473	1
54	1895	462	461	1
55	1897	467	466	1
56	1899	471	470	1
57	1901	466	466	0
58	1903	492	492	0
59	1905	500	500	0
60	1907	502	502	0
61	1909	504	504	0
62	1911	518	518	0
63	1913	554	554	0
64	1915	543	543	0
65	1917	566	566	0
66	1919	556	556	0
67	1921	559	559	0
68	1923	557	557	0
69	1925	548	548	0
70	1927	548	548	0
71	1929	566	565	1
72	1931	558	557	1
73	1933	550	549	1
74	1935	550	549	1
75	1937	555	554	1
76	1939	560	559	1
77	1941	562	561	1
78	1943	554	553	1
79	1945	566	564	2
80	1947	553	551	2
81	1949	554	552	2
82	1951	555	553	2
83	1953	555	553	2
84	1955	540	537	3
85	1957	545	541	4
86	1959	552	548	4
87	1961	559	555	4
88	1963	551	547	4
89	1965	549	543	6
90	1967	543	537	6
91	1969	555	544	11
92	1971	549	535	14
93	1973	545	528	17
94	1975	541	523	18
95	1977	544	526	18
96	1979	541	524	17
97	1981	544	525	19
98	1983	541	520	21
99	1985	543	522	21
100	1987	544	521	23
101	1989	551	527	24
102	1991	536	509	27
103	1993	531	491	40

SOURCE: Inter-University Consortium for Political and Social Research, and Carroll McKibbin. Roster of United States Congressional officeholders and biographical characteristics of Members of the United States Congress, 1788-1991: Merged Data. Eighth Ed. Ann Arbor, MI. The tabulations were produced using SAS.

APPENDIX D:
NORTH CAROLINA 12 VOTING-AGE POPULATION BY RACE, AND BY RACE AND TURNOUT

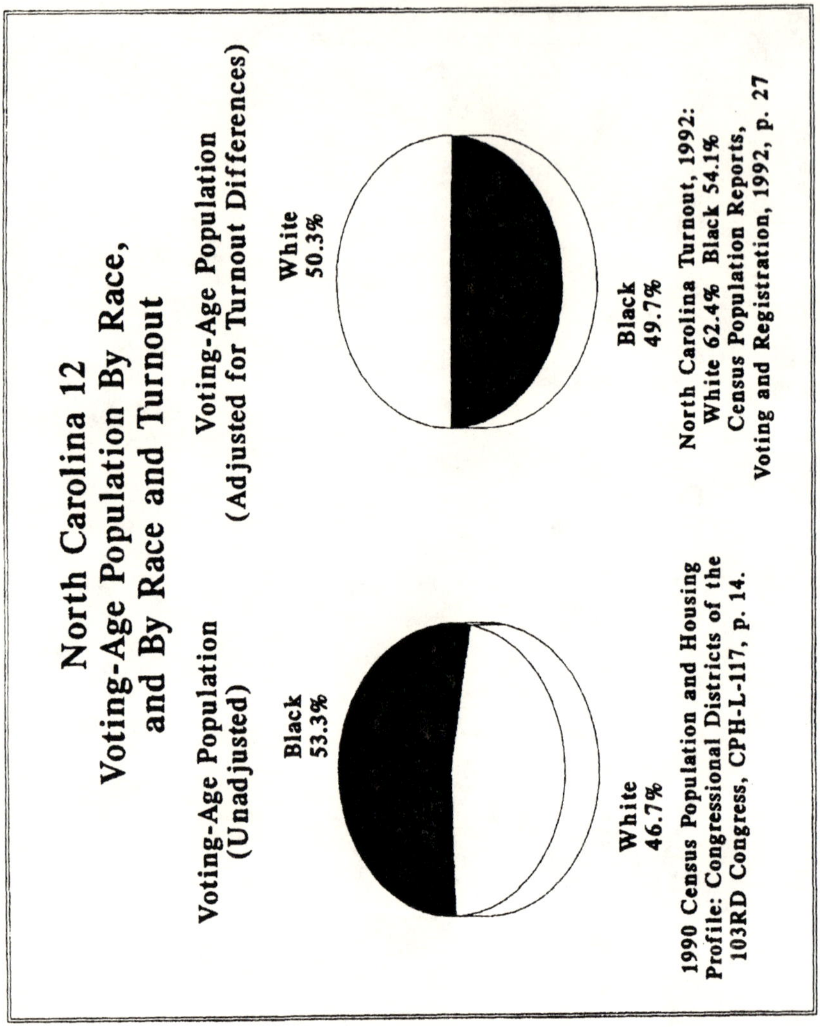

APPENDIX E:
VOTING SCORES, WHITE NONHISPANIC DEMOCRATIC CONGRESSMEN, SOUTHERN STATES BY DISTRICT BLACK AND HISPANIC VOTING-AGE POPULATIONS, 103RD CONGRESS, FIRST SESSION

TABLE A. Voting Scores, White NonHispanic Democratic Congressmen, Southern States By District Black and Hispanic Voting-Age Populations, 103RD Congress, First Session

District	Voting-Age Population		White Democratic Incumbent	Democrat Vote Share 1992	Voting Support Scores			Interest Group Ratings				National Journal's Liberal Ranking		
	Black	Hispanic			Conservative Coalition	Presidential (Clinton)	Party	ADA	AFL CIO	ACU	CCUS	Economic	Social	Foreign
Alabama 3	23.6	0.6	Browder	62	91	76	75	20	58	52	36	48	40	51
Alabama 4	5.9	0.3	Bevill	70	93	82	75	45	92	38	18	61	43	44
Alabama 5	13.7	0.7	Cramer	66	91	82	77	45	82	38	18	57	47	46
Arkansas 1	14.8	0.5	Lambert	70	50	72	86	65	75	25	45	52	56	79
Arkansas 2	15.2	0.7	Thornton	74	86	84	86	50	83	30	45	54	53	51
Florida 1	11.2	1.9	Hutto	55	100	64	53	25	25	67	64	44	29	44
Florida 2	21.0	2.0	Peterson	74	73	91	90	55	100	25	27	78	60	46
Florida 5	4.7	2.6	Thurman	53	57	74	88	80	100	17	18	78	54	70
Florida 11	14.5	13.7	Gibbons	57	48	93	86	75	83	17	45	59	72	74
Florida 15	6.3	3.0	Bacchus[Retiring]	51	49	97	87	60	83	25	36	55	67	59
Florida 19	2.2	5.5	Johnson	63	19	84	92	90	92	8	18	68	78	87
Florida 20	3.9	11.5	Deutsch	59	27	87	92	90	100	13	18	61	71	51
Georgia 7	11.7	1.0	Darden	57	89	92	87	45	75	25	45	55	56	51
Georgia 8	18.4	1.4	Rowland[Retiring]	56	89	71	73	20	42	58	82	42	45	59
Georgia 9	3.5	1.6	Deal	59	80	58	68	15	42	61	73	38	42	40
Georgia 10	16.5	1.1	Johnson	54	75	78	82	45	58	33	45	46	56	51
Louisiana 3	19.5	2.4	Tauzin	Unopposed[1]	88	47	48	35	42	78	73	40	27	33

cont'd....

TABLE A, *Continued*

District	Voting-Age Population		White Democratic Incumbent	Democrat Vote Share 1992	Voting Support Scores			Interest Group Ratings				National Journal's Liberal Ranking		
	Black	Hispanic			Conservative Coalition	Presidential (Clinton)	Party	ADA	AFL-CIO	ACU	CCUS	Economic	Social	Foreign
Louisiana 7	17.7	1.3	Hayes	Unopposed[†]	86	65	65	20	50	70	90	42	33	51
Mississippi 1	20.0	0.4	Whitten[Retiring]	60	87	80	67	45	82	27	36	54	48	51
Mississippi 3	27.9	0.5	Montgomery	81	95	75	72	30	42	50	55	45	40	47
Mississippi 4	36.5	0.4	Parker	72	95	67	59	20	33	67	73	42	31	44
Mississippi 5	17.5	1.1	Taylor	63	91	48	37	25	42	79	73	29	31	35
North Carolina 2	20.1	1.1	Valentine[Retiring]	55	76	66	72	30	30	48	45	45	40	47
North Carolina 3	19.6	1.4	Lancaster	56	79	81	79	50	67	46	45	49	52	47
North Carolina 4	18.9	1.2	Price	66	47	87	94	70	92	9	36	68	73	63
North Carolina 5	14.0	0.7	Neal[Retiring]	54	71	72	79	50	73	29	55	51	53	51
North Carolina 7	17.1	1.2	Rose	58	56	90	85	70	92	8	40	68	68	63
North Carolina 8	20.9	1.0	Hefner	61	67	79	88	65	92	13	27	66	59	51
South Carolina 3	18.8	0.5	Derrick[Retiring]	61	66	80	86	65	92	26	20	61	60	44
South Carolina 5	27.9	0.5	Spratt	61	82	82	85	55	83	25	45	54	58	59
Tennessee 3	10.5	0.6	Lloyd[Retiring]	51	93	83	73	50	83	30	45	59	48	47
Tennessee 4	3.5	0.4	Cooper[Running for Senate]	66	88	76	69	55	73	38	45	47	47	40
Tennessee 5	20.6	0.8	Clement	72	65	81	82	55	75	29	50	49	56	47
Tennessee 6	5.4	0.5	Gordon	58	70	83	87	60	83	21	27	61	56	63

cont'd....

TABLE A, *Continued*

District	Voting-Age Population		White Democratic Incumbent	Democrat Vote Share 1992	Voting Support Scores			Interest Group Ratings				National Journal's Liberal Ranking		
	Black	Hispanic			Conservative Coalition	Presidential (Clinton)	Party	ADA	AFL-CIO	ACU	CCUS	Economic	Social	Foreign
Tennessee 8	17.4	0.6	Tanner	84	91	71	70	50	75	50	36	50	45	43
Texas 1	16.4	2.7	Chapman	Unopposed[7]	90	78	75	45	83	25	50	53	54	44
Texas 2	15.4	4.9	Wilson	56	76	79	70	60	100	29	40	61	54	43
Texas 4	7.7	3.6	Hall	60	86	54	54	20	33	79	73	32	24	37
Texas 5	15.3	15.3	Bryant	61	30	82	92	90	91	4	27	68	79	93
Texas 9	19.8	8.5	Brooks	56	79	86	84	60	100	17	20	75	56	47
Texas 10	10.0	18.7	Pickle[Retiring]	72	63	90	78	65	75	9	45	52	67	46
Texas 11	14.6	10.4	Edwards	67	86	82	75	35	67	33	55	42	55	51
Texas 12	7.4	13.8	Geren	63	95	72	63	20	33	75	91	34	38	47
Texas 13	7.3	15.7	Sarpalius	60	95	72	69	40	75	46	45	49	34	59
Texas 14	10.4	20.4	Laughlin	72	93	78	70	20	45	52	45	42	48	51
Texas 16	3.6	66.4	Coleman	52	60	90	90	65	92	21	27	66	64	51
Texas 17	3.2	14.1	Stenholm	66	91	60	52	10	17	78	73	35	24	59
Texas 24	17.9	18.8	Frost	60	79	87	79	65	91	21	36	68	64	58
Texas 25	24.9	14.9	Andrews[Defeated in Primary]	59	90	87	72	55	83	25	36	47	53	50
Texas 29	9.8	55.4	Green	66	40	77	85	85	100	13	18	88	56	69
Virginia 2	15.5	3.0	Pickett	56	82	82	75	20	42	50	73	40	58	51

cont'd....

TABLE A, *Continued*

District	Voting-Age Population		White Democratic Incumbent	Democrat Vote Share 1992	Voting Support Scores			Interest Group Ratings				National Journal's Liberal Ranking		
	Black	Hispanic			Conservative Coalition	Presidential (Clinton)	Party	ADA	AFL-CIO	ACU	CCUS	Economic	Social	Foreign
Virginia 4	30.7	1.0	Sisisky	69	88	77	71	45	75	42	45	46	55	51
Virginia 5	22.9	0.5	Payne	69	82	86	79	30	50	42	45	47	52	51
Virginia 8	12.5	8.0	Moran	57	36	89	90	80	92	8	27	61	80	63
Virginia 9	2.4	0.5	Boucher	63	52	82	80	60	100	13	30	75	62	66
Virginia 11	7.5	7.0	Byrne	52	34	76	91	95	100	8	9	64	68	70
Average (N = 56)	14.6	6.6		64.2	73.9	77.9	76.6	49.8	72.1	35.1	43.9	54.0	52.5	53.3

SOURCES: 1990 U.S. Census, Population and Housing Profile, *Congressional Districts of the 103rd Congress, C.Q. Weekly Report*, V. 51, pp. 3473-3487, *National Journal*, Volume 26, pp. 170-189.

KEY: **Conservative Coalition Voting Support:** Percentage of member's votes in agreement with a majority of southern Democrats and a majority of Republicans against a majority of northern Democrats. **Presidential Voting Support:** Percentage of member's votes in agreement with President Clinton's stated position. **Party Voting Support:** Percentage of member's votes in agreement with a majority of Democrats against a majority of Republicans. **Americans for Democratic Action (ADA):** Liberal Democratic Group founded by Hubert Humphrey and Eleanor Roosevelt in 1947. **AFL-CIO:** Organized labor's official national organization. **American Conservative Union (ACU):** Conservative organization formed in 1964. **Chamber of Commerce:** National organization representing business, professional, and trade groups. **National Journal's Liberal Rankings:** Within each category, the number indicates that the member is more liberal than that percentage of the members of the U.S. House of Representatives.
‡ Missed more than half the rated votes. † Unopposed or no major party opposition (Democratic vote share is 100). All entries expressed in percentages.

This table was prepared by Dr. David A. Bositis of the Joint Center for Political and Economic Studies as part of the Joint Center's study, *Redistricting and Representation*.

JOINT CENTER FOR POLITICAL AND ECONOMIC STUDIES

APPENDIX F:
VOTING SCORES, CBC MEMBERS, SOUTHERN STATES BY DISTRICT BLACK AND HISPANIC VOTING-AGE POPULATIONS, 103RD CONGRESS, FIRST SESSION

TABLE C. Voting Scores, CBC Members, Southern States By District Black and Hispanic Voting-Age Populations, 103RD Congress, First Session

District	Voting-Age Population		Member	Democratic Vote Share 1992	Voting Support Scores			Interest Group Ratings				National Journal's Liberal Ranking		
	Black	Hispanic			Conservative Coalition	Presidential (Clinton)	Party	ADA	AFL-CIO	ACU	CCUS	Economic	Social	Foreign
Alabama 7	63.5	0.3	Hilliard	80	30	75	90	90	100	4	9	88	68	84
Florida 3	50.6	2.7	Brown	60	39	86	92	75	100	4	18	88	77	69
Florida 17	54.0	24.1	Meek	Unopposed †	43	91	90	75	92	9	18	78	87	50
Florida 23	45.7	9.1	Hastings	65	18	89	90	90	92	4	18	78	87	79
Georgia 2	52.3	1.6	Bishop	64	59	88	89	75	100	13	18	88	63	59
Georgia 5	57.5	1.8	Lewis	72	9	79	98	100	98	0	9	88	87	87
Georgia 11	60.4	1.0	McKinney	73	7	76	93	100	100	0	9	66	87	93
Louisiana 2	56.2	3.8	Jefferson	Unopposed †	23	83	91	95	92	4	18	64	87	93
Louisiana 4	62.6	0.9	Fields	74	20	80	94	95	100	4	9	68	87	79
Mississippi 2	58.1	0.5	Thompson	55	14	71	87	94	100	6	20	88	87	87
North Carolina 1	53.4	0.7	Clayton	68	14	76	93	100	100	0	9	88	87	87
North Carolina 12	53.3	0.8	Watt	72	7	79	97	100	100	12	9	88	87	87
South Carolina 6	58.3	0.5	Clyburn	65	45	82	90	90	100	13	27	88	77	63
Tennessee 9	54.1	0.7	Ford	67	7	54	64	80	86	5	20	‡	87	87
Texas 18	48.6	13.7	Washington	68	5	63	70	90	100	5	0	66	87	93
Texas 30	47.1	15.1	Johnson	74	34	90	94	90	92	0	27	78	87	79
Virginia 3	61.2	1.2	Scott	79	30	89	93	90	100	8	18	68	80	66
Average (N = 17)	55.1	4.6		72.7	23.8	79.5	89.1	89.9	97.2	5.4	15.1	79.4	82.9	78.9

SOURCES: 1990 U.S. Census. Population and Housing Profile, *Congressional Districts of the 103rd Congress, C.Q. Weekly Report* V. 51, pp. 3473-3487. *National Journal* Volume 26, pp. 170-189.
KEY: Conservative Coalition Voting Support: Percentage of member's votes in agreement with a majority of southern Democrats and a majority of Republicans against a majority of northern Democrats. **Presidential Voting Support:** Percentage of member's votes in agreement with President Clinton's stated position. **Party Voting Support:** Percentage of member's votes in agreement with a majority of Democrats against a majority of Republicans. **Americans for Democratic Action (ADA):** Liberal Democratic Group founded by Hubert Humphrey and Eleanor Roosevelt in 1947. **AFL-CIO:** Organized labor's official national organization. **American Conservative Union (ACU):** Conservative organization formed in 1964. **Chamber of Commerce:** National organization representing business, professional, and trade groups. **National Journal's Liberal Rankings:** Within each category, the number indicates that the member is more liberal than that percentage of the members of the U.S. House of Representatives. ‡ Missed more than half the rated votes.
† Unopposed or no major party opposition (for Democrats, Democratic vote share is 100 percent). All entries expressed in percentages.

This table was prepared by Dr. David A. Bositis of the Joint Center for Political and Economic Studies as part of the Joint Center's study of *Redistricting and Representation*

JOINT CENTER FOR POLITICAL AND ECONOMIC STUDIES

APPENDIX G:
EDUCATIONAL BACKGROUND OF CBC MEMBERS, 103RD CONGRESS

TABLE 4. Educational Background of CBC Members, 103RD Congress

Type of Degree		CBC Members	All Members
Doctoral		0[1] (0%)	26 (6%)
Law		16 (42%)	189 (43%)
Masters	MA/MS	8 (20%)	73 (17%)
	MBA	2 (5%)	20 (5%)
Bachelors		12 (32%)	100 (23%)
No College Degree		2 (5%)	28 (6%)

NOTES: The percentages for CBC members do not sum to 100% because Earl Hilliard (D-AL) has both a Law and an MBA degree. 1. Cynthia McKinney (D-GA) is a doctoral candidate.

SOURCE: *C.Q. Weekly Reports*.

JOINT CENTER FOR POLITICAL AND ECONOMIC STUDIES

APPENDIX H: ACKNOWLEDGEMENTS

The Congressional Black Caucus Foundation has had two meetings of scholars and practitioners who have given us considerable insight on these matters. They are:

Dr. David A. Bositis
Professor John Hope Franklin
Amelia L. Parker
Dr. Harry L. Watson
Barbara Arnwine, Esq.
Dr. Mary Frances Berry
Honorable Corrine Brown
Dr. Orville Vernon Burton
Professor Jerome Culp
Dayna Cunningham, Esq.
Dr. Helen G. Edmonds
James Ferguson, Esq.
Honorable Cleo Fields
Dr. Glenda E. Gilmore
Dr. David Goldfield
Rodney Gregory, Esq.
Professor Charles Hamilton
Tony Harrison
Wade Henderson, Esq.
Professor F. Michael Higginbotham
Anita Hodgkiss, Esq.
Professor Sherrilyn Ifill
Jeh C. Johnson, Esq.
Elaine Jones, Esq.
Professor Pamela S. Karlan
Dr. Robert Korstad
Quentin Lawson
Dr. Steven Lawson
Dr. Allan Lichtman
Laughlin MacDonald, Esq.
Dr. Percy E. Murray
Robin Nesbitt, Esq.
Hon. Eleanor Holmes Norton
Professor Charles Ogleetree
Professor Frank Parker
Dr. Julian M. Pleasants
Dr. H. Leon Prather
Theodore Shaw, Esq.
Michael P. Sistrom
Flora J. Hatley Wadlington
Dr. Ronald Walters
Honorable Mel Watt
Eddie Williams
Dr. Linda Williams
Brenda Wright, Esq.
Colleen Adams
Anton A. Bell
Erica Foster
Shirley Jones, Esq.

[E]RACING DEMOCRACY: THE VOTING RIGHTS CASES

*Lani Guinier**

> The American people are infected with racism — that is the peril. Paradoxically, they are also infected with democratic ideals — that is the hope.
>
> MARTIN LUTHER KING, JR.[1]

Race is an issue that continues deeply to divide American politics. Many Americans vote along racial lines[2] or identify themselves in racial terms.[3] Americans of color still suffer disadvantage in racial, as well as economic, terms.[4] Even Supreme Court Justices who condemn the assumption that race defines political interests acknowledge the practical importance of race in drawing election districts.[5] Despite this clear evidence that race matters, however, the Supreme Court's jurisprudence offers little direct guidance on how to structure democratic competition among racial groups that seek political power and influence.

The question of group representation plays out with particular acrimony in the voting rights arena because of two competing forces: the inescapable race consciousness of the Voting Rights Act[6] and the ideo-

---

* Professor of Law, University of Pennsylvania. I thank Harlon Dalton, Pamela Karlan, and Susan Sturm for their very helpful criticisms of an earlier draft. Professors Charles Beitz and John Ferejohn gave me invaluable feedback at the Sept. 2, 1994 American Political Science Association Roundtable on Group Representation.

[1] MARTIN L. KING, JR., *Showdown for Nonviolence*, *in* A TESTAMENT OF HOPE: THE ESSENTIAL WRITINGS AND SPEECHES OF MARTIN LUTHER KING, JR. 64, 71 (James M. Washington ed., 1991).

[2] *See, e.g.*, Peter Applebome, *From Atlanta to Birmingham, Blur of Progress and Stagnation*, N.Y. TIMES, Aug. 3, 1994, at A14 ("More often than not, [votes in the New South are] cast along racial lines . . . . [B]lacks and whites have political agendas as divergent as they were 30 years ago."); *U.S. District Court Upholds 'Gerrymander' for Blacks*, N.Y. TIMES, Aug. 3, 1994, at A12 ("[I]t's not just past discrimination. . . . We've got discrimination now. There is no way that a district 28 to 30 percent black is ever going to elect a black person to Congress. People . . . will always vote along racial lines. What difference does it make whether the district looks pretty?") (quoting La. State Sen. Dennis Bagneris) (internal quotation marks omitted); *see also* Stephen M. Feldman, *Whose Common Good? Racism in the Political Community*, 80 GEO. L.J. 1835, 1848 (1992) (arguing that racial intolerance and racial group interests influence political activity much more than individualistic interests).

[3] *See infra* note 100.

[4] *See, e.g.*, Johnson v. De Grandy, 114 S. Ct. 2647, 2656, 2658 (1994) (accepting the district court's finding that Hispanics continued to suffer adverse social, economic, and political effects as a result of historic discrimination) (citing De Grandy v. Wetherell, 815 F. Supp. 1550, 1573–74 (N.D. Fla. 1992)). Current discrimination in areas such as health care, education, or employment may be probative of a Voting Rights Act violation. *See* Thornburg v. Gingles, 478 U.S. 30, 36–37 (1986) (citing S. REP. NO. 417, 97th Cong., 2d Sess. 28–29 (1982), *reprinted in* 1982 U.S.C.C.A.N. 177, 205–07).

[5] *See infra* note 12.

[6] *See* 42 U.S.C. §§ 1971–1974e (1988).

logical aversion of many federal judges to race-conscious public policy. The language of the Voting Rights Act explicitly recognizes racial categories of voters,[7] whose behavior it measures against an ideal of political equality. The Voting Rights Act, especially as amended in 1982, acknowledges that race can function as an impediment to the expression by certain groups of voters of their political preferences; accordingly, its goal is to remedy voting practices that have discriminatory results, regardless of the purposes of the practices.[8] The Voting Rights Act also uses race to frame the remedy for group-based exclusion from the political process. Race-conscious districting is currently the judiciary's remedy of choice for minority vote dilution.[9] Such districts assure politically cohesive racial minorities the opportunity "to elect representatives of their choice,"[10] as guaranteed by section 2(b) of the Voting Rights Act.

The explicitly race-based approach of the statute and of judicial interpretations of it, however, directly conflicts with an emerging consensus among conservative and neoliberal commentators about the danger of any and all race-conscious decisionmaking by government.[11] Some apparently believe that a society once deliberately segregated by race cannot be deliberately integrated by race. The Supreme Court has implied that race consciousness is dangerously close to racial discrimination[12] and that racial classifications pose a "risk of lasting harm to our society" by "reinforc[ing] the belief, held by too many for too much of

---

[7] *See id.* § 1971(a) (protecting classes defined by race or color); *id.* §§ 1973b(f), 1973aa–1a(e) (protecting "language minorities," defined as individuals "who are American Indian, Asian American, Alaskan Natives, or of Spanish heritage").

[8] The 1982 amendments restored a discriminatory results standard for proof of discrimination, *see id.* § 1973(b), and thus eliminated the discriminatory intent standard imposed by the Supreme Court in City of Mobile v. Bolden, 446 U.S. 55, 66–68 (1980).

[9] *See, e.g.*, Johnson v. De Grandy, 114 S. Ct. 2647, 2658–59 (1994) (measuring the "proportionality" of minority political power by minority control of single-member districts); Growe v. Emison, 113 S. Ct. 1075, 1082–83 (1993) (explaining the district court's creation of a majority minority district and noting that a federal district court may sometimes be justified in adopting a redistricting plan that contains such districts); Thornburg v. Gingles, 478 U.S. 30, 46 n.11 (1986) (explaining that vote dilution results when minority group members are separated by district lines, causing an "ineffective majority," or are crowded into too few districts, resulting in an "excessive majority").

[10] 42 U.S.C. § 1973(b).

[11] *See, e.g.*, Richard A. Epstein, *Tuskegee Modern, or Group Rights Under the Constitution*, 80 Ky. L.J. 869, 875–76 (1992) (acknowledging that § 2(b)'s protection of specific classes makes it clear that the statute is not "colorblind" but suggesting that the focus of courts on maximizing protected groups' political participation constitutes reverse discrimination); Jim Sleeper, *Rigging the Vote by Race*, Wall St. J., Aug. 4, 1992, at A14 (criticizing "ethnic gerrymandering" because "[w]e're all diminished when government constrains us to see ourselves first as members of deprived ethnic groups and only second as citizens in a common American experience").

[12] In *Shaw v. Reno*, Justice O'Connor, writing for the Court, opined that segregating voters into separate voting districts because of their race and without regard to geographic and political boundaries resembles "political apartheid." Shaw v. Reno, 113 S. Ct. 2816, 2827 (1993). Justice O'Connor argued that race-conscious districting "may balkanize us into competing racial factions" even when used to remedy prior discrimination. *Id.* at 2832. However, Justice O'Connor did concede that race is relevant in drawing election districts. *See id.* at 2826.

our history, that individuals should be judged by the color of their skin."[13]

This hostility toward race-conscious decisionmaking is consistent with the growing tendency since the Voting Rights Act's passage thirty years ago to think about equal opportunity in purely individualistic terms.[14] It also follows from the assumption that race is inherently divisive, even when used to address the concrete results of past racial discrimination. For some, colorblindness, and not integration of legislative bodies, is the goal. The problem with this view is that the rhetoric of individualistic, colorblind decisionmaking is impossible to reconcile with a statute that explicitly singles out racial groups for protection from political marginalization.[15]

Two voting rights cases decided during the 1993 Supreme Court Term invited the Court to resolve the conflict between individualistic rhetoric and the race-conscious Voting Rights Act. These cases presented the Court the opportunity to answer the basic question underlying this tension: should racial groups be represented because of, not merely in spite of, their group identity?

In *Holder v. Hall*,[16] the Court confronted "the question whether the size of a governing authority is subject to a vote dilution challenge" under section two of the Voting Rights Act.[17] Justice Kennedy, writing for the Court, avoided the racial subtext by holding that the black plaintiffs could not maintain a section two challenge to a single-person commission because there were no "benchmarks" against which to measure

---

[13] *Id.* at 2832.

[14] *See* Howard Winant, *Difference and Inequality: Postmodern Racial Politics in the United States*, *in* RACISM, THE CITY AND THE STATE 108, 123–24 (Malcolm Cross & Michael Keith eds., 1993) (arguing that the political Right is "[a]ctively engaged in political projects that would deny the significance of race" in the name of individual rights); *see also* Kimberlé W. Crenshaw, *Race, Reform, and Retrenchment: Transformation and Legitimation in Antidiscrimination Law*, 101 HARV. L. REV. 1331, 1378, 1380 (1988) (arguing that the civil rights movement has been more successful at eradicating formal subordination than material or economic subordination because the latter is easier for whites to reconcile with the concept of individual equal opportunity).

[15] The Voting Rights Act is one such statute. *See supra* p. 111; *infra* note 17.

[16] 114 S. Ct. 2581 (1994).

[17] *Id.* at 2583–84. To show vote dilution, a Voting Rights Act plaintiff must demonstrate that the group to which she belongs is "politically cohesive." Thornburg v. Gingles, 478 U.S. 30, 51 (1986). Factors relevant to political cohesion include socio-economic similarity, agreement on important issues, bloc voting, and "whether the minorities consider themselves 'one' even in situations in which they could benefit independently." Nixon v. Kent County, 790 F. Supp. 738, 743–44 (W.D. Mich. 1992). Plaintiffs must also demonstrate that the local majority votes as a bloc, an element that may be proved by evidence that the racial majority consistently defeats the racial minority's representatives. *See Gingles*, 478 U.S. at 51; *see also* Voinovich v. Quilter, 113 S. Ct. 1149, 1155 (1993) (treating blacks implicitly as a cohesive voting bloc and considering the possibility that a districting plan violated the Voting Rights Act by depriving black voters of influence districts). Thus, the Court explicitly recognizes that racial bloc voting is the way in which a local majority can constitute itself as a "political group" to defeat the interests of the racial minority.

the dilutive voting practice.[18] In *Johnson v. De Grandy*,[19] the Court considered a vote dilution challenge to single-member legislative districts.[20] Justice Souter, writing for the Court, camouflaged the tension by holding that there can be no violation of section two when, "in spite of continuing discrimination and racial bloc voting, minority voters form effective voting majorities in a number of districts *roughly proportional*" to their percentage of the local, as opposed to the state population.[21]

The Court failed in both cases to seize the opportunity to address openly the conflict between the rhetoric of colorblindness and the statutory language of racial group empowerment. Thus, although the Court's pragmatic approach resolved the specific controversies of the moment, the Court did not resolve the larger policy questions about group representation. As a result of the Court's tentativeness, its entire voting rights jurisprudence remains subject to attack.[22]

For example, in a stunning concurrence in *Holder v. Hall*, Justice Thomas asserted that it is erroneous to read the Voting Rights Act to "cover claims of vote dilution."[23] Justice Thomas argued that racial groups should not "be conceived of largely as political interest groups."[24] He argued that the current case law should be overturned to eliminate claims for "proportional allocation of political power according to race."[25] Theoretical assaults — like the ones found in Justice Thomas's strongly worded concurring opinion in *Holder v. Hall* and in the amici briefs in *Johnson v. De Grandy*[26] — called for a powerful response grounded in a democratic theory of group representation. None was forthcoming. Instead, the Court left unexplored the volcanic core of the contemporary voting rights debate — whether groups should be represented.

---

18 *See Holder*, 114 S. Ct. at 2588.

19 114 S. Ct. 2647 (1994).

20 *See id.* at 2651.

21 *Id.* (emphasis added).

22 *See, e.g.*, Brief Amicus Curiae of Anti-Defamation League of B'nai B'rith in Support of Neither Party at 6 n.3, 7, *De Grandy* (Nos. 92-519, 92-593, 92-767) (arguing that recognizing and labeling a group as African American "unfairly equates the color of one's skin with a community of interest and creates unjustified stereotypes of culturally diverse minorities"). The Anti-Defamation League concluded that no racial or ethnic class is entitled to maximum "feasible" representation under the Voting Rights Act. *See id.* at 16. The American Jewish Congress, which filed an amicus brief in support of the State of Florida, argued that maximization of one group's power necessarily diminishes another group's power. *See* Motion for Leave to File a Brief Amici Curiae and Brief Amici Curiae of the American Jewish Congress and Community Relations Committee of the Greater Miami Jewish Federation in Support of Appellants at 21, *De Grandy* (Nos. 92-519, 92-593, 92-767).

23 *Holder*, 114 S. Ct. at 2592, 2618–19 (Thomas, J., concurring in the judgment).

24 *Id.* at 2598.

25 *Id.* at 2614; *see also* Epstein, *supra* note 11, at 884 (claiming that the principle of the Reconstruction Amendments was to "get race out of politics").

26 *See supra* note 22.

This Case Comment argues that the Voting Rights Act is a statute in search of a theory. Both *De Grandy* and *Holder* illustrate the inadequacy of current voting rights jurisprudence to articulate a principled and workable strategy for enforcing the Act. That Congress has passed, reenacted, and then amended the law[27] may provide the legal authority for judicial intervention to protect minority group voting rights. But neither the Congress that passed the statute, nor the Court that has consistently upheld it, has excavated the principles of democracy in which to locate a group's statutory right to an effective vote. Because the Supreme Court has not formulated a coherent theory on which to rest the Voting Rights Act, the Act remains vulnerable to ideological challenge every time a federal court is asked, or a state voluntarily seeks, to remedy racial minority group exclusion.

The goals of the Act can and should be defended by framing them philosophically within a theory of group representation. The premise of such an approach is that group representation, as a matter of democratic theory, is not about race but about democratic political community. Because of the confluence of historical discrimination and contemporary exclusion, racial and language minority groups enjoy an exclusive right under the Act to establish a legal violation.[28] Once a violation has been proved, however, the most acceptable way to empower the particular plaintiff class would be to move to a broader conception of group representation based on interests rather than race.

Framed by a theory of group representation, the Voting Rights Act could achieve its original goal: to enfranchise victims of racial discrimination. This theory of group representation could also answer those whose criticisms of the Act are based in democratic theory. The theory of group representation, at the remedial stage, would treat all politically cohesive groups alike. Informed by such a theoretical approach, judicial intervention may be popularly understood as a means of transforming the political process to benefit all voters. The Voting Rights Act could then be implemented as it was intended — to achieve more democracy, not less.

I. The 1993 Term Voting Rights Cases

Johnson v. De Grandy and *Holder v. Hall* posed the question whether section two of the Voting Rights Act of 1965, as amended in 1982, requires federal courts to maximize, or at least to ensure, the representation of minority groups. In *De Grandy*, the Court held that section two does not require maximization of minority group-domi-

---

[27] *See* Voting Rights Act of 1965, Pub. L. No. 89-110, 79 Stat. 437, *amended by* Act of June 19, 1970, Pub. L. No. 91-285, 84 Stat. 314; Act of Aug. 6, 1975, Pub. L. No. 94-73, 89 Stat. 400; Act of June 29, 1982, Pub. L. No. 97-205, 96 Stat. 131.

[28] *See* sources cited *supra* notes 7, 11.

nated districts.[29] Similarly, in *Holder* the Court construed section two to grant a minority group the right to representation within a governing body, but not the right to challenge the size of that body, and thus refused to require minimum levels of minority group participation in government.[30] Both holdings constrain the federal judiciary's ability to enforce the Voting Rights Act. The *Holder* case, in particular, undermines Congress's decision to override local majorities whose election structures result in minority group exclusion.[31]

A. Johnson v. De Grandy

In *De Grandy*, the district court consolidated three actions filed by African American plaintiffs, Latino plaintiffs, and the Department of Justice.[32] The African American and Hispanic plaintiffs separately alleged that Florida's 1992 districting plan[33] diluted their respective groups' voting strength.[34] The 1992 plan created twenty house districts and seven senate districts located at least partially within Dade County.[35] The district court held that, under the three-pronged test of *Thornburg v. Gingles*,[36] Latinos were entitled to be majorities in eleven instead of their existing nine house districts, and ordered the legislature to redraw the lines accordingly.[37] The district court also held that the senate districts proposed by the plan diluted both African American and Hispanic voting strength.[38] But the district court did not grant a remedy for the senate districts because it found it impossible

---

29 *See De Grandy*, 114 S. Ct. at 2659–60.

30 *See Holder*, 114 S. Ct. at 2584, 2588.

31 *See* 42 U.S.C. § 1973(b) (directing that a political process that is "not equally open to participation by members" of protected classes violates federal law).

32 *See De Grandy*, 114 S. Ct. at 2651–52.

33 On April 10, 1992, Florida's legislature passed Senate Joint Resolution 2-G, FLA. STAT. ch. 10.1001–10.1008 (1993), which redivided Florida into 40 single-member senate and 120 single-member house districts based on the 1990 Census. *See De Grandy*, 114 S. Ct. at 2652.

34 *See De Grandy*, 114 S. Ct. at 2652. There is some political animosity between African Americans and Hispanics in the Dade County area. *See* De Grandy v. Wetherell, 815 F. Supp. 1550, 1569 (N.D. Fla. 1992) ("Hispanics and African-Americans were each politically cohesive among themselves but were not at all cohesive — and were often at odds — in relation to each other.").

35 *See De Grandy*, 114 S. Ct. at 2658, 2663.

36 478 U.S. 30 (1986). *Thornburg v. Gingles* established that a § 2 vote dilution claim requires plaintiffs to meet a three-pronged test: first, that the minority group is "sufficiently large and geographically compact to constitute a majority single-member district"; second, that the minority group is "politically cohesive"; and third, that whites constitute a voting bloc that usually operates to defeat minority candidates. *Id.* at 50–51. *Gingles* involved multimember districts, but its test is also applicable to single-member districts. *See De Grandy*, 114 S. Ct. at 2654–55 (citing Growe v. Emison, 113 S. Ct. 1075, 1084 (1993)).

37 *See De Grandy*, 815 F. Supp. at 1563, 1580–82.

38 *See id.* at 1574.

to create an additional district for either group without diluting the voting strength of the other.[39]

The Supreme Court, in an opinion by Justice Souter,[40] found no statutory violation in either the house or senate districting under the 1992 plan and therefore did not reach the issue of remedies.[41] Holding that *Thornburg v. Gingles* requires a totality of the circumstances inquiry,[42] the Court affirmed the district court's decision to uphold the senate districting plan[43] and reversed the district court's holding that the house districting plan violated section two.[44] The Court's holding with respect to the house districting rested on its factual finding of rough proportionality on a local rather than a statewide basis, which it arrived at by disaggregating and comparing each protected group's *local* voting-age population with the number of arbitrarily designated *local* districts each group controlled.[45]

The Court reasoned that the State was under no duty to maximize minority districts for either blacks or Latinos.[46] Rather, the State fulfilled its obligation to give minorities an equal opportunity to participate in the political process because minority voters formed "effective voting majorities in a number of districts roughly proportional" to their respective shares of a state divined local population.[47] Thus, the *De Grandy* decision indicates that, once a majority subdivides its power or distributes decisionmaking power on a limited local basis, minorities are entitled to a fair, but not necessarily the most fair share.

---

[39] *See id.* at 1578–80. Specifically, the district court found that the Hispanic plaintiffs' plan, which added a Hispanic supermajority senate district in the Dade County area, and the NAACP plan, which added an African American majority district in the same area, were incompatible. *See id.* at 1574–78. The Court concluded more generally that the "ideal solution" of adding one African-American-dominated and one Hispanic-dominated senate district was "not a viable option," *id.* at 1577, because the remedies were "mutually exclusive," *id.* at 1578.

[40] Justice Souter was joined by Chief Justice Rehnquist and Justices Blackmun, Stevens, O'Connor, and Ginsburg. Justice O'Connor filed a separate concurring opinion. Justice Kennedy concurred in part and concurred in the judgment. Justice Thomas filed a dissenting opinion, in which Justice Scalia joined.

[41] *See De Grandy*, 114 S. Ct. at 2653.

[42] *See id.* at 2657; *supra* note 36.

[43] *See De Grandy*, 114 S. Ct. at 2663.

[44] *See id.* at 2662.

[45] *See id.* at 2651. The Court cautioned that "the degree of probative value assigned to proportionality may vary with other facts" but insisted that proportionality is relevant evidence under the totality of circumstances test. *Id.* at 2661–62. The United States government argued that measuring proportionality on a statewide basis would provide a "clear and objective measure of proportional representation," while a regional approach would allow a party to bolster its argument by adjusting regional boundaries. Brief for the United States as Appellee at 25, *De Grandy* (Nos. 92-519, 92-793, 92-567).

[46] *See De Grandy*, 114 S. Ct. at 2659–60.

[47] *Id.* at 2651; *cf. supra* note 45.

B. Holder v. Hall

The plaintiffs in *Holder v. Hall* belonged to a minority group (African Americans) that had never been able to elect any of its members to the single-person commission that governs Bleckley County, Georgia.[48] They challenged the county's sole-commissioner form of government under section two and under the Fourteenth and Fifteenth Amendments.[49] The district court applied the three-part *Gingles* test[50] to the section two claim and held that the plaintiffs met the compactness prong of the test but failed to establish that their minority group was politically cohesive or that whites usually voted as a bloc.[51] The Eleventh Circuit reversed on the statutory claim, finding that the plaintiffs satisfied all three *Gingles* factors.[52] The Supreme Court granted certiorari to review the statutory claim[53] and reversed and remanded.[54] In an opinion by Justice Kennedy, the Supreme Court held that Bleckley County's single-person county commission was not subject to challenge under section two.[55] The five-Justice majority, cobbled together in three separate opinions,[56] gave three different explanations for refusing to apply section two to Bleckley County's form of government. Justice Kennedy determined that section two does not cover the size of a governing body because sizes vary so widely that no standard exists for comparison.[57] Justice O'Connor agreed with this rationale but argued that a practice subject to scrutiny under section five of the Voting Rights Act[58] might also be sub-

---

48 *See* Holder v. Hall, 114 S. Ct. 2581, 2584 (1994). Bleckley County's black community leaders testified that, as a practical matter, it is futile to sponsor African American candidates for this post because blacks were only 20% of the county voting-age population. *See* Hall v. Holder, 955 F.2d 1563, 1571 (11th Cir. 1992). The plaintiffs, six black registered voters from Bleckley County and the Cochran/Bleckley Chapter of the NAACP, argued for a county commission large enough that African Americans would constitute a majority in one single-member district. *See Holder*, 114 S. Ct. at 2584–85. African Americans do have a clear majority in one of the five existing school board districts. *See Holder*, 955 F.2d at 1569 n.10.

49 *See Holder*, 114 S. Ct. at 2584–85.

50 *See supra* note 36.

51 *See* Hall v. Holder, 757 F. Supp. 1560, 1582 (M.D. Ga. 1991).

52 *See Holder*, 955 F.2d at 1568–69.

53 *See Holder*, 114 S. Ct. at 2585.

54 *See id.* at 2588.

55 *See Holder*, 114 S. Ct. at 2588. Justice Blackmun, dissenting, pointed out that Justice Kennedy's view in the Georgia case is inconsistent with 30 years of precedent, which broadly construed the Voting Rights Act to overcome "a wide variety of election- and voting-related practices." *Id.* at 2619–20 (Blackmun, J., dissenting).

56 Justice Kennedy was joined by Chief Justice Rehnquist in full and by Justice O'Connor in part. Justice O'Connor also filed a separate opinion, concurring in part and concurring in the judgment. Justice Thomas concurred in the judgment in an opinion joined by Justice Scalia. Justices Blackmun, Stevens, Souter, and Ginsburg dissented.

57 *See id.*

58 42 U.S.C. § 1973c (requiring preclearance for changes in voting procedures for covered jurisdictions).

ject to a section two dilution challenge.[59] Justice Thomas concurred but called for a "systematic reassessment" of the Court's interpretation of section two.[60] In dissent, Justice Blackmun responded that the proposed five-member commission presented a reasonable benchmark because such a commission was specifically authorized by the Georgia legislature, is the most common type of governing body in Georgia, and was adopted by Bleckley County itself for its school board.[61]

C. *Implications*

The opinions in these two cases are in tension. On the one hand, *De Grandy* suggests that proportionality of representation is "a relevant fact in the totality of circumstances" and is to be considered with regard to a section two claim.[62] On the other hand, according to *Holder*, if a jurisdiction sets the size of the governing body so low that it permits group representation only for the dominant racial group, unrepresented minorities have no cause of action under section two.[63]

In the prior Term's *Shaw v. Reno* decision,[64] the Court recognized the role of race in American democracy but sought, in the name of majoritarian democracy, to place limits on the use of race as a primary factor in allocating representation. Because the Court did explicitly take account of race in *De Grandy* and *Holder*, however, the 1993 Term undercuts critics of the Voting Rights Act who challenge any kind of race-consciousness in drawing districts or providing minority group representation.[65] Thus, if *Shaw v. Reno* marks the voting rights precipice, the Court blinked in its 1993 Term. In another sense, however, the Court continues to defer to the political chorus of local white majorities who underrepresent, or even refuse to represent, racial minorities. This indifference to the way racism undermines representa-

---

59 *See Holder*, 114 S. Ct. at 2588–89 (O'Connor, J., concurring in part and concurring in the judgment).

60 *Id.* at 2591 (Thomas, J., concurring in the judgment); *infra* Part II.

61 *See Holder*, 114 S. Ct. at 2622 (Blackmun, J., dissenting). Justice Blackmun acknowledged that dilution is a relative concept under which the challenged voting practice must be compared with a "reasonable and workable" alternative. *Id.* However, he argued that the problems with § 2 dilution claims in this context can be overcome by "flexible, fact-intensive" inquiries. *Id.* (quoting Thornburg v. Gingles, 478 U.S. 30, 46 (1986)). Justice Blackmun further argued that single-member commissions can be a dilutive practice. *See id.* at 2624. Justice Blackmun and the other dissenters also stressed the language of the statute, *see id.* at 2619; the many congressional reenactments that acknowledge judicial interpretations of the statute, *see id.* at 2621; *id.* at 2626–27 (Stevens, J., dissenting); the doctrine of stare decisis, *see id.* at 2628–29; and the function of federal judges to effectuate Congress's multiple, competing purposes, *see id.* at 2625 (Ginsburg, J., dissenting).

62 *De Grandy*, 114 S. Ct. at 2651.

63 *See Holder*, 114 S. Ct. at 2586–88.

64 113 S. Ct. 2816 (1993).

65 *See Holder*, 114 S. Ct. at 2586; *De Grandy*, 114 S. Ct. at 2651.

tive democracy contradicts the inclusive conception of democracy that informs the statute.[66]

Although the Court affirmed the general race-conscious thrust of voting rights jurisprudence,[67] the Court's opinions are impoverished by their failure to approach minority group representation from a more general understanding of representative democracy. The Court failed to answer directly the broader questions of democratic theory and the rhetoric of colorblindness that Justice Thomas raised in his provocative *Holder* concurrence.

II. JUSTICE THOMAS'S RADICAL RECONSTRUCTION

Concurring in *Holder*, Justice Thomas's goal was to reconstruct the Voting Rights Act, especially as amended in 1982, to remove the right to group representation from the statute.[68] Justice Thomas's project — to shrink the statutory meaning of voting to the single act of casting a ballot — was not a conventional attempt at statutory construction, but a radical reconstruction of the law.[69]

Justice Thomas acknowledged that courts have consistently interpreted the Voting Rights Act to protect more than the formal right to register and vote.[70] The statute refers to an "effective" vote and establishes the right of members of a protected class to enjoy the same "opportunity to participate" *and* "to elect" representatives of their choice as do other members of the electorate.[71] The Senate Report that accompanied the 1982 amendments to section two contains ninety-two references to vote dilution and the representation of minority groups in its 108 pages. The report explains:

---

66 *See supra* notes 7–10 and accompanying text.

67 *See De Grandy*, 114 S. Ct. at 2651.

68 By locating his attack on the Court's vote dilution jurisprudence in his concurring opinion in *Holder* rather than in his dissenting opinion in *De Grandy*, Justice Thomas sought to give his views more currency.

69 *See, e.g.*, *Holder*, 114 S. Ct. at 2625, 2628, 2629–30 (separate opinion of Stevens, J.) (describing the "radical character" of Justice Thomas's "suggested interpretation," which may be "best described as an argument that the statute be repealed or amended in important respects").

This approach is remarkable for judges such as Justice Thomas, and his fellow concurrer Justice Scalia, who presumably believe that the Court's role is constrained by the legislative choices already made by Congress. This approach is so unconventional that Justice Thomas lost the votes of other Justices who had elsewhere expressed substantive reservations about the statute. *See* Presley v. Etowah, 112 S. Ct. 820, 830 (1992) (Kennedy, J., joined by Rehnquist, C.J., and O'Connor, Scalia, Souter & Thomas, JJ.); Chisom v. Roemer, 501 U.S. 380, 404–11 (1991) (Scalia, J., dissenting, joined by Kennedy, J.); Thornburg v. Gingles, 478 U.S. 30, 94 (1986) (O'Connor, J., concurring in the judgment, joined by Burger, C.J., and Powell & Rehnquist, JJ.).

70 Justice Thomas recognized that current law includes the concept of vote dilution and that "a vote dilution claim necessarily depends on the assertion of a group right." *Holder*, 114 S. Ct. at 2605 (Thomas, J., concurring in the judgment).

71 42 U.S.C. § 1973(b); *see also id.* § 1973*l*(c)(1) (noting that the term "voting" includes "all action necessary to make a vote effective").

> There is more to the right to vote than the right to mark a piece of paper and drop it in a box or the right to pull a lever in a voting booth . . . . [The] federally protected right [to vote] suffers substantial dilution . . . [when a] favored group has full voting strength . . . [and] [t]he groups not in favor have their votes discounted.[72]

Although the legislation was passed by overwhelming bipartisan congressional majorities and signed into law by a conservative Republican President,[73] Justice Thomas dismissed such legislative history "gloss"[74] as "a series of partisan statements about purposes and objectives."[75]

Instead, Justice Thomas focused exclusively on the Act's text. According to Justice Thomas, reviewing courts have distorted the statutory definition of voting, which "include[s] all action necessary to make a vote *effective*," by "seiz[ing]" on the word "effective" and "pluck[ing]" it "out of context."[76] Justice Thomas did not say exactly what might be the proper context for understanding Congress's use of the word "effective." But he overlooked an obvious possibility: when Congress first passed the Act in 1965, the Supreme Court was using the term "effective" in its one person/one vote opinions. At the time, constitutional one person/one vote complaints alleged a systematic plan to "discriminate against a *geographical class* of persons."[77] Voters assigned to urban and suburban districts complained that, because of the *size* of their districts, their votes were less effective than votes cast in more sparsely populated rural districts.[78] In *historical* context, the

---

[72] S. REP. NO. 417, 97th Cong., 2d Sess. 19 (1982), *reprinted in* 1982 U.S.C.C.A.N. 177, 196 (quoting Reynolds v. Sims, 377 U.S. 533, 555 n.29 (1964) (quoting South v. Peters, 339 U.S. 276, 279 (1950) (Douglas, J., dissenting))) (internal quotation marks omitted). Even Senators initially opposed to the amendment of § 2 admitted that "vote dilution" is based on concerns for post-election rights of groups. For example, Senator Orrin Hatch, who voted for the committee bill but dissented from the Senate Committee Report, wrote: "Instead of directing its protections toward the individual citizen as did the original Act — and as does the Constitution — the amendments would make racial and ethnic *groups* the basic unit of protection." *Id.* at 94, *reprinted in* 1982 U.S.C.C.A.N. at 267. In addition, an amendment to prevent the existence of at-large elections from being considered evidence of a violation of § 2 failed in committee by a vote of 13–5. *See id.* at 77, *reprinted in* 1982 U.S.C.C.A.N. at 256. At-large elections are a classic vote dilution mechanism, in which all voters get to cast a formal ballot, but a minority of the voters may get no voice in selecting representatives.

[73] The 25-year extension of the Voting Rights Act of 1965, with an amendment of § 2, was passed in 1982 by an 85–8 vote in the Senate and by unanimous consent in the House. *See* Howell Raines, *Voting Rights Act Signed by Reagan*, N.Y. TIMES, June 30, 1982, at A16; *Voting Rights Measure Approved by Congress*, N.Y. TIMES, June 24, 1982, at B11.

[74] *See Holder*, 114 S. Ct. at 2607 (Thomas, J., concurring in the judgment).

[75] *Id.* at 2612.

[76] *Id.* at 2605.

[77] Baker v. Carr, 369 U.S. 186, 273 (1962) (Frankfurter, J., dissenting) (quoting Plaintiffs' Compl., *Baker* (No. 2724), *reprinted in* Tr. of R. at 12) (emphasis added). The dissenting opinions acknowledge the claim that the distribution of electoral strength among geographic units reflects a legislative judgment about the representation of interests. *See, e.g.*, *id.* at 334 (Harlan, J., dissenting).

[78] The concerns raised by the plaintiffs in one person/one vote constitutional dilution cases involved their inability to cast a "meaningful" or "effective" ballot. The plaintiffs did not com-

term thus referred to the post-election concern for the "weight" or "influence" of a geographic grouping of votes, and not merely to formal access to a voting booth.[79]

Nevertheless, Justice Thomas decided that an effective vote means simply the individual ability to cast a ballot. Justice Thomas justified his departure from thirty years of statutory construction primarily on political theory grounds.[80] In Justice Thomas's view, the Supreme Court opinions that construe the statutory language "all action necessary to make a vote effective"[81] are philosophically wrong-headed[82] and essentially reflect nothing more than a "political decision" that the purpose of a vote or, more precisely, of a fully effective vote, is to control seats in an elected body.[83] According to Justice Thomas, this measure of efficacy equates voting power with control of single-member districts.[84] This standard uses geographic districts to allocate political power, an approach that, to Justice Thomas, is "not a require-

---

plain about the difficulty of casting a ballot, but rather raised post-election concerns that the votes of urban and suburban voters were less "effective" or were "diluted" compared to the potential influence of votes cast by voters in less populous, rural districts. *See, e.g.*, Moore v. Ogilvie, 394 U.S. 814, 818–19 (1969) ("The idea that one group can be granted greater voting strength than another is hostile to the one man, one vote basis of our representative government."); Gray v. Sanders, 372 U.S. 368, 379 (1963) (expressing dissatisfaction with an electoral system that gives disproportionate weight to rural votes and to votes from less populous counties).

Justice Thomas cites approvingly Burns v. Richardson, 384 U.S. 73 (1966), which concerned a challenge under the Equal Protection Clause to the apportionment of the Hawaiian house and senate, *see id.* at 75. The plaintiffs in *Burns* challenged the legislative failure to take into account "community of interests, community of problems, socio-economic status, political and racial factors." *Id.* at 87 (quoting Holt v. Richardson, 240 F. Supp. 724, 730–31 (1965)) (internal quotation marks omitted). In *Burns*, the Court focused again on group representation, and not just on individual ballot access. The Court held that the constitutional requirement of proving invidious discrimination had not been met because the plaintiffs did not show that the scheme operated "to minimize or cancel out the voting strength of racial or political elements of the voting population." *Id.* at 87–88 (quoting Forston v. Dorsey, 379 U.S. 433, 439 (1965)) (internal quotation marks omitted).

[79] *See, e.g.*, Maryland Comm. for Fair Representation v. Tawes, 377 U.S. 656, 673 (1964); Reynolds v. Sims, 377 U.S. 533, 565 (1964); Wesberry v. Sanders, 376 U.S. 1, 7–8 (1964); Baker v. Carr, 369 U.S. 186, 207–08 (1962). These cases involved dilution of votes as a result of population disparities among legislative districts. They were not focused, as Justice Thomas claims Congress was, only on "citizens' access to the ballot." *Holder*, 114 S. Ct. at 2604 (Thomas, J., concurring in the judgment).

[80] *See Holder*, 114 S. Ct. at 2594 (Thomas, J., concurring in the judgment). "[I]t is only a resort to political theory that can enable a court to determine which electoral systems provide the 'fairest' levels of representation or the most 'effective' or 'undiluted' votes to minorities." *Id.* at 2592.

[81] 42 U.S.C. § 1973*l*(c)(1); *see id.* at 2626 (Stevens, J., dissenting) (citing Allen v. State Bd. of Elections, 393 U.S. 544, 565–66 (1969)).

[82] *See id.* at 2597–2600 (Thomas, J., concurring in the judgment). Although he does not tackle its implications, Justice Thomas makes use of an approach that would also dislodge the theoretical basis for constitutional one person/one vote cases. *See supra* notes 77–79 and accompanying text.

[83] *Holder*, 114 S. Ct. at 2595 (Thomas, J., concurring in the judgment).

[84] *See id.* at 2596.

ment inherent in our political system."[85] He also pointed out that, even within geographically districted governing bodies, votes that do not control a seat may nevertheless be an influential "'swing' group of voters"[86] or be cast in "minority 'influence' districts."[87]

The idea of vote dilution embodied in the Voting Rights Act — the concept that groups can be arbitrarily deprived of political clout by the way an election structures and allocates political power — is for Justice Thomas simply that: an idea. It is a question of political theory on which reasonable people may differ. For Justice Thomas, the Act is equally compatible with an alternative theory of democracy, one in which the right to vote conveys only symbolic, not necessarily real privileges.[88] In such a "republican arrangement," as long as minorities can vote, they have all the political power they are due; if voting is the extent of political rights, the government should not intervene when "numerical minorities lose."[89]

The professed jurisprudential virtue of Justice Thomas's formulation is that it avoids "immers[ing] the federal courts" in the "hopeless project" of choosing between competing political theories[90] and limits federal judicial intervention in local election matters. Justice Thomas's interpretation of the statute, however, itself rests on a particular political theory. Justice Thomas's political theory, or at least the theory he imputed to the Congress that enacted the Voting Rights Act, is that political equality is satisfied by the simple condition of universal suffrage.[91] His position — that the statute should be limited

---

85 *Id.* at 2601. Indeed, under the logic of current voting rights jurisprudence, geographic districts may be replaced by another voting structure. Justice Thomas specifically labels cumulative voting a non-districted election arrangement that is consistent with current judicial interpretation of the Voting Rights Act and the Constitution. *See id.* at 2601 n.17.

86 *Id.* at 2596.

87 *Id.* at 2596 n.8.

88 This is essentially the view that voting is an important ritual, which symbolizes membership in the political community. *See infra* notes 111–114. There is some support for such a view as a matter of democratic theory. *See, e.g.*, CHARLES R. BEITZ, POLITICAL EQUALITY 40–41, 133, 150 (1989) (arguing generally that the right to vote requires an equally weighted vote but not "an equally effective" vote). However, even Professor Beitz believes that special circumstances warrant judicial intervention to protect disadvantaged groups whose ability to exercise "an effective vote" is systematically thwarted because of prejudice. *See* Charles R. Beitz, Outline Prepared for American Political Science Association Roundtable on Group Representation (Sept. 2, 1994) (unpublished notes, on file at the Harvard Law School library).

89 *Holder*, 114 S. Ct. at 2596 (Thomas, J., concurring in the judgment).

90 *Id.* at 2592. Echoing Justice Frankfurter in Colegrove v. Green, 328 U.S. 549, 553–54 (1946), Justice Thomas concluded that questions of democratic political theory are beyond the capacity of the federal judiciary.

91 *See, e.g.*, *Holder*, 114 S. Ct. at 2592 (Thomas, J., concurring in the judgment) (arguing that the "terms [of the Voting Rights Act] reach only state enactments that limit citizens' access to the ballot").

to claims that challenge direct denial of the right to cast a ballot — rests on a political theory of individualized democracy.[92]

Thus, Justice Thomas must argue for more than a Frankfurter-like judicial abstention. If he wants courts to interpret the Act as consistent with one political theory rather than another, Justice Thomas must make a different case. This he tries to do by arguing that the conventional view of the Act as embodying the concept of group representation is not only a dangerous political choice;[93] it is also an immoral choice, because it treats racial groups as if they were political interest groups.[94] On this account, racial group representation emphasizes irrelevant differences, such as race, and suppresses relevant differences, such as the dissenting ideology of "double minorities."[95] For Justice Thomas, the immorality of group representation justified extreme judicial action: ignoring traditional rules of stare decisis,[96] Justice Thomas proposed overruling *Thornburg v. Gingles*,[97] the Supreme Court decision that established a vote dilution claim under the Voting Rights Act.[98]

Justice Thomas's approach neglects the fact that representative democracy is neither exclusively individual nor discrete but is relational

---

92 *See* JOSEPH A. SCHUMPETER, CAPITALISM, SOCIALISM AND DEMOCRACY 283 (1950) (calling individualized or direct democracy primitive mass action). Individualized democracy is best realized by referenda or initiatives in which each voter speaks for herself directly and exclusively by the way she casts a ballot. Aristotle termed direct democracy "perverted" because it fails to protect the rights and interests of the minority. *See* ARISTOTLE, POLITICS III.6.11, III.7.5 (B. Jowett trans., 1885). James Madison made a similar argument in *Federalist* No. 10. *See* THE FEDERALIST NO. 10, at 81 (James Madison) (Clinton Rossiter ed., 1961); *cf.* Jonathan Still, *Political Equality and Election Systems*, 91 ETHICS 375, 378 (1981) (noting that universal suffrage is simply a necessary but not a sufficient condition to realization of political equality).

93 Justice Thomas calls it a "disastrous misadventure in judicial policymaking." *Holder*, 114 S. Ct. at 2592 (Thomas, J., concurring in the judgment).

94 *See id.* at 2597. Allocating political power on the basis of race, for Justice Thomas, is the moral equivalent of requiring "registration on racial rolls." *Id.* at 2599.

Justice Thomas essentially challenges the way in which race functions as a political, not just a sociological category. For Justice Thomas, racial group representation is inherently divisive. *See id.* (quoting Wright v. Rockefeller, 376 U.S. 52, 66 (1964) (Douglas, J., dissenting)). It can only "serve to deepen racial divisions by destroying any need for voters or candidates to build bridges between racial groups or to form voting coalitions." *Id.* It encourages "racially based understanding of the representative function." *Id.* (citing Shaw v. Reno, 113 S. Ct. 2816, 2828 (1993) (stating that racial classification of voters signals "to elected officials that they represent a particular racial group rather than their constituency as a whole" and thereby threatens "to undermine our system of representative democracy")). Although Justice Thomas's tone is adamant, he provides no empirical evidence to support his assertions. *Cf. infra* note 100 (citing evidence that race may in fact coincide with political interests).

95 "Double minorities" are racial minority subsets who have views distinct from the majority of racial minority group members.

96 *See Holder*, 114 S. Ct. at 2591 (Thomas, J., concurring in the judgment) (arguing that "a systematic reassessment of our interpretation of the Act is required").

97 478 U.S. 30 (1986).

98 *See Holder*, 114 S. Ct. at 2619 (Thomas, J., concurring in the judgment).

and inherently group-based.[99] Further, although Justice Thomas offered a theory of exit for minority group members who choose to emphasize their individual identity, he offered nothing to explain or empower those whose *chosen* identity is group-based.[100]

In an ironic twist, Justice Thomas's approach, which repudiates racial minority group representation in the cause of race-neutrality, is not itself race-neutral. He posited that blacks and Latinos can serve as influential "swing votes" when in the minority. If true, this premise should also apply to double minorities, who dissent from the prevailing views of their racial group.[101] Yet Justice Thomas seems to assert, to the contrary, that minority racial group representatives will not represent all of their constituents, at least not to the same extent as white politicians elected from single-member, multi-racial districts.[102]

Implicit in Justice Thomas's argument that race is not a political category[103] may be the concern that racial group members who do not share the dominant political viewpoint of the racial minority group will be ignored by representatives chosen by the minority group. This is a claim that, even when racial groups are treated as political interest groups, they will function in contravention of their own political interests. They will refuse to bargain. They will refuse to form coalitions.

---

[99] *See infra* notes 111–114 and accompanying text.

[100] It seems clear that many people *do* believe that their interests coincide with group interests. The district court in *De Grandy* and the Court of Appeals in *Holder* found that the record in each case supported the claim that the plaintiff racial groups were politically cohesive. *See* Hall v. Holder, 955 F.2d 1563, 1573 (11th Cir. 1992); De Grandy v. Wetherell, 794 F. Supp. 1076, 1079 (N.D. Fla. 1992). Justice Thomas recognized that this claim, under the political cohesion threshold in *Thornburg v. Gingles*, *see* 478 U.S. at 51, requires proof of a correlation between voting behavior and race. *See Holder*, 114 S. Ct. at 2597 (Thomas, J., concurring in the judgment). He dismissed this requirement as extraneous window dressing because proof of political cohesion can be established by a simple bivariate regression analysis without demonstrating the cause of the correlation. *See id.* at 2598 n.13.

[101] In other words, the criticisms about racial representation expressed by Justice Thomas presumably disable any district winner from representing the district losers. *See* Lani Guinier, *Groups, Representation, and Race-Conscious Districting: A Case of the Emperor's Clothes*, 71 TEX. L. REV. 1589, 1611–16 (1993) (detailing my view that district representation unfairly and inaccurately assumes that the district losers are represented based on principles of virtual representation). I am skeptical that any voter is well represented by political opponents, in part because I view voting instrumentally and not merely symbolically. Justice Thomas apparently shares my concern only with regard to the internal politics within racial groups. He apparently does not share my concern with respect to other political groups or inter-racial group representation of people of color by whites.

[102] *See Holder*, 114 S. Ct. at 2599 (Thomas, J., concurring in the judgment) (noting that the formation of racial minority districts makes it unnecessary for elected officials to be responsive to the needs of citizens not of the same race as the elected official).

[103] For Justice Thomas, race is not a political category because not all blacks think or act alike. But neither do all members of a political party think or act alike. Indeed, members of the Court have commented on the absence of any real ideological ties connecting members of national political parties. *See, e.g.*, Democratic Party v. Wisconsin Democratic Party, 450 U.S. 107, 131–32 (1981) (Powell, J., dissenting) (noting that a national political party does not have a uniform political ideology or mission).

They will simply stamp their feet and demand racial group recognition but will not negotiate for racial group influence.

The political theory that underlies this reconstruction of the Voting Rights Act is not just race-conscious. It is similar to the patronizing attitude toward people of color associated with the first Reconstruction following the Civil War. It exploits many of the very stereotypes about blacks that Justice Thomas tried so hard to dislodge.

Alternatively, Justice Thomas may be arguing that dissenting racial minority voters deserve special protection from other minority voters. Yet given his views that numerical minorities lose in a majoritarian democracy, he can hardly argue that the jurisprudence of minority voting rights should be governed by special preferences to double minorities.[104]

Beyond these theoretical concerns, Justice Thomas's formalistic approach to political participation is an unpersuasive exercise in statutory construction, even to critics of the Voting Rights Act, and certainly to a majority of the Court.[105] Justice Thomas arrogated to himself the task of reconstructing current law and chose for the Congress a political theory of limited access. Notwithstanding Justice Thomas's discomfort with judges' implementing certain "political choices,"[106] Congress, by the terms of the Voting Rights Act, chose to involve the judiciary in precisely this way.

Despite the gaps in its reasoning, Justice Thomas's opinion is important for two reasons. First, Justice Thomas demonstrated the centrality of political theory to an understanding of minority vote dilution. As Justice Thomas argued, vote dilution claims require the federal judiciary to develop theories of the basic principles of democratic self-government. The question of defining minority vote dilution can only be answered by reference to a theory that defines effective participation in representative government. Second, Justice Thomas provided an enduring rationale for future challenges to the Act. Although the

---

104 If Justice Thomas is focused on members of the racial minority who choose to exit the group, he might claim instead that these double minorities cannot be heard because racial minorities will be perceived as monolithic whether or not they are. But this, too, singles out the racial minority for special exemption from principles of majority rule. In this way, Justice Thomas proves the power of David Strauss's claim that, because race is not irrelevant, "we do not have a choice between colorblindness and race-consciousness; we only have a choice between different forms of race-consciousness." David A. Strauss, *The Myth of Colorblindness*, 1986 SUP. CT. REV. 99, 114.

In contemporary discourse, colorblindness has come to mean that mere recognition of race, except to condemn intentional racial discrimination, is dangerous. Yet because of the recognition and support our political system gives to other, non-racial groups, colorblindness, although ostensibly race-neutral, singles out race for special treatment.

105 Justice Thomas gained only the vote of Justice Scalia for the proposition that Justice Stevens's opinion in Chisom v. Roemer, 111 S. Ct. 2354 (1991), means that § 2 only applies to ballot access cases.

106 *Holder*, 114 S. Ct. at 2596 (Thomas, J., concurring in the judgment).

dissents in *Holder* and the majority in *De Grandy* recognized the broad remedial goal of the statute, none of the other opinions in those cases took Justice Thomas's challenge to articulate a theory of democratic representation from which a principled and workable strategy for enforcing the Act might emerge.[107]

III. Toward a Theory of Interest Group Representation

This Case Comment argues that, in order to legitimate the Voting Rights Act within the contemporary discourse of race, the Act must be considered from the perspective of a broader theory concerning the democratic representation of groups.[108] First, group representation is not only consistent with, but is the very essence of representative democracy. Second, although race may be constitutive of identity, it should be treated as a political, not a biological category. Finally, in choosing remedies to guarantee representation opportunities for politically cohesive racial groups, courts should select remedies that also have the potential to empower other politically cohesive groups. This is especially true when successful voting rights challenges by racial minority groups expose more systematic problems with current political arrangements.

A. *The Essentially Democratic Character of Group Representation*

Group participation in political life is consistent with fundamental democratic principles. Theories of both communitarian democracy and democratic pluralism insist that democracy is sustained by the intermediate groups or associations that provide collective bases for political action.

Communitarianism posits that the very essence of democracy is community, a collection of individuals with a collective consciousness or common cultural and social experiences.[109] According to communitarianism, democracy is most fruitful when intermediate groups or local communities disseminate information, facilitate debate, and promote interaction among citizens.

Group participation is also essential to the pluralist conception of democracy as free competition among interest groups. Pluralism views the democratic process as a series of coalitions, negotiations, bargains,

---

[107] The validity of the Voting Rights Act and of vote dilution claims under the Act was not directly at issue in these cases, so the dissenting Justices in *Holder* were able to fulfill their decisional duties without gracing Justice Thomas's arguments with a theoretical response. But because there was no majority opinion, an opinion by four Justices providing an alternative to Justice Thomas's political theory would have been welcome.

[108] *Cf.* Iris M. Young, *Polity and Group Difference: A Critique of the Ideal of Universal Citizenship*, 99 ETHICS 250, 261, 273 (1989) (arguing that a democracy should assure the effective representation of its constituent groups).

[109] *See* Wendy Brown-Scott, *The Communitarian State: Lawlessness or Law Reform for African Americans?*, 107 HARV. L. REV. 1209, 1217–18 (1994); Young, *supra* note 110, at 261, 273.

and compromises among groups, which ultimately result in group winners and group losers.[110] In a pluralist analysis, shifting alliances between groups help ensure that no one dominant group monopolizes power.[111] Groups provide minorities an opportunity to organize effectively with other minorities to veto objectionable policies, or at least to moderate majority tyranny. In this way, collective political action can enhance the power and influence of the individual.[112]

Even if one accepts that group participation is central to American politics, the question remains whether group participation is or should be fundamental not only in the electoral process, but also in post-election politics. To answer affirmatively suggests an instrumental, rather than a merely symbolic conception of voting. In my view, the right to vote essentially consists of three different rights: the right to cast a ballot, the right to cast a ballot that "counts," and the right to cast a ballot that embodies a fair chance to influence legislative policy-making.[113] Despite the Supreme Court's frequent emphasis on the individual in voting rights jurisprudence, the Court has also recognized that electoral rights embody "a constellation of concepts," and that, as one moves from ballot access to influencing legislative policy, "voting loses its purely individual character."[114] In other words, the right to vote

---

110 *See generally* DANIEL A. FARBER & PHILIP P. FRICKEY, LAW AND PUBLIC CHOICE 1–37 (1991) (outlining the role of interest groups in the political process).

111 James Madison recognized the potential power of factions and sought, through separation of powers and federalism, to prevent them from becoming tyrannical. *See* THE FEDERALIST No. 48, at 310–11 (James Madison) (Clinton Rossiter ed., 1961). For similar reasons, the Framers chose to establish a representative rather than a direct democracy. *See* Julian N. Eule, *Judicial Review of Direct Democracy*, 99 YALE L.J. 1503, 1526–27 (1990) (quoting THE FEDERALIST No. 10, *supra* note 10, at 61–62; *see also supra* note 92 (discussing direct democracy).

112 *See, e.g.*, Epstein, *supra* note 11, at 879 (arguing that the rights of the individual are transferred to the group itself when individuals decide to come together through voluntary association); Michael Walzer, *Multiculturalism and Individualism*, DISSENT, Spring 1994, at 185, 187, 189 (arguing that it is only in the context of associational activity that individuals learn to deliberate, argue, make decisions, and take responsibility and that individuals who are participants in a common life are stronger, more confident, and more savvy).

113 These three distinct components of the right to vote are reflected in the different generations of voting rights litigation. *See* LANI GUINIER, TYRANNY OF THE MAJORITY 1–20 (1994). They are also described by Professor Karlan as separate, yet complementary interests in participation, aggregation, and governance. *See* Pamela S. Karlan, *The Rights to Vote: Some Pessimism About Formalism*, 71 TEX. L. REV. 1705, 1709–20 (1993). Participation, which involves the ability to take part in the formal electoral process by casting a ballot, is individualistic, symbolic, and outcome-independent. The aggregation interest, which means having one's preferences taken into account in choosing public officials, is collectivist, instrumental, and outcome-dependent. The governance interest, in which voting is a means for indirectly taking part in post-election decision-making, is also collectivist and outcome-dependent. *See id.*

114 Pamela S. Karlan, *All Over the Map: The Supreme Court's Voting Rights Trilogy*, 1993 SUP. CT. REV. 245, 247, 249; *see also* Davis v. Bandemer, 478 U.S. 109, 167 (1986) (Powell, J., concurring in part and dissenting in part) ("The concept of 'representation' necessarily applies to groups: groups of voters elect representatives, individual voters do not."); Alexander M. Bickel, *The Supreme Court and Reapportionment*, *in* REAPPORTIONMENT IN THE 1970s at 57, 59 (Nelson W. Polsby ed., 1971) ("We have, since Madison, realized that people tend to act politically not so

should be enjoyed both by individuals and by groups throughout the political process as well as at the ballot box.

Representative democracy is premised on the notion that one representative can assert the collective interests of a group of voters.[115] By anointing one individual to stand in for a group, representative democracy thus depends on the aggregation of voters. In America, voters are aggregated largely through single-member electoral districts, which subdivide the larger whole to empower local, geographically based groups.[116] Districts are geographic units represented by a single individual who is presumed to speak for and to serve a constituency with common interests defined by physical proximity.[117] Territorially based electoral districts are compatible with federalism which, as both a political principle and an institutional structure, seeks to balance competing group attachments and to facilitate geographically based political autonomy.[118] If it is consistent with democratic principles to allocate electoral representation to geographically defined groups, it should be consistent with democratic principles to base representation upon other types of groups as well. This is especially true given that geography may not be the most salient characteristic on which to base group representation.[119]

---

much as individuals as in groups . . . ."); T. Alexander Aleinikoff & Samuel Issacharoff, *Race and Redistricting: Drawing Constitutional Lines After* Shaw v. Reno, 92 MICH. L. REV. 588, 600–01 (1993) (arguing that "an individual-rights based view" has little relevance to voting rights analysis because meaningful participation in a democratic system is dependent on the power of the group to which the individual belongs). Indeed, the Court has upheld deliberate legislative manipulation of district size in pursuit of group-representation goals such as preserving the integrity of political subdivisions. *See* Mahan v. Howell, 410 U.S. 315, 329–30 (1973); Abate v. Mundt, 403 U.S. 182, 185–87 (1971).

[115] *See* Eule, *supra* note 111, at 1526–27.

[116] *See* Guinier, *supra* note 101, at 1592.

[117] Indeed, the focus on the shape of districts spawned by the Court's decision in Shaw v. Reno, 113 S. Ct. 2816, 2824–28 (1993), suggests that "compactness" is a proxy for normalcy and that those who live in relatively close proximity are "normally" treated as a community or group. Elsewhere I argue that geographically based single-member districts are imperfect electoral proxies for communities of interest. *See* Guinier, *supra* note 101, at 1593.

[118] *See* Lucas v. Forty-Fourth Gen. Assembly, 377 U.S. 713, 749–65 (1964) (Stewart, J., dissenting). Federalism concerns have led the Court to permit larger population deviations from the one person/one vote principle in state and local reapportionment than in congressional reapportionments, in part to recognize local group interests. *Compare Mahan*, 410 U.S. at 324–25 (holding that a state legislature redistricting plan should be judged according to an as equal "as is practicable" standard that is less stringent than the test for judging congressional reapportionment) *with* Kirkpatrick v. Preisler, 394 U.S. 526, 530–31 (1969) (holding that a state must make a "good faith effort to achieve precise mathematical equality" in a congressional reapportionment).

[119] *See* Hendrik Hertzberg, *Constitution 1: Let's Get Representative*, NEW REPUBLIC, June 29, 1987, at 16 ("The communities that count are communities of interest and belief . . . . Ideology, profession, class, even racial and sexual identity — these are the soil our roots grow in now, as much as or more than where we live."). Yet geography can still approximate the interests of some groups, such as blacks, because of their extreme spacial segregation. *Cf.* DOUGLAS S. MASSEY & NANCY A. DENTON, AMERICAN APARTHEID 9–16 (1993) (tracing the history of extreme racial segregation and explaining the reasons for its perpetuation).

In my opinion, one premise of the Voting Rights Act is the essential democratic role that minority racial group representation plays in dispersing authority throughout the political process. A violation of the Act can be established by a showing that "members of a [protected racial] class . . . have less opportunity than other members of the electorate to participate in the political process *and to elect representatives of their choice*."[120] A violation does not require evidence that an individual has been denied equal electoral participation; a violation can be based upon proof that members of a racial group have been given less political and electoral opportunity.

Justice Thomas's formalistic view of political participation is thus in tension with the apparent group-based, election and post-election focus of the Voting Rights Act. The Act's promise to minority racial groups that they will be protected from electoral systems that afford them "less opportunity . . . to elect representatives of their choice"[121] is vacuous if, as Justice Thomas suggests, it encompasses no more than protection of the right to cast individual ballots. Although the Act expressly states that there is no right to "descriptive" or proportional representation by the actual members of a racial group,[122] the Act provides that "[t]he extent to which members of a protected class have been elected to office in the State or political subdivision is one circumstance which may be considered."[123] This language is a strong indication that the foundation of the Voting Rights Act is a political theory that includes representation of, not just voting by group members.[124]

---

120 42 U.S.C. § 1973(b) (emphasis added).

121 *Id.*

122 *See id.* The statute defines proportional representation as the "right to have members of a protected class elected in numbers equal to their proportion in the population." *Id.*

As Justice Souter pointed out in *De Grandy*, the disclaimer denies the right to proportional descriptive representation, which is the correlation between the number of elected minority group members and voters. *See De Grandy*, 114 S. Ct. at 2658 n.11. Functionally proportional representation does not rely on the color or "description" of the elected representatives. It instead suggests a correlation between the number of representatives who are sponsored by and accountable to the minority group and the group's population percentage in the electorate. The Voting Rights Act is designed to ensure that racial minorities are fairly represented by minority-sponsored candidates of their choice although not necessarily by candidates of their race. *See id.*

123 42 U.S.C. § 1973(b).

124 Because the Act refers to "members" of a protected class, it is possible to read the statute in a way that resists the concept of group representation. Nevertheless, as Professor Ferejohn recently argued, although we may formally set up the electoral system by referring to individuals, groups of people use that system. John Ferejohn, Remarks at American Political Science Association Roundtable on Group Representation (Sept. 2, 1994). For example, Justice Souter's opinion in *De Grandy* affirms the importance of proportional representation of groups, although he repudiates the claim that the representational function should be performed exclusively by actual group members. *See supra* note 122.

B. Protecting Racial Group Representation

The Voting Rights Act enumerates certain protected classes and creates a cause of action whereby members of those classes can invoke the judicial process to help ensure equal representation for their groups.[125] Because the Act's provisions include only racial and language minorities, many of Justice Thomas's objections to the Act stem from his perception that the Act affords preferential treatment to those minority racial groups it protects. But such objections to preferential treatment do not go to the broader question: is group representation consistent with democratic principles? If the answer to that question is "yes" — and the Court's constitutional jurisprudence, as well as democratic theories of pluralism and communitarianism, suggests that it is — then the Act's protection of group representation is not inconsistent with democratic ideals. Moreover, if the empirical evidence, including the history of racial discrimination in the United States, demonstrates that racial minorities, as a group, have been traditionally underrepresented, then the special protections afforded to those groups under the Act are justified.[126]

In the Voting Rights Act, Congress did not create race as a category; Congress simply acknowledged its political salience.[127] Since race is a political cue for both whites and people of color, it is not surprising that race also correlates with voting behavior in many jurisdictions.[128] In light of America's racial history, in many parts of the country race functions as a proxy, albeit a crude one, for the political interests of disadvantaged groups.[129] Minority groups that have been discriminated against deserve representation. Intervention under the Act is justified when a minority group has been excluded *as a group* because of prejudice.

But racial group identity is not merely a reaction to disadvantage or oppression. Racial group members have an immutable characteristic that society uses as a basis to discriminate, which ties members

---

125 The protections of the Voting Rights Act apply only to racial and linguistic minority groups. *See* 42 U.S.C. §§ 1973, 1973b(f)(2).

126 If voting rights remedies accomplish some widely perceived social good, such as promoting participatory democracy by holding elected officials more accountable to all their constituencies, such remedies will enjoy more popular support. This is Professor Bell's "interest-convergence" thesis. *See* Derrick A. Bell, Jr., Brown v. Board of Education *and the Interest-Convergence Dilemma*, 93 HARV. L. REV. 518, 522–28 (1980); *infra* Part III.C.

127 Congress sought to resolve the political unfairness that results when, because of racial bloc voting, race matters as an empirical fact. *Cf.* S. REP. NO. 417, *supra* note 72, at 34, *reprinted in* 1982 U.S.C.C.A.N. at 212 (rejecting the notion that the Voting Rights Act interjects race into politics because that would be "like saying that it is the doctor's thermometer which causes high fever").

128 *See, e.g.*, Samuel Issacharoff, *Polarized Voting and the Political Process: The Transformation of Voting Rights Jurisprudence*, 90 MICH. L. REV. 1833, 1845–90 (1992) (describing the prevalence and function of racially polarized voting).

129 *See* Strauss, *supra* note 104, at 114–15.

together by common experience, and which encourages members to socialize and to marry each other. Providing equal representation for underrepresented minority groups would not only begin to remedy historical oppression of certain groups, but might also create incentives for their increased political participation. Such participation has the potential to diversify debate on issues of public importance and to legitimize democracy by presenting a greater range of views in the legislature to mirror or model an integrated society.[130] At their most compelling, claims for minority group representation seek to generate greater confidence in the fairness and accountability of government to the interests of all underrepresented citizens.

In other words, minority group representation is not purely cultural, historical, or biological; it also has a political component. Group members may identify collectively along a common axis and organize to promote common interests in ways similar to other political associations.[131]

Yet there are crucial differences between racial minorities and other political interest groups. A social or political interest group member comes to the group as a matter of choice. Identifying with the group is an affirmation, validation, or mirroring of a chosen identity. On the other hand, members of a racial, ethnic, or religious minority do not necessarily choose their minority group identity.[132] Racial or ethnic groups are relevant because, as a sociological fact, individuals define, understand, and identify themselves and their interests (and are defined, understood, and identified by others) in part in terms of their racial or ethnic group membership. Racial, religious, ethnic, or language minority group membership, however, does not exclusively form the person — the experience is complex.[133] Some group members prefer to deny or to disassociate from their group identity.

---

130 *See* Melissa S. Williams, Descriptive Representation With a Difference, Paper Presented at the American Political Science Association Roundtable on Group Representation (Sept. 2, 1994) (unpublished manuscript, on file with the Harvard Law School library).

131 *See* MARTIN L. KING, JR., WHERE DO WE GO FROM HERE: CHAOS OR COMMUNITY? 123–25 (1967) (arguing that blacks must "work passionately for group identity," meaning group unity and consciousness that enables meaningful political participation).

132 In this sense, the status of racial minorities is comparable to that of "constitutive" cultural communities. *See* Naomi M. Stolzenberg, *'He Drew a Circle That Shut Me Out': Assimilation, Indoctrination, and the Paradox of a Liberal Education*, 106 HARV. L. REV. 581, 648–49 (1993) (describing local communities, such as the Amish, that shape self-identity by endowing their members with values and attachments); *see also* Robert M. Cover, *The Supreme Court, 1982 Term — Foreword: Nomos and Narrative*, 97 HARV. L. REV. 4, 14–16 (1983) (describing a "paideia" or involuntary community into which members are socialized).

133 As Henry Louis Gates writes in his memoir, "I'm divided. I want to be black, to know black, to luxuriate in whatever I might be calling blackness at any particular time — but to do so in order to come out the other side, to experience a humanity that is neither colorless nor reducible to color." HENRY L. GATES, JR., COLORED PEOPLE: A MEMOIR at xv (1994).

Others dissent from the prevailing views of most group members but, at the same time, wish to affiliate as group members.

To return to the questions posed by the cases, should race be considered in determining the fair representation of minority groups? Some, such as Justice Thomas, say that racial minorities should not be treated as groups in the electoral process because their members are adequately represented as individuals when formal, legal barriers to ballot access have been eliminated. Historically, designating racial groups was both a barrier to their participation and a definition of their existence. Thus, on this account, to recognize racial minority groups formally creates the potential for reimposing discrimination.[134] While a racial group may choose to identity itself privately, publicly it should have no function or formal status.

Others might argue that there is no right to fair representation for any non-geographic group, and therefore that racial groups deserve no special protection. But to respond, as Justice Thomas seems to, that, because the experience of race is complex and potentially divisive, it simply does not exist — or should be ignored — is to forbid racial generalizations, whether or not they are accurate. Ultimately, this decision to ignore race treats racial minority groups differently from other groups, whose existence the political system encourages.

I propose an alternative view. I argue that the underrepresentation of racial and language minority groups is a problem because it disables groups that function politically from playing an important democratic role. Exclusion of a racial or language minority group exposes a deep fissure in the American democratic bargain, which purportedly reconciles majoritarian preferences with minority interests. The challenge is to remedy that flaw without necessarily requiring a single minority identity or reinforcing racial group boundaries as impenetrable.

However defined and redefined, contextualized and complicated, the almost irrefutable existence of something like a racial minority group identity suggests that a vital political system must accommodate those who *choose* that identity. To make room, however, does not mean to evict other identities. To this end, a racial minority group should be represented to the extent that its members in fact act collectively. Mere assumptions about alleged uniformity should be insufficient to justify measures to ensure group representation. This approach acknowledges that one's racial group is not the only club to which one belongs. Collective group preferences might be measured by using innovative electoral schemes like cumulative voting and pro-

---

[134] Conservative and neoliberal commentators fear that the state cannot be trusted to act benignly when it allocates benefits based on group identity. If such allocations are perceived as arbitrary, they could reinforce existing hostility or perpetuate feelings of racial superiority or inferiority. *See, e.g.*, ABIGAIL THERNSTROM, WHOSE VOTES COUNT? AFFIRMATIVE ACTION AND MINORITY VOTING RIGHTS 242–43 (1987).

portional representation.[135] In this view, unity is defined as collaboration rather than as sameness. Group representation becomes a dynamic, interactive process that makes political stability more likely.

The fundamental question posed by vote dilution cases is how much a minority citizen's vote should be worth in a representative democracy.[136] Given the increasing ambivalence with which the present Court treats the statutory basis for protection of racial and language groups, it may make sense to reframe the question more broadly. Rather than the implicitly preferential suggestion that racial minority groups should be represented, the question could be whether racial minorities should be treated like other political groups. In other words, can remedies be devised to allow voluntary interest groups to be represented in proportion to their electoral strength?

C. *Remedies Based on a Theory of Fair Representation for Voluntary Interest Groups*

In the debate about the fairness of the Voting Rights Act's protection of racial group representation, concerns about special treatment of minority racial groups can be alleviated if federal courts take care in constructing remedies for Voting Rights Act violations. Although only certain racial and language minority groups are statutorily entitled to allege a violation of the Voting Rights Act, court-imposed remedies for such violations can and should take into account the need to protect representation for non-racial minority groups as well. Just as the district court in *De Grandy* was unwilling to impose a plan that benefited either African Americans or Latinos at the expense of the other group's ability to achieve group representation,[137] courts devising vote dilution remedies would be within their authority to consider the representation needs of groups other than those entitled to protection under the Act.[138] Such remedies "value" every citizen's vote equally,

---

[135] I discuss cumulative voting below at p. 133.

[136] *See Holder*, 114 S. Ct. at 2593–94 (Thomas, J., concurring in the judgment) (stating that dilution cannot be evaluated until the court first defines how much a "vote should be worth" (quoting Baker v. Carr, 369 U.S. 186, 300 (1962) (Frankfurter, J., dissenting))).

[137] *See* De Grandy v. Wetherell, 815 F. Supp. 1550, 1578–80 (N.D. Fla. 1992).

[138] The Court in *Davis v. Bandemer* said this approach is constitutionally permissible as long as the electoral system is not consistently "arranged in a manner that will degrade a voter's or a group of voters' influence on the political process as a whole." Davis v. Bandemer, 478 U.S. 109, 131–33 (1986). Even Justice Thomas conceded that such remedies are consistent with statutory and constitutional law. *See Holder*, 114 S. Ct. at 2591–94 (Thomas, J., concurring in the judgment).

Non-districted electoral schemes would potentially empower a variety of politically cohesive groups. *See* GUINIER, *supra* note 113, at 114. Social and political groups can all be recognized in the remedial process, as inevitably they are in districting. This formulation of a remedial approach borrows liberally from the work of Professor Susan Sturm. *See, e.g.*, Susan P. Sturm, *A Normative Theory of Public Law Remedies*, 79 GEO. L.J. 1355, 1360–65, 1373–76 (1991).

meaning everyone's vote would presumably count toward the election of someone.[139]

I call this principle of democratic representation "one vote/one value."[140] When racial minority groups prove a violation of the Act, they essentially establish that the principle of one vote/one value has been thwarted; they are unable, because of prejudice, to elect representatives of their choice. However, the ideal of one vote/one value can only be realized in a system of universal group representation in which everyone is given the opportunity to identify with a "chosen" group based on real interests — not merely on geography or arbitrary racial characteristics.[141]

A violation can only be proved under the Act based on evidence of racial or language minority group exclusion. However, at the remedial stage, judicial intervention should be justified in terms of one vote/one value principles of democratic group representation.[142] Elsewhere I have explored alternative remedies that are consistent with a one vote/one value universal approach. For example, non-districted solutions, such as cumulative voting, recognize group identity only to the extent that voters choose to act upon it politically.[143] Each voter is given the same number of votes as open seats. In a multi-seat election, voters can aggregate their votes to reflect the intensity of their preferences. Because voters, depending on their interests, can form coalitions that cut across racial lines, this form of political arrangement diminishes the likelihood of reifying race as a fixed, political category. Members of different racial groups who enter into such alliances are more likely "to find confidence-building measures that build trust and overcome antagonism."[144]

---

139 *See* GUINIER, *supra* note 113, at 71–73, 122–23.

140 *See id.* One vote/one value seeks to combine universal suffrage and a fair probability of influencing legislative outcomes through the election of preferred representatives.

141 To be popularly understood, the remedial claim must appear to restore the racial minority to the position it would have been in absent the discrimination. However, if white political or numerical minority groups do not feel they have their "own" representative, giving one to racial minority groups seems preferential, not remedial. Like minority voters, white voters do not necessarily share a unity of interests and may enter into multiple, cross-cutting alliances that are not reflected simply because their elected official is "white." Whites *and* racial minorities should each enjoy the opportunity to assert their most salient interests and to hold their elected officials accountable for advocating those interests.

142 *Cf.* Tashjian v. Republican Party, 479 U.S. 208, 213–17 (1986) (finding unconstitutional a state statute limiting participation in political party primaries to party members); Epstein, *supra* note 11, at 877 (arguing that "all voluntary associations should be protected under the Constitution" without giving groups "any special status").

143 *See* GUINIER, *supra* note 113, at 94–95.

144 Daniel Goleman, *Amid Ethnic Wars, Psychiatrists Seek Roots of Conflict*, N.Y. TIMES, Aug. 2, 1994, at C1, C13 (noting that one way to reduce ethnic and racial conflict is to respect group differences and then to provide group members the opportunity to "express frankly their grievances, fears and anger to those in the other group").

Indeed, much of my work is dedicated to finding electoral arrangements that empower racial minorities by building cross-racial alliances. I have argued, for example, that a remediation strategy based on the principles of proportional representation for *all* politically cohesive groups is a less arbitrary means of recognizing race as a social and political category than is our current, geographically based system. Only racial groups that demonstrate actual political cohesion are represented, and then only to the extent that they in fact mobilize members of the electorate to cast their multiple votes in support of a common set of interests. These interests may or may not be racially based, and those who support them may or may not be racially similar. Race, in this sense, becomes a political, not a biological cue. It is chosen, not inherited.

No one needs to decide in advance what a group is. The voters make that decision by the way they cast their ballots. No one needs to decide between competing groups. The voters choose by the way they participate. No one needs to decide whether a minority group identity is the only or primary identity. The voters do that by the way they vote. In this way, a solution to the problem of the exclusion or underrepresentation of racial and language minority groups becomes an indirect opportunity to protect other groups. Such a solution is more likely to gain broad-based political support because it creates equal representative opportunities for all political interest groups. Group representation becomes the connective tissue linking *all* the people to their elected representatives.

Race-conscious redistricting — the conventional remedy under the Voting Rights Act — is problematic because it appears to give special protection only to racial minority groups. But if other groups, such as women, were to examine the way in which geographic districting underrepresents their interests, they might begin to understand that the exclusion of racial minorities is symptomatic of flaws in winner-take-all districting as a system for allocating representation of everyone.[145]

A balanced assessment of each potential judicial remedy would address the ensemble of its properties in the context of three criteria. First, does the court's plan fully remedy the violation of a protected group's statutory rights? Second, does the remedy protect the rights of all voters to gain representation? In other words, is the remedy consistent with a theory of fair representation for all politically cohe-

---

[145] *See* DOUGLAS J. AMY, NEW VOICES, REAL CHOICES 102–03 (1993) (noting that winner-take-all districts underrepresent women); ANNE PHILLIPS, ENGENDERING DEMOCRACY 80 (1991) (arguing that women fare comparatively better in proportional representation, multi-seat elections).

sive groups? Third, is the remedy consistent with concerns of federalism and local majority rule?[146]

I believe a conservative, majoritarian Supreme Court is more likely to respect the national majority's effort to protect racial minority voters when the enforcement effort proceeds in terms of universal remedies to protect all numerical minority groups, whether defined in terms of race, political affiliation, or geography. Federalism, after all, also empowers minority groups — regional or geographic minorities. Although the local minorities in Bleckley County, Georgia and Dade County, Florida are racial rather than geographic, the Court should begin to explain that protecting those minorities is not preferential treatment based on race but is similar, equal treatment based on numerical minority group status and is consistent with the universal one vote/one value principle.

In the cases at hand, dilution of the racial minority's voting strength was arguably the result of the ability of incumbent politicians to distribute power arbitrarily through a system of winner-take-all districts (*De Grandy*) and by the refusal to district at all (*Holder*). If so, it would be as anomalous to defer to incumbent politicians in denying any remedy to the racial minority plaintiffs as it would have been in *Baker v. Carr*, in which race was *not* an issue, to defer to legislators who were riveted to their seats and had refused to reapportion in the absence of judicial intervention.[147] Deference to such local majorities may simply pervert democracy in the name of inverted federalism. These local, geographic majorities are actually regional minorities, who deserve no special deference if they arbitrarily constitute themselves as a permanent, monolithic group or overrepresent themselves to avoid sharing power with other racial, regional, or political groups.[148]

If the Supreme Court had construed minority group representation as a fundamental tenet of democracy instead of as a special exception to it, it likely would have adopted a different approach in both *Holder* and *De Grandy*. In *Holder*, the Court might have found the plaintiffs'

---

146 *See* Daniel R. Ortiz, *Federalism, Reapportionment, and Incumbency: Leading the Legislature to Police Itself*, 4 J.L. & POL. 653, 658–59 (1988).

147 *See* Baker v. Carr, 369 U.S. 186, 259 (1962) (Clark, J., concurring).

148 Local majority rule is not consistent with either communitarian or pluralistic conceptions of democracy if the local majority hoards rather than disperses power. *See* Lani Guinier, *Lines in the Sand*, 72 TEX. L. REV. 315, 341 (1993) (noting that the theory behind separation of powers and checks and balances requires power-sharing to constrain the majority faction and to disperse power).

Size is itself a relative concept. But determining what is reasonable is inherent to the judicial, as well as the legislative project. Congress has delegated such reasonableness determinations to the courts by using "totality of the circumstances" language in the Voting Rights Act. 42 U.S.C. § 1973(b). Contrary to the opinions expressed by a majority of Justices in *Holder*, *see Holder*, 114 S. Ct. at 2588; *id.* at 2591 (O'Connor, J., concurring in part and concurring in the judgment); *id.* at 2619 (Thomas, J., concurring in the judgment), courts are authorized and competent to decide challenges brought against the size of a governing body.

claim to be covered by the Voting Rights Act had it viewed their attempt to expand the size of the commission as an effort to improve democracy rather than circumvent it. If the Court were to intervene in Bleckley County to effectuate the one vote/one value remedial goals of the Act, the result of its intervention would potentially benefit not only the racial minority plaintiffs, but other politically cohesive minority groups as well. Implementing the Voting Rights Act would thus preserve the democratic process within Bleckley County itself.

Likewise, in *De Grandy*, the Court need not have overruled the district court's finding of a violation in order to evade the messy problem of allocating political power between competing minority groups. Informed by a theory of fair representation, the Court might have realized that racial divisions would not have been exacerbated by enforcing the Voting Rights Act, but rather stemmed from the state majority's decision to award power by artificial geographic units such as winner-take-all single-member districts.[149]

The facts of *De Grandy* illustrate the underlying flaws in the Court's current approach to the Voting Rights Act. Both the black and Latino plaintiffs had competing, mutually exclusive, *but legitimate* claims for representation. This circumstance exposes the problems with incumbent-controlled, single-member districting as a means of apportioning political power. Instead of declaring a new standard of "rough proportionality," measured on an arbitrary regional basis, the Court should have affirmed the finding of a violation and then directed the lower court to seek a remedy for the affected areas that would have been less divisive and would have ensured greater political accountability to choices made by voters rather than to those made by elected officials.

Consistent with one vote/one value ideals, an alternative approach to allocating power might be a multi-seat district that uses cumulative or limited voting. Voters within that multi-seat district would essentially subdistrict themselves by the way they cast their ballots; the allocation of political power between blacks, Latinos, *and whites* would depend *at each election* on the organization and mobilization efforts of each group. Individual members of a racial group who did not feel aligned with that group in that particular election would be free to express their preferences by voting with other groups. Under universal group representation, local democracy would become a dynamic method of governance open to all significant groups rather than a bat-

---

[149] The Court's standard for demonstrating political cohesiveness also reinforces the insularity of the minority. A discrete and insular minority must be a majority of a district to be politically represented. The minority becomes visible only when it is a political category — in other words, a majority of the district. District boundaries then become "barriers" reinforcing the insularity of the minority because without those lines, the minority might become politically invisible. In this way, attempts to maximize minority majority districts both assume and potentially reinforce a monolithic minority viewpoint.

tle for total victory in the control of winner-take-all, single-member districts.

CONCLUSION

A remedial theory of fair representation for all groups based on the principle of one vote/one value is necessary to provide stability and coherence to current voting rights doctrine. On the one hand, historical prejudice against, and continued underrepresentation of cognizable, protected racial and language minority groups presently justifies judicial intervention under the Voting Rights Act. The statute is intended to remedy the exclusion of these minority groups. On the other hand, remedies that appear to give preferential treatment to racial groups threaten the so-called colorblind vision espoused by an increasingly conservative federal judiciary. In order to reconcile the race consciousness of the Act with the rhetoric of race-neutrality, I propose that courts embrace the concept of group representation as a universal remedial principle of democratic accountability and legitimacy. Specifically, at the remedy stage of a voting rights case, courts should prefer universal remedies that have the potential to empower all politically cohesive groups, instead of just the plaintiff class. In this way, intervention under the Act, although limited to historically justified claims brought by racial and language minorities, would also be forward-looking. By examining creative solutions beyond single-member geographic districting, voluntary interest group representation encourages remedies that increase the accountability of elected officials to all of their constituents and that allow the Court to respond to critics of the Act in a manner that is empirically accurate and theoretically coherent. Thus, the legal claims of racial minorities are not resolved to benefit racial minorities alone but to make politics better for everyone.

Race remains an important political affiliation in many parts of America, but it need not be the only important political affiliation. As Henry Louis Gates, Jr., has written, "I want to be black but not only black."[150] We can recognize race without reinforcing separatist, monolithic views of racial groups. We can recognize race without erasing democracy. Representing racial minority groups fairly need not be special treatment. Representing racial minority groups fairly can be to treat those groups the same as other viable community-based organizations and political constituencies. While this may require a rethinking of equal protection analysis,[151] on the other side of the equation lies the possibility of more democracy for all types of minority interest groups.

---

150 GATES, *supra* note 133, at xv.

151 *See* Stolzenberg, *supra* note 132, at 646–51.

THE NEW YORK TIMES
NEW YORK, NY
DECEMBER 7, 1994

Quotas Aren't The Issue

By Allan J. Lichtman

WASHINGTON

The body of the mighty Democratic Congress isn't even cold, and critics are already blaming the usual suspects: African-Americans. In a variant of the lament heard after every Democratic setback since 1968 — that support for black interests will consign the party to permanent minority status — we're told that the new predominantly black Congressional districts in the South helped Republicans by draining black Democrats from neighboring white districts.

The argument may sound plausible, but it's dead wrong. The current round of Congressional redistricting, based on the 1990 Census, was completed before the 1992 elections. The same districts that produced a 41-seat Democratic majority in 1992 yielded nearly a 15-seat G.O.P. majority in 1994.

The 1994 elections were a broad-based rejection of Democratic candidates and had nothing to do with the allegedly debilitating effects of black districts: weakening white Democratic districts, attracting stronger Republican challengers and strengthening marginal G.O.P. districts.

Democrats actually fared a bit better in the nine states with new black districts than in the 41 states with no such districts; they lost 19 percent of the seats they had held in the nine states (all Southern), as against 21 percent in the others. (This pattern does not change when corrected for variable factors like the partisan leaning of states and the retirement of Democratic incumbents.) Even if the Democrats had kept every one of their seats in the nine redistricted states, losses in the other states would still have cost them their majority in the House.

A study of Democratic Congressional losses by the NAACP Legal Defense and Education Fund late last month sustains the conclusions reached here. It found that in states with new black districts, as in other states, the main problem for Democrats was not the distribution of votes among districts but a statewide abandonment of the Democrats. In Georgia, for example, where Democrats have lost five seats since 1990, the party's share of the statewide Congressional vote plummeted from 61 percent in 1990 to 46 percent in 1994.

Democrats might have held on to a few more seats by gerrymandering certain swing districts to include more black voters. But in the changed politics of 1994, the strategy might have backfired; in Georgia, the Legal Defense Fund study found, spreading blacks among mainly white districts would probably have cost Democrats even more seats. And the price of such gerrymandering would have been to reduce African-Americans yet again to pawns in a power game played by whites.

Critics say the creation of black districts since the 1970's has "resegregated" an otherwise integrated politics in the South. Precisely the opposite is true. It was the absence of black districts in the South that produced segregated, nearly all-white government. As a result of white bloc voting, black candidates had (and still have) minimal prospects in majority-white districts, despite cohesive support from black voters. If white bloc voting did not exist and blacks were able to forge interracial coalitions, creation of black districts would not be required under the Voting Rights Act.

In 1970, the states of the old Confederacy had no black Congressional dis-

A familiar tale — blacks as Democratic scapegoats.

Allan J. Lichtman, professor of history at American University, has testified for plaintiffs and defendants in more than 50 Federal voting rights cases.

CONTINUED......

tricts and no blacks serving in Congress. Today, there are 17 black representatives from these states, all elected from districts with a black majority or plurality. Nationwide, there are 39 black representatives in Congress; only two are from majority-white districts.

Some people argue that the election of black officials is of little consequence because black interests were equally well represented by white legislators elected from white districts with substantial black populations.

But according to the journal Congressional Quarterly, members of Congress from the new black districts provided only 28 percent support for the "conservative coalition" of Republicans and right-leaning Democrats in 1993. A sample of white representatives elected in 1990 (before redistricting) from districts with the highest black percentages in the same states provided 63 percent support for the conservative coalition in 1992.

The scapegoating of black districts is not only wrong but pernicious. It threatens both the representation that blacks have achieved and the future of the Democratic Party, which can ill afford to be distracted from its real problems of defining a compelling message and rebuilding its base from the grass roots. Democratic problems in the South will be solved only by addressing the common economic concerns of whites and blacks — declining wages, job insecurity, the growing use of part-time workers — and not by trying to use African-Americans to stem a rising tide of white Republican votes. □

GERRYMANDER HYPOCRISY

Supreme Court's Double Standard

JAMIN B. RASKIN

Racial double standards are nothing new in American law, but the Supreme Court's voting rights jurisprudence has turned farcical. State legislators redrawing Congressional and state legislative districts in the 1990s now carry both a license and a warning from the Court. The license, granted for decades, is to draw far-flung squiggly lines all over the map in order to guarantee the legislators' re-election or the re-election of incumbent white U.S. House members. The warning, issued in the Court's 1993 *Shaw v. Reno* decision, is not to draw any such "bizarre" districts with the purpose of creating African-American or Latino political majorities.

These two Supreme Court positions are on a logical collision course. From the day it was decided, *Shaw* looked deeply suspicious, since it imposed strict scrutiny on only those oddly shaped districts where African-Americans or Latinos are in a majority. The Court had never before found that the Constitution required districts to have certain shapes, sizes or looks. District appearance was a question for the states. Now, in the name of tidy district lines and fighting what Justice Sandra Day O'Connor called "political apartheid" (a term never used by the Court to describe slavery, Jim Crow, poll taxes, literacy tests or white primaries), the Court cast doubt on dozens of racially integrated districts represented by blacks and Latinos.

In the wake of *Shaw*, the Court's disparate treatment of white incumbents and black and Latino majorities has only grown more glaring. Several federal courts have struck down oddly shaped districts with black and Latino majorities and representatives, while upholding oddly shaped districts next door where white majorities have elected white politicians to office. In the illustrative case of *Vera v. Richards* last August, a panel of three Republican judges threw out as racial gerrymanders two majority-black Congressional districts and one majority-Latino district in Texas, solemnly invoking Martin Luther King Jr. along the way.

Meanwhile, the same panel categorically rejected challenges to majority-white districts whose perimeters looked every bit as peculiar as those of the minority districts. The panel was not disturbed that House incumbents from Texas "were actively involved in the redistricting process" or that they were so influential in getting districts drawn for "incumbency protection" that all but one of them had been re-elected in 1992. Neither were the judges troubled by the fact that the minority districts appeared contorted precisely because white Democratic incumbents, looking for liberal

Jamin B. Raskin is a professor of constitutional law and associate dean at the Washington College of Law at the American University.

votes, took big geographic bites out of minority communities.

By blessing the entrenchment of white incumbents and wiping out black and Latino majority districts, the Texas court is only following the perverse logic of Supreme Court doctrine. The equal protection clause of the Fourteenth Amendment, enacted in 1868 to dismantle white supremacy, has been twisted by the Court to mean that African-Americans and other minorities may not form a numerical majority in any district unless they are in communities that are geographically compact and residentially isolated. Political apartheid, indeed.

As a matter of democratic theory, the couple of dozen districts drawn to facilitate black and Latino majorities are far more defensible than the hundreds of districts drawn to protect particular white incumbents. The former were brought into being under the 1982 Voting Rights Act amendments because racially polarized voting still enables white-dominated legislatures to manipulate district lines to dilute minority political power. Without consciously drawn minority districts, most states would continue to have lily-white House delegations. No black has ever been elected to Congress from the South in a majority-white district. Even today *with* the new districts (hanging on by a thread), minorities remain underrepresented in Congress and every state legislature. African-Americans are 12 percent of the population but have only 7 percent of the seats in Congress, while Latinos make up 10 percent of the population but have only 3 percent of Congressional seats. Furthermore, these districts discriminate against no one: The North Carolina district at issue in *Shaw* is 53 percent black and 47 percent white and permits all citizens to vote and run for office.

On the other hand, "incumbency protection" districts are deeply offensive to democratic values. In the *Vera* case, Representative Ronald Coleman from El Paso testified that, as head of his party delegation's redistricting committee in 1992, he was in constant contact with state legislators, urging them to adopt districts drawn by his colleagues in the House. As then-state legislator Eddie Bernice Johnson put it, the incumbents "have practically drawn their own districts. Not practically, they have." By fencing out unfriendly voters and potential rivals, incumbents make districts in their own image and turn elections into a formality. In our self-perpetuating incumbentocracy, voters don't really pick public officials on Election Day because public officials pick voters on redistricting day.

But in the Court's new racial Rorschach test, incumbent-friendly inkblot districts are lawful if the white race is in the majority. This arbitrary policy is untenable. Either the Court should define what it means by "bizarre" districts and strike all of them down, or it should take back one of the most poorly reasoned and most reactionary decisions of this century. But, with the Court's conservatives in the driver's seat, we probably have to brace ourselves this term for more color-conscious finger-painting on the Constitution. □

THE NEW CONSTITUTIONAL RORSCHACH TEST

Q. Which of the following four Congressional districts in Texas are unconstitutional gerrymanders, according to a district court decision implementing the Supreme Court's holding in *Shaw v. Reno*?

DISTRICT 18

DISTRICT 29

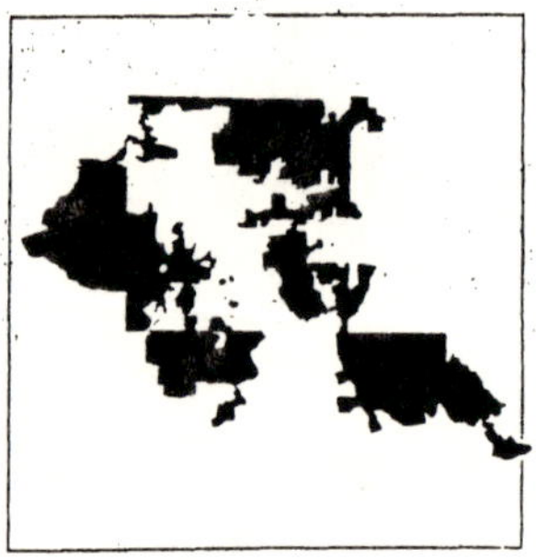

DISTRICT 6

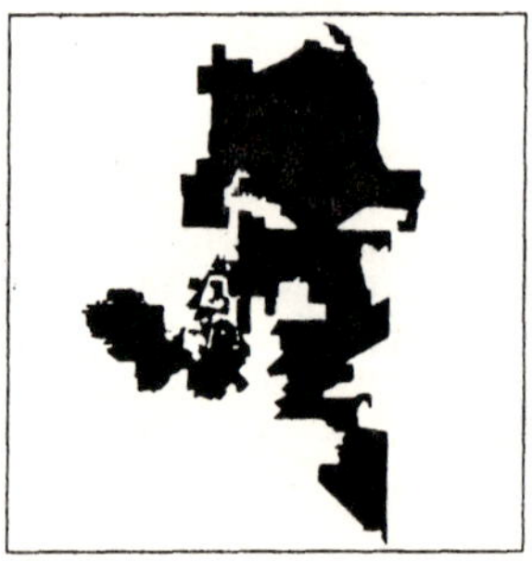

DISTRICT 3

A. On August 17, 1994, a three-judge panel of the U.S. District Court in the Southern District of Texas struck down district 18, which is 50.9 percent African-American and 15.3 percent Latino, and also struck down district 29, which is 60.6 percent Latino and 10.2 percent African-American. In the same decision, it upheld district 6, which is 90.9 percent white, and district 3, which is 89.3 percent white.

MORE NOTES FROM A POLITICAL THICKET

*Abigail Thernstrom**

INTRODUCTION

Cases involving minority voting rights are only partly about voting rights.[1] At issue between the opposing sides are radically different views of American society and the place of blacks and Hispanics in it. That makes them tough to resolve, and it makes them unusually important. The Supreme Court decided two redistricting cases this past June and has agreed to review two this term; these cases force the Court to take a stand on questions that lie at the very heart of our definition of ourselves as a multiethnic, multiracial society.

This past term's cases involved the constitutionality of majority-black congressional districts in Louisiana[2] and Georgia.[3] Both districts were drawn with the explicit purpose of creating safe black constituencies, and were thus subsequently challenged as unconstitutional racial gerrymanders—racial classifications that violate the Fourteenth Amendment.

The plans were defended by the two states, however, as reasonable: race-conscious, but not race-driven. But even if viewed as a racial classification, and thus subject to strict judicial scrutiny, the states argued, they could meet the test; they were narrowly tailored to remedy past discrimination and to further a compelling state interest in complying with the Voting Rights Act.

Although ostensibly constitutional cases, two interwined questions were, in fact, before the Supreme Court: what does the Fourteenth Amendment allow, and what does the Voting Rights Act demand? For even if the

---

* Senior Fellow, The Manhattan Institute; Adjunct Professor, Boston University.

[1] The Voting Rights Act of 1965 covers members of five protected groups, the most important of which are blacks and Hispanics. The cases discussed below, however, involve only blacks.

Much of the analysis of Shaw v. Reno, 113 S. Ct. 2816 (1993), is contained in Abigail Thernstrom, Shaw v. Reno*: Notes from a Political Thicket*, 1994 PUB. INTEREST L. REV. 35. A number of other sections of this Article are drawn from ABIGAIL M. THERNSTROM, WHOSE VOTES COUNT? AFFIRMATIVE ACTION AND MINORITY VOTING RIGHTS (1987) [hereinafter THERNSTROM, WHOSE VOTES COUNT?].

[2] Hays v. Louisiana, 862 F. Supp. 119 (W.D. La. 1994), *vacated*, 115 S. Ct. 2431 (1995).

[3] Miller v. Johnson, 115 S. Ct. 2475 (1995).

districting lines were race-driven, the Court could not resolve the question of their constitutional legitimacy without deciding what the Voting Rights Act requires. The states had a compelling interest in complying with the law, but not—obviously—with an erroneously interpreted statute.[4]

These are legal issues that involve basic questions about the nature of American society, the direction in which we want to go, and how we get there. Are blacks still (in Lani Guinier's words) a "pariah group"?[5] Is a color-blind Constitution the wrong idea?[6] Does race consciousness, permitted or encouraged by the law, just harden the lines of race and ethnicity that already divide us? Or is that consciousness a necessity in a society in which true racial equality is still a dream deferred?[7]

These are just some of the issues that have run through the line of decisions that began in 1993 with *Shaw v. Reno*,[8] which held that plaintifs who challenged race-based districts did indeed have a claim upon which relief could be granted. This past term, in ***Miller v. Johnson***,[9] the Court struck down Georgia's Eleventh Congressional District as an impermissible racial classification, while, in ***Hays v. Louisiana***,[10] it threw out the challenge to Louisiana's Fourth Congressional District on the ground that the white plaintiffs, who lived outside the district, lacked

---

[4] Nor clearly can the Supreme Court blindly accept as a compelling interest justifying a racial classification compliance with the law as interpreted by an executive department—whatever the merits of that interpretation. As Justice Kennedy noted, writing for the Court in *Miller*: "Were we to accept the Justice Department's objection itself as a compelling interest adequate to insulate racial districting from constitutional review, we would be surrendering to the Executive Branch our role in enforcing the constitutional limits on race-based official action. We may not do so." *Id.* at 2491.

[5] LANI GUINIER, THE TYRANNY OF THE MAJORITY 37 (1994).

[6] The Reverend Jesse Jackson has recently suggested substituting "color-caring" leadership for that which is color-blind, implying the two are mutually exclusive. *This Week with David Brinkley* (ABC television broadcast, July 23, 1995). Jackson is not alone in rejecting that traditional civil rights ideal. On the history of the color-blind ideal, see ANDREW KULL, THE COLOR-BLIND CONSTITUTION (1992).

[7] The inseparability of legal and political issues in voting rights cases has led Justice Thomas to argue—with respect, at least, to the question of vote dilution—that "[t]he matters the Court has set out to resolve in [these] cases are questions of political philosophy, not questions of law. As such, they are not readily subjected to any judicially manageable standards that can guide courts in attempting to select between competing theories." Holder v. Hall, 114 S. Ct. 2581, 2596 (1994) (Thomas, J., concurring). Thus, he would have the Court end its "disastrous misadventure in judicial policymaking," and embark on a "systematic reexamination" of its interpretation of the act. *Id.* at 2592, 2602.

[8] 113 S. Ct. 2816 (1993).

[9] 115 S. Ct. 2475 (1995).

[10] 862 F. Supp. 119 (W.D. La. 1994), *vacated*, 115 S. Ct. 2431 (1995).

standing to sue. Nevertheless, because *Hays* is likely to return with a new set of plaintiffs, both that case and *Miller v. Johnson*, in addition to *Shaw*, are discussed below.

I. What Does the Fourteenth Amendment Allow?

A. *Voting Rights and the Fourteenth Amendment*

The Fourteenth Amendment is no stranger to voting rights cases. From 1965 to 1982 a series of constitutional rulings explored the meaning of equal protection in the electoral context. When did a multimember district unconstitutionally "dilute" the voting power of blacks and Hispanics? Were minority citizens denied an equal opportunity to elect the representatives of their choice when black Democratic candidates regularly lost in a Republican-dominated county? Every method of voting affects the distribution of seats among partisan, ethnic, and other groups. And none can promise every citizen equal power; inevitably, some individuals, like some groups, will be better positioned and more politically skillful than others. But a democracy promises not that power itself will be shared, but only that every citizen is "a *potential* participant, a *potential* politician."[11] Democracies guarantee a fair political process, but no particular results. Opportunity, not outcome. But how to recognize proper electoral opportunity? How to know when adequate potential is there? That was the hard question that only the constitutional cases directly and legitimately raised in the years 1965 to 1982.[12]

Raised, but did not resolve. And in 1982 that important line of cases came to an end. In that year the Voting Rights Act was amended to allow minority plaintiffs to ignore the demands of Fourteenth Amendment litigation. Two years earlier, in 1980, the Supreme Court had held in *City of Mobile v. Bolden* that a successful constitutional attack on an at-large or other method of voting would have to demonstrate invidious *intent* in the adoption or maintenance of the electoral procedure in use.[13] As long as the method of voting had not been designed or perpetuated to keep minorities

---

[11] Michael Walzer, Spheres of Justice: A Defense of Pluralism and Equality 310 (1983) (emphasis added).

[12] Indirectly and illegitimately, particularly after 1980, the question was also addressed by the Justice Department in its review of submitted electoral changes in jurisdictions "covered" by § 5 of the Voting Rights Act. *See* Thernstrom, Whose Votes Count?, *supra* note 1, ch. 8.

[13] 446 U.S. 55 (1980).

from public office, blacks and whites stood on equal electoral footing, the Court concluded.[14] Their votes were not diluted. Ballots cast in an electoral system uncontaminated by racial purpose carried their full, constitutionally guaranteed weight. In the view of the civil rights groups, it was an unacceptable ruling, and representatives of those groups went to work immediately on a statutory amendment that would allow plaintiffs to circumvent the need to prove discriminatory intent. The fruit of their labor was a bold and radical revision of the Voting Rights Act.

Prior to 1982, the revised provision, section 2, was a seemingly insignificant preamble to the Act. It introduced a statute resting on the Fifteenth Amendment by simply restating the core of that Amendment, and with its clear link to the Constitution, it implicitly contained an intent test for electoral discrimination. A minor alteration in wording, however, solved the problem of proving racist intent. The provision was rephrased to contain a "results" test, allowing plaintiffs to challenge at-large elections, district lines, or other voting-related arrangements as discriminatory in their "result." The change left the constitutional test standing—yet idle.

To this day, vote dilution remains a question that now arises only in section 2 cases. Minority plaintiffs who challenge a districting plan or other electoral arrangement on the ground of unequal electoral opportunity predictably choose to rest their case on statutory, not constitutional, grounds.[15] But in 1993, in *Shaw v. Reno*, Fourteenth Amendment voting rights suits made a remarkable, unexpected comeback. In revised form, however. The constitutional question re-emerged—radically changed. The issue was no longer fair and effective representation for members of racial and ethnic minority groups. It had become, instead, the limits imposed by the Fourteenth Amendment on precisely that race-conscious districting that had been the remedy of choice in both Fourteenth Amendment and (after 1982) section 2 suits.

Until 1993, plaintiffs in voting rights cases had gone to court to assert the right of members of minority groups to have their race or ethnicity explicitly acknowledged. They demanded race-driven electoral arrange-

---

[14] *Id.* at 66.

[15] And, indeed, the impact of § 2 is greater than almost anyone in 1982 imagined possible. Its impact has been greatly heightened by the distorted reading given the provision by the Justice Department and courts. The revised § 2 was a gift to minority plaintiffs, but not initially of the magnitude it would come to have.

ments, most often race-based single-member districts that ensured minority officeholding. But *Shaw* raised a new question: was not that remedial arrangement itself constitutionally suspect? Race-based districting sorts citizens out by race. Didn't such sorting raise equal protection issues?

Race-based districting, the Court held in *Shaw*, is actually no different than other forms of discriminatory state action. "A plaintiff challenging a reapportionment statute under the Equal Protection Clause may state a claim by alleging that the legislation, though race-neutral on its face, rationally cannot be understood as anything other than an attempt to separate voters into different districts on the basis of race, and that the separation lacks sufficient justification."[16] Districts that constitute race-based classifications, in short, are not distinctive; they, too, are subject to strict judicial scrutiny.[17]

"In order to get beyond racism, we must first take account of race," Justice Blackmun said in 1978.[18] It was that highly dubious—and, by 1978, unoriginal—notion that had informed the first line of Fourteenth Amendment decisions. And it was that idea that *Shaw* implicitly challenged. Taking race into account—drawing race-conscious legislative districting lines—may not get us beyond race at all, Justice O'Connor suggested.[19] In fact, race-consciousness may widen the racial divide, heightening our sense of racial identity.[20] It was a point reiterated this past term by Justice Kennedy in *Miller v. Johnson*, who quoted at length from *Shaw*.[21]

If the very remedy for electoral discrimination so frequently ordered by courts and the Justice Department has now been questioned, the switch has to be seen as a sign of changed times. For roughly thirty years after the passage of the Voting Rights Act in 1965, the primary concern on the

---

[16] *Shaw v. Reno*, 113 S. Ct. 2816, 2828 (1993).

[17] *Id.* at 2830-32.

[18] Regents of the Univ. of Cal. v. Bakke, 438 U.S. 265, 407 (1978) (Blackmun, J., concurring).

[19] *Shaw*, 113 S. Ct. at 2832.

[20] Karlan and Goldstein argue that the Voting Rights Act "is explicitly race-conscious," and, thus, the Court's new-found concern over the constitutionality of race-conscious districting pits the statute against the Constitution. *On a Collision Course*, LEGAL TIMES (April 17, 1995), 24. But this point assumes that the race-based districting that plaintiffs in *Shaw* and subsequent cases challenged is mandated by the Voting Rights Act; that is far from the case. *See infra* pages 877-82.

[21] Miller v. Johnson, 115 S. Ct. 2475, 2483 (1995).

part of those who enforced the law was racial exclusion.[22] White racial attitudes, however, have been transformed in the intervening years, and the majority of blacks have joined the social and economic mainstream. Today, racism may not be our main problem, the Court implicity acknowledged in *Shaw*; racial and ethnic fragmentation, driven in part by racial districting and other public policies, may have become the greater danger.

B. A Racial Classification

Race-based districting raises constitutional questions, the Court held in *Shaw*. But when is a state in fact racially classifying voters in violation of the Equal Protection Clause? Justice O'Connor's answer in 1993 was neither altogether reassuring nor entirely clear. "This Court never has held that race-conscious state decisionmaking is impermissible in *all* circumstances," O'Connor wrote.[23] Sometimes it's okay, in other words—just your everyday, garden-variety "reasonable" racial classification. But problems clearly arise when a district is "so extremely irregular on its face that it rationally can be viewed only as an effort to segregate the races for purposes of voting, without regard for traditional districting principles and without sufficiently compelling justification."[24] "Bizarre" districts, "unexplainable on grounds other than race," were thus a source of concern.

Districts that look bad, in other words, are bad, Justice O'Connor seemed to suggest. "[R]eapportionment is one area in which appearances do matter," the majority opinion concluded.[25] Highly irregular contours obviously drawn with race in mind suggest racial stereotyping, reinforcing "the perception that members of the same racial group . . . think alike . . . ."[26]

And yet surely contours less "highly irregular" could also be drawn

---

[22] The primary concern of the Justice Department and the federal courts was racial exclusion, but in finding that type of exclusion they have relied on legal standards that are, in my view, highly questionable. Thus, they have frequently ordered remedies for an imagined wrong. *See* THERNSTROM, WHOSE VOTES COUNT?, *supra* note 1, ch. 8.

[23] Shaw v. Reno, 113 S. Ct. 2816, 2824 (1993) (emphasis added).

[24] *Id.*

[25] *Id.*

[26] *Id.* at 2827.

"with race in mind." Shape, as Justice Kennedy acknowledged in *Miller*, could not be the only test. In both the Louisiana and Georgia cases, the "looks bad" test was supplemented by essentially uncontroverted direct trial evidence that clearly established the overriding importance of race. In *Hays*, the contours of District Four could "only be explained credibly as the product of race-conscious decisionmaking," the trial court concluded;[27] twelve of the fifteen parishes the district contained had been split, as had four of the top seven cities in the state.[28] In the Georgia case, too, the contours of the Eleventh District were determined by "a far-flung search for black voters," as the trial court put it.[29] Its population was drawn from "four discrete, widely spaced urban centers that [had] absolutely nothing to do with each other, and stretch[ed] the district hundreds of miles across rural counties and narrow swamp corridors."[30]

Majority-black districts like those in Louisiana and Georgia are of course far from 100 percent black, and as a consequence, the Congressional Black Caucus (the "CBC"), in its brief, described them as "among the *least* segregated districts in the Nation."[31] The point was very misleading. Majority-minority districts are not "integrated." The white voters they contain are merely "filler people," as two proponents of race-based districting have acknowledged with refreshing candour.[32] Whites are simply included so as not to waste black ballots by excessive "packing."

That is, these are districts in which only black ballots are meant to count. They are designed to be safe black constituencies.[33] In effect, they

[27] Hays v. Louisiana, 862 F. Supp. 119, 122 (W.D. La. 1994), *vacated*, 115 S. Ct. 2431 (1995).

[28] *Id.* at 121.

[29] Johnson v. Miller, 864 F. Supp. 1354, 1377 (S.D. Ga. 1994), *aff'd*, 115 S. Ct. 2475 (1995).

[30] *Id.* at 1389. In her dissent, Justice Ginsburg argued that "[e]vidence at trial . . . shows that considerations other than race went into determining the Eleventh District's boundaries." Miller v. Johnson, 115 S. Ct. 2475, 2503 (1995) (Ginsburg, J., dissenting). Her denial that race was the overwhelming consideration in the configuration of that district is truly puzzling, given the evidence.

[31] Brief for the Congressional Black Caucus as Amicus Curiae at 19-20, Hays v. Louisiana, 115 S. Ct. 2475 (1995) (Nos. 94-558, 94-627).

[32] T. Alexander Aleinikoff & Samuel Issacharoff, *Race and Redistricting: Drawing Constitutional Lines After* Shaw v. Reno, 92 MICH. L. REV. 588, 630-31 (1993). Whites in majority-black districts, the authors write, "should not be expected to compete in any genuine sense for electoral representation" in those districts, "lest they undo the preference given to the specified minority group." *Id.* at 631.

[33] It is hardly a coincidence that the present occupant of the congressional seat from District Four was the chairman of the Louisiana State Senate reapportionment committee that drew its convoluted boundaries. The district he mapped out was designed as a safe black seat—for him. CONGRES-

have a sign pasted on them: "No white candidates need apply." And, in fact, almost no white candidates do come forward. None in the newly-created majority-minority congressional districts. Whites who think of running in a majority-black constituency are informed in no uncertain terms that the color of their skin disqualifies them; they are treading where they do not belong. Thus, as Lublin has pointed out, in 1992 several members of the U.S. House of Representatives chose to retire or move to other districts under pressure from black leaders to let blacks run racially uncontested races in the districts designed for them.[34]

As the Court made clear in *Miller*, Georgia's District Eleven and other majority-black constituencies thus constititute racial classifications not because they look bizarre (the emphasis in *Shaw*), but because the classification of voters by race is precisely their point.[35] Race, not community, has determined their contours. Race was "the predominant factor motivating the legislature's decision to place a significant number of voters within or without a particular district."[36] Indeed, these districts are intentionally race-based for a goal their proponents believe in: maximizing black officeholding.

SIONAL QUARTERLY'S POLITICS IN AMERICA, 1994: THE 103D CONGRESS 650 (Duncan ed., 1993).

[34] David Lublin, Gerrymander for Justice? Racial Redistricting and Black and Latino Representation 48, 90 (1994) (unpublished manuscript, on file with author).

[35] 115 S. Ct. 2475, 2487 (1995):

> Our observation in *Shaw* of the consequences of racial stereotyping was not meant to suggest that a district must be bizarre on its face before there is a constitutional violation. . . . Shape is relevant not because bizarreness is a necessary element of the constitutional wrong or a threshold requirement of proof, but because it may be persuasive circumstantial evidence that race for its own sake, and not other districting principles, was the legislature's dominant and controlling rationale in drawing its district lines . . . . [P]arties may rely on evidence other than bizarreness to restablish race-based districting.

Id. In her dissent, Justice Ginsburg argued that "[o]ur Nation's cities are full of districts identified by their ethnic character—Chinese, Irish, Italian, Jewish, Polish, Russian, for example." *Id.* at 2505 (Ginsburg, J., dissenting). What can be wrong, then, with black districts? The analogy doesn't hold. No legislature has strung Polish voters together from widely dispersed residential pockets in order to ensure Polish officeholding, nor has the Justice Department ever suggested than any legislature should.

[36] *Id.* at 2488. The Court in *Miller* made it very clear that plaintiffs must prove that "the legislature subordinated traditional race-neutral districting principles . . . to racial considerations." *Id.* It is thus not sufficient to assert that a legislature was "aware of racial demographics"; such awareness is normally part of "the complex interplay of forces that enter a legislature's redistricting calculus." *Id.*

II. What Does the Voting Rights Act Demand?

The Court in *Shaw* referred to the possibility that the state of North Carolina "went beyond what was reasonably necessary to avoid retrogression"—the discriminatory effect against which section 5 of the Voting Rights Act guards.[37] But, in fact, it was not the state that was out of bounds; it was the Department of Justice, which had directed North Carolina to create a second majority-black district. In the redistricting processes in Louisiana and Georgia as well the Attorney General insisted the states draw a maximum number of safe black districts.[38] In the case of Georgia, in fact, it was the American Civil Liberties Union's "max-black" plan—described by the trial court as a "triumph of demographic manipulation"—that became the Department's "guiding light."[39] At a meeting with voting section attorneys in Washington, Georgia legislators were "told to subordinate their economic and political concerns to the quest for racial percentages."[40] It is "disingenuous" to argue that the Department's objections to the proposed districting plans proposing fewer districts than the ACLU's max-black plan "were anything less than implicit commands," the district court concluded.[41] "No one in the General Assembly—including the Black Caucus—thought so, and DOJ lawyers did nothing to dissuade legislators of that notion."[42]

And yet neither sections 5 nor 2 of the Voting Rights Act, the relevant statutory provisions, required the drawing of every last possible majority-minority constituency, as the Supreme Court said in *Miller* and on numerous other occasions.[43] The Department of Justice enforces a law entirely of its own making.[44] This is not a new story; since the early 1980s, the voting rights section of the civil rights division has been distorting the

---

[37] Shaw v. Reno, 113 S. Ct. 2816, 2831 (1993).

[38] *See, e.g.*, Johnson v. Miller, 864 F. Supp. 1354, 1363-64 (S.D. Ga. 1994), *aff'd*, 115 S. Ct. 2475 (1995); Letter from Deval L. Patrick, Assistant Attorney General, Civil Rights Division, to Brenda Wright and Robert B. McDuff, dated April 29, 1994.

[39] *Johnson v. Miller*, 864 F.Supp. at 1363-64.

[40] *Id.* at 1364 n.8.

[41] *Id.* at 1364.

[42] *Id.* at 1364 n.16.

[43] *See, e.g.*, Thornburg v. Gingles, 478 U.S. 30 (1986); City of Lockhart v. United States, 460 U.S. 125 (1983); Beer v. United States, 425 U.S. 130 (1976).

[44] In *Shaw* the Court noted that states have an interest in complying with federal antidiscrimination laws, but only those "that are constitutionally valid as interpreted and applied." 113 S. Ct. 2816, 2830 (1993).

statute it is supposed to enforce.

A. *Section 5: The Retrogression Test*

The statute that Congress passed in 1965 set limits on the authority of the Justice Department that, in the main, remain in place today. Those limits were (and are) integral to the integrity of the act. The powers of the Attorney General under section 5 were extraordinary. Envisioned as an emergency measure, the provision allowed federal intrusion on constitutionally sanctioned local prerogatives and thus fundamentally altered federal-state relations. A town in a "covered" state could make no change affecting voting—not even a change in the location of a polling place—without Justice Department approval. Moreover, the burden was on the jurisdiction to prove the racial neutrality of its action beyond any doubt. Only a provision so narrowly drawn and carefully circumscribed could have withstood constitutional scrutiny.

The limits of section 5, in 1965, were set by section 4. One banned literacy tests in states and counties with a bad record on black enfranchisement.[45] The other made sure that the effect of that ban stuck. The demand that federal authorities preclear any new voting procedure in counties and states in which literacy tests had been suspended thus had an unambiguous and limited aim: guarding against renewed disfranchisement, or the use of the back door once the front one was blocked.

The ingenuity of racists had kept litigators who were attempting to secure the basic franchise always running and always behind, and those who shaped the Voting Rights Act could not be sure that eliminating the literacy test would do the trick. As the distinguished civil rights attorney Joseph Rauh explained, stopping southern states from inventing new ways around the basic enfranchising provisions of the Act was the point of preclearance; its aim was simply "self-defense."[46]

---

[45] Jurisdictions subject to the ban were identified by a statistical test. States and counties in which total registration or turnout in the presidential election of 1964 had fallen below 50%, and a literacy test had been used to screen potential registrants, were assumed to have engaged in electoral discrimination.

[46] Hearings before Subcommittee No. 5 of the Committee on the Judiciary, U.S. House of Representatives, 89th Congress, March-April 1965, 399.

In *Allen v. State Board of Elections*,[47] a broader view of the provision did emerge—one that protected against vote "dilution" and thus allowed the Justice Department to review annexations, new district lines, and other changes affecting minority voting strength. That broader view did somewhat muddy the legal waters. In 1965 the reference in section 5 to the discriminatory "effect" of a change in the method of voting was innocuous and thus unnoticed; "effect" and "purpose" were basically interchangeable terms. That is, the disfranchising impact of a sudden change in the method of registration or voting in a southern jurisdiction with a rotten history of civil rights violations made its purpose clear. But once annexations, redistrictings, and at-large voting were also subject to preclearance, effect and intent became two quite separate questions. A municipal annexation, for instance, may be undertaken for perfectly normal, nonracial reasons, even though its impact is to add proportionally more white voters to the city, thus diluting the black vote. The Court's decision in *Allen*, in short, in allowing section 5 objections to rest on disparate racial impact alone, began the process by which the statute became an instrument for affirmative action in the electoral sphere.

Not only the Court, but in both 1970 and 1975 when the temporary provisions of the statute were extended and revised, Congress too partially remade the preclearance provision. In extending the extraordinary protection of section 5 to ethnic groups without the extraordinary history of southern blacks, in covering places outside the South that had no comparable history of racism, and in agreeing to ignore the difference between disfranchisement and dilution, Congress gave the provision independent validity as an instrument to promote the election of minorities to public office in both the South and North.[48] Moreover, the District Court for the District of Columbia, which has sole jurisdiction in section 5 cases, made a consistent attempt to amend the statute through the process of judicial enforcement.[49] Nevertheless, the Supreme Court, in its decisions interpret-

---

[47] 393 U.S. 544 (1969).

[48] This complicated history of the way in which subtle and seemingly small statutory changes had big consequences is explored in THERNSTROM, WHOSE VOTES COUNT?, *supra* note 1, chs. 2 & 3.

[49] The lower court simply ignored Supreme Court rulings, and few of its decisions were appealed. In doing so, it was joined by the Justice Department and civil rights groups, both of which disliked the High Court's refusal to insist on the promise of proportional racial and ethnic representation as the standard which jurisdictions had to meet in submitting electoral changes for preclearance. *See* THERNSTROM, WHOSE VOTES COUNT?, *supra* note 1, chs. 7 & 8.

ing the preclearance provision, never abandoned the "self-defense" rationale. The point of section 5 remained protection from backsliding—from "retrogression." It was to protect electoral gains already in place—to stop measures that left blacks worse off, deprived of political power they already had.[60]

With respect to districting, the Court's no-retrogression test could not be simpler.[61] If there had been two majority-black congressional districts in Louisiana prior to the 1990 census, for instance, the state could not have chosen to eliminate one. But if the state had only one—as was the case—it was not legally obligated, under the effects test in section 5, to create another. As the Supreme Court stated in *Beer*, "It is . . . apparent that a legislative reapportionment that enhances the position of racial minorities with respect to their effective exercise of the electoral franchise can hardly have the 'effect' of diluting or abridging the right to vote on account of race within the meaning of section 5."[62]

In short, while neither Georgia nor Louisiana (nor other states that have engaged in race-based districting) misread the clear signals from the Department of Justice, those signals were at odds with the law. In insisting, in the post-1990 redistricting process, that states draw a maximum number of majority-minority districts, the Department ignored both the clear meaning of discriminatory "effect" under section 5 and the Supreme Court's decisions interpreting that provision.[63]

---

[60] *See* City of Lockhart v. United States, 460 U.S. 125 (1983); Beer v. United States, 425 U.S. 130 (1976).

[61] Annexations were a different question; a jurisdictional expansion that added more white than black voters to a city's electoral roll forced the municipality to adopt single-member districts that ensured (to the extent possible) minority officeholding in proportion to the minority population. The result was a double standard—one for districting, another for annexations—that encouraged the Justice Department (which needed little encouragement) to ignore the *Beer* test and simply, without explanation, lift the annexation standard out of context and apply it to redistricting submissions. The Act was pulled in conflicting directions by other Supreme Court decisions as well. *See, e.g.*, City of Rome, Ga. v. United States, 446 U.S. 156 (1980). Nevertheless, the Court has never abandoned the *Beer* standard in a redistricting case. On the record of the D.C. court and the Supreme Court's partial complicity in sanctioning an entitlement to proportionate racial and ethnic officeholding, see THERNSTROM, WHOSE VOTES COUNT?, *supra* note 1, ch. 7.

[62] 425 U.S. at 141.

[63] Dissenting in *Shaw*, Justice White stated that the "Attorney General's interposition of a § 5 objection 'properly is viewed' as 'an administrative finding of discrimination' against a racial minority." 113 S. Ct. 2816, 2838 (1993). But that finding rested on standards that the Supreme Court has never sanctioned.

B. *Discriminatory Purpose: More Definitional Games*

In its correspondence with Louisiana over an earlier districting plan for the state board of education, the Department of Justice acknowledged that the proposed lines "appear[ed] to have no retrogressive effect" and thus in large measure met the section 5 requirement. But it refused to preclear the plan because an allegedly better one could be drawn.[64] That "better" one contained another bizarrely-shaped majority-black district, and the failure to draw that district was viewed as a sin of omission that betrayed discriminatory intent. Louisiana thus logically assumed that the same rules would apply to congressional redistricting—that the Justice Department would refuse to preclear a proposed plan as long as another majority-black constituency could still be created. In the case of Georgia, too, the state's allegedly inadequate explanation for "its refusal in the first two submissions [of districting plans] to take the steps necessary to create a third majority-minority district" was read by the federal government as a violation of section 5's prohibition against purposefully discriminatory plans.[65]

In fact, the government's policy was legally indefensible.[66] Section 5 does contain both an effects and an intent test. In reviewing submissions, the Department of Justice is expected to ask two quite different questions: Will the proposed change leave minority voters with reduced electoral power? Or, alternatively, does it suggest hostility to minority voters? The latter question, clearly, could not be answered by counting the number of safe black districts. If such a count told the Justice Department all it needed to know, the question of discriminatory effect—to which the provision separately refers—would be superfluous. Every electoral plan with an allegedly insufficient number of safe black districts could be viewed as infected with racist intent.[67]

---

[64] Hays v. Louisiana, 839 F. Supp. 1188 (W.D. La. 1993) (three-judge court), *vacated*, 114 S. Ct. 2731 (1994).

[65] Miller v. Johnson, 115 S. Ct. 2475, 2492 (1995).

[66] *See, e.g.*, Georgia v. Reno, 881 F. Supp. 7, 14 (D.D.C. 1995); New York v. United States, 874 F. Supp. 394, 401 (D.D.C. 1994). The District Court for the District of Columbia's interpretation of the purpose prong of § 5 squares with legislative history. *See* THERNSTROM, WHOSE VOTES COUNT?, *supra* note 1, ch. 8.

[67] As O'Rourk notes, "[i]n essence, what the Justice Department appears to be doing is dressing a results analysis in the clothes of purpose." And, among other things, that strategy allows the Department to ignore the retrogression test, which (if properly applied) will often legitimize districting

Moreover, the Department's position turns the enforcement of a federal law over to civil rights groups and their allies. It gives every organization with a "preferable" districting scheme—one that seems to ensure more black officeholding—the power to veto a proposed districting plan. And, in the case of Georgia, as noted above, the Justice Department did in effect allow the American Civil Liberities Union to assume the government's job. Federal policy was literally driven by the ACLU: "an embarrassment," as the district court put it.[58]

The Georgia case provides the fullest record to date of the cozy relationship between the Justice Department's voting rights section and the civil rights community. But the basic facts of that relationship have been evident for some time. For instance, in 1984, in a section 5 case involving state senate redistricting in South Carolina, the NAACP tried to suggest that the plan it offered was the one a jurisdiction had to adopt—that the failure to do so would constitute evidence of discriminatory purpose in violation of the preclearance provision.[59] Throughout the 1980s, it was an argument that both the D.C. district court and the Justice Department came close to embracing.[60]

---

plans that do not guarantee a maximum number of safe minority seats. Timothy G. O'Rourk, *Shaw v. Reno: The Shape of Things to Come*, 26 RUTGERS L.J. 723, 752 (1995). This is not to say, of course, that there can be no circumstantial evidence of invidious purpose. As Butler points out, if a state has failed to recognize concentrations of minority voters that would naturally produce majority-minority districts using standard districting criteria, it could legitimately be said to have failed to carry its burden of proving an absence of discriminatory intent. But, unless a rejected plan clearly meets the state's own stated redistricting criteria and is superior in that regard to the plan actually adopted, the argument that rejection itself is a sign of unacceptable purpose amounts to nothing more than an insistence on a maximum number of majority-minority districts. Katharine Inglis Butler, *Affirmative Racial Gerrymandering: Fair Representation for Minorities or a Dangerous Recognition of Group Rights*, 26 RUTGERS L.J. 498, 510-11 (1995).

[58] "Succinctly put, the considerable influence of ACLU advocacy on the voting rights decisions of the United States Attorney General is an embarrassment," the district court concluded. Johnson v. Miller, 864 F. Supp. 1354, 1368 (S.D. Ga. 1994), *aff'd*, 115 S. Ct. 2475 (1995). That influence was evident even in the process by which the federal government notified the state of its decision. The Department of Justice told the ACLU of its impending objection; the ACLU notified the Black Caucus before the letter of objection arrived at the office of the Georgia Attorney General. *Id.* at 1360-63.

[59] South Carolina v. United States and the NAACP, Inc., Civil Action No. 83-3626, District Court for the District of Columbia, 1984, NAACP's-Defendant's Supplemental Response to Interrogatories, April 2, 1984, 3-4: "The redistricting plan as drawn avoidably and deliberately denies Blacks the equal opportunity to elect a candidate of their choice . . . . Moreover, the State . . . failed and or refused to implement suggestions for redistricting made by the NAACP Defendants, as well as other minority organizations."

[60] *See* THERNSTROM, WHOSE VOTES COUNT?, *supra* note 1, ch. 8.

C. *Section 2: A Different Question*

The Justice Department led Louisiana and Georgia to believe that preclearance required meeting the demands of both sections 5 and 2. Again, the policy is not new but it's wrong. By adminstrative fiat the preclearance provision has been rewritten.

Sections 2 and 5 "differ in structure, purpose, and application," the Supreme Court noted in *Holder v. Hall.*[61] As the D.C. District Court explained at length in two recent decisions, the two are quite separate provisions.[62] It was an overdue insight. In 1982, when section 2 was transformed from an inconsequential preamble into a powerful instrument for ridding the nation of methods of election with a discriminatory "result," there was literally no discussion of a consequent change in section 5. In fact, during the debates of 1981 and 1982, civil rights spokesmen directly and indirectly assured members of Congress that the amendment of section 2 would not alter the preclearance provision.[63]

Those assurances fell on deaf administrative ears. In January, 1987, the Justice Department "incorporated" section 2 into section 5. Revised districting lines, a new polling place, and other electoral changes submitted for federal review under section 5 were henceforth judged by section 2 standards as well. An objection would be lodged if the proposed change was arguably discriminatory in purpose, effect, or "result" (the latter being a section 2 question), with the burden on the submitting jurisdiction to prove the racial neutrality of its proposed action. Section 5 was thus changed—on the assumption, evidently, that Congress had acted without debate to give dramatic new force to a central provision in the Act.[64] And yet, in justifying such a radical overhaul of a key provision—one whose limits were clearly understood—the Department could point only to one

---

[61] 114 S. Ct. 2581, 2587 (1994).

[62] New York v. United States, 874 F. Supp. 394 (D.D.C. 1994); Georgia v. Reno, 881 F. Supp. 7 (D.D.C. 1995).

[63] *See, e.g.*, 128 CONG. REC. 14,938 (1982) (exchange between Reps. Don Edwards and Elliott H. Levitas).

[64] *See* Procedures for the Administration of Section 5 of the Voting Rights Act of 1965, as amended, 28 C.F.R. § 51.55(2):

> In those instances in which the Attorney General concludes that, as proposed, the submitted change is free of discriminatory purpose and retrogressive effect, but also concludes that a bar to implementation of the change is necessary to prevent a clear violation of amended section 2, the Attorney General shall withhold section 5 preclearance.

footnote, buried in the 1982 Senate Judiciary Committee Report and unsupported by the text to which it was appended.[65]

The change in section 5 not only had no basis in legislative history. The Justice Department had assumed an inappropriate role. Federal administrators, remote from the scene, became plaintiff, defendant, and judge, all rolled into one, with no reliable way of gathering information on race and politics in the local jurisdiction remotely comparable to that which opposing attorneys present at a trial. Cases resting on section 2 involve complex questions of electoral opportunity; courts are asked to judge whether the "totality of circumstances," for instance, in the city of Detroit suggests electoral inequality between minority and white citizens. Adjudicating competing claims about racial fairness requires, as the Supreme Court has noted, an "intensely local appraisal"—the specific detailed knowledge that only a court can obtain.[66] It was for that reason precisely that section 2 (as written and understood at the time) did not offer—as section 5 did—the option of administrative preclearance as an alternative to a full-scale court proceeding in which evidence and rebuttal evidence is fully presented.[67] Administrative procedures are no substitute for a trial.

D. *Access, Not Outcome*

There is another, perhaps more important point. Attached or unattached to section 5, section 2 does not mean what the Justice Department says it means. That is, compliance with section 2 does not, in any case, necessitate the drawing of any particular number of majority-minority districts. The provision guarantees equal electoral access, not racially fair outcomes. Opportunity is the "result" it ensures. And indeed, as Justice Kennedy noted in *Miller*, if the act did in fact compel race-based districting, by definition it would raise a serious constitutional question; such an interpretation would jeopardize the entire statute.[68]

The intimate link between section 2 and the pre-1980 legal standards

---

[65] The footnote states that: "In light of the amendment to section 2, it is intended that a section 5 objection also follows if a new voting procedure itself so discriminates as to violate section 2." S. REP. No. 417, 97th Cong., 2d Sess. 12 n.31 (1982) [hereinafter "*1982 Senate Report*"].

[66] White v. Regester, 412 U.S. 755, 769 (1973).

[67] The Justice Department itself, in its "comments" introducing the new 1987 guidelines, admitted that administrative review did not remotely resemble a judicial proceeding. 28 C.F.R. § 51.55.

[68] Miller v. Johnson, 115 S. Ct. 2475, 2492 (1995).

established in Fourteenth Amendment cases should alone make that clear. In amending section 2, Congress lifted language directly from two constitutional rulings: *Whitcomb v. Chavis*[69] and *White v. Regester*.[70] In both, the Court had directed trial courts judging the level of electoral opportunity in a jurisdiction to assess the political environment: the setting in which the voting took place. Judges had been asked to distinguish the failure of minority voters to elect candidates of their choice for reasons of race from normal electoral defeat—that to which every group, however defined, was vulnerable. It was, however, a very tall order. What were the criteria that distinguished the one setting from the other?

Unequal electoral opportunity was inevitably an elusive concept. Were black voters distinctively entitled to some degree of representation? Was black officeholding an important measure of opportunity? As Justice Frankfurter observed (dissenting in *Baker v. Carr*), we can only know if voters are improperly represented if we know what it means to be properly represented.[71] And yet we lack a theoretical framework to decide. The point still held twenty years later.

Nevertheless, if section 2 asked courts to measure an inadequately defined phenonenon—electoral inequality—it did not leave judges entirely clueless. Some guidance was provided. In *Whitcomb*, for instance, the Supreme Court unequivocally rejected the view that a showing of disproportionately low minority officeholding and evidence of black residential clustering would suffice to establish electoral discrimination.

By lifting language directly from that decision and from *White*, Congress thus rejected the notion that black voters had a right to even one legislative seat reserved for a black representative. Section 2, as Butler notes, is nothing but "standard remedial legislation."[72] Plaintiffs must establish a violation of their statutory right to an electoral process open to black political aspirations; only then are they entitled to a race-conscious remedy. Minority voters were guaranteed not their "fair share" of politi-

[69] 403 U.S. 124 (1971).

[70] 412 U.S. 755 (1973).

[71] Baker v. Carr, 369 U.S. 186, 300 (1962) (Frankfurter, J., dissenting).

[72] As Butler points out, "[a] jurisdiction that adopts extreme measures [stringing together black residential pockets] to create majority-black districts is akin to a manufacturer paying punitive damages to potential purchasers of its product prior to anyone suffering an injury or establishing a defect in the product." Butler, *supra* note 57, at 516.

cal offices, but only a "fair shake," a chance to play the electoral game by fair rules.[73] In fact, the language of section 2—guaranteeing minority voters an equal opportunity "to elect representatives of their choice"—plainly suggested a definition of representation broader than that which would have been conveyed had the phrase read, "*minority* representatives of their choice."

In addition, the concern was clearly with election contests in racist settings. Blacks, Congress concluded, lacked an equal chance to elect representatives of their choice where race had left them politically isolated—without potential allies in electoral contests. That focus was spelled out by numerous witnesses at the 1982 hearings and in the Senate Judiciary Committee Report as well.

The report thus listed "factors" to which courts were instructed to refer in judging the merits of a vote dilution suit. Those factors included a history of discrimination, racial polarization, a candidate slating process to which minorities were denied access, political campaigns characterized by racial appeals, and a lack of responsiveness on the part of public officials to minority interests.[74] The point of the list was clear: to help judges identify those situations in which either a history of discrimination or ongoing racism had left minority voters at a distinctive disadvantage in the electoral process. Not only the list, but other language in the report signalled the importance of past and present racism. The concern, it noted, was with those exceptional communities in which racial politics still dominated the electoral process.[75]

That was the message as well of a number of civil rights advocates who

---

[73] For the "fair share"/"fair shake" distinction, *see* James F. Blumstein, *Defining Discrimination: Intent vs. Impact*, NEW PERSPECTIVES, Summer 1984, at 29, 30.

[74] *1982 Senate Report*, *supra* note 65, at 28-29; Thernstrom, *supra* note 1, at 192-97.

[75] *1982 Senate Report*, *supra* note 65, at 32. The report also cited a South Carolina district court decision in *McCain v. Lybrand*, No 74-281, slip op. (D.D.C., April 17, 1980), as an illustration of the faithful application of the already familiar "results" test. The plaintiffs had prevailed in that decision because black candidates, the court found, tended to lose elections "not on their merits but solely because of their race." A report issued by the Subcommittee on the Constitution to the Senate Committee on the Judiciary expressed concern that precisely that distinction would be lost. Not so, retorted the full committee's own report. In "most" jurisdictions white voters give substantial support to black candidates. But "unfortunately . . . there are still some communities . . . where racial politics do dominate the electoral process." And in such communities "a particular election method can deny minority voters equal opportunities to participate meaningfully in elections." 1982 *Senate Report*, *supra* note 65, at 33.

testified at the 1982 hearings. For instance, Armand Derfner, a leading civil rights attorney and key witness, argued that single-member districts had no "precisely correct racial mix." The entitlement was not to districts that were, say, two-thirds black. Section 2 only promised an electoral process that was fluid—open to racial change, and thus not "frozen." Courts were expected to ask if minority voters would have "some influence."[76] Claims of dilution would rest, Derfner said, on "evidence that voters of a racial minority [were] isolated within a political system . . . 'shut out,' i.e. denied access . . . [without] the opportunity to participate in the electoral process."[77]

When were minorities "frozen" out, however? No witness offered a definition of that total electoral exclusion against which the Act protected, except to say that the test had been met when a group had "really been unfairly throttled."[78] "Unfairly throttled" that is, by racism, the Senate report—and the entire history of the Act—made clear.

Some will argue that an interpretation of section 2 that makes racist exclusion the test of electoral discrimination is at odds with the stated intent in 1982 to create a way around the demand that plaintiffs provide evidence of discriminatory intent. Not at all. The objection in 1982 to the decision in *Mobile* was to the demand that plaintiffs produce a "smoking gun." Advocates did not object, in other words, to the focus on racism, but only to the Court's alleged insistence on direct evidence of racist intent.

In sum, in revising section 2 Congress unequivocally and properly rejected the notion of group entitlement to even one legislative seat—however concentrated or dispersed black residential patterns were found to be. Had witnesses at the 1982 congressional hearings lobbied for an amended statute that would mandate race-based districting and thus guarantee legislative seats for members of designated minority groups, their arguments would have certainly fallen on deaf ears. Such a demand was not even remotely politically possible.

There is thus never any necessity on the part of a state (or its subdivisions) to maximize black officeholding by means of race-based districting.

---

[76] *Voting Rights Act: Hearings on S. 1992 Before the Subcommittee on the Constitution of the Committee on the Judiciary*, 97th Cong., 2d Sess. 803, 810 (testimony of Armand Derfner).

[77] *Id.* at 810 (prepared statement of Armand Derfner).

[78] *Id.* at 803.

Race-conscious districting is available only as a remedy for a proven section 2 violation, and then only if it adheres to standard districting criteria.[79] In the Louisiana and Georgia cases, both states (in creating a maximum number of safe black constituencies) hoped to avoid a costly and disruptive battle with the Department of Justice. Redistricting is a politically complex and laborious process, and to present a plan that won't be precleared is a waste of extensive political effort. That both states sought to avoid that rejection is understandable, but in their eagerness to do so, they engaged in a racial classification of voters that raised serious Fourteenth Amendment questions. A compelling state interest justifies a racial classification, but a preference for smooth bureaucratic sailing does not meet that test.

E. *A Coercive Distortion of the Law: Business as Usual*

The district courts in both the Louisiana and Georgia cases raised serious concerns over the Justice Department's coercive role in bending local jurisdictions to its will.[80] The circumstances were particularly egregious in the Georgia case, where Justice Department lawyers who have the responsibility to make impartial preclearance determinations worked in active concert with an outside group that wanted a maximum number of race-driven districts. As the trial court noted, the ACLU's attorney, Ms. Kathleen Wilde, developed a relationship with the voting section that was "informal and familiar; the dynamics were that of peers working together, not of an advocate submitting proposals to higher authorities."[81]

As noted above, the record of the Justice Department in these two cases is not abberational. The voting section of the Justice Department's Civil Rights Division has long assumed freewheeling power to object to districting plans that did not seem "right"—that is, racially "fair."[82] In 1981, for

[79] As Butler notes, only geographically compact minority groups may claim that a districting scheme dilutes their voting strength. It thus cannot be possible that a district that runs down an interstate highway collecting residentially scattered black voters is necessary if a state wishes to avoid violating the act. Butler, *supra* note 57, at 518 (referring to Thornburg v. Gingles, 478 U.S. 30, 50 (1986)).

[80] *See, e.g.*, Hays v. Louisiana, 839 F. Supp. 1188, 1196 n.21 (W.D. La. 1993), *vacated*, 114 S. Ct. 2731 (1994).

[81] *Johnson v. Miller*, 864 F.Supp. 1354, 1362 (W.D. La. 1994), *vacated*, 115 S. Ct. 2431 (1995).

[82] This criticism is developed in detail in THERNSTROM, WHOSE VOTES COUNT?, *supra* note 1,

instance, a Justice Department memo on county council districts for Barbour County, Alabama, explained that calculating what was "fair" was simple. "Since blacks constitute 40.5 percent of the voting age population, they would be entitled to 2.8 districts [that is, two viable districts plus a third influence district]." The voting section itself drew up the right plan. Such calculations—in Democratic and Republican administrations alike—became a routine part of the preclearance process.[83] Only one thing is new: with the post-1990 availability of sophisticated census software, the racial sorting of voters has become exquisitely precise.[84]

What is routine is obviously not necessarily right. The voting section of the Department of Justice has long had the aura of a law office; its files suggest attorneys at work constructing a case for minority plaintiffs.[85] And yet the interests of minority plaintiffs are not necessarily those of either the minority voters whom the Department purports to represent or the American public, its only legitimate client.

III. The Real Issue

At the heart of voting rights disputes, I noted at the outset, is an argument about the nature of American society. It is true of all conflicts over affirmative action policies. Deliberately drawn majority-minority districts are racial classifications for familiar affirmative action ends. The point of the race-conscious districting is precisely that of most such policies: to provide maximum protection for black candidates from white competition. Law school affirmative action programs, by setting separate admissions standards, pit black applicants primarily (sometimes only) against other blacks. Likewise, "safe" black legislative districts amount to protective racial sorting. Their aim is to ensure electoral contests in which black candidates compete only against other black candidates, eliminating potential white competitors.

Questions involving affirmative action in the electoral sphere are thus not simply about who ends up where on a districting map. At issue be-

---

ch. 8; and in Katharine Inglis Butler, *Reapportionment, the Courts, and the Voting Rights Act: A Resegregation of the Political Process?*, 56 Univ. of Colo. L. Rev. 1, 21 (1984).

[83] Thernstrom, Whose Votes Count?, *supra* note 1, at 172.

[84] On the impact of the changed technology in the crafting of districts, *see, e.g.*, Shaw v. Hunt, 861 F. Supp. 408 (E.D.N.C. 1994).

[85] *See* Thernstrom, Whose Votes Count?, *supra* note 1, ch. 8.

tween the opposing sides are entirely different views of white racial attitudes, black opportunity, the nature of democratic representation, and the costs of race-conscious policies.

A. *Bleak and Wrong*

Black candidates cannot get elected in majority-white settings, the brief for the Congressional Black Caucus argued in the Louisiana case. That is "contemporary reality."[86] The doors of political opportunity are still closed. Black candidates remain at the mercy of racist white opposition. Hence the need for protective policies—for race-based districts drawn to ensure black officeholding, an implicit statutory promise.

From the outset the Voting Rights Act did clearly promise more than simple access to the polling booth; the architects of the statute believed black ballots would mean black power. Not just black political influence, but blacks elected to public office. But the statute contained no guarantee of such electoral success, and, equally important, the CBC's portrait of the American racial landscape is much too bleak.[87]

Whites not only say they will vote for black candidates; they do so, often casting their ballots for an African-American running against a white opponent. That choice is most often available in mayoral contests. Conventional wisdom has it that the overwhelming majority of black mayors have been elected from majority-black cities. This is true but misleading. Most of those black "cities" are in fact tiny majority-black towns in the South. Eliminate those small urban dots on the southern map, focus on cities of 50,000 or more in population, and quite a different picture emerges. Sixty-seven percent of the black mayors elected in such cities over the last thirty years have not had the benefit of a majority-black constituency.[88]

---

[86] Brief for the Congressional Black Caucus at 1, Hays v. Louisiana, 862 F. Supp. 119 (W.D. La. 1994), *vacated*, 115 S. Ct. 2431 (1995).

[87] A concern that preferential policies rest on the arguably demeaning assumption that blacks require extraordinary protection from white competition in order to succeed in American society runs through a number of affirmative action cases. *See, e.g.*, Regents of the Univ. of Cal. v. Bakke, 438 U.S. 265, 298 (1978) ("[P]referential programs may only reinforce common stereotypes holding that certain groups are unable to achieve success without special protection based on a factor bearing no relationship to individual worth.").

[88] *See* Abigail Thernstrom & Stephan Thernstrom, *The Promise of Racial Equality*, *in* THE

Even in Maine, with a black population of just 0.4 percent, the mayors of two important cities are black. In the 1989 mayoral race in New York City (29 percent black), Rudolph Guiliani lost between 25 and 30 percent of the white vote to David Dinkins. At least 38 percent of whites deserted Jon Derus in Minneapolis (13 percent black) in 1993, and cast their ballots for the victor, Sharon Sayles Belton, the black president of the city council. That same year, 31 percent of the white electorate in St. Louis (48 percent African-American) voted for Freeman Bosely, Jr., despite the availability of three white candidates on the ballot; in fact, Bosely's overall vote total was precisely that of his white predecessor. Belton and Bosley were making their first try; incumbents (although not David Dinkins) generally do even better.

It is not only in races for a mayor's seat that white voters choose black candidates over those who are white. L. Douglas Wilder, in his successful gubernatorial run in 1989, got an estimated forty to forty-three percent of Virginia's white vote. Sceptics will say that figure still represents only a minority of the white electorate, but Charles Robb, the white Democratic governor who preceded Wilder, did only a shade better: forty-five percent. Illinois (11.6 percent black) elected Carol Moseley-Braun as its U.S. Senator in 1992. In 1994, Ohio elected J. Kenneth Blackwell as state treasurer, and New York chose H. Carl McCall as state comptroller. Also in 1994, J.C. Watts won a congressional seat in an eighty-three percent white Oklahoma district.

But what about Georgia and other southern states? Was Wilder's election in Virginia a fluke? Georgia, in fact, was one of the first states to send an African-American to Congress from a majority-white district. Andrew Young, elected in 1972, did not have the benefit of a majority-black constituency. Young, however, was the first and last from his state, and in Louisiana no black congressman from a majority-white constituency has ever been elected. Hence the need, the CBC argues, for safe black constituencies. In fact, for three reasons the record in neither state is particularly telling.

To begin with, the past is not the future. White racial attitudes have been changing fast, and the record of black electoral success in 1975 tells us little about the prospects for such success today. In addition, black can-

---

NEW PROMISE OF AMERICAN LIFE ch. 5 (Lamar Alexander & Chester E. Finn, Jr. eds., 1995).

didates cannot win contests they do not enter. And scholars who attempt to assess white willingness to support black candidacies on the basis of election returns cannot learn anything from elections in which no black candidate has been in the race.

Finally, congressional candidates—whatever their color—cannot win elections if their political views are at odds with the majority of voters in their district. California Representative Ronald V. Dellums is repeatedly elected from a constituency that includes Berkeley and like-minded suburbs, but few majority-white districts are as left-leaning as his. Particularly in the South, centrist and conservative candidates (whether white or black) will do better than those who are militantly liberal. J.C. Watts, a black Republican, would not have been elected in Oklahoma had he run as a liberal Democrat. As the Supreme Court recognized in ***Whitcomb***, when black Democratic candidates lose in conservative districts, it is not their race but their ideology that white voters are rejecting.[89]

Guinier, among others, has argued that centrist or conservative black candidates who can attract strong white support are not "authentically" black.[90] There is a political test for "blackness"; black constituents can lack representation even with blacks in office. If (in Guinier's words) those officeholders are not "community-based," "culturally-rooted," and "politically, psychologically, and culturally black,"[91] then they're tokens—contaminated by white support. In her view, as mayor of Atlanta, Andrew Young did not count as a black advocate;[92] the "authentic" leader need not "appeal to white voters in order to get elected."[93] "Authenticity" has "a distinctive voice"[94] and a level of group consciousness incompatible with white enthusiasm.

It's an accusation with a familiar ring. White civil rights sympathizers in the South were once regularly called "nigger-lovers." Governor Wilder,

---

[89] Since blacks in Indiana's largely Republican Marion County were Democrats, the Court concluded that the "dilution" of their voting strength was a "mere euphemism for political defeat." It was not race but party that had determined electoral outcome. 403 U.S. 124, 153 (1971).

[90] GUINIER, *supra* note 5, at 55-58.

[91] Lani Guinier, *The Triumph of Tokenism: The Voting Rights Act and the Theory of Black Electoral Success*, 89 MICH. L. REV. 1077, 1103 (1991).

[92] Andrew Young's record, Guinier asserts, was not much different from that of Atlanta's white business-oriented mayors. *Id.* at 1118 n.196.

[93] *Id.* at 1103-4.

[94] *Id.* at 1108.

Andrew Young, Justice Clarence Thomas, and other African-Americans against whom the charge of inauthenticity has been leveled are, in effect, "honky-lovers" and as such racial renegades.

But by that definition, a number of recently elected black mayors do not count as "black" for purposes of representation. Many are fiscal conservatives, tough on crime, and opposed to busing. Moreover, Jesse Jackson, whom the media treat as the authentic voice of black America, is actually to the left of the majority of black voters, recent polling data suggest.[95] If the data are correct, the point applies as well to the Congressional Black Caucus.

Conservative and moderate blacks can represent black voters—and so can elected whites. The Voting Rights Act was designed to protect black voters, not officeholders with a particular color or those who hold only certain political views. The members of the CBC and other black politicians are strong advocates of racial gerrymandering; such districting is in their interest. All elected officials like safe constituencies from which to run, and majority-black districts are safe constituencies. Almost inevitably, they elect a black legislator. In part, that is because white candidates, as discussed above, are not welcome in such districts, but in part it is the consequence of the fact that black voters, whose electoral power is still relatively novel, tend to vote as a bloc.

If safe black districts are a gift to black politicians, they are not so clearly in the interest of black voters. Such districts may marginalize the black elected officials upon whom the voters count to represent their interests effectively.[96] In fact, arguably, a greater dispersion of black voters over more "influence districts" would result in a better representation of black interests, since more public officials, both black and white, would owe their election in part to black support.[97]

---

[95] MICHAEL C. DAWSON, BEHIND THE MULE: RACE AND CLASS IN AFRICAN-AMERICAN POLITICS 137, fig. 6.3 (1994).

[96] *See* James F. Blumstein, *Racial Gerrymandering and Vote Dilution:* Shaw v. Reno *in Doctrinal Context*, 26 RUTGERS L.J. 517 (1995) [hereinafter Blumstein, *Racial Gerrymandering*]. As Blumstein points out, in Wright v. Rockefeller, 376 U.S. 52 (1964), two groups of black plaintiffs were at odds as to what would be in the best interests of African-Americans in Manhattan and, thus, urged different districting plans. *Id.* at 521-22.

[97] *See* Voinovich v. Quilter, 113 S. Ct. 1149 (1993), in which plaintiffs argued that black voters were being "packed" into districts in such a way as to lessen their overall influence. *Id.* at 1153.

That greater dispersion, however, depends on judicial action. Majority-minority districts are here to stay, unless courts intervene. In this important sense, legislative plans that protect black candidates from white competition are a distinctive form of affirmative action. Separate lists for black and white candidates for spots on a police force or for seats in a medical school class are, at least in theory, temporary measures; their life is due to expire when the need for such protective racial sorting ends.

The racial gerrymandering of legislative districts, on the other hand, if allowed to stand, is likely to be permanent for two reasons. Black incumbents are politically secure; few white political aspirants would want to risk a media thrashing for attempting allegedly to "disfranchise" black voters.[98] In addition, in the covered jurisdictions of the South and elsewhere, the retrogression test of section 5 forbids backsliding—a drop in the number of secure black legislative seats. Plans approved today become the absolute baselines against which subsequent districting changes are measured through at least 2007, when section 5 is now scheduled to expire.[99]

B. A People Apart

That in a racially fair political system blacks would hold office in proportion to their numbers in the population is a conviction that runs through all the writings by advocates of race-based districting.[100] In part, these advocates simply believe that disproportionately low minority officeholding can have only one explanation: white racism. In part, proportionality is the logical legal standard once a distinction is made between "meaningful" and "meaningless" black ballots.[101] For that distinction ne-

[98] And, indeed, as the district court noted in the Georgia case, it had "been placed in the unenviable position of depriving black citizens of a privilege [although one] the Justice Department never had the right to grant: maximization of the black vote, whatever the cost." It was a politically uncomfortable position for federal judges with lifetime job tenure, and clearly would have been even more so had they been up for election. Miller v. Johnson, 864 F. Supp. 1354, 1369 (S.D. Ga. 1994), *aff'd*, 115 S. Ct. 2475 (1995).

[99] "[A]ny redistricting plan designed for proportionality, that is upheld by the Court today, will not be easily uprooted in the foreseeable future." *Id.* at 1386.

[100] *See* Chandler Davidson, *Minority Vote Dilution, An Overview, in* MINORITY VOTE DILUTION 1, 12 (Chandler Davidson ed., 1984) ("[A]bout one-fifth as many blacks hold office as would be likely in a nonracist society."). More recently, see Brief for the United States at 12, United States v. Hays, 115 S. Ct. 231 (1995).

[101] The problem of defining "meaningful" votes did not first surface in the minority vote dilution

cessitates a determination as to when black votes "fully count," and the phrase itself invites a definition that gives those ballots maximum weight, defined as proportionate racial and ethnic officeholding. Anything less suggests a compromised right.

In addition, disproportionately low black officeholding, proponents of race-conscious districting clearly believe, denies representation to a group for whom members of no other group can speak.[102] "[B]lacks live in a different world from whites,"[103] Lani Guinier argues; "disagreements among blacks pale by comparison with the differences in political interest and philosophy between blacks and whites."[104] In severely divided societies, of which the United States is one, whites cannot speak for blacks, or (by logical extension) blacks for whites. Blacks—the assumption runs—are a nation within our nation, a people apart. And as such, they are entitled, as a matter of elementary fairness, to representation in proportion to their population strength.[105]

It may have been a legitimate argument in 1945; it isn't today. Fifty years ago, the novelist and social critic Richard Wright described his boyhood days in a South in which "whites had drawn a line over which we

---

cases. It had been fully apparent in the reapportionment decisions. *See* Reynolds v. Sims, 377 U.S. 533 (1964); Baker v. Carr, 369 U.S. 186 (1962).

[102] The notion that blacks are a group apart, sharing distinctive views, was directly attacked by Justice Kennedy in *Miller*. If redistricting, he wrote, often involves racial considerations, "it does not follow . . . that individuals of the same race share a single political interest. The view that they do is 'based on the demeaning notion that members of the defined racial groups ascribe to certain 'minority views' that must be different from those of other citizens,' . . . , the precise use of race as a proxy the Constitution prohibits." *Miller*, 115 S. Ct. at 2487 (citation omitted). *See also* Holder v. Hall, 114 S. Ct. 2581, 2597 (1994) (Thomas, J., concurring):

> [I]n resolving vote dilution actions we have given credence to the view that race defines political interest. We have acted on the implicit assumption that members of racial and ethnic groups must all think alike on important matters of public policy and must have their own 'minority preferred' representatives holding seats in elected bodies if they are to be considered represented at all.

[103] Lani Guinier, *No Two Seats: The Elusive Quest for Racial Equality*, 77 VA. L. REV. 1413, 1468 (1991) (quoting Jennifer L. Hochschild & Monica Herk, *"Yes, But . . .": Principles and Caveats in American Racial Attitudes*, *in* MAJORITIES AND MINORITIES: NOMOS XXXII 308, 319 (John W. Chapman & Alan Wertheimer eds., 1990)).

[104] *Id.* at 1468.

[105] Justice Ginsburg comes close to embracing this view in her dissent in *Miller*. "But ethnicity itself can tie people together, as volumes of social science literature have documented—even people with divergent economic interests." 115 S. Ct. at 2504 (Ginsburg, J., dissenting).

dared not step."[106] But that South has disappeared, and the position of African-Americans within American society has been transformed. More than eighty percent of blacks polled in national surveys report having whites as neighbors.[107] Few whites say that they wouldn't want to live next door to a black family, while 30 percent object to having a Fundamentalist as a neighbor.[108] African-Americans are permanent and influential political players in both North and South. They are partners in powerful law firms, and doctors at distinguished hospitals. An African-American model in an upscale Bloomingdale's clothing ad is now business as usual, as are black faces in TV commercials selling every sort of product. The Bill Cosby show, watched by twenty million viewers, earned NBC a billion dollars.

African-Americans still have incomes below the national average, are less likely than whites to have a college degree, have higher poverty rates, and rank behind whites in most measures of socio-economic status. But they are no longer a people apart in the way that they arguably were as recently as the early 1960s, before the Civil Rights Revolution. Since then they have become part of the American mainstream. As the district court noted in *Johnson v. Miller*, "[b]lacks in Georgia did indeed rise from a common heritage of slavery and oppression, but with the shedding of those burdens they have begun to follow myriad, distinctive paths."[109]

Until the 1960s almost all of the small numbers of blacks students attending college were to be found in historically black institutions; today the number in higher education has grown explosively, and six out of seven of them attend predominantly white institutions. "Buy Black" campaigns routinely flop. Black separatist parties go nowhere. This picture could obviously be enlarged, but the point should be clear. The United States is not yet a fully integrated society, but it has moved in that direction with impressive speed in the four decades since *Brown v. Board of Education*. A separate and excluded people may be entitled to legislative set-asides, seats reserved to ensure their political inclusion. In 1995, blacks

---

[106] RICHARD WRIGHT, BLACK BOY 251 (1966).

[107] William Feigelman & Bernard S. Gorman, *Blacks Who Live Near Whites: 1982 and 1987*, 74 SOC. & SOC. RES., July 1990, at 202-07.

[108] HOWARD SCHUMAN ET AL., RACIAL ATTITUDES IN AMERICA: TRENDS AND INTERPRETATIONS 106-07 (1985); 1989 Gallup poll cited in STEPHEN BATES, BATTLEGROUND 64 (1993).

[109] Johnson v. Miller, 864 F. Supp. 1354, 1390 (S.D. Ga. 1994), *aff'd*, 115 S Ct. 2475 (1995).

no longer need such an extraordinarily protective arrangement.

African-Americans are not a racially-defined nation within our nation. And yet if both they and whites believe they are, it may well become true. This is especially the case if that perception informs the law. Separate admissions procedures for whites and blacks, separate hiring processes, separate legislative districts: given a stamp of approval by Congress and the courts, they paint an official, influential, and perverse portrait of American society.

Two societies—one white and one black—is not a fact; it is what the columnist Robert J. Samuelson has called (in another context) a psycho-fact: it is not true, but we feel it is and thus it threatens to become so.[110] Perceptions can take on a life of their own, shaping the society that they purport to describe.

Racially gerrymandered districts are an attempt to provide racial and ethnic minorities, and only them, with representation free from the constraints that our geographically based districting system places on the representation of all group interests.[111] To impute to Congress an intent to permanently remove one group from the pluralism of American politics not only misreads the basic objectives of the Voting Rights Act, but would ensure the very segregation the act was intended to cure.

C. *A Shared Danger*

"All citizens are stigmatized by the notion that their 'interests' can be defined by race or will be represented adequately only if a member of their racial 'group' holds a particular office," the district court in the Louisiana case concluded.[112] It was true as well of the segregated institutions of the Jim Crow South. Both blacks and whites were harmed when drinking fountains carried "white" and "colored" signs.[113]

---

[110] Robert J. Samuelson, *The Triumph of the Psycho-Fact*, WASH. POST, May 4, 1994, at A25.

[111] *See* Butler, *supra* note 57, at 523-24. As Butler notes, Justice Stevens's observation in *Shaw* that "African Americans may [now] be the only group to which it is unconstitutional to offer specific benefits from redistricting" (113 S. Ct. 2816, 2845 n.4 (1993) (Stevens, J., dissenting)) is simply backwards. The Constitution permits the states to recognize group interests, but only those that can be furthered with a geographically based representational structure.

[112] Hays v. Louisiana, 862 F. Supp. 119, 125 (W.D. La. 1994), *vacated*, 115 S. Ct. 2431 (1995).

[113] As Justice Thomas put it in his concurrance in *Adrand Constructors, Inc. v. Pena*, 115 S.

Racial classifications, in short, deliver the message that skin color matters—profoundly. They suggest that white folks and black folks just are not the same, that race and ethnicity are the qualities that really matter. Individuals are defined by blood—not by character, social class, religious sentiments, age, or education. But categories appropriate to a caste system are a poor basis on which to build that community of equal citizens upon which democratic government depends. Equal citizens are free to define themselves, and do so differently in different contexts. A voter whose choice of a candidate in a presidential primary is shaped primarily by racial considerations might react to the issues in a school board contest as parents of other races do. It is precisely that fluidity of individual political identity that prevents the formation of castes, which are rigid and hierarchical by nature.

The danger posed by racial classifications, as the Court said in *Shaw*, is especially serious when the question is the distribution of political power—the good that ultimately determines the allocation of all other social goods. "Racial classifications" with respect to voting carry particular dangers," Justice O'Connor noted. "Racial gerrymandering, even for remedial purposes, may balkanize us into competing racial factions . . . [carrying] us further from the goal of a political system in which race no longer matters."[114] It is a point that Justice Thomas reiterated at length in *Holder v. Hall*: "Our drive to segregate political districts by race," he said, "can only serve to deepen racial divisions by destroying any need for voters or candidates to build bridges between racial groups or to form voting coalitions."[115]

No decisions this past term were more important than those involving race-driven districting. If the Supreme Court had overturned the judgments of the lower courts in the Louisiana and Georgia cases, it would have signed on to a badly mistaken notion of American society—one that sees white racial attitudes as little changed since the 1960s; a racial divide that creates two nations, separate and unequal; blacks as politically ex-

---

Ct. 2097 (1995), it is "irrelevant whether a government's racial classifications are drawn by those who wish to oppress a race or by those who have a sincere desire to help those thought to be disadvantaged." *Id.* at 2119 (Thomas, J., concurring). Blumstein's article contains a good discussion of the point that racial classifications are, in themselves, an evil; their impact is not the issue. Blumstein, *Racial Gerrymandering*, *supra* note 96, at 522.

[114] Shaw v. Reno, 113 S. Ct. 2816, 2832 (1993).

[115] Holder v. Hall, 114 S. Ct. 2581, 2599 (Thomas, J., concurring).

cluded and thus in need of extraordinary protection from white competition. If embraced by the law in subsequent decisions, that view will perpetuate and encourage group-think. Ours is still a nation of individual citizens, not a confederation of racial and ethnic groups. But we need the Court's help to stay the course.

OPINION/ESSAYS

Go Back to the Drawing Board To Make More Votes Count

By John B. Anderson

IN rejecting Rep. Cynthia McKinney's congressional district as a "racial gerrymander" in September 1994, two federal judges made a remarkable statement in their majority opinion: "The time has come to contemplate more innovative means of ensuring minority representation in democratic institutions... Georgia's [legislature] owes its citizens new solutions."

Now these same judges have imposed a new plan on Georgia that eliminates two of the state's three congressional districts with majorities of black voters. In a state that is more than one-quarter black, the number of blacks in the 13-member congressional delegation quite possibly will be reduced from three to one, as was true in the 1980s. With challenges to majority-minority congressional districts under way in New York, Illinois, Florida, Virginia, Louisiana, North Carolina, and Texas, the Georgia ruling opens the floodgates to changes in numerous congressional districts that would result in black and Latino representatives being replaced by whites.

Most Americans do not benefit from a two-party system in congressional elections.

The Georgia plan hardly suggests an "innovative" and "new" approach to minority representation, but then again, a 1967 law mandating that states use single-seat congressional districts prevented the judges from pursuing the only truly innovative approach: proportional-voting systems, as used in most of the world's established democracies and in many local elections in the United States.

Systems with multiseat districts (areas with more than one representative) can use various methods, including letting people vote for several candidates, concentrate several votes on one, or rank their preferences. These proportional systems ensure that most voters have a vote that contributes to the election of a candidate. In a five-seat district, the top five candidates would win, so 20 percent of like-minded voters are sure to elect one representative, 51 percent to elect three.

The Center for Voting and Democracy has drafted a plan for Georgia that creates three multiseat districts. It preserves all county lines, provides black voters with a realistic opportunity to help elect three candidates of their choice, and ensures that 70 percent of Georgians would directly elect a representative.

This last fact demonstrates how proportional-voting systems could be the foundation of a new *voters'* rights movement in which black and ethnic minorities would join with the many millions of discontented white voters to establish a lasting foundation for fair representation of those in the majority and the minority. Indeed, the irony of the political and judicial backlash against "voting rights" as now defined is that over 60 percent of eligible voters did not participate in the 1994 congressional elections; over 60 percent of Americans would welcome a viable third party to contest all levels of elections; and over 70 percent disapprove of how Congress is handling its job.

Part of this frustration stems from the

Keeping Things in Proportion

With the winner-take-all system, a 30% black population cannot elect its candidate of choice without significant white support. But if members of Congress were chosen through a proportional system, the top 3 vote-getters in a 3-seat district would win; black voters could elect a representative.

DISTRICT	A (3 seats)	B (3 seats)	C (5 seats)
Population	1,766,641	1,771,873	2,939,522
Pop. per seat	588,880	590,624	587,904
Winning percent*	25.1%	25.1%	16.7%
Nonwhite VAP**	32.6%	27.7%	24.6%

*Percentage of voters needed to elect one representative using cumulative voting or preference voting
**Voting-age population

Source: The Center for Voting and Democracy

fact that because of single-seat districts, most Americans do not experience congressional elections as a two-party system, let alone the multiparty system a majority wants. Rather, most districts simply are not competitive. We are taught the fiction that all elections are up for grabs, but in 1994 2 out of 3 House races were won by landslides of over 20 percent. The fewer than 1 in 7 seats that changed parties was the biggest such change in over 40 years.

This lack of competition is hardly an accident. The challenges to black-majority districts have forced district drawers in several states to explain the extreme steps taken to protect incumbents – steps that increased census data and computer technology make all the more precise. The Texas attorney general recently told the Supreme Court that incumbent protection was far more the cause of "bizarre" district shapes than racial factors, while Texas Rep. Eddie Bernice Johnson (R) testified last year, "[The incumbents] have practically drawn their own districts. Not practically. They have." Indeed, after the Texas redistricting in 1992, 26 of 27 incumbents were reelected. The three "open" seats went to state legislators who drew their districts, and only 1 of 30 races was closer than 10 percent.

Yet voting-rights advocates are forced to defend such gross distortions of the democratic process when they result in majority-minority districts. Instead, by taking what admittedly is a political gamble to support voters' rights through proportional-voting systems, they could seize the moral high ground and find political allies among the majority of voters fed up with their lack of choices in congressional elections. If successful, they would gain a lasting foundation for minority voting rights in a manner analogous to the way in which the universal Social Security coverage better secures the protection of the elderly poor. Giving all voters more credible choices would be far more popular than accepting the confines of an unfair and undemocratic electoral system in which line-drawers have more influence than voters.

Representative McKinney (D) has already taken this bold step. She introduced House Resolution 2545, the Voters' Choice Act, to amend the 1967 statute that mandates single-seat districts, restoring states' power to adopt proportional systems. Those who join McKinney in urging the US to consider proportional systems are impressively diverse, including Alvin Toffler, Ralph Nader, Kevin Philips, Lani Guinier, and the directors of US Term Limits and the National Women's Political Caucus.

Proportional-voting systems could help us build a stronger democracy. They could help avoid political gerrymandering and other methods that work at cross-purposes to the broader goal of national unity constructed on the base of a participatory democracy. They would be predicated more on what voters think and less on political geography and where they happen to live. This, I firmly believe, is the kind of true political reform that America needs.

■ *John B. Anderson is a former Republican member of Congress and independent presidential candidate. He is National Chair of the Center for Voting and Democracy in Washington.*

FACTUAL ERRORS AND CHILLING CONSEQUENCES: A CRITIQUE OF *SHAW V. RENO* AND *MILLER V. JOHNSON*[*]

FRANK R. PARKER[**]

In Mississippi in 1966, just after the Voting Rights Act was passed, there was a majority black congressional district that had been in effect for decades. Because black people in Mississippi could not register and vote, it didn't matter that there was a majority black district—it didn't matter to the white people that there was a majority black legislative district.

This district was called the Delta district. The Voting Rights Act became law in 1965. Black people could register and vote for the first time, and black registration in Mississippi increased from 6.7 percent to about 60 percent within a two year period. In 1966, just a few months after the Voting Rights Act was passed, the Mississippi legislature adopted a new congressional redistricting plan for Mississippi in which it sliced up the majority black Delta District and distributed parts of it among three white majority districts, thereby converting a majority black district into three majority white districts.

This is what *Miller v. Johnson*[1] requires, that the Eleventh Congressional District of Georgia, a majority black district, now has to be sliced up and eliminated. Not only is this result legal and permissible, but it's constitutionally required. The result is kind of like capital punishment. It's easy to be for capital punishment in the abstract, but how many people actually want to watch an execution? These decisions are very damaging for blacks and minority political participation in this country. The Supreme Court seems to be on a tear to eliminate majority black and majority Hispanic districts, and we've only seen the beginning.

Now that the Eleventh District, Cynthia McKinney's district in Georgia, has been declared unconstitutional, the Justice Department has conceded that the Second Congressional District in Georgia, Samford Bishop's district, will not meet the

---

[*] This essay is a revised and edited transcript of remarks delivered at the Conference Commemorating the 30th Anniversary of the Voting Rights Act of 1965 in Birmingham, Alabama on October 10, 1995.

[**] Visiting Professor of Law, American University, Washington College of Law. A.B., Oberlin College, 1962; LL.B., Harvard Law School, 1966.

[1] 115 S. Ct. 2475 (1995).

Shaw v. Reno,[2] *Miller v. Johnson* test. Additionally, the Georgia legislature has passed a new redistricting plan for the state legislature in which it has wiped out fifteen majority black districts—an action that has received very little publicity.

So we are now seeing the first reduction in minority representation in Congress and in state legislatures since the post-reconstruction period. That act is going to have a very chilling effect on race relations in this country, and a very damaging effect on democratic principles in this country.

Now, we must first examine how we got to where we are. How did these majority black districts get there in the first place? It is really a puzzle that North Carolina, Georgia, Louisiana, and Texas, which had been resisting the Voting Rights Act and resisting creating majority black districts for a long period of time, suddenly after the 1990 census would create large numbers of new majority black and Hispanic districts.

How did this happen? This was not a Republican plot. It was not a Justice Department plot, although the Justice Department played a role. It was the result of the Supreme Court's decision in *Thornburg v. Gingles,*[3] the efforts of legislative black caucuses that had become increasingly influential as time went on, Justice Department objections under Section 5 of the Voting Rights Act, the efforts of civil rights lawyers to persuade legislatures to create additional majority black and majority Hispanic districts, and in some cases, the press, which also exerted pressure on state legislators to create these districts.

How did *Thornburg v. Gingles* instigate these districts? Well, you will recall *Thornburg v. Gingles* was decided in 1986 by the Supreme Court, the first decision under Section 2 of the Voting Rights Act as it was amended in 1982.

Thornburg v. Gingles sets out three preconditions for proving a Section 2 violation: 1) can a majority-minority district be created; 2) are minority voters politically cohesive, defined as bloc voting by minority voters; and 3) are minority-preferred candidates usually defeated by white bloc voting?

Now, you don't have to be a rocket scientist to deconstruct that decision and convert it to an if-then statement. If factors two and three are satisfied—if minority voters are politically

---

[2] 113 S. Ct. 2816 (1993).

[3] 478 U.S. 30 (1986).

cohesive and bloc vote for minority-preferred candidates, and number three, if white voters usually bloc vote to defeat minority-preferred candidates—then the failure to create a majority-minority district where one can be created could be a violation of Section 2 of the Voting Rights Act.

Now, today the panelists have characterized this as a very bizarre, radical notion that has never been accepted by the Supreme Court or by anyone. The fact is that seven state legislatures after the 1990 census and federal and state courts in an additional seven states interpreted *Thornburg v. Gingles* to that very end. That, if there was racially polarized voting and minority preferred candidates usually were defeated by white bloc voting, Section 2 of the Voting Rights Act suggested that majority-minority districts should be created if additional ones could be created. Also, there was *Jeffers v. Clinton*[4] (yes, President Clinton, when he was the governor of Arkansas), a Section 2 decision that came down after *Thornburg v. Gingles*, in which a three judge district court supported this very interpretation of *Gingles*, and which was summarily affirmed by the United States Supreme Court.

So that's why state legislatures and federal and state courts doubled the number of majority-minority districts after the 1990 census, from twenty-six to fifty-two. That is why the membership of the Congressional Black Caucus increased 50 percent, the largest increase numerically in American history, and also why the membership of the Hispanic Caucus increased 38 percent.

That is the situation in which we found ourselves when these so-called reverse discrimination cases were filed.

Now, the voters who filed these cases did not file them as injured parties, but as spoilers who filed in order to establish a constitutional principle of colorblind redistricting. You know that this came out of a law school, right, because it was based on principle rather than anyone being injured. So these plaintiffs attempted to establish the principle of colorblind redistricting, and they have been largely successful.

Now, let me mention two fundamental factual errors of the *Miller v. Johnson* decision, which as far as I can tell, no one has pointed out, especially in print. I bring up these fundamental factual errors in *Miller v. Johnson* to show the haste with which the Supreme Court is deciding the cases, the lack of any

[4] 730 F. Supp. 196 (E.D. Ark. 1989), *aff'd mem.*, 498 U.S. 1019 (1991).

real deliberation, and the lack of any real understanding of what the Supreme Court is dealing with.

There are two fundamental factual errors of *Miller v. Johnson.* First, the Court in *Miller v. Johnson* says: "The State does not argue, however, that it created the Eleventh District to remedy past discrimination, and with good reason: there is little doubt that the State's true interest in designing the Eleventh District was creating a third majority-black district to satisfy the Justice Department's preclearance demands."[5] This assertion is wrong. The Eleventh District was not the "third majority-black district." The Second District was the third majority black district. Both of the prior plans that the Georgia state legislature submitted to the Justice Department, to which the Justice Department objected because the third majority-black district had not been created, created a majority-black Eleventh District in east-central Georgia. In both of those plans there was an Eleventh Congressional District, which was about sixty percent black and which occupied approximately the same territory that the final Eleventh District occupied.

There was one major difference. In the two previous plans, the second majority black district, that is, the Eleventh District, went over to Macon rather than Savannah. The only difference was that in the third plan, a third majority black district called the Second District was created out of the Macon area and the Eleventh District went over to Savannah.

But the black population percentage which the Supreme Court now says is the critical factor was essentially the same. I don't think anyone has really emphasized that this is a major factual error that fundamentally affects the decision.

The second major factual error has to do with the question of a community of interest. This is somewhat more debatable, but I think it's a major factual error. In *Miller v. Johnson,* the Supreme Court says basically that it is ridiculous to think of the Eleventh Congressional District as a community of interest.

The Court cites the testimony of Timothy O'Rourke, who is a repeat expert witness for defendants in voting rights cases: "The evidence was compelling 'that there are no tangible "communities of interests" spanning the hundred of miles of the Eleventh District.'"[6] Now, what this completely ignores is

---

[5] *Miller,* 115 S. Ct. at 2490.

[6] *Miller,* 115 S. Ct. at 2490 (quoting Miller v. Johnson, 864 F. Supp. 1354, 1389-90

the testimony of a black professor of history, Dr. Marsha Darling, who did an extensive study of the area encompassed by the Eleventh Congressional District and delivered a paper and expert testimony at the trial indicating that indeed the Eleventh Congressional District in Georgia did encompass a community of interest. She testified that black people who grew up in the rural areas of east-central Georgia, after they graduated from high school and went looking for jobs, would go to Atlanta and Savannah looking for jobs. They would still have family members in the rural counties where they grew up. They would sometimes come back to go to church there. But the population of the district, even though it encompassed urban areas in the Atlanta suburbs and Savannah and very rural counties, nevertheless had a community interest of black people that was very strong, and black people stayed in that particular area.

Her testimony was completely ignored by the District Court and completely ignored by the United States Supreme Court. This just shows that *Miller* is a result-oriented decision. The Supreme Court is not concerned about what the evidence is in these cases. They just want to reach a particular result.

Now, there is a dispute even among the panelists here today on what the harm is and what the injury is from creating majority-black and majority-Hispanic districts. I find it fascinating that even Katharine Butler and Professor Blumstein can't agree on what the injury is, or even if you need to show an injury at all. As I understand Professor Butler's comments,[7] she says that no showing of injury is required. Well, you have to read *United States v. Hays*,[8] because that decision denies standing to white voters who live outside the challenged congressional district because they weren't injured. So Professor Butler's position that no showing of injury is required is inconsistent, to say the least, with the Supreme Court's decision in *Hayes*.

Now, as I understand Professor Blumstein's position, it is that the injury is purposeful discrimination—that this is essentially the problem and the wrong under *Shaw v. Reno* and *Miller v. Johnson*. The problem I have with that explanation is

(S.D. Ga. 1994)).

[7] Katharine I. Butler, *Affirmative Racial Gerrymandering: Rhetoric and Reality*, 26 CUMB. L. REV. 313, 340-41 (1996).

[8] 115 S. Ct. 2431 (1995).

that in neither case did the plaintiffs allege or prove racially discriminatory purpose or effect. In fact, in *Shaw v. Reno*, the Supreme Court clearly said a showing of discriminatory purpose was not required. So I don't think that answers the question of what the harm is, or what the injury is.

Interestingly enough, neither of the panelists defending these two decisions argue that the injury is what the Supreme Court itself defined as the injury, and that is racial polarization. In both of these cases, the Supreme Court defined the injury as racial polarization. Both decisions said that the particular danger of racial redistricting is that it may Balkanize us into competing factions, and cause racially polarized thinking: that voters of a particular race "'think alike, share the same political interests, and will prefer the same candidates at the polls.'"[9] "By perpetuating stereotypical notions . . . racial gerrymander may exacerbate the very patterns of racial bloc voting, . . ."[10] and racially polarized representation, that elected members are more likely to represent only the members of one racial group rather than their constituency as a whole. That is the Supreme Court's definition of the injury or the harm in both *Shaw v. Reno* and *Miller v. Johnson*.

George Will has taken us a step further in a recent column in the Washington Post and shows how racial redistricting is actually related to the *O. J. Simpson* verdict. George Will in his column says that the *O. J. Simpson* verdict is the result of "the ravages of racial thinking." Will goes on to state that:

> For more than a generation now, public policies such as affirmative action, racial spoils systems and the cult of "diversity" have been teaching the nation that groupthink is virtuous. Such policies have taught this by encouraging identity politics—the politics of thinking that you are but a fragment of the racial or ethnic group to which you belong and you have few if any obligations beyond it.
>
> Such policies have taught this by making it admirable—and lucrative—to identify with grievance groups defined by their resentments of the larger society. Such policies have taught this by accommodating the doctrine of categorical representation—the doctrine that the interests of a group can be understood, empathized with and properly represented only by members of that group. Given all this, it is not surprising that the jurors had no pangs of conscience about regarding Simpson

[9] *Miller*, 115 S. Ct. at 2486 (quoting Shaw v. Reno, 113 S. Ct. 2816, 2827 (1993)).

[10] *Shaw*, 113 S. Ct. at 2818.

> merely as a member of a group—and not seeing his victims at all. People who think "race-conscious remedies" for this or that can be benign are partly to blame.[11]

Forget Rodney King, Denny's, Shoney's, the Aryan Nation, the Ku Klux Klan, and Mark Fuhrman. It is racial redistricting that caused the *O. J. Simpson* verdict. This, I think, is the *reductio ad absurdum* of the argument that racial polarization is caused by racial redistricting.

Ladies and gentlemen, "The Emperor has no clothes." There is no more proof that racial redistricting causes racially polarized thinking and racial stereotypes, racial bloc voting or representational harms than there is proof that racial redistricting caused the *O. J. Simpson* verdict. There is no empirical evidence that creating majority-black and majority-Hispanic districts has any impact on racial bloc voting, has any impact on whether whites vote for whites or blacks vote for blacks, or has any impact on how representatives elected from white and black districts represent or serve the members of their constituency.

Even the Supreme Court seems to concede this point by not stating categorically in positive statements that racial redistricting causes racial bloc voting or the other factors. But as Professor Karlan points out in her paper,[12] what the Supreme Court says is that racial redistricting may Balkanize us, separate us into competing factions, and may exacerbate patterns of racial bloc voting. The Supreme Court is not even sure that this is true. There is no evidence to support it, and when cases come along out of the racial context, the Supreme Court characterizes such allegations as conjectural, or wholly speculative; and says there is no injury, therefore there's no standing. Also, there is not even an Article III case or controversy because there's no injury.

It's interesting that neither Professor Butler nor Professor Blumstein, who are defending *Miller* and *Shaw*, has attempted to defend the notion that racial redistricting causes racial polarization in any way.

Now, the presumption of representational harm, which is imbedded in these decisions, is very interesting. You know that confused Supreme Court decisions sometimes have unintended consequences. I think Professor Karlan has brilliantly in her

---

[11] George F. Will, *Circus of the Century*, WASH. POST, Oct. 4, 1995, at A25.

[12] Pamela S. Karlan, *Still Hazy After All These Years: Voting Rights in the Post-Shaw Era*, 26 CUMB. L. REV. 287, 311 (1996).

paper shown how confused these Supreme Court decisions are. Let me simply talk about one of the unintended—I think—consequences of these confused decisions.

The Supreme Court in both *Shaw* and *Miller* says that racial redistricting raises the danger that elected officials are more likely to represent only the members of one racial group rather than their constituency as a whole. The Court says that there is a presumption or an assumption from racial redistricting that black or Hispanic members of Congress elected from black or Hispanic districts will represent only the black or Hispanic voters who voted for them. Now this is amazing, because this is the first time the Supreme Court has ever indulged this presumption, and the effect of the indulgence of this presumption is to completely re-open the debate on proportional representation. Lani Guinier, where are you when we need you? This assertion opens the debate on proportional representation. The reason is that in every prior case, including *Whitcomb v. Chavis*,[13] *White v. Regester*,[14] and *Davis v. Bandemer*,[15] the Supreme Court said again and again there is no constitutional right to proportional representation because we assume that the representative who is elected from a particular district will serve the constituency as a whole and not merely the voters who elected him or her.

Proportional representation must be rejected because there is no harm. Because if the member of Congress elected from the district is assumed to represent all of the people, there is no need for proportional representation. Only when plaintiffs can prove a lack of adequate representation is the Equal Protection Clause triggered. *Davis v. Bandemer* is the clearest statement of this, in which Justice White in his opinion said,

> An individual or a group of individuals who votes for a losing candidate is usually deemed to be adequately represented by the winning candidate, and to have as much opportunity to influence that candidate as other voters in the district. We cannot presume in such a situation, without actual proof to the contrary, that the candidate elected will entirely ignore the interests of those voters. This is true even in a safe district where the losing group loses election after election. Thus, a group's electoral power is not unconstitutionally diminished by the simple fact of an apportion-

[13] 403 U.S. 124 (1971).

[14] 412 U.S. 755 (1973).

[15] 478 U.S. 109 (1986).

> ment scheme that makes winning elections more difficult, and a failure of proportional representation alone does not constitute impermissible discrimination under the Equal Protection Clause.[16]

This is a fundamental argument against proportional representation.

Now the Supreme Court has gone the other way, and is now willing to indulge the presumption that a person elected from a congressional district will represent only the race of the voters who elected him or her. Therefore, we now must reexamine the whole issue of proportional representation. Now we need to have every racial group in this country represented because we are no longer willing to indulge the assumption that whoever is elected will represent the entire constituency rather than simply the group that elected him or her. Every district is racially identifiable; we have white districts, we have black districts, we have Hispanic districts, and every one is racially identifiable. If this presumption is correct, the Supreme Court now must require proportional representation. Only then can each political and racial group get representation that is responsive to its interests. I'm sure this is an unintended consequence, but it does re-open the debate in a major way.

We have discussed the damaging impact on state legislatures, who now don't know what to do. State legislatures don't know whether to create majority-black districts or not create majority black districts. If they follow *Thornburg v. Gingles* or follow the Justice Department's objections, they have to create majority black districts. If they do create majority black districts, then they are subjected to *Shaw v. Reno* lawsuits. So we have conflicting obligations. Professor Karlan described this as walking a tight rope.

In my article I use the term "double bind."[17] Now I don't know if you're familiar with the term double bind. It's actually a psychiatric term, double bind. It's approximately equivalent to a dilemma. Double binds occur in families and are characteristic of families containing schizophrenic members. The parent is perceived by the patient as emitting signals of an incongruent nature. "The parent will, for example, invite the patient to express a courageous opinion, and when that

---

[16] *Bandemer*, 478 U.S. at 132.

[17] Frank R. Parker, *The Constitutionality of Racial Redistricting: A Critique of* Shaw v. Reno, 3 D.C. L. REV. 1, 47 (1995).

opinion is expressed, will disparage it as unloving, disloyal, disobedient, etc."[18] The result is that it produces what is called schizo phrenogenic families, where everyone in the family is schizophrenic, because everyone is being subjected to conflicting duties and conflicting obligations.

You cannot treat only individuals for schizophrenia within that family, you have to treat the entire family. This is what the Supreme Court is doing. The Supreme Court is saying, create majority black districts. And you create majority black districts. And they say, no, no, no, that's unconstitutional, you're violating the Equal Protection Clause. So if you've been feeling a little schizophrenic recently, blame the Supreme Court.

---

[18] ROBERT J. CAMPBELL, PSYCHIATRIC DICTIONARY 93 (1989).

Commentary

Making sense out of the way we should vote

The first time Luis Gutierrez took me for a tour of his political turf we lunched, at his urging, not on *arroz y gandules* but on *pierogis* and *kolacky* at his favorite lunch counter just off Division Street. That told me Gutierrez realized the voters he wanted to put in his pocket were just as important as the ones who were already there.

He was the brand new alderman of the 26th Ward, the beneficiary of a federal court order that some wards be redrawn to boost Hispanic representation.

He is a congressman now, the beneficiary once again of favorable rulings from the court and the voters. His hold on his district seems secure, in part because he has been adept at reaching across ethnic constituencies.

Gutierrez could probably represent any Democratic district in the country. But face it — he is seen as an Hispanic congressman in a district that was drawn for the sole purpose of electing him, or someone like him.

Why else would a district take a big gulp of heavily Hispanic precincts on the Northwest Side, snake out west along a path no more than a few blocks wide until it touches the DuPage County border, turn around and follow forests and the Eisenhower Expressway—but avoid as many real people as possible—

R. Bruce Dold

safely reaches the heavily Hispanic precincts of the Southwest Side?

This cuts to one of the messiest unresolved issues in American politics. Is it constitutionally permissable, and morally proper, to create congressional districts solely to promote minority representation?

Last month, a panel of federal judges decided that Gutierrez' Rorschach test of a district met the standard. But it is a ruling written in sand. It will be appealed, and there is every reason to think that the U.S. Supreme Court will find that his district doesn't cut it at all.

Last year, the Supreme Court ruled 5-4 that race cannot be the predominant factor in crafting district boundaries without a compelling government reason. The court sort of hinted at what reasons would be compelling. This provided as much clarity on race and politics as Justice Potter Stewart once did on obscenity.

The Supreme Court might shed more light on its thinking when it rules later this year on remap cases out of Texas and North Carolina. But don't count on it. In the meantime, remap follies have reached epic proportions.

In Georgia, everyone except Jimmy Carter's barber seemingly has had a hand in drawing the lines. The legislature drew two maps, but the Justice Department rejected them. So the legislature drew a map that made the Justice Department happy, but it was shot down by the Supreme Court in that 5-4 ruling. When the legislature couldn't agree on another map, federal judges drew one themselves. The American Civil Liberties Union challenged that map, but the Supreme Court a couple of months ago turned a deaf ear to the challenge.

Confused? So is everybody else.

Now keep this in mind. In just a few years, a new census count will set off another round of mapmaking, and a new round of court fights. It will be particularly delicate in Illinois because the state is likely to lose another congressional district.

Two certainties emerge from this mess. Racial gerrymandering isn't serving well the people it is intended to serve, and the Supreme Court is heading, in fits and starts, toward abolishing it altogether.

Gerrymandering has modestly increased black and Hispanic representation in Congress, but at a cost. By packing blacks and Hispanics, traditionally Democrats, into certain districts, the Democratic hold on other districts has weakened. That contributed to the Democrats' recent loss of control of the House for the first time in 40 years.

It has also contributed to a Balkanization of national and local politics. One result is that politicians who have little or no minority presence in their districts are less likely to show much concern for minority issues.

The only thing worse than continuing the Balkanization of politics fostered by gerrymandering would be a Supreme Court-ordered wholesale disenfranchisement of minorities.

That's a very real possibility. The ridiculous lengths to which some states went to draw minority districts have given the Supreme Court the ammunition to force a halt. Even if the high court has a change of heart or membership, the deep divisions on the issue are likely to continue the legal uncertainty for years.

There's a way to protect minority interests and avoid these wild gyrations in mapmaking.

The Center for Voting and Democracy, headed by former U.S. Rep. John Anderson, is promoting a whole different way of voting. Congressional districts would be greatly enlarged and several

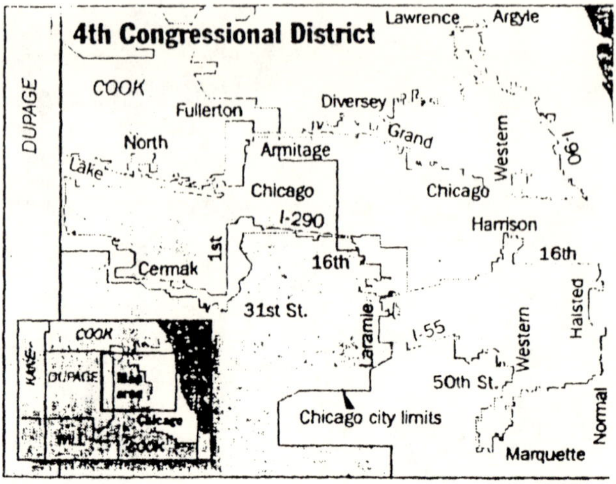

Chicago Tribune

members would be elected from each district through "cumulative" voting.

Illinois used to choose the legislature that way, and the system contributed some of the smartest, most independent legislators the state has ever had. Since cumulative voting was abandoned, the legislature has become more partisan, mean-spirited and prone to blindly follow the demands of its leadership.

Cumulative voting works like this. If five members were to be elected from a district, voters would have five votes to cast. They could parcel them out as they wish: five votes for one candidate, one vote for five candidates, or some mix in between.

Such a plan would recognize and reward ethnic and racial blo voting, but rid the country of gerrymandering schemes that one federal court panel likened to "racial apartheid."

And that would be a very healthy thing.

COMMENTARY

NOT "WRONGFUL" BY ANY MEANS: THE COURT'S DECISIONS IN THE REDISTRICTING CASES

Carol M. Swain[*]

It is an honor to be here at the University of Houston Law Center and to have been chosen to serve as a commentator for Professor Pamela Karlan's very incisive paper in which she criticizes the United States Supreme Court for its lack of a coherent theory of politics.[1] In keeping with the tenor of Professor Karlan's own work, I will try in my remarks to offer a few crisp, cogent arguments.

Professor Karlan by no means is alone in her concerns about the Court's inability to expound adequate theories to explain what many believe to be conflicting decisions. A number of other legal scholars are likewise troubled by the Court's decisions in the voting rights cases. Anthony Peacock, for example, argues that the Court is in a quandary because of its inability to reconcile the "results-oriented" Voting Rights Act with the protections afforded individuals under the more "race-neutral" Equal Protection Clause of the Fourteenth Amendment.[2] It is the Court's inability to reconcile competing notions of equality that has led to the string of five to four decisions against race-conscious districting that began with *Shaw v. Reno* (*Shaw I*).[3]

---

* Associate Professor of Politics and Public Affairs, Woodrow Wilson School, Princeton University; B.A., Roanoke College, 1983; M.A., Virginia Polytechnic & State University, 1984; Ph.D., University of North Carolina, 1989.

1. *See* Pamela S. Karlan, *Just Politics? Five Not So Easy Pieces of the 1995 Term*, 34 HOUS. L. REV. 289 (1997).

2. *See* Anthony A. Peacock, Shaw v. Reno *and the Voting Rights Conundrum: Equality, the Public Interest, and the Politics of Representation*, *in* AFFIRMATIVE ACTION AND REPRESENTATION: SHAW V. RENO AND THE FUTURE OF VOTING RIGHTS (forthcoming 1997).

3. 509 U.S. 630 (1993).

Professor Karlan is on the mark when she draws parallels between the issues at stake in *Romer v. Evans*,[4] the gay and lesbian rights case, and those that consumed the Court in *Gomillion v. Lightfoot*.[5] In these cases, the majority group was about to strip voters of political rights that they already had exercised under the law.[6] For the Court to have ruled against the plaintiffs would have led to major retrogressions in the political status of both groups.

While I agree with many of Professor Karlan's arguments, we part company on the redistricting issues. I do not agree that the redistricting cases have been decided wrongfully, that the Court has been as inconsistent on these matters as many hold, or that minority voters somehow have been harmed by the Court's decision to subject racial gerrymandering to strict scrutiny.[7] In my opinion, the Court has dealt no fatal blows to minority voters. On the contrary, I believe that its decisions in the voting rights area have enhanced the likelihood that blacks and Hispanics will obtain more meaningful representation from a much broader group of elected officials.

Indeed, there is much to applaud in the Court's recent voting rights decisions, and one fact must be established beyond a doubt: contrary to what many civil rights lawyers and activists have predicted, the Court has not moved to invalidate the Voting Rights Act of 1965.[8] Rather, in *Bush v. Vera*,[9] the Court explicitly affirmed its support for that legislation and for the creation of majority-minority districts that meet its criteria as outlined in *Thornburg v. Gingles*.[10] Under the *Gingles* criteria, states are compelled to create majority-minority districts whenever and wherever a geographical area contains a large, compact minority population of sufficient size to constitute a majority in a single-member district.[11] The group must vote in a politically cohesive

---

4. 116 S. Ct. 1620 (1996).

5. 364 U.S. 339 (1960).

6. *See Romer*, 116 S. Ct. at 1623-24 (addressing the constitutionality of Amendment 2 to the Colorado Constitution, which was passed essentially to overturn the voting successes of gays and lesbians "in various Colorado municipalities"); *Gomillion*, 364 U.S. at 340-42 (discussing the validity of Local Act No. 140, passed by the Alabama Legislature in 1957, which redefined the boundaries of the City of Tuskegee for the purpose of disenfranchising black voters).

7. *See Shaw I*, 509 U.S. at 644-49 (stating that Supreme Court precedent supports the conclusion "that redistricting legislation that is so bizarre on its face that it is 'unexplainable on grounds other than race'" requires strict scrutiny analysis (quoting Arlington Heights v. Metropolitan Housing Dev. Corp., 429 U.S. 252, 266 (1977))).

8. 42 U.S.C. § 1973 (1994).

9. 116 S. Ct. 1941 (1996).

10. 478 U.S. 30 (1986).

11. *See id.* at 50.

manner and be able to demonstrate that its candidates of choice have been defeated regularly by white voters who vote in blocs.[12]

In *Vera*, the Court reaffirmed its support for the nonretrogression standard articulated in *Beer v. United States*,[13] which has been interpreted to mean that an electoral change cannot leave minority voters worse off than they are now.[14] Therefore, *Vera*'s value to minority voters and incumbents is unmistakable. In those regions of the country where dwindling populations have meant the loss of congressional seats, minority incumbents are afforded an extra measure of protection from being redistricted out of their seats, even when their districts have lost significant population. Far from striking down the Voting Rights Act, the Court majority in *Vera* reaffirmed its support for that legislation and for the nonretrogression standard that serves to protect minority incumbents.[15]

Beginning with the first *Shaw* case, the Court has struck down majority-minority districts that have failed the first prong of the *Gingles* test. The districts invalidated have been those that have sprawled for miles and miles, from one end of the state to the other, collecting pockets of minority voters while carefully avoiding enclaves of whites.[16] The jagged contours of the invalidated districts indicated to the Court that a compact minority population simply was not present.[17]

Proponents of the invalidated districts have tried unsuccessfully to sway the Court with "yes, but" arguments—yes, the challenged districts are not geographically compact, they have argued, but, if it were not for our desire to adhere to other districting criteria, we might have drawn more compact districts that could have met the *Gingles* test.[18]

12. *See id.* at 51.

13. 425 U.S. 130 (1976).

14. *See* Miller v. Johnson, 115 S. Ct. 2475, 2483 (1995).

15. *See Vera*, 116 S. Ct. at 1963 (plurality opinion) (interpreting the nonretrogression standard to require "that the minority's *opportunity* to elect representatives of its choice not be diminished . . . by the State's actions").

16. *See Vera*, 116 S. Ct. at 1954-60 (plurality opinion) (describing three unusually shaped legislative districts in Texas); Shaw v. Hunt (*Shaw II*), 116 S. Ct. 1894, 1900-01 (1996) (stating that North Carolina's District 12, which was drawn on the basis of race, was "dubbed the least geographically compact district in the Nation"); Miller v. Johnson, 115 S. Ct. 2475, 2484-85 (1995) (noting that a Georgia redistricting plan "split" and "gouged" certain voting populations in an effort to create majority-black districts).

17. *See, e.g.*, *Vera*, 116 S. Ct. at 1958-59 (plurality opinion).

18. *See, e.g.*, *id.* at 1960-64. In *Vera*, the State of Texas proffered "three compelling interests" to justify its creation of three majority-minority districts: "[T]he interest in avoiding liability under the 'results' test of VRA § 2(b), the interest in remedying past and present racial discrimination, and the 'nonretrogression' principle of VRA § 5 (for District 18 only)." *Id.* at 1960. In a plurality opinion, the Court

Professor Karlan points out that minorities confront a special disadvantage in drawing compact districts because other interests control the redistricting process. "Within the political sphere," she argues, "the Court's decisions in *Vera* and *Shaw II* do to blacks and Hispanics something very much like what Colorado tried to do to gays."[19] Because minorities traditionally have not controlled the redistricting process, it is unlikely, she fears, that they will be positioned to draw their districts before other more powerful interests intervene.[20] I am sympathetic with her concerns on this matter. Still, they may be overblown.

The Court's ruling in *Vera* gives minorities stronger standing to assert their claims for compact minority districts. By ruling that state governments have a "compelling state interest" to comply with section 2 of the Voting Rights Act,[21] the Court has established a basis for accountability in those geographical areas where districts can be drawn that will meet the *Gingles* criteria. In the next round of redistricting, therefore, minority voters should be able to assert their legal rights and demand that states comply with the law by drawing reasonably compact minority districts in places where the size and distribution of the minority population warrants it. The incumbency protection crowd that dominated the redistricting process in states like North Carolina and Texas, and prevented the drawing of minority districts, should lose much of its force in the future. State governments that desire to comply with the law of the land will draw their minority districts first. Drawing minority districts first should not be a major problem in the South, where Republicans, now in control of many state governorships and legislatures, are especially fond of minority districts.[22]

Voting rights activists, I believe, have overstated their case against the Court. African-Americans and Hispanics have not been harmed by the Court's redistricting decisions. Despite dire predictions to the contrary, Congress has not been "'bleach[ed].'"[23] Minority legislators, in fact, performed much

---

rejected these arguments and struck down the Texas districts as unconstitutional. *See id.* at 1964.

19. *See* Karlan, *supra* note 1, at 308.

20. *See id.*

21. *See Vera*, 116 S. Ct. at 1960 (plurality opinion).

22. *See GOP Victory Will Keep DOJ in Mainstream*, DOJ ALERT, Dec. 5, 1994, at 7, 7-8.

23. *See* Kevin Sack, *Victory of 5 Redistricted Blacks Recasts Gerrymandering Disputes*, N.Y. TIMES, Nov. 23, 1996, at Y1, Y8 (1996) (quoting Laughlin McDonald, the director of the Southern regional office of the ACLU, who predicted that the Supreme Court's decisions in *Shaw II* and *Vera* would cause a "'bleaching of Con-

better than was predicted during the 1996 elections, as black Democrats who stood for re-election in invalidated districts were returned to office by respectable margins. It is significant that Georgia Representatives Cynthia McKinney and Sanford Bishop avoided runoff primaries and garnered a third of the white vote in their general elections;[24] indeed, Bishop and McKinney won about the same percentage of the white vote that other Georgia Democrats won.[25] According to University of Georgia political scientist Charles Bullock III, black Georgia Democrats now perform about as well as white Georgia Democrats.[26] Louisiana Representative Cleo Fields, the only black Democrat not to be re-elected,[27] chose not to run for re-election in his new district.[28]

Every indication suggests that racial polarization in the United States is declining, even in the South. Given the predominance of black voters in Democratic primaries, black candidates stand a realistic chance of winning Democratic nominations and attracting enough white votes to win general elections. The prospects, therefore, of electing additional minority candidates from majority-white constituencies is anything but dismal.

There is, indeed, reason for optimism. Despite the ugly history of race relations in the South, the first blacks to serve in Congress from that region during this century were elected in majority-white districts. In the early 1970s, Tennessee Representative Harold Ford and Georgia Representative Andrew Young were elected in districts that had clear white majorities, and Texas's Barbara Jordan and her successors were elected in a district that was not majority black.[29] In fact, Barbara Jordan's district had almost equal percentages of blacks, Hispanics, and whites, with no single group constituting a majority.[30] And

---

gress'").

24. *See* Salim Muwakkil, *Holding Pattern*, IN THESE TIMES, Dec. 9, 1996, at 18, 19.

25. *See* Charles S. Bullock, *Incumbency, Not Race, Wins in the South*, NEWSDAY, Nov. 13, 1996, at A41.

26. *See* Charles S. Bullock, *The South in the House*, Extension of Remarks, Dec. 1996 (unpublished paper on file with author).

27. *See* Clarence Page, *Results Are Deceptive in Redrawn Black Districts*, HOUS. CHRON., Dec. 1, 1996, at 3C.

28. *See id.*

29. *See* Jamie B. Raskin, Comment, *Affirmative Action and Racial Reaction*, 38 HOW. L.J. 521, 533 (1995) ("[I]n the history of the United States from the post-Reconstruction era through 1990, only three African Americans—Andrew Young, Barbara Jordan, and Harold Ford—have been elected to the House from a southern district in which whites were in a majority.").

30. *See* Laughlin McDonald, Holder v. Hall*: Blinking at Minority Voting Rights*, 3 D.C. L. REV. 61, 92 & n.219 (1995).

although the eighteenth district of Texas has consistently sent blacks to Congress, voting rights activists sought to increase its black voting-age population to fifty-one percent.[31] No wonder the Court rejected the contention of the voting rights activists that the district needed a black majority to continue to elect black politicians.

Some activists are clinging to the hope that President Clinton will have an opportunity to appoint a liberal judge to the Supreme Court who will help reverse the trend of what they see as a string of hostile antiminority rulings. If this happens, instead of the spate of five to four decisions against affirmative action and racial gerrymandering, we might all look forward to five to four decisions in their favor. Whatever the courts do in regard to redistricting, it is clear that minorities need options that extend beyond the limited number of additional majority-minority districts that can be drawn.

One of these options is to elect more minority politicians in nonpacked minority districts. Policy makers have some latitude concerning the size of the minority population that they place in particular districts. Often districts are packed in a manner that wastes black votes and black influence.[32] Recent research by Columbia University Professors Charles Cameron, David Epstein, and Sharyn O' Halloran demonstrates that black representation in Congress can be maximized by creating districts that are less than fifty percent black.[33] These authors calculated the optimal level of black voting-age population (BVAP) needed to give black candidates and black voters a realistic chance to increase their descriptive and substantive representation.[34] According to their findings, the optimal level of BVAP is forty-seven percent in the South, with the excess voters distributed across other districts;[35] only a twenty-eight BVAP was needed in the northeast.[36] Their findings suggest that creative districting strategies exist that can comply with *Gingles* and simultaneously augment minority representation.

---

31. *See Vera*, 116 S. Ct. at 1950-51, 1958 (plurality opinion) (stating that, in response to the 1990 census, "the Texas Legislature promulgated a redistricting plan that, among other things . . . reconfigured District 18 . . . to make it a majority-African-American district").

32. *See* CAROL M. SWAIN, BLACK FACES, BLACK INTERESTS: THE REPRESENTATION OF AFRICAN AMERICANS IN CONGRESS 210-11 (1993).

33. *See* Charles Cameron et al., *Do Majority-Minority Districts Maximize Substantive Black Representation in Congress?*, 90 AM. POL. SCI. REV. 794 (1996).

34. *See id.* at 794, 800-10.

35. *See id.* at 808.

36. *See id.*

Minority representation itself should be viewed by the voting rights community as something much broader than the representation that takes place when voters and legislators share skin pigmentation. The Supreme Court and the Justice Department have never stated that representation requires that politicians share the same skin color as the district majority. Instead, the Court has spoken of enhancing the ability of minorities to impact public policies by electing candidates of their choice. When representation is defined more broadly than shared race, then there is evidence to suggest that political party or, more specifically, whether a Democrat is in office, is as important as the race of the representative. In fact, there is evidence to suggest that this is more important. Given the way minorities define their policy preferences, their substantive interests are best served by the election of more Democrats.[37]

In short, minorities are in a win-win situation when they are positioned to influence more legislators than the handful they can elect when packed in oversized majority-minority districts. Their ability to influence more legislators has been enhanced by the Court's decisions in the redistricting cases. Put simply, the Court's redistricting decisions have not been wrongly decided.

37. *See* SWAIN, *supra* note 32, at 207-25 (discussing "[t]he dependence of African Americans on Democrats for representation of their interests . . . ."); L. Marvin Overby & Kenneth M. Cosgrove, *Unintended Consequences? Racial Redistricting and the Representation of Minority Interests*, 58 J. POL. 540, 540 (1996) (opining that "since the 1960s [the Republican party] has been less sensitive to civil rights issues than has the Democratic party").

THE CASE FOR PROPORTIONAL REPRESENTATION

ROBERT RICHIE AND STEVEN HILL

Nearly all elections in the United States are based on the winner-take-all principle: voters for the candidate who gets the most votes win representation; voters for the other candidates win nothing. This system is unjust and unnecessary. It is unjust because it leaves minorities (whether racial or political) unrepresented. As John Stuart Mill said, "It is an essential part of democracy that minorities should be adequately represented. No real democracy, nothing but a false show of democracy, is possible without it."[1] It is unnecessary because we have immediate opportunities, at local, state, and national levels, to join the vast majority of mature democracies that have already adopted systems of proportional representation.

Proportional representation (PR) is based on the principle that any group of like-minded voters should win legislative seats in proportion to its share of the popular vote. Whereas the winner-take-all principle awards 100 percent of the representation to a 50.1 percent majority,

• Page number 3 bp0156$$$1 02-14-01 13:21:06

PR allows voters in a minority to win their fair share of representation.

How does this work? A typical winner-take-all system divides voters into "one-seat districts," represented by one person. With PR, voters in a constituency instead have several representatives: ten one-seat districts might, for example, be combined into a single ten-seat district. A party or group of voters that wins 10 percent of the popular vote in this district, then, would win one of the ten seats; a party or slate of candidates with 30 percent of votes would win three seats, and so forth. Various mechanisms work to provide proportional representation, and the details of different systems matter. But the principle of full representation is fundamental. Acceptance of it changes the way one sees electoral politics.

What's the Problem?

Consider three current failures of our winner-take-all system of representation:

- Members of racial and ethnic minorities are underrepresented;
- Voters' choices are restricted to candidates within the two-party, Republican/Democratic monopoly;
- Most legislative elections are effectively "no-choice" contests in districts dominated by a single party.

By restricting voters' choices and underrepresenting voters from minority groups, winner-take-all elections devalue the right to vote, our fundamental democratic right. Correcting these failures requires PR. No other political reform currently on the table—public financing of elections, term limits, fusion, or universal voter registration—will suffice to correct these deficiencies in our democracy.

Representation of Racial Minorities

At every level of government, the proportion of black, Latino, and Asian-American elected officials lags far behind these groups' share of the electorate. When members of a racial or ethnic group make up a majority of the electorate in a winner-take-all election, they tend to elect a member of their racial or ethnic group. Every majority-black U.S. House district has a black representative; and in the 49 white-majority states, 144 of 147 U.S. senators and governors are white (as we write, in September 1998). Most racial minorities clearly prefer representatives of their race, but winner-take-all elections often deny them a realistic opportunity to elect candidates of their choice. A quarter of our population is black or Latino, but these groups are in the minority in every state and as a consequence hold only one of 100 U.S. Senate seats. The fact of such underrepresentation throughout our legislatures undercuts their legitimacy and effectiveness in addressing issues of concern to racial and ethnic minorities.

Two Parties

Winner-take-all elections prop up our two-party monopoly. Since 1960, new parties have formed at comparable rates in the United States and in European democracies using PR. But new parties in the United States are almost completely shut out of representation, whereas half the new parties in the European systems eventually have won seats—and the influence and organizing ability that comes from electoral viability.[2] Polls show most Americans would like to see a third party electing candidates at every level of government, but only three of our nearly eight thousand state and congressional legislators were elected on a minor-party ticket—all of them in Burlington, Vermont.

Minor parties by definition begin with minority support, which wins nothing in winner-take-all elections unless it is geographically concentrated. With little chance to win, minority party candidates cannot build or sustain support. Ross Perot's well-financed independent candidacy in 1992 won 19 percent of the vote, but he did not finish first in any congressional district. In 1996, his vote was reduced by more than half, although one voter in ten still voted for minor-party presidential candidates, and half of all eligible voters saw no reason to participate.

"No-Choice" Elections

One-party dominance of most American legislative districts provides a more subtle, but more sweeping, indictment of our winner-take-all system. Most Americans, most of the time, experience "no-choice" elections for city council, state legislature, and the U.S. House of Representatives. In the last ten House elections, for example, more than 90 percent of incumbents were reelected. The average margin of victory in House races is consistently over 30 percent. More than one-third of state legislative races in the 1990s were not even nominally contested by both major parties; fully 68 percent were not contested in Massachusetts in 1996. So-called "swing" legislative districts feature genuine competition and a chance for voters to cast a meaningful vote, but they are exceptions.

The dominance of one-party districts should be no surprise: gerrymandering allows legislators to choose their constituents in redistricting before their constituents go to the polls to choose representatives. Even though political intentions can be removed from the redistricting process—as in Iowa's criteria-driven procedure, for example—its political effects are unavoidable. Given that some (perhaps most) districts will be noncompetitive in winner-take-all elections, all districting ends up as some form of gerrymandering.

The ramifications of our fundamentally lopsided political landscape are often ignored in debates over term limit proposals and campaign finance reform. The real culprit for noncompetitive elections is winner-take-all elections, not incumbency and inequities in campaign spending. In most districts, a clear majority of voters prefers one party's political philosophy to that of the other party. Consider open-seat elections, with no incumbent competing for the seat, and none of the financial advantages that come with incumbency. In 1996, Republicans won 29 of 35 open House seats in districts where Bill Clinton ran behind his national average, despite being outspent in a third of their victories. Yet Republicans won none of the 18 districts where Clinton ran ahead of his national average, despite being financially competitive in half of those defeats. This trend is not confined to elections in presidential years. Overall, Democrats hold 99 of the 100 U.S. House districts where Clinton ran most strongly in 1996. Of the 150 districts where he ran most weakly, Republicans hold 134.

To be sure, congressional winners usually outspend their opponents. But that is because money follows power: to gain access, most major campaign contributors invest in candidates they expect to win. The great majority of voters are consistent in their voting patterns both between and within elections. We should be relieved that voters are well-grounded in a political philosophy, but frustrated that this consistency leads to most of them experiencing no-choice elections.[3]

Why PR?

Support for PR as an alternative to winner-take-all politics has come from a diverse and distinguished group, including Alexis de Tocqueville, Charles Beard, Walter Lippman, Jane Addams, A. Philip Randolph, Robert Kennedy, and, quietly, Franklin Roosevelt. The most outspoken early supporter of PR was John Stuart Mill, in his *Representative Government* (1861)—written less than two decades after the first works detailing possible PR systems.

The Majoritarian Argument

Perhaps Mill's most important contribution to the case for PR was his argument that majority rule itself is improved by full minority representation. By maximizing the number of voters who elect candidates, he pointed out, PR increases the chances that a legislative majority has support from a majority of voters; it is required for full representation, with voters having the power to elect representatives reflecting a range of opinion; and it fosters a deliberative legislative process which improves the majority view by ensuring that minority opinions are represented and heard.

As Mill observed, any particular majority is a collection of minorities, not a monolithic bloc. Once some voters are excluded from representation, policy can be passed without the support of a majority of the electorate. Suppose, for example, that all representatives win their elections with only 50.1 percent of votes. A law passed with support from only 50.1 percent of the legislators then would have backing from only a quarter of votes cast. Mill's point is no mere theoretical concern. In the 1994 "Republican revolution," in which Democrats lost their 40-year stranglehold on the U.S. House of Representatives, fewer than one in four eligible voters voted for a winning House candidate. As a result, House passage of any particular bill in 1995 required the votes of representatives elected by only 13 percent of eligible voters.

By contrast, legislation in democracies with PR generally requires the support of representatives elected by a far higher percentage of the electorate. In Germany's 1994 elections with PR—with a high turnout and a high percentage of effective votes typical of European PR elections—more than three in four eligible voters elected candidates. (Four in five eligible Germans participated, and 19 in 20 voters elected a representative.) So passage of a bill required the votes of representatives elected by nearly 40 percent of eligible voters.

Majority rule also is undercut by winner-take-all elections because they drive voters into two camps. But two-choice elections obscure shades of difference and create the illusion of majority support for the winner. Mill stressed the importance of voters having a full range of choices and representation of their different communities of interest. "I cannot see," he wrote, "why the feelings and interests which arrange mankind according to localities, should be the only ones thought worthy of being represented." The notion that geography should be the primary basis of representation is even more antiquated now, given the increased mobility of our population, ease of communication across distances, and importance of economic, social, and political associations without geographic definition.

Finally, PR is important for majority interests because, as Mill argued, it provides represented minorities with a platform to challenge conventional wisdom. An advocate of universal suffrage, Mill still was sympathetic to conservative concerns about educated minorities being outvoted by newly enfranchised, less-educated voters. Assuring a voice to the minority eliminated his fears because of his faith in the results of a fully democratic process, with open and organized discussion among competing political ideas and projects. By allowing dissenters to win representation, PR fosters ongoing challenges to majority opinion, and thus complements our First Amendment freedoms.

In conjunction with attack ads, polling, and focus groups, the system of winner-take-all elections has made it extremely difficult to have reasoned political debate on certain contentious issues. These issues can assume great symbolic weight for swing voters—ironically, because they are among the relatively few voters with so little political grounding that they will support either party. The death penalty, for example, has come to represent "toughness" on crime. Because winner-take-all elections make nuanced positions difficult, and require that candidates win the support of politically indifferent swing voters, opponents of the death penalty find it hard to run credible campaigns for president or for most legislative offices. On a whole range of issues—from drug policy to abortion rights to welfare reform—debate in political campaigns tends to be highly stylized, making it that much more difficult to challenge public opinion.

Mill's majoritarian argument for PR gains empirical support from a recent statistical comparison of 12 democracies in Europe.[4] John Huber and G. Bingham Powell contrast a "Proportionate Influence Vision" of democracy, in which "elections are designed to produce legislatures that reflect the preferences of all citizens," with the "Majority Control Vision," in which "democratic elections are designed to create strong, single-party majority governments that are essentially unconstrained by other parties in the policy-making process." They conclude that "governments in the Proportionate Influence systems are on average significantly closer to their median voter than are governments in the Majority Control and Mixed systems. . . . If voters are presented with a wide range of choices and electoral outcomes are proportional, governments tend to be closer to the median."

In short, governance is more likely to take place at the

center of the political spectrum with PR, since the electorate is fully represented and voters are able to express a wider range of preferences. At the same time, fair representation of the margins provides a mechanism to transform policy by shifting the political center. Opposition voices will be heard, and their ideas will be far more likely to be debated. If those ideas win growing support, the major parties will adjust accordingly in order to hold onto their supporters.

Other Reasons for PR

Mill's majoritarian argument is not the only case for PR. Four other claims are commonly offered in its support:

1. PR increases voter turnout. Voter turnout is generally estimated to be 10 to 12 percent higher in nations with PR than in similar nations using winner-take-all elections.[5] This difference is understandable. In the United States, as we indicated, relatively few legislative elections are competitive, and our analysis of recent House elections demonstrates a strong correlation between the degree of competition and the level of participation.[6] People in noncompetitive districts—whether supportive of the majority or minority—might better invest their time and resources by supporting candidates in competitive races elsewhere than by voting in their own. In PR systems, winning fair representation is depen-

dent on voter turnout. Because nearly every vote will help a party win more seats, voters have more incentive to participate, and parties have incentives to mobilize their supporters. Moreover, parties and other electoral organizations have strong incentives to keep their supporters informed, and informed citizens are more likely to vote.

2. PR provides better representation for racial minorities. The 1982 amendments to the Voting Rights Act resulted in more districts drawn with majorities of racial and ethnic minorities. This increase in "majority-minority districts" produced a remarkable leap in representation of people of color in the U.S. House in 1992. Between 1990 and 1992, the number of black and Latino House members jumped from 35 to 55.

In a series of recent rulings against so-called "racial gerrymandering," the Supreme Court has made it much harder to establish majority-minority districts; the result is almost certain to be a decrease in the number of elected black legislators. Lani Guinier, Jesse Jackson, and other civil rights leaders have argued for PR as an alternative, and already more than 75 localities have adopted semi-proportional systems to settle voting rights cases.[7] By building from a fundamental principle of political fairness, PR could secure voting rights of racial minorities, without specifically targeting minority voters (just as Social Security protects low-income seniors by providing benefits for all).

In addition to winning a fair share of seats, minorities would have greater opportunities to negotiate for influence because they could "swing" among parties. South Africa used PR in its first all-race elections in 1994, and the two leading parties—the African National Congress and the National Party—ran multiracial slates with messages of inclusion. When New Zealand had its first PR election in 1996, the first Asian citizen was elected, and Pacific Islanders and indigenous Maoris tripled their representation. A Maori-backed party formed a coalition government with the governing party—a party whose relationship with Maoris had been analogous to Republicans' post-1960 relationship with American blacks.

By improving representation, PR in turn encourages minority communities to mobilize and win access to power. From 1925 to 1955, Cincinnati used the "choice voting" form of PR to elect a nine-seat city council. (See appendix for an explanation of choice voting.) In 1929, when blacks were barely 10 percent of the population, a black independent candidate ran a strong campaign. In the next election, he was added to the Republican party's slate and was elected. In 1947, when blacks were 15 percent of the population, a former president of the Cincinnati NAACP ran in large part to defend the choice voting system that was under attack from Republicans seeking to restore their old domination of the council. In an indication that any substantial group of voters cannot be ignored with PR, the other major party slate supported him in 1949. He was elected, resulting in black representatives holding two of nine seats.[8]

3. PR increases the number of women in office. The percentage of women elected to office in the United States—only 11 percent of the U.S. Congress—is scandalously low, particularly in light of the relative strength of the American women's movement compared to other nations with far higher percentages of women legislators. Studies show that women representatives make a qualitative and quantitative difference in the type of legislation introduced and passed, yet the growth of women in state legislatures and Congress has stalled since 1992 despite relatively high turnover and the historic high in women's candidacies in 1996.

In state legislative elections, women win seats in significantly higher percentages in multiseat districts than in one-seat districts.[9] The major reasons for this difference are that women are more likely to run and voters are more likely to seek gender balance when there is more than one seat to fill. Because PR expands options, PR systems give women additional leverage to force the major parties to support more women candidates. In 1994, a threat by women supporters of the major parties in Sweden to form a new women's party led to women winning 41 percent of seats in 1994 because the major parties recruited more women candidates. New Zealand, Italy, and Germany are among a growing number of democracies that use systems with a mix of winner-take-all districts and PR seats.[10] It is instructive that women in all three countries are three times more likely to win seats elected by PR than to win in one-seat districts.

4. PR ends gerrymandering. Drawing district lines for political purposes has occurred from the first redistricting: the term "gerrymander" refers to a Massachusetts district plan drawn in 1812. But gerrymandering has become far more potent in an era of powerful computers, more detailed census information, and better techniques for measuring voter preferences.

As one example, Democrats in control of the redistricting process in Texas in 1991 placed the eight Republican incumbents in districts that were packed to be among the most conservative in the nation. These incumbents were easily reelected in 1992, but Democrats won 21 of the remaining 22 seats with only 50 percent of the statewide vote. Only one race was won by less than 10 percent, and the three open seats went to state legislators serving on redistricting committees. Congresswoman Eddie Bernice Johnson, the primary architect of the plan, admitted in 1997 that the redistricting process "is not one of kindness. It is not one of sharing. It is a power grab."

PR makes gerrymandering of any sort far more difficult. The smaller the percentage of votes that can be "wasted" on losing candidates—49 percent in a winner-take-all race, but less than 20 percent in a five-seat PR election and less than 10 percent in a 10-seat PR election—the harder it is for legislators to manipulate electoral outcomes.

Progressives Need Multiparty Politics

The case for PR is fundamentally nonpartisan. Voters across the spectrum can support greater democracy or feel poorly represented by winner-take-all elections. But American political progressives have a particularly urgent need to support PR because of the growing problems created by the lack of a serious electoral vehicle to the Democrats' left. Many progressives overrate their current degree of support in the electorate, while others leap in equal error to desperate conclusions about the electorate's likely conservatism. The more complicated reality is disguised by winner-take-all elections, which divide voters into two camps and leave much progressive thought on the margins of political dialogue and influence.

A progressive party that won 5 to 10 percent of legislative seats in PR elections could have a great impact on public discourse, cross-issue organizing, and the policies of the Democratic Party. Electorally, this party could check the Democrats' rightward drift. It would give the base of the Democratic Party—labor, African-Americans, feminists, environmentalists, defenders of civil liberties—a credible alternative, and thus an influence within the Democratic Party similar to that now held by the relatively few "swing" Democrats willing to vote for Republicans. When all voters, not just the centrist fringe, can swing their votes, the major parties must pay more attention to their base.

In addition, a progressive party would provide an opportunity for progressive activists to join together to build an infrastructure of independent politics—work that is very difficult to pursue in a two-party system that pushes activists into single-issue politics.[11] It would give progressives greater access to media and an ongoing means to challenge conventional wisdom. It is one thing for the media to ignore activists who have no strong supporters in Congress; it would be more difficult to ignore a congressional contingent that consistently demonstrated a credible level of national support.

A progressive party would force healthy, if difficult, policy debates among progressives. Winning 10 percent of the vote in a PR system is hard work. The German Greens have never reached 10 percent nationally, yet have had a remarkable impact on German policy and the environmental positions of both major parties. They are partners in governing coalitions in several German states and may soon be part of the national government. At the same time, Greens have made great strides in building coalitions among their members. Organizing a party need not replace other grassroots organizing: a study of German Greens found that over 80 percent of members were active with an organization outside the Greens. But having the Green Party as a unifying electoral presence has made their other work more effective. American progressives urgently need PR to create a similar unifying electoral vehicle.

With PR, a progressive party also could find unexpected allies. Progressives might not outdo conservatives in winning over the majority. But a winner-take-all, two-party system facilitates "divide-and-conquer" strategies in which a conservative party can cut into the potential economically progressive majority with such wedge social issues as gun control, gay rights, affirmative action, and abortion.

In a two-party system, conservatives can create an electoral majority with a set of positions that can be opposed by the majority of voters, but bring together fervent minorities willing to accept positions they oppose in exchange for support for their issue: social liberals seeking low taxes, blue-collar Catholics opposing abortion, labor union members opposing gun control, and so on. With electable choices across the spectrum, a multiparty system based on PR would allow us to find out where the American people really stand—and on many issues, they arguably will stand to the left of current policy. The political center of most of Europe, with its policies on health care, welfare, worker rights, and the environment, is where American progressives would love to be.

The Washington Post

FRIDAY, APRIL 17, 1998 A23

William Raspberry

Superdistricts in North Carolina

DURHAM, N.C.—Remember the North Carolina congressional district denounced by Justice Sandra Day O'Connor as unconstitutionally "bizarre"?

Well, things just got a little bizarrer—perhaps so bizarre that it may finally be possible to do something sensible about a serious issue of electoral equity.

The state legislature's redistricting panel redrew the problem 12th District—the one that used to run 175 miles from Durham to Gastonia and, for a part of that way, was no wider than I-85—in a patent effort to put together enough black voters to elect a member of Congress.

The modified 12th was wider, 73 miles shorter and significantly less black—47 percent as opposed to the 57 percent of the old district. A three-judge federal panel approved it unanimously.

But then Robinson O. Everett, the Duke law professor whose challenge led to the Supreme Court's overturning of the old 12th, challenged the newly drawn one. He won earlier this month, throwing the legislature, the voters and prospective candidates for Rep. Mel Watt's seat into confusion and forcing the postponement of the primary election scheduled for May 5.

Time, emphatically, is not the only problem. The drafters are supposed to satisfy a Justice Department mandate to draw the district boundaries in a way that redresses past anti-black discrimination (Watt and Rep. Eva Clayton, both elected under the plan thrown out by the Supreme Court, were the first blacks elected to Congress from North Carolina since 1901), while also satisfying the court's instruction not to be self-consciously racial about it. And, oh, the districts mustn't look too bizarre on the map.

One more thing: The legislative panel charged with the task is under party pressure not to disturb the present balance of six Republicans and six Democrats now in the North Carolina delegation.

That's the bad news. The good news is that it is possible to achieve political and racial equity while satisfying all the parties and increasing the prospects for civility and cooperation.

The magic? Proportional voting. Under the simplest plan I've seen (from the Center for Voting and Democracy), North Carolina would be divided into four three-member superdistricts instead of the present 12 single-member districts. Voters would be "cumulative"—that is, each voter would have three congressional ballots, one for each seat in the superdistrict. A voter could cast one ballot for each of three candidates, split the three votes between two candidates, or give them all to a single candidate.

The superdistricts would be nicely compact, would avoid any hint of racial (or other) gerrymandering and make quite likely the election of *three* black members to Congress. There's more: Robinson Everett and Mel Watt both like the plan.

I like it too, and for a special reason: It makes interparty cooperation not just possible but almost necessary, because it allows for the coexistence of Republicans and Democrats in the same constituency. Illinois chose its legislature through cumulative voting for some 90 years, ending in 1980, Rob Richie of the Center for Voting and Democracy told me, and—well, listen:

"The fact that you could have both major parties representing the same district was powerfully important. There used to be Republicans representing (largely Democratic) Chicago, for instance, and Democrats elected in the (largely Republican) suburbs. Cooperation was a natural. But look at what's happening now: Chicago voters only elect Democrats, so Republicans are free to demagogue the city on things like support of the schools, knowing it won't cost them anything. You get a lot of city-against-suburb fights that are totally unnecessary. Cumulative voting helps to avoid most of that."

The system, applied to congressional elections, might go a long way toward promoting cooperation across party, racial and other lines, since candidates would have to appeal to a much wider electorate. Demagogues would have a tough time winning.

One little problem: In 1967, Congress enacted legislation requiring single-member districts. But similar legislation had been enacted—and repealed—at least four times in the past. Rep. Cynthia McKinney (D-Ga.), whose district was one of those thrown out by the Supreme Court and redrawn, has introduced legislation to make superdistricts an option. Mel Watt is a co-sponsor.

Maybe it's too much to expect that something so sensible could be done, requiring, as it does, both federal and state action. But when I look at the mess in North Carolina's 12th District, I have to think it's worth a shot.

The Charlotte Observer

rlotte.com FRIDAY, APRIL 24, 1998 + E CAROLINAS EDITION

EDITORIALS

Redistricting

Look beyond political fighting over single-member districts

If you've kept up with the congressional redistricting roller coaster in North Carolina for the past few years, no doubt you're feeling a little queasy. So are we, thanks to the constant turmoil that the federal courts and the U.S. Justice Department have created in their yes-you-can, no-you-can't approach to district sizes, shapes and demographics.

It was the Justice Department under President George Bush that pushed states to draw congressional districts with black majorities wherever possible, requiring the N.C. legislature to draw new districts likely to elect black members of Congress. And it was federal judges who last year said that approach relied too much race in drawing districts. Now the courts have spoken several more times, branding the current set of districts invalid because the legislature still relied too heavily on race when redrawing the 12th District, stretching from Charlotte to Greensboro.

The courts postponed the May 5 congressional primaries and this week gave the legislature until May 22 to redraw districts for a primary to be held Sept. 15. Unless the state and the Justice Department agree by June 24, the court will step in and draw the new districts.

We can think of few things worse than allowing the courts, which have contributed mightily to the confusion over redistricting and to voter disenchantment with politics, to redraw these districts. North Carolina has been caught in the middle of a battle bewtween the Justice Department and the federal courts. The resulting fiasco should persuade legislators that there's a better way to draw congressional districts. They should seriously consider a plan by Rep. John Weatherly, R-Cleveland, to set up an independent redistricting commission to handle legislative and congressional redistricting.

And, for the future, they might look beyond the single-member districts that are at the root of the current fight. Consider the proportional voting plans used with court approval in other states. Such a system could, for example, create four three-member congressional districts to replace the current 12 single-member districts. Voters in the four districts would have three votes each, and could cast all for one candidate or split their votes among two or three candidates.

The districts could be compact and logical, and they could avoid the complications related to trying to satisfy the Justice Department by having enough black residents and the courts by not having too many. The districts wouldn't be drawn with race in mind at all. They would let voters define their interests, even when geography didn't, opening the door to such groups as women, environmentalists, religious conservatives and others who can't be lumped together in single-issue districts.

Granted, it would be a very different congressional redistricting plan — to some voters, bordering on the weird. But given the contradictory directives that have come down from federal judges and federal bureaucrats, it might give voters a much better way to speak up. Like a redistricting commission, some sort of proportional voting sounds radical, but it's worth studying before the 2000 Census starts the fight all over again.

Dred Scott's Unwon Freedom: The Redistricting Cases as Badges of Slavery

By James U. Blacksher

In a half dozen cases decided over the last three terms, beginning with *Shaw v. Reno* (1993) and, most recently, *Abrams v. Johnson* (1997), the Supreme Court has held that congressional districts in North Carolina, Texas, and Georgia, drawn for the predominant purpose of producing black voter majorities, violated the Fourteenth Amendment.

The Court ruled that the states cannot use race in drawing these districts without satisfying new onerous legal burdens that the Supreme Court has decided to impose.The redistricting process is an especially important opportunity for black political association and participation in democratic government. Redistricting legislation is not merely another act of state government. In a real sense, it is not state action at all, so much as it is a bargain struck among the state's democratic constituents. The constitutional requirement that after every decennial census members of the legislature undertake negotiations to reconstitute their electoral base, like the Supreme Court recently said about party conventions, is a state-created framework for the exercise of private political rights. Representatives of the many political associations which constitute the state's body politic are supposed to agree on the new shape of their democratic compact, with the explicit understanding that the resulting district lines will have a powerful effect on the outcomes of elections for the next decade. Arguably, the federal judiciary bears an even greater burden of justifying oversight of the foundationally political redistricting process than its oversight of party activity.

The ability to consent to the laws under which one is governed has always been the essential difference between a free man (women not gaining the franchise until 1919) and a slave in American political tradition and constitutional jurisprudence. This was the principle on which the Supreme Court rested its infamous decision in *Dred Scott v. Sandford*, (1857), that neither black slaves nor their descendants are eligible to be citizens of the United States. The Civil War and adoption of the Thirteenth, Fourteenth and Fifteenth Amendments to the Constitution during Reconstruction reversed the *Dred Scott* ruling that black persons may never be citizens, but they did not reject Chief Justice Taney's basic point, that until African Americans are recognized as equally free peoples and are allowed to consent to the terms of the constitutional covenant they will not be full members of the sovereign nation.

To this day, the Supreme Court perpetuates the constitutional doctrine that the Reconstruction Amendments extended to blacks only equal legal rights, not equal social status and equal political freedom. According to this principle, only a negotiated consent to the constitutional compact can make the citizen a real partner in the democratic enterprise, a full member of the sovereign people, and a coheir of national institutions. The mere grantee of citizenship rights, while entitled to the protection of law, is not recognized as an equal member of the sovereign people or as an author of those rights.

After Reconstruction, in the *Civil Rights Cases* (1883), the Court ruled that the Enforcement Clauses of the Thirteenth and Fourteenth Amendments had not given Congress the authority affirmatively to force whites to accept blacks as social equals, that is, to "establish a code of municipal law regulative of all private rights between man and man in society." Even more importantly, the Court did not consider the exclusion of blacks from private places of business to be one of the badges and incidents of slavery. The Civil War Amendments extended to the freedmen and their descendants only the right to be free from the most onerous legal disabilities. In the Court's view, this was all that was necessary for blacks to enjoy the essence of citizenship, and thus the essential distinction between freedom and slavery.

The dominion of whites was safe, because "Congress did not assume, under the authority given by the Thirteenth Amendment, to adjust what may be called the social rights of men and races in the community . . ." Of course, in that day as in this one, no white American would have accepted a bundle of legal rights as a substitute for freedom from domination by even a benign government not consented to. The first Justice John Marshall Harlan—grandfather of Justice John Marshall Harlan II who served from 1955 - 1971—acknowledged what the Court's majority chose to ignore: the status of blacks, nonmembers of the sovereign community was a badge of slavery more hateful and enduring than any restriction of merely legal privileges. White Americans would retain the exclusive power to decide what citizenship for blacks would mean.

Justice Harlan's famous dissent a decade later in *Plessy v. Ferguson* (1896) is rightly praised for its eloquent defense of the American ideal and the Reconstruction radicals' aspirations that the Civil War Amendments be used to remove all "legal discriminations, implying inferiority in civil society."

But it is important to understand why Harlan advocated this seemingly more magnanimous view. Justice Harlan did not disagree with the *Plessy* majority's basic proposition that even aggressive legal enforcement of all the civil rights of black people could not, by itself, produce social equality, for "social equality," said Justice Harlan, "no more exists between two races when travelling in a passenger coach or a public highway than when members of the same races sit by each other in a street car or in the jury box, or stand or sit with each other in a political assembly, or when they use in common the streets of a city or town, or when they are in the same room for the purpose of having their names placed on the registry of voters, or when they approach the ballot-box in order to exercise the high privilege of voting." Harlan did not doubt that whites were "the dominant race in this country," and that white America would "continue to be for all time, if it remains true to its great heritage and holds fast to the principles of constitutional liberty." Harlan's view was that white dominance in this country should last forever, but only if it respected the legal rights of blacks to the fullest. It was in this context, for this purpose, indeed in the same paragraph, that he wrote the famous phrase, "[o]ur Constitution is color-blind." What Justice Harlan was proposing was a wiser real politik, a more beneficent strategy for preserving white rule and maintaining social order.

Supreme Court decisions in the Shaw cases would make interracial legislative dialogue constitutionally illegitimate and black political influence once again impotent.

Brown v. Board of Education (1954) essentially adopted the first Justice Harlan's position that it is impossible to justify legal segregation of the races without openly endorsing white supremacy. This was the argument Chief Justice Warren used to win unanimity for the Court's opinion. Legal scholars still debate whether the Warren Court, as the chief legitimator of the Civil Rights Movement, wanted merely to remove all the official structures states had developed to prop up separate white and black societies, or whether it intended to use its constitutional power and moral authority to revolutionize America's social order and actually move blacks into the white "mainstream."

We know the Warren era soon ended. Bit by bit, case by case, an increasingly conservative Supreme Court shifted its leadership policy from promoting racial integration to defending white Americans' freedom to associate in racially separate societies defined by both class privilege and ethnic identity.

Today, the Court has come full circle to renounce the Reconstruction social integration agenda for the second time, restoring its view in the *Civil Rights Cases* that blacks should not be "special favorite[s] of the laws." As the Supreme Court eased away from any pretensions of overseeing the integration of black and white societies, it struggled to find new constitutional justifications for what might now be called white superiority. The old laissez faire conception of equal opportunity, as determined by social and economic markets, was still at hand. It would be used first to limit anti-discrimination laws in the name of associational freedom, then to denounce as preferential affirmative action any legal attempts to modify the institutional structure of the marketplace.

The Supreme Court has rebuffed the efforts of the black community to deploy more legal equality in its struggle to transform its subordinate status in civil society. Since they reclaimed the franchise through the Voting Rights Act of 1965, African Americans have turned to the political forums of civil society itself, seeking the opportunity as legally coequal members of a democratic republic to negotiate practical arrangements that might lead to true equality in the American nation. The Voting Rights Act of 1982 reflected this new black electoral influence and the political compromise it was able to achieve with representatives of America's white majority. The *Shaw* cases, however, threaten not only the redistricting deals African Americans have been able to make, but also the constitutional legitimacy of their ability to bargain politically at all.

The victim perceived by the *Shaw* majority is not the white plaintiffs but their nation. In this light, the plaintiffs are properly viewed as members and subjects of a collective nation, rather than as citizens and rights-bearers in a democratic republic. In the *Shaw* cases, the Court found a majority of justices who want to define late twentieth-century American national identity in terms of colorblind individualism. The problem, however, is that in the group-defining context of redistricting, colorblind individualism will perpetuate the primary badge of slavery instead of removing it. Entrenched as constitutional principle, colorblind individualism threatens to prohibit black Americans and other ethnic groups from negotiating collectively with white Americans over basic democratic structures, foreclosing the possibility that African Americans as a people eventually might achieve the ability to consent to the form of government and to become coequal members of the nation. This poses a unique problem for African Americans in that they have never been given the opportunity to consent.

The *Shaw* cases are an attempt to synthesize the judge-made desegregation and one-person, one-vote constitutional principles into an analytically-distinct constitutional cause of action that can trump the deal African Americans thought they had made in 1982 for a broad group-based regime of rights based on political fairness, which takes into account all the historical and social realities that African Americans confront. As constitutional history, *Shaw's* definition of national identity is worse than disingenuous; as constitutional change, it serves only to perpetuate the American nation's historical refusal to negotiate with the descendants of slaves.

Two original constitutional pillars of American national identity were nonblackness and nonsectarianism, the one to define Americans as white, the other to prevent white Americans from fighting among themselves. Both nationalist principles remain embedded in our constitutional jurisprudence. Since the beginning of the Republic, white Americans, in the name of national unity, have always been able to turn to the Supreme Court for constitutional protection against efforts to include blackness in the sovereign people's own understanding of who they are.

Today the Supreme Court is moving toward relaxing nonsectarianism, acknowledging that religious differences among white Americans no longer present the dangers of communal faction they once did, expressing a growing willingness to approve government support of religious communities, and tolerating more open involvement of organized religion in political activities.

The *Shaw* cases, along with their affirmative action cousins, represent the Supreme Court's countervailing strategy for keeping querulous whites united around their nonblackness. The *Shaw* cases exercise the presumed finality of constitutional edicts to outlaw the efforts of those white Americans who, with pressure from the federal government, have demonstrated some willingness to deal with African Americans as negotiating partners in state democracies. These openly black-white redistricting bargains are seen by the *Shaw* majority as threats to colorblind paradigms of whites, which have become crucial to the national and personal identities of some other Americans.

There is a genuinely painful irony in this historical situation: In 1857, a Supreme Court dominated by Southerners declared that a unified nation could not tolerate treating even free blacks as coequal political agents; in 1995, a Court on which no white Southerner sits has declared that the American nation cannot tolerate Southern white legislators openly negotiating with African Americans as free political agents. The irony is not surprising, however, because the question of how free blacks fit in the American national identity has always transcended sectional differences.

White America did not intend that the recent implementation of blacks' voting rights would lead to any renegotiation of national identity, and it is moving to cut off this route to fundamental change as well. This is the function of colorblind rhetoric. The same Court that resoundingly repudiated the incursion of civil rights in "amorphous" social affairs now is moving to bar the doors of political venues to blacks. The American nationalists who succeeded in keeping civil society out of bounds for constitutional courts are reversing their position and asking the judiciary to set strict limits on the ability of blacks to engage in free political bargaining. Colorblindness as a judicial justification for outlawing vital political negotiations between white Americans and peoples of color is not only hypocritical, it is rationally insupportable by any democratic theory.

We should recall how in the late 1850s, proslavery forces converted "nonintervention" into intervention, contending that Congress could not interfere with the local institution of slavery, while at the same time insisting that the federal government act affirmatively to protect slaveholders in the territories and free states. In the 1990s, proponents of colorblindness are arguing simultaneously that the Supreme Court has no power to interfere with associational rights in civil society and that the Court must enjoin state legislatures from allowing free negotiations between representatives of white and black communities over the basic structures of government. They would make interracial legislative dialogue constitutionally illegitimate and black political influence once again impotent. Dred Scott would recognize a familiar American theme were he to return today. ■

James Blacksher is a voting rights attorney practicing in Alabama.

Enforcing Voting Rights in the Clinton Administration As We Approach the New Millenium

by Todd A. Cox

Introduction

The fairness of any legal system can be measured by the availability of adequate remedies to protect one's rights. Thus, the essential question is, does one have free access to a court or legislative body to obtain vindication where a human right has been infringed?

A. Leon Higginbotham, Jr., *In the Matter of Color, Race and the American Legal Process: The Colonial Period* (1978).

As the next century approaches, the voting rights of the nation's minorities are at an important crossroads. At the beginning of the first Clinton Administration, lawsuits challenging redistricting plans that contained minority-opportunity districts (i.e., districts providing minorities an equal opportunity to elect candidates of their choice) threatened to eliminate the electoral gains won following the 1990 redistricting.[1] As the first half of the second Clinton Administration draws to a close, there are continued threats to minority voting rights from new *Shaw* challenges, as well as new questions raised in the enforcement of both the Voting Rights Act of 1965[2] and the National Voter Registration Act of 1993 (NVRA).[3] The Administration will have to be proactive in its law enforcement and creative in developing responses to the challenges that have become inevitable in enforcing voting rights laws. Depending on the enforcement strategies implemented by the Administration, minority electoral gains will either be protected or suffer severely as we near the next century and the next redistricting cycle. With the first two years of the second term of the Clinton Administration as a backdrop, this chapter will briefly examine the burgeoning and continuing threats to minority voting rights that the Administration will have to confront in the following areas: (1) enforcement of section 2 of the Voting Rights Act[4] in the wake of *Shaw* and its progeny; (2) enforcement of section 5 of the Voting Rights Act[5] in the wake of *Shaw* and recent Supreme Court rulings; and (3) enforcement of the NVRA in light of recent legislative attacks, as well as the persistent resistance by states, and potential obstacles relating to changes in the laws that affect the agencies through which the NVRA is implemented.

I. Continuing to Ensure Electoral Opportunities in the Post-*Shaw* Era

Although the country is fast approaching the 2000 census and a new redistricting cycle, the courts are still resolving battles over redistricting plans developed after the 1990 census. In the wake of *Shaw v. Reno*,[6] and *Miller v. Johnson*,[7] several Supreme Court rulings on Fourteenth Amendment Equal Protection challenges to majority-black or Hispanic congressional districts have helped clarify the criteria for creating minority-opportunity districts. Through these decisions, the Supreme Court has made a definitive statement that the Voting Rights Act is still valid, and that there is a compelling justification for creating majority-minority districts to remedy violations under the Act.

In *Shaw v. Hunt*[8] and *Bush v. Vera*,[9] the Court once again addressed the constitutional standards that apply to congressional districts that were drawn to create equal electoral opportunities for minority voters. In *Shaw v. Hunt*, the Court reviewed North Carolina's 1990 congressional plan, following a full trial on the merits regarding the constitutionality of North Carolina's Twelfth and First Congressional districts.[10] Similarly, *Bush v. Vera* involved a challenge to three congressional districts in Texas. In both cases, the Court ruled that all of the challenged districts were unconstitutional under the Fourteenth Amendment because they were not narrowly tailored to further a compelling governmental interest.[11]

However, the Supreme Court's rulings in the *Shaw* line of cases have not eroded the need for states and local jurisdictions to be sufficiently "race conscious" in their redistricting processes so as to avoid diluting minority voting strength. Indeed, in *Bush*, the Court stated that "[s]trict scrutiny does not apply merely because redistricting is performed with consciousness of race.... Nor does it apply to all cases of intentional creation of majority-minority districts."[12] As Justice O'Connor observed:

> *States may intentionally create majority-minority districts and may otherwise take race into consideration, without coming under strict scrutiny. Only if traditional districting criteria are neglected, and that neglect is predominantly due to the misuse of race, does strict scrutiny apply.*[13]

Moreover, Justice O'Connor has made clear that nothing in *Shaw* or its progeny should be interpreted as calling into question the continued importance of complying with section 2 of the Voting Rights Act:[14]

> *The results test of § 2 is an important part of the apparatus chosen by Congress to effectuate this Nation's commitment "to confront its conscience and fulfill the guarantee of the Constitution" with respect to equality in voting. S. Rep. No. 97-417, p. 4 (1982).*[15]

Justice O'Connor recognized that "it would be irresponsible for a State to disregard the § 2 results test,"[16] concluding that states have a compelling interest in complying with section 2 of the Voting Rights Act and, more specifically, in complying with "the results test as this Court has interpreted it."[17] Justice O'Connor's opinion confirms that reasonably compact majority-minority districts are not inevitably subject to challenge under the constitutional claim recognized in *Shaw*, and that jurisdictions continue to have a compelling interest in complying with the Voting Rights Act.[18]

The most recent Supreme Court decision in this area is instructive. In *Lawyer v. Department of Justice*,[19] the Court upheld the constitutionality of a majority-minority state senate district in the Tampa Bay, Florida, region. In this case, the district court approved a settlement plan that reduced the total minority voting-age population in the challenged district from an original 55.3% to 51.2% through reconfiguration of the district to one that was characterized as still somewhat oddly shaped, albeit "less strained and irregular."[20] In determining whether it would approve the new boundaries, the district court placed primary importance on the fact that the new plan "offers to any candidate, without regard to race, the opportunity to seek elective office and both a fair chance to win and the usual risk of defeat."[21]

The Supreme Court upheld the settlement, finding that race, while a factor, did not predominate and subordinate Florida's traditional redistricting criteria.[22] Although the new district splits three counties and several municipalities and is irregularly shaped, the Court held that none of these factors required a finding that the district was unconstitutionally race-based. The Court relied on the district court's finding that Florida has traditionally drawn districts that encompass more than one county and cross bodies of water, and that the district at issue therefore was not a dramatic departure from Florida's traditional redistricting principles. It thus acknowledged for the first time an important limit on the Shaw doctrine: a majority-minority district's adherence to "traditional redistricting principles" should be judged according to the principles the state itself applies in drawing districts rather than abstract concepts of ideal compactness and shape. In another case, *King v. State Board of Elections*, the Court affirmed without an opinion a district court ruling that Illinois' Fourth Congressional District, drawn after the 1990 census, is constitutional.[23] Lower courts have applied the principles of these and prior Supreme Court rulings and determined that the creation of majority-minority districts under the Voting Rights Act is valid.[24]

In view of the affirmances in *Lawyer* and *King*, as well as the Supreme Court's repeated assurances that the use of race in drawing district lines does not automatically render districts unconstitutional, it appears evident that jurisdictions have a compelling justification for complying with the strictures of section 2 of the Voting Rights Act, and may be sufficiently race-conscious in redistricting to avoid diluting minority voting strength.

This term, the Supreme Court will again have an opportunity to provide further guidance on these issues, taking for review *Cromartie v. Hunt*.[25] *Cromartie* challenges the new Twelfth and First Congressional districts, drawn after the Court struck the old Twelfth in *Shaw v. Hunt*. The new Twelfth was only 47% African American, reduced from the original 53% minority district that the Supreme Court struck down in *Shaw v. Hunt*. *Cromartie* will give the Supreme Court perhaps its final opportunity prior to the 2000 census to clarify its original *Shaw* ruling and to further develop the limits for redrawing districts found to be unconstitutional under the *Shaw* standard.

Over the past two years, the U.S. Department of Justice has intervened in some of these *Shaw* challenges and has been named as a defendant in several of them.[26] The Department's involvement in these cases has had an impact on its enforcement record. A number of federal court decisions in recent years have been harshly critical of the Department's section 5 enforcement policies.[27] Also, in a number of cases, lawyers for the plaintiffs who are challenging the majority-minority districts have successfully sought to take the depositions of the Department's Voting Section personnel, and even of the Assistant Attorney General of the Civil Rights Division, concerning the Department's decision-making process in section 5 preclearance determinations. These inquiries are often time-consuming and demoralizing for the Civil Rights Division and Voting Section staff. Moreover, these probes have threatened the confidentiality between Department staff and the outside community that has been a hallmark of the Division's ability to gather information for, and execute its responsibilities under, the section 5 preclearance process.

Despite these obstacles, the Division must continue to intervene in these challenges. Defense of these challenges has borne fruit not only in ultimate victories, but also in the successful settlement of cases and redrawing of districts that still provide minorities an equal opportunity to elect candidates of choice. In this regard, *Lawyer*, in which the Department was a party-defendant, is instructive, for the presence of the Department at settlement negotiations and on appeal was an important part of the success of that case. As a party, the Department is in a position to instruct courts directly about its enforcement role, as well as shape settlements and court decisions.

However, while defense of challenged majority-minority districts is an important priority, it is equally important for the Voting Section to employ its substantial personnel and resources in bringing affirmative cases under section 2 of the Voting Rights Act. As discussed above, section 2 is recognized by the Supreme Court to be constitutional, and jurisdictions have a responsibility to comply with its strictures; in other words, the *Shaw* line of cases has not erected a bar to section 2 lawsuits.[28] Thus, the Voting Section must invigorate its program of investigating and filing cases under the Act. A proactive and vigorous strategy for bringing cases under section 2 will help bolster the credibility of the Department and the Voting Rights Act's validity before the courts and before otherwise recalcitrant jurisdictions. The Department must become a leader in this important effort, as it is critical for courts and jurisdictions alike to understand that section 2 compliance is still required and that the Department will hold jurisdictions accountable for any discrimination against minority voters during the next redistricting process.

Also, since census data is essential in the redistricting process, this Administration's decision to permit individuals to designate multiple racial and ethnic categories on the 2000 census forms presents particular issues for the post-2000 redistricting process. In order to ensure an accurate count of individuals during redistricting and reapportionment, it will be critically important to report these multiple categories in a format that is useful for enforcing civil rights law and creating redistricting plans. The Department will need to take the lead in coordinating this Administration's efforts to determine and implement the methods for tabulating and reporting the census data collected, and to ensure consistent enforcement and compliance across the agencies that use this data.

II. Enforcing Section 5 of the Voting Rights Act

Confronted with "unremitting and ingenious defiance of the Constitution,"[29] Congress enacted the Voting Rights Act of 1965 to "banish the blight of racial discrimination in voting,"[30] concluding that "the unsuccessful remedies which it had prescribed in the past would have to be replaced by sterner and more elaborate measures in order to satisfy the clear commands of the Fifteenth Amendment."[31] The Voting Rights Act and, specifically, section 5 of the Voting Rights Act, represents the culmination of Congress's efforts to establish these new remedies designed to "rid the country of racial discrimination in voting."[32]

Section 5 prohibits the enforcement or administration by covered jurisdictions of "any voting qualification or prerequisite to voting, or standard, practice, or procedure with respect to voting" without first receiving preclearance from the United States Attorney General or the United States District Court for the District of Columbia.[33] Covered jurisdictions can meet this burden by showing that the voting change is not tainted, even in part, by an invidious racial purpose[34] and will not have a retrogressive effect.[35] For several reasons, including cost and convenience, jurisdictions tend to seek preclearance through the administrative process conducted by the Department of Justice, rather than through litigation in the district court. Therefore, the Department has a unique, critical role in preventing the implementation of discriminatory electoral practices. The Administration, however, must confront several issues related to its section 5 enforcement responsibilities.

First, the district court decision in *Bossier Parish v. Reno*[36] threatens to significantly alter the fundamental standard for reviewing voting changes submitted pursuant to section 5. The Supreme Court in *Village of Arlington Heights v. Metro Housing Development Corp.* held that the assessment of whether purposeful discrimination was a motivating consideration "demands a sensitive inquiry into such circumstantial and direct evidence of intent as may be available."[37] The Supreme Court also identified several factors that may provide evidence of invidious purpose in the context of official action taken by governing officials, including: (1) the historical background of the decision; (2) the sequence of events leading up to the action taken; (3) procedural departures from the normal process; (4) substantive departures from the normal process; and (5) the legislative or administrative history, including contemporary statements by the members of the governing body, minutes of their meetings, and any testimony by the decision-makers regarding their intent.[38]

In the first *Bossier* decision, however, a sharply divided three-judge district court granted preclearance to the Bossier Parish, Louisiana, school board redistricting plan, holding that circumstantial evidence of discriminatory intent may not be considered in a section 5 proceeding if such evidence would also be admissible in a proceeding under section 2 of the Voting Rights Act.[39] In a vigorous dissent, District Judge Gladys Kessler pointed out that the majority's standards for determining discriminatory intent departed sharply from Supreme Court precedents such as *Arlington Heights*, and stated that the record "demonstrates overwhelmingly that the School Board's decision . . . was motivated by discriminatory purpose."[40] The district court also refused to apply a

Justice Department regulation under which section 5 preclearance would be denied if a voting change would constitute a clear violation of the "results" test of section 2 of the Voting Rights Act.[41]

On appeal, the Supreme Court upheld the district court's unanimous conclusion that a section 2 violation could not be an independent justification for a denial of preclearance under section 5.[42] However, the Court remanded, instructing the lower court to apply the standard set out in *Arlington Heights* to the evidence of discriminatory purpose in the record, and directing the district court to consider the parish's argument that section 5's discriminatory purpose prong was limited to voting changes adopted with an intent to retrogress, and did not extend to a more general intent to limit minority voting strength.[43] On remand, the district court panel did not address the question of the scope of section 5's purpose prong. It applied the *Arlington Heights* standard only to the issue of whether the parish intended to retrogress when it made the decision to adopt the redistricting plan, with a majority of the court determining that the parish did not intend to retrogress.[44] The case is again pending before the Supreme Court on appeal.

Following the initial Supreme Court ruling in *Bossier*, the Department of Justice made a change in its regulations governing the section 5 administrative process. This change removed the provision authorizing the Department to deny section 5 preclearance if a voting change would constitute a clear violation of the "results" test of section 2 of the Voting Rights Act.[45] It is thus critically important that the Department be prepared to bring affirmative section 2 lawsuits against jurisdictions whose voting changes may not violate section 5's purpose or effect prongs, but nevertheless violate section 2. In addition, depending upon the outcome of the *Bossier Parish* case in the Supreme Court, the Department may have to determine how it will further modify its method of evaluating voting changes under section 5.

Second, the Supreme Court's decisions in the *Shaw* line of cases present certain challenges to the Department's section 5 enforcement. Specifically, the Department must evaluate its section 5 decision-making process in light of these rulings to determine if further guidance should be provided to submitting jurisdictions. For example, the Department will have to determine how it will respond to a redistricting submission in which members of the community have alleged that the plan violates the standard set out in *Shaw* and subsequent cases.[46] Similarly, the Department will have to prepare for the possibility that a jurisdiction itself will use compliance with the *Shaw* standard as a reason for seeking to implement a redistricting plan that other evidence indicates was adopted with the intent to discriminate against minority voters or would have a discriminatory effect against minority voting rights.

In addressing these and other issues regarding section 5 law enforcement, the Department should be aware of several concerns. First, current regulations, policy directives, and administrative decision precedents already accommodate these various contingencies, obviating the need for any changes in formal policy. It is understandable that the Department is sensitive to the critiques of its policies leveled by the courts and may wish to be responsive to changes in the law. Nevertheless, the Department should seek other methods to assure the courts and covered jurisdictions that it is complying with the governing laws, short of radical changes to its section 5 regulations or procedures that could have the unintended result of weakening section 5 enforcement.

Second, in addressing these and any other issues, the Department should consult the stakeholders in the section 5 process, including the minority voters whom the process is intended to protect.[47] Timely input from all parties with a stake in the section 5 process will not only help ensure that the purposes of the process are preserved, but will also enhance the credibility of the process with those groups.

III. Enforcement of the National Voter Registration Act

A. Responding to Legislative Attacks on the National Voter Registration Act, and the Erection of Electoral Barriers and Voter Intimidation

The National Voter Registration Act is approaching its fifth anniversary. It has been enormously successful in enlarging the pool of voters by requiring states to provide voter registration materials in a variety of offices providing various public services, such as drivers' licenses, public assistance, and services to the disabled. Indeed, the Federal Election Commission, the agency charged with reporting the impact of the NVRA on the administration of elections, reports that in 1996, more than 27 million people were registered to vote pursuant to the statute.[48] Specifically, the Federal Election Commission (FEC) noted that "[t]he mail registration provisions of the NVRA [under which voters are permitted to register to vote by mail] caused very few problems for the States and accounted for nearly one third of all voter registration applications from 1995 through 1996."[49] Despite the success and the relative ease in implementing the statute, there have been legislative attempts over the years to amend the NVRA to remove many of the features that have made it most successful. The most recent iteration of these efforts occurred during the last Congress.

At the beginning of the 105th Congress, California Congresswoman Loretta Sanchez's electoral victory was challenged in the House by former Representative Robert Dornan, whom she defeated. At the heart of the former Congressman's challenge were allegations that noncitizens had voted in the election and had provided the margin for victory in the race. In the wake of these allegations of vote fraud and the subsequent House investigations into them, the House considered several bills—termed "ballot security" measures—which, while purportedly designed to address issues regarding vote fraud, actually threatened to undermine or effectively to repeal provisions of the NVRA and, ultimately, the Voting Rights Act.

Beginning in 1997, the House first considered H.R. 1428, which would have established a federal program to "confirm" the citizenship of registered voters and voter registration applicants at the discretion of state or local election officials, allowing them to drop registered voters from the rolls and reject registration applications if their citizenship could not be confirmed. Under the bill, the local registrars were given the discretion to use the databases of the Social Security Administration (SSA) and the Immigration and Naturalization Service (INS) to confirm the citizenship status of would-be and current registrants. However, at the June 25, 1997, hearing before the House Judiciary Subcommittee on Immigration and Claims, both agencies testified that it was not possible to verify a person's citizenship using either agency's database.[50] The bill was defeated in February 1998.

Proponents of NVRA amendments next made several failed attempts to incorporate these amendments into various campaign finance proposals. First, before the 1998 Easter recess, the House considered and defeated a "campaign finance reform" bill, H.R. 3485, which incorporated the language of H.R. 1428. Second, the House considered a new campaign reform bill, H.R. 2183, and permitted members to offer a number of amendments to the legislation, including amendments: (1) eliminating the Voting Rights Act requirement that jurisdictions provide bilingual voting materials and bilingual assistance;[51] (2) establishing, similar to H.R. 1428, a federal pilot program to allow state and local election officials to "verify" citizenship of voters in, "at a minimum," California, Texas, Florida, New York, and Illinois, by using INS and SSA data; and (3) repealing the NVRA's mail-in registration requirement, requiring proof of citizenship and Social Security numbers to register to vote, allowing states to purge voters from the rolls for nonvoting, and permitting states to require photo identification at the polls.

Of course, these amendments had nothing to do with campaign finance. They were introduced without any congressional findings or proof of *any*, let alone any widespread, fraud or problems with the

NVRA procedures. Significantly, where there have been allegations of fraud in an electoral process, the existing system—under state *and* federal law—has operated to address the complaints and adjudicate the matters.[52]

Rather than addressing vote fraud, these proposals posed serious threats to the voting rights of all Americans. Requiring "proof of citizenship to register or to vote" and requiring photo identification would have a disparate impact on low-income citizens who are disproportionately racial minorities, as they would be forced to purchase documents to prove identity and citizenship in order to vote, tantamount to a poll tax.[53] Moreover, repealing the mail-in registration would undermine the NVRA. The FEC Report indicated that approximately 27 million people had registered under the NVRA, with more than 12 million registering through mail-in.[54] If enacted, these bills would have eroded protections guaranteed by the NVRA and the Voting Rights Act, erecting additional, unnecessary barriers and hurdles to voter registration that, in principle, the NVRA was designed to eliminate, and against which the Voting Rights Act was designed to protect.

We should expect similar measures to be introduced as bills or amendments in Congress in the coming years. As in past debates over these issues, the Department of Justice and other agencies should continue to advise Congress that the federal government does not have the ability to create data systems that would facilitate these various proposals. In addition, the Department should point out the potential for discrimination raised by proposals such as the ones discussed, particularly by those that would eliminate the Voting Rights Act's bilingual provisions or erect barriers at the polls that would render the provisions of the NVRA a nullity. It will be critical not only to defeat such proposals in the future, but also to ensure such an overwhelming defeat that the proponents of these measures do not continue to reintroduce them and states and private parties are not further empowered to replicate these measures locally.

Through its legislative advocacy and the section 5 process, the Department of Justice must continue to be vigilant and work to prohibit the implementation of electoral requirements that would intimidate or disproportionately impact the electoral participation of minority voters, such as requiring the presentation of photo identification at the polls. In addition, through its election monitoring, the Department should work to preempt intimidation in the electoral process. Even before specific complaints and allegations are lodged, the Department should investigate areas with a prior history of discriminatory or intimidating electoral practices. When allegations of intimidating activity are presented, the Department must act *promptly* and *systematically* to investigate allegations and then act aggressively to preempt the intimidation by instructing private and public parties that the intimidating behavior constitutes a violation of the Voting Rights Act. Finally, if necessary, the Department must in due course litigate to prevent or cause the cessation of voter intimidation, integrating this litigation strategy into its process of pre-election investigation and its federal observer program. While the Department currently conducts pre-election investigations and sends federal observers when specific allegations are raised, the threshold for Department intervention tends to be quite high. A lower threshold would permit the Department to intervene earlier and preempt discriminatory activity, perhaps even obviating the need for further federal involvement.

B. The Next Generation of NVRA Litigation and the Need to Expand Agency Coverage

At this stage of the NVRA's enforcement, most questions concerning the statute's constitutionality have been resolved and lawsuits against states that had simply refused to comply with the NVRA have been successfully concluded.[56] However, enforcement of the NVRA in public assistance agencies and disability benefits offices in many states has been much less systematic than its enforcement at drivers' license bureaus. It is thus still necessary to pursue aggressively the remaining jurisdictions that have failed to designate the broad spectrum of agencies necessary to provide all the voter registration opportunities contemplated by the NVRA. This should be a priority for the Voting Section, requiring a next generation of NVRA lawsuits to ensure that where the NVRA has been implemented, states are complying with the strictures of the law fully and fairly, particularly in public assistance and disability agencies. It is essential, therefore, for the Department of Justice to conduct ongoing investigations of NVRA compliance nationwide, including the development of a comprehensive strategy for the extensive and thorough collection of data concerning NVRA implementation in the state agencies.[66]

In addition, as a result of welfare law changes, many public assistance recipients may not currently be offered the chance to register to vote which the NVRA offers. Many states are adopting programs under which prior AFDC (Aid to Families with Dependent Children)[67] recipients are diverted from the new Temporary Assistance to Needy Families (TANF)[68] program to job training and job service programs. These diverted individuals may not be provided opportunities to register to vote pursuant to the NVRA during this process. As the principal NVRA law enforcer, the Department of Justice should take the lead in researching and collecting data on the effects of these diversion programs and on voter registration. The Department should also coordinate with other agencies, such as the Department of Health and Human Services, to ensure that state agencies are still fulfilling their obligations under the NVRA.

IV. Conclusion

In order to facilitate the sharing of information and views, the Department should consider establishing formal working groups composed of Department personnel and members of the voting rights advocacy community and holding periodic meetings to discuss issues of concern. Such working groups could help to foster trust between the community and the Department on these issues and help everyone stay informed of policy changes and trends. They also would provide an informal means for the community to share ideas and give feedback to the Department.

The Voting Rights Act and the NVRA are the primary statutes that guarantee the voting rights of this country's citizens. As the principal agency charged with enforcing them, the Department of Justice stands at the intersection of these statutes, ensuring that these rights continue to be protected in the face of a changing legal and legislative landscape. The strategies which this Administration develops to address the new issues confronting voting rights law will shape the future of the government's voting rights enforcement and impact minority voting rights in the next century.

Endnotes

[1] The gains in minority representation resulting from the redistricting following the 1990 census were dramatic. For example, prior to 1990, there were still five southern states with substantial African American populations which had not elected a single African American to Congress since the end of Reconstruction: Alabama, Florida, North Carolina, South Carolina, and Virginia. In 1992, those five states elected eight African Americans to Congress because each of those states for the first time created one or more majority African American congressional districts. Overall, African American representation in the House of Representatives increased from 26 in 1991, prior to redistricting, to 39 in 1992, following redistricting.

[2] 42 U.S.C. § 1973, *et seq.*

[3] 42 U.S.C. § 1973gg, *et seq.*

[4] 42 U.S.C. § 1973, as amended.

[5] 42 U.S.C. § 1973c.

[6] 509 U.S. 630 (1993).

[7] 515 U.S. 906 (1995).

[8] 517 U.S. 899 (1996).

[9] 517 U.S. 952 (1996).

[10] In the original 1993 *Shaw v. Reno* decision, the Court did not address the constitutionality of the challenged districts; the Court addressed only whether the plaintiffs had a cause of action to challenge the districts under the Constitution.

[11] In *Shaw*, however, the Court ruled the plaintiffs in the case did not have standing to challenge the First Congressional district and, therefore, the Court did not decide the constitutionality of that district.

[12] *Bush*, 517 U.S. at 958 (citations omitted).

[13] *Id.* at 993. (O'Connor, J., concurring) (emphasis in original). See also *United States v. Hays*, 515 U.S. 737, 745 (1995) ("We recognized in *Shaw*. . . that the 'legislature always is *aware* of race when it draws district lines, just as it is aware of age, economic status, religious and political persuasion, and a variety of other demographic factors. That sort of race consciousness does not lead inevitably to impermissible race discrimination'") (citation omitted) (emphasis in original).

[14] Section 2 of the Voting Rights Act of 1965, 42 U.S.C. § 1973, as amended, prohibits any practice that has the intent or result of denying a citizen of the United States the right to vote on account of race, color, or status as a language minority. Section 2 states in pertinent part:

> *Sec. 2(a) No voting qualification or prerequisite to voting or standard, practice or procedure shall be imposed or applied by any State or political subdivision in a manner which results in a denial or abridgement of the right of any citizen of the United States to vote on account of race or color, or in contravention of the guarantees set forth in section 4(f)(2), as set forth in subsection (b).*
>
> *(b) A violation of subsection (a) is established if, based on the totality of the circumstances, it is shown that the political processes leading to nomination or election in the state or political subdivision are not equally open to participation by a class of other citizens protected by subdivision (a) in that its members have less opportunity than other members of the electorate to participate in the political process and to elect representatives of their choice. . . .*

[15] *Id.* at 992 (O'Connor, J., concurring).

[16] *Id.* at 991-992 (O'Connor, J., concurring).

[17] *Id.* Justice O'Connor's opinion on this issue is particularly important given that four other members of the

117

Court, who dissented from the rulings striking down the North Carolina and Texas plans, clearly agree that states have a compelling interest in avoiding diluting minority voting strength and in complying with section 2 of the Voting Rights Act. See *Bush*, 517 U.S. at 1003, 1011 (Stevens, J., joined by Ginsburg and Breyer, JJ., dissenting); *id.* at 1045, 1050-51 (Souter, J., joined by Ginsburg and Breyer, JJ., dissenting).

[18] See also *Lawyer v. Department of Justice*, 521 U.S. 567, 117 S. Ct. 2186 (1997) (upholding the constitutionality of a Florida state legislative districting plan that was drawn with conscious consideration of race to settle litigation challenging a prior plan, creating a majority-minority district that afforded minority voters the opportunity to elect candidates of their choice that was somewhat irregularly shaped and that split county and city boundaries); *Abrams v. Johnson*, 521 U.S. 74 (1997) (approving congressional districting plan for Georgia having majority-black district); *King v. State Board of Elections*, __ U.S. __, 118 S. Ct. 877 (1998) (*per curiam*) (summarily affirming district court ruling upholding the constitutionality of Illinois' Fourth Congressional District); *DeWitt v. Wilson*, 856 F. Supp. 1409, 1413-14 (E.D. Cal. 1994) (finding that intentional creation of majority-minority districts does not violate Constitution when redistricting plan "evidences a judicious and proper balancing of the many factors appropriate to redistricting, one of which was the consideration of the application of the Voting Rights Act's objective of assuring that minority voters are not denied the chance to effectively influence the political process"), *aff'd*, 515 U.S. 1170 (1995).

[19] 521 U.S. 567, 117 S. Ct. 2186 (1997).

[20] *Scott v. United States*, 920 F. Supp. 1248, 1255 (M.D. Fla. 1996), *aff'd sub nom. Lawyer v. Department of Justice*, 521 U.S. 567, 117 S. Ct. 2186 (1997).

[21] *Id.* at 1256.

[22] See *Lawyer*, 117 S. Ct. at 2195.

[23] *King v. State Bd. of Elections*, __ U.S. __, 118 S.Ct. 877 (1998). See also *Abrams v. Johnson*, __ U.S. __, 117 S. Ct. 1925 (1997) (upholding the constitutionality of a Georgia district court's decision to maintain one urban majority-black congressional district and to eliminate two nonurban majority black districts).

[24] See *Clark v. Calhoun County, Mississippi*, 88 F.3d 1393, 1407 (5th Cir. 1996) (the Supreme Court in its recent decisions did not alter the *Gingles* proof, nor did the "Court suggest that a district drawn for predominantly racial reasons would necessarily fail the *Gingles* test [for majority-minority districts]"); *Cane v. Worcester County*, 35 F.3d 921, 926-27 n.6 (4th Cir. 1994), *cert. denied*, 115 S. Ct. 3616 (1995) (holding that *Shaw* is not implicated in section 2 challenge to at-large election scheme where proposed majority-black remedial district was comparable to other election districts drawn by the county); *Addy v. Newton County, Mississippi*, 2 F. Supp. 2d 861 (1997) (dismissal of Fourteenth Amendment challenge to majority-minority district created to remedy section 2 violation).

[25] *Cromartie v. Hunt*, No. 4:96CV104-BO(3) (E.D.N.C. April 14, 1997), *prob. juris. noted*, 119 S. Ct. 28 (1998).

[26] See, e.g., *Hays v. State of Louisiana*, 936 F. Supp. 360 (W.D. La. 1996); *Scott v. United States*, 920 F. Supp. 1248 (M.D. Fla. 1996), *aff'd sub nom. Lawyer v. Department of Justice*, 521 U.S. 567, 117 S. Ct. 2186 (1997).

[27] See, e.g., *Smith v. Beasley*, 946 F. Supp. 1174 (D.S.C. 1996); *Johnson v. Miller*, 863 F. Supp. 1354 (S.D. Ga. 1994), *aff'd*, 115 S.Ct. 2475 (1995).

[28] See *Barnett v. City of Chicago*, 141 F.3d 699 (7th Cir. 1998), *cert. denied*, 118 S. Ct. 2372 (1998); *Johnson v. Hamrick*, 1998 WL 476186 (N.D. Ga. June 12, 1998); *Goosby v. Town of Hempstead*, 956 F. Supp. 326 (E.D.N.Y. 1997).

[29] *South Carolina v. Katzenbach*, 383 U.S. 301, 309 (1986).

[30] *Id.* at 308.

[31] *Id.* at 309.

[32] See *id.* at 315.

[33] 42 U.S.C. § 1973c. Section 5 reads in pertinent part:

Whenever a State or political subdivision with respect to which the prohibitions set forth in section 4(a) based upon determinations made under the first sentence of section 4(b) are in effect shall enact or seek to administer any voting qualification or prerequisite to voting, or standard, practice, or procedure with respect to voting different from that in force or effect on November 1, 1964, . . . such State or subdivision may institute an action in the United States District Court for the District of Columbia for a declaratory judgment that such qualification, prerequisite, standard, practice, or procedure does not have the purpose and will not have the effect of denying or abridging the right to vote on account of race or color, or in contravention of the guarantees set forth in section 4(f)(2), and unless and until the court enters such judgment no person shall be denied the right to vote for failure to comply with such qualification, prerequisite, standard, practice, or procedure: Provided, That such qualification, prerequisite, standard, practice, or procedure may be enforced without such proceeding if the qualification, prerequisite, standard, practice, or procedure has been submitted by the chief legal officer or other appropriate official of such State or subdivision to the Attorney General and the Attorney General has not interposed an objection within sixty days after such submission, or upon good cause shown, to facilitate an expedited approval within sixty days after such submission, the Attorney General has affirmatively indicated that such objection will not be made.

[34] See *City of Richmond v. United States*, 422 U.S. 358, 378-379 (1975); *City of Rome v. United States*, 422 U.S. 156, 172 (1980); *Busbee v. Smith*, 549 F. Supp. 494, 516-517 (D.D.C. 1982), *aff'd*, 459 U.S. 1166 (1983); *Wilkes County v. United States*, 450 F. Supp. 1171, 1177 (D.D.C. 1978).

[35] See *Beer v. United States*, 425 U.S. 130, 140-142 (1976); 28 C.F.R. § 51.54.

[36] 7 F. Supp. 2d 29 (D.D.C. 1998).

[37] *Village of Arlington Heights v. Metropolitan Housing Development Corp.*, 429 U.S. 252, 266 (1977).

[38] *Arlington Heights*, 429 U.S. at 267-68.

[39] *Bossier Parish School Board v. Reno*, 907 F. Supp. 434 (D.D.C. 1995).

[40] *Id.* at 463.

[41] *Id.* at 442.

[42] *Reno v. Bossier Parrish School Board*, 520 U.S. __, 117 S. Ct. 1491 (1997).

[43] *Id.* at 1494.

[44] *Bossier Parish School Board v. Reno*, 7 F. Supp. 2d 29 (D.D.C. 1998).

[45] Effective May 1, 1998, the Attorney General amended the Procedures for the Administration of section 5 of the Voting Rights Act of 1965, deleting paragraph (b)(2) of 28 C.F.R. § 51.55.

[46] Similar issues would be raised, during the course of litigation, when a jurisdiction submits a redistricting plan that is challenged under the *Shaw* standard.

[47] In a speech to the National Conference of State Legislatures Annual Meeting in 1997, Acting Assistant Attorney General for the Civil Rights Division Isabelle Katz Pinzler spoke of the Department's deep concern over the criticism of the Department's policies in *Shaw* and *Miller*, and that as a result of developments in redistricting and section 5 law, the Department was beginning the process of studying whether the guidelines governing its section 5 administrative process needed to be revised. Subsequently, the Department has met with officials from jurisdictions covered by section 5 to discuss the section 5 process and possible changes to the current administrative guidelines.

[48] Federal Election Commission, *The Impact of the National Voter Registration Act of 1993 on the Administration of Elections for Federal Office, 1995-1996, a Report to the 105th Congress*, 27.

[49] *Id.* at 1.

[50] Statement of David W. Ogden, Associate Deputy Attorney General, before the Subcommittee on Immigration and Claims, Committee on the Judiciary, United States House of Representatives, concerning H.R. 1428 Voter Eligibility Verification Act, at 4-8 (June 25, 1997) ("DOJ Testimony"); Statement by Sandy Crank, Associate Com-

missioner for Policy and Planning, before the House Judiciary Subcommittee on Immigration and Claims, at 1-3 (June 25, 1997).

[61] This amendment mirrored earlier attempts to remove this provision. See H.B. 351, 104th Congress, 1st Session (introduced Jan. 9, 1995).

[62] In particular, there is no evidence that the registration and voting of noncitizens, a concern that the citizenship confirmation process was purportedly designed to address, is a significant or widespread national problem. For example, a Grand Jury convened in Orange County to investigate allegations that noncitizens had illegally registered to vote in the Dornan/Sanchez 46th Congressional District election refused to return indictments against anyone.

[63] See, e.g., Statement of Becky Cain, President, League of Women Voters of the United States, before the House Judiciary Subcommittee on Immigration and Claims, at 2 (June 25, 1997); DOJ Testimony, *supra* note 50, at 8-9.

[64] Federal Election Commission, *supra* note 48, at 27.

[65] See, e.g., *Association of Community Organization for Reform Now v. Edgar*, 56 F.3d 791 (7th Cir. 1995); *Condon v. Reno*, 913 F. Supp. 946 (D.S.C. 1995).

[66] Of course, these strategies will be developed in the context of the district court decision in *United States v. State of New York*, 3 F. Supp. 2d 298 (E.D.N.Y. 1998), holding that New York was not required by the NVRA to designate public and private hospitals, nursing homes, and community-based organizations that process Medicaid applications as voter registration agencies.

[67] 42 U.S.C. § 601.

[68] Personal Responsibility and Work Opportunity Reconciliation Act of 1996, Public Law No. 104-193, 110 Stat. 2105, 2110.

A Report on Issues Relating to African American History and "Communities of Interest" in Georgia's Eleventh Congressional District

Prepared for Johnson v. Miller by Marsha J. Darling, Ph.D., May 27, 1994; revised July 14, 1994

Credentials

Marsha J. Darling
Georgetown University
Department of History

Introduction

Recently, attorneys and historians at the Department of Justice have asked me to investigate and analyze the social and cultural history of Black Americans living in the counties that comprise what is now the 11th Congressional District of Georgia. In the context of the court's concerns in Shaw v. Reno (1993), I am providing a report that explores the historical development of social and cultural traditions and organizations that demonstrate the strength and persistence of a community defining and organization building tradition of organized self-help among Black Americans in the counties of Georgia now included in the 11th Congressional District. For want of a better familiar frame of reference, I will refer to the 11th Congressional District as a "community of interest."

Several major factors emerged as significant variables regarding the legal arguments about Georgia's 11th Congressional District. To begin with, a history of skin color based exclusion had defined access to public accommodations and group rights in the state of Georgia for most of the decades in this century. However, in addition to what has become referenced as race based exclusion, another compelling rationale for defending and legitimizing districts like the eleventh congressional district was to be found in an argument for the recognition of culturally cohesive communities that have derived from shared and similar historical experiences, particularly when it come to patterns of self-help organization building and mutual assistance. It is in this light that Black American "communities of interest" should be considered.

As broad and potentially obtuse a concept used so commonly in the past to embrace a political entity drawn for varying considerations from geography to political affiliations and party interests, to culturally homogenous interests such as religious affiliations, community of interest offers promise as a complement and addition to other important arguments on behalf of redistricting criteria. Culture, and not just skin color is the important additional, and usually overlooked variable in the argument that Black Americans share in "something" that binds many together. Mutual assistance and benevolence have been vital cultural constructions in Black American communities in the South as well as the North, dating to the 18th century. It is the assumption that Black Americans are only a racial group, that is, persons bound together by white constructions of "race" (as subsumed entirely in the meanings ascribed to skin color), that unfortunately have dominated much of white scholarly writing about Black Americans.

The argument that I make in this report is that the racial constructions that dominated pre-revisionist historical scholarship reduced Black American identity to a racial designation, and therefore for racist reasons, whether intentional or not, denied the recognition of Black American culture, particularly in the South. The documentary evidence for Black American mutual assistance and benevolence, organizational development and infrastructure building in the South, and in Georgia in particular, are there in the historical records. By and large, and until fairly recently, mainstream American historians have used race and not culture as a defining categorization for discussing African American history.

Many white scholars wrote history through their representations and most often defenses and elevations of the history of white Americans. Since Black Americans were cast in oppositional terms and definitions, as the undeserving "other," that left only a depraved, undeserving of the exercise of rights place in history for the nation's brown skinned people. One story was a history of racial achievement, freedom and cultural supremacy, while the other story presented as the opposite of white skinned racial and cultural achievement, justified as racial subordination, enslavement, and second class citizenship.

The ill conceived logic of racism that has been sustained by many white scholars, and more recently, by black neoconservative scholars is that people of African descent have no culture, and are only a skin color group. Having been trained at some of the nation's best schools in this distortion of denial of accurate information and scholarly interpretation about Black American culture and history, it is not surprising that some of the Court's justices are misinformed. Cast in this manner, it is little wonder that the Court in its <u>Shaw</u> opinion suggested the inappropriateness of efforts to place Black Americans together in voting districts.

I was asked whether there was a basis in historical documents and scholarship for an assertion that African American communities in

Georgia's black belt have constitute "communities of interest." As an historian of southern social history, particularly African American History, I was asked to address two very important issues that are significant among a number of other issues, namely, the assumptions about "race" and "culture" likely to be operating as the backdrop for the Court's thinking in Shaw v. Reno, and two, the scholarly evidence for organized African American self-help traditions and "communities of interest" in the blackbelt counties east of Atlanta that comprised the 11th Congressional District represented by Ms. Cynthia McKinney when Johnson v. Miller went before the Court.[1]

Rationale for this Essay

Both the United States District Court and the Supreme Court decided Johnson v. Miller (1994) on behalf of the white litigants who challenged the 11th Congressional District as it was configured in 1994. Although it is not always foremost in the language of the Court, the two issues addressed by this essay continue to be an issue for the Court because its concerns in Shaw v. Reno have failed to come to terms with the extent and meaning of African American culture and not just the social construction of "race" as it relates to African Americans in the South. It is obvious that a challenge for the Court is to see a tradition of African American "race-uplift" self-help across and within counties in Georgia's black belt help during much of this century. It must be said that a focus on a tradition of African American self-help actually helps to explain the scale of white opposition to black progress that is everywhere evident in the South. In addition, a concern for African American self-help does not obliterate a concern for distributive justice based on how the social construction of "race" has been used by many whites and often the state itself, to deprive Black Americans of their rights.

By way of illustrating how tricky is the "social construction of race" when it comes to Black Americans, consider that fortunately, we are clear about why it is important to redistrict so as to put Hasidic Jews together in voting districts because they share a commonality made possible by a shared religion, and participation in organizations, institutions, customs, and traditions. Why then is it, that many of us don't get it about Black Americans? Is it because the construction of American History has not presented Hasidic Jews as bereft of any culture.

A Word about Constructions

As an historian I accepted the task primarily because in reading the

Court's majority opinion in Shaw v. Reno,[2] it seemed to me that some of the assumptions made about "race" and "culture" were derived in large measure from an acceptance of social constructions of Black American group identity that were fashioned from racist historical and social science scholarship written in the 19th and 20th centuries. Much of the historiography and social science scholarship written earlier in this century derived from ideas and beliefs about the presence and vitality of white skin people's cultures, and the total absence of brown skinned people's cultures. Hence, much of what passed as cutting edge scholarship actually reflected the subjective biases of writers living in an age of the ideology of white supremacy, and race and gender based marginalization and exclusion.

Many scientists, scholars, and legal thinkers sought to explain oppositional rights and privileges, and apartheid like structures and operations within a democracy, by according cultural presence and greatness to people of European ancestry, and cultural negation and moral depravity to people of African, Native American and Asian ancestry. Essentially, whether reading the scholarship of some of the preeminent historians of American History, or the assumptions inherent in the minds of many social science scholars, public health officials, medical doctors, eugenics doctors, or practitioners of "pseudo-scientific" protocols and practices, social definitions were constructed that reinforced already existing racist and sexist beliefs about African Americans.[3]

At the very center of a discourse about racism's role in shaping social science scholarship and legal theory, is the fact that American society has been saturated with white ideological construction that deny or disclaim Black American culture. Where in reality, according to documents dating as far back as the colonial era, culture has always been defining for many, many Black Americans, the social construction of racism has been responsible for instilling the assumption that Black Americans are people who share only skin color and have no culture. Whether as the "one-drop" blood rule used as the basis for constructing laws about miscegenation, or "racial medicine" used as the basis for the infamous Tuskegee experiment, or the "pseudo-sciences" that started with the assumption that biological difference is inherently linear and unequal when it is racial and sexual, racist ideology constructed a definition of "skin color" in place of culture. In this manner, the social construction of "race" was used to supercede ethnicity, because those of African descent were legislated out of the exercise of human rights. Also, "race" was a definitional category invented to mute African ethnicity and deny the existence of especially African influenced culture in the minds of many people. Since culture became a basis for the entitlement of rights, those without a culture were all the more ineligible.

While there is a legitimate claim Black Americans can invoke that seeks redress for exclusionary treatment received based on being treated as a biological rather than cultural group, that in an of itself does not preclude our addressing what may arguable be a more fundamentally manageable, substantive, geographically and politically organized, and viable unit or measure of political analysis. Black Americans in Georgia are not just a group of folk who share skin color, and little if any other interests, activities, etc. Historically, Black Americans in some of Georgia's counties have organized themselves into organizations, institutions, and movements that reflect shared interests, agendas and goals. There is a legitimate and politically compelling reasons for recognizing the above-mentioned organized activity as reflective of shared political values, ideals and objectives. In addition, Black Americans have also found themselves confronting contemporary issues like environmental pollution.

In the context of Johnson v. Miller, it is important to remember that there are historical and cultural factors that validate a claim for "communities of interest". All construction derive in part from what we want to see, and scholars have a responsibility to construct African American History from a fuller range of primary documents and sources than has been used in the past. Indeed, much of the writing of earlier American History used no Black American sources at all. Sometimes that was unavoidable, but often the assumption of Black inferiority determined that white scholars did not seek out sources culled from Black life and culture. With the exception of African Americans scholars like W. E. B. Du Bois, Charles Chestnut, Carter G. Woodson, Charles Johnson, and white scholars like Arthur Raper, Melville Herskovits, Franz Boas, Herbert Aptheker, much of earlier accounts of Black Americans were explicitly racist, or avoided the sources, research and scholarship of black and white scholars who were not racist towards Black Americans.

The fact that skin color has been defining in the minds of whites is not a social construction of African Americans, it is a "mind set" of the accumulation of ideas and beliefs about the absence of any culture amongst Black Americans. The consequence of culturally negating ideas has often rendered Black Americans as an assortment of brown skinned folks who happen to be the same skin color, but who have not fashioned cultural markers that organize ideas, beliefs etc. into mutual aid, benevolence and organized institutions. It is important to say that such a "skin color equals culture" equation derives not from the machinations of Black political thought, but rather from the fixation many whites have had with constructing racial explanations for depriving African Americans of rights.

While some Black Americans have been cut off from learning or understanding the evolution of cultural traditions and institutions that have organized many Black American people around shared values and beliefs, it remains true that during those decades in this century when most white scholars and most white Americans dismissed any cultural legacy among Black Americans because racial segregation deprived whites of ever seeing and really understanding the internal workings of self-help concepts, that a strident self-help movement continued evolving, despite sometimes seemingly insurmountable odds defined by white racial bigotry.

I am suggesting a very focused, historically accountable use of the term "communities of interest." We must be accountable to how amorphous a term like "communities of interest" can become when it is used in a manner that suggests the absence of very clear boundaries. Hence, in the context of this essay, the primary focus of my inquiry is to identify and assess those historical aspects of rural and urban African American culture that provide a "community of interest" among African American citizens in Georgia, including specifically the 11th Congressional District. In particular, I was asked to evaluate whether African Americans living in the urban communities within the district, Savannah, Augusta, and the southern portions of DeKalb County, share a common historical experience with African American persons residing in the rural counties within the congressional district as it was drawn by the Georgia State Legislature.

While the concept of "communities of interest" is broad and encompassing of much that is not invoked as relevant in this essay, the concept is useful, relevant and accurate for conveying information that has too seldom been deemed important except to Black scholars. This information should therefore more accurately serve to debunk the racist renderings of Black history that have throughout this century reinforced the invisibility of African American culture, self-help movements, and hence specific affiliations and cultural, social, political constructions within African American communities that constitute discernible, politically meaningful units of political and social analysis.

The particular discussion of "communities of interest" that is used in this paper serves to correct the myopia that has for decades skewed discourses about Black Americans into narrowly drawn constructions identifiable only as a skin color designation. Because the social construction of race has been given power, it now exists, but arguably, it is not more important as a basis for constructing "community of interest" than cultural traditions, organizations and institutions. It is culture that holds people together.

The majority opinion in Shaw cautions against mere assumptions that persons of a particular race or color have a common interest:

> A reapportionment plan that includes in one district individuals who belong to the same race, but who are otherwise widely separated by geographical and political boundaries, and who may have little in common with one another but the color of their skin, bears an uncomfortable resemblance to political apartheid. It reinforces the perception that members of the same racial group - regardless of their age, education, economic status, or the community in which they live - think alike, share the same political interests, and will prefer the same candidates at the polls. We have rejected such perceptions elsewhere as impermissible racial stereotypes.[4]

A racial stereotype is a set of assumptions, most often pejorative, about the beliefs and behaviors of members of an ethnic group that is not based on value-free observations or firsthand knowledge, but rather on misinformation and predetermined prejudices. Thus, the challenge set forth in this caveat by the Shaw majority is to determine based on observation and knowledge whether African American citizens in a congressional district share a common historical experience, a common folk culture, a common set of values, beliefs, traditions and customs, or a common set of political interests.

Enduring Assumptions about Culture and "Race"

Despite impressive social changes in race relations in this century pejorative stereotypes and racist beliefs about Black Americans often continue to exercise a significant social force in contemporary society.

This enduring legacy of denying or misrepresenting African American culture as nonexistent is still with us now, but its roots extend back into earlier decades of this and the previous century. Many patterned and learned beliefs, racial in origin, and limiting and negative in their characterizations of Black Americans have survived to date because they have been given cultural sanction and intellectual protection. The most tenacious and pernicious assumption is that Black Americans have no culture, and therefore do not comprise a community of people with shared, common and unifying values, beliefs and actions and commitments. The idea that Black Americans have no culture is very much rooted in racial, biological and cultural theories that historically have represented the majority of African Americans as bereft of values, institutions, organizations, or sustaining ideals and beliefs about obligation, reciprocity, responsibility, the basis for human worthiness, self-help, and a morality and ethics of charitable and philanthropic giving. As it has done in previous decades in this century, the belief that Black Americans lack a culture encourages and even predisposes many to regard Black Americans as a "race," not a cultural group.

In this vein, a few scholars have researched the evolution of white segregationist thought. In his classic text on the evolution and legitimization of segregationist thought Professor I. A. Newby relates that:

> History was the other basic element of segregationist thought. From it segregationists derived two of their most elemental beliefs: first, Negro Africa never produced a civilization worthy of the name and remained even yet a land of savagery and cannibalism; and second, the history of Negroes in America demonstrates the race's incapacity for responsible citizenship. In their effort to prove the latter, segregationists received substantial assistance from historians, many of whom believed explicitly in Negro inferiority. The views of James Ford Rhodes [in History of the United States, (N.Y.: 1909), Vol. IV, p. 556], one of the most distinguished historians of his generation, were not untypical....Reading the historians' works one gets no inkling of the horrors of white supremacy, or the hopes and accomplishments of Negroes. When Negroes are not a problem for white men, they disappear entirely from the historians' accounts, leaving a distinct impression that the race made no worthwhile contribution to the nation's history.[5]

The idea and belief that Black Americans lack a culture was initially crafted as an ideological justification for slavery, and later as a rationale and justification for Jim Crow segregation, with its emphasis on citizenship exclusion, economic marginalization, social subjugation and physical repression. It has been passed along from one generation to another, primarily via written, oral, and visual stereotypes. In racist circles across the country the idea that Black Americans have no culture has served as further justification for why racist whites did not want to associate with blacks. Being perceived as lacking a culture in such circumstances meant that at the level of popular culture very often blacks have been judged culturally inferior, labeled primitive, represented as being without civilization or "cultivation."

Jim Crow laws were written and enforced to exclude blacks from inclusion in society, and to allow discrimination in the workplace or factory. Sharecropping contracts very often used coercion and bigotry to deny Black agricultural workers just wages and compensation. In such a system, the disparate and unequal treatment Blacks received rested on racist ideas about Black American worthlessness. In most instances, the racist views held by many local law enforcement officials precluded Black Americans from seeking legal intervention or remedy for even the most blatant violations of fair and just practices.

Educational appropriations were apportioned unequally, and Black workers and professionals were often treated with a slight of hand, never paid the same wage for the same work as a white worker or professional. Books and articles were written, speeches were given, and movies were made that denigrated African Americans, derided, belittled or dismissed them as culturally indistinguishable in any way, except of course as social pariah. [6]

Of central importance, the assumption that African Americans are a "race" -- just a group of folk with shades of brown skin -- and not a cultural group, precluded any analysis of whether there was a more far reaching Black American historical and cultural record than had been cited or published by white scholars. The vital challenge to document, assess and analyze Black American culture was most often undertaken by W. E. B. Du Bois, Charles S. Johnson of Fisk University, Arthur F. Raper of the Commission on Interracial Cooperation, T. J. Woofter, John Hope Franklin, Melville Herskovits, Franz Boas, C. H. Wesley and the pioneering work of Carter G. Woodson in founding the Journal of Negro History.[7] However, while not all of the above authors are Black Americans, it bears noting that "Negro scholars" were largely discredited as intellectuals and much of what they wrote went unread by the majority of white scholars. Often Black scholars were given the not so subtle message that the scholarship they produced was not really scholarship unless it focused on white or European history, traditions and society. Much of the work of these social scientists and historians failed to be integrated into the mainstream of academic thinking, legal and social policy interpretation, and race relations at the level of popular culture.

Thus, during the decades of the early 20th century in which public education became available, much of what appeared as knowledge and scholarly insight represented Black Americans as "inherently inferior" and lacking any culture. The consequence of such racially derived thinking was that most often African Americans were depicted as a "racial" group. In their classic study of race relations in the 1930s deep South, Anthropologists Allison Davis and Burleigh Gardner assessed white beliefs about the "subordination of Negroes." The authors observed that:

> The subordinate position of the Negroes is generally interpreted by the whites as being due to inherent differences between the two groups. Thus, to the whites, the subordination of the Negroes is not

> merely a characteristic of the social structure, which might conceivably be subject to change, but isbased upon immutable factors, inevitable and everlasting. To them, the Negro is a lower form of organism, biologically more primitive, mentally inferior, and emotionally undeveloped. He is insensitive to pain, incapable of learning, and animal-like in his behavior."[8]

In the process of diminishing Black Americans to the point where only their skin color was thought relevant, scholars and laypersons alike lost an opportunity to explore and assess the cultural ethos of Black Americans. The mythology that there is no Black American culture, and that Blacks are only a "race" obscures the very clear historical record of Black American cultural history that extends so far back as to predate the Revolutionary War.

Ideas, even bad ideas often have a life of their own, particularly if they can be used to perpetuate the role that beliefs about biological determinism have served in this century. The consequence of all of this is that many people who thought themselves well educated were taught to see African Americans only in terms of the social construction of something that has been labeled "race," and not in terms of the multi-faceted ethnic cultural legacy that has very clearly informed and shaped much of Black American belief and behavior. The enduring legacy of the misrepresentation of Black Americans often continues in many ways to obstruct a clear vision of the fact and significance of a series of historical cultural experiences, values, beliefs, organizations, institutions, leadership, folklore and traditions, often shared and common to even spatially separate communities of African Americans.

Historical Understanding of Black "Communities of Interest"

There are several important issues that relate to the concept of "communities of interest" amongst African Americans in the South, and particularly in Georgia's 11th Congressional District. The first issue has to do with assessing the consequence of a shared range of historical experiences of social, political, economic and cultural subjugation, and racial discrimination that link African Americans one with another. In this regard, it is important to acknowledge the challenges to African American freedom, equality and self-determination. The second issue has to do with assessing the impact, specificity and continuity of African American cultural responses to marginalization and exclusion, and to the challenges of creating organizational infrastructures and prompting legal enforcement proceedings that have articulated and actualized the citizenship rights of participatory democracy for African Americans. In this regard, it is important to examine African American responses to oppression, inequality and second class citizenship. A third issue has to do with assessing the initiatives created by African Americans that testify to a tradition of African Americans establishing self-help institutions. Dating from the colonial period, the black population of Georgia, like that in the rest of the South, lived overwhelmingly in rural areas.

Africans were imported into Georgia in the 18th century primarily to work as agricultural plantation laborers. Indeed, the African and African American population remained overwhelmingly rural throughout the 19th century as well, working first as slaves and, after emancipation, as sharecroppers, tenants, or small farmers. In addition, according to scholars of the 19th century, by the year 1860, an estimated 250,000 free Blacks lived, worked and created institutions in the South. [9]

There is a rich record of primary documents that establishes evidence of these active self-help institutions in free Black communities. Such institutions included: dues paying mutual aid societies, and participant-payment benevolent associations (the early precursors to African American insurance companies), Masonic lodges, fellowship societies that raised monies for education, literary societies that taught basic literacy skills, burial societies that also paid survivor's benefits to widows and children, orphanages, anti-slavery societies, the Black press, social action churches, banks started with capital raised by churches, fraternal orders that raised monies for needy projects, female educational societies, and philanthropic organizations that dispensed charitable giving to those unable to pay their own dues.[10] Self-help organizational and institutional leadership, prevalent throughout the decades of the 19th and 20th century, used the social structures and institutions that were under some measure of black control to solidify their presence. The needs of most free Black families required of the self-help movement that it embrace values that adopted and supported an extended and expanded social and cultural extension of what family meant. In addition, self-help institutions were used to provide essential material support to a wide range of folks across generational and socioeconomic lines. Essentially, much that was said and written about in the Black press in terms of definitions of African American kinship embraced not only the cultural value of one's own family, but also expanded the definition of "deservability" to include adoptive and non-blood kin as "deserving and worthy" family members. Often referenced as "race uplift" in the African American press, self-help organizational and institutional leadership often derived its emphasis on collective self-help and representation and reciprocity and obligation, from the structure and operation of extended kinship networks in most African American communities.[11]

The demise of slavery brought about the ability of Black Americans to choose what kinds of social structures to form and validate. Many longstanding African American institutions that date to the early 19th century were reaffirmed and validated, and the family, the church and the rural schools were the three socializing vehicles for the inculcation of values and beliefs predicated on self-help and one's social responsibility for one's own uplift and for improving the lot of others less fortunate. The self-help institutions that served the needs of free Black communities in the South, and in Georgia, were called upon to meet the needs of newly freedpersons in the decades following emancipation. Quickly and effectively Black colleges and institutions grew and expanded their involvement in African American communities within their regions. Training teachers, doctors, nurses, ministers, administrators, and many vocational occupations, historically Black colleges like Tuskegee, Atlanta University, Spelman College, Morehouse College, and Meharry Medical College were often at the forefront of uplifting African American communities.

The establishment and support for historically black colleges and universities have been central to the hope for better access to quality-of-life enhancing opportunities. In the 11th congressional district, Paine College, a private historically black college, is located in Richmond County, in the city of Augusta. Paine College, founded in the late 1800s by a diverse group of African Americans associated with the self-help and missionary work of the Colored Methodist Church, has functioned as an institution of higher learning in the 11th Congressional District. The graduates of Paine College, many of whom became schoolteachers and preachers during the Jim Crow segregation era, would normally send their children, students or parishioners to Paine College. Often, the college, churches or community-based organizations would provide scholarships for young people from the rural counties comprising the 11th Congressional District, to enroll as students at Paine College. According to officials at Paine College, the alumni association was one of the chief vehicles for maintaining contact with graduates and for recruiting potential new students. To this day, many of Paine College's graduates become professionals who remain in the 11th Congressional District and who involve themselves in any number of issues, like health care, environmental social justice, and political participation. Hence, some of the issues that Paine College's graduates involve themselves in constitute self-interest issues that impact African Americans across class lines.

Paine College brings many urban and rural African Americans from the counties that comprise the 11th Congressional District together around shared educational interests. Paine College presently draws close to 50% of its students from the 11th Congressional District, which indicates that the socio-cultural networks established from the College's inception, continue to operate today. The Christian Methodist Church and the United Methodist Church support Paine College. Historically, Paine College has been inseparable from the religious affiliations that have influenced the college's recruitment and enrollment of many African American students drawn primarily from the rural counties in the 11th Congressional District. According to school authorities, African American students at Paine College come from Sandersville, Waynesboro, Greensboro, Augusta, Savannah, and towns such as Milledgeville.

Just as African American mutual aid societies and benevolence associations assisted communities with burial, widows and orphans benefits, longstanding and newer African American voluntary organizations proved invaluable in providing a range of resources and services that were essential to the self-help capacity of rural and urban southern communities. Importantly, many of the African American lodges, fraternities, sororities, women's clubs, and youth clubs had local as well as national chapters that span the decades of the 19th and 20th centuries.

In the decades immediately following slavery, before African Americans were politically disenfranchised, political self-help organizations like the Union League, and local and regional populist organizations were sustained as self-help efforts by many African Americans. Beginning in the early 20th century political organizations like the NAACP provided support for constitutional and political rights for African Americans. Significantly, in the 20th century, organizations like the NAACP grew out of local efforts in counties where there were substantial numbers of African Americans needing and wanting to organize effective efforts at political inclusion and protection of civil rights. Hence, African American participation in the NAACP in Georgia grew from small chapters organized in some of the rural counties as well as urban areas of the state. Those chapters sent delegates and representatives to regional and national meetings. In this vein, the Negro Convention Movement, dating from the 19th century helped to serve as a predecessor to the political and civil rights organizations like the NAACP. The NAACP was everywhere promoted as a vehicle for actualizing shared civil rights, human rights and literacy goals and objectives.

The Black American Protestant denominational churches stand out as significant self-help and philanthropic institutions in both the 19th and

20th centuries. History records a significant difference between black and white Protestant churches. African American churches have been distinctly different in their emphasis on promoting social activism through a social gospel orientation. African American churches have focused on using sermons, music, worship services, instructional services in the churches, mentoring and leadership training, and church activism in the communities surrounding the church as a part of their mission and efforts on behalf of sustaining hope and optimism at the same time as pursuing just and righteous redress for social wrongs. Indeed, from local churches that participate as chapters of organized national church conferences and conventions, the Black Church has been the institution that has consistently identified and articulated the compelling ethical and moral issues around which civil and human rights efforts have been organized. In this manner, the African American church has been fashioned into a vehicle for the representation of commonly held and unifying African American cultural values.

It is important to note the context of how this tradition has evolved within the 11th Congressional District, as the following African American churches are located in the 11th Congressional District: the African Methodist Episcopal, the Christian Methodist Episcopal (formerly Colored Methodist), the Baptist, and the Church of God in Christ. Importantly, while the worship services of some of the above cited churches have divergent roots, almost all exhibit similar worship styles, indicating the existence of common cultural patterns. There is a common and shared emphasis on the importance of the spiritual and social action gospel music and singing. Music with a message is deeply rooted in the oral history, spoken narrative culture, folklore, and oral traditions of rural Georgians. "Singings" or black gospel concerts are often held across the region. These events often produce an exchange of entertainment styles that can lead to new song movements and cultural patterns that have and continue to influence American popular culture.

Within the 11th Congressional District, a very strong African American presence is also well established in the following mainline Christian churches: the Presbyterian and the United Methodist. It is important to note that blacks and whites do not typically worship together. Thus even though African Americans are a subset of the larger denominations cited above, for the most part, their churches operate differently from the larger congregations. For instance, in most cases, the cultural traditions are expressed differently, including the order of worship. Hence, the social functioning of the churches are different, and reflect the evolution of issues and problems that form a common area of concern for African Americans who have experiences that unite and bond them together around common goals, and also around common challenges and problems (i.e., racial discrimination in employment, environmental social justice issues, disparate treatment in banking practices, and access to quality and reasonably priced health care, housing and social services). Pastors conferences, and other occasions where ministers travel to provide guest lectures also afford the various church leaders an opportunity to share information, issues, and intervention efforts at the local level. Interviews with African American church leaders indicate that it is normal for ministers in the 11th Congressional District to travel from Savannah to preach in Augusta, or from Decatur to Keysville. In this way, African American communities of interest are maintained despite spatial distances.

The Black American family has long been the repository of values and beliefs that have served to mold individual character, inculcate values about obligation, reciprocity, mutual assistance, deference to elders, responsibility for dependent children -- whether one's own or others, hard work, charity to those in need, spiritual growth, and respect for one's mother. The Black American family operates as an extended kinship network of spatially linked households, or if you will, what I call "familial clusters." The presence of African American rural and urban familial clusters has been so important to Black family resource sharing and basic survival, that it calls into question whether the Census Bureau's basis for evaluating household structure as the measurement of the "family" is as useful as would be a multiple-household measurement that assessed not only family structure, but also individual familial functions, as opposed to "status bearing" roles, in the familial cluster.

Scholars have documented that extended family kinship systems amongst African Americans very often transcend class, residential, occupational, and educational differences. My own extensive research on southern rural and urban Black American families confirms the presence and significance of "familial clusters." These Black American familial clusters have operated in rural, suburban and urban communities across the country, and they have been an especially important and organizing part of Black life and culture in the South where the physical proximity of Black households in rural areas very often establishes a small social nucleus, organized within a small physical radius so as to permit members of different households to assist one another in establishing a network of support based on shared and mutual obligations and reciprocity.[12]

It is important to note that the familial network described above has been mentioned in interviews with contemporary Georgians who live in the 11th Congressional District. For instance, Representative Tyrone

Brooks has commented on the cultural links and familial obligations that transcend county lines and rural/urban spatial distances in his own experience.

One of the most important legacies of the self-help movement is the chronicle of black land acquisition, particularly in the decades following the end of slavery. Forty acres and a mule were also a Black American aspiration. [13] While there is little question but that the majority of southern rural Black Americans worked the land as sharecroppers under the peonage conditions of the crop-lien system, many African American acquired farms and property. According to the 1920 Census of Agriculture African Americans living in the South owned 15 million acres of land. It is important to note that the Census enumeration of Black owned land provides a significant undercount. The Census reports only on land that is in cultivation, and that produces certain levels of sales. In my research I found that for decades many aging African American couples or widows remain living in houses on small farms that have been in their family for years, even decades. Because their land does not bring sales that meet the minimum commercial sales limits, the agricultural Census does not count their farmland. Essentially, that means that outside of undertaking land title searches and totaling all of the acreage as given on deeds, there is no reliable number to correct the obvious undercount that is present in the Census Bureau's "minimum sales" requirement. From available data we know that the apex of Black landownership occurred in the early decades of this century. In the context of Georgia, Arthur F. Raper has examined the development and extent of landownership amongst rural southern African Americans. In his now classic study of Macon and Greene counties in Georgia in the 1930s, Dr. Raper devotes a full chapter to an exploration of the significance of rural African American landownership.[14]

Political disfranchisement, physical repression, the lack of available credit, the crushing force of the boll weevil on the region's cotton markets, extralegal means of expropriating Black owned land, and the depression were all factors that contributed to the decline of Black landownership in the decades since 1920. [15] Even though their numbers have diminished significantly, many Black belt counties still contain sizeable numbers of African American landowners. [16] Landowners have been important to the economic and institutional development of rural communities, as have been financially independent businesspersons.

The growth of Black businesses in the rural, suburban and urban South has provided a greater degree of financial security to Black persons who, together with black landowners, have exercised a greater degree of independence. It is also clear from the research that I have conducted in rural African American southern communities in the upper and lower South over the course of twenty years that Black landowners, merchants, and church denomination supported ministers were amongst the people most actively involved persons in the movement for voting and civil rights.

During the 20th century an increasing percentage of African Americans migrated out of the plantation regions of Georgia into cities such as Atlanta, Augusta, Savannah, Macon, or Albany within the state or to urban areas in other states.[17] Most Black American citizens in the cities of the 11th Congressional District, like those in urban communities throughout the United States as a whole, trace their lineage back to a rural setting. In the majority of cases, black urban residents in DeKalb County, Augusta, and Savannah are either the children or the grandchildren of persons who grew up as agricultural laborers in rural counties of Georgia. Arguably, extended kinship networks operate to maintain and support many urban and rural African Americans.

Whether rural or urban, black persons who grew up during the period of segregation and disfranchisement in Georgia shared a common historical experience of second-class citizenship. They were all subject to the same racially discriminatory laws enacted by the Georgia General Assembly, they all suffered in varying degrees from racial disparities in educational expenditures by the public school systems of Georgia, and they all experienced in varying degrees the same difficulties in registering and voting. These are all well-known aspects of racial discrimination in Georgia's past.

Whether rural or urban, African Americans who participated in the civil rights movement during the quarter century following World War II shared a common historical experience as well. Although the civil rights organizations of the 1960s may have been strongest in the cities, they sought to help rural blacks mobilize for both protest and political activity. The desegregation of public accommodations and public schools after the 1964 Civil Rights Act, and the elimination of most restrictions to the registration rolls and the ballot box after adoption of the 1965 Voting Rights Act, affected African Americans in the rural counties of the 11th Congressional Districts just as it did those in Augusta, Savannah, or DeKalb County.

For both those black citizens who continue to reside in the poor rural counties of the district and those who live in the poor urban neighborhoods of the district, the effects of past racial discrimination lingered at least as late as the 1980s. The percentage of blacks living below the poverty level, according to data from the 1980 Census, was three times as great as among whites. In both rural and urban areas, between 40 and 50 percent of all blacks lived below the poverty level.[18] Whether rural or urban, blacks living within the district who share these effects of past discrimination have a common interest in programs that provide financial assistance or job training to the unemployed, that enable the poor to purchase food at a lower cost, that aid in the purchase or rental of low cost housing, that provide early childhood education, that support an effective public health system, and that ease the traditional difficulties placed in the path of voter registration.

Many of the adult Black American citizens of the district, both rural and urban, were educated in segregated public schools where the per-pupil expenditures for blacks were, as a rule, substantially lower than for whites. Public schools in Georgia were racially segregated by law until desegregated by federal court orders.[19] Not only were blacks and whites sent to separate schools, but funding for black schools was dramatically inferior to that provided white schools. In 1940, for example, per-pupil expenditures for white students in Georgia were $46.70, three times as high as the $14.61 spent on average for black students. As late as 1952, when the state was trying to narrow the gap between funding for black and white schools as a defense of the "separate but equal" system, Georgia still spent $163.76 per pupil for whites and $110.59 for blacks.[20]

These same adults grew up in households where both family income and per capita income were substantially lower on average than among whites in their communities, whether rural or urban. These disparities in educational and economic status continue to inhibit black political participation within the 11th Congressional District.[21] The 11th congressional district is home to three of the four cities that have served as Georgia's capital (Savannah, Milledgeville, and Augusta). In 1990 the population of the district was 586,195. Whites numbered 202,129 (34%), Blacks numbered 375,585 (64%). The median age was 30 and the 62 and over population was 12% of the districts total. From an economic point of view, the 11th congressional district will have more sites of Olympic competition than any other district with events scheduled for Atlanta, Savannah and Augusta.

Between the urban pockets of the 11th are miles of agricultural acreage. This area was once known as Georgia's cotton belt, but today many of the people depend more on other crops, including corn, soybeans and peanuts. Much of the central portion of the district is part of Georgia's black belt, contiguous counties heavily populated with African Americans. Also prominent in the 11th is the kaolin mining industry, which provides the white clay for use in white paint, china and stationery. In the context of economic and political African American communities of interest, environmental social justice issues as well as civil rights issues comprise areas of concern for increasing numbers of African Americans living in the counties in the 11th congressional district.

In many areas of the South, environmental social justice issues link many African Americans across education and socio-economic income levels in a community of interest that focuses on obtaining equity and social fairness in the context of economic, political and environmental development issues. This is true of many African American communities at the local level in the 11th Congressional District. The Environmental Protection Agency has determined that race more than class is the determining factor in the siting and location of hazardous waste that endangers the quality of life. In many communities in the South, including the 11th Congressional District, environmental toxic waste is disproportionately sited and located in or near African American communities.

The extent to which a broad range of African American citizens are adversely affected by environmental degradation is in the main responsible for environmental justice citizen action groups. There are organizations working in Savannah to promote environmental justice. These organizations enjoin a broad base of support in many African American communities in the 11th congressional district. Some of the issues that are endangering the quality of life in spatially and economically different communities link communities together. These organizations are working on environmental issues with the Savannah River Site, nuclear weapons production, local and state landfills and incinerators, area water contamination, air pollution concerns, the paucity of health impact studies related to environmental toxicity, uneven enforcement of federal regulations, and lack of community representation in the public policy process. It is even the case that one of these organizations works at the community level across race and class lines, and is a member of the Environmental Protection Agency's Region IV Environmental Justice Task Force.

Richmond County has often been cited by environmental activists as one of the most polluted areas in the state of Georgia. One of the key environmental justice issues for African Americans is located in Augusta's Hyde Park community. The Piedmont Wood Preserving Company manufacturing process utilizes an array of chemicals to treat wood products. The chemical residue is later discarded and transported by water, directly through the Hyde Park community area. There are African American residents who maintain that water contamination has caused severe illnesses and is a cause of premature deaths among African American citizens. Hence, environmental social justice issues link communities of African Americans together around shared environmental concerns and problems, and voters often poll political candidates about their positions on these and other pressing matters of racial and social equity.

At a time when many legal experts and social science scholars in the country are seeking ways to bring insights to the Court's assumptions and reasoning in many of the Shaw cases, construction that will withstand the test of time and history should be held close to heart, even if the temperament mind set of the majority of the Court still cannot see past deeply problematic constructions that deprive the Court of a legitimate basis for defending the VRA's role in bringing about participatory democracy for African Americans.

---

1 My interdisciplinary research on African American "familial clusters," obligation/reciprocity networks, and the growth of African American self-help traditions and organizations amongst rural Black Americans in the black belt counties between Atlanta and Savannah extends back more than a decade ago. This essay was delivered as a written report "Communities of Interest, African American History and the Courts" to the Department of Justice and the Supreme Court, and served as the basis for my oral testimony as an expert witness before the United States District Court for the Southern District of Georgia, plaintiffs, Johnson et.al. v. Miller, Howard, Murphy, Cleland (officials of the State of Georgia). I gratefully acknowledge the research assistance of Mr. Keith Jennings of Clark Atlanta University, and Ms. Joy Gaines of Georgetown University Law School.

2 See, 113 S.Ct. 2816 (1993).

3 See, Stephen Jay Gould, The Mismeasure of Man (New York: Norton, 1996) and Daniel Kevles, In the Name of Eugenics: Genetics and the Uses of Human Heredity. (Cambridge: Harvard University Press, 1985).

4 See, 113 S.Ct. 2816, 2827 (1993).

5 See, especially I. A. Newby, Ed., The Development of Segregationist Thought (Homewood, Illinois: The Dorsey Press, 1968), pp. 6, 8.

6 See, especially, Rayford W. Logan, Ed., The Attitude of the Southern White Press Toward Negro Suffrage, 1932-1940 (Washington, D.C.: The Foundation Publishers, 1940), and Donald Bogle, Toms, Coons, Mammies, Mulattoes and Bucks (N.Y.: Continuum Press, 1992).

7 See, especially, W.E.B. Dubois, Ed., Some Efforts of American Negroes for Their Own Social Betterment (Atlanta: Atlanta University Press, 1898, 1906), and, Economic Cooperation Amongst the Negroes in Georgia (Atlanta: 1917), and, The Negro in Business (Atlanta: 1899), and, The Negro American Family (Atlanta: 1908), and, Morals and Manners Among Negro Americans (Atlanta: 1914), and The Common School and the Negro American. See also, Charles S. Johnson's work on Georgia in Growing Up in the Black Belt: Negro Youth in the Rural South (New York: Schocken Books, 1941), and, Shadow of the Plantation (Chicago: University of Chicago Press, 1934); Charles H. Wesley, Negro Labor in the United States: 1850-1925 (N.Y.: Russell & Russell, 1927). For more

recent scholarship, see, John Sibley Butler, Entrepreneurship and Self-Help Among Black Americans (Albany: SUNY Press, 1991), and, Marsha J. Darling, "We Have Come This Far By Our Own Hands: A Tradition of Black Self-Help and Black Philanthropy, and the Growth of Corporate Philanthropic Giving to African Americans," in Marilyn E. Lashley and Melanie Njeri Jackson, Eds., African Americans and the New Policy Consensus: Retreat of the Liberal State? (Westport, CT.: Greenwood Press, 1994).

8 See, especially Allison Davis, Burleigh B. Gardner and Mary R. Gardner, Deep South: A Social Anthropological Study of Caste and Class (Chicago: University of Chicago Press, 1941), p.15-16.

9 See, especially, Ira Berlin in Slaves Without Masters: The Free Negro in the Antebellum South (New York: Random House Inc., 1974).

10 See, generally, James Oliver Horton & Lois E. Horton, Black Bostonians (New York: Holmes and Meier Publishers, 1979); James B. Browning, "The Beginnings of Insurance Among Negroes," Journal of Negro History 22 (October, 1937): 417-432; Emmett Carson, "Despite Long History, Black Philanthropy Gets Little Credit as `Self-Help' Tool" Focus (June: 3-4) 1987; St. Clair Drake, "Churches and Voluntary Associations," Mimeographed. (Chicago: Work Projects Administration, 1940); Robert L. Harris, Jr., "Early Black Benevolent Societies, 1780-1830," The Massachusetts Review 20 3 (603-625), 1979; George W. Hines & George W. Cook, "Negro Insurance," Howard University Record 9 (6), 1915; James Jackson, "Fraternal Societies Aid Race Progress," Crisis 45, July, 1939; N. F. Mossell, The Work of the Afro-American Woman (New York: Oxford University Press, 1988) reprint; John L. Rury, "Philanthropy, Self-Help, and Social Control: The New York Manumission Society and Free Blacks, 1785-1810," Phylons, XLVI (3), 231-240, 1985; C. A. Spencer, "Black Benevolent Societies and the Development of Black Insurance Companies in Nineteenth Century Alabama," Phylons XLVI (3), 251-261, 1985.

11 See, Martin Dann, The Black Press - 1827-1890: The Quest for National Identity (East Rutherford, N.J.: Putnam Publishing Group, 1971).

12 See, generally, Elmer P. Martin and Joanne Mitchell Martin, The Black Extended Family (Chicago: University of Chicago, 1978); Harriette Pipes McAdoo, Ed., Black Families (Beverly Hills, CA.: Sage Publications, Inc., 1981); Robert B. Hill, The Strengths of Black Families (New York: National Urban League, 1971); Theodore R. Kennedy, You Gotta Deal With It: Black Family Relations in A Southern Community (New York: Oxford University Press, 1980); Carol Stack, All Our Kin: Strategies for Survival in a Black Community (New York: Harper & Row, 1974); Herbert G. Gutman, The Black Family in Slavery and Freedom, 1750-1925 (New York: Random House, 1976); Marsha J. Darling, "The Disinherited as Source: Rural Black Women's Memories," in Michigan Quarterly Review XXVI, No. 1, Winter, 1987.

13 See, especially Loren Schweninger, Black Property Owners in the South, 1790-1915 (Urbana: University of Illinois Press, 1990).

14 See, Arthur F. Raper, Preface to Peasantry: A Tale of Two Black Belt Counties (Chapel Hill: University of North Carolina Press, 1936).

15 See, generally George B. Tindall, The Emergence of the New South, 1913-1945

(Baton Rouge: Louisiana State University Press, 1967).

[16] See, especially Leo McGee and Robert Boone, Eds., The Black Rural Landowner - Endangered Species: Social, Political, and Economic Implications (Westport: Greenwood Press, 1979).

[17] See, generally Daniel M. Johnson and Rex R. Campbell, Black Migration in America: A Social Demographic History (Durham: Duke University Press, 1981), and Everett Lee, Hortense L. Bates and Douglas C. Bachtel, "Georgia's Black Population," in Issues Facing Georgia, 2, (December, 1986). Also see Appendix A, which shows the changes in the black population for each county in the Eleventh Congressional District from 1910 to 1990.

[18] Douglas Bachtel, Marylou Mandell, and Everett S. Lee, "Georgia's Changing Social, Economic, and Demographic Environment: A Historical Perspective," Issues Facing Georgia, 2 (December, 1988).

[19] See Joint Statement of Undisputed Facts, Paragraph Nos. 104-126.

[20] Harry S. Ashmore, The Negro and the Schools, 153 (1954).

[21] A report by Dr. Allan J. Lichtman, expert witness in Johnson v. Miller, includes quantitative analyses of political participation and voting behavior by black and white persons in the 11th Congressional District. See, also Gerald David Jaynes and Robin M. Williams, Jr., Eds., A Common Destiny: Blacks and American Society (National Academy Press, Washington, DC, 1989).

Copyright Acknowledgments

Cook, Rhodes. "Map Drawers Must Toe the Line in Upcoming Redistricting." *Congressional Quarterly Weekly Report* 48 (Sept. 1, 1990): 2786-2794. Reprinted with the permission of Congressional Quarterly Inc.

Still, Edward. "Voluntary Constituencies: Modified At-Large Voting as a Remedy for Minority Vote Dilution in Judicial Elections." *Yale Law & Policy Review* 9 (1991): 354-369. Reprinted by permission of Yale Law & Policy Review, Vol. 9, No. 1991, pp. 354-369.

Karlan, Pamela S. "Undoing the Right Thing: Single Member Offices and the Voting Rights Act." *Virginia Law Review* 77 (Feb. 1991): 1-45. Reprinted with the permission of the University of Virginia, School of Law.

Aleinikoff, T. Alexander. "A Case for Race-Consciousness." *Columbia Law Review* 91 (June 1991): 1060-1125. Reprinted with permission. This article originally appeared in the Columbia Law Review.

"Redistricting of the Mississippi State Legislature 1991-1992: The Impact of the Grassroots Community on the Formation of Public Policy," excerpt from the Southern Echo Training Manual. *Advancing Community Organizing Skills, Part 1: The Fundamentals* (April 1998): 123-140. Reprinted with the permission of Southern Echo, Inc.

Higginbotham, Jr., A. Leon, Clarick, Gregory A., and David, Marcella. "*Shaw v. Reno*: A Mirage of Good Intentions with Devastating Racial Consequences, w/ Appendices." *Fordham Law Review* LXII, 6 (April 1994): 1593-1659. Reprinted with the permission of the Fordham Law Review.

Guinier, Lani. "The Supreme Court, 1993 Term: [E]racing Democracy: The Voting Rights Cases." *Harvard Law Review* 108 (Nov 1994): 109-142. Copyright 1994 by the Harvard Law Review Association. Reprinted with permission.

Lichtman, Allan. "Quotas Aren't the Issue." *New York Times* (December 7, 1994): A23. Reprinted with the permission of the New York Times.

Raskin, James B. "Gerrymander Hypocrisy: Supreme Court's Double Standard," *The Nation* (February 6, 1995): 167-168. Reprinted with permission from *The Nation* Magazine. Copyright The Nation Company, L.P.

Thernstrom, Abigail. "More Notes from a Political Thicket." *Emory Law Journal* 44 (Summer 1995): 911-936. Reprinted with the permission of Emory Law Journal.

Anderson, John B. "Go Back to the Drawing Board to Make More Votes Count." *Christian Science Monitor* (January 12, 1996): 18. Reprinted with the permission of the Christian Science Publishing Society.

Parker, Frank. "Factual Errors and Chilling Consequences: A Critique of *Shaw v.*

Reno and *Miller v. Johnson*." *Cumberland Law Review* 26 (1996): 527-537. Reprinted with the permission of the Cumberland Law Review.

Dodd, R. Bruce. "Making Sense Out of the Way We Should Vote." *Chicago Tribune* (April 5, 1996): I, 11. Reprinted with the permission of the Chicago Tribune.

Swain, Carol M. "Commentary: Not 'Wrongful' By Any Means: The Court's Decisions in the Redistricting Cases." *Houston Law Review* (Summer 1997): 315-321. Reprinted with the permission of the University of Houston Law Center.

Richie, Robert, and Hill, Steven. "The Case for Proportional Representation." *Boston Review* 23, 1 (February/March 1998): 3-20 Reprinted with the permission of Boston Critic, Inc.

Raspberry, William. "Superdistricts in North Carolina." *Washington Post* (April 17, 1998): A23. Reprinted with the permission of the Washington Post Company.

"Redistricting: Look Beyond Political Fighting Over Single-Member Districts." *The Charlotte Observer* (April 24, 1998). Reprinted with permission from The Charlotte Observer. Copyright owned by The Charlotte Observer.

Blacksher, James U. "Dred Scott's Unwon Freedom: The Redistricting Cases as Badges of Slavery." *Southern Changes* 20, 3 (Fall 1998): 28-30. Reprinted with the permission of Southern Regional Council Inc.

Cox, Todd A. "Enforcing Voting Rights in the Clinton Administration As We Approach the New Millennium," in Corrine M. Yu and William L. Taylor, eds. *Test of Our Progress: The Clinton Record on Civil Rights. A Report of the Citizen's Commission on Civil Rights:* 109-120.

Darling, Marsha J. "Issues Relating to African American History and 'Communities of Interest' in Georgia's 11th Congressional District." Expert Witness Report in *Miller v. Johnson* submitted to the United States District Court (1994).